The American Presidency

The American Presidency

Origins and Development, 1776-2011

SIXTH EDITION

SIDNEY M. MILKIS
University of Virginia

MICHAEL NELSON
Rhodes College

Los Angeles | London | New Delhi
Singapore | Washington DC

CQ Press
2300 N Street, NW, Suite 800
Washington, DC 20037

Phone: 202-729-1900; toll-free, 1-866-4CQ-PRESS (1-866-427-7737)

Web: www.cqpress.com

Photo credits: 24, 28, 64, 77, 101, 101, 136, 142, 143, 170, 175, 188, 208, 252, 258, 267, 278 Library of Congress; 190, National Portrait Gallery/Smithsonian Institution; 222, 236, Theodore Roosevelt Collection, Harvard College Library; 300, National Archives; 326, The John F. Kennedy Presidential Library; 342, Cecil Stoughton/The Lyndon Baines Johnson Presidential Library; 363, The Gerald R. Ford Presidential Library; 370, Bill Fitz-Patrick—The White House; 380, Pete Souza—The White House; 395, David Valdez—The White House; 401, Bush Presidential Materials Project; 413, MTV; 421, 506, Scott Ferrell—Congressional Quarterly; 426, 426, 442, 446, 467, 472, 506, Reuters; 455, AP; 497, Abbie Rowe—National Park Service, courtesy of Harry S. Truman Library; 505, The Jimmy Carter Presidential Library.

Cover design: Malcolm McGaughy
Cover photos: George Washington Silhouette at UW: David Hogan, Getty Images
Composition: C&M Digitals (P) Ltd.

∞ The paper used in this publication exceeds the requirements of the American National Standard for Information Sciences—Permanence of Paper for Printed Library Materials, ANSI Z39.48-1992.

Printed and bound in the United States of America

15 14 13 12 11   1 2 3 4 5

Library of Congress Cataloging-in-Publication Data

Milkis, Sidney M.
  The American presidency : origins and development, 1776-2011 / Sidney M. Milkis, Michael Nelson.—6th ed.
      p. cm.
  Includes bibliographical references and index.
  ISBN 978-1-60871-281-6 (alk. paper)
  1. Presidents—United States—History. 2. Executive power—United States—History. 3. Constitutional history—United States. 4. United States—Politics and government.
I. Nelson, Michael, 1949- II. Title.

  JK511.M56 2011
  352.23'50973—dc22

                                                                    2011015137

Dedicated, with love and gratitude, to

Carol Milkis   *Linda E. Nelson*
Lauren Milkis   *Michael C. L. Nelson Jr.*
David Milkis   *Samuel M. L. Nelson*
Jonathan Milkis   *McClain Alexander Nelson*

Contents

Preface   xi

CHAPTER 1
The Constitutional Convention   1
    Antecedents   2
    The Constitutional Convention   8

CHAPTER 2
Creating the Presidency   27
    The Making of the Presidency: An Overview   27
    Number of the Executive   30
    Selection and Succession   32
    Term of Office   35
    Removal   36
    Institutional Separation from Congress   39
    Enumerated Powers   41
    The Vice Presidency   55
    Ratifying the Constitution   59

CHAPTER 3
Bringing the Constitutional Presidency to Life: George Washington and John Adams   70
    The Election of George Washington   71
    Making the Presidency Safe for Democracy   73
    Forming the Executive Branch   75
    Presidential "Supremacy" and the Conduct of the Executive Branch   77
    Presidential Nonpartisanship and the Beginning of Party Conflict   80
    Washington's Retirement and the Jay Treaty: The Constitutional Crisis of 1796   87
    The 1796 Election   90
    The Embattled Presidency of John Adams   91
    The Alien and Sedition Acts   94

CHAPTER 4

The Triumph of Jeffersonianism   100

The "Revolution" of 1800   101
Jefferson's War with the Judiciary   104
The Democratic-Republican Program and the Adjustment to Power   105
The Limits of "Popular" Leadership   109
The Twelfth Amendment   111
Jefferson's Mixed Legacy   112
The Presidency of James Madison and the Rise of the House
    of Representatives   113
The Presidencies of James Monroe and John Quincy Adams   117

CHAPTER 5

The Age of Jackson   126

Jacksonian Democracy   127
The Rise of the Party Convention   130
Jackson's Struggle with Congress   131
The Aftermath of the Bank Veto   133
The Decline of the Cabinet   134
The Limits of the Jacksonian Presidency   136
Martin Van Buren and the Panic of 1837   139
The Jacksonian Presidency Sustained   140
John Tyler and the Problem of Presidential Succession   143
The Presidency of James K. Polk   145
The Slavery Controversy and the Twilight of the Jacksonian Presidency   150

CHAPTER 6

The Presidency of Abraham Lincoln   158

Lincoln and the Slavery Controversy   160
The Election of 1860   162
Lincoln and Secession   164
Lincoln's Wartime Measures   166
The Emancipation Proclamation   170
The Election of 1864   173
Lincoln's Legacy   176

CHAPTER 7

The Reaction against Presidential Power: Andrew Johnson to William McKinley   181

Reconstruction and the Assault on Executive Authority   183
The Impeachment of Andrew Johnson   188
Ulysses S. Grant and the Abdication of Executive Power   189

The Fight to Restore Presidential Power   195
Congressional Government and the Prelude to a More Active Presidency   205

CHAPTER 8
Progressive Politics and Executive Power: The Presidencies of Theodore
    Roosevelt, William Howard Taft, and Woodrow Wilson   218
Theodore Roosevelt and the Expansion of Executive Power   219
The Troubled Presidency of William Howard Taft   234
Progressive Politics and the Elections of 1912   240
Woodrow Wilson's Theory of Executive Leadership   243
Wilson and Party Reform   245
The Art of Popular Leadership   245
Wilson's Relations with Congress   247
Wilson as World Leader   250

CHAPTER 9
The Triumph of Conservative Republicanism   265
The Harding Era   267
The "Silent" Politics of Calvin Coolidge   275
Herbert C. Hoover and the Great Depression   278
The Twentieth Amendment   283

CHAPTER 10
The Consolidation of the Modern Presidency: Franklin D. Roosevelt
    to Dwight D. Eisenhower   288
Franklin D. Roosevelt and the Modern Presidency   289
The Modern Presidency Sustained: Harry S. Truman and
    Dwight D. Eisenhower   307

CHAPTER 11
Personalizing the Presidency: John F. Kennedy to Jimmy Carter   333
John F. Kennedy and the Rise of the "Personal Presidency"   334
Lyndon B. Johnson and Presidential Government   341
The Twenty-Fifth Amendment   348
The Presidency of Richard Nixon   351
Gerald R. Ford and the Post-Watergate Era   363
A President Named Jimmy   366

CHAPTER 12
A Restoration of Presidential Power? Ronald Reagan and
    George H. W. Bush   377
The Reagan Revolution   377
Reagan's Legacy and the Accession of George H. W. Bush   391
The Bush Presidency   397

CHAPTER 13

Bill Clinton and the Modern Presidency   410

The Election of 1992   411

The First Year of the Clinton Presidency   414

The 1994 Elections and the Restoration of Divided Government   418

The Comeback President   420

Balanced Budgets, Impeachment Politics, and the Limits of the Third Way   426

CHAPTER 14

George W. Bush and Unilateral Presidential Power   437

The 2000 Election   438

Bush v. Gore   440

The Early Months of the Bush Presidency   442

September 11 and the War on Terrorism   445

An Expanded Presidency   446

Bush and the Republican Party   451

Courts and Parties   456

CHAPTER 15

Barack Obama and the Dilemma of Modern Presidential Leadership   462

The 2008 Elections   464

Ideology, Partisan Politics, and the Democratic Party   465

The New Foundation and Partisan Rancor   469

Obama, Partisanship, and the War on Terrorism   473

Obama and the Administrative Presidency   475

The 2010 Midterm Elections   478

Barack Obama, the Modern Presidency, and American Democracy   479

CHAPTER 16

The Vice Presidency   486

The Founding Period   487

The Vice Presidency in the Nineteenth Century   490

Theodore Roosevelt to Harry S. Truman   493

The Modern Vice Presidency   497

Conclusion   510

Appendix   515

Constitution of the United States   517

U.S. Presidents and Vice Presidents   536

Summary of Presidential Elections, 1789–2008   539

Index   549

Preface

Encouraged by the strong response to the first five editions of *The American Presidency: Origins and Development*, we have undertaken a sixth edition with three important objectives in mind. First, we wanted to take account of recent events and developments: George W. Bush's entire two terms as president, the 2008 and 2010 elections, and the first two years of the Obama presidency. Second, we sought to refine the writing and analysis throughout the book. And third, we wanted to incorporate the best of the new scholarship on the origins and development of the presidency.

At its launch, *The American Presidency* was the first comprehensive one-volume history of the presidency to be written by political scientists in more than fifty years. Not since Wilfred E. Binkley published *The Powers of the President: Problems of American Democracy* in 1937 had a similar effort been undertaken.

One advantage of a historical approach to the presidency is that it fills the enormous gap that has arisen in the education of most contemporary students of the office. Because the historical profession (with notable exceptions) has in recent years deemphasized political history in favor of social history, we political scientists have had to step into the breach. So be it: the historians' self-inflicted misfortune has become our good fortune.

Another reason for political scientists to approach the presidency with an eye to history is that in doing so we supplement the approach taken by most standard textbooks. Instead of artificially segregating the presidency into its discrete parts—the president and Congress, presidential elections, party leadership, and so on—a historical approach necessarily integrates every aspect of the office in a way that accurately reflects the dynamic interaction of the various parts. We see, for example, how Franklin D. Roosevelt's attempt to seize control of the Supreme Court in 1937 simultaneously affected—and was affected by—his relations with Congress, his party, the public, and the media. The same can be said of Barack Obama's election in 2008, the financial crisis and wars in Afghanistan and Iraq that he inherited, his health care reform and other legislative initiatives, and the Republican resurgence in the 2010 mid-term election.

In this edition, we continue to tell the history of how the institution of the presidency was created and how it has developed during its more than two centuries of existence. We describe what has remained constant in the office, mostly because of its constitutional design. We also discuss those historical innovations that have endured.

We are less concerned about describing either the cyclical patterns in the history of the presidency or what is idiosyncratic about particular presidents. Abraham Lincoln and Millard Fillmore, for example, receive a chapter and a few paragraphs, respectively, but more because of how they affected the presidency than because of the kinds of people they were. We believe that the institutional history of the presidency is a sufficiently important and neglected topic to merit a book all its own.

Some readers may ask: How pertinent is the presidency's first century and a half to its most recent eight decades? The answers of many political scientists, at least until recently, have ranged from "hardly" to "not at all." Students of the modern presidency typically mark 1933, the year of FDR's first inauguration, as year one of presidential history.

Our argument—and our evidence—is different. Many of the most important institutional characteristics of the presidency date from the Constitutional Convention and the earliest days of the Republic, which we chronicle in Chapters 1–3. During the nineteenth century, highly significant patterns and practices of presidential conduct took shape; these we discuss in Chapters 4–7. As for the era of the modern presidency—that is, the era in which the president has replaced Congress and the political parties as the leading instrument of popular rule—we trace its origins to Theodore Roosevelt and Woodrow Wilson as much as to Franklin Roosevelt and his successors (Chapters 8–15). Put simply, TR and Wilson began the practices that strengthened the president as the nation's popular and legislative leader; FDR then consolidated, or institutionalized, the president's new leadership roles in ways that subsequent presidents have continued.

This book is an interpretive political history of the presidency (and, in Chapter 16, the vice presidency) as well as a factual one. We have worked hard to get our facts straight and to make our interpretations sound. Research scholars, we think, will continue to be stimulated by much of what we report about the deep roots of modern American political institutions. Students will gain a solid undergirding for their study of the presidency, the Constitution, political development, and contemporary American politics and government. We also hope that this book will find its home not only in reading rooms and classrooms but also in living rooms. After all, in a system of republican government such as ours, political history means our politics, our history.

We take pleasure and pride in the friendship and colleagueship that underlie our continuing collaboration on *The American Presidency*. The book is truly a joint intellectual endeavor.

We have many thanks to offer, not least to our wives and children, to whom this book is dedicated. Kenneth Stevens of Texas Christian University, Darren Wheeler of Ball State University, and John White of Catholic University of America reviewed the fifth edition and provided several helpful suggestions for improvement. We also thank Jesse H. Rhodes of the University of Massachusetts, Amherst, and Emily Charnock of the University of Virginia for sharing with us their excellent research and penetrating insights on President Obama. We are indebted to Judy Hunt for her excellent index. For their work or encouragement (or, in most instances, both) on previous editions, we thank these members of CQ Press's extraordinarily able staff: David Tarr, Joanne Daniels, Margaret Sewell, Shana Wagger, and freelance manuscript editor Sabra Bissette Ledent. For their work and encouragement on this edition, we thank Brenda Carter, director of college publishing; Charisse Kiino, sponsoring editor; Carolyn Goldinger, freelance manuscript editor; and Elizabeth Kline, production editor.

Sidney M. Milkis and Michael Nelson

CHAPTER 1

The Constitutional Convention

T he Constitutional Convention of 1787 was, as Connecticut governor Samuel Huntington told the delegates to his state's ratifying assembly, "a new event in the history of mankind. Heretofore, most governments have been formed by tyrants and imposed on mankind by force. Never before did a people, in time of peace and tranquility, meet together by their representatives and, with calm deliberation, frame for themselves a system of government."[1] In the midst of this "new event," nothing was newer than the American presidency, an invention unlike any other national executive in history. In designing the office, the fifty-five convention delegates drew on their personal and professional experience, study of history and philosophy, understanding of political reality, and individual and collective wits.

The constitutional presidency that the convention created may be regarded as, in a sense, the office's genetic code. Because of the Constitution, the presidency is a one-person office, and the president, who is elected for a fixed four-year term by the entire country, shares virtually all the powers of the national government with an equally distinct and independent Congress. The constitutional presidency contains, as does an individual's configuration of DNA molecules, some ingredients whose meaning has been clear and unchanging from the moment of conception, such as the sex of a baby and the thirty-five-year minimum age requirement for the president. The Constitution also includes sentences and phrases that are the legal equivalent of genetically rooted baldness: their meaning, although determined at the very beginning, could only be discovered later. For example, "He shall take Care that the Laws be faithfully executed" first appeared as a passing constitutional reference— the fifth of six clauses in the single sentence that constitutes Article II, section 3. But in later years this provision afforded the president a strong legal claim to powers as varied as acting against secession by the southern states and directing the activities of the extensive federal bureaucracy. Finally, there are those attributes whose meaning could only be found in the vagaries of individual choice and environmental circumstance. Just as the relation of physical strength to well-being varies from person to person and situation to situation, so, for example, has the president's constitutional power to "recommend to

[Congress's] consideration such Measures as he shall judge necessary and expedient" been of varying importance to different presidents at different times.[2]

ANTECEDENTS

As is true of any invention, the presidency had antecedents, all of which influenced the form the office took in the Constitution. The delegates to the Constitutional Convention had long experience with British executives—namely, the king in London and his appointed governors in the American colonies. And ever since independence was declared in 1776, delegates had the benefit of a decade's worth of experience with governments of their own design, both the various state constitutions and the Articles of Confederation, which created and defined a national government. These experiences, more than anything else, set the stage for the calling of the convention and the creation of the presidency in the summer of 1787.

BRITISH AND COLONIAL EXECUTIVES

During their long years as colonists of Great Britain, Americans became well-acquainted with the British form of government, which is best described as a constitutional monarchy. Great Britain was headed by a king (or, less frequently, a queen) who assumed the throne through inheritance and reigned for life. The monarch's power was limited by Parliament, the British legislature. Although the king could order the nation into war, his order prevailed only if Parliament was willing to appropriate the funds needed to finance the effort. Conversely, Parliament could pass laws, but the king could veto them. Parliament, a bicameral legislature, consisted of the House of Commons, an elected body, and the House of Lords, which was made up of hereditary peers with lifetime tenure.

The British form of government was more than just the most familiar one to the American colonists. Many of them also regarded it as the best that human beings ever had devised. Basic liberties seemed better safeguarded by Great Britain's constitutional monarchy than by any other government in history. British wealth and power were first among the nations of the world. Indeed, Great Britain seemed to have solved what traditionally had been regarded as an insoluble problem of classical political philosophy—that is, the inherent limitations of each of the three basic forms of government identified by Aristotle: monarchy (rule by one person), aristocracy (rule by an elite group), and democracy (rule by the people).[3] As the problem usually was formulated, because those who were entrusted to govern on behalf of the whole society ended up using power for their own selfish ends, monarchy soon degenerated into despotism, aristocracy into oligarchy, and democracy into anarchy, then tyranny. The British remedy, developed over several centuries, was to ameliorate these tendencies by blending elements of all three forms of government into one—monarchy in the king, aristocracy in the House of Lords, and democracy in the House of Commons—and then allowing each element to check and balance the others.

The governments of most of Great Britain's American colonies resembled the British government—that is, they had a governor appointed by the king and a legislature composed of an upper house, which in most colonies was appointed by the governor, and a lower house, which was elected by the people. Royal governors were armed with substantial powers, including the right to cast an absolute veto over colonial legislation, the right to create courts and appoint judges, and even the right to prorogue, or dissolve, the legislature. But politically astute governors exercised these powers cautiously, because only the legislature was empowered to appropriate the funds required to finance a colony's government and pay the governor's salary.

For all their virtues, the British and colonial governments were prone to abuse by executives who were hungry for power. King George III, who reigned during the American Revolution, used government contracts, jobs, and other forms of patronage as bribes to ensure the support of members of Parliament. Some colonial governors employed similar practices to influence their legislatures.[4] In 1776 the colonists' anger about these abuses of power was expressed fervently in the Declaration of Independence. The Declaration is best known for its ringing preamble ("all men are created equal," "Life, Liberty and the pursuit of Happiness"), but it consists mainly of a long, detailed indictment of executive "injuries and usurpations, all having in direct object the establishment of an absolute Tyranny over these States."

The lesson many Americans learned from their experience with the British and colonial governments was that liberty is threatened by executive power and safeguarded by legislative power. As James Wilson, a Scottish-born Pennsylvanian who signed the Declaration, fought in the Revolutionary War, and later served as a delegate to the Constitutional Convention, observed:

> Before [the Revolution], the executive and judicial powers of the government were placed neither in the people, nor in those who professed to receive them under the authority of the people. They were derived from a different and a foreign source: they were regulated by foreign maxims; they were directed to a foreign purpose. Need we be surprised, then, that they were objects of aversion and distrust? . . . On the other hand, our assemblies were chosen by ourselves: they were guardians of our rights, the objects of our confidence, and the anchor of our political hopes. Every power which could be placed in them, was thought to be safely placed: every extension of that power was considered as an extension of our own security.[5]

STATE CONSTITUTIONS

During the course of the Revolutionary War, seventeen constitutions were written by the thirteen newly independent states. (Some states began with one constitution, then replaced it with another.) Revulsion against their experience with the British executive—the king in London and his royal governors in the colonial capitals—led almost all the authors of state constitutions to provide for weak governors and strong legislatures. As Wilson wryly observed, under independence "the executive and the judicial as well as the legislative authority was now the child of the people; but to the two former, the people behaved like stepmothers. The legislature was still discriminated by excessive partiality; and into its lap, every good and precious gift was profusely thrown."[6]

In the decade after independence was declared, state governors typically were elected by the legislature for a brief term (one year, in most cases) and were ineligible for reelection. They were forced to share their powers with a council whose members were appointed by the legislature or elected by the people. This arrangement made them, in the assessment of historian Gordon S. Wood, "little more than chairmen of their executive boards."[7] Indeed, at the Constitutional Convention, Virginia governor Edmund Randolph would oppose the proposal to make the presidency a unitary office by saying that as governor, he was merely "a member of the executive."

The powers the governors did have were meager. Most state constitutions made vague grants of authority to their executives and by specifically denying them the right to veto legislation and make appointments rendered them incapable of defending even that modest power from legislative encroachment. In his *Notes on the State of Virginia,* Thomas Jefferson described the result in his home state: "All the powers of government, legislative, executive and judiciary, result to the legislative body. The [state constitutional] convention, which passed the ordinance of government, laid its foundation on this basis, that the legislative, executive and judiciary departments should be separate and distinct, so that no person should exercise the powers of more than one of them at the same time. But no barrier was provided between these several powers. The judiciary and executive members were left dependent on the legislative for their subsistence in office and some of them for their continuance in it."[8]

The constitution of the historically pro-British state of New York offered a striking exception to the general practice of weak governors and strong legislatures. New York's governor was elected by the people, not the legislature, for a term of three years, not one, and, rather than being confined to a single term, could be reelected as often as the voters wanted. George Clinton, the first governor to be chosen under the New York constitution, was elected seven times, for a total of twenty-one years. The executive power in New

York's government was unitary, exercised by the governor alone and not shared with a council. The governor was empowered to veto legislation, subject to override by the legislature, and to make appointments, subject to legislative confirmation. Finally, these and other powers of New York's governor (which were extensive) were defined by the state's constitution in detail.

THE ARTICLES OF CONFEDERATION

The decision by the Continental Congress to declare independence from Great Britain in the summer of 1776 was accompanied by another equally important decision. Congress adopted the Virginian Richard Henry Lee's motion that "a plan of confederation be prepared and transmitted to the respective Colonies for their consideration and approbation." Such a step was militarily necessary. Although the Declaration of Independence made each of the states, in effect, an independent nation, they could not fight a common war against the British without some sort of common government.

The states, however, jealous of their independence and reluctant to substitute even a homegrown central government for the British government they had just rejected, surrendered power grudgingly. They stipulated to their delegates in Congress that the confederation was to be no stronger than was absolutely necessary to wage the war for independence. Reacting against their experience with British rule, the states also made clear that the confederation's executive component must be minimal. Nothing remotely resembling a king would be tolerated.

On June 11, 1776, the Continental Congress formed the Committee of Thirteen (one delegate from each state) to draft a plan of confederation. The committee acted expeditiously, submitting its recommendation on July 12. More than a year later, on November 15, 1777, Congress adopted a revised version of the plan, calling it the Articles of Confederation and Perpetual Union. Ratification by the states came slowly, with the last state not voting its approval until March 1, 1781. But because the articles so much resembled the ad hoc arrangement the states were already using under the Continental Congress, the delay in ratification made little difference.

The Articles of Confederation more than embodied the states' dread of central government and executive power. Indeed, they created less a government than an alliance or, as the articles themselves put it, a "league of friendship." Each state, regardless of wealth or population, was represented equally in Congress. The president, chosen by Congress, was merely its presiding officer. Eventually, after the burden of making all financial, diplomatic, and military decisions and executing all legislative enactments became more than the legislators could handle, Congress created small executive departments headed by appointed officials. The activities of these departments, however, were closely monitored by Congress. In truth, Congress enacted few laws of consequence, because passage required the support of nine of the thirteen states. Amendments to the articles had to be approved by all the states.

In addition to setting forth a weak institutional structure, the Articles of Confederation undermined the power of the national government in other ways. Technically, Congress was empowered to declare war, make treaties and enter alliances, raise an army and navy, regulate coinage and borrow money, supervise American Indian affairs, establish a post office, and adjudicate disputes between states. Funds and troops were supposed to be supplied by the states according to their wealth and population. But Congress had no power to tax the states or to enforce its decisions. When, as often happened, one or two states balked at meeting an obligation, other states followed suit. "Each state sent what was convenient or appropriate," historians Christopher Collier and James Lincoln Collier have observed, "which usually depended on how close to home the fighting was."[9] After the Revolutionary War was won and the common threat from the British was ended, states felt even less reason to honor Congress's requests.

NATIONAL PROBLEMS

For all its weakness, the Articles of Confederation did not prevent the United States from winning independence. The Revolutionary War effectively ended on October 17, 1781, when Gen. George Washington's American army and a French fleet, anchored off Yorktown, Virginia, forced the British forces led by Charles Lord Cornwallis to surrender.

The problems of a weak, purely legislative national government became more apparent in the half-decade after victory. No longer bound together by the threat of a common foe, the states turned their backs almost completely on Congress and on each other.

Overlapping claims to western lands brought some states into conflict. Connecticut settlers and Pennsylvania troops clashed violently in one disputed area. The western territories, which extended as far as the Mississippi River, were the nation's most valuable resource, but until the states' rival claims were settled, it was difficult to develop and profit from them. On the Atlantic coast, some states with port cities, such as New York, Massachusetts, and South Carolina, placed taxes on goods imported from overseas by merchants in neighboring states.

The new nation was burdened by a crippling debt. By 1789 foreign creditors held more than $10 million in promissory notes and were owed $1.8 million in unpaid interest. Unless paid, they were unwilling to engage in further trade with the United States. Yet Congress was unable to persuade the states to contribute to the Treasury. The total income of the national government in 1786 was less than one-third of the interest due that year on the national debt.

The United States also faced numerous problems on its borders. The nation's northern, southern, and western boundaries were under siege, with only an ill-equipped, poorly financed army of seven hundred to defend them. British soldiers continued to occupy two Great Lakes forts that their government had promised to vacate under the Treaty of Paris, which formally ended the Revolutionary War in 1783. Similarly, Spain closed the Mississippi River to American ships and made claim to land east of the river that according to the treaty belonged to the United States. Both Spain and Great Britain encouraged American Indian tribes to raid frontier settlements. (Spain, in particular, roused the Creeks in Florida to harass settlers in Georgia.) Abroad, American ships were preyed on by pirates in the Mediterranean Sea and were denied entry by Great Britain to its colonies in Canada and the West Indies, two lucrative markets for trade.[10]

In the midst of foreign and domestic difficulties, another problem developed that mixed elements of both. A currency crisis engulfed the United States, largely because Americans had gone on a buying spree, importing luxury items such as clocks, glassware, and furniture from Great Britain that they had been unable to get during the war. As specie—gold and silver, the only American currency acceptable to foreign creditors—flowed out of the country to pay for these goods, it became scarce at home. Meanwhile, many debtors, especially farmers who had left the land to fight for independence and still had not been paid by the financially destitute national government, faced bankruptcy or foreclosure. In response, these debtors pressured their state legislatures to print vast sums of paper money that they could use to pay their debts. Creditors, unwilling to be reimbursed in depreciated currency, fought back politically, but with limited success. The highly democratic state legislatures often were more responsive to the greater number of debtors among their constituents than to the smaller number of creditors.

LESSONS OF EXPERIENCE

Fear of executive power remained strong among Americans during the decade after independence was declared. But the problems that beset the United States under the strong legislative governments of the states and the weak legislative government of the Articles of Confederation taught certain lessons, particularly to people of property.[11] As political scientist Charles C. Thach Jr. has written, "Experience with the state governments during the period following the cessation of hostilities served . . . to confirm the tendencies toward increasing confidence in the executive and increasing distrust of the legislature." Experience also taught several things about the proper design of an effective executive:

> It taught that executive energy and responsibility are inversely proportional to executive size; that, consequently, the one-man executive is best. It taught the value of integration; the necessity of executive appointments, civil and military; the futility of legislative military control. It demonstrated the necessity of the veto as a protective measure . . . [for] preventing unwise legislation. . . . It demonstrated the value of a fixed executive salary which the legislature could not reduce. It discredited choice [of the executive] by the legislature, though without teaching clearly the lesson of popular choice. . . . And, above all, it assured the acceptance of, if it did not create, a new concept of national government—the fundamental principles of which were the ruling constitution, the limited legislature, and the three equal and coordinate departments.[12]

THE CONSTITUTIONAL CONVENTION

Of all the problems that plagued the new nation after independence, none seemed more amenable to solution than those involving commerce among the states. Few benefited and many suffered from the protectionist walls that individual states had built around their economies. The Virginia Assembly, at the urging of James Madison, one of its youngest members, called for a trade conference to be held at Annapolis, Maryland, in September 1786 and urged all the other states to send delegations.

The Annapolis Convention was a failure. Only Virginia, New Jersey, and Delaware sent full delegations, and seven states, suspicious of Virginia's intentions, boycotted the meeting altogether. The convention proposed no remedies to the nation's trade difficulties. But the delegates who did come to Annapolis, notably Madison and Alexander Hamilton of New York, rescued the enterprise by issuing a bold call to Congress to convene an even more wide-ranging meeting. They urged that the states be enjoined to choose delegates to "meet at Philadelphia on the second Monday in May next [1787], to take into consideration the situation of the United States, to devise such further provisions as shall appear to them necessary to render the constitution of the Federal Government adequate to the exigencies of the Union."

Initially, Congress was cool to the summons of the Annapolis Convention. But within weeks an event occurred that lent urgency to the nationalist cause. A mob of farmers in western Massachusetts, saddled with taxes and debts and unable to persuade the state legislature to ease credit, closed down courts and stopped sheriffs' auctions to prevent foreclosure orders from being issued and executed against their lands. Although similar outbreaks had occurred in other states, they had been suppressed easily. This one, dubbed Shays's Rebellion after one of its leaders, Revolutionary War hero Daniel Shays, threatened for a time to rage out of control. The reaction around the country among people of property and, more generally, those worried about social disorder was one of shock and horror, both at the class warfare that seemed to be erupting and at the inability of the national government to help states maintain the peace. Thomas Jefferson's private comment to Madison that "a little rebellion now and then is a good thing" was very much the exception in this regard. "What, gracious God, is man! That there should be such inconsistency and perfidiousness in his conduct," declared the usually stoic George Washington after hearing of the Massachusetts riots. "We are fast verging to anarchy and confusion." [13]

On February 21, 1787, Congress decided to act on the Annapolis Convention's request by passing a resolution: "RESOLVED, That in the opinion of Congress it is expedient that on the second Monday in May next a Convention of delegates who shall have been appointed by the several states be held in Philadelphia for the sole and express purpose of revising the Articles of Confederation and reporting to Congress and the state legislatures such alterations and provisions therein as shall when agreed to in Congress and confirmed by the states render the federal constitution adequate to the exigencies of government and the preservation of the Union."

The states were no more compelled to follow this congressional summons than to follow any other. But when a sufficient number—whether frightened by the prospect of further uprisings, concerned about the nation's growing domestic and international weakness, or inspired by the example of the nationally revered George Washington, who decided to attend as a delegate from his native Virginia—selected delegations, all the other states but Rhode Island fell into line for fear of having their interests ignored.

THE DELEGATES

The Constitutional Convention has been variously described as an "assembly of demigods" (Jefferson), a "miracle at Philadelphia" (author Catherine Drinker Bowen), and a "nationalist reform caucus" (political scientist John P. Roche), to cite but three descriptions.[14] The convention may have been all of these things. But, mundanely, it also was a gathering of fifty-five individuals.

Who were the delegates? Self-selection had much to do with determining who was chosen by the various states to represent them at the convention and who actually went. Political leaders who were committed to the idea that the national government had to be dramatically improved embraced the opportunity to attend. Most of those who were basically satisfied with the status quo—including prominent Americans such as Patrick Henry and Richard Henry Lee of Virginia, Samuel Adams of Massachusetts, and George Clinton of New York—stayed away. (Henry, a strong defender of the Confederation, reputedly said that he "smelt a Rat."[15]) If they had attended and fought stubbornly for their position, observed political scientist Clinton Rossiter, the convention "would have been much more perfectly representative of the active citizenry of 1787. It would also, one is bound to point out, have been crippled as a nation-building instrument."[16]

The fifty-five delegates were generally united in their belief that a stronger national government was vital to the health of the new American nation. In part, this agreement stemmed from their similar experiences in the national arena. Forty-two were current or former members of Congress. Twenty-one had risked life and livelihood by fighting in the Revolutionary War. Eight had signed the Declaration of Independence. All were republican, at least to the extent that they opposed a hereditary monarchy and supported some form of representative government.

Collectively, the convention was young. Many of the delegates were, in the words of historians Stanley Elkins and Eric McKitrick, "the young men of the Revolution," who had come of age during the revolutionary decade of the 1770s, when the idea of building a nation was more inspiring than traditional state loyalties.[17] Madison, at thirty-six, was older than eleven other delegates, including Gouverneur Morris of Pennsylvania (thirty-five), Edmund Randolph of Virginia (thirty-three), and Charles Pinckney of South Carolina, who was twenty-nine but said he was twenty-four so he could claim to be the youngest delegate. (That distinction belonged to Jonathan Dayton of New Jersey, who was twenty-six.) The average age of the delegates—even counting Benjamin Franklin of Pennsylvania, who at age eighty-one was sixteen years older than the next-oldest delegate—was forty-three.

Other shared characteristics contributed to the delegates' common outlook on many fundamental issues. Almost all lived in the long-settled coastal regions of their states; the backcountry frontier was hardly represented at the convention. Almost all were prosperous—about half were lawyers and another quarter owned plantations or large farms. Only two delegates were small farmers, a group that accounted for 85 percent of the nation's white population. The wealth of most of the delegates derived from personal property—government securities and investments in manufacturing, shipping, and land speculation. The prosperity of other delegates lay in real property, notably large farms and, in the South, slaves.[18]

RULES AND PROCEDURES

Congress had summoned the convention to assemble on Monday, May 14, 1787. But not until Friday, May 25, were the seven state delegations needed for a quorum present in Philadelphia. Although most of the other delegations arrived within a few days, some came much later.

The first order of business on May 25 was to elect a president, a word that, in the usage of the day, suggested a "presiding officer" more than a "leader" or "chief executive." Not surprisingly, George Washington was the delegates' unanimous choice. Washington spoke on only one issue during the convention—he rose on the last day to support a proposal requiring that each member of the House of Representatives represent at least thirty thousand people rather than forty thousand.[19] The delegates agreed unanimously. But clearly Washington played more than a ceremonial role. According to the Colliers, "during that long, hot summer, this gregarious man was constantly having dinner, tea, supper with people, and one must assume of course that he was actively promoting his position"—namely, a strong national government and a strong executive within that government.[20] Even Washington's last-minute speech on the minor point of representation was meaningful in symbolic terms. As Gordon Wood points out, "It was his way of saying to his colleagues that he favored the Constitution."[21]

After Washington was elected president of the convention, a secretary was chosen—Maj. William Jackson of Pennsylvania. Jackson kept the convention's official journal, which was little more than a record of motions and votes. Fortunately, James Madison decided to keep a more extensive record of the delegates' debates and deliberations. Madison had been frustrated in his studies of other governments by the near-impossibility of determining what their founders had intended when creating them. Although he was acting on his own initiative, the other delegates knew what he was doing because he sat up front, next to Jackson, instead of with the Virginia delegation so that he would not miss a word. In fairness to his colleagues, Madison decided to keep his notes secret until the last delegate died. That delegate turned out to be him: Madison died in 1836, at the age of eighty-five. Along with the rest of Madison's papers, his notes on the Constitutional Convention were purchased by Congress in 1837 and published in 1840.

The only other business of the convention's first day was to accept the credentials of the various state delegations. In doing so, the delegates implicitly agreed to follow the then-customary procedure of having each state cast one vote. James Wilson was displeased by this arrangement (he felt the more populous states should have a greater voice), but he was persuaded by Madison and others that to alienate the small-state delegates at such an early stage could abort the entire proceeding.

On Monday, May 28, the delegates adopted additional rules and procedures. None was more important to the success of the convention than the rule of secrecy. The rule was simple: no delegate was allowed to communicate anything to anyone except a fellow delegate about the convention's discussions and deliberations.

Thomas Jefferson, then the U.S. ambassador to France, wrote John Adams, the ambassador to Great Britain, that he was appalled by "so abominable a precedent. . . . Nothing can justify this but the innocence of their intentions and ignorance of the value of public discussions." But in a letter to Jefferson, Madison explained the delegates' decision: "It was thought expedient in order to secure unbiased discussion within doors, and to prevent misconceptions & misconstructions without, to establish some rules of caution which will for no short time restrain even a confidential communication of our proceedings."[22] In other words, secrecy permitted the delegates to think out loud about issues and even to change their minds without appearing weak or vacillating. It also kept opponents of a stronger national government from sensationalizing particular proposals or decisions as a means of discrediting the whole undertaking. Years later, Madison told historian Jared Sparks that "no Constitution would ever have been adopted by the Convention if the debates had been made public."[23]

Another important rule the convention adopted was to permit any of its decisions to be reconsidered at the request of even a single delegate. Because issues could always be raised and decided again, those who were on the losing side of a crucial vote were encouraged to stay and try to persuade the other delegates to change their minds rather than to walk out and return home in protest.

AN OVERVIEW OF THE CONVENTION

The Constitutional Convention was not a scripted or even an especially orderly proceeding. The delegates' decision to allow issues to be reconsidered, reinforced by their twin desires to build consensus among themselves and to create a government whose parts would mesh with one another, meant that the convention "could not, and did not, proceed in a straight line, neatly disposing of one issue after the next until all were dealt with. It moved instead in swirls and loops, again and again backtracking to pick up issues previously debated."[24] Historian Jack N. Rakove has compared the constitution-writing process to "the solution of a complex equation with a large number of dependent variables: change the value of one, and the values shift throughout."[25]

Students of mathematics know that not all such equations are solved. Once the convention was called, the risk of failure was great. As Franklin wrote to Jefferson on April 19, 1787, "If it does not do good it will do harm, as it will show that we have not the wisdom among us to govern ourselves."[26] Nor did the delegates' work proceed smoothly. Near the midway point, Washington wrote, "I almost despair of seeing a favourable issue to the proceedings of the Convention, and do therefore repent having had any agency in the business."[27] Nevertheless, from May to September the delegates used drafts and debates, compromises and committees to organize their deliberations and help them work through the many issues that faced them. These plans and committees structured the work of the convention into seven main stages:

- Introduction of the Virginia Plan (May 29)
- Decision by the convention to recast itself as the Committee of the Whole, originally for the purpose of considering the Virginia Plan in detail but later to evaluate the New Jersey Plan and Alexander Hamilton's plan as well (May 30–June 19)
- Clause-by-clause debate by the delegates of their decisions when meeting as the Committee of the Whole (June 20–July 26)
- Work of the five-member Committee of Detail, which was appointed by the convention to produce a draft of the new Constitution that reflected the delegates' manifold decisions on particular issues (July 24–August 6)
- Consideration by the delegates of each provision of the report of the Committee of Detail (August 7–31)
- Recommendations of the eleven-member Committee on Postponed Matters, which was created to propose acceptable solutions to problems that continued to divide the delegates (August 31–September 8)
- Final adjustments, including the work of the Committee of Style, which was charged to write a polished draft of the Constitution, and last-minute tinkering by the delegates, culminating in their signing of the proposed plan of government (September 9–17)

VIRGINIA PLAN (MAY 29). The Virginia Plan, introduced on May 29 by Governor Randolph but written mainly by Madison, offered a radical departure from the Articles of Confederation. The plan proposed to create a three-branch national government and to elevate it to clear supremacy over the states, partly by grounding its authority squarely in the sovereignty of the people.[28]

According to the Virginia Plan, the heart of the national government would be a bicameral legislature, with the lower house apportioned according to some combination of wealth and population and elected by the people and the upper house elected by the lower house from a list of candidates nominated by the states. The legislature's powers would include broad authority not just to pass laws but also to conduct foreign policy and to appoint most government officials, including judges.

A national judiciary, organized into "one or more supreme tribunals" and various "inferior tribunals" and appointed with life tenure by the legislature, would form the second branch. One of its broad-ranging powers was "impeachments of any National officers."

The government also would have an executive branch, although it was vaguely defined in the Virginia Plan. The "national executive" (the plan left unresolved the question of whether this would be a person or group of people) was "to be chosen by the National Legislature for a term of ——— years." Its powers were obscure: "besides a general authority to execute the National laws, it ought to enjoy the Executive rights vested in Congress by the [Articles of] Confederation." No one knew exactly what the phrase "Executive rights" meant.

Another element of the proposed new government was a "Council of revision" consisting of "the executive and a convenient number of the National Judiciary." The council would be empowered to veto laws passed by the national legislature, subject to override if a vetoed law was passed again by an unspecified legislative majority.[29]

Finally, the new government would have the power to veto state laws that were in conflict with the Constitution or with national legislation. For Madison, argues Gordon Wood, the worst thing about the Articles of Confederation was not the weakness of the national government but "the vices within the several states" that had produced an abundance of unjust and inconsistent laws. When the convention later rejected this provision of the Virginia Plan, Madison was for a time "convinced that the Constitution was doomed to fail."[30]

The delegates' response to the Virginia Plan was remarkably placid, especially considering that it proposed to transform the weak national government into such a strong one. "So sharp a break was Virginia asking the other states to make with the American past that one wonders why at least one stunned delegate . . . did not rise up and cry havoc at the top of his lungs," Rossiter wrote. "Instead, the delegates ended this [May 29] session by resolving to go into a 'committee of the whole house' " on the next day to "consider the state of the American union."[31]

COMMITTEE OF THE WHOLE (MAY 30–JUNE 19). In becoming the Committee of the Whole, the convention was, in a sense, simply giving itself a different name. The same group of delegates made up the committee as made up the convention. But as the Committee of the Whole they could operate more informally. To symbolize this change, Washington temporarily stepped down as president and Nathaniel Gorham of Massachusetts was chosen to preside. In addition, any decision made by the delegates while meeting as the committee would be in the form of a recommendation to the convention that would be debated and voted on at least once more.

From May 30 to June 13 the Committee of the Whole spent most of its time going over the Virginia Plan, clause by clause. Much of the plan was accepted, but parts of it were altered, and some ambiguous provisions were clarified.[32] The executive was defined as a unitary, or one-person, office. This person would be elected by the legislature for a single, seven-year term and would be subject to impeachment and removal on grounds of "malpractice or neglect of duty." The executive alone, not a council of revision, was empowered to veto laws passed by the legislature, subject to override by a two-thirds vote of both houses. The requirement for a supermajority here and elsewhere in the new plan of government was an American invention, unknown to the British Parliament, but used widely in the states.[33]

In deference to the states, the Committee of the Whole decided that members of the upper house of the national legislature (who had to be at least thirty years old) would be chosen by the various state legislatures. They would serve seven-year terms and be eligible for reelection. Members of the lower house, also eligible for reelection, would serve three-year terms. All members of the national legislature would be barred from holding any other government office, mainly to prevent the emergence of conflicts of interest. As for the courts, there would be one "supreme tribunal," and the judges who served on it or on such "inferior tribunals" as the national legislature might create would be appointed by its upper house for a lifetime term.

The New Jersey Plan. One plank of the Virginia Plan was especially controversial: the provision that both houses of the national legislature be apportioned according to population. Delegates from the states that thought of themselves as large (Virginia, Massachusetts, Pennsylvania, and the three states whose populations were growing most rapidly—Georgia, North Carolina, and South Carolina) favored the idea. They fought sharply with the delegates from the other states, who feared that their constituents would be hopelessly outnumbered in the legislature and wanted to preserve the existing arrangement of equal representation in Congress for each state. A compromise plan, proposed by Roger Sherman of Connecticut on June 11, would have apportioned the lower house of the legislature according to population and the upper house on the basis of one state, one vote. But few delegates were ready yet for compromise. Instead, small-state delegates responded to the Virginia Plan with a sweeping counterproposal. It was introduced on June 15 by William Paterson of New Jersey.

The New Jersey Plan came in the form of amendments to the Articles of Confederation rather than as a new constitution. It proposed to add two branches to the one-branch national government of the Articles: a plural, or committee-style, executive, to be elected by Congress for a single term and "removeable by Cong[ress] on application by a majority of the Executives [governors] of the several States," and a supreme court, with its judges appointed by the executive for lifetime terms. The plan also declared national laws and treaties to be "the supreme law of the respective States" and authorized the executive to use force if necessary to implement them. In addition, Congress would be empowered to regulate interstate and international commerce and impose taxes. But the main purpose of the New Jersey Plan was unstated: to preserve the structure of Congress under the Articles as a single-house legislature in which each state, regardless of size, cast one vote.[34]

Hamilton's Plan. On June 18 Alexander Hamilton delivered a four-to-six-hour speech to the delegates in which he urged them to consider his plan for an avowedly British-style government.[35] "He had no scruple in declaring," according to the notes kept by Madison, "supported as he was by the opinions of so many of the wise & good, that the British Government was the best in the world: and that he doubted much whether any thing short of it would do in America."[36]

Specifically, Hamilton proposed that, as in Great Britain, the national government would be supreme in every way to the states. Governors would be appointed by the national legislature and granted the right to veto laws passed by their own state assemblies. Members of the upper house of the national legislature, like members of the British House of Lords, would serve for life. As for the executive, "the English model is the only good one on this subject," Hamilton asserted.[37] Although he did not suggest that the United States create a hereditary monarchy, Hamilton did propose that the executive be chosen by electors and granted lifetime tenure and vast powers, including "a negative on all laws about to be passed, . . . the direction of war when authorized or begun, the sole appointment of the heads of the departments, the power of pardoning all offences except Treason," and, along with the Senate, the treaty-making power. In truth, argues biographer Ron Chernow, Hamilton's proposal was for "a new hybrid form of government that would have the continuity of a monarchy combined with the civil liberties of a republic."[38]

Hamilton's speech was dismissed by most of the delegates as being far beyond the bounds of what the people or the states would accept. Some scholars have suggested that his real purpose was to offer a plan so extreme that the Virginia Plan would seem moderate by comparison.[39] Yet several of his specific proposals were adopted later in the convention, notably those concerning the president's power to grant pardons and to negotiate treaties. As for the New Jersey Plan, it was defeated on June 19 by a vote of seven states to three. Later that day, the Virginia Plan, as already modified, was approved by the Committee of the Whole and referred to the convention for further consideration. But the conflict between the delegates from the large states and the small states over apportionment in the national legislature was far from resolved.

CONVENTION DEBATE (JUNE 20–JULY 26). On June 20, with Washington again in the chair as president of the convention, the delegates began their clause-by-clause evaluation of the plan of government they had laid out while meeting as the Committee of the Whole. Among the changes they voted in the plan were these:

- Members of the lower house of the legislature would be elected for a term of two years, not three, and would have to be at least twenty-five years old.
- Members of the upper house would serve a six-year rather than a seven-year term. Terms would be staggered so that one-third were elected every two years.

- The national legislature would not have the power to veto state laws, much to Madison's dismay. But, borrowing a plank from the New Jersey Plan, national laws and treaties would be "the supreme law of the respective States."
- A property requirement for members of the executive, legislative, and judicial branches would be established. (This idea later was abandoned.)
- Delegates expressed enough displeasure with the provision for legislative election of the president to a single, seven-year term to guarantee that it would not remain in the final document, but they failed to agree on an alternative.

More than any other issue, deciding how the legislature would be apportioned consumed the convention's time, attention, and endurance during these five weeks of debate. Delegates from the small states pressed relentlessly for equal representation of the states in Congress. Large-state delegates just as adamantly insisted on representation according to population, wealth, or some combination of the two.

A special committee, with members from every state, was appointed on July 2 to propose a compromise. On July 5, after a break to celebrate Independence Day, the committee recommended a plan of equal representation for each state in the upper house and apportionment according to population in the lower house. As a sop to delegates from the large states who feared that the small state–dominated upper house would push for spending programs that would impoverish the large states, the committee vested exclusive power in the lower house to originate all legislation dealing with money. This happy mixture of principle and practicality was tarnished by a dreadful, if unavoidable, compromise with America's "peculiar institution": in one of the three constitutional clauses that protected forced servitude, each slave counted as three-fifths of a person. These three clauses, which also included a guarantee that slaves could continue to be imported and a fugitive slave provision requiring states to return escaping slaves to their owners, would cast a long dark shadow over the Republic.

For more than a week the delegates engaged in a complex and sometimes bitter debate about the compromise over representation. New questions were raised about whether states yet to be admitted to the Union should receive as much representation as the original thirteen, how often a national census should be taken to measure population changes, and whether apportionment in the lower house should reflect a state's wealth as well as its population. On July 16 the convention voted narrowly to approve the main points of the special committee's proposal, sometimes called the Connecticut Compromise in honor of its author, Roger Sherman of Connecticut. One week later the delegates undermined the idea that the upper house would represent the states in the new government by deciding that every state would have two members, each of them free to vote independently of each other and of their state governments.

COMMITTEE OF DETAIL (JULY 24–AUGUST 6). On July 24 the convention voted to appoint a Committee of Detail to review all of its decisions and then draft a plan of government that incorporated them. The five-member committee included representatives of the three main regions of the country— Nathaniel Gorham of Massachusetts and Oliver Ellsworth of Connecticut (a protégé of Sherman) from New England, James Wilson of Pennsylvania from the middle states, and Edmund Randolph of Virginia and John Rutledge of South Carolina from the South. The committee worked while the rest of the convention adjourned until August 6.

One indication of the committee's influence is that it took convention-passed resolutions amounting to 1,200 words and transformed them into a draft constitution of 3,700 words.[40] The committee also drew from a wide range of other sources in compiling its report: the New Jersey Plan, the Articles of Confederation, the rules of Congress, some state constitutions (notably those of New York and Massachusetts), and a plan of government proposed by Charles Pinckney of South Carolina.[41]

Most of the memorable phrases in the Constitution were written by the Committee of Detail, including "state of the Union" and "We the People." Institutions were named. The executive became the president; the national tribunal, the Supreme Court; and the legislature, Congress, with its upper house called the Senate, and its lower house the House of Representatives.

For the most part, the committee, in keeping with its name, simply fleshed out the details of earlier convention decisions. It established procedures for the president's veto, defined the jurisdiction of the courts, and adjusted certain relations between the states. In some instances, however, the committee substituted its own judgment for the convention's. For example, it vested the power to impeach in the House and omitted the property requirement for officeholders.

Perhaps the most important decision by the Committee of Detail was to transform general grants of power into specific ones. What had been Congress's broadly stated authority "to legislate in all cases for the general interests of the Union" became instead a list of eighteen enumerated powers, including the power to lay and collect taxes, regulate interstate commerce, establish post offices, make war, elect a national treasurer, and create inferior courts—all culminating in a sweeping grant "to make all Laws that shall be necessary and proper for carrying into Execution" these and "all other Powers vested" in the new government. The states were forbidden certain powers—notably to make treaties with other nations, to print money, and to tax imports.

The committee granted the president the authority to recommend legislation to Congress, make executive appointments, receive ambassadors from other nations, issue pardons, "take care" that the laws be executed, and command the armed forces. An oath to "faithfully execute the office" of president also was included, as was a provision that the president of the Senate would exercise the powers and duties of the presidency if the president died, resigned, or became disabled. The judiciary—the Supreme Court and the other "inferior courts" to be created by law—was given jurisdiction in cases arising under the laws of the national government as well as in controversies between states or between citizens of different states.

Finally, responding to a threat to walk out by Gen. Charles Cotesworth Pinckney of South Carolina (an older cousin of Charles Pinckney), the committee not only forbade Congress to tax or ban the importing of slaves and the exporting of goods, but also placated southern delegates' fears that Congress might enact navigation laws requiring that American exports be transported on American ships (a boon to northern shipbuilders but a burden to southern agricultural exporters). The committee decided that Congress would have to pass such laws by a two-thirds vote in both houses.

CONVENTION DEBATE (AUGUST 7–31). As they had with the Virginia Plan and the report of the Committee of the Whole, the delegates reviewed the draft constitution proposed by the Committee of Detail clause by clause. Much of the draft was approved. Some parts, however, were modified, and others became matters of serious controversy.

Modifications. The delegates tinkered with several provisions of the Committee of Detail's draft:

- They enacted citizenship requirements for members of Congress (seven years for members of the House, nine years for senators), along with a requirement that legislators be inhabitants of the states they represent.
- They raised the majority needed in both houses of Congress to override a president's veto from two-thirds to three-fourths. (Near the end of the convention, the delegates restored the two-thirds requirement.)
- They judged Congress's power to "make war" too sweeping to protect the nation if it was attacked when Congress was out of session. The clause was revised to read "declare war."
- They forbade Congress to pass ex post facto laws (retroactive criminal laws) or bills of attainder (laws that declare a person guilty of a crime without a trial).
- They barred the government from granting "any title of nobility" to any person and forbade government officials to receive "any present,

emolument, office, or title of any kind whatever from any king, prince, or foreign state."
- They empowered Congress to activate the militia of any state "to execute the laws of the Union, suppress insurrections, and repel invasions."
- They dropped the two-thirds requirement for Congress to pass navigation acts.
- They created a procedure to amend the Constitution: "on the application of the legislatures of two-thirds of the states in the Union for an amendment of this Constitution, the legislature of the United States shall call a convention for that purpose."
- They prohibited any religious test as a requirement for holding office.
- They expanded the president's oath to include these words: "and will to the best of my judgment and power preserve, protect, and defend the Constitution of the United States." (Later, "to the best of my judgment and power" became "to the best of my ability.")
- The Committee of Detail had proposed that the new constitution take effect when ratified by a number of state conventions (not state legislatures) but did not specify the number. The delegates now voted to set it at nine, a number "familiar to the people" from the Articles of Confederation.

Controversies. The draft constitution's slavery provisions came under fierce assault from several northern delegates, especially the three-fifths rule for counting slaves as part of the population and the prohibition against laws banning the importation of slaves. The North's concern derived less from moral considerations than from fear of slave rebellions, which might attract foreign invaders and, in any event, probably would require northern arms and money to put down. Southern delegates not only defended the provisions to protect slavery but also declared that their states would not ratify any constitution that placed slavery in jeopardy.

Adopting the same approach used to settle the controversy between the large and small states, on August 22 the convention appointed a special committee to find a compromise solution. Two days later, the committee proposed that Congress be authorized, if it so decided, to end the importation of slaves after 1800. In the meantime, Congress could tax imported slaves at a rate no greater than ten dollars each. (A euphemism—"such Persons," not "slaves"— was used in the Constitution.) General Pinckney persuaded the convention to change 1800 to 1808. The committee's recommendation, as amended, was passed.

Controversies over two other matters caused the convention to bog down: the powers of the Senate, which delegates from the large states wanted to minimize and delegates from the small states wanted to maximize, and a cluster of issues concerning presidential selection. On August 31, nearing the end of its labors, the convention appointed a Committee on Postponed Matters, with a member from each state delegation, to propose solutions to these vexing problems.

COMMITTEE ON POSTPONED MATTERS (AUGUST 31–SEPTEMBER 8). Beginning on September 4, the Committee on Postponed Matters, chaired by David Brearley of New Jersey, made several recommendations about the presidency.[42] The committee, sometimes referred to as the Committee on Unfinished Parts or, because it had one member from each state delegation at the convention, the Committee of Eleven, proposed a presidential term of four years rather than seven, with no restriction on the president's eligibility for reelection. The president was to be chosen, not by Congress, but by the Electoral College. To constitute the Electoral College, each state would select, by whatever means it chose, electors equal in number to its representatives and senators in Congress. The candidate who received the largest majority of electoral votes would become president. The candidate who finished second would become vice president. (This was the first mention of the vice presidency at the convention.) If no candidate received a majority, the Senate would select the president and vice president from among the five candidates who received the greatest number of electoral votes.

As a corollary to its proposal for the Electoral College, the committee recommended that certain responsibilities be assigned to the vice president: to preside over the Senate, with the right to cast tie-breaking votes, and to act as president if the office became vacant before the president's term expired. Finally, the committee recommended that qualifications for president be stated in the Constitution. The president would have to be at least thirty-five years old, a natural-born citizen of the United States or a citizen at the time of the Constitution's enactment, and a resident of the United States for at least fourteen years.

For several days the delegates carefully considered the committee's complex and surprising proposal for presidential selection. On September 7 they passed it after making only one substantial change: the House of Representatives, not the Senate, would choose the president in the event of an Electoral College deadlock, with each state delegation casting one vote. The Senate still would choose the vice president if the electoral vote for that position was tied.

Having approved the Electoral College, the convention quickly took other actions to reduce the powers of the Senate, mostly in response to demands by the large states. The president was granted the authority to make treaties and to appoint ambassadors, public ministers, consuls, Supreme Court justices, federal judges, and all other officers whose appointments were not otherwise provided for. Senate confirmation would be required for all of these appointments. A two-thirds vote by the Senate was stipulated for ratifying treaties.

On September 8 the convention approved the final proposals of the Committee on Postponed Matters. The president was to be impeached by the House on grounds of "treason or bribery or other high crimes and misdemeanors against the United States" and removed from office if convicted by the Senate. The delegates added the vice president and other civil officers to the roster of those who were subject to impeachment, but they raised the majority needed for Senate conviction from a simple majority to two-thirds. In addition, the House was empowered to originate "all bills for raising revenue."

Having completed (or so they believed) their work on the Constitution, the delegates ended their business later that day by voting to create a five-member Committee of Style to write a polished final draft for them to sign. The committee's leading members were Madison, Hamilton, and Gouverneur Morris, who seems to have done most of its work.

FINAL ADJUSTMENTS (SEPTEMBER 9–17). Even as the Committee of Style labored, the convention continued to modify its earlier decisions. On September 10 Madison urged that special constitutional conventions not be a part of the process of amending the Constitution. Instead, he argued, amendments should be initiated by a two-thirds vote of Congress or by two-thirds of the state legislatures, with approval by three-fourths of the states needed for ratification. Two days later, Hugh Williamson of North Carolina successfully moved that the requirement for overriding a presidential veto be reduced from a three-fourths vote of each house of Congress to a two-thirds vote. The Committee of Style incorporated these changes into its draft.

Meanwhile, some delegates were expressing more fundamental reservations about the Constitution. Randolph worried that the convention had gone far beyond its original charge from Congress to propose revisions in the Articles of Confederation. He urged that the proposed constitution be approved not just by state ratifying conventions but also by Congress and the state legislatures, even if this process necessitated a second constitutional convention. His fellow Virginian, George Mason, and Elbridge Gerry of Massachusetts objected to the absence of a bill of rights from the Constitution. So convinced were the other delegates that such an enumeration was unnecessary, observes historian Richard Beeman, that "not a single state delegation in the Convention supported the idea of a federal bill of rights."[43]

The Committee of Style reported to the convention on September 12.[44] Its draft not only reduced the number of articles from twenty-three to seven but also included some significant innovations. The most memorable of these was the preamble: "We the People of the United States, in Order to form a more perfect Union, establish Justice, insure domestic Tranquility, provide for the common defence, promote the general Welfare, and secure the Blessings of Liberty to ourselves and our Posterity, do ordain and establish this Constitution for the United States of America."[45] The committee also added a provision that barred states from passing laws to impair the obligations of contracts. Finally, it wrote vesting clauses for Congress and the president that, intentionally or not, suggested that the president might have executive powers beyond those enumerated in the Constitution.

The committee's draft met with widespread approval from the delegates, but they continued to tinker. Congress was stripped of its power to choose the national treasurer in favor of the president. A provision was added that the Constitution could not be altered to deprive a state of equal representation in the Senate without the state's consent. And, at the initiative of Gouverneur Morris and Elbridge Gerry, a compromise procedure for amending the Constitution was created that incorporated both the Committee of Detail's recommendation and Madison's plan. As finally agreed, a constitutional amendment could be proposed by either a two-thirds vote of both houses of Congress or a convention that Congress was required to call if two-thirds of the state legislatures requested one. In either case, three-fourths of the states would have to ratify an amendment for it to become part of the Constitution.

Despite these alterations, Randolph, Gerry, and Mason remained unhappy, expressing doubts about the magnitude of the changes that the convention was recommending. But their motion for another constitutional convention to consider any objections and recommendations that might be offered by the state ratifying conventions was defeated by a vote of eleven states to none. As Rakove has noted, the delegates realized from experience that "a second federal convention would assemble encumbered by proposals for amendments of all kinds and bound by instructions that would make it impossible to replicate the process of persuasion, compromise, and bargaining from which the completed Constitution had so laboriously emerged."[46]

The convention's work finished, the delegates assembled on September 17 to sign an engrossed, or final, copy of the Constitution. Forty-two of the original fifty-five delegates were still present in Philadelphia, and all but Randolph, Mason, and Gerry signed the document. Even then, the delegates could not resist some fine-tuning, unanimously approving a Washington-supported motion to alter slightly the apportionment formula for the House of Representatives.

Speaking first before and then during the signing ceremony, Benjamin Franklin offered the convention's most memorable benedictions. To the delegates, he presented a long speech that— as read by Wilson because of Franklin's frailty—said in essence:

George Washington presiding at the signing of the Constitution in Philadelphia on September 17, 1787.

Mr. President, I confess that there are several parts of this constitution which I do not approve, but I am not sure that I shall never approve them. For having lived long, I have experienced many instances of being obliged by better information, or fuller consideration, to change opinions even on important subjects, which I once thought right, but found to be otherwise. . . . I doubt too whether any other convention we can obtain may be able to make a better constitution. . . . It therefore astonishes me, Sir, to find this system approaching so near to perfection as it does; and I think it will astonish our enemies. . . . Thus I consent, Sir, to this constitution because I expect no better, and because I am not sure it is not the best.[47]

Later, as the last few delegates waited to affix their signatures to the Constitution, Franklin gestured to Washington's chair and said to those standing nearby: "Painters have found it difficult to distinguish in their art a rising from a setting sun. I have often in the course of this session and the vicissitudes of my hopes and fears as to its issue, looked at that sun behind the President without being able to tell whether it was rising or setting. But now, at length, I have the happiness to know that it is a rising and not a setting sun."

NOTES

1. Max Farrand, ed., *The Records of the Federal Convention*, 3 vols. (New Haven: Yale University Press, 1911), 2:641–643.

2. The idea is elaborated on in Erwin C. Hargrove and Michael Nelson, *Presidents, Politics, and Policy* (Baltimore: Johns Hopkins University Press, 1984), chap. 2.

3. Aristotle, *The Politics*, trans. Carnes Lord (Chicago: University of Chicago Press, 1984), bks. 3.14–18 and 4.

4. Jack P. Greene, *Peripheries and Center: Constitutional Development in the Extended Politics of the British Empire and the United States, 1607–1788* (Athens: University of Georgia Press, 1986), chap. 2.

5. Quoted in Charles C. Thach Jr., *The Creation of the Presidency, 1775–1789* (Baltimore: Johns Hopkins University Press, 1969), 27.

6. Ibid.

7. Gordon S. Wood, *The Creation of the American Republic, 1776–1787* (Chapel Hill: University of North Carolina Press, 1969), 138.

8. Thomas Jefferson, *Notes on the State of Virginia*, ed. William Peden (Chapel Hill: University of North Carolina Press, 1955).

9. Christopher Collier and James Lincoln Collier, *Decision in Philadelphia: The Constitutional Convention of 1787* (New York: Ballantine, 1986), 5.

10. To a large degree, British hostility to the United States was caused, or at least rationalized, by the American failure to comply with two provisions of the Treaty of Paris. One provision compelled the United States to reimburse British loyalists for property that had been seized from them during the war; the other required that prewar debts to British merchants be paid. Individual states actively resisted both of these requirements, and the national government was powerless to enforce them.

11. Wood, *Creation of the American Republic*.

12. Thach, *Creation of the Presidency*, 49, 52–53.

13. George Washington to David Humphries, December 26, 1786, http://gwpapers .virginia.edu/documents/constitution/1784/index.html; George Washington to James Madison, November 5, 1786, http://www.loc.gov/teachers/classroommaterials/connec tions/george-washington/file.html.

14. Lester Cappon, ed., *The Adams-Jefferson Letters* (Chapel Hill: University of North Carolina Press, 1959), 1:196; Catherine Drinker Bowen, *Miracle at Philadelphia* (Boston: Little, Brown, 1966); and John P. Roche, "The Founding Fathers: A Reform Caucus in Action," *American Political Science Review* 55 (December 1961): 799–816.

15. Quoted in Collier and Collier, *Decision in Philadelphia*, 74.

16. Clinton Rossiter, *1787: The Grand Convention* (London: MacGibbon and Kee, 1968), 141.

17. Stanley Elkins and Eric McKitrick, "The Founding Fathers: Young Men of the Revolution," *Political Science Quarterly* 76 (June 1961): 181–216.

18. Historian Charles A. Beard believed that the enactment of the Constitution, more than anything else, was a triumph of the "personality"—that is, financial and commercial—interests over the "realty," or landed interests. See Beard, *An Economic Interpretation of the Constitution* (New York: Macmillan, 1913). A powerful critique of this once-influential theory was offered by Forrest McDonald in *We the People: Economic Origins of the Constitution* (Chicago: University of Chicago Press, 1958).

19. Washington was right: Anti-Federalist opponents of the proposed Constitution attacked it severely during the ratification debates for requiring each House member to represent too many people.

20. Collier and Collier, *Decision in Philadelphia*, 108.

21. Gordon S. Wood, *Revolutionary Characters: What Made the Founders Different* (New York: Penguin Press, 2006), 46.

22. Cappon, *Adams-Jefferson Letters*, 1:196; Farrand, *Records*, 3:35. All of Madison's notes on the convention are included in Farrand. A one-volume edition is James Madison, *Notes of Debates in the Federal Convention of 1787* (Athens: Ohio University Press, 1966).

23. Roche has argued that the preservation of secrecy by the delegates testifies to their sense of shared enterprise: even when they disagreed strongly about particular issues, they were sufficiently committed to the effort to keep their objections within the convention's walls. See Roche, "Founding Fathers."

24. Collier and Collier, *Decision in Philadelphia,* 120.

25. Jack N. Rakove, *Original Meanings: Politics and Ideas in the Making of the Constitution* (New York: Knopf, 1996), 14.

26. Walter Isaacson, *Benjamin Franklin: An American Life* (New York: Simon and Schuster, 2003), 445.

27. Quoted in Joseph J. Ellis, *His Excellency, George Washington* (New York: Knopf, 2004), 178.

28. The Virginia Plan can be found in Farrand, *Records,* 1:20–22.

29. The Virginia Plan was one of two that were offered to the convention on May 29. Madison recorded in his notes for that day that Charles Pinckney of South Carolina also introduced a plan. But because Madison (who had long loathed Pinckney from their days together in Congress) neither described the Pinckney Plan nor included its text, scholars have had to reconstruct it as best they could from other documents—in particular, some notes found in the papers of James Wilson.

The Pinckney Plan probably resembled the Virginia Plan in many ways. It, too, provided for a strong, three-branch national government. It seems to have been more specific regarding the executive, however. The executive was to consist of a single person (called "president") who would serve a seven-year term and be empowered, among other things, to recommend laws to the legislature, oversee the executive branch, and act as commander in chief of the military.

Pinckney borrowed most of the elements of his plan from the Articles of Confederation, the Massachusetts Constitution, and, especially, the New York Constitution. Even though his plan was rejected, somewhere between twenty-one and forty-three specific contributions to the U.S. Constitution (depending on how one does the counting) seem to have been made by Pinckney.

See S. Sidney Ulmer, "James Madison and the Pinckney Plan," *South Carolina Law Quarterly* 9 (Spring 1957): 415–444; Ulmer, "Charles Pinckney: Father of the Constitution?" *South Carolina Law Quarterly* 10 (Winter 1958): 225–247; and Collier and Collier, *Decision in Philadelphia,* 97.

30. Wood, *Revolutionary Characters,* 157, 160.

31. Rossiter, *1787,* 171.

32. The resolution of the Committee of the Whole can be found in Farrand, *Records,* 1:235–237.

33. Richard J. Ellis, ed., *Founding the American Presidency* (Lanham, Md.: Rowman and Littlefield, 1999).

34. The New Jersey Plan can be found in Farrand, *Records,* 1:242–245.

35. Hamilton's Plan can be found in ibid., 1:291–293.

36. Ibid., 1:288.

37. Ibid., 1:289.

38. Ron Chernow, *Alexander Hamilton* (New York: Penguin Press, 2004), 232.

39. Clinton Rossiter dismisses this view in *Alexander Hamilton and the Constitution* (New York: Harcourt, Brace and World, 1964).

40. The Committee of Detail report can be found in Farrand, *Records,* 2:177–189.

41. See note 29.

42. The recommendations of the Committee on Postponed Matters can be found in Farrand, *Records,* 2:497–499, 508–509.

43. Richard Beeman, *Plain, Honest Men: The Making of the American Constitution* (New York: Random House, 2009), 342. James Wilson of Pennsylvania argued that any attempt to enumerate the rights of the people would necessarily be incomplete, posing the risk that "everything not expressly mentioned will be presumed to be purposely omitted" (343).

44. The Committee of Style draft can be found in ibid., 2:590–603.

45. The preamble it replaced was blander and more state-centered: "We the people of the states of New Hampshire, Massachusetts," etc.

46. Rakove, *Original Meanings,* 107.

47. Farrand, *Records,* 2:641–643.

CHAPTER 2

Creating the Presidency

D uring the course of the Constitutional Convention, the presidency developed along two main lines. First, the loosely designed executive of the Virginia Plan took on greater clarity and specificity. Second, the weak executive, which was subordinate to the legislature and initially seemed to be favored by most delegates, was made stronger. These two developments manifested themselves at the convention in a variety of specific issues of executive design. The issues included the number of the executive, the methods of executive selection and succession, the length and character of the term of office, the means of removing the executive in extraordinary circumstances, the institutional separation of the executive from the legislature, and the enumerated powers of the executive.

THE MAKING OF THE PRESIDENCY: AN OVERVIEW

The design of the executive was one of the most vexing problems of the Constitutional Convention, and solving it was the convention's most creative act. Other issues were more controversial, but they typically lent themselves to compromise solutions, such as the small states agreeing to split the difference with the large states and provide for a bicameral legislature and northern and southern delegates working out the three-fifths rule for counting slaves. When it came to the nature and powers of the executive, however, the delegates labored in a realm of such intellectual and political uncertainty that the politics of compromise was largely irrelevant. The result, although long in coming, was that "the presidency emerged not from the clash of wills to gain a long-contested point, but from a series of ingenious efforts to design a new institution that would be suitably energetic but safely republican."[1]

One problem the delegates encountered was that their experience offered several models of what they did not want in an executive but few models that they found attractive. The British monarch and the royal colonial governors had been, in their eyes, tramplers of liberty. The constitutions that the states wrote after independence provided for governors who were unthreatening but also weak to the point of impotence. The national government of the Articles of Confederation, such as it was, had no chief executive at all.

George Washington, hero of the American Revolution and presiding officer of the Constitutional Convention, was to many people the personification of the new republic and of the presidency.

A second problem that stymied the delegates derived from their general ambivalence about executive authority. They wanted an executive that was strong enough to enforce the law and check a runaway legislature, but not so strong as to become despotic. This ambivalence was shared by the American people, whose hatred of monarchy existed side by side with their longing to make George Washington king. As political scientist Seymour Martin Lipset has shown, Washington was a classic example of what the German sociologist Max Weber called a charismatic leader, one "treated as endowed with supernatural, superhuman, or at least specifically exceptional powers or qualities."[2] Historian Marcus Cunliffe records:

> Babies were being christened after him as early as 1775, and while he was still President, his countrymen paid to see him in waxwork effigy. To his admirers he was "godlike Washington," and his detractors complained to one another that he was looked upon as a "demigod" whom it was treasonous to criticize. "Oh Washington!" declared Ezra Stiles of Yale (in a sermon of 1783). "How I do love thy name! How have I often adored and blessed thy God, for creating and forming thee into the great ornament of humankind!"[3]

But the public's longing for Washington was just that: a longing for Washington, not for a hereditary monarchy. As Stanley Elkins and Eric McKitrick have pointed out, Washington's wide-ranging responsibilities as commander in chief during the Revolutionary War meant that "he had in a certain sense been acting as President of the United States since 1775."[4] Delegates and citizens alike knew that Washington would wield power responsibly and relinquish it voluntarily—he had already done so once. But would his successors? "The first man put at the helm will be a good one," Benjamin Franklin told the convention. "No body knows what sort may come afterwards."[5]

Despite the delegates' difficulties, the presidency gradually took shape as the convention wore on. For all their intellectual uncertainty, the delegates moved steadily in the direction of a more clearly defined executive. For all their ambivalence about power, they made the executive stronger than they were initially inclined to do.

GREATER CLARITY

Charles Thach noted in his classic book *The Creation of the Presidency* that Virginia delegate James Madison "has with much justice been called the father of the Constitution." But even as admiring a scholar as Thach conceded that "the claims for his paternity do not extend to the fundamentals of Article II."[6]

Madison himself claimed no role in creating the presidency. As he wrote to George Washington on April 16, 1787, less than a month before the scheduled opening of the convention, "I have scarcely ventured as yet to form my own opinion either of the manner in which [the executive] ought to be constituted or of the authorities with which it ought to be cloathed."[7] Madison's Virginia Plan offered the convention a shadowy and vaguely defined national executive. Even the basic structure of the executive—whether it would be a single person, a chaired board, or a committee—was unclear. In addition, the length of the executive's term was not specified, and its powers were not enumerated.[8]

Madison's fellow delegates seem to have shared his uncertainty. The only issues they resolved to their satisfaction during the convention's first two months were the unitary nature of the executive and its power to veto laws passed by the legislature, subject to override. The Committee of Detail, which began its work on July 24, helped matters some: it gave the executive the name *president,* provided for succession, and enumerated the powers of the office. But the main issues that divided the delegates—the president's selection, term, and reeligibility—were not resolved until September, when the Committee on Postponed Matters proposed selection by an Electoral College, a four-year term with no limit on eligibility for reelection, and the creation of the vice presidency.

GREATER STRENGTH

For all the vagueness of its conception, the national executive of the Virginia Plan generally accorded with what most delegates at the start of the Constitutional Convention seem to have been seeking: an agent of restraint in a basically legislative government. The executive in Madison's proposal was weak (it was bound by a council and devoid of enumerated powers), but it certainly was stronger than in the one-branch government of the Articles of Confederation. The executive also was subordinate to the legislature, which was empowered to elect it. But it was not subservient, as demonstrated by its fixed term, the veto power, and the bar on legislative reductions of the executive's salary.

Dissatisfied with the convention's early inclination toward a subordinate executive, a coterie of committed and talented delegates worked diligently and effectively to strengthen the office's constitutional power. They were led by two Pennsylvania delegates: James Wilson, who envisioned the executive as "the man of the people," and Gouverneur Morris, who regarded a properly constituted executive as "the great protector of the Mass of the people."[9] Although Wilson and Morris both favored a strong executive, they did so for different reasons. Morris thought that a strong executive would restrain public opinion.[10] Wilson thought that such an executive would enhance the influence of public opinion in government. Historian Richard Beeman accurately describes Wilson as the only delegate who envisioned presidents "much like those we have today—vigorous and powerful, but based firmly on the will of the people."[11] Despite these differences, during the course of the convention the pro-executive group won victory after victory. Once the architects of the Constitution had resolved to strengthen the national government—to create self government on a grand scale—they had no recourse, it seemed, but to attempt to reconcile popular government and an executive power.

NUMBER OF THE EXECUTIVE

The number of the executive was the first issue to rouse the delegates. The debate on number followed two tracks. First, should the executive be unitary or plural—that is, a single person or a board? Second, should the executive be forced to consult with a council before exercising some or all of its powers?

UNITARY OR PLURAL?

The Virginia Plan said nothing about the number of the executive, perhaps because Madison had no clear opinion on the matter or perhaps because, like Roger Sherman of Connecticut, he initially felt that the legislature should be free to define and then redefine the shape of the executive as it saw fit.

On June 1 the convention, meeting as the Committee of the Whole, heard a motion from Wilson that the executive be a single person. According to Madison's notes, "a considerable pause ensu[ed]" as the usually talkative delegates lapsed into silence.[12] They were discomforted by the prospect of discussing the issue in the presence of George Washington, whom everyone assumed would be the leader of whatever executive branch they created.[13] After Franklin admonished his colleagues to speak freely, however, the debate was joined. The issue became an early test for the pro-executive delegates at the convention.

Edmund Randolph of Virginia and Sherman led the fight against Wilson's motion. Randolph, arguing that a single executive, by its nature, would be the "foetus of monarchy," proposed instead a three-person committee, with one member from each region of the country. Sherman, who regarded the ideal executive "as nothing more than an institution for carrying the will of the Legislature into effect," said he "wished the number might not be fixed, but that the legislature should be at liberty to appoint one or more as experience might dictate."[14] Franklin argued that the policies pursued by an executive board would be less easily changed, and therefore more stable and consistent, than those of an individual. In addition, he pointed out that the death or disability of an executive board member would not pose problems of succession, unlike the death or disability of a single executive.[15]

Wilson defended his motion shrewdly. To be sure, he argued, a single executive would be a source of "energy" and "dispatch"—that is, of consistent and timely action—in the new government. But Wilson also claimed that a single executive was indispensable to controlling executive power— how could responsibility for incompetence or abuses of power be assigned to a committee?[16] These arguments were persuasive to most delegates. They feared monarchy, but they also realized how much the national government had suffered under the Articles of Confederation from the diffuseness of executive responsibility. As property owners, they worried about threats to the social order such as Shays's Rebellion and regarded a single executive as more likely than a committee to respond quickly and effectively to riot and discord.

On June 4 the convention voted strongly for a unitary executive. One of Washington's few recorded votes was in favor of this motion. Washington's concern to unify executive responsibility was born of his experience as commander in chief of the revolutionary forces. Lacking clear administrative authority, even in the appointment of his own officers, he complained bitterly of having "power without the means of execution when these ought to be coequal at least."[17]On average, the most vocal proponents of a unitary executive were nearly fifteen years younger than the opponents. The reason for this discrepancy, political scientist Richard J. Ellis has argued, is that "the views of executive power of the older delegates were colored by their battles against the royal governors. The younger delegates who had come of age during the 1770s and 1780s were more worried about the weakness of executive power in the state constitutions and the Articles of Confederation."[18]

A COUNCIL?

The Virginia Plan provided that a "council of revision" consisting of the executive and "a convenient number of the National Judiciary" would be empowered to veto laws passed by the legislature. All thirteen state constitutions provided for councils of various sorts, most of which were legislatively selected. Sherman, who voted in the end for the single executive, said that he had done so only because he assumed it would be forced to share power with a council. Wilson, however, opposed a council, because he believed that such a body would dilute the virtues of the unitary executive—energy, dispatch, and responsibility.

The proposal for a council was tabled on June 4 after two Massachusetts delegates, Elbridge Gerry and Rufus King, injected a new argument into the debate. Gerry and King questioned the wisdom of having judges participate in making laws on which they later would be asked to rule. Delegates also wondered what effect a council would have on executive power. Some saw it as a check on the executive, but others, including Madison, thought a council would buttress the executive with the support of the judiciary, thereby strengthening it in its relations with the legislature.

The council idea recurred in several guises throughout the convention. Morris and others tried to persuade the delegates to enact a purely advisory council, consisting mainly of the heads of the executive departments.[19] As late as September 7, George Mason of Virginia suggested that the House of Representatives or the Senate be charged to appoint an executive council with members from all regions of the country. "The Grand Signor himself had his Divan," Mason noted, drawing from Ottoman history.[20] But because no consensus ever formed about either the wisdom of having a council or the form it should take, the idea was abandoned.

SELECTION AND SUCCESSION

Wilson was as much opposed to the clause in the Virginia Plan that provided for the executive "to be chosen by the National Legislature" as he was in favor of a unitary executive. Legislative selection would make the executive a creature of (and therefore subservient to) the legislature, Wilson believed. On June 1 he proposed instead that the executive be elected by the people. Wilson said he realized that his idea "might appear chimerical," but he could think of no better way to keep the executive and legislative branches "as independent as possible of each other, as well as of the states."[21]

The delegates dismissed Wilson's proposal for popular election. To some, the idea was just too democratic. (They thought democracy was suited only for small communities.) In addition, by requiring voters to pass judgment on candidates from distant states of whom they knew little or nothing, popular election seemed impractical. Mason stated both of these objections cogently: "It would be as unnatural to refer the choice of a proper character for chief Magistrate to the people, as it would, to refer a trial of colours to a blind man."[22] Speaking on behalf of the southern delegates, Madison added a more overtly political point: in direct elections candidates from the more populous North almost always would win.[23]

Undiscouraged, Wilson returned to the convention on June 2 with a proposal for an Electoral College to select the executive. For purposes of election, each state would be divided into a few districts. The voters in these districts would choose electors, who in turn would gather at a central location to choose the executive. A plan similar to Wilson's was accepted in principle on July 19 and ultimately was adopted in September. But in the early days of the convention it still seemed too novel.[24] Delegates feared the mischief that might ensue, perhaps instigated by agents of foreign governments, when the electors met. They also doubted whether "men of the 1st nor even of the 2d. grade" would be willing to serve as electors.[25] The delegates voted instead to affirm the legislative selection provision of the Virginia Plan.

The convention's decision to adopt legislative selection of the executive, although it was reaffirmed in several votes taken in July and August, was not a happy one. The source of the unhappiness was that, in the delegates' minds, a legislatively selected executive could not be allowed to stand for reelection lest executive powers and patronage be used, in effect, to bribe legislators for their votes. But the delegates also believed that eligibility for reelection was a valuable incentive to good performance in office and regretted that legislative selection ruled out executive reeligibility. The result was an ongoing search for a selection process that was desirable in its own right and allowed for reelection. This was no easy task. In the memorable description of political scientist Robert A. Dahl, "The Convention twisted and turned like a man tormented in his sleep by a bad dream as it tried to decide."[26] Of the ideas the delegates considered and rejected, wrote Clinton Rossiter, some were rather far-fetched:

> election by the state governors or by electors chosen by them, neither a scheme that could muster any support; nomination by the people of each state of "its best citizen," and election from this pool of thirteen by the national legislature or electors chosen by it, an unhelpful proposal of John Dickinson; election by the national legislature, with electors chosen by the state legislatures taking over whenever an executive sought reelection, a proposal of [Oliver] Ellsworth that found favor with four states; and, most astounding of all, election by a small group of national legislators chosen "by lot."[27]

The search for an alternative to legislative selection became more urgent after August 24. Until that day, no consideration had been given to how the legislature was to choose the president. Now, by a vote of seven states to four, the convention approved a motion that Congress would elect the president by a "joint ballot" of all the members of the House of Representatives and Senate, following the practice most states used to elect their governors. This decision, by giving the large states a clear majority in the presidential selection process, threatened to reignite the controversy between large and small states that had already split the convention once. To avert this catastrophe, Sherman, the author of the Connecticut Compromise between the large and small states on legislative apportionment, moved on August 31 to refer the whole issue of presidential selection to the Committee on Postponed Matters.

On September 4 the committee proposed the Electoral College as a method to elect the president, with no restriction on the president's right to seek reelection. The president would be selected by a majority vote of the electors, who would be chosen by the states using whatever methods each state decided to adopt. (The delegates expected that in time most states would entrust the selection of electors to the people.[28]) Every state would receive electoral votes equal in number to its representation in Congress. If no presidential candidate won the votes of a majority of electors, the Senate would elect the president from among the five highest electoral vote recipients. To prevent a cabal from forming in the Electoral College, electors would never meet as a national body—instead, they would vote in their state capitals and then send the results to the Senate for counting. Finally, to ensure that the electors would not simply support a variety of home-state favorites, each was required to vote for two candidates for president from two different states (an idea first proposed by Gouverneur Morris on July 25), with the runner-up in the presidential election filling the newly created office of vice president.

The proposal for an Electoral College was generally well received by the delegates. As political scientist Andrew Rudalevige has noted, "The Electoral College [was] very much a salesman's straddle, allowing proponents of popular election and legislative selection both to tout its provisions."[29] Fred Barbash has listed several ways in which the proposal was "baited" with something for virtually every group at the convention:

> For those in the convention anxious for the President to be allowed reelection, the committee made him eligible without limit.
>
> For those worried about excessive dependence of the President on the national legislature, the committee determined that electors chosen as each state saw fit would cast ballots for the presidency.
>
> For the large states and the South, the committee decided that the number of electors would be proportioned according to each state's combined representation in the House and Senate. . . .
>
> For the small states, the committee determined that when no candidate won a majority of electoral votes, the Senate would choose the president from among the leading contenders.[30]

Only one aspect of the proposed Electoral College proved controversial among the delegates: Senate selection of the president in the absence of an Electoral College majority for any candidate. Large-state delegates objected because the Senate underrepresented them in favor of the small states. Moreover, not foreseeing the development of a two-party system, some delegates believed that after Washington (the obvious choice as the first president), majorities seldom would form in the Electoral College and the Senate would choose most presidents. George Mason estimated that the Electoral College would fail to reach a majority "nineteen times in twenty."[31]

Sherman proposed what historian Carol Berkin has called "a brilliant solution": let the House of Representatives elect the president if the Electoral College failed to produce a majority, but assign each state's House delegation a single vote.[32] The Senate would still choose the vice president in the event of a tie vote. Quickly, on September 6, the convention agreed.

One issue that the creation of the vice presidency resolved, at least partially, was what would happen if the president died, resigned, became disabled, or was impeached and removed. The Committee of Detail was the first to deal with the matter. It recommended that the president of the Senate "discharge the powers and duties of [the Presidency] . . . until another President of the United States be chosen, or until the disability of the President be ended." When Madison and other delegates objected that this proposal might give the Senate an incentive to remove the president in favor of one of its own members, the issue was referred to the Committee on Postponed Matters.

The committee proposed that the vice president, not a senator, be president of the Senate. It also designated the vice president as the person to step in if a vacancy occurs in the presidency. The convention agreed, but only after passing an additional motion, discussed later in this chapter, that seemed to call for a special presidential election before the expiration of the departed president's term. Somehow this intention was lost when the Committee of Style wrote its final draft of the Constitution. No one caught the error. As a result, the convention left the Constitution vague on two important matters. First, in the event of the president's death, resignation, disability, or removal, did the vice president become president or merely assume the powers and duties of the presidency? Second, would the vice president serve out the unexpired balance of the president's term or only fill in until a special election could be held to pick a new president?

TERM OF OFFICE

Questions about length of term, eligibility for reelection, and selection were so interwoven in the minds of the delegates that they could not resolve any one of them without resolving the others. Indeed, one political scientist has compared their efforts to sort out these questions to a game of "three-dimensional chess."[33]

The Virginia Plan left the length of the executive's term of office blank— literally: "Resolved, that a National Executive be . . . chosen by the National Legislature for the term of ———— years." The plan also stipulated that the executive was "to be ineligible a second time." When these provisions came before the Committee of the Whole on June 1, a variety of alternatives were proposed, including a three-year term with no limit on reeligibility, a three-year term with two reelections allowed, and a seven-year term with no reeligibility at all. Although the delegates approved the single seven-year term, the vote was close, five states to four.

Underlying the delegates' uncertainty was the relationship between two aspects of the executive that they eventually came to regard as incompatible: eligibility for reelection and legislative selection. Mason explained why the Constitution could not include both: if the legislature could reelect the executive, there would be a constant "temptation on the side of the Executive to intrigue with the Legislature for a re-appointment," using political patronage and illegitimate favors to buy legislators' votes.[34]

Nevertheless, on July 17 the convention voted for both legislative selection and reeligibility. When James McClurg of Virginia pointed out the contradiction between these two decisions, the one-term limit on the executive was reinstated. McClurg, supported by Morris and by Jacob Broom of Delaware, offered a different way out of the dilemma: election of the executive by the legislature for a life term. But this proposal smacked too much of monarchy to suit the other delegates.

On July 24 and 26 the convention voted again to have the legislature select the executive for a single seven-year term. But the advantages the delegates saw in reeligibility were so powerful that the issue remained alive. Reeligibility would allow the nation to keep a good executive in office and give the executive what Morris called "the great motive to good behavior, the hope of being rewarded with a re-appointment."[35] As Alexander Hamilton later argued in *Federalist* No. 72, even an executive whose behavior was governed by personal motives such as "avarice," "ambition," or "the love of fame" would do a good job in order to hold on to the office that could fulfill those desires.[36] More ominously, Morris warned: "Shut the Civil road to Glory & he may be compelled to seek it by the sword."[37]

To complicate their task further, the delegates' choice between legislative selection and reeligibility implied a related decision between a short term and a long term. If the executive were chosen by the legislature for a single term only, the delegates believed, the term should be long. If the executive were eligible for reelection, it should be short.

In late August the convention changed course for the last time. Effectively deciding against legislative selection of the president, the delegates created the Committee on Postponed Matters to propose an alternative. The committee's recommendation, adopted by the convention, was that the Electoral College choose the president for a four-year term, with no limit on reeligibility.

REMOVAL

As the convention unfolded, the delegates realized they should provide for situations in which the executive had to be removed from office before the four-year term expired. Serious abuse of power was one such situation, and the remedy was impeachment. Disability was the other but, even at convention's end, the delegates were less than clear about what ought to happen if the executive became disabled.

IMPEACHMENT

Impeachment, a traditional practice of the British political system, has deep historical roots. During the seventeenth century, as Richard Ellis has written, impeachment of the king's ministers and councilors by the House of Commons, with trial by the House of Lords, "became a tool in Parliament's struggle to rein in the power of the monarchy and to make ministers of the Crown accountable to Parliament."[38] In the eighteenth century, when the House of Commons gained the power to force ministers to resign after a vote of no confidence, impeachment waned in importance. But the tradition of executive accountability remained.

Although the Virginia Plan made no detailed provision for impeaching the executive (it merely said that the "supreme tribunal" would "hear and determine . . . impeachments of any National officers"), most of the delegates agreed that some mechanism should be included in the Constitution. Even proponents of a strong executive realized that their goal could be achieved only if the other delegates were assured that an out-of-control president could be removed from office.

The convention's consensus on impeachment became apparent on June 2, when the Committee of the Whole passed North Carolina delegate Hugh Williamson's motion that the executive be "removable on impeachment and conviction of malpractice or neglect of duty."[39] (Impeachment is analogous to indictment by a grand jury; it must be followed by a trial and conviction for the impeached official to be removed from office.) The consensus was confirmed and strengthened on July 19, when Gouverneur Morris suggested that if the executive were assigned a short term of office, there would be no need for impeachment—the passage of time would lead to the executive's removal soon enough. Morris was answered the next day by Gerry, Randolph, Franklin, and Mason, all of whom made clear that they regarded impeachment not only as a vital safeguard against and punishment for abuses of power, but also (at least in Franklin's view) as a way to remove tyrants without having to resort to assassination. Morris retreated, declaring that he was persuaded by his colleagues' arguments.

The Committee of Detail tried to clarify Williamson's definition of the grounds for presidential impeachment, changing it from the vague "malpractice or neglect of duty" to the more specific "treason, bribery, or corruption." It also created a mechanism for removal: "impeachment by the House of Representatives and conviction in the Supreme Court." The convention did not take up the impeachment provision of the committee's report until

August 27, when Morris asked that it be tabled. He argued that if, as still seemed possible, the convention decided to create a council of revision for the president that included the chief justice of the United States, the Court should not be involved in the impeachment process. The delegates agreed to Morris's motion without objection. Later that week, on August 31, the Committee on Postponed Matters was formed and took charge of the impeachment issue.

The committee made its three-part recommendation on September 4: first, impeachment by the House; second, trial by the Senate, with the chief justice presiding; and third, impeachment and conviction on grounds of treason or bribery, but not the broad offense of "corruption." On September 8 Mason complained that to bar only treason and bribery "will not reach many great and dangerous offenses," including certain "attempts to subvert the Constitution." Drawing from the constitutions of six states, including his own state of Virginia, Mason proposed that "maladministration" be added to the list of impeachable actions.[40] After Madison objected that in practice maladministration would mean nothing more than unpopularity with Congress, Mason moved to substitute "other high crimes and misdemeanors," a term from fourteenth-century English common law that referred to serious abuses of constitutional authority. This definition passed, despite Madison's continuing objection to its breadth.

The delegates made three other modifications to the committee's impeachment proposal on September 8. The majority required for Senate conviction was raised to two-thirds. The vice president and "all civil officers of the United States" were made subject to impeachment in the same way as the president. Finally, to remind senators that they should vote impartially, the delegates decided that "they shall be on Oath or Affirmation" during impeachment trials.

DISABILITY

Although the delegates were thorough and deliberate in considering the grounds for and process of impeachment, they treated presidential disability cavalierly. The matter was first put before the convention on August 6 as part of a provision of the Committee of Detail report that dealt mainly with succession. It read: "In the case of his . . . disability to discharge the powers and duties of his office, the President of the Senate shall exercise those powers and duties, until another President of the United States be chosen, or until the disability of the President be removed."

On August 27, when this provision of the committee's report came before the convention, John Dickinson of Delaware complained that "it was too vague. What is the extent of the term 'disability' & who is to be the judge of it?"[41] The delegates decided to postpone their discussion of disability until another time, presumably intending to supply answers to these questions. But that time never came. Disability was left undefined in the Constitution, and no process was created either to determine if a president is disabled or to transfer the powers and duties of the presidency to a successor. Instead, the Committee on Postponed Matters merely named the vice president, rather than the president of the Senate, as the successor to a disabled president and substituted "inability" for "disability," without explaining what difference, if any, this substitution made.

INSTITUTIONAL SEPARATION FROM CONGRESS

Many of the delegates were strongly influenced by the idea that, to preserve liberty, government should incorporate the principle of separation of powers. Various political philosophers of the Enlightenment, including England's John Locke, had articulated this idea, but no version was more familiar to the delegates than that of French writer Baron de Montesquieu. As the author of *L'Esprit des lois* (The Spirit of the Laws) in 1748, Montesquieu was "the oracle who is always consulted and cited" on the subject of separation of powers, wrote Madison in *Federalist* No. 47. One passage in Montesquieu's book, which the delegates knew well and Madison quoted, stated: "When the legislative and executive powers are united in the same person or body, there can be no liberty because apprehensions may arise lest *the same* monarch or senate should enact *tyrannical laws to execute* them in a tyrannical manner. . . . Were the power of judging joined with the legislative, the life and liberty of the subject would be exposed to arbitrary control, for *the judge* would then be *the legislator.*"[42]

As applied in the Constitution, the separation of powers principle did not require a strict division of labor in which each branch of the government was assigned complete and exclusive power to perform certain functions. Indeed, the Constitution assigns few powers to the federal government that are not shared by two or more branches. To the delegates, separation of powers actually meant something more like "separated institutions sharing powers"—that is, a separation in which the membership of one branch does not overlap and cannot dominate another.[43]

From the beginning, the convention imposed two prohibitions to preserve institutional separation within the government. The first banned alterations in the incumbent executive's salary. The second forbade simultaneous membership in the legislative and executive branches. Both prohibitions were in the Virginia Plan and remained substantially unaltered in the final Constitution.

SALARY

Immediately after the clause stating that the executive shall be chosen by the legislature, the Virginia Plan provided that the executive shall "receive punctually at stated times, a fixed compensation for the services rendered, in which no increase or diminution shall be made so as to affect the Magistracy existing at the time of increase or diminution." In view of the Virginia Plan's brevity and generality, the level of detail in this provision is remarkable, as is the priority Madison assigned to it. Clearly, Madison feared that the legislature might either infringe on executive independence by lowering the executive's salary or reward or entice the executive by increasing the salary.

During the course of the convention, the provision for executive salary was modified only slightly. The delegates eventually added a stipulation that "he shall not receive within [his term of office] any other Emolument from the United States, or any of them." On June 2 Franklin urged that the executive not be compensated at all. To attach a salary to the position, Franklin said, "united in view of the same object" two "passions which have a powerful influence on the affairs of such men. These are ambition and avarice, the love of power, and the love of money. . . . Place before the eyes of men a post of *honor* that shall be at the same time a place of *profit,* and they will move heaven and earth to obtain it."[44] The delegates gave Franklin's words courteous attention but no more. Their concern was to protect the executive from the legislature, not to create an office that only the rich could afford to occupy.

MEMBERSHIP

The delegates' commitment to separating membership in Congress from the executive branch did not waver. The Virginia Plan said that legislators were "ineligible to any office established by a particular State, or under the authority of the United States, except those peculiarly belonging to the functions of the first branch [the legislature], during the term of service, and for the space of ———— after its expiration." The final document, although lifting the restriction on legislators holding executive office after they left Congress, included essentially the same provision: "no Person holding any Office under the United States, shall be a Member of either House during his Continuance in Office." The Constitution also prohibited members of Congress from serving as electors in presidential elections.

The delegates wanted to keep the membership of the legislative and executive branches separate to prevent the executive from, in effect, bribing members of Congress with jobs and salaries. On June 22 Pierce Butler of South Carolina, supported by Mason, "appealed to the example of G[reat] B[ritain] where men got into Parl[iamen]t, that they might get offices for themselves or their friends. This was the source of corruption that ruined their Govt."[45] On

June 23 Butler added: "To some of the opposers he [George III] gave pensions—others offices, and some, to put them out of the house of commons, he made lords. The great Montesquieu says, it is unwise to entrust persons with power, which by being abused operates to the advantage of those entrusted with it."

The office-holding issue was raised again on August 14, when John Mercer of Maryland took the opposite side of the question. He argued that because "governments can only be maintained by *force* or *influence*" and the president lacks force, to "deprive him of influence by rendering the members of the Legislature ineligible to Executive offices" would reduce the president to "a mere phantom of authority."[46] Unpersuaded, the delegates did not alter their earlier decision, either then or on September 3, when Wilson and Charles Pinckney argued that honorable people would be reluctant to serve in the new government if the constitutional presumption was that they were too corrupt to fulfill faithfully the responsibilities of more than one office.[47]

Nothing was said during the convention about judges holding executive offices. The New Jersey Plan would have prohibited them from doing so, but the subject never was discussed on the convention floor. Indeed, most of the proposals that delegates made for a council of revision included one or more federal judges as members. Political scientist Robert Scigliano has argued that allowing judges to hold executive office was not an oversight on the delegates' part. Instead, they regarded the executive and judicial powers as joined because both involved carrying out the law. According to Scigliano, the delegates also believed that Congress would be the most powerful branch in the new government unless the executive and the judiciary could unite when necessary to restrain it.[48]

ENUMERATED POWERS

The convention was slow to enumerate the powers of either the presidency or the other branches of the government. Indeed, the delegates' initial inclination seems to have been to give each branch a general grant of power rather than a specific list. The Virginia Plan empowered the legislature simply "to legislate in all cases to which the separate states are incompetent, or in which the harmony of the United States may be interrupted by the exercise of individual [state] Legislation." The executive, in addition to sharing the veto with a council, was to execute the national laws.

The advantage the delegates saw in a general grant of powers (which they approved both while meeting as the Committee of the Whole and soon afterward in convention) was that the alternative, a specific enumeration, risked limiting the government to a list of powers that the passage of time would render obsolete. But the convention was uneasy with its choice. "Incompetent" was a vague word, easily subject to abuse, and so was any other word or phrase they might devise for a general grant.

Reading the delegates' mood, the Committee of Detail enumerated each branch's powers in the draft constitution that it presented to the convention. The delegates' reaction confirmed the committee's judgment. Although they debated each proposed power separately, they never questioned the decision to enumerate.

All the powers of the presidency are detailed in Article II of the Constitution except the veto power, which is in Article I, section 7. The powers are discussed below in the order they appear in the Constitution. So are three other provisions of Article II: the president's title, oath of office, and qualifications.

VETO

The right to veto acts passed by the legislature was the only specific grant of power to the executive proposed in the Virginia Plan. The states' recent experience with weak governors and powerful legislatures was proof enough to most delegates that the veto was indispensable to executive self-defense against legislative encroachments. Even so, they were initially reluctant to cede too much responsibility to the executive.

The Virginia Plan provided that the executive could cast a veto only with the cooperation of a council of judges. Madison believed that support from such a council would buttress the executive's willingness to cast vetoes. He based this belief on the contrasting experiences of New York, where the governor alone had the veto power and almost never used it, and Massachusetts, where council-supported governors vetoed bills freely.[49] The plan also stipulated that a vetoed act would become law if an unspecified majority of both houses of the legislature voted to override it.

On June 4 Wilson and Hamilton urged the delegates, then meeting as the Committee of the Whole, to grant the executive an absolute veto—that is, a veto not subject to legislative override. Franklin, Sherman, Mason, and others rose in opposition to this suggestion, invoking their own and the public's memories of the British king and his royal governors, who had cast absolute vetoes against acts passed by colonial legislatures. "We are not indeed constituting a British Government, but a more dangerous monarchy, an elective one," warned Mason, who wanted to empower the executive merely to postpone the enactment of an offensive law in the hope that the legislature would decide to revise it.[50] Elbridge Gerry found a middle ground that was acceptable to most of the delegates: an executive veto, subject to override by a two-thirds vote of each house of the legislature. The recommendation that the executive share the veto power with a council was tabled.

In its report of August 6 the Committee of Detail, although faithfully reflecting the decisions of the Committee of the Whole on the veto, also sought to settle an unresolved issue. The committee stipulated that after a bill was passed and presented, the president would have seven days in which to respond. If the president neither signed nor vetoed the bill during that week, it would become law. But the committee made an important exception to prevent Congress from getting its way by adjourning before the president had a chance to cast a veto. If Congress adjourned during the seven-day period, the president had merely to ignore the bill in order for it to be vetoed. Such vetoes later became known as "pocket vetoes."

On August 15 and 16 the convention voted to modify the Committee of Detail's report in ways that strengthened the president's veto power. The two-thirds requirement for congressional override of a veto was raised to three-fourths. In addition, the period in which a president could cast a veto was lengthened from seven days to ten days, not including Sundays. Finally, to prevent Congress from evading a veto by passing legislation and calling it something other than a "bill," the veto power was extended to "every order, resolution, or vote" of Congress.

Only one further modification was made in the veto. On September 12, in a gesture designed to persuade delegates suspicious of presidential power to sign the Constitution, the convention voted to make veto overrides easier by restoring the two-thirds requirement.

"THE EXECUTIVE POWER"

The Virginia Plan introduced the executive article by stating "that a national Executive be instituted." The Committee of the Whole modified this provision of the plan by adding "to consist of a single person." The Committee of Detail, however, proposed "vesting" clauses for all three branches of government:

> The legislative power shall be vested in a Congress. . . .
>
> The Executive Power of the United States shall be vested in a single person. His stile shall be, "The President of the United States of America," and his title shall be, "His Excellency."
>
> The Judicial Power of the United States shall be vested in one Supreme Court, and in such inferior courts as shall, when necessary, from time to time, be constituted by the Legislature of the United States.

The vesting clause that the Committee of Detail proposed for the president was particularly important because it made clear that the powers of the presidency derive directly from the Constitution, not from discretionary grants by Congress. But the clause was less instructive on another important aspect of presidential power. As political scientist Richard M. Pious has noted, " 'Executive Power' was a general term, sufficiently ambiguous so that no one could say precisely what it meant. It was possible that the words referred to more than the enumerated powers that followed, and might confer a set of unspecified executive powers."[51] First among these unspecified powers was prerogative, which philosopher John Locke had discussed at length in a book that was widely familiar among the delegates, *Second Treatise of Government*. Locke had argued that in times of crisis laws that were inadequate to the challenges at hand should temporarily "give way to the executive power, viz., that as much as may be, all the members of society are to be preserved." Prerogative, according to Locke, was "the people's permitting their rulers to do several things of their own free choice, where the law was silent, or sometimes, too, against the direct letter of the law, for the public good, and their acquiescing in it when so done."[52]

The theory that the powers of the presidency extend beyond those listed in the Constitution is supported by the language of the document itself, thanks to a "joker," as Charles Thach has called it, that Morris, the chief drafter for the Committee of Style, tossed into the final version. The committee's charge was merely to put the Constitution into polished language. "Positively with respect to the executive article," noted Thach, Morris "could do nothing." His pro-executive biases were so well known that any changes would have been quickly detected. Morris left the vesting clause for the presidency unaltered ("the executive Power shall be vested in a President of the United States of America"), but he changed the vesting clause for Congress to read: "All legislative Powers *herein granted* shall be vested in a Congress of the United States" (emphasis added).

Thach suspects that Morris did his tinkering "with full realization of the possibilities"—that is, presidents could later claim that the different phrasing of the two branches' vesting clauses implies that there are executive powers beyond those "herein granted." Otherwise, why would the Constitution not apply those restricting words to the president in the same way it does to Congress? "At any rate," Thach concluded, "whether intentional or not, it [the difference between the two vesting clauses] admitted an interpretation of executive power which would give the president a field of activity wider than that outlined by the enumerated powers."[53]

COMMANDER IN CHIEF

Because the Virginia Plan said nothing about who would direct the armed forces, the delegates took it for granted during the early stages of the convention that Congress would be the controlling branch, as it had been under the Articles of Confederation. The issue did not come up for debate in the Committee of the Whole. The Committee of Detail, however, suggested a military role for the president in its enumeration of the powers of each branch.

The committee proposed that the president "shall be commander in chief of the Army and Navy of the United States, and of the Militia of the several States." But it also recommended that Congress be empowered "to make war; to raise armies; to build and equip fleets; to call forth the aid of the militia, in order to execute the laws of the Union; enforce treaties; suppress insurrections, and repel invasions." The meaning of these provisions confused the delegates when they took them up for consideration on August 17. Clearly, Congress's power to "make" war included directing the actual conduct of the fighting, but so did the president's power as "commander in chief of the Army and the Navy." Which branch would actually order soldiers and sailors into action? Which would tell them where to go and what to do when they got there?

The debate on the convention floor about the powers of war was brief and went only part way toward resolving the ambiguities created by the Committee of Detail. Pierce Butler, doubting that Congress would be able to act quickly enough on military matters if an urgent need should arise, urged the convention to vest the power to make war in the president, "who will have all the requisite qualities, and will not make war but when the Nation will support it." Madison and Gerry agreed that Congress might be unable to respond to foreign invasions promptly, perhaps because it was not in session. But, unwilling to entrust the president with such vast military powers, they "moved to insert 'declare' [war], striking out 'make' war; leaving to the Executive the power to repel sudden attacks." Sherman agreed: "The Executive shd. be able to repel and not to commence war." [54] Madison and Gerry's motion passed.

As for control of the various state militia, on August 27 the convention approved without discussion a motion by Sherman that the president act as commander in chief of the militia only "when called into the actual service of the U.S." The clause as finally written in the Constitution reads: "The President shall be Commander in Chief of the Army and Navy of the United States, and of the Militia of the several States, when called into the actual Service of the United States."

"REQUIRE THE OPINION"

The Constitution authorizes the president to "require the Opinion, in writing, of the principal Officer in each of the executive Departments, upon any Subject relating to the Duties of their respective Offices." [55] This curious provision (Hamilton described it in *Federalist* No. 74 "as a mere redundancy in the plan, as the right for which it provides would result of itself from the office" [56]) was proposed on September 4 by the Committee on Postponed Matters and adopted by a unanimous vote on September 7. But the clause's origin lay in the Virginia Plan's proposal for an executive council, an idea that recurred frequently during the convention.

Although most delegates seem to have favored some sort of council, they never created one because they held such varied opinions about who should be on it and whether its relationship to the president should be merely advisory or involve the shared exercise of executive powers. One version of the council idea was included in a sweeping plan for the organization of the executive branch that Gouverneur Morris and Charles Pinckney introduced on August 20. The Morris-Pinckney plan provided for the creation of five departments: domestic affairs, commerce and finance, foreign affairs, war, and marine. The "principal officers" of each department would be appointed by the president and serve at the president's pleasure. Together with the chief justice of the United States, they would constitute a Council of State whose purpose would be to "assist the President in conducting the Public affairs. . . . The President may from time to time submit any matter to the discussion of the Council of State, and *he may require the written opinions of any one or more of the members:* But he shall in all cases exercise his own judgment, and either Conform to such opinions or not as he may think proper; and every officer abovementioned shall be responsible for his opinion on the affairs relating to his particular Department" (emphasis added).[57]

The Morris-Pinckney plan was not debated by the delegates, but the proposal to empower the president to require written opinions from individual department heads on matters relating to their responsibilities seems to have been the basis for the September 4 recommendation of the Committee on Postponed Matters. Although on September 7 Mason, Franklin, Wilson, Dickinson, and Madison again urged that a council be created, their colleagues, frustrated by their inability to agree on a specific proposal and eager to conclude the convention's business, approved the committee's recommendation as written.

PARDON

Alexander Hamilton was the first delegate to suggest that the delegates grant the president the power to pardon criminals. In his long speech to the convention on June 18, he urged that the executive "have the power of pardoning all offences except Treason; which he shall not pardon without the approbation of the Senate."[58] Perhaps persuaded by Hamilton's proposal, the Committee of Detail recommended that the president "shall have power to grant reprieves and pardons; but his pardon shall not be pleadable in bar of an impeachment" (that is, to prevent an impeachment).

The pardon power is a power of kings. In Great Britain all crimes were regarded as offenses against the Crown. Accordingly, the power to forgive was a royal prerogative. Crimes in the United States were regarded as offenses against the law, not the executive, which is why no state constitution allowed governors a unilateral pardon power.[59]

It is therefore remarkable that the delegates resisted efforts to modify the committee's recommendation in any substantial way. Sherman's August 25 motion to require the president to gain the Senate's consent for a pardon was defeated by a vote of eight states to one. Two days later Luther Martin of Maryland moved to allow pardons only "after conviction." He withdrew the motion when Wilson, using the crime of forgery as an example, objected that "pardon before conviction might be necessary in order to obtain the testimony of accomplices." On September 12 the Committee of Style clarified one aspect of the pardon power by limiting it to "offences against the United States"—that is, to violations of federal rather than state law. A September 15 motion by Randolph to disallow pardons for treason ("The President may himself be guilty. The Traytors may be his own instruments.") was defeated by a vote of eight states to two after Wilson argued that if the president "be himself a party to the guilt he can be impeached and prosecuted."[60] The pardon entered the Constitution as the president's only unchecked power.

Although no thorough case for granting the pardon power to the president was ever offered at the convention, Hamilton's defense of it in *Federalist* No. 74 may reflect the delegates' thinking. Hamilton began by pleading the need for leeway in the criminal justice system to "make exceptions in favor of unfortunate guilt." As to pardons for treason, he wrote, perhaps with Shays's Rebellion in mind, "The principal argument for reposing the power of pardoning in this case in the Chief Magistrate is this: in seasons of insurrection or rebellion there are often critical moments when a well-timed offer of pardon to the insurgents or rebels may restore the tranquility of the commonwealth; and which, if suffered to pass unimproved, it may never be possible afterwards to recall."[61]

"MAKE TREATIES"

At the start of the convention, most delegates seemed to assume that the power to make treaties with other countries would be vested in Congress. That had been the practice under the Articles of Confederation and, although the Virginia Plan said nothing specific about treaties, it did provide that "the National Legislature ought to be impowered to enjoy the Legislative Rights vested in Congress by the Confederation."

The first suggestion that the treaty power be shared between the legislative and executive branches came from Hamilton. One provision of the plan of government he proposed on June 18 was that the executive should "have with the approbation and advice of the Senate the power of making all treaties."[62] The delegates did not discuss Hamilton's suggestion on the convention floor, and it appeared to be dead when the August 6 report of the Committee of Detail provided instead that "the Senate shall have power to make treaties."

The committee's proposal sparked heated debate, much of it spawned by changes in the design of the Senate that had occurred during the convention.

The conclave of national statesmen envisioned by the Virginia Plan had become a states-dominated body, a smaller and perhaps more easily manipulated version of the Continental Congress.[63] Mason argued that an exclusive treaty-making power would enable the Senate to "sell the whole country by means of treaties."[64] Madison thought that the president, who would represent the entire country, should make treaties. Regional concerns also were expressed. Southern delegates worried that their states' right to free navigation of the Mississippi River might be surrendered in a treaty. New Englanders expressed similar fears about their right to fish in the waters near Newfoundland. Having reached an impasse, the delegates referred the treaty issue to the Committee on Postponed Matters.

On September 4 the committee recommended that the president, "with the advice and Consent of the Senate," be granted the treaty-making power and that no treaty be approved "without the consent of two-thirds of the members [of the Senate] present." The provision for a two-thirds vote, which was designed to assuage the separate concerns of southerners and New Englanders that they would be outnumbered on issues of regional importance, was highly controversial and provoked numerous motions to revise. One proposal would have deleted the two-thirds requirement for ratification in favor of a simple majority. Another would have strengthened the requirement by stipulating two-thirds approval by the entire membership of the Senate, not just those who were present for the vote. Another would have included the House of Representatives in the treaty ratification process. Yet another proposal— which initially passed and then was rejected—would have applied the simple majority rule to treaties whose purpose was to conclude a war. In the end, however, the committee's recommendation of a two-thirds vote of the senators present was accepted.

The proposal to involve the president with senators in treaty making was relatively uncontroversial, reflecting the occasional alliance between pro-executive delegates and small-state delegates that had formed after the convention decided that the states would be represented equally in the Senate. Only one motion was made to modify the president's role: Madison moved to allow two-thirds of the Senate, acting alone if it chose to do so, to conclude peace treaties. Madison worried that the president, who inevitably would derive unusual power and prominence from a state of war, might be tempted to "impede a treaty of peace." His motion failed when Nathaniel Gorham of Massachusetts pointed out that Congress could end a war by simply refusing to appropriate funds to continue the fighting.[65]

APPOINTMENT AND COMMISSIONING

Article II, section 2, of the Constitution provides three methods for appointing federal judges and other unelected government officials: presidential appointment with Senate confirmation (the ordinary method); presidential appointment without Senate confirmation (when the Senate is in recess); and, when Congress so determines by statute, appointment of certain "inferior Officers" (that is, officers subordinate to the heads of the departments or the courts of law) by the department heads or the courts. Clearly, the delegates had moved a long way from both the Articles of Confederation, which vested the appointment power entirely in Congress, and the Virginia Plan, which proposed to continue that practice.

The appointment power was one of the first, last, and (in between) most contentious issues at the convention. Although, as Richard Ellis has shown, no delegate doubted that "it was the legislature and not the executive that should have the power to create offices, there the agreement ended."[66] On June 1 the delegates, meeting as the Committee of the Whole, approved Madison's motion to modify the Virginia Plan slightly by adding to the then-limited powers of the executive the ambiguous phrase "to appoint to offices in cases not otherwise provided for."[67] But this decision simply opened the door to stronger advocates of executive power, such as Wilson and Hamilton, who wanted to make the appointment of judges, ambassadors, and other government officials a purely executive responsibility, with no involvement at all by the legislature.

Heated debate erupted periodically in June and July about issues such as which branch of government would be most prone to favoritism in appointments and which would know best the qualifications of prospective appointees. Many delegates, mindful of how George III and his royal governors in the colonies had used government appointments as patronage plums to curry support among legislators, dreaded giving this power to even a home-grown executive.

On July 21 the delegates voted to confer on the Senate sole responsibility for judicial appointments. The Committee of Detail added the appointment of ambassadors to the Senate's list of powers, and then stipulated that Congress as a whole should elect the national treasurer. The committee also confirmed the convention's earlier decision that the president "shall appoint officers in all cases not otherwise provided for by this Constitution" and authorized the president to "commission all the officers of the United States." It remained unclear, however, where responsibility would lie for appointing the heads of the departments and other departmental officials and employees.

On August 24, at a time in the convention when the delegates generally were trimming back the power of the Senate, they passed a motion that, although not altogether clear, seemed to expand the president's right to make most appointments while still leaving complete responsibility for choosing judges and ambassadors in the Senate's jurisdiction. The motion, which was offered by John Dickinson, stated that the president "shall appoint to all offices established by this Constitution, except in cases herein otherwise provided for, and to all offices which may hereafter be created by law."[68] But the delegates did not revisit their August 17 rejection of Delaware delegate George Read's motion to allow the president to appoint the treasurer. They still wanted anything to do with money firmly in Congress's hands.

As it had for the treaty power, the Committee on Postponed Matters proposed in early September to extend even further the president's role in the appointment process. Judges, ambassadors, ministers, and officers that the delegates had not already provided for would be appointed by the president with the advice and consent of the Senate. A simple majority vote of the senators present would suffice to confirm a presidential appointment. Wilson tried again to persuade the delegates to make appointments a unilateral power of the president. To involve the Senate, he argued, would foster "a dangerous tendency to aristocracy." But his motion failed.[69]

The convention accepted the committee's recommendation after making three additions: the president was given the power to fill vacancies that occur while the Senate is in recess (September 6); the power to appoint the treasurer was transferred from Congress to the president (September 14); and control of certain forms of patronage was distributed between the two branches by giving Congress the power to "vest the appointment of such inferior officers as they think proper" in the president, the courts, or the heads of the departments (September 15).

ADVISORY LEGISLATIVE POWERS

In enumerating the proposed powers of the presidency, the Committee of Detail specified: "He shall, from time to time, give information to the Legislature, of the state of the Union: he may recommend to their consideration such measures as he shall deem necessary, and expedient." The latter of these two provisions, both of which were uncontroversial, was modified slightly in response to an August 24 motion by Morris. He argued that the Constitution should make it "the *duty* of the President to recommend [measures to Congress], & thence prevent umbrage or cavil at his doing it." In other words, Congress would be less likely to resent presidential recommendations if the president had no constitutional choice but to offer some.

The convention approved Morris's suggestion that the words "he may" be replaced by "and."[70] The Constitution as finally written reads, "He shall from time to time give to the Congress Information of the State of the Union, and recommend to their Consideration such Measures as he shall judge necessary and expedient."

CONVENE AND ADJOURN CONGRESS

The Committee of Detail recommended that the president be allowed to "convene them [the House and Senate] on extraordinary occasions"—that is, to call Congress into special session. Furthermore, "in case of disagreement between the two Houses, with regard to the time of adjournment, he may adjourn them to such time as he thinks proper."

James McHenry of Maryland was among those who wanted to grant the president the flexibility to call only the Senate back into session, presumably to consider a treaty or an urgent presidential appointment. He persuaded the delegates to amend the special session clause to that effect on September 8. The Constitution therefore reads: "he may, on extraordinary Occasions, convene both Houses, or either of them."

"RECEIVE AMBASSADORS"

The president's power to "receive Ambassadors" was proposed by the Committee of Detail. The committee joined this power to another—permission to "correspond with the supreme Executives of the several States" (the state governors)—which the convention rejected on August 25 as being, according to Morris, "unnecessary and implying that the president could not correspond with others."[71] As for receiving ambassadors, the absence of debate or discussion by the delegates leaves unclear whether they meant this power to be substantive or merely ceremonial. In practice, the power to receive or, in particular cases, to refuse to receive ambassadors has made the president the sole official recipient of communications from foreign governments and the sole determiner of which governments the United States recognizes diplomatically.

"TAKE CARE"

According to the Virginia Plan, the executive was to have "general authority to execute the National Laws." On June 1 Madison sought to revise this provision to read: "power to carry into effect the national laws . . . and to execute such other powers not Legislative nor Judiciary in their nature as may from time to time be delegated by the national Legislature." The stipulation about legislative and judicial powers reflected Madison's acceptance of a suggestion by Charles Cotesworth Pinckney, who felt it was important to explicitly prohibit "improper powers" from being delegated to the executive. The other South Carolina Pinckney (Charles) persuaded the delegates to strike the amendment as "unnecessary."[72] No further controversy over the "take care" clause ensued. The Committee of Detail's formulation—"he shall take care that the laws of the United States be duly and faithfully executed"—was adopted without discussion by the convention and survived virtually intact in the final Constitution: "he shall take Care that the Laws be faithfully executed."

TITLE

During the first two months of their deliberations, the delegates usually referred to the head of the executive branch as the "national executive," "supreme executive," or "governor." On August 6 the Committee of Detail included the term "president" in its report to the convention. The title had been used for the presiding officer of Congress and many other legislative bodies, including the convention itself. It was familiar and reassuring to those who feared that the delegates might be creating a monarchical or tyrannical office. Once proposed by the committee, the title "president" was accepted without debate by the convention.

OATH OF OFFICE

"Before he enter on the Execution of his Office," the Constitution requires the president to "take the following Oath or Affirmation:—'I do solemnly swear (or affirm) that I will faithfully execute the Office of President of the United States, and will to the best of my Ability, preserve, protect and defend the Constitution of the United States.'" Although another provision of the Constitution states that all legislators, judges, and other officials of both the national government and the various state governments "shall be bound by Oath or Affirmation, to support this Constitution," the language of only the president's oath is included in the document. Some regard the wording of the presidential oath (it pledges the president to execute "the office" rather than the laws) as further support for the claim that there are implied powers of presidential prerogative in the Constitution.

Virtually no debate or discussion accompanied the writing of the president's oath by the Constitutional Convention. The first half of the oath was proposed by the Committee of Detail on August 6: "I —— solemnly swear (or affirm) that I will faithfully execute the office of President of the United States of America." On August 27 Mason and Madison moved that the phrase "and will to the best of my judgment and power preserve, protect and defend the Constitution of the U.S." be added. Wilson objected that a special presidential oath was unnecessary, but Mason and Madison's motion passed handily.[73] On September 15 the delegates substituted "abilities" for "judgment and power," but no discussion was recorded that explains this alteration.

Departing from the practice that prevailed in most of the states at the time, the convention barred the imposition of a religious oath on the president and other officials of the national government. Some state constitutions required public adherence to Christianity as a condition for serving as governor, others an adherence to the Protestant form of Christianity. North Carolina insisted that its governor affirm the existence of God and the truth of Protestantism and hold no religious beliefs that were inimical to the "peace and safety" of the state. On August 30 Charles Pinckney moved that "no religious test shall ever be required as a qualification to any office or public trust under the authority of the U. States." Sherman said he thought the proposal was "unnecessary, the prevailing liberality being a sufficient security agst. such tests." Nevertheless, Pinckney's motion was approved.[74]

QUALIFICATIONS

No statement of qualifications for president was included in the Constitution until September 7, just ten days before the convention ended. In all likelihood, the lateness of the convention's actions on presidential qualifications was the result of deliberation, not neglect. Throughout their proceedings, the delegates seem to have operated on the principle that qualifications for an office needed to be established only if qualifications for those choosing the person to fill the office were not.[75] Therefore, qualifications, which were not stated for voters, were included for members of the national legislature: members of the House of Representatives must be at least twenty-five years old, seven years a citizen, and an inhabitant of the state they represented; and senators must be at least thirty years old, nine years a citizen, and an inhabitant of the state. Conversely, qualifications for judge hips and other appointed offices never were included in the Constitution because these officials are selected by other government officials for whom qualifications were stated.[76]

Through most of the convention's deliberations, the majority of delegates remained wedded to the idea that Congress, a body of constitutionally qualified members, would elect the president. The delegates thus saw no need to include qualifications for president in the Constitution. By mid-August, however, it was obvious that most had changed their minds about legislative selection of the executive. Although they had not yet decided on an alternative, whatever procedure they eventually devised to choose the president clearly would involve selection by an unqualified body because members of Congress were the only officials for whom constitutional qualifications were stated. This new election procedure, in turn, would necessitate the writing of qualifications for president. These qualifications would have to be high, because the delegates also seem to have agreed that the greater the powers of an office, the more stringent the qualifications for it should be.

On August 20 Gerry moved successfully that the Committee of Detail be revived for the purpose of proposing a list of qualifications for president. Two days later, the committee did so: the president was to be thirty-five years old or older, a U.S. citizen, and an inhabitant of the United States for at least twenty-one years. On September 4 the Committee on Postponed Matters submitted a revised statement of qualifications: at least thirty-five, a natural-born citizen or a citizen at the time of the Constitution's adoption, and fourteen years a resident. The delegates approved the revised recommendation on September 7.

Each element of the presidential qualifications clause was grounded in its own rationale. The age requirement had two justifications. First, the delegates presumed, age would foster maturity. As Mason said in the debate on establishing a minimum age for members of the House of Representatives, "Every man carried with him in his own experience a scale for measuring the deficiency of young politicians; since he would if interrogated be obliged to declare that his political opinions at the age of 21 were too crude & erroneous to merit an influence on public measures."[77] Second, the passage of years left in its wake a record for the electorate to assess. According to John Jay, the author of *Federalist* No. 64, "By excluding men under 35 from the first office [president], and those under 30 from the second [senator], it confines the electors to men of whom the people have had time to form a judgment, and with respect to whom they will not be liable to be deceived by those brilliant appearances of genius and patriotism which, like transient meteors, sometimes mislead as well as dazzle."[78]

The residency and citizenship requirements for president were grounded less in principles of good government than in the politics of the moment. The stipulation that the president must be at least fourteen years a resident of the United States was designed to eliminate both British sympathizers who had fled to England during the Revolutionary War and popular foreign military leaders, notably Baron Frederick von Steuben of Prussia, who had emigrated to the United States to fight in the Revolution. As for the length of the residency requirement, the Committee of Detail's recommendation of twenty-one years probably was reduced to fourteen because the longer requirement—but not the shorter one—might have been interpreted as barring three of the convention's delegates from the presidency: Alexander Hamilton, Pierce Butler, and James McHenry.

The reason for requiring that the president be a natural-born citizen also was tied to contemporary politics. Rumors had spread while the convention was meeting that the delegates were plotting to invite a European monarch to rule the United States. Prince Henry of Prussia and the Duke of Osnaburgh, who was King George III's second son, were the most frequently mentioned pretenders.[79] The practice of importing foreign rulers was not unknown among the European monarchies of the day and would not have seemed preposterous to Americans who heard the rumor. The delegates, aware that the mere existence of an independent executive in the Constitution was going to provoke attacks by opponents who suspected that the presidency was a latent monarchy, seem to have believed that they could squelch at least the foreign king rumor by requiring that the president be a natural-born citizen of the United States.[80]

No property qualification for president was included in the Constitution, even though most state constitutions required that the governor own property and the delegates had approved a similar requirement for the president more than a month before they enacted the presidential qualifications clause. On July 26, the convention adopted a motion by Mason and the Pinckneys that a property qualification be stated for judges, legislators, and the executive. The Committee of Detail neglected the motion in its proposed draft of the Constitution, which provoked both a complaint and another motion from Charles Pinckney on August 10. John Rutledge of South Carolina, the chair of the committee, apologized and seconded Pinckney's motion. He said the committee had made no recommendation about property "because they could not agree on any among themselves, being embarrassed by the danger on one side of displeasing the people by making them high, and on the other of rendering them nugatory by making them low."[81] Pinckney suggested $100,000.[82]

In response, Franklin rose to attack the very idea of property qualifications. As Madison paraphrased Franklin's argument in his notes, "Some of the greatest rogues he was ever acquainted with, were the richest rogues." Pinckney's motion, Madison recorded, quickly "was rejected by so general a no, that the States were not called."[83] In truth, the practical difficulty of establishing an acceptable property requirement, more than the belief that such a requirement should be rejected as a matter of principle, seems to explain why the Constitution was silent about property ownership by the president.

THE VICE PRESIDENCY

The idea of an office like the vice presidency was not unknown among the delegates to the Constitutional Convention. During the period of British rule, several colonies had lieutenant governors (sometimes known as deputy governors or by another title) whose ongoing duties were minor but who stood by to serve as acting governor if the governor died, was removed from office, was ill, or was absent from the colony.

After independence, five states—Connecticut, Massachusetts, New York, Rhode Island, and South Carolina—included lieutenant governors in their constitutions. Each lieutenant governor was elected in the same manner as the governor and was charged to act as governor when needed. New York's lieutenant governor was also the ex officio president of the state senate and was empowered to break tie votes. Other states handled the matter of gubernatorial death, absence, or inability differently. In Georgia and Virginia the head of the privy council, a cabinet-style body, was the designated gubernatorial successor; in Delaware and North Carolina it was the Speaker of the upper house of the legislature; in New Hampshire, the senior member of the state senate.[84]

It is difficult to say whether the experience of the states had much influence on the convention's decision to create the vice presidency. No one referred to the state lieutenant governors in the debates. Nor was any proposal made to include a vice president in the Constitution until very late in the proceedings. Indeed, the invention of the vice presidency seems to have been an afterthought of the convention, a residue of its solution to the problem of presidential selection.

As noted earlier, the delegates initially decided that the legislature should choose the executive, but they eventually replaced legislative selection with the Electoral College, providing that each state pick presidential electors, who in turn would elect the president by majority vote. A possibly fatal defect of this procedure was that the electors would simply vote for a variety of local favorites, preventing the choice of a nationally elected president. But the committee remedied this potential problem by assigning each elector two votes for president, requiring that they cast at least one of their votes for a candidate who "shall not be an inhabitant of the same State with themselves," and attaching a consequence to both votes: the runner-up in the election for president would be awarded the newly created office of vice president.

As Hugh Williamson, a member of the Committee on Postponed Matters, testified, "Such an office as vice-President was not wanted. He was introduced only for the sake of a valuable mode of election which required two to be chosen at the same time."[85] But, having invented the vice presidency, the committee proposed that the office be used to solve two other problems that had vexed the convention.

SENATE PRESIDENT

The first problem was the role of president of the Senate. Some delegates had fretted that if a senator were chosen for this position, one of two difficulties would arise. If the senator were barred from voting except in the event of a tie (which was customary for presiding officers because it guaranteed that tie votes would be broken), the senator's state would be denied half its representation on most issues. If the senator were allowed to vote on all matters, the state would be effectively overrepresented in the Senate, occupying two voting seats and the presiding officer's chair. As a way around this dilemma, the Committee on Postponed Matters recommended that the vice president serve as president of the Senate, voting only to break ties. An exception was made for presidential impeachment trials, when the chief justice of the United States presides. In an oversight, vice presidents were not barred from presiding at their own impeachment trials.

SUCCESSION

The second problem that the committee used the vice presidency to solve was succession when the presidency unexpectedly became vacant. This, too, was a matter to which the convention turned rather late. The Virginia Plan and the New Jersey Plan were silent about succession. On June 18, as part of his sweeping proposal for a national executive chosen by electors to serve for life, Hamilton suggested that in the event of the executive's death, resignation, impeachment and removal, or absence from the country, the senator who served as president of the Senate should "exercise all the powers by this Constitution vested in the President, until another shall be appointed, or until he shall return within the United States, if his absence was with the Consent of the Senate and Assembly [House of Representatives]." But Hamilton's plan received little consideration from the delegates and was never formally discussed.

Sustained attention was first given to the succession question by the Committee of Detail. Knowingly or not, the committee followed Hamilton's lead in its August 6 report to the convention, providing that "in the case of his [the president's] removal as aforesaid, death, resignation, or disability to discharge the powers and duties of his office, the President of the Senate shall exercise those powers and duties, until another President of the United States be chosen, or until the disability of the President be removed." When the delegates discussed this provision on August 27, considerable dissatisfaction was voiced. Madison, who feared that the Senate would have an incentive to create presidential vacancies if its own president was the designated successor, suggested instead that "the persons composing the Council to the President" fill that role.[86] Morris offered the chief justice as successor. Finally, Williamson asked that the question be postponed. The convention agreed, placing the issue in the hands of the Committee on Postponed Matters.

The committee, which reported to the convention on September 4, proposed that "in the case of his [the president's] removal as aforesaid, death, absence, resignation, or inability to discharge the powers or duties of his office the Vice President shall exercise those powers and duties until another President be chosen, or until the inability of the President be removed." Three days later Randolph, in an effort to supplement the committee's proposal with one that provided a method of presidential succession if there were no vice president, moved: "The Legislature may declare by law what officer of the United States shall act as President in the case of the death, resignation, or disability of the President and Vice President; and such Officer shall act accordingly until the time of electing a President shall arrive." Madison then moved to replace the last nine words of Randolph's motion with "until such disability be removed, or a President shall be elected." The motion passed, as amended.[87]

Madison's reason for amending Randolph's motion is clear: he wanted Congress to call a special presidential election to replace a departed president or, in his words, to permit "a supply of vacancy by an intermediate election of the President." Other evidence from the records of the convention suggests that most of the delegates intended that the president's successor serve merely as acting president and only until a special election could be called.[88] But sometime in the period September 8–12, when the Committee of Style was working to fulfill its charge to produce a smooth, final draft of the Constitution, that intention was lost, probably unwittingly. The committee took the September 4 motion of the Committee on Postponed Matters and Randolph's September 7 motion and merged them into one provision, which, with minor modification, became paragraph 6 of Article II, section 1, of the Constitution: "In Case of the Removal of the President from Office, or of his Death, Resignation, or Inability to discharge the Powers and Duties of the said Office, the Same shall devolve on the Vice President, and the Congress may by Law provide for the Case of Removal, Death, Resignation or Inability, both of the President and Vice President, declaring what Officer shall then act as President, and such Officer shall act accordingly, until the Disability be removed, or a President shall be elected."[89]

Clearly, the delegates' intentions regarding succession were obscured by the Committee of Style. Grammatically, it is impossible to tell—and in its rush to adjournment, the convention did not notice the ambiguity—whether "the Same" in this provision refers to "the said office" (the presidency) or, as the delegates intended, only to its "powers and duties." Nor can one ascertain if "until . . . a President shall be elected" means until the end of the original four-year term or, again as intended, until a special election is held.[90]

The vice presidency was not a controversial issue at the Constitutional Convention. On September 4, when the delegates were considering the Committee on Postponed Matters' proposal for the Electoral College, Nathaniel Gorham worried that "a very obscure man with very few votes" might be elected because the proposal required only that the vice president be the runner-up in the presidential election, not the recipient of a majority of electoral votes. Sherman replied that any of the leading candidates for president would likely be distinguished.

The role of the vice president as president of the Senate was discussed on September 7. Gerry, seconded by Randolph, complained about mixing legislative and executive elements: "We might as well put the President himself at the head of the Legislature. The close intimacy that must subsist between the President & vice-president makes it absolutely improper." Morris responded wryly that "the vice president then will be the first heir apparent that ever loved his father." Sherman added that "if the vice-President were not to be President of the Senate, he would be without employment." He also reminded the convention that for the Senate to elect a president from among its own members probably would deprive that senator of a vote. Mason ended the brief debate by branding "the office of vice-President an encroachment on the rights of the Senate; . . . it mixed too much the Legislative & Executive, which as well as the Judiciary departments, ought to be kept as separate as possible."[91]

Despite these minor objections, the convention voted overwhelmingly to approve the vice presidency. The delegates, however, gave no serious attention to the vice president's responsibilities as successor to the president.

RATIFYING THE CONSTITUTION

Congress's original call for a convention in Philadelphia had charged the delegates only to propose amendments to the Articles of Confederation, not to design an entirely new system of government. By itself, the delegates' decision to ignore this charge ensured that controversy would ensue when, having met so long in secret, they published their proposed plan of government in September. In addition, several provisions of the draft Constitution, including the enhanced powers of the national government and the design of the legislative branch, were certain to be controversial. But nothing astonished the nation more than the convention's decision to recommend that a strong national executive be established—unitary, independently elected for an unrestricted number of terms, and entrusted with its own substantial grant of powers.

In the debates that the various state ratifying conventions held on the Constitution, Anti-Federalists (the label that was attached to those who opposed the plans) concentrated much of their fire on the presidency. Federalists rose to the office's defense. Most state conventions debated at least one aspect of the proposed executive.[92]

THE ANTI-FEDERALIST CRITIQUE OF THE PRESIDENCY

Anti-Federalists attacked the presidency as a disguised monarchy that, in collaboration with an allegedly aristocratic Senate, eventually would rule the United States much as the British king, assisted by the House of Lords, was said to rule England.

The most strident opposition to the presidency was registered by Patrick Henry of Virginia. On June 7, 1788, speaking with unvarnished fervor, Henry voiced the Anti-Federalists' fears of a presidential monarchy to his state's ratifying convention:

> This Constitution is said to have beautiful features, but when I come to examine these features, Sir, they appear to me to be horridly frightful: Among other deformities, it has an awful squinting; it squints towards monarchy: And does this not raise indignation in the breast of every American?
>
> Your President may easily become a King; . . . if your American chief, be a man of ambition, how easy it is for him to render himself absolute: The army is in his hands, and if he be a man of address, it will be attached to him; . . . I would rather infinitely, and I am sure most of these Convention are of the same opinion, have a king, Lords, and Commons, than a Government so replete with such insupportable

evils. If we make a King, we may prescribe the rules by which he shall rule his people, and interpose such checks as shall prevent him from infringing them: But the President, in the field, at the head of his army, can prescribe the terms on which he shall reign master, so far that it will puzzle any American ever to get his neck from under the galling yoke. . . . And what have you to oppose this force? What will then become of you and your rights? Will not absolute despotism ensue?[93]

Other Anti-Federalists focused their attack on the close relationship they thought the Constitution fostered between the "monarchical" president and the "aristocratic" Senate, the two bodies that, without the involvement of the "democratic" House of Representatives, shared the powers of appointment and treaty making. A group of delegates at the Pennsylvania ratifying convention published a report on December 18, 1787, asserting that the Constitution's treaty-making provisions virtually invited foreign meddling. The Senate would consist of twenty-six members, they noted, two from each of the thirteen states. Fourteen senators would constitute a quorum for that body, of whom only ten were needed to provide a two-thirds vote to ratify a treaty proposed by the president. "What an inducement would this [small number] offer to the ministers of foreign powers to compass by bribery *such concessions* as could not otherwise be obtained," the Pennsylvania dissenters warned.[94]

Although monarchy was the Anti-Federalists' main fear, few features of the presidency were immune from their attack. The North Carolina and Virginia ratifying conventions urged the enactment of a constitutional amendment that would limit each president to no more than eight years in office in any sixteen-year period. The Anti-Federalist Cato (he is often identified as New York governor George Clinton, but there is no solid evidence of that), writing in the *New York Journal* in November 1787, argued that the president's term was too long and cited Montesquieu's endorsement of annual elections. In addition, Cato charged, the absence of a council meant that the president would "be unsupported by proper information and advice, and will generally be directed by minions and favorites." Instead of direct election by the people (which Cato said he favored), the president "arrives to this office at the fourth or fifth hand."[95]

Some of the most pointed criticisms of the proposed constitution came from disaffected delegates to the Constitutional Convention. George Mason told the Virginia ratifying convention that the "mode of [presidential] election is a mere deception . . . on the American people." Because, after George Washington's certain election as the first president, the Electoral College almost never would produce a majority for a candidate, the House of Representatives would end up selecting nearly all presidents.[96] Luther Martin complained to the Maryland convention that the veto allowed the president to prevail over all but a two-thirds majority of both houses of Congress.[97]

The presidency also drew criticism from two future presidents. Thomas Jefferson observed archly in a letter to Madison that a president who could be reelected indefinitely and who commanded the armed forces "seems a bad edition of a Polish king." James Monroe fretted about the possibility of a president being reelected into life tenure.

THE FEDERALIST DEFENSE OF THE PRESIDENCY

Article II posed a political problem to Federalists who were trying to persuade the states to ratify the Constitution. Not only was the presidency the most obvious innovation in the new plan of government, but its unitary nature roused fears of a British-style monarchy. The Anti-Federalists fanned these fears.

Proponents of the Constitution at the state ratifying conventions stressed both the virtues of the presidency and the restraints the Constitution placed on the office. In doing so, they relied heavily on the explanations and defenses of the Constitution that Hamilton, Madison, and Jay were putting forth in a series of eighty-five newspaper articles that Hamilton, who conceived the project, had commissioned. These articles, later gathered in a book called *The Federalist Papers,* appeared pseudonymously in several New York newspapers under the name "Publius," after the Roman statesman Publius Valerius who is celebrated in Plutarch's *Parallel Lives* for stabilizing the nascent republic.[98] Hamilton wrote about fifty of the articles, Madison about twenty-five, and Jay, who became ill after writing four of the first five numbers in the series, five. Hamilton and Madison collaborated on the rest. The articles were reprinted and disseminated widely throughout the states.[99]

In March 1788 Hamilton wrote *Federalist* Nos. 69–77, which dealt with the presidency.[100] *Federalist* No. 69 squarely addressed the Anti-Federalist charge that the presidency was a latent monarchy. Hamilton argued that in contrast to the British king, who secured his office by inheritance and served for life, the president is elected for a limited term. The king had an absolute veto on laws passed by Parliament; the president's veto could be overridden by Congress. The king could both declare war and raise an army and navy; the president could do neither. The king could prorogue Parliament for any reason at any time; the president could adjourn Congress only when the House of Representatives and the Senate could not agree on an adjournment date. The king could create offices and appoint people to fill them; the president could not create offices and could fill them only with the approval of the Senate. Finally, Hamilton noted that the president, unlike the king, could be impeached and removed. In *Federalist* No. 65, he described impeachable offenses as "the abuse or violation of some public trust. They are of a nature which may with peculiar propriety be denominated POLITICAL, as they relate chiefly to injuries done immediately to the society itself."

Hamilton dissembled to some degree in drawing these contrasts. The powers he ascribed to the British monarch were more characteristic of the seventeenth century than of the eighteenth century, during which the influence of Parliament and the prime minister had grown. For example, the last British monarch to veto an act of Parliament was Queen Anne in 1707. But *Federalist* No. 69 was effective in deflating the Anti-Federalists' caricature of the presidency. Indeed, Hamilton deftly argued that in many cases the president's power was less than that wielded by the governor of New York, the staunch Anti-Federalist Clinton.

Federalist No. 70, less defensive in tone than No. 69, described the virtues of the presidency. Its theme was "energy," a quality that, according to Hamilton, is requisite to good government: "It is essential to the protection of the community against foreign attacks; it is not less essential to the steady administration of the laws; to the protection of property against those irregular and high-handed combinations which sometimes interrupt the ordinary course of justice; to the security of liberty against the enterprises and assaults of ambition, of faction, and of anarchy."

Energy in the government created by the Constitution was provided by the president, Hamilton argued, mostly because of the office's unitary character. Unity provided the presidency with a whole host of virtues—"decision, activity, secrecy, and dispatch . . . vigor and expedition." In contrast, a plural executive would be riven by disagreements among its members that would render it slow to act and prone to faction. It also would be hard for the people to hold a plural executive responsible for failures, because each member could blame the others.

In *Federalist* Nos. 71–73, Hamilton defended the presidency as having additional qualities indispensable to energy. "Duration," the theme of No. 71, was one. The four-year term provided the president with enough time to act firmly and with resolve but was not so long as "to justify any alarm for the public liberty." Hamilton added in No. 72 that the provision for reelection shrewdly acknowledged that "the desire of reward is one of the strongest incentives of human conduct." Without that incentive, a president would be tempted either to slack off or, at the opposite extreme, to usurp power violently; with it, Hamilton anticipated, a national leader might be prompted "to plan and undertake extensive and arduous enterprises for the public benefit." Presidential reeligibility also allowed the nation to keep a president in office if it so desired. "There is an excess of refinement in the idea," he insisted, " of disabling the people to continue in office men who had entitled themselves, in their opinion, to approbation and confidence."

"Adequate provision for its support" was a third energy-inducing quality of the presidency, according to Hamilton. He attached great importance to the prohibition that the Constitution placed on Congress not to raise or lower an incumbent president's salary. In the first part of No. 73, Hamilton argued that without such a bar, Congress could "reduce him by famine, or tempt him by largesse," which would "render him as obsequious to their will as they might think proper to make him."

Later in No. 73, and continuing in Nos. 74–77, Hamilton defended the enumerated powers of the presidency, which, along with unity, duration, and adequate support, were for him the indispensable ingredients of presidential energy. Far from being threatening, Hamilton argued, the office's constitutional powers were modest and essential to the operations of good government.

VETO. "The propensity of the legislative department to intrude upon the rights, and to absorb the powers, of the other departments has been already more than once suggested. . . . [Without the veto, the president] might gradually be stripped of his authorities by successive resolutions or annihilated by a single vote. . . . But the power in question has a further use. It not only serves as a shield to the executive, but it furnishes an additional security against the enaction of improper laws."

COMMANDER IN CHIEF. "Even those [constitutions] which have in other respects coupled the Chief Magistrate with a council have for the most part concentrated the military authority in him alone. Of all the cares or concerns of government, the direction of war most peculiarly demands those qualities which distinguish the exercise of power by a single hand."

TREATIES. "With regard to the intermixture of powers [between the president and the Senate] . . . the essence of the legislative authority is to enact laws, or, in other words, to prescribe rules for the regulation of the society; while the execution of the laws and the employment of the common strength, either for this purpose or for the common defense, seem to comprise all the functions of the executive magistrate. The power of making treaties is, plainly, neither the one nor the other. . . . It must indeed be clear to a demonstration that the joint possession of the power in question, by the President and Senate, would afford a greater prospect of security than the separate possession of it by either of them."

APPOINTMENT. "I proceed to lay it down as a rule that one man of discernment is better fitted to analyze and estimate the peculiar qualities adapted to particular offices than a body of men of equal or perhaps even of superior discernment. The sole and undivided responsibility of one man will naturally beget a livelier sense of duty and a more exact regard to reputation. He will, on this account, feel himself under stronger obligations, and more interested to investigate with care the qualities requisite to the stations to be filled, and to prefer with impartiality the persons who may have the fairest pretensions to them. . . . To what purpose then require the co-operation of the Senate?

Alexander Hamilton, one of the authors of **The Federalist Papers,** *defended the Constitution's provisions for a strong executive office.*

I answer, that the necessity of their concurrence would have a powerful, though, in general, a silent operation. It would be an excellent check upon a spirit of favoritism in the President, and would tend greatly to prevent the appointment of unfit characters.... The possibility of rejection would be a strong motive to care in proposing."[101]

OTHER POWERS. "The only remaining powers of the executive are comprehended in giving information to Congress on the state of the Union; in recommending to their consideration such measures as he shall judge expedient; in convening them, or either branch, upon extraordinary occasions; in adjourning them when they cannot themselves agree upon the time of adjournment; in receiving ambassadors and other public ministers; in faithfully executing the laws; and in commissioning all the officers of the United States. Except some cavils about the power of convening *either* house of the legislature, and that of receiving ambassadors, no objection has been made to this class of authorities; nor could they possibly admit of any."

THE VICE PRESIDENCY IN THE RATIFICATION DEBATES

"Post-convention discussion of the vice presidency was not extensive," legal scholar John D. Feerick has noted.[102] The only mention of the office in *The Federalist Papers* is in No. 68, written by Hamilton. Like the delegates' debate at the Constitutional Convention, this passage is concerned mainly with the vice president's role as president of the Senate:

> The appointment of an extraordinary person, as Vice-President, has been objected to as superfluous, if not mischievous. It has been alleged, that it would have been preferable to have authorized the Senate to elect out of their own body an officer answering to that description. But two considerations seem to justify the ideas of the Convention in this respect. One is, that to secure at all times the possibility of a definitive resolution of the body, it is necessary that the President should have only a casting [tie-breaking] vote. And to take the Senator of any State from his seat as Senator, to place him in that of President of the Senate, would be to exchange, in regard to the State from which he came, a constant for a contingent vote. The other consideration is, that, as the Vice-President may occasionally become a substitute for

the President, in the supreme Executive magistracy, all the reasons which recommend the mode of election prescribed for the one, apply with great if not with equal force to the manner of appointing the other.[103]

Hamilton may have been responding in part to concerns raised by the Anti-Federalist Cato, who argued that the vice presidency was both "unnecessary" and "dangerous." "This officer," warned Cato, "for want of other employment is made president of the Senate, thereby blending the executive and legislative powers, besides always giving to some one state, from which he is to come, an unjust preeminence."[104]

Luther Martin of Maryland, who opposed ratification, expressed concern that large states like Pennsylvania and Virginia typically would benefit from the vice president's Senate role:

> After it is decided who is chosen President, that person who has the next greatest number of votes of the electors, is declared to be legally elected to the Vice-Presidency; so that by this system it is very possible, and not improbable, that he may be appointed by the electors of a *single large state;* and a very undue influence in the Senate is given to that State of which the Vice-President is a citizen, since, in every question where the Senate is divided, that State will have two votes, the President having on that occasion a casting voice.

George Mason, another convention delegate who opposed ratification, also complained about the vice president's right to vote in the Senate and the office's mix of legislative and executive responsibilities. His fellow Virginia Anti-Federalist Richard Henry Lee worried about the absence of stated qualifications for the vice president.[105]

Defenders of the vice presidency made a virtue of the office's role as Senate president. In their view, the vice president's election by the nation as a whole would be good for the Senate. "There is much more propriety to giving this office to a person chosen by the people at large," urged Madison, "than to one of the Senate, who is only the choice of the legislature of one state." William R. Davie of North Carolina expressed confidence that a nationally elected vice president would cast tie-breaking votes "as impartially as possible." Answering another argument of the Constitution's critics, Connecticut delegates Oliver Ellsworth and Roger Sherman wrote separately that the vice president did not wield a mix of legislative and executive powers, but rather that the vice presidency was part of the legislative branch except in the event of a succession, at which time it entered the executive branch.[106]

In all, as Feerick has concluded, the vice presidency "received scant attention in the state ratifying conventions. . . . The discussion of the vice-presidency that did occur centered mostly on the fact that the office blended legislative and executive functions."[107] As at the Constitutional Convention, little was said in the state debates about the vice president's duties as successor to the president.

NOTES

1. Jack N. Rakove, *Original Meanings: Politics and Ideas in the Making of the Constitution* (New York: Knopf, 1996), 82.
2. Seymour Martin Lipset, *The First New Nation* (New York: Basic Books, 1963), chap. 1; Max Weber, *The Theory of Social and Economic Organizations* (New York: Oxford University Press, 1947), 358.
3. Marcus Cunliffe, *George Washington: Man and Monument* (New York: New American Library, 1958), 15.
4. Stanley Elkins and Eric McKitrick, *The Age of Federalism: The Early American Republic, 1788–1800* (New York: Oxford University Press, 1993), 34.
5. Max Farrand, ed., *The Records of the Federal Convention*, 3 vols. (New Haven: Yale University Press, 1911), 1:103. Contemporaries often compared Washington to Cincinnatus, the ancient Roman who left his plow when called to lead Rome against Carthage and then returned to it as soon as the victory was won. See Garry Wills, *Cincinnatus: George Washington and the Enlightenment* (Garden City, N.Y.: Doubleday, 1984), 36–37.
6. Charles C. Thach Jr., *The Creation of the Presidency, 1775–1789* (Baltimore: Johns Hopkins University Press, 1969).
7. Robert A. Rutland and William M. E. Rachal, eds., *The Papers of James Madison* (Chicago: University of Chicago Press, 1975), 9:385.
8. Political scientist Calvin C. Jillson argues that Madison's fellow Virginia delegates, not Madison himself, brought what little clarity there was to the executive provision of the Virginia Plan. See Jillson, *Constitution Making: Conflict and Consensus in the Federal Convention of 1787* (New York: Agathon Press, 1988), 42–47.
9. Farrand, *Records*, 2:52, 523.
10. Richard J. Ellis, ed., *Founding the American Presidency* (Lanham, Md.: Rowman and Littlefield, 1999), 12–13.
11. Richard Beeman, *Plain, Honest Men: The Making of the American Constitution* (New York: Random House, 2009), 129.
12. Farrand, *Records*, 1:65.
13. Charles L. Mee Jr., *The Genius of the People* (New York: Harper and Row, 1987), 118.
14. Farrand, *Records*, 1:66, 65.
15. Ibid., 1:102.
16. Ibid., 1:65.
17. W. B. Allen, ed., *George Washington: A Collection* (Indianapolis, Indiana: Liberty Classic, 1988), 230.
18. Ellis, *Founding the American Presidency*. See also Beeman, *Plain, Honest Men*, 27.
19. See, for example, Farrand, *Records*, 2:487–488.
20. Ibid., 2:541.
21. Ibid., 2:68, 69.
22. Ibid., 2:30.
23. Ibid., 2:57.
24. Ibid., 2:100.
25. Indispensable to the eventual adoption of the Electoral College was Wilson's conversion of Madison, who declared on July 19 that "it is essential then that the appointment of the Executive should either be drawn from some source, or held by some tenure, that will give him a free agency with regard to the Legislature. This could not be if he was appointable from time to time by the Legislature" (ibid., 2:56).
26. Robert A. Dahl, *Pluralist Democracy in the United States: Conflict and Consent* (Chicago: Rand-McNally, 1967), 84.
27. Clinton Rossiter, *1787: The Grand Convention* (London: MacGibbon and Kee, 1968), 199.
28. Richard P. McCormick, *The Presidential Game: The Origins of American Presidential Politics* (New York: Oxford University Press, 1982), 25. In many ways, Shlomo Slonim has

argued, the Electoral College was "a second round of the Connecticut Compromise in settling large state-small state differences." Slonim, "The Electoral College: The Evolution of an Ad Hoc Congress for the Selection of a President," *Journal of American History* 73 (June 1986): 55.

29. Andrew Rudalevige, *The New Imperial Presidency: Renewing Presidential Power after Watergate* (Ann Arbor: University of Michigan Press, 2005), 25.

30. Fred Barbash, *The Founding: An Account of the Writing of the Constitution* (New York: Linden Press/Simon and Schuster, 1987), 182.

31. Farrand, *Records*, 2:500.

32. Carol Berkin, *A Brilliant Solution: Inventing the American Constitution* (New York: Harcourt, Brace, 2002), 143–144.

33. John P. Roche, "The Founding Fathers: A Reform Caucus in Action," *American Political Science Review* 55 (December 1961): 810.

34. Farrand, *Records*, 1:68.

35. Ibid., 2:33.

36. Alexander Hamilton, James Madison, and John Jay, *The Federalist Papers,* with an introduction by Clinton L. Rossiter (New York: New American Library, 1961), 437–448.

37. Farrand, *Records*, 2:53.

38. Ellis, *Founding the American Presidency,* 233.

39. Farrand, *Records*, 1:88.

40. Ibid., 2:550.

41. Ibid., 2:427.

42. Hamilton, Madison, and Jay, *Federalist Papers,* 301, 303.

43. Richard E. Neustadt, *Presidential Power* (New York: Wiley, 1960), 35.

44. Farrand, *Records*, 1:82.

45. Ibid., 1:376.

46. Ibid., 2:284.

47. The bar to overlapping membership strongly distinguishes the American system of government from parliamentary systems, in which executive offices are customarily held by legislators. James Sundquist, *Constitutional Reform and Effective Government,* rev. ed. (Washington, D.C.: Brookings, 1992), 232–244.

48. Robert Scigliano, "The Presidency and the Judiciary," in *The Presidency and the Political System,* 3rd ed., ed. Michael Nelson (Washington, D.C.: CQ Press, 1990), 471–499.

49. Robert J. Spitzer, *The Presidential Veto: Touchstone of the American Presidency* (Albany: State University of New York Press, 1988), 10.

50. Farrand, *Records*, 1:101.

51. Richard M. Pious, *The American Presidency* (New York: Basic Books, 1979), 29.

52. John Locke, *Second Treatise of Government* (Indianapolis: Bobbs-Merrill, 1952), 91–96.

53. Thach, *Creation of the Presidency,* 138–139.

54. Farrand, *Records*, 2:318.

55. Political scientist Anthony J. Bennett has interpreted the phrase "their respective Offices" to mean that the convention did not intend for the department heads to constitute a cabinet. See Bennett, *The American President's Cabinet: From Kennedy to Bush* (New York: St. Martin's Press, 1996), 2.

56. Hamilton, Madison, and Jay, *Federalist Papers,* 447.

57. Farrand, *Records*, 2:343–344.

58. Ibid., 1:292.

59. Ellis, *Founding the American Presidency,* 220–221.

60. Farrand, *Records*, 2:426, 626.

61. Hamilton, Madison, and Jay, *Federalist Papers,* 447, 449.

62. Farrand, *Records*, 1:292.

63. Rakove, *Original Meanings,* 89, 267.

64. Farrand, *Records*, 2:309.

65. Ibid., 2:540.

66. Ellis, *Founding the American Presidency,* 190.

67. Farrand, *Records,* 1:67.

68. Ibid., 2:405.

69. Ibid., 2:522.

70. Ibid., 2:405.

71. Ibid., 2:419.

72. Ibid., 1:67.

73. Ibid., 2:427.

74. Ibid., 2:468. In 1853 Franklin Pierce affirmed—rather than swore—to faithfully execute the office of president. At the first inaugural ceremony, on April 30, 1789, George Washington began the practice of adding the words "so help me God" at the conclusion of the oath. See Charles C. Euchner and John Anthony Maltese, *Selecting the President* (Washington, D.C.: CQ Press, 1997), 142.

75. Michael Nelson, "Constitutional Qualifications for the President," *Presidential Studies Quarterly* 17 (Spring 1987): 383–399.

76. During most of the convention, the appointment power belonged mainly to senators; toward the end the president's role in appointments was enhanced substantially.

77. Farrand, *Records,* 1:375.

78. Hamilton, Madison, and Jay, *Federalist Papers,* 391.

79. Richard Beeman attributes the latter rumor to an anonymous pamphleteer in Fairfield, Connecticut. Beeman, *Plain, Honest Men,* 263.

80. Another reason the convention decided to include a requirement of natural-born citizenship for the president may be found in a letter John Jay sent to George Washington on July 25. "Permit me to hint," Jay wrote, "whether it would not be wise and reasonable to provide a strong check on the admission of foreigners into the administration of our National Government, and to declare expressly that the command in chief of the American Army shall not be given to, nor devolve upon, any but a natural *born* citizen." On September 2, two days before the Committee on Postponed Matters proposed the natural-born citizen requirement to the convention, Washington replied to Jay, "I thank you for the hints contained in your letter." See Farrand, *Records,* 4:61, 76.

81. Ibid., 2:249.

82. Beeman, *Plain, Honest Men,* 280.

83. Farrand, *Records,* 2:249.

84. John D. Feerick, *From Failing Hands: The Story of Presidential Succession* (New York: Fordham University Press, 1965), chap. 2.

85. Farrand, *Records,* 2:537.

86. Ibid., 2:427.

87. Ibid., 2:535.

88. See ibid., 2:137, 146, 163, 172.

89. On September 15, 1787, delegates discovered a clerical error in the committee's draft and changed "the period for chusing another president arrive" to "a President shall be elected."

90. For a thorough comparison of the convention's decisions on succession with the Committee of Style's rendering of them, see Feerick, *From Failing Hands,* 48–51. Feerick speculates that the committee may have omitted presidential "absence" from the list of situations that require a temporary successor because it was covered by the term *inability.*

91. Farrand, *Records,* 2:537. In truth, it still is constitutionally unclear whether the vice president is part of the legislative branch, the executive branch, both branches, or neither. See Michael Nelson, *A Heartbeat Away* (Washington, D.C.: Brookings, 1988), chap. 4.

92. Pauline Maier, *Ratification: The People Debate the Constitution* (New York: Simon and Schuster, 2010), passim.

93. Quoted in Ralph Ketcham, ed., *The Anti-Federalist Papers and the Constitutional Convention Debates* (New York: New American Library, 1986), 213–214.

94. Ibid., 251.

95. "Letters of Cato, No. 4," in *The Evolving Presidency: Landmark Documents, 1787–2010,* 4th ed., ed. Michael Nelson (Washington, D.C.: CQ Press, 2012), 10–14.

96. Ellis, *Founding the American Presidency,* 117.

97. Ibid., 145.

98. Plutarch, *Lives,* vol. 1 (New York: Modern Library, 2001).

99. Voices of other famous people were raised in defense of the Constitution as well. See, for example, Tenche Cox, "An American Citizen I," and Noah Webster, "A Citizen of America," in *The Debate on the Constitution,* part 1 (New York: Library of America, 1993), 20–25 and 129–163, respectively.

100. All quotations from the *Federalist* may be found in Hamilton, Madison, and Jay, *Federalist Papers,* 415–464.

101. In a passage in *Federalist* No. 77 that would prove embarrassing a year later, Hamilton wrote that the Senate's consent "would be necessary to displace as well as to appoint" an executive official.

102. Feerick, *From Failing Hands,* 51.

103. Hamilton, Madison, and Jay, *Federalist Papers,* 414–415.

104. Quoted in Cecelia M. Kenyon, ed., *The Antifederalists* (Indianapolis: Bobbs-Merrill, 1966), 305.

105. Feerick, *From Failing Hands,* 52–54.

106. Quotes are drawn from ibid., 52–55.

107. Ibid., 5.

CHAPTER 3

Bringing the Constitutional Presidency to Life: George Washington and John Adams

T he Constitution provided a broad outline of the powers and duties of the president, leaving considerable leeway for individual presidents and future events to shape the executive office. By stating that "the executive Power shall be vested in a President of the United States of America" and that "he shall take Care that the Laws be faithfully executed," without in most instances stipulating what those executive responsibilities would be, the Constitution gave rise to unending conflict about the proper scope of presidential authority. "The executive article fairly bristles with contentious matter," Charles Thach has written, "and, until it is seen what decision was given to these contentions, it is impossible to say just what the national executive meant."[1]

From the words of the Constitution alone, one cannot determine what the relationship of the chief executive to the chief officers of the executive departments was supposed to be, or that of Congress to the executive branch. Similarly, the Constitution left unclear the extent of the powers that were implied by the president's responsibilities in war, peace, and diplomacy.[2]

In large measure, presidents have been able to fill the interpretive void, as "presidentialists" at the Constitutional Convention such as James Wilson, Gouverneur Morris, and Alexander Hamilton had hoped. As Richard Pious has written, "The president claims the silences of the Constitution."[3] The expansion of executive power did not come easily, however. The institutional design of the Constitution created congressional as well as presidential partisans, including influential political leaders such as Thomas Jefferson and James Madison. This chapter and those that follow chronicle the major developments that have shaped both the idea of presidential power, including some furious debates about the proper definition of executive authority, and the institutional changes that have occurred in the presidency.

THE ELECTION OF GEORGE WASHINGTON

Many of the most important questions about the character and breadth of presidential authority were settled during the two terms served by George Washington. The nation's first chief executive was very much aware that his actions could establish enduring precedents. "Few who are not philosophical spectators," Washington wrote early in his first term, "can realize the difficult and delicate part which a man in my situation has to act. . . . In our progress towards political happiness my station is new; and, if I may use the expression, I walk on untrodden ground. There is scarcely any part of my conduct which may not hereafter be drawn into precedent."[4]

Significant precedents for the proper conduct of the executive office were settled not only by the first president but also by the First Congress. Its work from 1789 to 1791, Thach has observed, "was simply the continuation of that done at the Constitutional Convention two years before."[5] Many of those who had framed the Constitution in Philadelphia were on hand in New York, the government's first temporary capital, to put the new instrument into operation. The First Congress included eighteen delegates to the convention: eight in the House of Representatives, including Madison, and ten in the Senate. "It is safe to say," historian Charles A. Beard has written, "that four-fifths of the active, forceful leaders of the Convention helped to realize as a process of government the paper constitution they had drafted."[6]

The election of George Washington as the first president was never in doubt. Still, as one historian has written, "Never was the election of a president so much a foregone conclusion and yet so tortuous in consummation."[7] Although the Electoral College met in the various state capitals on February 4, 1789, its unanimous vote for Washington was not official until the president of the Senate, temporarily elected for the purpose, opened the ballots in the presence of both the House and the Senate. One of the final acts of the outgoing Congress of the Articles of Confederation had been to summon the new Congress to convene in New York on March 4. But the newly elected legislators were slow to arrive, and a quorum still had not been reached by the end of the month. Anyone other than Washington might have been in the capital in time for the opening of Congress, which finally occurred when the House obtained a bare quorum on April 1 and the Senate on April 6. But Washington wanted to fulfill the strictest requirements of correct behavior. Because he would not be officially elected until a joint session of Congress tallied the votes of the electors, he waited for formal notification at his Mount Vernon, Virginia, home and worried about the "stupor or listlessness" being displayed by the members of the new Congress on whom the success of the Constitution would largely depend.[8]

Ironically, the start of the new government was further delayed by Washington himself who, when he finally received official notice of his election on April 14 from Secretary of the Congress Charles Thompson, took his time riding from Virginia to New York "lest unseemly haste suggest that he was improperly eager for the office."[9] Because the president-elect believed that the future of the government required its acceptance by the people, he was concerned with how his progress through the states to the capital would be received.

Washington's caution, however, went deeper than an awareness of the American people's fear of executive power. As Gordon Wood has written, Washington, both as general and as president, sought to fulfill the "Cincinnatus myth of Roman legend," which celebrates the disinterested patriot who devotes his life to his country. Washington's diffidence, although studied, was not disingenuous. Self-denial came naturally to him: in 1783, toward the end of the Revolutionary War, Washington had faced down the Newburgh Conspiracy, a cabal of army officers who were prepared to act against Congress for failing to meet its financial obligations to the military. Although the exact plans of the conspiring officers were never stated clearly, they apparently discussed displacing Congress and ruling the country themselves. Revered by most of the officers and soldiers, Washington could have emulated famous generals-turned-dictator such as Julius Caesar, Oliver Cromwell, and Napoleon by taking advantage of this uprising to advance his personal power. Instead, at a hastily called meeting he prevailed on the conspirators to reaffirm their loyalty to Congress. At a time when the relationship between the army and the legislature was still unsettled, Washington established a critical precedent that strengthened the still-fragile tradition of military subordination to civilian authority. The Newburgh incident also enhanced Washington's reputation for honesty and unshakable devotion to republican government and the ideals of the Revolution.[10] Thomas Jefferson expressed the general feeling when he observed that "the moderation and virtue of a single character had probably prevented this revolution from being closed as most others have been by a subversion of that liberty it was intended to establish."[11]

After the signing of the peace treaty that ended the Revolutionary War and secured British recognition of American independence, Washington surrendered his sword to Congress on December 23, 1783, and retired to Mount Vernon. His retirement from power had a profound effect throughout the Western world. "It was extraordinary, it was unprecedented in modern times," Wood has written, for "a victorious general [to surrender] his arms and [return] to his farm."[12] English military heroes such as William of Orange and the Duke of Marlborough had all sought political rewards commensurate with their military achievements. In contrast, Washington sincerely wanted, both for himself and his soldiers, to "return to our Private Stations in the bosom of a free, peaceful and happy country."[13] The American people recognized Washington's sincerity and responded with respect, admiration, even awe. As classicist Garry Wills has noted, Washington "gained power from his willingness to give it up."[14]

The popular adulation that greeted Washington in every hamlet as he traveled to New York to become president revealed his country's devotion. As he entered Philadelphia, surrounded by military horsemen who had formed an escort fifteen miles from the city, some twenty thousand citizens "lined every fence, field, and avenue." At the city limits, infantry wheeled and artillery fired their cannon. The units then fell into line behind Washington, as did squads of citizens on every block until, as one newspaper account had it, "the column swelled beyond credibility itself." The parade finally reached the City Tavern, where Washington was honored with "a very grand and beautiful banquet." The evening was topped off by fireworks.[15] The nation's first president arrived at last in New York in time to be inaugurated on April 30, 1789.

The long and complicated business of Washington's election and his assumption of the responsibilities of the presidency foretold the major task of his administration: "to make the government which had been adopted, often by the thinnest of majorities, and in only eleven out of thirteen states, happily acceptable to the overwhelming majority of the entire population."[16] This was an ambitious task. It required the construction of a unified and energetic national government in a political landscape that was traditionally inhospitable to strong central authority. That the "more perfect Union" promised by the Constitution included a strong presidency was particularly notable, even radical, in the American context, in which executive power had long been the object of public distrust. In view of this tradition, bringing the constitutional presidency to life may have been an impossible task without Washington's great popularity and propriety. Indeed, Washington was, or so James Madison wrote in 1789, the only aspect of the government that really caught the imagination of the people at the outset.[17]

MAKING THE PRESIDENCY SAFE FOR DEMOCRACY

As America's first "republican monarch," historian Joanne B. Freeman has written, "Washington had an exceedingly difficult role: somehow he had to embody the new government's dignity and authority without rising to monarchical excess."[18] Washington's awe-inspiring personality and popularity made him an indispensable source of unity and legitimacy for the newly formed government. At the same time, those who were suspicious of strong executive power found these qualities dangerous. The result was that many of the conflicts that arose during Washington's administration and that of his successor, John Adams, involved efforts to make executive power compatible with republican government.

Some of these conflicts concerned the most routine matters. For example, Washington's schedule became the subject of controversy at the start of his administration, prompting him to distribute queries to trusted advisers "on a line of conduct most eligible to be pursued by the President of the United States." The challenge, as Washington understood it, was to establish precedents for presidential conduct that would allow the executive enough privacy to get his work done and enough distance to retain the dignity of the office, without giving the impression that he disdained contact with the people. The course that Washington decided on satisfied neither those, such as Vice President Adams and Treasury Secretary Alexander Hamilton, who wanted to insulate the president from excessive popular influence, nor zealous republicans who wished to see an open executive office. Nevertheless, Washington revealed his great sensitivity to the importance of attaining public support and respect for the presidency through activities that, no matter how mundane, were of great symbolic importance:

Washington established two occasions a week when any respectably dressed person could, without introduction, invitation, or any prearrangement, be ushered into his presence. One was the President's "levee," for men only, every Tuesday from three to four. The other was Martha's tea party, for men and women, held on Friday evenings. Washington would also stage dinners on Thursdays at four o'clock in the afternoon. To avoid any charges of favoritism or any contests for invitations, only officials and their families would be asked to the dinners, and these in an orderly system of rotation.[19]

Washington's effort to strike the right balance between "courtly formality and republican simplicity" was broadly, but not universally, successful.[20] As historian Catherine Allgor has written, "To Jefferson these entertainments embodied European practices characteristic of the court systems that republicanism meant to overthrow . . . the deep corruption of monarchies."[21]

An even more controversial issue of etiquette was how the president should be addressed on formal occasions. A committee of the House of Representatives wanted to address him simply as "the President of the United States." But in May 1789 the Senate, at the urging of Vice President Adams, who was presiding over the upper chamber, rejected the House report. Adams, believing that "titles and politically inspired elegance were essential aspects of strong government," supported a title such as "His Elective Majesty," "His Mightiness," or even "His Highness the President of the United States and Protector of the Rights of the Same."[22] But this proposal proved controversial. Madison led the opposition in the House to what he perceived as the Senate's effort to apply nomenclature to the executive that would be "dangerous to republicanism."

At first, Washington favored a title for the president as grand as Adams's suggestions: "His High Mightiness, the President of the United States and Protector of Their Liberties."[23] But when he realized the extent of the controversy, Washington threw his support to Madison, even expressing annoyance at Adams's efforts "to bedizen him with a superb but spurious title." On

May 27, in a letter to Jefferson, Madison reported with relief that calm had been restored in Congress; the episode's only result was the facetious presentation to the heavy-set Adams of the title "His Rotundity."[24] Thereafter, it was agreed that the chief executive should have no more elaborate title than president of the United States.

Beneath all the bickering over etiquette and nomenclature lay serious matters of state. Some political leaders, such as Adams and Hamilton, believed that a strong executive was necessary to make the American experiment in self-government successful. Other important figures in the new government, especially Jefferson and Madison, were concerned that too much reliance on the presidency would undermine the delicate system of checks and balances that had been worked out in Philadelphia in 1787. Madison had led the effort to strengthen the national government at the convention, and he played a critical role during Washington's presidency in fighting off some early legislative attempts to encroach on the executive domain. Yet concern about the domestic policies and international objectives that Hamilton pursued as Washington's secretary of the Treasury spurred Madison to join Jefferson in opposing the expansion of executive power after 1790.

Even minor controversies became important when they touched on the central principles of how a republican government ought to work. The fundamental issues that animated battles over such matters underlay virtually all of the conflicts that made the task of forming a new government so delicate. It was to Washington's great credit that he was able to mediate effectively the disputes that surrounded the creation of the American presidency and, in doing so, to build a strong foundation for national unity.

FORMING THE EXECUTIVE BRANCH

During Washington's first term, Congress passed bills to establish three major executive departments: State, Treasury, and War. In accordance with the Constitution, the heads of these departments were nominated by the president and confirmed by the Senate. For secretary of state, Washington chose Jefferson, who as minister to France had shown himself to be an excellent diplomat. Hamilton, a widely recognized expert on finance and commerce, became secretary of the Treasury. Henry Knox, a diligent administrator who had served General Washington reliably as chief of artillery during the Revolutionary War, was President Washington's choice to be secretary of war.

Washington selected Edmund Randolph of Virginia as the first attorney general. At that time, the office of attorney general occupied a unique position in the executive branch. It did not yet possess the status and dignity of a department, but the attorney general attended cabinet meetings and served as legal adviser to the president and the department heads.[25]

In forming the executive branch, the Washington administration employed highly informal procedures. No rigid division of labor was established between the departments, nor did formal rules or strictly defined codes of behavior govern their internal operations. In general, executive administration was ad hoc and personal. Indeed, the notion of a "President's Cabinet" did not take form during the early years of Washington's tenure. Washington did not even use the word *cabinet* until April 1793, and he did not convene formal meetings of "the Heads of the Great Departments" and the attorney general until almost the end of his first term.[26]

Administrative informality did not mean, however, that no purpose animated the appointments and procedures of Washington's presidency. Recognizing the need to invest his administration with talented and respected leaders whose presence would advance the acceptability of the new government, Washington sought the most admired people available to carry out its functions. His three principal counselors—Hamilton, Jefferson, and, in Congress, Madison—formed a remarkable constellation of advisers, and the latter two later were elected president in their own right. Nevertheless, strong disagreements arose among them, with Madison and Jefferson often allied against Hamilton. Washington recognized the varied talents of these three independent-minded leaders and, for a time, was able to yoke them in a "single harness." His ability to do so and the general success that he achieved as an administrator helped "to plant in the minds of the American people the model of a government which commanded respect by reason of its integrity, energy, and competence."[27]

Washington's appointments to other jobs were also intended to enhance the legitimacy of the fledgling national government. As the bills to create the various departments became law during his first term, the president found himself with nearly a thousand offices to fill. Considering all of these appointments to be important, Washington devoted an enormous amount of time to them. According to administrative historian Leonard D. White, "No collector of customs, captain of a cutter, keeper of a lighthouse, or surveyor of revenue was appointed except after specific consideration by the President."[28]

Although besieged by applicants, directly or through intermediaries, Washington "scrupulously declined to exploit the opportunity to create a patronage system." His appointments were made with little regard to personal relations or family connections. They were partisan only in the sense that he chose persons "of known attachment" to the Constitution. Especially during the first two years of his administration, Washington took care not to appoint former British loyalists or other persons whose support for the Constitution was doubtful.[29]

In general, White has written, "Washington's rules of selection shone in statesmanlike splendor. The dominating standard was the rule of fitness."[30] In

The first cabinet, selected by President George Washington, far left, included Secretary of War Henry Knox (on Washington's left), Secretary of the Treasury Alexander Hamilton, Secretary of State Thomas Jefferson, and Attorney General Edmund Randolph.

screening applicants for jobs, however, Washington did not employ the criteria of "merit" and "neutral competence" that have dominated civil service procedures since the early twentieth century. He was concerned less with his appointees' expertise than with their reputation for good character. Apart from personal integrity, standing in one's local community was a principal ingredient of fitness, reflecting Washington's desire to cultivate a favorable opinion of the national government in the far-flung sections of the Union. As Stanley Elkins and Eric McKitrick have observed, Washington routinely referred to his appointees as "first Characters . . . who by virtue of their abilities and records of public service stood first, as it were, in the respect of their neighbors."[31] In every way, Washington's personnel policies manifested his concern for the requirements of building a nation.

PRESIDENTIAL "SUPREMACY" AND THE CONDUCT OF THE EXECUTIVE BRANCH

In addition to his hiring policies, Washington established the critical precedent that authority over the executive branch belongs primarily to the president. He subscribed to a theory of administration that viewed members of the cabinet as "assistants or deputies" of the president. As Hamilton had written in *Federalist* No. 72, such persons "ought to derive their offices from his appointment, at least from his nomination, and ought to be subject to his superintendence." Washington's theory of national administration prevailed against competing views that foresaw either the Senate or individual cabinet officers sharing fully in the direction of the executive departments.[32]

The belief that the upper house of the legislature should be involved in the details of administration was especially strong in the American tradition, reaching far back into the colonial era. Indeed, a bill nearly passed Congress during Washington's first term that would have severely restricted the president's administrative authority. The bill, which involved the creation of the Department of State, raised the issue of where the power to dismiss an executive official should lie. Significantly, Hamilton's advocacy of the "deputy" theory of administration did not extend to the removal of executive office-holders. In *Federalist* No. 77, he had cited the principle of "steady administration" to contend that the Senate's approval was needed to remove an official, just as it was to appoint one.

Washington and Madison, his chief congressional ally in this matter, responded to *Federalist*-quoting critics of a strong executive by arguing that presidents would be rendered powerless if they were not master of their own domain. As Madison argued during the House debate on the State Department bill, "Vest [the removal power] in the Senate jointly with the President, and you abolish at once the great principle of unity and responsibility in the executive department, which was intended for the security of liberty and the common good."[33] In other words, how could the president be held responsible for the actions of incompetent or disobedient executive officials if he had no authority to fire them?

Madison successfully led the fight in the House against senatorial interference with presidential removals, but in the Senate the final vote was tied. Vice President Adams, as president of the Senate, broke the tie in favor of the president's unilateral power to remove executive appointees from office. From then on, the First Congress followed Madison's lead by passing laws establishing the other major departments of the government that were carefully designed to minimize legislative influence in the executive branch.[34]

The decision to vest the removal power in the president was a critical prelude to Washington's dominance of administration. As the most comprehensive account of public administration in the early days of the Republic concludes, "All major decisions in matters of administration, and many minor ones, were made by the President. No department head, not even Hamilton, settled any matter of importance without consulting the President and securing his approval."[35]

Congress's eventual acquiescence to presidential supremacy over the departments was probably a tribute to Washington's demonstrated devotion to the principle of separation of powers. The president shared Madison's conviction that the chief executive should be supreme in matters pertaining to the conduct of the executive branch but restrained in matters that are rightfully the legislature's. Washington did recommend legislation to Congress, albeit sparingly, but he applied no pressure to get his program enacted. "Nor," Washington biographer James Thomas Flexner has observed, "did he attempt during his first term to achieve by executive orders any matter that the strictest interpretation of the Constitution could regard as within the legislative domain."[36]

Hamilton had argued in *Federalist* No. 73 that aggressive use of the veto was essential for the president to protect the office from legislative usurpation and to "furnish security against the enaction of improper laws." But Washington believed that the president's veto power should be applied only to bills of doubtful constitutionality, not unwise policy.[37] His caution was understandable in the context of the times. As Richard Beeman has observed, "The first three grievances listed in the Declaration of Independence had been directed at the abuse of the royal governors' veto power.[38]

Washington's circumspect use of the veto did not mean that he was a weak president, intent on avoiding conflict with the legislature at all costs. Rather, the first president sought to win the trust of Congress and the people so that he and future presidents would be able to exercise power forcefully when it seemed most appropriate—that is, when managing the affairs of the executive branch, conducting foreign policy, and upholding the law. In view of the inherently uneasy relationship between executive power and popular rule, Washington feared that aggressive presidential efforts to dominate the legislative process might vindicate the fears of the Anti-Federalists that the presidency would tend toward monarchy. Washington's respect for Congress won him the trust of most legislators, which eventually enabled him to carve out significant spheres of presidential influence in his own domain. Just as Washington's self-denial at the end of the revolution set the stage for his ascent to the presidency, so did his restraint as the first president bestow legitimacy on the office he occupied.[39]

Washington's propriety in executive-legislative relations extended even to foreign policy. The president did not hesitate to assert his primacy in diplomatic affairs, but he worked hard to develop a line of communication with the Senate, which he believed was required by the Constitution's stipulation that the president seek that body's "Advice and Consent" on treaties. Washington initially interpreted this requirement to include consultation with the Senate before treaty negotiations with another country began. But his first effort to involve the Senate fully in the making of a treaty occasioned an awkward and embarrassing incident that caused a very different precedent to be established.

After Washington drafted instructions for a commission he had appointed, with Senate approval, to negotiate a treaty with the Creek Indians, he accompanied acting secretary of war Knox to the Senate chamber in August 1789 to seek the senators' "Advice and Consent." Vice President Adams began the session by reading the proposed treaty to the Senate. But the president's appeal for consultation was greeted with an awkward silence that was broken only reluctantly by the senators, who proceeded to engage in a confused and tentative discussion of the treaty. Finally, Sen. William Maclay of Pennsylvania, certain that there was "no chance of a fair investigation of subjects while the President of the United States sat there, with his Secretary of War, to support his opinions and overawe the timid and neutral part of the Senate," spoke in favor of a motion that the papers of the president be submitted to a Senate committee for study. As the senator sat down, Washington started up in what Maclay described as a "violent fret" and cried out: "This defeats every purpose of my coming here."[40] Although Washington achieved his purpose in the end—the Senate later ratified the treaty with only minor changes—he had to sit for a long time, listening to what seemed to him a dull and irrelevant debate. When the president left the Senate chamber, he reportedly was overheard saying that he would "be damned if he ever went there again."

The Creek Indian treaty incident revealed the great difficulty of establishing a forum for formal personal encounters between the chief executive and the legislature within the constitutional system of "separated institutions sharing powers." Washington in effect "slammed the door" on similar encounters in the future and, as a result, neither he nor any later president ever consulted the Senate in the same way.[41] Most significant, Washington's failure to obtain the Senate's active cooperation in the preliminary work of making treaties ended up firmly establishing the president's supremacy in matters of diplomacy. To be sure, presidents never did come to possess an unhampered treaty-making power. But the Washington administration created a precedent that relegated the Senate to approving or rejecting treaties that the executive already had negotiated.

PRESIDENTIAL NONPARTISANSHIP AND THE BEGINNING OF PARTY CONFLICT

Washington's conduct as president embodied his understanding that the presidency was a nonpartisan office. Like most of the framers of the Constitution, he disapproved of "factions" and did not regard himself as the leader of any political party. Washington believed that Article II of the Constitution encouraged the president to stand apart from the jarring conflict that was inherent in a legislative body. As such, the president could provide a strong measure of unity and stability to the political system. This was a task that, by temperament and background, Washington was well suited to perform. Although he insisted on being master of the executive branch, it was contrary to his principles to try to influence either congressional elections or the legislative process. The primary duty of the president, he believed, was to execute the laws.[42]

Washington's conception of the presidency did not survive even his own administration. Disagreements within his brilliant constellation of advisers led to the early demise of the nonpartisan presidency. Party conflict arose from the sharp differences between Hamilton and Jefferson that emerged during Washington's first term and became irreconcilable during his second term. These differences became obvious in the reaction to Hamilton's financial measures for the "adequate support of public credit," which he proposed, at the behest of the House of Representatives, in a series of reports to Congress in 1790 and 1791. In the reports, Hamilton called on Congress to assume the war debts of the states, to create a national bank, and to enact a system of tariffs to protect infant manufacturing industries in the United States.

All of these proposals, save for the protectionist tariff, were supported by Washington and passed by Congress. Once implemented, Hamilton's program allowed the United States, so lately on the verge of bankruptcy, to establish sounder credit and a more stable financial system than all but a few European nations. Yet these measures, successful as they were, pushed Jefferson into barely disguised opposition to the Washington administration's domestic program, sowing seeds of formal party conflict that blossomed as soon as Washington retired from the presidency.

Jefferson did not oppose all of Hamilton's measures; indeed, he approved of the plan to pay the national government's domestic and foreign debts. Although Jefferson also had grave reservations about the national government assuming the states' debts, believing that such a policy would unduly benefit securities speculators, he acquiesced even to this policy as part of a deal he worked out with Hamilton. The two agreed that the nation's capital would be transferred from New York to Philadelphia in 1790 for ten years, pending permanent removal in 1800 to the new federal city of Washington, which would be built on the Potomac River between Maryland and Jefferson's home state of Virginia. But Jefferson, and eventually Madison, opposed Hamilton's proposal for a national bank, which was contained in the Treasury secretary's December 1790 report to Congress. According to Jefferson and Madison, Hamilton's plan would establish national institutions and policies that exceeded the constitutional powers of the new government.

Furthermore, Hamilton's initiatives presupposed a principal role for the president in formulating public policies and carrying them out. This view,

Jefferson and Madison believed, made the more decentralized and republican institutions—Congress and the states—subordinate to the executive, thereby undermining popular sovereignty and starting the United States down the path toward a British-style monarchy. In 1791 Madison warned, "The incompetency of one Legislature to regulate all the various objects belonging to the local governments would evidently force a transfer of many of them to the executive department; whilst the increasing splendor and number of its prerogatives supplied by this source, might prove excitements to ambition too powerful for a sober execution of the executive plan, and consequently strengthen the pretext for an hereditary designation of the magistrate."[43]

NEUTRALITY PROCLAMATION 1793

When war broke out in 1793 between Great Britain and France, a difference of opinion about the executive's proper role in foreign affairs aggravated the growing rift between Hamilton and Jefferson. Convinced that the French Revolution of 1789 had gotten out of hand, degenerating into mob rule, Hamilton and his "Federalist" supporters took the side of England, a nation for which they had deep sympathies. Jefferson and Madison endorsed what they believed to be the sacred republican cause of the French Revolution. They and their fellow "Democratic-Republicans" regarded Hamilton's support of England as evidence of his supposed preference for monarchy.

Conflicts over foreign affairs, like those over domestic policy, were inextricably joined to contrasting beliefs about the proper extent of presidential power. As political scientist Fred Greenstein has observed, Washington was supremely confident of his ability to chart the new nation's course through dangerous international waters because, as commander in chief during the Revolutionary War, he had "perfected his political and diplomatic skills in the course of his dealings with the [independent] state governments, Congress, and France."[44] But when Washington issued the Neutrality Proclamation of 1793, the Anglo-French question provoked a bitter exchange of views about the executive's proper role in foreign policy. The proclamation declared that the duties and interests of the United States required the government to "with sincerity and good faith adopt and pursue a conduct friendly and impartial to the belligerent powers." It prohibited Americans from "committing, aiding, or abetting hostilities against any of the said powers, or by carrying to them any of those articles which are deemed contraband by the modern usage of nations."[45]

Even before Washington's policy was announced, Hamilton and Jefferson took predictable stands on the merits of the Neutrality Proclamation. In private councils, Jefferson advised the president against it on two grounds. First, he believed such a unilateral executive action to be unconstitutional. A declaration of neutrality was, in effect, a declaration that there would be no war, a decision that rightfully belonged to Congress. Second, the 1778 treaty that secured French support for the American Revolution obligated the United States to provide France with any necessities of war that had to be brought across the Atlantic. In reply, Hamilton told the president that in the absence of a declaration of war by Congress, the executive had full power to proclaim and enforce American neutrality. Moreover, he defended neutrality between Great Britain and France on its merits, claiming that the tumultuous events in France had deprived that nation of any permanent government, thereby abrogating the obligations of the 1778 treaty.

Washington sided with Hamilton on the neutrality issue, but he took pains to unify his administration in public support of the proclamation. To mollify Jefferson, the word *neutrality* was not used in the text, although the sense clearly was there. Jefferson won a more substantial concession when Washington, against Hamilton's recommendation, decided to receive France's ambassador to the United States, Edmond Genet, which made the United States the first nation to receive an emissary from the new Republic of France. These concessions to the secretary of state notwithstanding, the proclamation was a victory for Hamilton. It boldly asserted the president's power of initiative in the conduct of foreign affairs.[46]

The controversy over the neutrality proclamation became public after Washington announced his policy, prompting Hamilton to write a series of newspaper articles under the pseudonym "Pacificus." Madison, at Jefferson's urging, replied to these articles in articles written as the "Helvidius." The issues that therstwhile coauthors of *The Federalist Papers* broached in this exchange illuminate the fundamental nature of a conflict that has occupied the nation's attention time and time again, not only in foreign affairs but also in other matters pertaining to the president's authority.

In defending the neutrality proclamation, Hamilton offered a sweeping justification for discretionary presidential power that sharply distinguished between the Constitution's separate "vesting clauses" for legislative and executive authority. Article I, Hamilton pointed out, states that "all legislative Powers herein granted shall be vested in a Congress of the United States," while Article II seems to provide a much more general grant: "The executive Power shall be vested in a President of the United States of America." The absence from Article II of the words "herein granted," he argued, meant that the executive power was both wide-ranging and vested exclusively in the president, "subject only to the exceptions and qualifications which are expressed in the Constitution."[47]

In foreign affairs, the explicit constitutional restrictions on presidential power extended no further than the right of the Senate to ratify treaties and of Congress to declare war. These rights of the legislature, Hamilton insisted, did not hinder the executive in other matters of foreign policy, which "naturally" were the domain of the president.[48] Indeed, Hamilton set forth a theory of presidential power that not only delegated to the executive nearly absolute discretion in the conduct of foreign affairs, but also proposed a broad conception of emergency powers that later presidents, especially those in the twentieth and twenty-first centuries, would draw on generously.[49]

Madison, replying in a rival newspaper as Helvidius, denied that foreign policy was "naturally" an executive power. The tasks of foreign policy—to declare war, to conclude peace, and to form alliances—were among "the highest acts of sovereignty; of which the legislative power must at least be an integral and preeminent part." In foreign as in domestic matters, Madison argued, republican government required that the president's power be confined to executing the laws. To suggest, as Hamilton did, that foreign policy was within the proper definition of executive power was to imply that the executive branch had a legislative power. Such an argument was "in theory an absurdity—in practice a tyranny."[50]

Important as it was, the precedent Washington established that the president can unilaterally enunciate a policy of neutrality was less significant than the larger issue in the debate between his leading advisers: whether the president is limited by the letter of the Constitution or is a sovereign head of state, with discretion to act independently unless the Constitution specifically spells out exceptions and limitations. The debate between Pacificus and Helvidius signaled that Washington's hope of establishing a presidency above parties was unrealistic, thwarted by fundamental conflicts about the constitutional interpretation of presidential power.

THE WHISKEY REBELLION

The strains created by the controversy over the neutrality proclamation led inevitably to an outbreak of open party conflict. The Federalists shared Hamilton's support for commerce and manufacturing, a strong executive in a strong national government, and, in foreign policy, Great Britain. In contrast, the Democratic-Republicans shared Jefferson's devotion to agriculture, a strong legislature in a weak national government, and France. The full implications of this conflict became clear during the presidency of John Adams, who took office in 1797. But even Washington, during his second term, was confronted with serious problems born of partisan differences. These problems culminated in the first significant test of the president's constitutional power to "take Care that the Laws be faithfully executed."

In 1794 militant opposition to a national excise tax on the production of whiskey arose in several parts of the country, particularly in the four westernmost counties of Pennsylvania, where whiskey was so important to the local economy that it was used, like money, as a medium of exchange. Backcountry Pennsylvanians had avoided paying the hated whiskey tax since it was first levied in 1791.[51] In the summer of 1794 resistance turned into mass defiance, stimulated at least in part by a local Democratic-Republican organization, the Mingo Creek society. A federal marshal and an excise inspector were forced to flee the area in July, and for two weeks western Pennsylvania was agitated by impassioned meetings, radical oratory, threats to drive all federal authority from Pittsburgh by force, and occasional acts of violence.

President Washington's response to the so-called Whiskey Rebellion was to issue a stern proclamation on August 7, 1794, demanding that the rebels "disperse and retire peaceably to their respective abodes" and warning "all persons whomsoever against aiding, abetting, or comforting the perpetuators of the . . . treasonable acts."[52] Almost simultaneously, after satisfying the law by securing from Supreme Court justice James Wilson a certification that the situation was beyond the control of federal marshals and courts, Washington asked the governors of Maryland, New Jersey, Pennsylvania, and Virginia to supply a militia army to put down the rebellion.

The governors complied with Washington's request. An army of thirteen thousand was assembled in Harrisburg, Pennsylvania, in September. It promptly marched into western Pennsylvania, with Washington himself in command—"the first and only time," historian Joseph J. Ellis has pointed out, "a sitting American president led troops in the field."[53] Pennsylvania governor Thomas Mifflin had argued against federal intervention, insisting that his state's authority was adequate to cope with the outbreak of lawlessness. But Washington was persuaded by Hamilton to suppress the insurrection with a massive display of force.

Hamilton was convinced that Washington had to assert unequivocally the supremacy of the national government when in conflict with local claims of independence and to establish the president's leadership in such situations. But the secretary of the Treasury and leader of the Federalists also was motivated by partisan considerations. Hamilton viewed the insurrection in rural Pennsylvania as an opportunity to discredit and crush his political enemies by branding them as traitors. Referring to local Democratic-Republican societies, Hamilton averred in a letter to Washington on August 2, 1792, that "formal public meetings of influential individuals" had "fomented" the "general spirit of opposition" that produced the violence in the western counties.

Democratic-Republican leaders such as Jefferson and Madison did not actively oppose the national government's intervention in the insurrection; indeed, many members of the Democratic-Republican societies in Philadelphia and Baltimore volunteered to join the federal force against the Whiskey Rebellion. Nevertheless, the Democratic-Republicans found themselves in a politically vulnerable position because of the activities of their brethren in the West. Most Americans seemed convinced that treason and rebellion had arisen from the opposition societies. "The[ir] game," wrote Madison of the

Federalists' strategy, "was to connect the Democratic societies with the odium of insurrection, to connect the Republicans in Congress with those societies," and to place President Washington "in opposition to both."[54] The immediate result was that the Federalists won control of Congress in the 1794 midterm election.[55]

For his part, Washington delayed using federal force in Pennsylvania until his protracted efforts to conciliate the rebels were rejected, reflecting "his earnest wish to avoid a resort to coercion."[56] In the face of a Washington-led army, the rebellion dissolved. Only twenty rebels were found; they were taken to the state capital in Philadelphia and charged with treason. Two were convicted, but Washington, with his usual determination to show that a strong executive need not be despotic, pardoned them.[57]

Although his display of force in Pennsylvania ended anticlimactically, Washington reported to Congress on November 19, 1794, that suppressing the insurrection had demonstrated that the prosperity of the United States rested "on solid foundations, by furnishing an additional proof that [citizens embraced understood] the true principles of government and liberty."[58] "The first president clearly understood that a government which cannot enforce its laws is no government at all," historian William M. Goldsmith has written, "and he also realized that within the framework of our complex political system, with its deliberate distribution of power, it is the responsibility of the executive to see that the laws are obeyed."[59]

Nevertheless, the Whiskey Rebellion and Washington's response exacerbated rather than ended the political conflicts that divided Americans in the 1790s. Jefferson and Madison became even more convinced that Hamilton intended to establish an overweening executive, including a standing army, that would subvert the Constitution. Moreover, as word of the actual events in western Pennsylvania spread throughout the country, the prestige of the Federalist Party began to erode. Jefferson wrote to Madison on December 28, 1794, that "the information of our militia, returned from the Westward, is uniform, that tho the people there let them pass quietly, they were objects of their laughter, not of their fear; . . . that their detestation of the excise law is universal, and has now associated to it a detestation of government." Jefferson added that the time was coming when the Democratic-Republicans would "fetch up the leeway of our vessel."[60]

Fortunately, the conflict between the Federalists and the Democratic-Republicans never became as raw and disruptive as the framers of the Constitution had feared partisan strife would be. The enduring restraint on factionalism in the United States may be attributed in part to the forceful example of nonpartisanship that was offered by George Washington at a time when maintaining unity was critical to the survival of the new government. To some extent, Washington sought to deal with the divisions between the Hamiltonians and the Jeffersonians by avoiding them, choosing to preside over the government rather than to dominate it.[61] As his response to the Whiskey Rebellion makes clear, Washington at times took stands on controversial issues, usually on the Hamiltonian side. Yet his extraordinary stature and popularity, combined with his commitment to a strong and independent legislature, restrained partisan strife for as long as he was president. Moreover, Washington's renunciation of party leadership left his successors a legacy of presidential impartiality that has never been eclipsed. Even after a formal two-party system emerged, the precedent set by Washington demanded that the chief executive strive to lead the nation, not just the party that governs the nation.

WASHINGTON'S RETIREMENT AND THE JAY TREATY: THE CONSTITUTIONAL CRISIS OF 1796

Near the end of 1795, the paramount political question for most public figures in the United States was whether Washington would accept a third term as president. The Constitution imposed no limit on presidential reeligibility, and, although Washington's political reputation was slightly tarnished by the partisan animosities that divided his cabinet, he could easily have remained in office had he chosen to do so.

Washington, however, was eager to return to Mount Vernon. In September 1796 he announced his retirement, marking the event by releasing his Farewell Address, which was published rather than spoken to an audience. Washington did not want his voluntary retirement to set a precedent limiting future presidents to two terms. Rather, he wanted the country to learn that the Constitution would function without him as president.

Washington's decision to retire eased somewhat the Jeffersonians' concerns about the dangerous aggrandizement of executive power. So did the absence of an heir: George and Martha Washington had no children. As biographer Richard Brookhiser has pointed out, to a nation as familiar with monarchy and besotted with Washington as the United States was in its early years, "The dynastic temptation was very real. The country was lucky that there was so little material for temptation to work with. Of the first five presidents, only John Adams had sons who survived to adulthood. . . . As it was, John Adams's eldest son, John Quincy Adams, became the sixth president." [62]

Washington's retirement cleared the way for a more partisan form of presidential politics. As long as he was president, Washington was able by dint of his prestige to restrain open party conflict. But Vice President Adams, although a distinguished and respected political leader, lacked Washington's stature as well as his reputation for impartiality. In the division between Federalists and Democratic-Republicans, Adams was clearly identified with the Federalists. His role in the controversy over the president's title and his well-known admiration for the British form of government marked him as a "monarchist" in the eyes of Jeffersonians. When Washington's decision to retire became known and Adams stepped forward as the heir apparent, the presidential campaign of 1796 began in earnest.

The 1796 election is generally regarded as one of the bitterest and most acrimonious in American history. The election matched John Adams and Thomas Pinckney, the Federalist candidates for president and vice president, against the Democratic-Republican ticket of Thomas Jefferson and Aaron Burr. The divisions between the parties were crystallized by the controversial Jay Treaty, which had been signed in London in November 1794.

In the Jay Treaty, Great Britain pledged that it would evacuate the north-west military posts that had sustained British power on American soil since the Revolution. The treaty also won a limited right for American vessels to trade with the British West Indies. As such, it promised to secure the territorial integrity of the United States and to ameliorate dangerous conflicts at sea. (Several skirmishes, the by-product of Great Britain's ongoing war with France, had brought the United States and Great Britain to the brink of war.) Yet when some secret terms of the Jay Treaty were leaked to the Democratic-Republican press in late June 1795, a political firestorm ensued that made John Jay (the chief justice of the United States who, acting as a presidential envoy, had negotiated the treaty) and, by implication, Washington the targets of vicious partisan attacks.

Democratic-Republican opposition to the Jay Treaty was animated by an intense dislike of the British, which was reinforced by Great Britain's use of its eight northwestern posts to stir American Indian tribes to attack settlers in the Northwest Territory. Democratic-Republicans, who were strongest in the South, also were enraged because the treaty provided no compensation to slave owners for the slaves seized by the British at the end of the Revolution. Nor did it create a mechanism to settle the pre–Revolutionary War debts that Americans owed to British citizens, which placed southerners, especially, in jeopardy of having to repay loans of long standing. In effect, then, the Jay Treaty became the issue through which the emerging polarization between Hamiltonians and Jeffersonians was hardened into organized two-party conflict.[63]

The Constitution required a two-thirds vote of the Senate to ratify a treaty. On June 24, 1795, the Federalist-dominated majority ratified the Jay Treaty by 20 to 10, with not a vote to spare. What made the treaty an election issue in 1796 was Madison's subsequent battle to undermine it in the House of Representatives. Because the treaty required that arbitration commissions be established to settle disagreements between the United States and Great Britain that were not resolved by the document itself, it could not be carried into effect without congressional appropriations. "Money bills," as the Constitution clearly specified, could originate only in the House. Whether the House, by virtue of its power over appropriations, was meant to share the Senate's role in foreign affairs was a constitutional issue that had not yet been settled. Madison sought to weld the widespread popular opposition to the treaty to Congress's own resentment of executive power. In doing so, he enjoyed the full support of Jefferson, who wrote on November 30, 1795, in a letter to Edward Rutledge, a friend in the South Carolina legislature: "I trust the popular branch of our legislature will disapprove of it [the Jay Treaty], and thus rid us of this infamous act, which is really nothing more than a treaty of alliance between England and the Anglomen of this country, against the legislature and people of the United States." [64]

On March 24, 1796, the Democratic-Republicans succeeded in passing a House resolution requesting the president to provide the House with all papers pertaining to the negotiation of the Jay Treaty. Albert Gallatin, one of the party's most persuasive leaders, argued that representatives had the authority to make this request "because their cooperation and sanction was necessary to carry the Treaty into full effect, to render it a binding instrument, and to make it properly speaking, a law of the land; because they had full discretion either to give or to refuse that cooperation; because they must be guided, in the exercise of that discretion, by the merits and expediency of the treaty itself, and therefore had a right to ask for every information which could assist them in deciding the question." [65]

Gallatin's aim was not merely to see the papers, or even to defeat the Jay Treaty and pave the way for the election of a Democratic-Republican president in 1796. [66] Along with Madison and Jefferson, he also wanted to assert the House's right to participate in the treaty-making process. They believed that if this power belonged exclusively to the president and two-thirds of the Senate, the president conceivably could act in concert with just twenty-two of the then–thirty-two senators to usurp all the powers of the House. Treaties, they noted, had the same constitutional status as the laws enacted by Congress.

In view of the Jay Treaty's unpopularity, the Democratic-Republicans had a real chance to scuttle it, which would have severely limited the president's power to conduct foreign affairs. But Washington, on the verge of retirement, chose to make the House's request for papers the last great constitutional issue of his presidency. He replied to the resolution with "a thunderous refusal," as historian Forrest McDonald has described it. [67] "To admit . . . a right in the House of Representatives to demand . . . papers respecting a negotiation with a foreign power," Washington asserted, "would be to establish a dangerous precedent." Except in matters pertaining to impeachment, "it does not occur that the inspection of papers asked for can be relative to any purpose under the cognizance of the House of Representatives."

Washington also lectured Congress on the Constitution. "Having been a member of the General Convention and knowing the principles on which the Constitution was formed," he observed pointedly, "the power of making treaties is exclusively vested in the President, by and with the advice and consent of the Senate, provided two-thirds of the senators present concur; and . . . every treaty so made and promulgated thenceforward became the law of the land." [68]

A constitutional impasse had been reached. The House claimed a right to see the papers, but it had no means to pry them loose from the president. A debate followed, consuming the entire month of April 1796, about whether the House would appropriate the funds (roughly $90,000) that were needed to carry the treaty into effect. In the end, Washington's resolute stand eroded the Democratic-Republicans' initial House majority. The enabling legislation for the treaty was approved at the end of April by the narrow vote of 51–48.

The Democratic-Republicans' effort to transform hostility to the Jay Treaty into a central campaign issue backfired. Their opposition to the treaty probably contributed to Adams's election as president in 1796 and to the Federalist gains in that year's congressional elections. The only solace the Democratic-Republicans could find in this latest defeat was that it rested on George Washington's influence, not the Federalist Party's. Even the Federalists must have realized, wrote Jefferson, "that nothing can support them but the colossus of the President's merits with the people, and the moment he retires, that his successor, if a monocrat, will be overborne by the republican sense of his Constituents." [69]

With the final enactment of the Jay Treaty, a constitutional crisis, underlain with bitter partisan strife, was averted. The incident did not settle permanently the question of the House's proper role in foreign affairs. More than two centuries later, the right of the House of Representatives to participate in all aspects of foreign policy is still a matter of serious debate. "But the precedent and correlative implications of the decision that Washington established in 1796," William Goldsmith has observed, "would be difficult to erase." [70]

THE 1796 ELECTION

In spite of the strong disagreements that divided Democratic-Republicans from Federalists, the contestants in the partisan strife of the 1790s were reluctant warriors. Partisanship was still not considered respectable in American politics, and candidates for president were not expected to seek the office actively. "Neither Adams nor Jefferson," historian John Ferling has noted, "left their farms that autumn, and neither issued public statements or wrote so much as a single letter in an effort to round up support." [71]

Nevertheless, party organizations dominated the election, conducting their campaigns through newspaper polemics, pamphlets, and political rallies. The issues that the parties raised so divided the country that the hard-won national unity the Constitutional Convention and the Washington administration had achieved was threatened. The Federalists branded Jefferson an atheist who would destroy all organized religion. He was accused of being a radical democrat who as president would allow republican government to deteriorate into the sort of mob rule that had recently brought the Reign of Terror to France. Democratic-Republicans excoriated Adams as a monarchist who neither believed in democracy nor respected the Constitution.

The 1796 election ended with a narrow Federalist victory. Adams was elected president with seventy-one electoral votes. He swept New England and, except for Pennsylvania, the Mid-Atlantic states while losing the South. Jefferson's sixty-eight electoral votes made him the vice president, because the avowedly nonpartisan constitutional mechanism for selecting the president and vice president had not yet been changed to accommodate the emergence of partisan competition. Until the Twelfth Amendment was enacted in 1804, the Constitution directed that every elector vote for two persons for president, with the second-place candidate becoming vice president. Because this mechanism was not designed to allow a party ticket to be chosen, the election of 1796 yielded an administration that was headed by the leaders of two hostile political organizations.

THE EMBATTLED PRESIDENCY OF JOHN ADAMS

John Adams became president in extraordinarily difficult circumstances. No other chief executive would ever have the unenviable task of succeeding a leader of Washington's stature. More significant, the international situation that Adams faced in 1797 was perilous. The Jay Treaty had greatly worsened American relations with an aggressive French government that was, after Napoleon Bonaparte defeated Austria in October 1797, at the height of its power. French harassment of American commerce at sea made Great Britain's interference with U.S. shipping in 1793 seem mild. As Jefferson said about George Washington, "The President is fortunate to get off just as the bubble is bursting, leaving others to hold the bag."[72]

The naval war with France escalated when Adams's diplomatic attempts to maintain Washington's policy of neutrality received an insulting and humiliating response from the French foreign ministry. The American mission to France, composed of John Marshall, Charles Cotesworth Pinckney, and Elbridge Gerry, a Democratic-Republican whom Adams chose to convince the opposition of his good intentions, was subjected to high-handed manipulation by Talleyrand, the French foreign minister. Talleyrand dispatched three representatives of the French government, referred to in secret dispatches as "X, Y, and Z," to meet with Adams's emissaries. Their mission was to discover how much the United States was willing to pay in bribes to French officials and loans to the French government to secure a treaty.

When the so-called XYZ Affair became public in early 1798, a furor erupted in the United States that seemed to make war with France inevitable. The more extreme Federalists, the "Arch-Federalists" or "Ultra-Federalists" as they were known, urged that a large army be created to deter an invasion by France. Although Adams was far more moderate than the extremists in his party, he also supported war preparations, especially the development of a larger navy. Meanwhile, war fever prompted Americans to "rally 'round the flag" in support of their president. Historian Sean Wilentz has noted that "Adams suddenly became, for the only time in his life, the focus of popular enthusiasm as the heroic American commander-in-chief."[73] He even took to wearing a full military uniform, adorned by a sword.

Adams's surge of popularity was short-lived, deflated by the higher taxes he and Congress imposed to pay for the expanded military. The resentment triggered by these taxes, especially the increased tax on whiskey, became a potent political issue for the Democratic-Republicans. Growing animosity between Federalists and Democratic-Republicans even led to rumors of civil discord and southern secession. At the end of June 1797, an alarmed Jefferson wrote to Edward Rutledge: "The passions are too high at present, to be cooled in our day. You and I have formerly seen warm debates and high political passions. But gentlemen of different politics would then speak to each other, and separate the business of the Senate from that of society. It is not so now. Men who have been intimate all their lives, cross the street to avoid meeting, and turn their heads another way, lest they should be obliged to touch their hats."[74]

Adams's efforts to deal with the domestic and international crises of the late 1790s were hindered as much by members of his own party as by the opposition. Although everyone expected the Democratic-Republicans, led behind the scenes by Vice President Jefferson, to oppose Adams's actions, "the Federalists were often as recalcitrant or bitter toward the president."[75] The president's most influential critic within the party was Hamilton, who regarded Adams as too moderate politically and therefore incapable of dealing with the nation's problems.

Although Adams was a Federalist, he intended to follow Washington's example of remaining above party as much as possible. The president was willing to accept a war declared by France, but he hoped to avoid one. His primary objectives were to protect American commerce, through diplomacy and an expanded navy, and to force the French to respect the American flag. Hamilton and his Arch-Federalist allies, however, wanted to exploit the conflict with

France, not to contain it. Ultimately, these differences caused an irreconcilable split within the Federalist Party. Jefferson noted in May 1797 that the "Hamiltons" were "only a little less hostile [to Adams] than to me."[76]

Hamilton severely tested Adams's authority as chief executive in several ways.[77] He was determined to guide the policy of the administration, even though he was not part of it. Hamilton had retired from the Treasury Department at the end of January 1795, but during the latter days of Washington's second term and throughout Adams's tenure he remained the dynamic center of the Federalist Party as a private citizen. Indeed, Hamilton's influence was enhanced in 1797 by Adams's decision to retain Washington's cabinet, a policy that the new president pursued both in deference to his predecessor and because he believed that good government required able and experienced administrators.[78]

Three members of Washington's final cabinet—Secretary of State Timothy Pickering, Secretary of War James McHenry, and Oliver Wolcott, who succeeded Hamilton as secretary of the Treasury—owed their positions in the government mostly to Hamilton, who had persuaded Washington to appoint them. In all important matters they looked to Hamilton, not to President Adams, to guide their actions. Only Charles Lee, who as attorney general was the least powerful member of the cabinet, and Benjamin Stoddert, who joined the cabinet as the secretary of the newly established Navy Department in 1798, were Adams loyalists. Disunity prevailed in executive policy except on those rare occasions when the president happened to agree with Hamilton.

As a result, the Adams administration suffered "an extraordinary situation in which the control of public policy became the prize of a struggle between a New York lawyer and a president who apparently was not fully aware of the activity of his rival."[79] The situation was aggravated by Adams's tendency to take retreats lasting as long as seven months from the capital (still in Philadelphia) in the erroneous belief that he could manage the affairs of government from his home in Quincy, Massachusetts.[80]

The conflict between Adams and the Arch-Federalists culminated in 1799, when the president decided to send a second mission to France in an effort to avoid war. In February, without consulting the cabinet or even the secretary of state, he nominated William Vans Murray, the American minister to the Netherlands, as minister plenipotentiary to the French Republic. Adams chose Murray because of his good relations with France; it was through Murray, in fact, that Adams had learned France was willing to receive a new American mission and wanted to avoid war with the United States. The Federalist-controlled Senate, which was sympathetic to Hamilton's views, probably would have rejected the nomination, but Adams's quick, unilateral action caught its members by surprise. Instead, senators compromised by asking for a three-member mission. The president consented.

Thwarting attempts by Secretary of State Pickering and others to postpone the sailing of the second mission, Adams first indicated that he was not opposed to a delay and then hurried the peace mission aboard an American frigate. The mission arrived in time to take advantage of France's uncertain political situation in the aftermath of a series of military defeats by the British. Although Adams's bold course aggravated his problems with the cabinet and the Federalist Party, it achieved a commercial agreement with France that removed the threat of war, thereby preserving the principle of neutrality toward Europe that he had inherited from George Washington.

More significant, Adams rescued the authority of the presidency. His political position was shaken by the peace mission controversy. In all likelihood it cost him any chance for reelection. But as Leonard White has written, "The outcome was a resounding affirmation of the authority of the President as chief executive and of the subordination of the department heads to his leadership and direction. Adams confirmed the character of the presidency as the Constitutional Convention had outlined it and as Washington had already formed it—but only after events which stirred grave doubts concerning its future."[81]

Solidifying his leadership in the aftermath of the peace mission, Adams rid the cabinet of the two men who were most disloyal to him. In May 1800 he asked for the resignation of McHenry, who gave it, and summarily fired Pickering when he refused to resign because "incredibly," according to John Ferling, "he expected Jefferson to be elected in the fall and wished to remain in charge of the last gasp of Federalist foreign policy."[82] Pickering was the first cabinet officer to be removed from office by a president. Adams appointed John Marshall to replace him as secretary of state.

THE ALIEN AND SEDITION ACTS

Scholars frequently praise John Adams for upholding the authority of the presidency in the face of a badly divided cabinet and party. But Adams also is widely condemned for his part in the passage and enforcement of the Alien and Sedition Acts of 1798. The Alien Act gave the president authority to expel foreigners who were suspected of subversion. The Sedition Act made it a crime, punishable by fine or imprisonment, to bring "false, scandalous and malicious" accusations against the president, Congress, or the government. Both acts were the product of war fever, which the Ultra-Federalists in Congress regarded as an opportunity to discredit Democratic-Republicans as anti-American. But Adams signed them into law without demurral.

The Sedition Act, in particular, was widely denounced as unconstitutional. To be sure, the act was not as oppressive as similar European statutes: it imposed on the prosecution the burden to prove an "intent to defame" and required a jury trial to convict. But the law was enforced in ways that treated legitimate political opposition as if it were a conspiracy against the government. As such, the Sedition Act violated the First Amendment to the Constitution, which had been added in 1791 as part of the Bill of Rights and which, among other things, forbade Congress to pass any law abridging freedom of speech or press.

The passage and enforcement of the Sedition Act was an unhappy chapter in American history. Although a much more drastic sedition law, the Espionage Act, was passed during World War I and enforced by sentences far more severe than those of Adams's day, the 1798 statute was marred, even motivated by partisan intolerance. Fourteen people were sentenced under the act, and suits were filed against five of the six leading Democratic-Republican newspapers. Indeed, most sedition cases came to trial in 1800 and were tied directly to the presidential election. The law degenerated into a Federalist instrument to stifle and even to destroy the Democratic-Republican Party.

But the Sedition Act was not simply an opportunistic partisan campaign tool. It represented a clash of views about the foundation of executive authority.[83] Was the personal reputation and character of the president the ultimate source of the office's authority, as the Federalists claimed? Or did the executive office's legitimacy properly rest in public opinion, as the Democratic-Republicans argued? The Federalists insisted that they were not attempting to restrict free speech, properly understood, but only false and malicious opinions that would destroy the reputation of national leaders. As President Adams put the Federalists' case, "The man or the nation without attachment to reputation, or honor, is undone."[84]

Democratic-Republicans warned that it was all too easy in the heat of political combat to exploit restrictive measures like the Sedition Act for partisan purposes. More fundamentally, they argued that opinions about government were intrinsically contentious and that judges and juries were incapable of distinguishing between legitimate and seditious points of view. Jefferson and his Democratic-Republican allies believed that all political opinions had a right to be heard, even those that were "false, scandalous, and malicious" or might "dissolve the Union or change its republican form." Such opinions should be allowed to "stand undisturbed as monuments of the safety with which the error of opinion may be tolerated where reason is left free to combat it."[85]

The partisan and intellectual dispute about the fundamental basis of presidential authority would have been much more damaging to the Union had Adams not resisted the most militant inclinations of his fellow Federalists. The president had little sympathy for the more extreme purposes of the Alien and Sedition Acts. He resisted Secretary of State Pickering's desire to use the alien laws to deport large numbers of immigrants. He also opposed the

Arch-Federalists' proposal to establish a large army. Adams's restraint was not unimportant. As historian Richard Hofstadter has written, "If we can imagine a determined High Federalist President in the White House seizing upon the most intense moment of Anti-French feeling to precipitate a war, we can imagine a partisan conflict that would have cracked the Union."[86] Nevertheless, although Adam's efforts to rise above partisan politics helped to prevent civil discord, they did not save him from defeat in the election of 1800. The Democratic-Republican victory sealed the fate of the Federalist Party and the Federalists' hope of withstanding the growing influence of popular opinion on the executive office.

NOTES

1. Charles C. Thach Jr., *The Creation of the American Presidency, 1775–1789* (Baltimore: Johns Hopkins University Press, 1969), 140.

2. Richard M. Pious, *The American Presidency* (New York: Basic Books, 1979), 38.

3. Ibid., 333.

4. *The Writings of George Washington*, ed. John C. Fitzpatrick, 39 vols. (Washington, D.C.: Government Printing Office, 1931–1944), 30:496. For a comprehensive account of Washington's contribution to the constitutional presidency, see Glen A. Phelps, "George Washington: Precedent Setter," in *Inventing the American Presidency*, ed. Thomas E. Cronin (Lawrence: University Press of Kansas, 1989).

5. Thach, *Creation of the American Presidency*, 141.

6. Charles A. Beard, *The Economic Origins of Jeffersonian Democracy* (New York: Macmillan, 1915), 105.

7. James Thomas Flexner, *George Washington and the New Nation: 1783–1793* (Boston: Little, Brown, 1970), 171.

8. *Writings of George Washington*, 30:280.

9. Forrest McDonald, *The Presidency of George Washington* (Lawrence: University Press of Kansas, 1974), 24.

10. Richard H. Kohn, "The Inside History of the Newburgh Conspiracy: America and the Coup d'Etat," *William and Mary Quarterly* 28 (April 1970): 187–220.

11. Jefferson is quoted in Gordon S. Wood, *Revolutionary Characters: What Made the Founders Different* (New York: Penguin Press, 2006), 42.

12. Gordon S. Wood, "The Greatness of George Washington," *Virginia Quarterly Review* 68 (Spring 1992): 196–197.

13. Quoted in ibid., 197.

14. Garry Wills, *Cincinnatus: George Washington and the Enlightenment* (Garden City, N.Y.: Doubleday, 1984), 23.

15. This description of Washington's journey is based on the account provided in Flexner, *George Washington and the New Nation*, 174–181.

16. Ibid., 398. North Carolina and Rhode Island did not ratify the Constitution until November 21, 1789, and May 29, 1790, respectively. See also "George Washington's First Inaugural Address," in *The Evolving Presidency: Landmark Documents, 1787–2010*, 4th ed., ed. Michael Nelson (Washington, D.C.: CQ Press, 2012), 41–44.

17. Flexner, *George Washington and the New Nation*, 193.

18. Joanne B. Freeman, *Affairs of Honor: National Politics in the New Republic* (New Haven: Yale University Press, 2001), 43.

19. Flexner, *George Washington and the New Nation*, 196.

20. Joseph J. Ellis, *His Excellency, George Washington* (New York: Knopf, 2004), 193.

21. Catherine Allgor, *Parlor Politics, in Which the Ladies of Washington Help Build a City and a Government* (Charlottesville: University Press of Virginia, 2000), 20–21.

22. Ellis, *His Excellency, George Washington,* 193.

23. Wood, *Revolutionary Characters,* 54.

24. Flexner, *George Washington and the New Nation,* 182–183; McDonald, *Presidency of George Washington,* 29–31; John Zvesper, *Political Philosophy and Rhetoric: A Study of the Origins of the American Party System* (New York: Cambridge University Press, 1977), 66; James Madison to Thomas Jefferson, May 27, 1789, in *The Writings of James Madison,* 9 vols., ed. Gaillard Hunt (New York: Putnam's, 1904), 5:370–372. See also Madison's letter to Jefferson of May 23, 1789, in 5:369–370.

25. On the early history of the office of attorney general, see Leonard White, *The Federalists: A Study in Administrative History* (New York: Macmillan, 1948), 164–172. The Department of Justice was established as an executive department of government in 1870.

26. McDonald, *Presidency of George Washington,* 39; Flexner, *George Washington and the New Nation,* 400.

27. Flexner, *George Washington and the New Nation,* 399; White, *Federalists,* 101.

28. White, *Federalists,* 106.

29. McDonald, *Presidency of George Washington,* 39.

30. White, *Federalists,* 258–259.

31. Stanley Elkins and Eric McKitrick, *The Age of Federalism: The Early American Republic 1788–1800* (New York: Oxford University Press, 1993), 54.

32. McDonald, *Presidency of George Washington,* 39.

33. "James Madison's Defense of the President's Removal Power," in Nelson, *Evolving Presidency,* 45–50.

34. Flexner, *George Washington and the New Nation,* 222; Thach, *Creation of the American Presidency,* 140–165. See also "James Madison's Defense of the Removal Power," in Nelson, *Evolving Presidency,* 45–50.

35. White, *Federalists,* 370.

36. Flexner, *George Washington and the New Nation,* 221.

37. Washington made one exception to the rule that the veto power should be confined to bills of doubtful constitutionality. Claiming only that it was bad military policy, he vetoed legislation to reduce the size of the army by dismissing two specific companies serving at outposts on the western frontier. Washington thereby implicitly claimed that presidential deference to Congress was less appropriate in foreign affairs and military policy than in domestic matters. See Phelps, "George Washington: Precedent Setter," 268–269.

38. Richard Beeman, *Plain, Honest Men: The Making of the American Constitution* (New York: Random House, 2009), 137.

39. Phelps, "George Washington: Precedent Setter," 266.

40. "Account by William Maclay of President George Washington's First Attempt to Obtain the Advice and Consent of the Senate to a Treaty," August 22, 1789, in *The Growth of Presidential Power: A Documented History,* 3 vols., ed. William M. Goldsmith (New York: Chelsea, 1974), 1:392–396.

41. Flexner, *George Washington and the New Nation,* 215–218.

42. Ibid., 398–399.

43. "Consolidation," from the *National Gazette,* December 5, 1791, in Hunt, *Writings of James Madison,* 6:67. As political scientist John C. Koritansky has noted, Jefferson's and Madison's fears about Hamilton's thoughts and practices were not without foundation: "The picture of the United States government that emerges from reflecting on Hamilton's thoughts is that of a constitutional monarchy. Jefferson [and Madison] knew whereof they spoke when they branded Hamilton a 'monarchist' and 'monocrat,' even if Hamilton never himself referred to his own thought in those words after he had respectively repudiated the avowedly monarchical stance he had taken in the Philadelphia convention." Koritansky, "Alexander Hamilton and the Presidency," in Cronin, *Inventing the American Presidency,* 296.

44. Fred I. Greenstein, *Inventing the Job of President: Leadership Style from George Washington to Andrew Jackson* (Princeton: Princeton University Press, 2009), 15.

45. Printed in *Letters of Pacificus and Helvidius on the Proclamation of Neutrality of 1793* (Washington, D.C.: Gideon, 1845), 3. See also "The Pacificus-Helvidius Letters," in Nelson, *Evolving Presidency,* 50–58.

46. McDonald, *Presidency of George Washington,* 126–127.

47. As described in Chapter 2, the framers probably did not intend for the vesting clauses to differ in this way.

48. *Letters of Pacificus and Helvidius,* 5–15.

49. Goldsmith, *Growth of Presidential Power,* 1:398.

50. *Letters of Pacificus and Helvidius,* 53–64.

51. The discussion of the Whiskey Rebellion relies heavily on McDonald, *Presidency of George Washington,* 145–147.

52. President George Washington, Proclamation of August 7, 1794, "Final Warning of a Resort to Force," in Goldsmith, *Growth of Presidential Power,* 1:246–248.

53. Ellis, *His Excellency, George Washington,* 225.

54. Quoted in Sean Wilentz, *The Rise of American Democracy: Jefferson to Lincoln* (New York: Norton, 2005), 65.

55. Alexander Hamilton to George Washington, August 2, 1794, in *The Papers of Alexander Hamilton,* ed. Harold C. Syrett (New York and London: Columbia University Press, 1986), 15–19. See also Thomas P. Slaughter, *The Whiskey Rebellion: Frontier Epilogue to the American Revolution* (New York: Oxford University Press, 1986), 163, 190–229; and Leland D. Baldwin, *Whiskey Rebels: The Story of a Frontier Uprising* (Pittsburgh: University of Pittsburgh Press, 1939), 259–272.

56. James D. Richardson, ed., *Messages and Papers of the Presidents,* 20 vols. (New York: Bureau of National Literature, 1897), 1:156.

57. McDonald, Presidency of George Washington, 145.

58. President George Washington, "Report to Congress on Success of Operation," November 19, 1794, in Goldsmith, *Growth of Presidential Power,* 1:253–255.

59. Ibid., 1:255.

60. *The Writings of Thomas Jefferson,* 10 vols., ed. Paul Leicester Ford (New York: Putnam's, 1895), 6:516–519; Wilfred E. Binkley, *President and Congress* (New York: Knopf, 1947), 287–288.

61. McDonald, Presidency of George Washington, 114.

62. Richard Brookhiser, *Founding Father: Rediscovering George Washington* (New York: Free Press, 1996), 164–165.

63. McDonald, *Presidency of George Washington,* 160.

64. Jefferson to Edward Rutledge, November 30, 1795, in Ford, *Writings of Thomas Jefferson,* 7:39–40.

65. *Annals of the Congress of the United States* (Washington, D.C.: Gales and Seaton, 1849), 4th Cong., part 1 (1795–1796), 465.

66. McDonald, *Presidency of George Washington,* 173.

67. Ibid., 173.

68. Richardson, ed., *Messages and Papers of the Presidents,* 1:186–188.

69. Jefferson to James Monroe, July 10, 1796, in Ford, *Writings of Thomas Jefferson,* 7:88–90.

70. Goldsmith, *Growth of Presidential Power,* 1:420–421. The power of the House in foreign affairs become especially controversial since the Vietnam War, which undermined confidence in the presidency and prompted a rise in congressional assertiveness during the 1970s and 1980s. The Carter administration learned, to its dismay, that it could not ignore the House in the pursuit of its diplomatic initiatives. Although House approval was not necessary to ratify treaties, the lower chamber influenced treaty making during the Carter years through both the appropriations process and committee investigations, thereby raising concerns about illegitimate House intrusion into the president's right to

conduct foreign affairs. During the ratification process for the two Panama Canal treaties in 1977 and 1978, for example, three House committees held hearings that served as an important and controversial forum to generate support for and opposition to the treaties.

The debate over House intervention in the details of foreign affairs intensified during the Reagan years as partisan differences sharpened the constitutional struggles between the executive and legislative branches. The House's "micromanagement" of foreign policy toward Central America, especially, became the subject of considerable political conflict and public controversy. The Boland Amendment, a prohibition on the expenditure of federal funds to aid the contra rebels in Nicaragua, was a House rider to an appropriations bill, which the Reagan administration considered an abuse of Congress's budgetary power.

By the 1990s the House had come to play a routine part in the treaty-making process, requiring presidents to take greater care in building political support for important or controversial treaties. As political scientist Robert Spitzer has observed, "The president cannot ignore the House. Through the appropriations process, committee investigations, and the ability to gain public attention, the House (especially the key committees) can have a profound effect on the treaty process." Robert Spitzer, "The President and Congress," in *Congressional Quarterly's Guide to the Presidency*, 2nd ed., ed. Michael Nelson (Washington, D.C.: Congressional Quarterly, 1996), 1301.

71. John Ferling, *Adams v. Jefferson: The Tumultuous Election of 1800* (New York: Oxford University Press, 2004), 85.

72. Jefferson to James Madison, January 8, 1797, in Ford, *Writings of Thomas Jefferson*, 7: 104–105.

73. Wilentz, *Rise of American Democracy*, 77.

74. Jefferson to Edward Rutledge, June 24, 1797, in Ford, *Writings of Thomas Jefferson*, 7:152–155.

75. Ralph Adams Brown, *The Presidency of John Adams* (Lawrence: University Press of Kansas, 1975), 25.

76. Jefferson to Elbridge Gerry, May 13, 1797, in *The Portable Thomas Jefferson*, ed. Merrill D. Peterson (New York: Viking Press, 1975), 471–474.

77. Leonard White, *The Federalists: A Study in Administrative History* (New York: Macmillan, 1948), 237–252.

78. Brown, *Presidency of John Adams*, 26–27.

79. White, *Federalists*, 241.

80. See, for example, David McCullough, *John Adams* (New York: Simon and Schuster, 2001), 508–514, 526–529.

81. White, *Federalists*, 237.

82. John Ferling, *John Adams: A Life* (Knoxville: University of Tennessee Press, 1992), 394.

83. Freeman, *Affairs of Honor*.

84. John Adams, Address to New Jersey College, 1798, in John Morton Smith, *Freedom's Fetters: The Alien and Sedition Laws and American Civil Liberties* (Ithaca: Cornell University Press, 1956), 99.

85. "Thomas Jefferson's First Inaugural Address," in Nelson, *Evolving Presidency*, 68–73.

86. Richard Hofstadter, *The Idea of a Party System: The Rise of Legitimate Opposition in the United States* (Berkeley: University of California Press, 1969), 110. For a balanced account of Adams's role in the passage and enforcement of the Alien and Sedition Acts, see Brown, *Presidency of John Adams*, 122–127.

CHAPTER 4

The Triumph of Jeffersonianism

L
ike George Washington, Thomas Jefferson would be counted among
the greatest Americans in history even if he had never been president.
French writer Alexis de Tocqueville celebrated the author of the
Declaration of Independence "as the greatest democrat ever to spring from
American democracy."[1] Jefferson's contributions as president deepened his
reputation as the first champion of popular rule to occupy the executive office.
Neither Washington nor Adams considered himself a democratic leader;
instead both understood the president's constitutional responsibility as
requiring them to stand above the clashes of opinion and partisan conflict
that jarred American politics during the 1790s.

Although Jefferson presided over much of the democratization of the
country's norms and institutions, his commitment to popular rule was far
from complete. With the indispensable support of James Madison, Jefferson
formed and led America's first great democratic political party, but he never
acknowledged the legitimacy of party government. As political scientist Harvey Mansfield has observed, Jefferson "never intended the public coexistence,
permanent establishment, and occasional alternation of two parties."[2] Rather,
Jefferson defended the Democratic-Republican Party as a temporary instrument of the people, its purpose being to defeat the Federalist attempt to
impose centralized "consolidation" on a fundamentally decentralized nation.
Once the Federalists and their program of executive aggrandizement were
beaten, Jefferson hoped, his own party could safely wither away, restoring the
nonpartisan character of the government created by the Constitution. The
country, he assured an anxious political ally, would then see a "rapid return of
general harmony," and its people would move "in phalanx in the paths of
regular liberty, order, and sacrosanct adherence to the constitution."[3] The
Democratic-Republican Party, as historian Richard Hofstadter argued, was to
be a "party to end party."[4]

In practice, however, Jefferson proved a better builder than architect. His
party did not bring an end to partisanship. Instead, it endeavored to use partisanship to strengthen the decentralizing, supposedly more democratic institutions of the Constitution—that is, Congress and the states. Once in office

100

The House of Representatives decided the outcome of the election of 1800 after Thomas Jefferson (left) and Aaron Burr received the same number of electoral votes for president. The Twelfth Amendment, which required that separate ballots be cast for president and vice president, was subsequently passed to avoid similar deadlocks.

the Democratic-Republicans tried, at least initially, to constrain the power of the executive and to limit the scope of the national government's authority so that it rarely intersected with the lives of the people.

With the triumph of the Jeffersonians, the national government shrank and remained small until the Civil War. Even today, despite its size, the United States retains qualities that are unique, at least in degree, among modern democracies: a constitutional commitment to the rights of individuals, a mistrust of elites, and a lack of centralized rule. Jefferson's contribution to American governance was both stylistic and substantive: he made the presidency look democratic, and he championed policies that moved the new nation in an anti-elitist direction. By the end of his eight years in office, Jefferson had severed the connection between presidential governance and economic privilege that the Federalists had sought to establish.

THE "REVOLUTION" OF 1800

The engine of Jefferson's victory in the presidential election of 1800 was the Democratic-Republican Party. Creating the party had been the work of many hands, but Jefferson was its undisputed leader. Although Jefferson disavowed partisan ambitions, his public stature and behind-the-scenes maneuvers were vital for maintaining the unity and commitment that made the Democratic-Republican triumph over the Federalists possible. But the coming of the Democratic-Republican Party to power was preceded by an odd set of occurrences that precipitated a constitutional crisis and nearly abrogated the results of the presidential election.

As noted in Chapter 2, the original Constitution, which was written without political parties in mind, provided that the candidate with the largest majority of electoral votes would become president and the runner-up in the presidential election would become vice president. In 1796 Federalists and Democratic-Republicans understood that Adams and Jefferson were the heads of their respective party tickets, and widespread agreement existed about the identity of each party's candidate for vice president. But the nominating process that the parties had devised was not yet sufficiently developed to enforce party discipline in support of a complete ticket. Adams was elected president in 1796, but his opponent, Jefferson, became the vice president when Adams's running mate, Thomas Pinckney, received fewer votes than Jefferson.

By 1800, however, formal party organizations were fully in place. Each party's members of Congress caucused to choose its nominees for president and vice president. The caucus's decision was then coordinated with party organizations in the various states so that electors were selected as instructed agents of the party, pledged to cast their two ballots for president for its presidential and vice-presidential candidates. The 1800 election broke along the same North-South divide as in 1796, but this time the Democratic-Republicans carried New York, giving them seventy-three electoral votes to the Federalists' sixty-five. Jefferson expected that one or two of Georgia's electors would cast their votes for him and for someone other than Aaron Burr of New York, the party's vice-presidential candidate.[5] When that did not happen, Jefferson and Burr ended up with the same number of electoral votes for president. According to the Constitution, it then fell to the lame-duck Federalist majority in the House of Representatives to decide which Democratic-Republican—Jefferson or Burr—would become president.[6]

Federalist leaders in Congress saw some advantage in making Burr president: he was a less-principled and, therefore, a more pliable politician than the "fanatic," Jefferson. Burr, for his part, refused to take the honorable steps required to correct the results of the Electoral College, even though everyone clearly understood that Jefferson was the head of the ticket. Instead, as historian Sean Wilentz has written, when Burr "fully realized that he had a credible chance to win the presidency, he decided to play out the string, come what may."[7] The result was a deadlock. Under the Constitution, a majority of the representatives from nine of the sixteen states was needed to elect the president, and neither party could produce the votes. The stalemate lasted through thirty-five ballots. Not until February 17, 1801, on the thirty-sixth ballot, was Jefferson elected.

Perversely, Jefferson's leading Federalist supporter in the House election was Alexander Hamilton, who not many months before had urged Gov. John Jay of New York to change the state's election laws in the Federalists' favor "to prevent an *atheist* in religion and a fanatic in politics from getting possession of the helm of State." Faced with a choice between Burr and Jefferson, however, Hamilton assured Federalist House members that Jefferson was the safer man. Writing to Delaware senator James A. Bayard in January 1801, Hamilton portrayed Jefferson in remarkably astute terms, foretelling much about the Virginian's presidency: "I admit that his politics are tinctured with fanaticism; that he is too much in earnest with his democracy; that he has been a mischievous enemy to the principal measures of our past administration." But, Hamilton added, Jefferson was neither an enemy of executive authority nor a slave to his principles. On the contrary, he was likely "to temporize" and to acquiesce in the prevailing, mainly Federalist, governing arrangements. Jefferson was also incapable of being corrupted, unlike Burr, whom Hamilton regarded as "the most unfit man in the U.S. for the office of President."[8] With tacit assurances from Jefferson that he would neither scuttle the navy nor summarily purge Federalist officeholders from the executive branch, Bayard, Hamilton, and few other Federalist leaders were able to persuade enough Federalist members of the House to abstain that Jefferson was elected by a vote of ten states to four.[9]

Jefferson's victory in the 1800 election marked the beginning of a critical realignment in American politics. Sweeping the congressional as well as the presidential elections, the Democratic-Republicans became the nation's leading political party and remained so until 1828. During the last decade of his life, in a letter to Spencer Roane, an eminent lawyer and legal scholar, Jefferson said that the "revolution of 1800," although it came about peacefully through a national election, was "as real a revolution in the principles of our government as that of 1776 was in its form."[10] As historian Joanne B. Freeman has pointed out, the peaceful revolution may have forestalled a violent one. If the Federalists in Congress had persisted in their efforts to deny him the presidency, Jefferson wrote, "the certainty is that a legislative usurpation would be resisted by arms."[11]

In Jefferson's view, the principles of the Revolutionary War had been perverted by the Federalists in their ardent commitment to expanding the responsibilities of the national government. The Federalists' domestic and international initiatives required that the executive assume so dominant a role in formulating and implementing public policy that the president eventually would be transformed into a monarch. The task of the Democratic-Republican revolution was to restore republican government by casting off the Federalist institutions and, according to Forrest McDonald, by "instill[ing] the people with the historical knowledge and true principles that would prevent them from losing their liberties again."[12]

The importance of the Democratic-Republican task was revealed clearly in Jefferson's first inaugural address, which pronounced a party program of reform that included a strictly limited role for the national government and, concomitantly, "support of the state governments in all their rights"; a "frugal" administrations, dedicated to economy in public expenditures; and the encouragement of agriculture over commerce. In laying out this program, Jefferson stressed that it commanded the allegiance of a majority of the people. Although he took care to pay homage to the rights of the minority against the "unreasonable will of the majority," Jefferson called for "a jealous care of the right of election by the people" and "absolute acquiescence in the decisions of the majority." [13]

JEFFERSON'S WAR WITH THE JUDICIARY

Jefferson's desire to pursue majority rule by his party animated his war with the federal judiciary. In a desperate attempt to maintain a foothold in the national government, the Federalists had packed the courts with judges of their own party before Adams left office. The Judiciary Act of 1801, enacted by the Federalist Congress and signed by Adams shortly before Jefferson was inaugurated, created dozens of new federal judgeships, which were hurriedly filled through so-called midnight appointments by the outgoing Adams administration. To the Jeffersonians, the judiciary constituted "the final barrier to be assaulted in the advance of popular government and political liberty." To the Federalists, the courts represented "the last bastion of moderation and sanity arresting the progress of mob rule and anarchy." [14]

More was at stake in this dispute than partisan power. The Democratic-Republicans opposed the doctrine that the Constitution implicitly vests the courts with broad authority to overturn the actions of elected officials on constitutional grounds. The Federalists supported the judiciary's claim to be the ultimate arbiter of the Constitution. Although Jefferson and his followers did not challenge the courts' right of judicial review, they insisted that each branch of the government shares equally the responsibility to decide matters of constitutionality.

These issues of power and principle came to a head in the case of *Marbury v. Madison* (1803).[15] The case involved a request by one of the Federalists' midnight appointees, William Marbury, that the Supreme Court issue a writ of mandamus forcing Jefferson's secretary of state, James Madison, to deliver Marbury's commission as a justice of the peace in the new capital, Washington, D.C. Although the commission had been ratified by the Senate and signed by John Marshall, who was Adams's secretary of state at the time, it was never delivered to Marbury. Madison, scorning the midnight appointments as part of a Federalist plot to control the government, simply held on to it. The unenviable task of mediating this bitter and symbolically important dispute fell to Marshall, himself an ardent Federalist and a late appointee as chief justice of the United States.

The Jefferson administration expected the Supreme Court to lay itself open to political attack by issuing the writ that Marbury had requested. But in a brilliant piece of judicial statecraft, Marshall outmaneuvered the Democratic-Republicans, sidestepping the case's narrow partisan issues to establish the authority of the Supreme Court. Writing for a unanimous Court, all of whose members had been appointed by Washington or Adams, Marshall scolded the administration for refusing to deliver the commission to which Marbury was legally entitled, noting that even the president is not above the law. But Marshall denied Marbury his writ of mandamus by ruling that Section 13 of the Judiciary Act of 1789, under which Marbury had brought his suit, was unconstitutional because it presumed to give the Supreme Court original jurisdiction in the matter, even though the Constitution provided that the Court's jurisdiction is purely appellate in all but a few kinds of cases. In effect, Marshall gave Jefferson a free hand to bar a few Federalist appointees from office, but only on the condition that the president accept the Court's power to judge the constitutional validity of acts of Congress.[16]

Jefferson was reluctant to accept victory on these terms. But so adroit was Marshall's ruling that the president could find no way to disobey the Court, as he had hoped to do. When he failed in a subsequent effort to impeach and remove the highly partisan but indisputably competent justice Samuel Chase, Jefferson's war with the judiciary came to an end. In any event, developments during his first term seemed to make the war unnecessary. By 1804 much of the Democratic-Republican program that Jefferson had heralded in his inaugural address was completed. The judiciary weathered the storm of Jefferson's first term, but the question that had given rise to the conflict between the president and the Court was never fully resolved. That question—whether ultimate authority on matters of constitutionality rests with elected officials in Congress and the White House or in the interpretations of the judiciary—has arisen time and time again in American history.[17]

THE DEMOCRATIC-REPUBLICAN PROGRAM AND THE ADJUSTMENT TO POWER

In important respects, the Democratic-Republican program was negative. A great deal of it aimed at repealing Federalist policies that the Jeffersonians believed had undermined the Constitution. In 1801 Congress, which also was captured by the Democratic-Republicans in the elections of 1800, removed the last vestiges of the Sedition Act (see Chapter 3). The act expired the day before Jefferson took office but, wanting to underscore his fierce opposition to it, he pardoned everyone (mostly Democratic-Republican newspaper publishers) who had been convicted of sedition. Moreover, at Jefferson's request Congress voted to repay with interest all the fines that were levied as part of their sentences. During Jefferson's first term, Congress also abolished most of the internal taxes, including the unpopular whiskey and direct property taxes, that the Federalists had enacted in 1798 to prepare for a possible war with France, and it reduced the size of the already small military establishment by severely cutting army and naval appropriations.[18]

Although Jefferson emphasized the importance of restraining the national government, he was not narrowly doctrinaire about government's proper limits. His main concern was to make Washington more responsive to the will of the people. "His faith in the people," historian Robert M. Johnstone Jr. has written, "gave to his views on power a flexibility that permitted the use of power in positive ways to emphasize the freedom *from* government."[19] In those areas in which actions by the national government were proper—that is, in matters pertaining to foreign affairs and the relations among the states—Jefferson believed that the government's powers should be exercised energetically.

When circumstances required, Jefferson was even willing to tolerate government actions that seemed to contradict his stated principles. In 1803 he purchased the massive Louisiana Territory from France, even though, as he conceded in a letter to Sen. John Breckinridge of Kentucky, he did not think the Constitution provided "for our holding foreign territory, still less for incorporating foreign nations into our union."[20] In 1807, seeking to preserve the long-standing American commitment to neutrality between Great Britain and France, Jefferson imposed an embargo on all foreign commerce. Enforcing the embargo involved coercion by the federal government on a scale rivaling the notorious Alien and Sedition Acts. As Jefferson argued in a September 1810 letter, written seventeen months after leaving the presidency: "A strict observance of the written laws is doubtless *one* of the high duties of a good citizen, but it is not the *highest*. The laws of necessity, of self-preservation, of saving our country when in danger, are of higher obligation. To lose our country by a scrupulous adherence to written law, would be to lose the law itself, with life, liberty, property and all those who are enjoying them with us; thus absurdly sacrificing the end to the means."[21]

Jefferson's actions as president reflected a "duality that was to underlie the whole of the [Democratic-Republican] era and to account for many of its frustrations."[22] Opposing conceptions of executive power had once been at the heart of the bitter conflict between the Federalists and the Democratic-Republicans. The Federalists had invested the president with broad responsibilities, fretted about legislative encroachments on executive power, and, especially in matters pertaining to foreign affairs, tried to minimize the checks on the president that the Constitution had granted to Congress. In contrast, the Democratic-Republicans, at least when out of power, had placed their faith in the people's representatives, believing that important decisions should originate in Congress. They also sought to restrict executive discretion severely, not only in domestic matters but in foreign affairs as well. As noted in Chapter 3, during the battle over the Jay Treaty, Democratic-Republicans had asserted the right of the House of Representatives to deny the funds necessary to implement treaties, thereby claiming for the lower house of Congress a virtual veto in foreign policy making.

In view of these differences, one might have expected important changes to occur in the conduct of the presidency when Jefferson and his party took control in 1801. But the Democratic-Republicans soon realized that a wholesale dismantling of executive power would make governing virtually impossible. Jefferson, with able support from his secretary of the Treasury, Albert Gallatin, exercised as much control of domestic policy as Alexander Hamilton had during the Washington administration. Hamilton's assurance to his Federalist colleagues in 1801 that Jefferson was "no enemy to the power of the executive" predicted accurately how Jefferson would act as president. To enforce his embargo policy, Jefferson secured authority from a Democratic-Republican Congress that exceeded any grant of executive power ever made by the Federalists. Moreover, Jefferson used this power with the kind of executive energy he once had denounced as the mark of tyranny.[23] In important respects, then, the "revolution of 1800" brought no sweeping alterations of the government's institutional arrangements.

Nevertheless, Jefferson's presidency marked an important change in the relationship between the president and the people.[24] His predecessors, Washington and Adams, had believed that the power of the presidency derived from its constitutional authority. Jefferson, although not rejecting this view, maintained that the strength of the office ultimately depended on the "affections of the people." He strongly implied in his first inaugural address that the program of the Democratic-Republican Party should be enacted simply because a majority of the voters had endorsed it in the 1800 election.[25]

Washington and Adams believed that some distance from the people was essential if presidents were to perform their proper task, which was to moderate the clash of parties and interests that inevitably would occur in Congress. But Jefferson felt that the most effective and responsible way for the president to lead the national government was by guiding the institutions that were rooted most firmly in a popular base—the House and, to a lesser extent, the Senate. Rather than stand apart from developments in Congress, Jefferson sought to direct them. In contrast to Hamilton's concept of a strong presidency, which emphasized the need for independent executive initiatives, Jefferson assumed the mantle of party leader in an effort to yoke the separate branches of the government in service to his and the Democratic-Republican Party's agenda.

Informed by a clear conception of the presidency, Jefferson's administration wrought other important institutional changes in pursuit of a closer relationship between the president and the people. One such change was to reduce the ceremonial trappings of the executive office. Jefferson stripped away much of the pomp and ceremony to which Washington and Adams had adhered; he regarded excessive formality in the conduct of the presidency as incompatible with a popularly based government. Unlike Washington, Jefferson rode around the capital not in a coach attended by liveried outriders, but on his own horse, with only one servant in attendance. He was the first president not to strap on a sword at his inauguration and powder his hair.[26] His clothing expressed republican simplicity, even to the point of offending some who regarded his appearance as unsuitable for a head of state. As one critic described Jefferson, "The President was in an undress—Blue coat, red vest . . . white hose, ragged slippers, with his toes out, clean linen, but hair disheveled."[27]

Jefferson's interest in removing the "monocratic" features from the executive led him to simplify his relationship with the legislature. His decision to submit his first annual message to Congress in writing rather than deliver it as a speech was "a calculated political act, designed to . . . reduce the 'relics' left by the Federalists and underline the return to sound republican simplicity."[28] (It also reflected his acute discomfort at public speaking.) Jefferson began what turned out to be the century-long practice of presidents sending their State of the Union messages to Congress in writing, to be read aloud by the clerk of the House.

Jefferson's adoption of a simpler presidential etiquette corresponded nicely with the transfer of the capital from Philadelphia to Washington in 1800. As secretary of state in the Washington administration, Jefferson had insisted on this transfer as the price for supporting Secretary of the Treasury Hamilton's plan to have the national government pay off the states' debts. The move left members of Congress, executive officials, judges, and foreign diplomats, who were accustomed to Philadelphia's culture and comforts, feeling stranded on the muddy banks of the Potomac. Historian Merrill D. Peterson has described the new city of Washington as "a village pretending to be a capital, a place with a few bad houses, extensive swamps, hanging on the skirts of a too thinly peopled, weak and barren country."[29] Yet Jefferson, who was seldom comfortable in cities, appreciated the change in setting. His informal style was compatible not just with his view of the presidency but also with Washington's relatively rustic character.

The move to the new capital also symbolized the growth in people and territory under way in the United States. The nation's population increased by more than one-third between 1800 and 1810. Geographically, the acquisition of the Louisiana Territory almost doubled the country's size. Jefferson's Democratic-Republican successors continued to support territorial expansion, committed as they were to encouraging agriculture over manufacturing. The nation had to expand whenever the opportunity arose "to make room for the generation of farmers yet unborn."[30] Furthermore, the political ascendance of the Democratic-Republican Party represented the rise of the agrarian and frontier interests of the South and West to political parity with the older commercial and financial interests of the East, which had controlled national politics under the Federalists.

The close relationship between territorial expansion and the Democratic-Republican program explains Jefferson's willingness to make the Louisiana Purchase in disregard of his oft-expressed commitment to a strict construction of the Constitution. After reading the deal with France, he pushed the Louisiana Treaty through the Senate, certain that constitutional niceties were less important than the opportunity to contribute on such a scale to the public good. The purchase of Louisiana, and the overwhelmingly favorable reaction it received around the country, sustained the Democratic-Republican effort to define the president as the agent of the people's best interests.[31]

Jefferson's "empire of liberty" was indifferent to the rights of African Americans. One unfortunate consequence of the move to Washington was that it embedded the seat of government in the heart of slave country. Indeed, Jefferson felt comfortable bringing slaves into the White House. As Fred Greenstein has observed, the Constitution's three-fifths rule for counting disenfranchised slaves for purposes of representation in Congress "already gave the South disproportionate influence in the Electoral College." (In the absence of that rule, Adams would have defeated Jefferson in the 1800 election.)[32] Of the four Jeffersonian presidents, only John Quincy Adams was not a slaveholder. The others—Jefferson, James Madison, and James Monroe—faced less criticism in Washington than they would have in the nation's previous capitals, especially Philadelphia, New York, and Trenton, and therefore less reason to consider the justice of slavery as an institution.

THE LIMITS OF "POPULAR" LEADERSHIP

Important as it sometimes was, popular presidential leadership had its limits during the Jeffersonian era. Neither Jefferson nor his three Democratic-Republican successors—Madison (1809–1817), Monroe (1817–1825), and Adams (1825–1829)—tried to enhance their power by bartering patronage or other favors for legislation in Congress. Indeed, until Andrew Jackson took office in 1829, presidents seldom used the spoils of federal appointments either to enhance party unity or to obtain legislation.

In spite of the bitter competition between the Federalists and the Democratic-Republicans, Jefferson did not purge all of his partisan opponents from the executive branch. The rate of turnover in federal jobholders was only one-third during his first two years in office and one-half during his entire first term. On the whole, the Democratic-Republicans continued to use Federalist methods of administration. As Leonard D. White has written, "After a brief period of transition, during which new men took over the most important posts, the same expectation of nonpartisan, lifetime service prevailed."[33] In appointing the heads of the executive departments, Jefferson valued steadiness of administration so highly that, after choosing his team with unusual care, he experienced the least turnover in the cabinet of any two-term president in history.[34]

Nor was it considered appropriate during the Jeffersonian era for the president to appeal over the heads of Congress to the people.[35] Until the twentieth century, presidents who tried to arouse popular support usually did so indirectly, through their influence on the party mechanisms in Congress and the state governments.

Jefferson's refusal to "go public" on the controversial embargo issue illustrates the limits on the era's acceptable techniques of presidential persuasion.[36] Initially, he was able to persuade Congress to enact the embargo by using his enormous popularity to exert influence indirectly on Democratic-Republican leaders. Yet during the course of its fourteen-month existence, the embargo began to unravel. The severe restrictions it placed on foreign trade wreaked havoc on businessmen in New England and planters in the South. The embargo also deprived the government of millions of dollars in revenue by barring nearly all imports. Perhaps most significant, it made a travesty of the Democratic-Republicans' traditional opposition to a broad constitutional interpretation of the regulatory powers vested in the national government and, especially, in the executive. By its unprecedented concentration of power in the president, by its deployment of the navy for law enforcement, and by its disregard of the Fourth Amendment's protection against unreasonable searches and seizures, the embargo "carried the administration to the precipice of unlimited and arbitrary power as measured by any American standard then known."[37]

Even after the embargo became hotly controversial, Jefferson never took the issue directly to the people. Democratic-Republican leaders received behind-the-scenes presidential directives, but to the nation Jefferson presented a stoic forbearance. To have done otherwise would have violated the custom that presidents not use oratory to influence public opinion directly. But Jefferson did not face the growing opposition to his policy with an "an imperturbable, almost sphinxlike silence."[38] Instead, as presidential scholar

Mel Laracey has noted, from late 1807 to early 1809, Jefferson sent at least nineteen public letters to citizen groups, Democratic-Republican party meetings, and state legislatures explaining and defending his unpopular embargo policy and urging continued support for it. Jefferson's most strongly worded letter was published on March 1, 1809, the same day he reluctantly signed the Non-Intercourse Act, which ended the embargo and replaced it with a bill that forbade trade only with Great Britain and France.[39] "Thus we were driven from the high and wise ground we had taken," Jefferson complained privately.[40]

THE TWELFTH AMENDMENT

The paragraphs in Article II, section 1, of the Constitution that created the Electoral College were among the document's least controversial provisions, both during the late stages of the Constitutional Convention and in the ratification debates that followed. "The mode of appointment of the Chief Magistrate of the United States," wrote Alexander Hamilton in *Federalist* No. 68, "is almost the only part of the system of any consequence, which has escaped without severe censure, or which has received the slightest mark of approbation from its opponents." It is all the more ironic, then, that the Electoral College was the first institution of the new system of government to undergo a major constitutional overhaul.

The source of the irony was the convention's faulty assumption that political parties would not arise to contest presidential elections. Instead, the delegates believed that states and ad hoc groups would nominate candidates for president. Individual electors would then vote for two of these candidates, one of them perhaps a local favorite but the other a leader of national stature. The most respected and, presumably, the best-qualified candidate would be elected as president and the second most respected as vice president.

The delegates' expectations were soon disappointed. The two political parties that formed during the Washington administration began within a very few years to nominate complete national tickets. As noted earlier, in 1800 the inevitable happened: the perverse tie vote in the presidential election between Jefferson and his Democratic-Republican running mate, Burr. To make matters worse, partisan mischief in the House almost overturned the voters' intentions. Some disgruntled Federalists then began hatching plots for the 1804 election. If the Democratic-Republican ticket won, they resolved, Federalist electors would cast one of their votes for the opposition party's vice-presidential nominee, thereby electing him instead of the presidential nominee as president and the presidential nominee as vice president.[41]

Aware of both the unsuitability of the original Constitution's presidential election process to the new realities of party politics and the Federalists' willingness to exploit the process's weaknesses, the Democratic-Republican–controlled Congress voted in December 1803 to propose the Twelfth Amendment. All but Connecticut, Delaware, and Massachusetts, the most ardent Federalist states, quickly voted to ratify, and the Twelfth Amendment became part of the Constitution in June 1804, just in time for the presidential election. No amendment except the Twenty-sixth, which in 1971 gave eighteen-year-olds the right to vote, has been ratified as rapidly.

The main effect of the Twelfth Amendment was to change a system in which electors cast two votes for president, with the candidate receiving the largest majority elected as president and the second-place finisher as vice president, to a system in which the electors were charged to vote separately for president and vice president, with a majority of electoral votes required to win each office. The amendment also reduced the number of candidates from which the House would elect the president in the event that no one received a majority of electoral votes. The reduction from the five highest electoral vote recipients to the three highest was an acknowledgment that a two-party system had developed in which even three candidates were unlikely to receive electoral votes in most elections, as well as that the parties had taken charge of the presidential nominating function.

The authority to select a vice president in the event of an Electoral College failure was lodged exclusively in the Senate, not partially as in the original Constitution. The amendment empowered the Senate to choose from the two highest electoral vote recipients for vice president, with a majority of the entire membership of the Senate required for election. The Constitution's age, residency, and citizenship requirements for the president were extended to the vice president, correcting an oversight in the original document. Finally, the new amendment stated that if a vice president, but not a president, has been chosen by the March 4 following the election, "the Vice President shall act as President as in the case of the death or other constitutional disability of the President."

The Twelfth Amendment reinforced the unitary character of the executive by eliminating the possibility that the vice president would be the leader of the opposition party.[42] For reasons discussed in Chapter 16, the amendment also severely diminished the prestige that the original Constitution had conferred on the vice presidency.

JEFFERSON'S MIXED LEGACY

Like the Federalists, Jefferson understood the need for presidential power. But Jefferson altered the tone and manner of executive authority to make it

consistent with popular rule. In place of the wide-ranging unilateral authority the Federalists had found for the executive in Article II of the Constitution, Jefferson substituted a party program that would be implemented by
the president but shaped by Congress and sanctioned by popular election.[43]

Unlike Washington and Adams, therefore, Jefferson de-emphasized the
constitutional powers of his office, governing instead through his extraconstitutional role as party leader. The Jefferson administration encouraged the
development of a disciplined party organization in Congress, with the president relying on his floor leaders in the House and Senate to advance his program. Another source of presidential influence was the party caucus, which
was created by the Federalists but used more extensively by the Democratic-
Republicans. During Jefferson's tenure as president, conclaves of leaders from
the executive and legislative branches formulated policy and encouraged party
unity. Secretary of the Treasury Gallatin played an important role in these
caucuses, and the president himself occasionally presided. Jefferson, in short,
constructed a highly centralized political party within the government, but
one that operated for the most part through conference, consultation, and free
discussion rather than through harsher political methods.[44]

The development of a party machinery made possible, as legislative historian Ralph Volney Harlow has written, "a radical change in the relationship
between executive and legislature." Should the party's leaders in Congress
ever take charge of the machinery, they would be in a position to control
the executive.[45] That is precisely what happened when Jefferson left office. The
institutions he developed for presidential leadership were turned to the
advantage of Congress. Ironically, then, it was only after Thomas Jefferson's
administration that the presidency shrank to the limited constitutional office
that long had been prescribed by the Democratic-Republican Party's chief
theorist, Thomas Jefferson.

THE PRESIDENCY OF JAMES MADISON AND THE RISE
OF THE HOUSE OF REPRESENTATIVES

The decline of presidential influence was especially evident during James
Madison's administration. While he was president, major institutional developments transferred power from the executive to the legislative branch, especially the House of Representatives. One such development was the evolution
of the congressional party caucus into an independent bastion of power.

The Democratic-Republican caucus's nomination of Jefferson for president in 1800 and 1804 had been a foregone conclusion, but the caucus of 1808
had a real decision to make. Although Secretary of State Madison generally
was regarded as Jefferson's heir apparent, the leader of the small anti-Jefferson
faction in the Democratic-Republican Party, Rep. John Randolph of Virginia,

tried to secure the nomination for James Monroe. In the end, Madison was nominated with strong support from Jefferson and was elected in a 122–47 electoral vote landslide that reduced his opponent, Charles Cotesworth Pinckney, to the Federalist Party's New England base. But the promises Madison had to make to his party's members in Congress to win their endorsement suggested that subsequent presidential nominations might well become occasions "to make explicit executive subordination to congressional president-makers." Indeed, some scholars believe that Madison's renomination by the Democratic-Republican Party in 1812 was delayed until he assured the "War Hawks" in the congressional caucus that he supported their desire for war with Great Britain.[46]

The emergence of the Speaker of the House as an important leader in Congress and Kentuckian Henry Clay's extraordinary use of the office during the Madison presidency further reduced executive power in relation to Congress. Until Clay's election as Speaker in 1811, party leadership in the House had been shared among several members. Clay was able to change this practice dramatically. According to Leonard White, "Clay was chosen Speaker on an issue that President Madison was unable to grip, and with the intention of forcing national action despite the president's incapacity to act—war with Great Britain. Clay succeeded in this purpose, and until the last day of Madison's administration the initiative in public affairs remained with Clay and his associates in the House of Representatives."[47]

Under Clay's direction, the House strengthened its capacity to meet its broader legislative obligations by expanding the number and influence of its standing committees, which enabled each representative to specialize in an area of interest. Because the committees' activities were coordinated by the Speaker, the House became an effective legislative instrument. Indeed, from 1811 to 1825 Clay was arguably the most powerful man in Washington.

The decline of presidential influence was demonstrated most dramatically during the War of 1812. War sentiment had been aroused by evidence that the British were supplying arms to American Indians, who were already angry about frontier settlers encroaching on historic tribal lands in the Indiana and Michigan territories; by British seizure of American ships and impressment (that is, conscription) of crew members; and, to some degree, by a desire to acquire territory in British Canada and Spanish Florida. The War Hawks, most of them Democratic-Republican members of Congress from the South and West whose constituents were suffering from Indian attacks and falling agricultural prices, fanned the flames of anti-British feeling. New England Federalists, traditionally pro-British and commercially tied to Great Britain through shipping and trade, opposed war but were severely outnumbered in Congress and around the country.

Madison's message of June 1, 1812, which urged Congress to declare war against Great Britain, was the first war message by an American president and commanded the least support: the vote to declare war was only 79–49 in the House and 19–13 in the Senate, with every Federalist member opposed. Later historical developments would establish formidable wartime powers for the presidency, but Madison's command of the nation's military effort was singularly undistinguished. He was hampered not only by his inability to influence Congress but also by personal qualities that were poorly suited to the tasks at hand. Madison's figure was slight, his speaking voice was weak, and the force of his personality was, at best, moderate. As Gaillard Hunt, a generally sympathetic Madison biographer, has written of the president's war leadership, "The hour had come but the man was wanting. Not a scholar in governments ancient and modern, not an unimpassioned writer of careful messages, but a robust leader to rally the people and unite them to fight was what the time needed, and what it did not find in Madison."[48]

From a military standpoint, the War of 1812 was the least successful in American history. Congress and the president rushed into war with a small, poorly trained army of less than seven thousand men and a sixteen-vessel navy, partly because Madison assumed that Canadians, many of them of French origin, would happily abandon their status as a British colony in favor of the United States. Jefferson predicted that the conquest of Canada would be "a mere matter of marching."[49] Far from it: at the beginning of the war, a relatively small British detachment stationed in Canada administered a series of disastrous defeats to the disorganized American army. The low point of the conflict occurred in August 1814, when Madison had to evacuate the capital for three days to escape a small British force that had moved unchallenged up the Chesapeake Bay and marched with little resistance into the heart of Washington, burning the Capitol, the White House, the Navy Yard, and most other public buildings.

Only Great Britain's decision not to prosecute the war on a massive scale saved the nation from further disaster. Public morale was boosted belatedly by Gen. Andrew Jackson's victory in the Battle of New Orleans on January 8, 1815. Although the battle had no effect on the outcome of the war (a peace treaty—the Treaty of Ghent—had been concluded two weeks earlier), it enabled Madison to retire as president in 1817 with some measure of honor. New Orleans also rendered a fatal political blow to the New England–based, pro-British Federalists, many of whom had opposed the war from the beginning and some of whom had even threatened to secede from the Union. "The confident nationalist party of Washington, Hamilton, and Adams," Wilentz has observed, "had shriveled into [a] phobic sectional party."[50]

Federalist defeat did not translate automatically into Democratic-Republican triumph. In important respects, Madison's failures as president transcended his personal limitations—they were attributable not just to him but also to the legacies he inherited from the Jefferson administration and from the Democratic-Republican tradition of which he had been one of the major architects. By opposing the creation of anything more than a minimal army and navy, Madison and Jefferson, preaching economy in government, had undone many of the military preparations that the Adams administration had undertaken. Their foreign policy depended on diplomacy to solve America's problems with France and Great Britain. When negotiations failed, the Democratic-Republicans were forced to rely on the 1807 embargo, an impractical attempt at peaceful coercion that proved disastrous for the economy without causing either Great Britain or France to stop interfering with American ships. The collapse of Madison's own embargo, enacted in 1812, left him no alternative but war when the British provocations continued, even though he knew that the country was neither prepared nor united for battle.

Years later, Madison recounted that he had hoped to overcome the nation's obvious unpreparedness by "throw[ing] forward the flag of the country, sure that the people would press onward and defend it."[51] Yet the rapid decline in the status of the presidency after Jefferson's tenure left Madison in a poor position to rally either Congress or the American people. Contrary to his expectations, Democratic-Republican legislators did not abandon their party's traditional doctrine of hostility to centralized power, even in wartime. Congress was willing to declare war but not to raise enough money to fight it. Moreover, the Madison administration's plan to use the state militia was scuttled by some state governments' lack of cooperation. The governors of Connecticut and Massachusetts, for example, refused to release their militia to fight in the war. The president, long an advocate of states' rights, "offered no suggestion for stopping so grave a defiance of federal authority."[52]

Madison faced up to the limitations of Democratic-Republican principles in his seventh annual message in December 1815, which recommended several measures to solidify the national resolve, including chartering the Second Bank of the United States. (The Democratic-Republicans had allowed the first bank to expire in 1811.) With no national bank in operation during the War of 1812, the federal government had lacked a convenient and stable source of currency, exacerbating a financial crisis that saw the national debt grow from $45 million in 1811 to $127 million in 1815. Believing that a national bank was a necessary evil without which a sound currency was unattainable, Madison signed the bank bill into law in 1816. As political scientist James D. Savage has observed, it took the severe economic dislocations of the war to persuade Madison and his party to embrace "the ghostly presence of Hamilton's national bank, with all its potential for corrupting the republic."[53]

Madison never ceased to express profound concern, however, about the potential abuses of executive power that he believed Hamilton had committed during the 1790s. According to historian Ralph Ketcham: "in every one of his critical relationships and decisions—in bringing the nation face to face with war, in dealing with Congress, in arranging his Cabinet and in enduring near-treasonable dissent—[Madison] acted in view of [Democratic-Republican] principles of executive leadership."[54] In the final analysis, these principles simply were not conducive to effective presidential initiative.

THE PRESIDENCIES OF JAMES MONROE AND JOHN QUINCY ADAMS

Madison's Democratic-Republican successors, James Monroe and John Quincy Adams, were unable to restore to the presidency the strength that the office had lost after Jefferson retired. Monroe, although a forceful man, was prone to formality and a stiffness of manner that ill qualified him for party leadership. Monroe also was hindered by a growing split within his party between "old" Democratic-Republicans, who inclined toward a strict construction of the Constitution, and "new" Democratic-Republicans, or National Republicans, who were more nationalist in outlook. Monroe was identified with the former group. The latter, which was led by prominent figures such as Henry Clay, John C. Calhoun, and Monroe's successor, John Quincy Adams, dominated the party after the War of 1812, even when Monroe was president.

Monroe, like Madison, was a protégé of Jefferson and therefore was regarded as the legitimate heir of the "Virginia Dynasty" that had supplied every president since 1801. Like both Madison and Jefferson, Monroe had served as secretary of state, which was the main stepping-stone to the presidency throughout the Democratic-Republican era. But the fragmentation of the Democratic-Republican Party ensured that he would also be the last of the Jeffersonians. Monroe's nomination was a difficult affair. Two other contenders, Clay and Secretary of the Treasury William Crawford of Georgia, were closely identified with the nationalist wing of the party. Although Monroe was nominated and easily elected in 1816, the trouble he had winning the endorsement of his party's congressional caucus foretold the difficulties that he would face as president.

One of the major domestic issues during the Monroe administration was "internal improvements." The president informed Congress that, in his view, a constitutional amendment was required before the national government could construct roads and canals. Congress, led by Clay, defied Monroe by passing a bill to repair the main east-west highway, known as the Cumberland Road. The president's veto of this bill signaled the breakdown of Democratic-Republican unity that was to plague him throughout his two terms.[55]

Monroe's strong response to the Cumberland Road controversy was the exception rather than the rule. Following the practice of presidents since Washington, he vetoed only legislation that he deemed unconstitutional. Indeed, Monroe's deference to Congress went beyond custom. More than any of his predecessors, Monroe practiced as well as preached legislative supremacy. As a result, he mostly abstained from involvement in the greatest issue of the day: the admission of Missouri as a state, which for the first time forced Congress to debate the status of slavery in the Louisiana Territory.

As a private citizen, Jefferson observed the bitter debate about Missouri with great concern. Writing to Rep. John Holmes of Maine, he said, "This momentous question, like a fire-bell in the night, awakened and filled me with terror. I considered it at once the knell of the Union."[56] Congress allayed Jefferson's fears by enacting the Missouri Compromise of 1820. In effect, this compromise perpetuated the Constitution's original compromise with slavery: it admitted Missouri to the Union as a slave state, allowed Maine to enter as a free state, and temporarily resolved the issue of slavery in the Louisiana Territory by banning it from all western territories north of Missouri's southern border, whose latitude is 36°30'. Monroe had little hand in the Missouri Compromise, save for signing the final bill. As Leonard White has written, "His course of action was perhaps politically wise, perhaps politically inevitable, but it abdicated leadership."[57] Indeed, the passive character of the Monroe administration prompted Supreme Court justice Joseph Story to remark in 1818 that "the Executive has no longer a commanding influence. The House of Representatives has absorbed all the popular feeling and all the effective power of the country."[58]

THE MONROE DOCTRINE

Justice Story's lament was not as pertinent to foreign as to domestic affairs. The Constitution conferred powers on the president in foreign policy that remained essentially untarnished. Previous service as secretary of state made all the Jeffersonian presidents confident and for the most part confidence-inspiring in the international arena.[59]

Monroe reinforced the president's right to take the initiative in foreign affairs by issuing the Monroe Doctrine, which became one of the pillars of American foreign policy in the nineteenth and twentieth centuries. The revolt of Spain's Latin American colonies between 1815 and 1823 had nearly liquidated the Spanish empire. The Monroe administration was alarmed by reports that other European powers, France in particular, had designs on several of the newly independent Latin American nations. Simultaneously, Tsar Alexander I of Russia, noting the presence of a Russian trading station in Bodega Bay, near San Francisco, issued a decree claiming exclusive trading rights for Russia in the area north of the fifty-first parallel, including all of modern-day Oregon and Washington. Responding to these threats, on December 2, 1823, President Monroe included in his annual message to Congress a sweeping statement that proclaimed the Americas independent from European interference: "The occasion has been judged proper for asserting, as a principle in which the rights and interests of the United States are involved, that the American continents, by the free and independent condition which they have assumed and maintain, are henceforth not to be considered as subjects for future colonization by any European powers."[60]

Although the Monroe Doctrine was neither confirmed by Congress nor enforced by President Monroe, it was a significant document. Like the Declaration of Independence, the Monroe Doctrine codified the aspirations of the American people. As historian W. P. Cresson has written, "It was a sincere expression of the belief in the superiority of American institutions and ideals, and the right of self-preservation, grounded in the conviction that the extension of European principles was dangerous to the peace and safety of the American system."[61]

The Monroe Doctrine was also an important statement, at a time of general executive weakness, that the president was paramount in the making of foreign policy. Monroe's defiant expression of hemispheric independence committed the United States to more burdensome diplomatic and military responsibilities, most of which inevitably would fall on the executive. For a time, this commitment was without important effect, but its potential to become a guiding influence on foreign policy was fulfilled in the late nineteenth and early twentieth centuries (see Chapters 7 and 8).[62]

The end of the Monroe presidency in 1825 also marked the end of a quarter-century–long political dynasty. Monroe was the last member of the Virginia "triumvirate"—Jefferson, Madison, Monroe—to serve as president. Each of these men played an important role in the formation and early history of the Republic. During the 1790s, the country's first decade under the Constitution, each had been a founder of the Democratic-Republican opposition to the Federalists and a leader during its rise as a governing party. Each served two full terms. Monroe was also the last president from the generation that had won the War of Independence. With the end of the Virginia dynasty, the Democratic-Republicans no longer were led by national figures who could hold the party together.

Ironically, political unity became all the more difficult to achieve because of the extraordinary electoral success of the Democratic-Republican Party. Mobilizing popular support for a governing coalition requires a credible opponent.[63] But during Monroe's first term as president, the Federalist Party disappeared as a national organization. The Federalists had grown so weak by 1816 that they stopped fielding a ticket in presidential elections. As a result, Monroe was unopposed for reelection in 1820.

For a time, Jefferson's claim that the Democratic-Republicans would some-day embody a new national consensus, a politics without parties, seemed justified. Their complete triumph over their Federalist rivals appeared to restore the nonpartisan character of the Constitution, this time on terms favored by Democratic-Republicans. But as political scientist James Roger Sharp has written, the Democratic-Republican Party did not wither away; instead it "became bloated and shapeless."[64] Triumph brought dissolution. Even as Monroe was inaugurated for the second time, his party was being torn apart by the ambitions of the many candidates who wanted to succeed him as president. In fact, as Catherine Allgor has pointed out, the 1824 campaign may have begun as early as 1817.[65] In 1818 John Quincy Adams, Monroe's secretary of state, observed that "political, personal and electioneering intrigues are intermingling themselves with increasing heat and violence." The result, Adams lamented, was that the government was "assuming daily more and more a character of cabal, and preparation, not for the next presidential election, but for the one after."[66]

POLITICS WITHOUT PARTIES: THE CONTROVERSIAL ELECTION OF 1824

With the Federalists vanquished and the Democratic-Republicans fragmented, the 1824 presidential election became a contest of individuals rather than of issues. For the first time, no Virginian was in the race, further evidence that an era had passed. Rival leaders from New England, the Deep South, and the West, each supported by his own organization and regional following, ran for president in one of the bitterest and most confusing campaigns in American history. The results of the election stirred a storm of controversy, prompting a revolt against the congressional caucus nominating process that had been used for a quarter century. John Quincy Adams, the eventual winner of the 1824 election, inherited an impossible governing situation. It was not improved by a personality that, in his own words, was "reserved, cold, forbidding, and austere."[67] When his one term in office was over, the Democratic-Republican era also came to an end amid conflicts so acrimonious that they endured for a generation.

In 1824, for the second time in twenty-five years, an election was decided not by the Electoral College but by the House of Representatives. Adams felt that as secretary of state he was the logical heir to the presidency. In contrast to his predecessors as secretary, however, Adams had no experience wooing voters, and he finished second with eighty-four electoral votes. Monroe's secretary of the Treasury, William Crawford, was the nominee of the Democratic-Republican caucus in Congress. But the party machinery had run down badly by 1824, and its support no longer was tantamount to election. Crawford came in third with forty-one electoral votes. The powerful Speaker of the

House, Henry Clay of Kentucky, was fourth with thirty-seven votes. Sen. Andrew Jackson of Tennessee, the hero of the Battle of New Orleans, received the most electoral votes, but with 99, he fell short of the 131 needed for a majority and election. Jackson also won a strong plurality of popular votes in the eighteen states (all but six in the now twenty-four-state union) that in 1824 allowed voters to choose the electors.

Under the Twelfth Amendment, when any candidate fails to secure a majority of electoral votes, the House of Representatives chooses the president from among the three highest vote-getters. This procedure eliminated Clay as a candidate. If the fourteen delegations from the states in which Jackson finished either first or second to Clay in the election had supported the Tennessean, he would have become president.[68] But Clay used the influence he still had with his fellow representatives to help secure Adams's election. The new president, in turn, appointed Clay as secretary of state. Jackson's supporters were furious, charging that Adams and Clay had made a "corrupt bargain" to thwart the will of the people. Jackson himself branded Clay "the *Judas* of the West" and prophesied that "his end will be the same."[69] Although the charge of conspiracy probably was unfounded, the controversial election of 1824 ensured the demise of what critics had come to call "King Caucus."

John Quincy Adams, the last president of the Jeffersonian era, was severely constrained by the general view that he was a minority president. But Adams was a statesman of considerable talent and accomplishment. Not content to stand in the shadow of Congress, he undertook to renew the strength of his office. In fact, Adams was the first president in history to openly attempt to lead Congress toward an active program of legislative achievement.

In his first annual message to Congress, Adams recommended a broad array of internal improvements, a national university, an observatory, scientific exploration, and voyages of discovery. His three Democratic-Republican predecessors had held strong reservations about the constitutional power of Congress to create and fund such enterprises. Madison and Monroe had followed Jefferson in believing that a constitutional amendment was needed before anything could be done. But Adams rejected both this narrow construction of the Constitution and the deference his recent predecessors had shown to Congress in domestic affairs. He also dismissed the reservations of his cabinet, whose members believed that his ambitious plans were impractical. After recounting the cabinet's resistance, Adams wrote in his diary, "Thus situated, the perilous experiment must be made. Let me make it with full deliberation, and be prepared for the consequences."[70]

Adams was the first president "to demonstrate the real scope of creative possibilities of the constitutional provision to 'recommend to their [Congress's] consideration such measures as he shall judge necessary and expedient.'"[71] But the combination of a disputed election, a divided party, and a stern and formal manner ill suited Adams for the task of building a political coalition. So, as Fred Greenstein has argued, did his failure to "moderate his proposals, establish priorities among them, and set about building support for the measures he deemed most important."[72] A quarter century of Jeffersonian presidents had not prepared the country for the sort of openly assertive executive leadership that Adams was attempting. Congress either ignored or ridiculed most of his proposals.

Adams's influence, never very great, was effectively ended by the midterm congressional elections of 1826. His political foes, championing Andrew Jackson's opposition to the administration, won control of both the House and Senate. "General Jackson will be elected," Adams wrote in his diary, looking ahead to 1828.[73] The Democratic-Republican era ended with Congress, not the presidency, at the center of the national government power, but with the strongest president to date poised to seize control of Washington at the head of a new, democratic army.[74]

NOTES

1. Alexis de Tocqueville, *Democracy in America,* ed. J .P. Mayer (Garden City, N.J.: Doubleday, 1969), 203. Originally published in 1835 and 1840.

2. Harvey Mansfield, "Thomas Jefferson," in *American Political Thought: The Philosophic Dimensions of Statesmanship,* ed. Morton J. Frish and Richard G. Stevens (New York: Peacock, 1983), 49.

3. Jefferson to James Sullivan, February 9, 1797, in *The Writings of Thomas Jefferson,* ed. Paul Leicester Ford (New York: Putnam's, 1895), 7:118.

4. Richard Hofstadter, *The Idea of a Party System: The Rise of Legitimate Opposition in the United States* (Berkeley: University of California Press, 1969), 122.

5. John Ferling, *Adams v. Jefferson: The Tumultuous Election of 1800* (New York: Oxford University Press, 2004), 161.

6. The method of voting added to the uncertainty of the House election. The Federalists controlled the House but did not control the congressional delegations of a majority of states. Of the sixteen states, eight could be counted on to support Jefferson, while six were controlled by the Federalists. The remaining two states were evenly divided. For a full account of the national trauma caused by the electoral gridlock of 1801, see ibid.; and James Roger Sharp, *American Politics in the Early Republic* (New Haven: Yale University Press, 1993), 250–275.

7. Sean Wilentz, *The Rise of American Democracy: From Jefferson to Lincoln* (New York: Norton, 2005), 93.

8. Hamilton to James A. Bayard, January 16, 1801, in *The Papers of Alexander Hamilton,* 27 vols., ed. Harold C. Syrett (New York: Columbia University Press, 1977), 25: 319–324. For a discussion of Hamilton's role in the 1800 election, see Hofstadter, *Idea of a Party System,* 136–140. See also Ferling, *Adams v. Jefferson,* 180.

9. Gordon S. Wood, *Empire of Liberty: A History of the Early Republic, 1789–1815* (New York: Oxford University Press, 2009), 285.

10. Jefferson to Spencer Roane, September 6, 1819, in *The Writings of Thomas Jefferson,* 20 vols., ed. Albert Ellery Bergh (Washington, D.C.: Thomas Jefferson Memorial Association, 1903), 15:212–216.

11. Joanne B. Freeman, *Affairs of Honor: National Politics in the New Republic* (New Haven: Yale University Press, 2001), 243.

12. Forrest McDonald, *The Presidency of Thomas Jefferson* (Lawrence: University Press of Kansas, 1976), 34.

13. "Thomas Jefferson's First Inaugural Address," in *The Evolving Presidency: Landmark Documents, 1787–2010,* 4th ed., ed. Michael Nelson (Washington, D.C.: CQ Press, 2012), 68–73.

14. Robert M. Johnstone Jr., *Jefferson and the Presidency* (Ithaca: Cornell University Press, 1978), 162.

15. *Marbury v. Madison,* 1 Cranch 137 (1803).

16. McDonald, *Presidency of Thomas Jefferson,* 50–51.

17. Indeed, for the rest of his life Jefferson regretted his failure to subdue the Marshall Court. As he told Spencer Roane, "The nation declared its will by dismissing functionaries of one principle, and electing those of another, in the two branches, executive and legislature, submitted to their election. Over the judiciary department, the Constitution deprived them of their control. That, therefore, has continued the reprobated system, and although new matter has been occasionally incorporated into the old, yet the leaven of the old mass seems to assimilate to itself the new, and after twenty years' confirmation of the federated system by the voice of the nation, declared through the medium of elections, we find the judiciary on every occasion, still driving us into consolidation." Jefferson to Roane, September 6, 1819, in Bergh, *Writings of Thomas Jefferson,* 5:212.

18. McDonald, *Presidency of Thomas Jefferson,* 41.

19. Johnstone, *Jefferson and the Presidency,* 46 (emphasis in original).

20. Jefferson to John Breckinridge, August 12, 1803, in *The Portable Thomas Jefferson,* ed. Merrill D. Peterson (New York: Viking Press, 1975), 494–497.

21. Thomas Jefferson, "The Higher Law of Necessity," in *The President, Congress, and the Constitution: Power and Legitimacy in American Politics,* ed. Christopher H. Pyle and Richard M. Pious (New York: Free Press, 1984), 62–63 (emphasis in original).

22. Leonard D. White, *The Jeffersonians: A Study in Administrative History, 1801–1829* (New York: Macmillan, 1951), 3.

23. Ibid., 551.

24. The discussion of the change in the presidency during the Jeffersonian era is based on James Ceaser, *Presidential Selection: Theory and Development* (Princeton: Princeton University Press, 1979), 88–122; Johnstone, *Jefferson and the Presidency,* 52–75; and Jeremy Bailey, *Thomas Jefferson and Executive Power* (New York: Cambridge University Press, 2007).

25. Ceaser, *Presidential Selection,* 102.

26. John Ferling, *A Leap in the Dark: The Struggle to Create the American Republic* (New York: Oxford University Press, 2003), 477.

27. Quoted in Johnstone, *Jefferson and the Presidency,* 58.

28. Ibid., 58–59. See also Jefferson to Nathaniel Macon, May 14, 1801, in Ford, *Writings of Thomas Jefferson,* 8:51–52.

29. Merrill D. Peterson, *Thomas Jefferson and the New Nation: A Biography* (New York: Oxford University Press, 1970), 653.

30. McDonald, *Presidency of Thomas Jefferson,* 22.

31. Johnstone, *Jefferson and the Presidency,* 67–75.

32. Fred Greenstein, *Inventing the Job of President: Leadership Style from George Washington to Andrew Jackson* (Princeton: Princeton University Press, 2009), 5–6.

33. White, *Jeffersonians,* 547.

34. Joyce Appleby, *Thomas Jefferson* (New York: Times Books, 2003), 41–42.

35. Jeffrey Tulis, *The Rhetorical Presidency* (Princeton: Princeton University Press, 1987).

36. Samuel Kernell, *Going Public: New Strategies of Presidential Leadership,* 3rd ed. (Washington, D.C.: CQ Press, 1997).

37. Leonard W. Levy, *Jefferson and Civil Liberties: The Darker Side* (Cambridge: Harvard University Press, 1963), 102.

38. Ibid., 96.

39. Mel Laracey, "Dear America: Public Letters as an Early Form of Presidential Mass Communication," (paper prepared for delivery at the 2009 Annual Meeting of the American Political Science Association, September 4, Toronto, Canada).

40. Jefferson to Thomas Mann Randolph, February 7, 1898, cited in Wilentz, *Rise of American Democracy*, 134.

41. Richard P. McCormick, *The Presidential Game: The Origins of American Presidential Politics* (New York: Oxford University Press, 1982), 82–87.

42. David E. Kyvig, *Explicit and Authentic Acts: Amending the U.S. Constitution, 1776–1995* (Lawrence: University Press of Kansas, 1996), 115–116.

43. On Jefferson's effort to recast executive power in a more popular form, see Gary J. Schmitt, "Thomas Jefferson and the Presidency," in *Inventing the American Presidency*, ed. Thomas E. Cronin (Lawrence: University Press of Kansas, 1989); and Ralph Ketcham, "The Jefferson Presidency and Constitutional Beginnings," in *The Constitution and the American Presidency*, ed. Martin Fausold and Alan Shank (Albany: State University of New York Press, 1991).

44. White, *Jeffersonians*, 48–59.

45. Ralph Volney Harlow, *The History of Legislative Methods in the Period before 1825* (New Haven: Yale University Press, 1917), 192; and White, *Jeffersonians*, 52.

46. White, *Jeffersonians*, 53–54. A Madison biographer, Gaillard Hunt, exonerates Madison of striking any bargain with party leaders in Congress to secure his renomination. But there is no doubt that the Democratic-Republican caucus sought assurances about Madison's willingness to send a war message to Congress before agreeing to his renomination. See Hunt, *The Life of James Madison* (New York: Russell and Russell, 1902), 316–319.

47. White, *Jeffersonians*, 55.

48. Hunt, *Life of James Madison*, 325.

49. Wood, *Empire of Liberty*, 659–660, 677.

50. Wilentz, *Rise of American Democracy*, 165.

51. Hunt, *Life of James Madison*, 318–319.

52. Ibid., 329–330.

53. James D. Savage, *Balanced Budgets and American Politics* (Ithaca: Cornell University Press, 1988), 98–99. See also Robert Allen Rutland, *The Presidency of James Madison* (Lawrence: University Press of Kansas, 1990), 68–70, 195–203.

54. Ralph Ketcham, "James Madison and the Presidency," in Cronin, *Inventing the American Presidency*, 360–361. Ketcham has argued that contemporary scholarly judgments of Madison as a weak president—such as his failure to be a dynamic leader, even during wartime—miss the philosophical and practical grounds of the president's conduct:

> It was not only uncongenial personally and in principle for Madison to move harshly against [the resistance to the war]; it was very nearly practically impossible as well. The federal system, which in Madison's own theory was the *only* republican way to govern a nation as large as the United States, gave state officials a multitude of ways to obstruct the national conduct of the war. Furthermore, republican theory forbade stifling the opposition or summarily denying civil liberties even during wartime; to do so was tantamount to losing the essential point (a free society) at the beginning and by default. (Ibid., 357–358 [emphasis in original].)

55. White, *Jeffersonians*, 38–41.

56. Jefferson to John Holmes, April 22, 1820, in Peterson, *Portable Thomas Jefferson*, 567–569.

57. White, *Jeffersonians*, 39. For a different, more appreciative view of Monroe as president, see Greenstein, *Inventing the Job of President*, chap. 6.

58. Quoted in ibid., 39.

59. William M. Goldsmith, ed., *The Growth of Presidential Power: A Documented History*, 3 vols. (New York: Chelsea, 1974), 1:378–386.

60. "The Monroe Doctrine," in Nelson, *Evolving Presidency,* 75–79.

61. W. P. Cresson, *James Monroe* (Chapel Hill: University of North Carolina Press, 1946), 448.

62. Goldsmith, *Growth of Presidential Power,* 1:455–456.

63. Ceaser, *Presidential Selection,* 102–103.

64. Sharp, *American Politics in the Early Republic,* 284.

65. Catherine Allgor, *Parlor Politics, in Which the Ladies of Washington Help Build a City and a Government* (Charlottesville: University Press of Virginia, 2000), chap. 4.

66. Charles Francis Adams, ed., *Memoirs of John Quincy Adams: His Diary from 1795 to 1848,* 12 vols. (Philadelphia: J. B. Lippincott, 1874–1877; New York: AMS Press, 1970), 4:193.

67. Ibid., 7:63.

68. Wilentz, *Rise of American Democracy,* 250.

69. Quoted in Sean Wilentz, *Andrew Jackson* (New York: Times Books, 2005), 49.

70. Adams, *Memoirs of John Quincy Adams,* 7:63.

71. Goldsmith, *Growth of Presidential Power,* 1:325.

72. Greenstein, *Inventing the Job of President,* 80.

73. Quoted in Wilentz, *Rise of American Democracy,* 294.

74. White, *Jeffersonians,* 42.

CHAPTER 5

The Age of Jackson

T he presidency of John Quincy Adams took on the character of a long and acrimonious political campaign. Adams's own reelection effort began even before he was inaugurated in 1825 and continued for four years. As the president struggled in Washington with a recalcitrant Congress, a well-organized opposition formed around the country in support of Andrew Jackson, who was intent on rectifying the so-called corrupt bargain between Adams and Henry Clay that he believed had denied him the presidency in 1824.

By 1828 the confused political situation that underlay the previous presidential campaign, in which there were four candidates, had been replaced by a new party alignment. The Federalist Party was long defunct, and the Democratic-Republicans, who had dominated American politics since 1801, were now divided into two major factions. Adams and Clay, who stood for the national aspirations of the National Republicans, as they sometimes were called, formed one group. Jackson and John C. Calhoun, who was vice president during Adams's administration, led the opposition, which dedicated itself to the traditional Democratic-Republican principles of states' rights and a narrow interpretation of the national government's constitutional powers. By 1832 these factions had developed further into, respectively, the Whig Party and Democratic Party. These two parties dominated the American political landscape until the eve of the Civil War.

The Jacksonian Democrats had the better of this rivalry. From 1828 until 1856 Democratic control of the presidency was interrupted only by the election of two Whig generals, William Henry Harrison in 1840 and Zachary Taylor in 1848, whose popularity as military heroes transcended party. Jackson's victory in the 1828 election was the culmination of a trend that had begun during the Jeffersonian era: the triumph of the emerging agrarian and frontier interests of the South and West over the commercial and financial interests of the Northeast. The purchase of the Louisiana Territory from France in 1803 and of Florida from Spain in 1819 had not only added millions of acres to the United States but also afforded greater influence to many Americans who previously had stood outside the regular channels of political power.

Jackson, in fact, was the first political "outsider" to become president. All of his predecessors had undergone extensive apprenticeships in national politics and diplomacy as vice president, secretary of state, or both. The hero of the Battle of New Orleans had little experience in Congress and none in executive administration. He was also, according to Sean Wilentz, "a social outsider, with an unpolished plebeian sensibility unlike any yet seen in an American president."[1] Jackson was a self-made man who had risen from a small cabin in the piney woods of South Carolina to a plantation near Nashville, Tennessee, and, eventually, to the White House. A powerful symbol of his times, Jackson embodied political principles and personal qualities that held sway in the country for nearly three decades. Appropriately, this period in American history has been called the "Age of Jackson."[2]

JACKSONIAN DEMOCRACY

The most important political theme of the Age of Jackson was the widespread desire for equality of opportunity, born of the conviction that no one should have special privileges at the expense of anyone else. Jackson followed Jefferson in believing that to eliminate privilege from society political leaders must strictly limit the role of the national government. Rapid territorial expansion had been accompanied by dynamic economic growth, which seemed to foster unbounded opportunity in all parts of the country. Within that expansive environment, Jacksonians wanted to confine power as much as possible to the less obtrusive state governments. As Jackson's Democratic successor in the presidency, Martin Van Buren, stated in his first annual message to Congress in 1837, "All communities are apt to look to government for too much. . . . But this ought not to be. . . . [T]he less government interferes with private pursuits the better for the general prosperity. . . . [I]ts real duty . . . is . . . to leave every citizen and every interest to reap under its benign protection the rewards of virtue, industry, and prudence."[3]

To be sure, the Jacksonian Democrats' concern for expanding equality of opportunity was limited to white males, especially those who previously had been barred from voting because they did not own enough property. As historian Richard John has written, "The Jacksonians fully endorsed the post-Missouri [Compromise] consensus—sustained by nonslaveholders and slaveholders alike—that it was imperative to keep the slavery issue off the national political agenda."[4] The Jacksonians' political philosophy encouraged a much bolder assault on national institutions and programs than the generally more flexible Jeffersonians had undertaken. Jackson withdrew the federal government from the realm of internal improvements such as subsidized highways and canals. He kept the armed forces, especially the army, to a minimum.

Jackson's fiscal policy was to hold down expenditures. The Bank of the United States, which Jeffersonians had learned to live with, was dismantled, and its deposits were reinvested in selected state banks.[5]

Yet the Age of Jackson had its contradictory and compensating aspects when it came to the authority of the national government. The Jacksonians regarded the president as the "tribune" of the people, an idea that invested the executive, in a period of democratic aspiration, with tremendous influence. During the Jeffersonian era, presidents had sometimes tried to develop a closer relationship with the people. But their modest efforts were made in the context of political principles and institutional arrangements that generally supported the supremacy of the legislature. Jackson tried to establish a direct connection between the president and the people, thereby challenging Congress's status as the national government's principal branch of representation. As historian Major L. Wilson has observed, "This gave him [Jackson] independent power and made the presidency rather than the Congress, the true organ of the nation's will."[6] The Jacksonians' strengthened presidency "gave voice in a new age to the rising spirit of democratic nationalism," which sustained and strengthened the Union in the face of serious sectional conflicts over issues such as protective tariffs and slavery.[7]

Jackson's commitment to national sovereignty was never more apparent than in the nullification crisis that arose near the end of his first term. In an effort to compel the federal government to accede to its demand for a lower tariff, South Carolina's legislature summoned a state convention on November 24, 1832, to declare that the new 1832 tariff law was "null and void." South Carolina cited the nullification doctrine of its native son, Vice President John C. Calhoun. The doctrine held that a state could declare any federal law that it deemed unconstitutional to be inapplicable within its borders. The ordinance of nullification that the South Carolina convention passed forbade federal officials to collect custom duties in the state after February 1, 1833, and threatened that South Carolina would secede from the Union if the federal government responded by attempting to blockade Charleston or otherwise use force.

In the face of this threat, Jackson issued a ringing proclamation that vigorously rejected South Carolina's claim of a right to disobey a federal statute. For a state to presume to annul a law of the United States, the president argued, was "incompatible with the existence of the Union, contradicted expressly by the letter of the Constitution, unauthorized by its spirit, inconsistent with every principle on which it was founded, and destructive of the great object for which it was formed."[8] In 1861 President Abraham Lincoln would base his response to southern secession on the same argument.

Jackson placed the responsibility to defend the Union squarely on the president's shoulders. It was the people, he believed, acting through the state ratifying conventions, who had formed the Union in 1787–1788, and the president—not Congress or the states—embodied most fully the will of the people. Jackson's conception of the presidency "transcended the older categories of nationalism versus states' rights" and offered a new understanding of national sovereignty.[9]

The idea that the president is the direct representative of the people lay at the heart of Jacksonian democracy. Although more supportive of popular rule than the Federalists, the Democratic-Republicans had demonstrated a restrained faith in democracy. The ongoing disputes between Democratic-Republicans and Federalists about the meaning of the Constitution overshadowed their basic agreement about the need to moderate democracy through various kinds of formal institutional relationships: among the legislative, executive, and judicial branches; between the state and national governments; and between the people and their representatives. The Jacksonians sought to reverse this equation by making the Constitution and its institutions the servant of public opinion. A leading Jacksonian journalist, John L. O'Sullivan, dismissed the founders' fears of democracy: "We are opposed to all self-styled 'wholesome restraints' on the free action of popular opinion and will." O'Sullivan believed in a system of checks and balances that prevented "precipitate legislation." But, he argued, all the branches of government, including the executive, "should be dependent with equal directness and promptness on the influence of public opinion."[10]

Alexis de Tocqueville, writing in the 1830s, identified this expanding doctrine of popular sovereignty as the cornerstone of Jacksonian democracy: "The people reign over the American political world as God rules over the universe. It is the cause and the end of all things; everything rises out of it and is absorbed back into it."[11] The dramatic surge of political reform in the 1830s had a profound effect on the presidency. Jackson's election in 1828 coincided with changes in state laws that replaced legislators with voters in the selection of presidential electors. In the first three presidential elections, most electors had been chosen by the state legislatures. But by 1832 electors were selected by popular vote in every state except South Carolina, which retained legislative selection until the Civil War. More than four times as many people voted in both 1828 and 1832 as in 1824. As a result, Jackson was the first president who could plausibly claim to have been elected by the people, strengthening his and his supporters' conviction that his mandate came directly from the source of all sovereignty.[12]

The president's claim to be the direct representative of the people also gained credence from the expansion of the electorate. The Jacksonians worked successfully to persuade the states to eliminate property qualifications for voting, which meant that universal white manhood suffrage was virtually established by 1832. This development brought into the electorate farmers, mechanics, and laborers—"the humble members of society," as Jackson called them—who regarded the presidency under Old Hickory's superintendence as a rallying point. Their support rescued the executive office from the congressional domination that had characterized presidential administrations from James Madison to John Quincy Adams. Indeed, with the collapse of the congressional nominating caucus in 1824, Jackson became the first president since George Washington to be chosen in a contest that did not involve Congress. In the general election, Jackson defeated Adams by 178–83 in the Electoral College and won 56 percent of the popular vote, the latter figure unsurpassed by any presidential candidate until Theodore Roosevelt in 1904. Taking office in 1829, Jackson found himself in a position to revitalize the presidency with a new independence and energy.

THE RISE OF THE PARTY CONVENTION

The advent of the Jackson presidency was accompanied by important developments in the party system. The demise of "King Caucus" left a vacuum in the presidential nominating process that soon was filled by national party conventions.[13] In 1832 the Democrats began using a convention to nominate their candidates for president and vice president, followed by the Whigs after the presidential election of 1836. National convention delegates were selected by state-level conventions made up of local party members. Implicit in the idea of the national convention was the premise that the delegates' authority sprang directly from the rank and file or, as Jackson put it, "fresh from the people."[14] Taken together, the new and elaborate Whig and Democratic organizations reached far beyond the halls of Congress and eventually penetrated every corner of the Union. Sustained by his party's far-reaching political network, Jackson became the first president to appeal to the people over the heads of their legislative representatives.[15]

Party reform did not by itself ensure a strong presidency. The national party apparatus on which presidents depended for support was little more than a loose confederation of state and local organizations. Yet because the president and the national convention rather than Congress were at the heart of the party's identity and mission, strong leaders such as Jackson enjoyed an added source of political influence. Even though their organizational structure and practices were decentralized, the parties orchestrated presidential campaigns. As a consequence, their representatives in Congress muted, to some extent, sectional or local interests and supported national policies as expressed in the party platform. Moreover, with the formation of a stable two-party system during the Jacksonian era, partisan loyalties sank deep roots in the minds and habits of the American people. Presidents became the beneficiaries of a stable foundation of popular support, enabling them to compete effectively with Congress for the public's attention.[16]

JACKSON'S STRUGGLE WITH CONGRESS

The transformation of the presidency from a congressionally to a popularly based office did not take place without a tremendous political struggle. The Whig Party, although it won only two of eight presidential elections between 1828 and 1856, offered vigorous opposition to the Democrats. Proclaiming the ideas of leaders such as Henry Clay and John Quincy Adams, the Whigs took a national approach to national problems. They advocated Clay's program, known as the American Plan, to recharter the Second Bank of the United States, enact a protective tariff, and foster internal improvements. This program challenged the states-centered policies of the Democrats, resting instead on a broad, Hamiltonian construction of the Constitution.

Yet the Whigs, who originally formed as the party of opposition to Jackson, resisted the expansion of executive power and defended Congress's traditional status as the principal instrument of republican government. Jackson and the Democratic Party firmly controlled the House, but the Senate, led by forceful Whigs such as Clay and Daniel Webster, often challenged both the president's policies and his claims to executive primacy. Although the Whigs were seldom the majority party in the Senate, they forged a coalition with Calhoun and some other states' rights–oriented southern Democrats, who resented Jackson's defense of the Union in the nullification crisis of 1832.

The conflict between the president and the Whigs came to a head in July 1832, when Jackson vetoed a bill to recharter the national bank four years before the existing charter expired. A generation earlier, as a central element of Alexander Hamilton's domestic program, the Bank of the United States had been a major point of contention between the Federalists and the Democratic-Republicans. Although Jefferson had attacked the bank as an unconstitutional expansion of the national government, he and his Democratic-Republican successors became reconciled to it once they were in office, viewing the bank as a necessary evil to sustain a stable national currency. In 1816 the Second Bank of the United States had received a twenty-year charter from Congress, but its president, Nicholas Biddle, decided to apply for an early recharter in 1832 at the urging of Clay and Webster. Clay, the Whigs' likely nominee for president in 1832, expected Jackson, whose dislike of the bank was well known, to veto the measure and thereby weaken his prospects for reelection. A considerable number of Democrats—especially in Pennsylvania, the home of the bank—supported the recharter legislation.

Jackson's veto of the bank bill on July 10, 1832, was, according to historian Robert V. Remini, "the most important veto ever issued by a president."[17] Certainly the veto established a precedent that significantly strengthened the presidency. Beginning with Washington, Federalist and Democratic-Republican presidents alike had agreed that a veto should be cast only when the president believed that a piece of legislation was unconstitutional. In forty years under the Constitution, presidents had vetoed only nine acts of Congress, and of these only three dealt with important issues. Jackson, in contrast, successfully vetoed twelve bills in eight years, even using the "pocket veto" for the first time. In his 1832 bank veto message to Congress, Jackson declared that a president should reject any bill he felt would injure the nation.

One implication of Jackson's interpretation of the veto power was that Congress now had to consider the president's opinions about bills before enacting them or else risk a veto. Even though the rechartering of the bank had involved an "agent of the Executive branch of government," Jackson complained in his veto message, "neither upon the propriety of the present action nor upon the provisions of this act was the executive consulted."[18] In demanding the right to be involved in the development of important legislation, Jackson "essentially altered the relationship between the executive and legislative branches of government."[19]

Two other aspects of Jackson's veto message were significant. First, the message rearticulated Jefferson's belief that the president and Congress each possess coordinate power with the courts to determine questions of constitutionality. Jackson argued that the national bank was unconstitutional as well as unwise, a claim that his Whig opponents regarded as outrageous in view of Chief Justice John Marshall's decision in *McCulloch v. Maryland* (1819) that Congress had the constitutional power to charter a bank.[20] Webster charged that Jackson had claimed, in effect, "a universal power of judging over the laws and over the decisions of the judiciary" that was "nothing else but pure despotism."[21]

Jackson insisted, however, that in matters of constitutional interpretation the president was no more bound by judicial rulings than by acts of Congress. Congress, the executive, and the Court, he asserted, "must each for itself be guided by its opinion of the Constitution." To rely solely on judicial precedent was to allow for "a dangerous source of authority, and should not be regarded as deciding questions of constitutional power except where the acquiescence of the people and the states can be considered as well settled."[22] Jackson's veto message dramatically reopened the controversy, which seemed to have been resolved in 1803 by *Marbury v. Madison,* over the authority of the federal courts. His claim that the president and Congress, the popularly elected branches, could reach their own judgments about the Constitution expressed his determination to forge a stronger connection between the people and their government.

The other notable aspect of Jackson's bank veto was the manner in which he laid the controversy between himself and Congress before the American people. The last paragraph of Jackson's veto message, anticipating his campaign for reelection, stated that if he were "sustained by his fellow citizens," he would be "grateful and happy."

Concerned about the political effects of the bank war, Congress failed to override the president's veto. Jackson's 219–49 electoral vote defeat of Clay in the 1832 election, which was fought in large measure on the bank issue, convinced even his political opponents, as the respected Whig newsweekly *Niles' Register* reported, that when the president "cast himself upon the support of the people against the acts of both houses of Congress," he was sustained. Never before had a chief executive appealed to the people over the heads of their elected legislators. Jackson's victory confirmed his conviction that the president, not Congress, was the people's true representative in Washington.[23]

THE AFTERMATH OF THE BANK VETO

The Jacksonian revolution was extended in the aftermath of the bank veto. Vindicated by his reelection in 1832, Jackson decided to kill off the bank once and for all by withdrawing the national government's deposits and placing them in selected state banks. But because Congress refused Jackson's request for authority to remove the bank's funds, the power to do so remained with the secretary of the Treasury, who had been granted this authority in the law that chartered the Second Bank of the United States in 1816.

When Secretary of the Treasury Louis McLane refused the president's request to transfer the deposits from the national bank to the state banks, Jackson nominated him to be secretary of state and replaced him at the Treasury with William J. Duane. But Duane also resisted Jackson's request and was dismissed within four months of taking office. His replacement, Roger B. Taney, formerly the attorney general, finally gave Jackson the cooperation he was looking for, which provoked the Senate to pass a censure resolution that accused the president of assuming "authority and power not conferred by the Constitution and laws."[24] Never before (or since) had a house of Congress voted to censure a president.

On April 15, 1834, Jackson countered the Senate's challenge with a written "Protest." In this message, which the offended Senate refused to enter in its journal, Jackson plainly stated his belief that "the President is the direct representative of the American people," not the Senate, which he dismissed as "a body not directly amenable to the people" because its members were elected by the state legislatures. Jackson further declared that the censure resolution was "wholly unauthorized by the Constitution, and in derogation of its entire spirit." He had been accused and, in effect, found guilty of an impeachable offense without the benefit of a trial, Jackson complained. Although the Senate's censure did not remove Jackson from office, it subjected him to a "solemn declaration" that threatened to undermine his authority and usurp the powers of the executive. The president concluded:

I do hereby *solemnly protest* against the aforementioned proceedings of the Senate as unauthorized by the Constitution, contrary to its spirit and to several of its expressed provisions, subversive of that distribution of the powers of government which it has ordained and established, destructive of the safeguards by which those powers were intended on the one hand to be controlled and the other to be protected, and calculated by their character and tendency, to concentrate in the hands of a body not directly amenable to the people a degree of influence and power dangerous to their liberties and fatal to the Constitution of their choice.[25]

Taken together, Duane's dismissal, Taney's removal of public deposits from the national bank, and the Senate's censure of Jackson raised a fundamental constitutional question: May the president, by firing someone, dictate how a discretionary power that Congress has vested exclusively in the head of a department shall be exercised? Whig leaders, notably Clay and Webster, defended Congress's right to vest independent authority in the Treasury secretary. Jackson claimed in response that the president was responsible "for the entire action of the executive department."

The Senate censure controversy—one battle in the long war between the president and Congress for control of executive administration—was won decisively by Jackson. His protest message became the leading issue in the next round of Senate elections, and Jackson's Democratic allies gained nine seats and took control of the upper house in 1837. At once, as historian H. A. Wise has written, the work of expunging from the record the Senate resolution of censure began, "which hurled senators from their seats in order to fill them with the pliant and supple tools of executive power to draw black lines on that journal around that resolution which dared to censure President Jackson!"[26]

On January 16, 1837, weeks before leaving office, Jackson had the satisfaction of seeing the Resolution of Censure formally expunged from the Senate journal. The Senate's decision to recant not only signified a personal political triumph for Jackson, but also confirmed his broad interpretation of the president's power to control the executive branch.[27]

THE DECLINE OF THE CABINET

Within the executive branch, Jackson reduced the status of the cabinet. His dismissal of William Duane, in fact, merely capped the administration's unprecedented record of cabinet instability. During Jackson's two terms as president, he had four secretaries of state, five secretaries of the Treasury, two secretaries of war, three attorneys general, three secretaries of the navy, and three postmasters general.

Much of this turnover took place in 1831 when, for the first and only time in American history, the president forced an entire cabinet to resign. Jackson issued the resignation order in frustration over his inability to resolve the so-called Petticoat Affair.[28] The affair involved unsubstantiated rumors of scandal and immorality concerning Margaret Eaton, the wife of Secretary of War John Eaton, and the refusal of all the cabinet members' wives to associate with her. These snubs infuriated Jackson, who was a longtime friend of both Eatons, and whose own recently deceased wife, Rachel, had also been the victim of vicious rumors. Jackson spent considerable time during his first two years as president establishing Margaret Eaton's innocence to his own satisfaction. He even presented a report of his findings to the cabinet—to no avail.

The impasse, which was poisoning both Washington society and the Jackson administration, was not resolved until Secretary of State Martin Van Buren, like Jackson a widower and a friend of the Eatons, persuaded the president to let him and Secretary Eaton resign as a way of triggering a wholesale turnover in the cabinet. Jackson's initial reaction to Van Buren's suggestion was "Never, sir! Even you know little of Andrew Jackson if you suppose him capable of consenting to such a humiliation of his friend by his enemies."[29] But the president soon came to see the political shrewdness of Van Buren's idea. Jackson told the other department heads that because he had formed the cabinet as a unit, the resignation of two members meant that he needed to replace them all. Van Buren's political star ascended in the eyes of the grateful president and his legions of devoted supporters. In contrast, the star of Van Buren's main rival to succeed Jackson as president, Vice President Calhoun, fell, in part because Calhoun's wife was among those who had persisted in snubbing Margaret Eaton.

The cabinet's status in the Jackson administration also was diminished by the president's reliance on his "kitchen cabinet," a group of unofficial advisers with whom he conferred confidentially. They included Andrew J. Donelson, Jackson's ward and private secretary; Maj. William B. Lewis, a longtime friend whom Jackson invited to live in the White House; Van Buren, whom a grateful Jackson named as his second-term vice president; Amos Kendall, formerly a newspaper editor; and Francis P. Blair, the editor of the *Globe,* a newspaper whose pages he used from 1830 to 1845 to support Democratic policies and denounce the Whigs. The kitchen cabinet was depicted by Jackson's political enemies as slipping into the president's study by way of the kitchen stairs. In contrast, the traditional cabinet was sometimes called the "parlor cabinet."

According to critics of the administration, the kitchen cabinet consisted of men who were gifted in the arts of political manipulation but advised the president badly on matters of policy and government. Yet Jackson's reliance on informal advisers signified more the dominant sway he held over public affairs than any undue dependence on shadowy sources of influence. The only permanent member of the kitchen cabinet was Jackson himself. Membership in the group shifted from month to month and from issue to issue. The decline of the formal cabinet during the Jackson administration marked

BORN TO COMMAND.

OF VETO MEMORY.

HAD I BEEN CONSULTED.

KING ANDREW THE FIRST.

Jackson's extension of executive power led his opponents to caricature him in this 1832 cartoon by an unknown artist as a monarch trampling the Constitution, a ledger of Supreme Court decisions, and the watchwords "Virtue," "Liberty," and "Independence."

the unprecedented prominence of the presidency between 1829 and 1837, not the rise of a new advisory body.[30]

THE LIMITS OF THE JACKSONIAN PRESIDENCY

According to the Whigs, the main legacy of Jackson's presidency was a dangerous expansion of presidential power. The bank controversy demonstrated, they argued, that the chief executive now possessed powers that dwarfed those of Congress and the judiciary, thereby undermining the constitutional separation of powers. Indeed, it was during this controversy that the anti-Jackson National Republican Party assumed the name of "Whig." Historically, the label derived from the British political party that opposed the power of the king and supported parliamentary supremacy. Whigs in the United States meant by their name to imply that the Jackson wing of the Democratic-Republican Party—the Democrats—had abandoned Jeffersonian principles in favor of an elected monarch, whom Whigs dubbed "King Andrew the First."[31]

Jackson's attitude toward the courts lent support to this indictment. His bank veto message had asserted that he reserved the right to question a Supreme Court decision if he thought it was based on an erroneous interpretation of the Constitution. Jackson's response to the Supreme Court's ruling in *Worcester v. Georgia* (1832) nearly led to a direct clash between the president and the justices, especially Chief Justice Marshall.[32] In this case, the Supreme Court struck down a Georgia law banishing the Cherokee Indians from the state's western territories on the ground that the law violated a federal treaty with the tribe. The issue was brought to the Court by two Christian missionaries, Samuel Worcester and Elizur Butler, who had ignored a provision in the Georgia law that prohibited whites from living in Cherokee territory without first obtaining a state license. Jackson, a vociferous defender of states' rights in matters of Indian policy, maintained a deafening public silence in the face of the Court's ruling. Newspaper editor Horace Greeley later reported that Jackson's private response was, "Well: John Marshall has made his decision: now let him enforce it!"[33] Although the authenticity of this statement has been questioned by some historians, Jackson certainly encouraged Georgia in its intransigence. His public actions, however, were more cautious. The president neither criticized the decision nor openly expressed support for Georgia's refusal to comply. Instead, with the help of Vice President–elect Van Buren, he maneuvered behind the scenes to orchestrate a compromise. The two missionaries received a gubernatorial pardon, in exchange for which they agreed to withdraw their legal challenge.[34]

Significantly, the *Worcester* controversy occurred during the national crisis aroused by South Carolina's passage of the ordinance of nullification. Jackson's cautious resolution of the case enabled him to ask Congress for authorization to use force to suppress nullification in South Carolina without being embarrassed by his support of Georgia in its own clash with the national government.[35] In the debate on the Nullification Proclamation, Jackson's loud voice had been heard in support of democratic nationalism. His public silence in the *Worcester* controversy revealed not just the limits of Jacksonian democracy, but also the constraints that bound the "tribune" of the people.

In truth, the institutional legacy of Jackson's two terms as president was much more ambiguous than his political opponents believed. Jackson did not simply expand the opportunities for unilateral executive action. His extension of executive power depended on the president's emergence as a popular leader, a role that was mediated in critical ways by his party. "More than any other American," Wilentz has written, Jackson oversaw the decline and fall of the elitist, gentry order established by the Framers, and its replacement with the ruder conventions and organization of democracy."[36] Van Buren and other members of Jackson's kitchen cabinet built the first national party organization that was extensive enough to constrain any excesses of personal ambition that might arise among Jackson's presidential successors. As Van Buren wrote to Thomas Ritchie, the editor of the *Richmond Inquirer,* the ultimate objective was to "substitute party principle for personal preference."[37]

THE PARTY PRESS

The bank war and other political struggles during the Jackson presidency were carried on through the party press that emerged during the 1830s. Jackson's relationship with Democratic journalists such as Amos Kendall and Francis Blair added an important dimension to his leadership. These editors provided the president with an acceptable tool for political influence by translating "White House decisions into forceful language and announc[ing] them with persuasive eloquence to the American people."[38] Blair's *Globe,* in fact, became the official organ of both the Jackson administration and its successor, the Van Buren administration. The newspaper enjoyed special access to official political circles as well as financial support from government printing contracts that were distributed by the administration. Its articles were reprinted in pro-Jackson state and local newspapers around the country, fanning the flames of grassroots support for the president and his agenda.[39]

Every Democratic president from Jackson to James Buchanan secured the solid support of at least one important newspaper. The *Globe* and other official White House organs made clear that they were speaking on behalf of the president. Yet the "administration press" was also a Democratic press, dedicated to the party's program and organization.[40] Thus, a more assertive presidency was bound inextricably to a more aggressive and popular party press.

THE "SPOILS SYSTEM"

Jackson implanted a system of rotation into government personnel practices, using the president's power of appointment and removal to hire and fire employees for partisan reasons. Until Jackson became president, the prevailing belief was that the government workforce should be stable and, to a large extent, politically neutral. Beginning in 1829, however, Jackson and his successors rejected this principle and either removed or sanctioned the removal of thousands of subordinates for political reasons. The credo of the new patronage system among Democratic Party activists was, as New York senator William L. Marcy put it, "to the victor belong the spoils of the enemy."[41] Jackson was hardly insensitive to the partisan advantages of "rotation in office," but he also had a deeper purpose in mind. Unless government jobs changed hands regularly, Jackson believed, the resulting "stasis bred corruption in the executive, . . . just as it bred the odious belief that ordinary men lacked the experience necessary to master the mysteries of government service."[42]

In theory, the new principle of rotation in office (or the "spoils system," as Jackson's opponents lastingly called it) expanded the powers of the executive enormously. The president was now in a position, as Jackson's dismissal of Duane during the bank controversy illustrated, to enforce conformity to administration policies within the executive branch. This was in keeping with how Jackson thought constitutional democracy ought to work. As summarized by biographer Jon Meacham, "He wanted a political culture in which a majority of the voters chose a president, and a president chose his administration, and his administration governed by its lights in full view of the people, and the people decided four years hence whether to reward the president with another term."[43] In time, however, most federal patronage came to be controlled by local party organizations in a manner that actually circumscribed presidential leadership. When party leaders demanded offices as a reward for rallying voters to the national ticket in congressional and presidential elections, even powerful chief executives were not inclined to refuse them. Moreover, to keep their jobs, many federal officeholders, particularly those who served in the widely scattered land offices, customhouses, and post offices, were required to return part of their salaries to the local party organization, to work for party at election time, and to "vote right."[44]

The postal system became the primary source of partisan favors. Beginning with Jackson and continuing well into the twentieth century, it was common practice for the president to appoint as postmaster general someone who would serve as the administration's principal patronage officer, representing the interests of the party to the president. Presidents who were insensitive to the demands of partisanship paid a severe political price. James Buchanan was attacked by many Democratic leaders when he removed loyal Democratic officeholders who had been appointed by his predecessor, Franklin Pierce.[45]

The powers of the presidency that Jackson brought to life were constrained not only by the party system but also by the fundamental political doctrine that he espoused: to limit the activities of the national government. "General Jackson's power is constantly increasing," Tocqueville wrote, "but that of the president grows less. The federal government is strong in his hands; it will pass to his successor enfeebled."[46]

MARTIN VAN BUREN AND THE PANIC OF 1837

As Tocqueville prophesied, Jackson's successor, the able and politically shrewd Martin Van Buren, took office in difficult circumstances. Indeed, Van Buren became the first president to have to deal with a nationwide domestic crisis. No sooner was he inaugurated in 1837 than the economy began a steep downward spiral, a decline that was in part the legacy of Jackson's assault on the national bank.

The Panic of 1837, as the crisis was called, was caused in large measure by speculation. A boom in western land and in manufacturing, transportation, banking, and other enterprises, which had begun in 1825, caused credit to become overextended in the national economy. By removing federal deposits from the financially prudent Second Bank of the United States and placing them in politically favored state banks, the Jackson administration had contributed to the rapid expansion of credit. In July 1836, conscious of the problems created by an overextended economy, Jackson issued a Treasury order, the so-called Specie Circular, requiring that hard currency (specie) be used to pay for all federal lands. This order aroused fears that Jackson and his successor would do all they could to shrink the money supply, causing privately owned banks to call in loans, many of which could not be paid. Financial panic ensued. In early 1837 mercantile houses began to fail, New Yorkers rioted to protest the high cost of flour, and almost every bank in the country suspended specie payments. The state banking system that the Jacksonians had encouraged to replace the national bank collapsed, costing the Treasury some $9 million.

Van Buren was a more pragmatic politician than Jackson, but he was sufficiently wedded to Jacksonian principles to resist government-sponsored solutions to the economic crisis. The new president rejected any proposal to revive the national bank. He also rejected the idea that the Treasury should provide a paper currency to facilitate domestic commerce. Like Jackson, Van Buren believed that the Treasury should attend to its own affairs and let businesses do the same.

Spurning the "constant desire" of the Whigs "to enlarge the power of government," Van Buren's response to the Panic of 1837 was modest. He proposed to establish an independent subtreasury, which would keep federal funds in federal vaults instead of depositing them in state banks. The subtreasury, however, was to have limited powers, leaving state banks free from federal regulation. Van Buren's proposal was not implemented until 1840; it was resisted for most of his term by a coalition of conservative Democrats and Whigs, many of whom wanted the national government to become more active in the economy.[47]

THE JACKSONIAN PRESIDENCY SUSTAINED

The presidential election of 1840 took place in the midst of an economic crisis for which many voters held the Democratic Party responsible. The triumph of the Whig candidate, William Henry Harrison, posed a challenge not only to the Jacksonians' domestic program but also to their institutional achievements. The victorious Whig Party was united above all else by opposition to the expansion of executive power that had taken place during the Jackson administration. Accordingly, Whig leaders such as Henry Clay and Daniel Webster saw the Panic of 1837 as an opportunity to reassert the powers of Congress.

Clay was the obvious candidate to head the Whig ticket in 1840. He was both the architect of the anti-Jackson program and the real founder of the Whig Party. But, believing General Harrison to be more electable, the Whigs nominated the aged (he was sixty-seven years old at the time of the election) hero of the War of 1812's Battle of Tippecanoe. Perhaps it consoled Clay and his allies to know that the general had proclaimed his support for the Whig assault on the executive in 1838, dedicating himself to a program that would limit the president to one term, free the Treasury from presidential control, and confine the exercise of the veto power to legislation that the president deemed unconstitutional.[48]

Although the 1840 campaign was not distinguished by a serious discussion of the issues, Harrison did pledge publicly to step down after one term. In a speech delivered on September 10, 1840, at Dayton, Ohio, he declared:

> In the Constitution, that glorious charter of our liberties, there is a defect, and that defect is, the term of service of the President,—not limited. This omission is the source of all the evil under which the country is laboring. If the privilege of being President of the United States had been limited to one term, the incumbent would devote all his time to the public interest, and there would be no cause to misrule the country. . . . *I pledge myself before Heaven and earth, if elected President of the United States, to lay down at the end of the term faithfully that high trust at the feet of the people!* [49]

Harrison's inaugural address, which Webster and Clay helped to write, provided further reason to believe that the Whig victory in 1840 might undo Jackson's reconstruction of the presidency. Indeed, when Harrison deemed "preposterous" the idea that the president could "better understand the wants and wishes of the people than their representatives," Jacksonians suspected that designing Whig leaders had persuaded the politically inexperienced general to accept the status of a figurehead, delegating the powers of his office to Congress.[50]

Yet the Jacksonian executive survived the Whig challenge. The importance of the presidency was so firmly established in the popular mind by 1840 that the executive no longer could be restored to the weak position it had occupied during the latter part of the Jeffersonian era. The Whigs, in fact, unwittingly contributed to the permanent transformation of the presidency by their conduct of the 1840 campaign. Jackson's partisan opponents had looked with disfavor on the popular campaign tactics that the Democratic Party had employed during the three previous presidential elections. But, having lost all of them to Jackson and Van Buren, the Whigs did everything in their power to rouse the people in 1840. They bought newspapers to publish party propaganda, held great rallies, sent popular party leaders on speech-making tours, and worked to mobilize as many voters as possible.

So intent were the Whigs on outdoing the Democrats' campaign in 1840 that they subordinated serious attention to principles and issues to slogans, songs, and symbols. Not only did "Tippecanoe and Tyler too" catch on (an alliterative catchphrase made possible by the nomination of Virginia's John Tyler for vice president), but a great deal of rabble-rousing occurred that for the first time made the log cabin an important symbol in presidential politics. A Democratic journalist had scornfully said of the rough-hewn Harrison,

"Give him a barrel of hard cider and . . . a pension of $2,000, and . . . he will sit the remainder of his days in his log cabin by the side of a . . . fire and study moral philosophy." Clever Whig propagandists pounced on this remark, turning it to their candidate's advantage. In no time, Harrison became "the log cabin and hard-cider candidate," an image that endeared him to many farmers and workers. Log cabin badges, log cabin songs, log cabin newspapers, and cider barrels were seen everywhere.

In the face of such campaigning, Martin Van Buren, whose origins actually were humbler than Harrison's but whose tastes, as displayed in the White House and in his attire, were ostentatious, never stood a chance. In one attack, Whig publicists circulated a speech by Rep. Charles Ogle of Pennsylvania, who charged that the president was such a degenerate that he had ordered the construction, just behind the White House, of "a number of clever sized hills, every pair of which, it is said, was designed to resemble and assume the form of AN AMAZON BOSOM, with a miniature knoll or hillock at its apex, to denote the n—ple."[51] Harrison received 234 electoral votes to 60 votes for Van Buren.[52]

This 1840 campaign cartoon shows Andrew Jackson leading Martin Van Buren to the White House for a second term. Van Buren, known as "Old Kinderhook" after his New York home, lost to the "log cabin and hard-cider" candidate, William Henry Harrison. But his partisan rallying cry, "OK," entered the language as an expression of agreement or approval.

The log cabin, hard-cider campaign stimulated tremendous interest and enthusiasm around the
country. Electoral turnout increased
substantially: the 2.4 million voters
who cast their ballots in 1840 constituted 80.2 percent of the eligible
electorate, a percentage that has
been surpassed only twice, in 1860
and 1876.[53] Ironically, by accepting
and expanding on the Democrats'
successful campaign techniques,
the Whigs unwittingly ratified the
Jacksonian concept of the president
as popular leader. The Whig Party's
anti-executive doctrine notwithstanding, it was no longer possible
for the presidency to be restored to
its late Jeffersonian status, however
unassuming a particular president
might be.[54]

John Tyler, as the first vice president to succeed to the presidency, faced the constitutional question of whether he succeeded to the office for the rest of the term or only succeeded temporarily to the responsibilities of the office. His decisive actions preempted debate and established a firm precedent for succession to the presidency.

JOHN TYLER AND THE PROBLEM OF PRESIDENTIAL SUCCESSION

The consolidation of the Jacksonian presidency became more pronounced
when Harrison, who caught pneumonia after delivering a ninety-minute
inaugural address in Washington's freezing rain on March 4, 1841, died only a
month later. Vice President Tyler quickly took the oath as president and vowed
to complete the remaining three years and eleven months of Harrison's term.
In doing so, Tyler imposed a solution on the unresolved constitutional problem of the vice president's right to assume the full status of the presidency
when the office becomes vacant. Tyler also proved to be a less enthusiastic
proponent of Whig theories of government than Harrison, particularly with
regard to the executive. Whig leaders were disappointed to discover that Tyler
was no ally in their effort to dismantle the Jacksonian presidency.

Tyler's constitutional right to become president was far from certain. The
succession clause of Article II was vague, stipulating only that in case of the
president's death, resignation, removal, or inability to discharge the powers
and duties of the office, "the Same" shall "devolve on the Vice President." Did
"the Same" refer to the "Office" or to its "Powers and Duties"? Specifically, did

Tyler remain vice president, merely acting as president until a special election could be held, or had he succeeded fully to the office and title of president for the remainder of Harrison's four-year term.

Tyler wasted no time asserting that he was the president in every sense of the word. Soon after hearing that Harrison was dead and despite some rumblings from Congress, he had a judge swear him in, and within ten days moved into the White House. Leaving no doubt that he intended to be his own man as president, on April 9, 1841, Tyler went before "the people" and gave an inaugural address to an audience assembled in the Capitol. Tyler's "exposition of the principles" that would govern his administration was a signal to the country that he would not be content to stand in Harrison's shadow. The address was also a warning to Whigs that Tyler did not intend to be a compliant subordinate of Clay and other party leaders. By acting boldly and decisively in an uncertain situation, Tyler established, in the absence of clear constitutional guidance, the firm precedent that an "accidental" president enjoys the same status as an elected president.[55] Congress's acquiescence became clear when a motion in the House of Representatives to address him officially in correspondence as "Vice President, on whom, by the death of the late President, the powers and duties of the office of President have devolved" was defeated overwhelmingly.[56] After all, not much was to be gained politically by alienating the person who, whether as president or acting president, wielded "the Powers and Duties of the said Office."

The difficulties that Tyler faced as president went beyond the constitutional doubts shrouding his succession. His elevation also created a political impasse. Tyler, a former Democrat, represented a faction of the Whig Party that dissented from many of the nationalist views preached by its leaders. In accordance with the practice common in American party politics, his nomination as vice president had stemmed from an effort to balance the Whig ticket—it was a gesture of reconciliation by the ascendant National Republican wing of the Whig Party to the smaller southern states' rights wing. Yet in this case, ticket balancing backfired. Tyler not only seized the reins of office decisively after Harrison's death, but also exercised the powers of the Jacksonian presidency in a way that thwarted the Whigs' efforts to enact Clay's American Plan for government-sponsored economic development.[57] Tyler was, in the apt phrase of political scientists Matthew Crenson and Benjamin Ginsberg, "a lapsed Democrat who relapsed after assuming the responsibilities of the president."[58]

Tyler's opposition to much of the Whig domestic program prompted him to cast more vetoes than any of his predecessors except Jackson. In 1841 Tyler vetoed two successive bills that resembled the old bank legislation Jackson had killed. The outburst of fury against the president after his second veto was extraordinary, expressing the Whigs' frustration at their inability to enact their program even after winning a presidential election. Effigies of Tyler were burned across the country, and the president received hundreds of letters threatening assassination. In Washington, every cabinet member except Secretary of State Daniel Webster resigned. Expressing nostalgia for the era of Democratic-Republican ascendancy, especially for the heir-presumptive role the secretary of state enjoyed during that period, Webster stayed on for another year and a half, trying to work with the new president.[59] Had Webster not resisted pressure from Clay to endorse a Senate scheme to prevent Tyler from appointing a new cabinet, Tyler himself may have had no choice but to resign.

The bank battles were only the beginning of the long struggle between Tyler and his party. Tyler's veto of a tariff measure in 1842 provoked the first attempt in history to impeach a president. His assertive exercise of the veto power was irreconcilable with the Whig theory of executive subordination to Congress. Clay even proposed a constitutional amendment that would permit Congress to override a veto by a simple majority vote.[60]

Tyler, claiming for the president a right to participate in the legislative process that was reminiscent of Jackson, defended his veto of the tariff bill on programmatic rather than constitutional grounds. Responding to Congress's accusation that he had misused the veto power and to the talk of impeachment, Tyler issued a strongly worded public message, stating that he represented "the executive authority of the people of the United States" and in "their name" protested "against every attempt to break down the undoubted constitutional power" of the presidency.[61] Like Jackson, Tyler also argued that when a conflict developed between the president and Congress, it was for the people to decide who was right. When the Whigs were defeated in the congressional elections of 1842, Tyler believed that he had been vindicated. Nothing came of the effort to impeach him, and the public greeted Clay's proposal for a constitutional amendment to weaken the veto power with indifference.

Although Tyler lost his party's support and with it any chance to be nominated for president in 1844, he prevented a potentially damaging setback to the executive office. As presidential scholar Wilfred E. Binkley has written, Tyler "prepared the way for the completion of the movement toward executive leadership started by Andrew Jackson."[62]

THE PRESIDENCY OF JAMES K. POLK

Few would have guessed as Tyler's term came to an end in 1845 that his relatively unknown Democratic successor, James K. Polk, would lead a successful administration. Yet Polk strengthened the office, successfully asserting executive responsibilities that were either unsought by his predecessors or denied to them. Polk's achievements did not come easily. He headed a Democratic Party that was beginning to break apart over the slavery issue. He also faced militant Whig minorities in both houses of Congress.

THE FIRST "DARK HORSE" CANDIDATE

Former president Martin Van Buren was widely expected to receive the 1844 Democratic nomination. But then the issue of Texas, and its annexation to the United States, intervened. Just before the Whig and Democratic nominating conventions, Tyler's secretary of state, John C. Calhoun, concluded an annexation treaty with the Republic of Texas, which had fought for and won its independence from Mexico in 1836. As a result, the two major parties' leading presidential candidates, Van Buren and Clay, were forced to announce their views on the treaty. Texas was an issue that aroused serious disagreements between North and South about the desirability of expanding the cotton-growing and slave-holding section of the United States.

Clay's opposition to annexation caused little controversy in the Whig Party, which increasingly was dominated by northerners.. But when Van Buren took the same position, a firestorm erupted among Democrats. They and their hero, Andrew Jackson, had long supported territorial expansion, a cause that was sacred to the emerging frontier interests of the South and the West. To defeat the Whigs, the Democrats needed strong support in the South, where states' rights advocates such as Calhoun looked westward to expand slavery. Yet Van Buren, belying his reputation as a pragmatic politician, chose to follow "the path of duty" and resisted the extension of slavery. His principled decision cost him any chance to return to the White House.

With Van Buren's candidacy seriously wounded, former governor Polk of Tennessee, so close an associate of Jackson that he was known as "Young Hickory," emerged at the deadlocked Democratic convention as a compromise choice between North and South, the first "dark horse" candidate in the history of American presidential elections. Polk did not even receive his first vote for the nomination until New Hampshire was polled on the eighth convention ballot. But New York's support on the ninth ballot started a stampede, as delegation after delegation rushed to transfer its votes to Polk and thereby demonstrate its loyalty to the winner.[63] In the election, Polk defeated Clay by 170–105 electoral votes, and the Democrats turned a six-seat deficit in the Senate into a twelve-seat majority.

REASSERTING PRESIDENTIAL POWER

Through a combination of shrewd political maneuvering and forceful statesmanship, Polk was able to overcome the centrifugal forces that dominated

American politics during the mid-1840s. After winning the Democratic nomination, he stole one of the Whigs' main issues by disclaiming any intention to seek a second term. Yet during his four years in office, Polk vigorously and effectively asserted executive functions that reinforced, even expanded, the Jacksonian conception of presidential power. Most significant, he was the first president to exercise close and daily supervision of the executive departments.

Consistent presidential influence had been especially absent from previous administrations' relations with the Treasury Department. Presidents had never been granted legal responsibility to oversee the various departmental budget estimates submitted annually to Congress. Instead, in the Treasury Act of 1789 Congress had assigned to the secretary of the Treasury the duty to prepare and report estimates of government expenditures for the coming year. George Washington's Treasury secretary, Alexander Hamilton, did not even consult the president in this matter. Both Hamilton and Albert Gallatin, who served in the Jefferson and Madison administrations, were distinctive among Treasury secretaries mainly in the initiative they took in budgetary policymaking. Their successors in the office simply gathered the departmental estimates and submitted them to Congress in one package. In 1839, for example, Van Buren's secretary of the Treasury, Levi Woodbury, refused to take any responsibility for making a composite budget or for reviewing the estimates that were submitted to him by the other departments.[64]

One of Polk's major achievements was to coordinate the budget: for the first time in history, the president oversaw the formation of a fiscal policy. Not only did Polk review all budget requests, but he also insisted that the department heads revise their planned expenditures downward. Polk was forced to tighten fiscal control after he launched the Mexican-American War in 1846, especially when the government began operating under the reduced revenues of the Walker Tariff, which he considered one of the major accomplishments of his administration.[65] Furthermore, Polk, like his fellow Tennessean and political mentor Jackson, hated public debt and was philosophically committed to limiting government spending. Polk's success in directing the budget was demonstrated by the tight fiscal rein he imposed on the War Department at the end of the Mexican-American War. Polk directed his reluctant secretary of war, William Marcy, to force the department's bureau chiefs to accept a return to the prewar level of expenditures.[66]

The precedents that Polk tried to establish in fiscal policymaking were not followed by his nineteenth-century successors. (Abraham Lincoln, another wartime president, was an exception.) But Polk's assertion of the president's right and duty to control personally the activities of the executive departments implanted the Jacksonian concept of the presidency more deeply in the

American constitutional order. In the face of belligerent Whig opposition, Polk's last message to Congress proclaimed that "the people, by the Constitution, have commanded the President, as much as they have commanded the legislative branch of government, to execute their will." Indeed, Polk argued, the president occupied a special place as the people's representative because "the President represents in the executive department the whole people of the United States, as each member of the legislative department represents portions of them."[67]

According to historian George Bancroft, who served the Polk administration as secretary of the navy, Polk succeeded "because he insisted on being its [the administration's] center and in overruling and guiding all his secretaries to act as to produce unity and harmony."[68] To some extent, this unity was the fortunate by-product of Polk's decision to try to hold his ever more fractious party together by excluding from his cabinet nearly every leading Democrat who actively coveted the presidency. "The virus of competing presidential ambitions must not be allowed to infect Polk's inner circle," biographer Robert W. Merry has written. "Hence there would be no offers to Van Buren, [Thomas Hart] Benton, [Lewis] Cass, Old Dick Johnson, or Calhoun." Polk's one exception demonstrated the rule: he named James Buchanan as secretary of state and then spent all four years ruing Buchanan's "self-interested maneuvers."[69]

Unity within the administration also was fostered by Polk's relentless and successful focus on achieving four specific goals: settling with Great Britain which country owned which parts of the Oregon Territory (accomplished by treaty in 1846); tariff reduction (the Walker Tariff of 1846, the measure named after Polk's secretary of the Treasury, Robert J. Walker); the reestablishment of an independent national Treasury (a Jacksonian mainstay passed by the Democratic Congress in 1846); and the acquisition of California from Mexico. The last of these took a war.

Perhaps Polk's most important contribution to the development of the presidency was his forceful performance as commander in chief during the Mexican-American War. The war had become inevitable after the United States annexed Texas, then admitted it as the twenty-eighth state in 1845 even though Mexico still claimed Texas and considered the annexation a hostile act. Polk's determination to secure New Mexico and California from Mexico provoked further territorial disputes. Unable to negotiate a purchase, Polk resolved to gain these territories by force. He sent an army led by Gen. Zachary Taylor insultingly close to Mexico. Playing into Polk's hands, Mexican cavalry forces attacked the American troops on May 9, 1846, only four hours after the president and his cabinet decided to ask Congress to declare war. Congress endorsed Polk's request on May 13, 1846. The army in New Mexico and the navy on the California coast brought the war to a successful conclusion in eighteen months.

As Leonard D. White has observed, "Polk gave the country its first demonstration of the *administrative* capacities of the presidency as a war agency."[70] To be sure, Polk did not push the executive's power as commander in chief to its limits—that task awaited Lincoln during the Civil War. Unlike Madison in the War of 1812, however, Polk did establish that a president without previous military experience could provide decisive wartime leadership. Polk insisted on being the final authority on all significant military matters. According to White,

> He determined the general strategy of military and naval operations; he chose commanding officers; he gave personal attention to supply problems; he energized so far as he could the General Staff; he controlled the military and naval estimates; and he used the Cabinet as a major coordinating agency for the conduct of the campaign. He told the Secretaries of War and Navy to give their personal attention to all matters, even of detail, and to advise him promptly of every important step that was to be taken. The President was the center on which all else depended; Hamilton's doctrine of the unity of the executive power was seldom more truly exemplified.[71]

Polk's efforts as commander in chief were neither mistake-free nor wholly nonpartisan. A loyal Democrat, he was disturbed that the war was making a hero of General Taylor, a Whig and potentially a formidable presidential candidate in 1848. In a petty partisan action, Polk refused to sign an order for the troops to fire a salute in honor of Taylor's victory at Buena Vista, a settlement in the northeastern part of Mexico. The president's relationship with the army's top commander, Gen. Winfield Scott, also a Whig, was similarly governed by partisanship. Polk urged Congress to create the post of lieutenant general for a Democratic senator, Thomas Hart Benton, so that a Democrat would supersede Scott as the commanding officer in the field. But Benton's military experience was so limited that the Democratic Senate narrowly rejected the president's recommendation.[72]

Polk's problems with his generals can be traced in part to the close relationship between the Jacksonian presidency and the newly institutionalized party system. Partisan practices that had become embedded in presidential politics during the 1830s and 1840s could not easily be put aside even in wartime. Because Scott and Taylor were regular army officers, Polk could do little about them. But volunteer regiments of state militia, which did much of the soldiering, fought principally under Democratic officers. The decision to call up the militia conformed to the Democratic Party's principled opposition to a large standing army, which it regarded as contrary to the character of free government. But the dependence on volunteers plagued Polk throughout the war. The president eventually was forced to recognize his error and, in December 1846, to ask for an increase in the size of the regular army. Until Congress granted his request in February 1847, critical military operations near Mexico City were halted.[73]

Notwithstanding his partisan practices and doctrine, Polk achieved his main goal as commander in chief during the Mexican-American War by acquiring New Mexico and California for the United States. Polk thereby became, except for Jefferson, the president who brought the most territory into the national domain. By demonstrating that the president could plan and oversee the execution of a wartime strategy, Polk effectively asserted the principle that the president is responsible for American military operations.[74]

THE SLAVERY CONTROVERSY AND THE TWILIGHT OF THE JACKSONIAN PRESIDENCY

Polk was the last president of the Jacksonian era whose administration was not consumed by the slavery question. The annexation of Texas and the Mexican-American War greatly expanded the southwest region of the United States. Most northerners objected strongly to the extension of slavery into the new territories. Meanwhile, southern whites were unwilling to distinguish the North's "free soil" position from outright abolitionism, interpreting every effort to bar slavery from the territories as a threat to slavery where it already existed.

The slavery issue had almost divided the Democratic Party in 1844, but it was papered over by the convention's compromise nomination of Polk. The rancorous debate about what to do with the spoils of the Mexican-American War made a similar rapprochement impossible in 1848. Van Buren, the organizational genius who had done so much to bring the original Democratic coalition together during the late 1820s, now abandoned his party to run as the Free Soil Party candidate. Although Van Buren received only 10 percent of the popular vote, he drained support from the Democratic candidate, Lewis Cass, thereby helping to elect the Whig nominee, Zachary Taylor.

Taylor, the hero of the Mexican-American War, probably would have won the presidential election in any event, but the Free Soil Party also drew enough votes to affect the outcome of many state elections. And Van Buren's campaign made it difficult for Democrats and Whigs to ignore the slavery issue any longer. In less than a decade, the party system that had dominated the Jacksonian era would collapse, and a new governing coalition would emerge.

THE PRESIDENCY OF ZACHARY TAYLOR

Because of its strong base in the South, the Democratic Party survived the slavery controversy and the Civil War, although in a greatly weakened condition. But Taylor's election in 1848 was the last major victory for the Whig Party, which endured only a few more years. The Whigs stood for national unity, an ideal that was rendered politically marginal by the slavery question.

Moreover, the Whigs' opposition to an active presidency was proven unwork-able by the last Whig to be elected president. Taylor's inaugural address was replete with Whiggish declarations about the need to limit executive power, but the new president's brief tenure (he died in the cholera epidemic that swept Washington in July 1850, just sixteen months into his term) was hardly true to his promise of political self-restraint.[75] The slavery controversy and Jackson's legacy of presidential leadership had made a hands-off presidency impossible.[76]

More than anything else, Taylor is remembered for his consistent and unyielding opposition to the Compromise of 1850, a congeries of legislative measures designed to preserve a temporary peace on the slavery issue. Taylor's opposition to the compromise, which imposed no restrictions on slavery in the former Mexican southwest territories and strengthened the federal Fugitive Slave Law, nevertheless still angered slaveholders by admitting Cali-fornia to the Union as a free state and ending the slave trade in the District of Columbia. Yet the president stood firm against southern threats of disunion. Although he was a southern slaveholder himself (like seven of his eleven pre-decessors as president), Taylor told congressional leaders that he would per-sonally lead the army into the field to restore the Union and would hang rebels "with as little mercy as he had hanged deserters and spies in Mexico."[77]

THE PRESIDENCY OF MILLARD FILLMORE

Taylor died before the crisis provoked by the Compromise of 1850 matured. His successor, Vice President Millard Fillmore of New York, restated tradi-tional Whig assurances about executive restraint, yet proved no more will-ing than Taylor to leave critical domestic matters to Congress. Fillmore, however, was as determined to see the compromise enacted as his predeces-sor had been to defeat it. The president's endorsement was politically important: one member of the House reported that between twenty and thirty representatives who before Taylor's death were adamantly opposed to the compromise did a dramatic about-face in response to Fillmore's support.[78] With unwonted confidence, the president exulted in September 1850 that "a final settlement" of the nation's sectional differences had been achieved.[79]

Having seen the Compromise of 1850 through to enactment, Fillmore was determined to enforce the new and stringent Fugitive Slave Act vigorously. When Massachusetts refused to cooperate in the prosecution of citizens who violated the act, Fillmore declared that his administration would admit "no right of nullification North or South." In practice, however, the president was never able to impose compliance with the law on those parts of the country where fugitive slaves were protected.[80]

Although Fillmore's tenure demonstrated again that the Jacksonian era had transformed the presidency irrevocably, even the strengthened executive was no match for the crisis engendered by the slavery question. The last two presidents of the Jacksonian era, Franklin Pierce of New Hampshire and James Buchanan of Pennsylvania, were nominated by the Democrats in part because they were "inoffensive . . . northerners with a high regard for the political sensibilities of southern slaveholders."[81] Each proved to be an irresolute leader who sought vainly to hold the northern and southern wings of the Democratic Party together. In doing so, each tried to defuse, rather than come to terms with, slavery as a political issue. But it was too late for temporizing. The nation's polarization over slavery was only aggravated by the efforts of Pierce and Buchanan to dispel the issue.

The Kansas-Nebraska Act of 1854 was the most telling of Pierce's failures to allay sectional conflict. The brainchild of Stephen A. Douglas, the influential Democratic senator from Illinois, the act once again tried to remove slavery from the national political agenda by resting its status in the territories on the principle of "popular sovereignty." According to this principle, as soon as the people of a territory received the right to choose a legislature, their elected representatives would decide whether to allow or forbid slavery. Because the act applied popular sovereignty to the Great Plains territories of Kansas and Nebraska, the central ingredient of the Missouri Compromise of 1820, which prohibited slavery north of Missouri's southern boundary line, would be repealed.

The debate on Douglas's popular sovereignty bill dragged on for three months. Pierce used all the powers of his office, including patronage, to help ensure its passage. In the end, party discipline among Democrats prevailed, buttressed by the president's insistence on making support for his bill "an absolute test of loyalty within the Democratic Party."[82] On May 25, 1854, the Kansas-Nebraska Act passed the Senate by a comfortable margin after narrowly passing the House, and Pierce signed it into law. Within six months, however, it became apparent that the repeal of the Missouri Compromise had aggravated, not quelled, the slavery controversy and had divided the Democratic Party irrevocably. Perversely, Pierce's forceful leadership of his party hastened its demise as a governing institution.

The elections of 1856 revealed the emergence of a new national political alignment. The Whigs' collapse after their landslide defeat in 1852, along with the northern crusade against slavery in Kansas (Nebraska's vote to become a free territory was never in doubt), prompted a new party to form. Offering a platform that stood squarely against the expansion of slavery beyond its existing borders, the Republican Party nominated John C. Frémont, a celebrated explorer of the American West, for president in 1856. Although the Republicans made a good showing in the election, they received no support in the South and were not yet sufficiently organized in the North to overcome this handicap. Winning Indiana, New Jersey, California, Illinois, his home state of Pennsylvania, and the entire South, the Democratic candidate, James Buchanan, was elected president by an electoral vote majority of 174–114.

THE PRESIDENCY OF JAMES BUCHANAN

Buchanan, who was just as anxious as Pierce to defuse the slavery controversy, was also determined to avoid the political damage that Pierce had suffered by fighting for a legislative solution. In his inaugural address, Buchanan associated himself with an as-yet-unannounced Supreme Court decision, arguing that the proper resolution of the slavery question in the territories belonged to the federal judiciary. Referring to the pending suit by Dred Scott, a sixty-two-year-old slave who claimed that extended residence with his owner on free soil had made him a free man, Buchanan pledged that he would "in common with all good citizens . . . cheerfully submit" to the decision of the Supreme Court "whatever [it] might be."[83]

Such a pledge, Binkley has noted, "was a strange abdication of executive claims by a member of the party of Jackson, who . . . had emphatically denied the right of the judiciary thus to determine public policies through the medium of court opinions."[84] In truth, Buchanan's avowed deference to the Supreme Court was disingenuous. He had already privately urged Justice Robert C. Grier, a fellow Pennsylvanian who held a critical swing vote on the Court, to side with colleagues who wanted to deny both Congress and the territorial legislatures the right to prohibit slavery.[85]

Buchanan's attempt to end the agitation over slavery in surreptitious alliance with the Supreme Court failed miserably. The Court's decision in *Dred Scott v. Sandford* opened the entire West to slavery, regardless of what the people in the territories might decide.[86] This aggressive foray into the slavery controversy not only severely damaged the prestige of the Court, but also opened the floodgates to a new outpouring of sectional strife that further fractured the Democratic Party and catapulted an obscure Illinois Republican, Abraham Lincoln, into the presidency in the election of 1860. Lincoln was among the many Whigs-turned-Republicans who strongly believed that the president should oppose Supreme Court decisions like *Dred Scott* when his own interpretation of the Constitution differed from the justices'. Lincoln did not go quite as far as Jackson in challenging the power of judicial review; he granted that the decision was binding on the parties to the suit. But he and many former Whigs turned Republicans were determined that *Dred Scott* would not determine the future course of slavery policy.

NOTES

1. Sean Wilentz, *Andrew Jackson* (New York: Times Books, 2005), 8.

2. Robert V. Remini, *Andrew Jackson and the Course of American Democracy, 1833–1845* (New York: Harper and Row, 1984), 7.

3. James D. Richardson, ed., *Messages and Papers of the Presidents*, 20 vols. (New York: Bureau of National Literature, 1897), 4:1561.

4. Richard R. John. "Affairs of Office: The Executive Departments, the Election of 1828, and the Making of the Democratic Party," in *The Democratic Experiment: New Directions in American Political History*, ed. Meg Jacobs, William J. Novak, and Julian E. Zelizer (Princeton: Princeton University Press, 2003), 67.

5. As historian Marvin Meyers has written, Jackson's political philosophy called for a return to the principles set forth in Jefferson's first inaugural address: "a wise and frugal government, which shall restrain men from injuring one another, which shall leave them otherwise free to regulate their own pursuits of industry and improvement, and shall not take from the mouth of labor the bread it has earned. This is the sum of good government, and this is necessary to close the circle of our felicities." As such—and here the bank war was the critical case—the strengthening of the executive office during the Jacksonian period "mobilized the powers of government for what was essentially a dismantling operation." Meyers, *The Jacksonian Persuasion* (Stanford: Stanford University Press, 1957), 20–21.

6. Major L. Wilson, *The Presidency of Martin Van Buren* (Lawrence: University Press of Kansas, 1984), 13.

7. Ibid.

8. Richardson, *Messages and Papers of the Presidents*, 3:1206.

9. Wilson, *Presidency of Martin Van Buren*, 13.

10. John L. O'Sullivan, "An Introductory Statement of the Democratic Principle," *United States Magazine and Democratic Review* (October 1837), in *Social Theories of Jacksonian Democracy: Representative Writings of the Period, 1825–1850,* ed. Joseph L. Blau (New York: Liberal Arts Press, 1954), 22–23.

11. Alexis de Tocqueville, *Democracy in America,* ed. J. P. Mayer (Garden City, N.Y.: Doubleday, 1969), 60. Originally published in 1835 and 1840.

12. Wilfred E. Binkley, *President and Congress* (New York: Knopf, 1947), 67.

13. See "The Tennessee General Assembly's Protest against the Caucus System," in *The Evolving Presidency: Landmark Documents, 1787–2010,* 4th ed., ed. Michael Nelson (Washington, D.C.: CQ Press, 2012), 80–84.

14. Jackson to James Gwin, February 23, 1835, cited in *Niles' Register,* April 4, 1835, 80.

15. Edward S. Corwin, *The President: Office and Powers, 1787–1957,* 4th ed. (New York: New York University Press, 1957), 20–21.

16. Ibid.; see also Leonard D. White, *The Jacksonians: A Study in Administrative History, 1829–1861* (New York: Macmillan, 1954), 24–25.

17. Robert V. Remini, *Andrew Jackson and the Course of American Freedom, 1822–1832* (New York: Harper and Row, 1981), 369.

18. "Andrew Jackson's Veto of the Bank Bill," in Nelson, *Evolving Presidency,* 89–93.

19. Remini, *Andrew Jackson and the Course of American Freedom,* 370.

20. *McCulloch v. Maryland,* 17 U.S. 316 (1819).

21. Quoted in Binkley, *President and Congress,* 72.

22. Richardson, *Messages and Papers of the Presidents,* 3:1144–5. On Jackson's view of the courts, see Robert V. Remini, "The Constitution and the Presidencies: The Jackson Era," in *The Constitution and the American Presidency,* ed. Martin Fausold and Alan Shank (Albany: State University of New York Press, 1991), 37–40.

23. Richardson, *Messages and Papers of the Presidents,* 3:1154; *Niles' Register,* November 17, 1832, quoted in White, *Jacksonians,* 23; Remini, *Andrew Jackson and the Course of American Freedom,* 373.

24. Quoted in Binkley, *President and Congress,* 79.

25. Richardson, *Messages and Papers of the Presidents,* 3:1311 (emphasis in original).

26. H. A. Wise, *Seven Decades of Union* (Philadelphia: Lippincott, 1872), 137.

27. Binkley, *President and Congress,* 82–85; White, *Jacksonians,* 33–44.

28. John F. Marszalek, *The Petticoat Affair: Manners, Mutiny, and Sex in Andrew Jackson's White House* (New York: Free Press, 1997).

29. Ibid., 159.

30. White, *Jacksonians,* 92–95; Remini, *Andrew Jackson and the Course of American Freedom,* 315–330.

31. Binkley, *President and Congress,* 80.

32. *Worcester v. Georgia,* 31 U.S. 515 (1832).

33. Horace Greeley, *The American Conflict: A History of the Great Rebellion in the United States of America,* vol. 1 (Hartford, Conn.: O. D. Case, 1867), 106 (emphasis in original).

34. Remini, *Andrew Jackson and the Course of American Freedom,* 275–279. Historian Edwin Miles has observed that the decision never really reached a point that required enforcement. The Supreme Court had merely remanded the case to the Georgia Superior Court for reversal of its earlier decision, and then recessed. Therefore, no further action in the matter could take place until the Court's next session in January 1833. By that time, the issue had been resolved. See Miles, "After John Marshall's Decision: *Worcester v. Georgia* and the Nullification Crisis," *Journal of Southern History* 39 (November 1973): 527.

35. Miles, "After John Marshall's Decision," 533–544.

36. Wilentz, *Andrew Jackson,* 152.

37. Van Buren to Thomas Ritchie, January 13, 1827, Martin Van Buren Papers, Library of Congress, Washington, D.C. For a discussion of Van Buren's concept of political leadership, see James W. Ceaser, *Presidential Selection: Theory and Development* (Princeton: Princeton University Press, 1979), 157–166.

38. Remini, *Andrew Jackson and the Course of American Freedom,* 325.

39. Fred I. Greenstein, *Inventing the Job of President: Leadership Style from George Washington to Andrew Jackson* (Princeton: Princeton University Press, 2009), 94.

40. On the development of the "administration press," see White, *Jacksonians,* chap. 15; and Melvin C. Laracey, *Presidents and the People: the Partisan Story of Going Public* (College Station: Texas A&M University Press, 2002).

41. Quoted in ibid., 320. On the theory and practice of rotation during the Jacksonian era, see ibid., 33–44 and chaps. 16–17.

42. Sean Wilentz, *The Rise of American Democracy: Jefferson to Lincoln* (New York: Norton, 2005), 325.

43. Jon Meacham, *American Lion: Andrew Jackson in the White House* (New York: Random House, 2008), 82.

44. Wilentz, *Rise of American Democracy,* 332–343.

45. Ibid., 313. The deleterious effects of the spoils system have often been exaggerated. As Leonard White writes in *Jacksonians,* "The consequences of rotation on the public service were unfortunate as a whole, but they were balanced in part by democratic gains, and because both Whigs and Democrats looked for character and competence among their partisans, and often found these qualities." Moreover, although the number of removals during the Jacksonian era was unprecedented, less than 10 percent of the federal workforce was affected. Wilentz, *Rise of American Democracy,* 308, 343.

46. Tocqueville, *Democracy in America,* 394.

47. On Van Buren's response to the Panic of 1837, see Wilson, *Presidency of Martin Van Buren,* chaps. 3–7; and Donald B. Cole, *Martin Van Buren and the American Political System* (Princeton: Princeton University Press, 1984), chaps. 10 and 11.

48. Gen. William Henry Harrison to Rep. Harmar Denny, December 2, 1838, in *The Growth of Presidential Power: A Documented History,* 3 vols., ed. William M. Goldsmith (New York: Chelsea, 1974), 2:637–641.

49. In Arthur M. Schlesinger Jr. and Fred I. Israel, eds., *History of American Presidential Elections, 1789–1968*, 4 vols. (New York: Chelsea, 1971), 1:737–744 (emphasis in original).

50. Binkley, *President and Congress*, 89.

51. Quoted in Ted Widmer, *Martin Van Buren* (New York: Times Books, 2005), 134.

52. For a description of the 1840 campaign, see Stefan Lorant, *The Presidency: A Pictorial History of Presidential Elections from Washington to Truman* (New York: Macmillan, 1951), 143–162.

53. Goldsmith, *Growth of Presidential Power*, 2:647.

54. Binkley, *President and Congress*, 108.

55. Robert J. Morgan, *A Whig Embattled: The Presidency under John Tyler* (Lincoln: University of Nebraska Press, 1954), 16–21.

56. Leonard Dinnerstein, "The Accession of John Tyler to the Presidency," *Virginia Magazine of History and Biography* 70 (October 1962): 447–458; Stephen W. Stathis, "John Tyler's Presidential Succession: A Reappraisal," *Prologue* 8 (Winter 1976): 223–236.

57. Morgan, *Whig Embattled*, chap. 2; Binkley, *President and Congress*, 92–99.

58. Matthew Crenson and Benjamin Ginsberg, *Presidential Power: Unchecked and Unbalanced* (New York: Norton, 2007), 91.

59. Daniel Walker Howe, *The Political Culture of the American Whigs* (Chicago: University of Chicago Press, 1979), 222–223.

60. Binkley, *President and Congress*, 98.

61. President John Tyler, Protest Message to the House of Representatives, August 30, 1842, in Goldsmith, *Growth of Presidential Power*, 2:710.

62. Binkley, *President and Congress*, 99.

63. Van Buren probably would have been nominated in spite of his opposition to the annexation of Texas, save for the two-thirds rule that governed Democratic conventions until it was repealed in 1936. The need for Democratic nominees for president and vice president to win support from two-thirds, rather than a majority, of national convention delegates gave the South a de facto veto over party nominations. On the nomination of Polk as the first dark horse candidate, see Charles A. McCoy, *Polk and the Presidency* (Austin: University of Texas Press, 1960), chap. 2; on Van Buren's actions in 1844, see Cole, *Martin Van Buren and the American Political System*, chap. 13.

64. McCoy, *Polk and the Presidency*, 74–75; White, *Jacksonians*, 77–79.

65. Polk and the Democrats had long been committed to passing a tariff reform act. As Speaker of the House, Polk had supported presidents Jackson and Van Buren in their attempts to enact low tariffs, and he devoted several pages of his first State of the Union address to a proposal for lowering tariff rates and placing rates on an *ad valorem* basis. Polk's dedication to tariff revision did not falter as war with Mexico approached. Instead, he pressured Congress to pass the Walker Act in 1846. He considered this assault on protectionism his most important domestic accomplishment, a vital measure for codifying the Jacksonian idea of economic justice. "Just as [Jacksonians] interpreted territorial expansion as a way to diminish the threat of industrialization and urbanization," historian Paul H. Bergeron has written, "so they also perceived protective tariffs as beneficial only to manufacturers and therefore detrimental to the working classes and to the vision of an agrarian America." Bergeron, *The Presidency of James K. Polk* (Lawrence: University Press of Kansas, 1987), 185–186. See also McCoy, *Polk and the Presidency*, 148–153.

66. White, *Jacksonians*, 81–82.

67. Quoted in Richardson, *Messages and Papers of the Presidents*, 6:2514–5.

68. Quoted in Binkley, *President and Congress*, 100–101.

69. Robert W. Merry, *A Country of Vast Designs: James K. Polk, the Mexican War, and the Conquest of the American Continent* (New York: Simon and Schuster, 2009), 114, 135.

70. White, *Jacksonians*, 50 (emphasis in original).

71. Ibid., 51.

72. Ibid., 55–56; McCoy, *Polk and the Presidency*, 103.

73. McCoy, *Polk and the Presidency*, 119–120; White, *Jacksonians*, 66.

74. McCoy, *Polk and the Presidency*, 140.

75. Attending a long, hot Fourth of July celebration in Washington, the president consumed large quantities of ice water, chilled milk, and fresh cherries—all items that Washingtonians had been warned away during the cholera epidemic. The circumstances of Taylor's illness and his death just five days later were unusual, so much so that rumors he had been poisoned endured for more than a century. The rumors were laid to rest only after Taylor's body was exhumed from its Louisville, Kentucky, grave and autopsied in 1991.

76. Binkley, *President and Congress*, 103–105; White, *Jacksonians*, 48.

77. The first seven slaveholding presidents were George Washington, Thomas Jefferson, James Madison, James Monroe, Andrew Jackson, John Tyler, and James K. Polk. Zachary Taylor was the eighth and last.

78. Binkley, *President and Congress*, 106.

79. Quoted in Wilentz, *Rise of American Democracy*, 643.

80. White, *Jacksonians*, 522, 529.

81. Crenson and Ginsberg, *Presidential Power*, 87.

82. Wilentz, *Rise of American Democracy*, 672.

83. Richardson, *Messages and Papers of the Presidents*, 7:2962.

84. Binkley, *President and Congress*, 107.

85. Elbert B. Smith, *The Presidency of James Buchanan* (Lawrence: University Press of Kansas, 1975), 23–29.

86. *Dred Scott v. Sandford*, 60 U.S. 393 (1857).

CHAPTER 6

The Presidency of Abraham Lincoln

braham Lincoln was the last nineteenth-century president to make an important contribution to the theory and practice of the executive. Lincoln's accomplishments were born of a national crisis that threatened to destroy the foundations of constitutional government in the United States. The leadership he displayed in navigating the uncharted waters of emancipation and total war has won him the enduring esteem of Americans as one of the finest presidents. The scholarly community has shared in the celebration of Lincoln's statesmanship. Most recent polls of American historians have rated Lincoln the "greatest" president in history.[1]

Whether Lincoln's talents and achievements strengthened or weakened constitutional government in the course of saving it is a matter of some dispute. Indeed, Lincoln's record as president has led at least a few critics to adjudge him not only a forceful leader but also a dictator, albeit a benevolent one in most accounts.[2] As commander in chief, especially, Lincoln demonstrated the presidency's great potential to assume extraordinary powers during a national emergency. The Civil War began in April 1861 while Congress was in recess, and for nearly four months every act of Union resistance to the seceding states of the South was a presidential act, performed without legislative authorization. To be sure, Lincoln considered his early measures to be temporary, emergency actions that would require ratification by Congress to become fully valid. Yet, as the challenges of emancipation and reconstruction emerged later in his presidency, it became clear that Lincoln "believed the rights of war were vested in the President and that as president he had extraordinary legal resources that Congress lacked."[3] Lincoln also acted in ways that preempted normal judicial functions, suspending the writ of *habeas corpus* and declaring martial law in various places.

Conceding that Lincoln went far beyond the normal bounds of presidential power during the Civil War, constitutional scholar James Randall nevertheless has argued that the president showed notable restraint and leniency in administering his wartime measures, befitting his high regard for individual liberty. By doing so, Lincoln used his extraordinary powers not to subvert democracy but to save it.[4] Lincoln certainly did not regard his presidency as a dictatorship. He defended his conduct by invoking a conception of the Constitution that respected procedural regularity and formal legality, but was concerned above all with fulfilling the president's responsibility to preserve the Union and uphold the basic principles of the constitutional order. Lincoln's presidency not only marked a critical moment in political history, but also raised anew, under conditions of unprecedented urgency, questions about the appropriate place of executive power in the American system of government.

It is ironic that Lincoln was the president who so forcefully extended the boundaries of executive power. Until 1854, when the Kansas-Nebraska Act was passed and the Republican Party was founded, Lincoln had been a Whig. His early political career was distinguished by his eloquent and forceful expression of the Whig Party's opposition to the Jacksonian Democrats' expansion of presidential power in the 1830s and 1840s. Significantly, Lincoln's first important speech, delivered in January 1838 to the Springfield (Illinois) Young Men's Lyceum, took the form of an allegory against great political ambition. Although the framers of the Constitution were ambitious for fame and influence, he argued, their passion for personal achievement benefited the country because it found outlet in a great and constructive enterprise: writing, ratifying, and implementing the Constitution. But what of succeeding generations?

The twenty-nine-year-old Lincoln warned in his speech that the "perpetuity of our free institutions"—that is, the survival of the Constitution—would be threatened by other leaders of great ambition who would not be content merely to uphold the work of the founding generation. Such men would disdain the well-worn path of constitutional government, Lincoln feared. They were members of the "family of the lion, or the tribe of the eagle" who would seek to use public office to remake politics and government in their own image. Then, in words that could only be understood as an attack on the Jacksonians' aggrandizement of executive power, Lincoln foretold the danger of demagogy, a danger made greater by the rise of the slavery controversy. "It thirsts and burns for distinction," he said of excessive ambition, "and if possible, it will have it, whether at the expense of emancipating the slaves, or enslaving free people."[5] In the peroration of his Lyceum address, Lincoln urged that "a reverence for the constitution and laws" become the civil religion of the nation and thereby serve as a bulwark against immoderate political ambition.[6]

In the mid-1840s Lincoln's devotion to settled, standing law informed his opposition to James K. Polk's assertive leadership in initiating and prosecuting the war with Mexico. As a Whig member of the House of Representatives, Lincoln argued that the Constitution gave the "war making power to Congress," and that "the will of the people should produce its own result without executive influence."[7] Nor did Lincoln give any indication during his rise to political prominence in the Republican Party in the late 1850s that he viewed bold presidential leadership as the appropriate means to resolve the slavery controversy.

Despite Lincoln's prepresidential commitment to executive restraint, as president he joined the "tribe of the eagle" against which his Lyceum appeal for reverence toward the law had been directed. As Garry Wills has argued, Lincoln imparted a new meaning to the Constitution that allowed little room for states' rights and none for slavery. According to Wills, "Lincoln not only put the Declaration [of Independence] in a new light as a matter of founding *law*, but put its central proposition, equality, in a newly favored position."[8] Still, Lincoln did not transcend the work of the framers. He was, according to Civil War historian James M. McPherson, a "conservative revolutionary" who wanted to preserve the Union as the nation's revolutionary heritage. For Lincoln, preserving this heritage was the primary goal of the Civil War. "My paramount object in this struggle," Lincoln wrote in a public letter addressed to New York newspaper editor Horace Greeley in the summer of 1862, "*is* to save the Union, and is *not* either to save or destroy slavery."[9] Yet Lincoln believed that to save the Union not just for the moment but enduringly, slavery would have to be placed on the road to eventual extinction in law and policy. Drawing on a verse in the Book of Proverbs—"A Word Fitly Spoken is like apples of gold in pictures of silver"—Lincoln praised the Declaration's principle of "liberty to All" as the essence of American political life. "The assertion of that principle, at that time," he wrote, "was the word 'fitly spoken,' which has proved an 'apple of gold' to us. The Union, and the Constitution, are the pictures of silver subsequently framed around it. The picture was made, not to conceal, or destroy the apple; but to adorn and preserve it."[10]

It took the Civil War to generate the radical momentum that led to a redefinition of politics and government in the United States. But Lincoln's words and actions directed the course of events during the fight for emancipation and union. In this sense, he really was a conservative revolutionary, committed to preserving, rather than abolishing, the heritage of American constitutional government.

LINCOLN AND THE SLAVERY CONTROVERSY

Lincoln was no abolitionist. Indeed, his relative moderation on the slavery issue helped him to wrest his party's 1860 presidential nomination away from the avowedly pro-emancipation William H. Seward, the former governor of New York and the most prominent Republican leader.[11] Although Lincoln consistently proclaimed himself "naturally antislavery," he believed that the national government lacked the authority to abolish slavery where it already existed. As he wrote to his closest friend, Kentuckian Joshua A. Speed, in 1855, "I acknowledge *your* rights and my obligations, under the Constitution, in regard to your slaves. I confess I hate to see the poor creatures hunted down, and caught, and carried back to their stripes, and unrewarded toils; but I bite my lip and keep quiet." [12]

At the same time, Lincoln believed that the extension of slavery into new states carved out of the western territories should not be permitted. In his view, extension threatened to perpetuate and expand the vile institution as a "positive good." With the enactment of the Kansas-Nebraska Act in 1854, Lincoln could no longer "bite his lip." In opening new land to slaveholders, Congress had violated the framers' understanding that slavery was a "necessary evil" that must be contained and allowed to die a "natural death." This constitutional impropriety was compounded in 1857 by the *Dred Scott* decision, in which the Supreme Court declared unconstitutional any act by Congress or the territorial legislatures to abolish slavery.

Lincoln was especially distressed because the Kansas-Nebraska Act and *Dred Scott* decision overturned the Missouri Compromise of 1820, which had prohibited slavery in the northern part of the Louisiana Territory. The spirit animating the Missouri Compromise, Lincoln claimed, was true to the principles of the Declaration of Independence, as well as to the Constitution. The Declaration's main author, Thomas Jefferson, had first given form to this spirit when he conceived the policy embodied in the Northwest Ordinance of 1787's ban on slavery in the old Northwest Territory, which later became Illinois, Indiana, Michigan, Ohio, and Wisconsin. Lincoln wanted to restore the Missouri Compromise for the sake not only of the Union but also of the "sacred right of self government" and the restoration of "the national faith." As he said in his Peoria address of 1854, "Our republican robe is soiled, and trailed in the dust. Let us repurify it. Let us turn and wash it white, in the spirit, if not in the blood, of the Revolution. Let us turn slavery from its 'moral rights' back upon its existing legal rights and its argument of 'necessity.' Let us return it to the position our fathers gave it, and there let it rest in peace." [13]

Lincoln's respect for the limits imposed on the national government by the Constitution deterred him from attacking slavery in the southern states, but unlike Stephen Douglas, his Democratic opponent in the 1858 Illinois Senate election and the author of the Kansas-Nebraska Act, Lincoln was unwilling to save the Union at the price of slavery's extension into the territories. To do so would detach the Constitution from its moral foundation in the Declaration. Lincoln argued that the South should join the North in restoring the long-standing national compromise on slavery that was embedded in the Northwest Ordinance and the Missouri Compromise.

The logic of Lincoln's position on slavery could not be satisfied by the political compromise for which he called, however. In portraying his opposition to slavery as a call to restore the country's basic values, Lincoln had shifted the terms of national debate. His plea for a new and explicit connection between the Declaration and the Constitution made a struggle over the existence of slavery all but inevitable. As he said in his speech accepting the Illinois Republican Party's nomination for the Senate in 1858,

> A House divided against itself cannot stand.
> I believe this government cannot endure, permanently, half *slave* and half *free*.
> I do not expect the Union to be *dissolved*—I do not expect the House to *fall*—but I do expect it will cease to be divided.
> It will become *all* one thing, or *all* the other.[14]

THE ELECTION OF 1860

The 1860 election did not provide Lincoln with a mandate to resolve the moral crisis created by the slavery controversy. He was a minority president who received almost no votes in the South. With the old Whig and Democratic coalitions supplanted by fiercely sectional politics, the presidential election became a fragmented contest among four candidates. The northern vote was split between Lincoln and Stephen Douglas, the official Democratic nominee. The southern electorate was divided between John C. Breckinridge of Kentucky, the standard-bearer of southern Democrats, and John Bell of Tennessee, who was nominated by the National Constitutional Union, a party formed from the remnant of southern Whiggery. The balloting yielded a decisive Electoral College victory for Lincoln, whose 180 votes easily outnumbered Breckinridge's 72, Bell's 39, and Douglas's 12 combined. Lincoln earned this victory by sweeping every northern state but New Jersey with 54 percent of the North's popular vote. But because he was virtually blanked in the South, his popular vote nationwide was slightly less than 40 percent, the smallest share earned by any successful presidential candidate in history.[15] Lincoln's victory was greeted throughout the South with ominous threats of secession. In bidding farewell to the citizens of Springfield on the eve of his journey to the nation's capital, Lincoln said, "I now leave, not knowing when, or whether ever, I may return, with a task before me greater than that which rested upon Washington."[16]

Lincoln's likening of his task to the one faced by the first president bespoke not only the troubles he anticipated, but also his hope of igniting a renewed faith in freedom and equality. "Washington fought for National Independence and triumphed," Charles Sumner, the Republican senator from Massachusetts, wrote in an 1865 eulogy of Lincoln. "Lincoln drew his reluctant sword to save those great ideas, essential to the character of the Republic, which unhappily the sword of Washington had failed to place beyond the reach of assault."[17]

Lincoln seldom received such fulsome praise from his Republican colleagues during his lifetime. Indeed, the troubles he faced on his arrival in Washington were aggravated by the doubtful regard that many of his party's leaders had for him. Seward had led on the first two ballots at the 1860 Republican convention in Chicago. "His claims to the nomination," historian Allan Nevins has written, "on grounds of governmental experience, long service to the free soil cause, and tested ability, seemed to outweigh those of anybody else."[18] But the delegates had turned to Lincoln on the third ballot, believing that his humble birth, homely wit, skill in debate, and geographical and political centrism would attract votes in midwestern states, especially Illinois and Indiana, which the Democrats usually won. The Republicans had shown in 1856 that they could count on Seward's Northeast (he was from New York), but they needed to add Lincoln's Midwest to elect a president.

Seward and his allies disdained Lincoln, whose experience in national affairs was limited to one term in the House of Representatives in the mid-1840s and a strong but unsuccessful Senate campaign against Douglas in 1858. "A profound student of the Constitution and the writings of the Founding

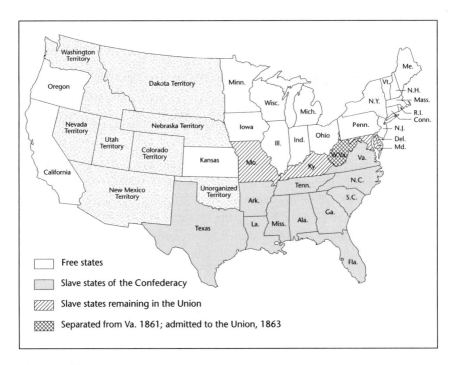

Alignment of the states, 1861.

Fathers," historian David Herbert Donald has observed, "Lincoln had limited acquaintance with the government they had established."[19] Republican leaders in the populous East regarded him as a "prairie lawyer," an upstart who had taken the nomination away from the Republican who was most fit to govern. After the election, Lincoln placated Seward by inviting him to become secretary of state. Indeed, Lincoln constituted his cabinet as a "team of rivals." In addition to Seward, he appointed Salmon P. Chase of Ohio as secretary of the Treasury and Edward Bates of Missouri as attorney general, each of whom had a political base of his own and thought he was more qualified to be president than Lincoln.[20] In doing so, Lincoln embraced the challenge of persuading the established leaders of his party that the man they had dismissed as a "backwoods president" could rise to the challenge of southern secession.[21]

LINCOLN AND SECESSION

In the face of such dire political circumstances, Lincoln's inaugural address on March 4, 1861, sought to reassure the South that his would be a policy of forbearance, not coercion.[22] He pointed out that despite white southerners' widespread fear that the election of a Republican president threatened "their property and their peace and personal security," there was no "reasonable cause for such apprehension."[23]

The "only substantial dispute" that faced the country, Lincoln said, was over the extension of slavery. "One section of the country believes slavery is *right* and ought to be extended," he said, "while the other believes it is *wrong* and ought not to be extended."[24] This moral dispute was not a matter that could be settled by "legal right," despite the Supreme Court's claim in the *Dred Scott* case that Congress could not prohibit slavery in the territories. Rather, the new president argued, slavery was an issue to be resolved only in the court of public opinion, through the regular course of elections. Otherwise, "the people will have ceased to be their own rulers, having to that extent practically resigned their government into the hands of an eminent tribunal."[25]

Lincoln's words fell on deaf southern ears. Ten weeks earlier, on December 20, 1860, South Carolina had become the first state to secede from the Union. Echoing the ordinance of nullification it issued during the 1832 tariff controversy, South Carolina claimed that secession was each state's constitutional right and declared itself restored to a "separate and independent place among nations." By the time of Lincoln's inauguration, six other Deep South states— Alabama, Florida, Georgia, Louisiana, Mississippi, and Texas—also had seceded. Lincoln, following Jackson's example, used his inaugural address to pronounce secession unacceptable: "I hold that in contemplation of universal law and of the Constitution the Union of these states is perpetual . . . , that no state upon its own mere notion can lawfully get out of the Union."[26] The new president declared that he would defend and maintain the Union and would enforce federal laws in all the states, as the Constitution enjoined him to do.

Lincoln's appeal for a peaceful resolution of the slavery controversy was quickly rejected by secessionist leaders.[27] Southern whites were unwilling to distinguish his call for compromise from outright abolitionism. They were at least half right: Lincoln's plea was a thinly veiled expression of his own moral indignation against slavery. Holding firmly to this belief, Lincoln rejected Seward's importunings immediately after the 1860 election that, while still president-elect, he seek to avert war with a compromise on the extension of slavery into the territories. When word arrived that Congress was considering a plan presented by Sen. John J. Crittenden of Kentucky to protect slavery south of the Missouri Compromise's 36°30' line, Lincoln intervened to defeat it. To surrender, under threat, what Lincoln defined as the Republican bedrock—no expansion of slavery in the territories—would have been disastrous not only for his party, but also for constitutional democracy. His fellow Republicans in Congress agreed. Despite Seward's talk of a negotiated settlement, not a single Republican in Congress voted for the Crittenden Plan.[28]

Lincoln's determination to carry out his party's platform and the Republicans' rejection of any compromise on their pledge to prohibit slavery in the territories reinforced concerns among southern leaders that they were engaged in a struggle to preserve slavery from extinction. On March 5, 1861, the day after Lincoln's inauguration, rebel batteries in South Carolina surrounded Fort Sumter in Charleston harbor, making war all but inevitable. As soon as secession became violent and irrevocable, Lincoln believed, his oath to uphold the Constitution allowed, even compelled him to take extraordinary measures to restore the Union, ultimately including emancipating the slaves. As he wrote in an 1864 letter to Albert G. Hodges, a Kentucky newspaper editor, the rebellion imposed on him the obligation to use "every dispensable means" to preserve "the nation, of which the Constitution was the organic law." It was senseless, Lincoln argued, to obey legal niceties while the very foundation of the law was threatened: "Was it possible to lose the nation and yet preserve the Constitution? By general law, life and limb must be protected, yet often a limb must be amputated to save a life; but a life is never wisely given to save a limb. I felt that measures otherwise unconstitutional might become lawful by becoming indispensable to the preservation of the nation."[29]

Even more than Lincoln's words, the reaction of the southern states to his election dramatically confirmed the transformation of the presidency that had occurred during the Jacksonian era. Although a few southern leaders counseled against secession, arguing that Lincoln's authority over slavery would be limited, such advice meant nothing to people who had witnessed the expansion of executive power since 1829. To be sure, the extent of the president's authority was exaggerated in the popular mind. But the myth that the presidency was the vital organ of the national government was symptomatic of the important precedents that had made the office so powerful.

LINCOLN'S WARTIME MEASURES

Lincoln did not hesitate to resort to "otherwise unconstitutional" measures after the rebels bombarded Fort Sumter on April 12, 1861. From that day until Congress convened in a special session called by Lincoln on July 4, everything that was done to protect the Union and prosecute the war was done by the president or on his authority.

The early stages of the Civil War marked the clearest instance of a chief executive taking the law into his own hands. To that extent, Lincoln waged a "presidential war."[30] Some of his actions, such as mobilizing seventy-five thousand state militia, were clearly within the proper bounds of the president's constitutional authority. Yet Lincoln went well beyond these bounds. Hoping to bring the insurrection to a speedy end, he imposed a naval blockade on the southern coast, enlarged the army by twenty-two thousand and the navy by eighteen thousand, and suspended the writ of *habeas corpus* in northern and border states where rebellious activity was high. This suspension broadly empowered government officials who were acting under the president's authority. They could make arrests without a warrant, for offenses undefined in the law, without having to answer for their actions before the regular courts.

Several of Lincoln's measures raised grave doubts about the constitutionality of his prosecution of the war. For example, his unauthorized enlargement of the military seemed to disregard blatantly Congress's constitutional power "to raise and support Armies." Indeed, in referring to his executive order of May 3, 1861, which called for enlistments in the regular army far beyond the existing legal limit, Lincoln frankly admitted that he had overstepped his authority. The president's critics also argued that because the power to suspend the writ of *habeas corpus* during a national emergency appears in Article I of the Constitution, which defines the authority of the legislature, the right to exercise the power belongs to Congress. Lincoln's suspension of *habeas corpus* was especially controversial because it struck at what constitutional scholar Edward S. Corwin has called "the greatest of all muniments of Anglo-American liberty."[31]

The severity of Lincoln's war measures prompted charges of "military dictatorship," even from some Republicans. The president's decision not to call a special session of Congress until Independence Day lent support to these charges.

In 1863 the constitutionality of Lincoln's conduct as president became an issue before the Supreme Court in the *Prize Cases*.[32] The Union navy had been capturing ships for violating the president's executive orders of April 19 and 27, 1861, which imposed the blockade along the southern coast. In determining whether it was lawful for the navy to obtain these "prizes," the Court decided the whole issue of the war's legality in its early stages. Shipping interests argued that a war begins only when Congress declares war, which it did not do until July 13, 1861. By this logic, the actions Lincoln took to suppress the southern insurrection before convening the legislature, including the blockade, were not valid.

Considering the urgent circumstances that prevailed in 1863, the Court brushed aside the shipping interests' constitutional claims. It upheld the legality of the war from the moment of Lincoln's blockade order, sustaining completely the president's actions while Congress was in recess. In rendering this decision, the Court drew attention to legislation Congress passed on July 13 to ratify Lincoln's orders, even while refusing to declare that this legislation was necessary to validate his course of conduct.

The Court's decision in the *Prize Cases* supported Lincoln's claim that his actions were justified by both the threat the southern rebellion posed to the public safety and his expectation that Congress eventually would approve what he had done. As Lincoln said in his Special Session Message to Congress on July 4, 1861, "These measures, whether strictly legal or not, were ventured upon under what appeared to be a popular demand and a public necessity, trusting then as now, that Congress would readily ratify them. It is believed that nothing has been done beyond the constitutional competency of Congress."[33]

The extraordinary powers that were accorded to Lincoln can be understood only in terms of the extraordinary conditions he faced. It was of considerable legal significance that the Civil War began as an "insurrection," not as a war.[34] Constitutionally, the president may not declare war but may proclaim the existence of a domestic rebellion, or insurrection. Lincoln believed, and Congress and the Supreme Court generally agreed, that an organized and violent rebellion at home requires quick, unilateral presidential action of a sort that might not be permissible during a formally declared war fought on foreign soil. An internal rebellion, Lincoln proclaimed, may impose a special burden on the legal process because the execution of the laws is "obstructed . . . by combinations too powerful to be suppressed by the ordinary course of judicial proceedings."[35]

Lincoln's conception of the president's responsibility to suppress treasonous activity justified the suspension of *habeas corpus* and the establishment of martial law in many areas of the country. As such, he claimed sweeping powers to arrest and detain those who were suspected of rebellious activity and then try them before military tribunals. As commander of the American revolutionary army, Gen. George Washington, too, had used military tribunals. These military courts, created to try enemy combatants during wartime, had operated outside the rules of evidence and other conventional codes of judicial conduct that apply in civilian courts. Lincoln was the first president to authorize their use.

As the Civil War progressed, Lincoln proclaimed even more comprehensive powers for the military authorities, without any apparent thought of seeking authorization from Congress.[36] On September 24, 1862, he issued an executive order declaring that all rebels and insurgents and all persons who discouraged enlistment in the Union army, resisted the draft, or engaged in any disloyal practice were subject to martial law and to trial by either a court-martial, which observes rules of evidence similar to those in the civilian courts, or a military tribunal.[37] This order provoked sharp controversy in the North. The draft, which was imposed for the first time during the Civil War, was very unpopular. As Horace Greeley warned the administration, "The people have been educated to the idea of individual sovereignty and the principle of conscription is repugnant to their feelings and cannot be carried out except at great peril to the free states." Greeley's words proved prophetic. In July 1863 draft riots broke out in New York City, sparking the greatest civil disorder in the nation's history, save for the Civil War itself. Yet resistance to the draft convinced the president that military justice and the suspension of *habeas corpus* were necessary, not only where the war was being fought but also in certain peaceful regions of the country.[38]

The Supreme Court eventually disapproved Lincoln's more far-reaching martial law measures, but not until the Civil War was over. In *Ex parte Milligan,* which was decided in 1866, the Court declared illegal the use of military tribunals to try citizens in places that were remote from the fighting.[39] Lambdin P. Milligan had been arrested on October 5, 1864, by order of Gen. Alvin P. Hovey, the Union commander at Indianapolis. Along with certain associates, Milligan was brought before a military tribunal and convicted of conspiracy to free rebel prisoners and smuggle them into Kentucky and Missouri, where they could rejoin the Confederate army. After the tribunal sentenced Milligan to be hanged, the case was brought to the Supreme Court on appeal.

In his opinion for the Court, Justice David Davis noted the significance of deciding *Milligan* after the war was over. "*Now* that the public safety is assured," Davis wrote, "this question, as well as others, can be discussed and decided without passion or the admixture of any element not required to form a legal judgment."[40] "During the war," Matthew Crenson and Benjamin Ginsberg have noted, "the justices would likely have hesitated to protect a Confederate sympathizer and thwart the president and military authorities."[41] But a year after the Confederate surrender, the Court confidently declared that Milligan's trial and conviction by a military tribunal had been illegal, ruling that the constitutional right to a fair trial cannot be swept aside even during a state of insurrection. Instead, conditions had to be so grave as to close the courts and depose the civil administration. Martial law, the Court stated, "could never exist where the Courts are open" but had to be "confined to the locality of actual war."[42]

The *Milligan* case diluted somewhat the legal significance of Lincoln's wartime precedents. But the powers and prerogatives that he assumed during the Civil War demonstrated conclusively, as Corwin has written, "that in meeting the domestic problems that a great war inevitably throws up an indefinite power must be attributed to the president to take emergency measures."[43]

Although Lincoln took extreme measures, neither Congress nor the Court restrained him very effectively. Congress did challenge the president's suspension of *habeas corpus* in an 1863 statute, which directed that prisoners be released unless they were indicted in a civil court. But the law was ineffective. It did not put an end to extralegal imprisonments, nor did it succeed in shifting control over punishment from military to civilian tribunals. Moreover, while the war was still in progress the Court refused to interfere with a military tribunal in a case that resembled *Milligan*.[44] In legal terms, the Civil War stands out as an exceptional period in American history, "a time when constitutional restraints did not fully operate and the rule of law largely broke down."[45]

The distinguished presidential scholar Clinton Rossiter described Lincoln's conduct as a "constitutional dictatorship," an apparent oxymoron that was meant to capture Lincoln's impressive if not fully persuasive argument that constitutional government has an unqualified power of self-preservation and that this power is centered in the office of the president. Although Lincoln's use of power in time of supreme crisis was eminently defensible, Rossiter warned, it might set a damaging precedent, allowing "some future President less democratic and less patriotic . . . to assert the same thing."[46] But other aspects of Lincoln's leadership demonstrated his faithfulness to the purposes for which the Union and the Constitution had been ordained.[47] Although the powers that Lincoln claimed were far-reaching, offering ample opportunity for abuse, his exercise of these powers was restrained. In most cases, a short military detention was followed by release or parole. As for martial law, military tribunals almost always were used only to try citizens in military areas for military crimes. Cases like *Milligan* that involved military trials for nonmilitary crimes in peaceful areas were few. Finally, and most remarkably, Lincoln did nothing to obstruct the conduct of free and fair elections during the war.

Building on the precedent established by James K. Polk in the Mexican-American War, Abraham Lincoln not only closely supervised his field commanders, but sometimes did so in person.

The Constitution, although stretched severely, was not subverted during the Civil War. It is a "striking fact," as Randall has noted, "that no life was forfeited and no sentence of fine and imprisonment [was] carried out in any judicial prosecution for treason arising out of the 'rebellion.'"[48] Lincoln was driven by circumstances to exercise power more arbitrarily than any other president. Yet he was criticized for leniency as often as for severity.

THE EMANCIPATION PROCLAMATION

Lincoln's concern for maintaining the integrity of the Constitution underlay his cautious handling of emancipation.[49] The president had argued consistently that to abolish slavery where it existed was beyond the constitutional authority of Congress. Yet, believing that the president's duties as commander in chief allowed him to grasp in war much that lies beyond legal reach in peace, Lincoln issued the Emancipation Proclamation on January 1, 1863.[50] Most presidential proclamations have been ceremonial pronouncements, such as the annual Thanksgiving Proclamation, which was first issued by George Washington.[51] But some proclamations, such as Washington's Neutrality Proclamation of 1793, are hard to distinguish from executive orders of the kind that Lincoln issued after the outbreak of the Civil War—that is, they require the federal government to take an action.

Lincoln's 1863 proclamation appeared to add the abolition of slavery to the restoration of the Union as the primary objectives of the Civil War. Even so, the Emancipation Proclamation was a more limited, cautious measure than Lincoln's cabinet and the so-called Radical Republicans in Congress had hoped it would be. The proclamation did not establish a comprehensive and sweeping policy of emancipation; indeed, Lincoln earlier had declared unauthorized and void the declarations by two of his generals that slaves in captured Confederate territory were free. Instead, Lincoln, who based the proclamation solely on what he called the "war power" and regarded it as "a fit and necessary war measure for suppressing rebellion," abolished slavery only in the unconquered parts of the Confederacy.[52] The proclamation also declared that the door was open for African Americans "to be received into the armed services of the United States."

As an act of "military necessity," the Emancipation Proclamation had important practical effects. Emancipation struck at the heart of the South's war effort in two ways: by disrupting its labor force and by converting part of that labor force into a northern military asset. More than one hundred thousand former slaves stopped bringing in crops on southern plantations, escaped north, and became Union soldiers. "Some of the commanders of our armies in the field who have given us our most important successes, believe the emancipation policy, and the use of colored troops, constitute the heaviest blow yet dealt to the rebellion," Lincoln wrote to the former mayor of Springfield, James C. Conkling, in August 1863.[53] To be sure, there was grumbling and dissent by some northern soldiers, who said they had enlisted to fight for the Union, not for abolition. But most soldiers understood and accepted the policy. As a colonel from Indiana put it, whatever their opinions about slavery and race, his men "desire to destroy everything that gives the rebels strength." Therefore, "this army will sustain the emancipation proclamation and enforce it with the bayonet."[54]

Although emancipation became a critical part of Union war strategy, Lincoln's proclamation neither condemned slavery as immoral nor guaranteed that it would be abolished after the war was over. Lincoln later vetoed the Wade-Davis Bill of 1864, which included the sort of sweeping emancipation and reconstruction measures that he believed the federal government had no constitutional authority to impose on the states. Yet the president realized that to return emancipated African Americans to slavery was unthinkable. When urged to do so by some northern Democrats, who argued that coupling emancipation with restoration of the Union would be an obstacle to peace negotiations with the Confederacy, Lincoln countered that "to announce such a purpose, would ruin the Union cause itself." Why would African American soldiers risk their lives for the Union, he asked, "with the full notice of our purpose to betray them?" The morality of such an act was even more troubling. If he were "to return to slavery the black warriors," Lincoln stated plaintively, "I should be damned in time and eternity for so doing."[55]

In fact, Lincoln had long believed that slavery was incompatible with the Union and that the nation was threaded together by a set of principles that required equality before the law. Those who signed the Declaration of Independence "did not mean to assert the obvious untruth, that all were actually enjoying that equality, nor yet, that they were about to confer it immediately upon them," Lincoln had said in criticizing the *Dred Scott* decision. "They meant simply to declare the *right,* so that *enforcement* of it might follow as fast as circumstances should permit."[56] The Civil War created the circumstances. Lincoln's presidential Reconstruction policy, which he announced in December 1863, therefore offered pardon and amnesty to any white southerner who took an oath of allegiance not only to the Union but also to all the administration's wartime policies concerning slavery and emancipation. Reconstructed governments sponsored by Lincoln freed the slaves in the Union-controlled areas of Louisiana, Arkansas, and Tennessee even before the war ended.[57]

Still, Lincoln was too respectful of procedural regularity and formal legality to completely abolish slavery by executive fiat. Instead, he worked to achieve abolition by constitutional amendment. In 1864 Lincoln took the lead in persuading the Republican national convention to adopt a platform calling for an amendment prohibiting slavery everywhere in the United States. Because slavery was "hostile to the principles of republican government, justice, and national safety," the platform declared, the Republican Party vowed to accomplish its "utter and complete extirpation from the soil of the Republic." Full emancipation became an end as well as a means of Union victory.[58] In 1864 and 1865, "intervening more directly in the legislative process than at any other point in his presidency," Lincoln pushed the Thirteenth Amendment through a reluctant Congress.[59] Ratification of the amendment in 1865 abolished slavery "within the United States or any place subject to their protection."

In sum, Lincoln's disregard for constitutional restrictions on the war power went hand in hand with a deep and abiding commitment to constitutional principles and institutions. His ability to reconcile his devotion to the Constitution with his desire to eliminate slavery helped to focus the will and resources of the Union on defeating the Confederacy. As historian Phillip Shaw Paludan has written, "Without Lincoln's unmatched ability to integrate egalitarian ends and constitutional means he could not have enlisted the range of supporters and soldiers necessary for victory. His great accomplishment was to energize and mobilize the nation, affirming its better angels by showing the nation at its best: engaged in the imperative, life-preserving conversation between structure and purpose, ideal and institution, means and ends."[60]

Lincoln did not become the tyrant he had warned against a quarter-century earlier in his speech to the Young Men's Lyceum. Instead, he invested his talent and ambition in strengthening the law by rooting it more firmly in morality. As Lincoln said in his Gettysburg Address, the great purpose of the war was that the American "nation, under God, shall have a new birth of freedom."[61]

THE ELECTION OF 1864

The free and full party competition that marked the 1864 election further demonstrates that Lincoln did not conduct the war in a dictatorial manner.[62] The stakes were great. Democrats charged that the war was hopeless: the Union army was losing battles and the Confederacy was persisting in rebellion because Republicans were elevating blacks over whites and the nation over the states. With enthusiastic support from the entire convention, the 1864 Democratic platform declared

> that after four years of failure to restore the Union by the experiment of War, during which under a pretense of a military necessity of war power higher than the Constitution, the Constitution itself has been disregarded in every part, and public liberty and private right alike trodden down, and the material prosperity of the country essentially impaired, justice, humanity, liberty, and the public welfare demand that immediate efforts be made for a cessation of hostilities, with a view of an ultimate convention of the States, or other peaceable means, to the end that, at the earliest practical moment, peace may be restored on the basis of the Federal Union of the states.[63]

Although the Democratic candidate for president, Gen. George B. McClellan, disavowed his party's "peace before reunion" plank, he opposed the Emancipation Proclamation and wanted the Union to continue fighting only until the presecession status quo could be restored. The Republicans held "the reasonable conviction," historian Harold M. Hyman has written, "that a Democratic triumph would mean . . . the perpetuation of slavery, and the further fragmentation of the dis-United States."[64]

Lincoln and most other Republican leaders believed that a Democratic victory was likely in 1864. Not only was there widespread public opposition to Lincoln's conduct of the war, but also the custom of the previous three decades had been for the president to serve only one term. Since Jackson's victory in 1832, no president had been reelected. Indeed, with the exception of Martin Van Buren in 1840, none had even been nominated by his party for a second term. Six days before the Democratic convention, Lincoln was resigned to defeat, hoping only to defuse the rising pressures for an immediate compromise with the Confederacy. "This morning, as for some days past," he wrote privately, "it seems exceedingly probable that the Administration will not be reelected. Then it will be my duty to so cooperate with the President-elect, as to save the Union between the election and inauguration; as he will have secured his election on such ground that he cannot possibly save it afterwards."[65]

In allowing the 1864 elections to take place, historian Herman Belz has argued, Lincoln "accepted a risk and permitted his power to be threatened in a way that no dictator, constitutional or not, would have tolerated."[66] During the campaign, rumors spread that if Lincoln was defeated, he would refuse to accept the verdict of the people and instead try to "ruin the government." Responding to these rumors at a public gathering in October, Lincoln stated that he was "struggling to maintain the government, not overthrow it." He then pledged that whoever was elected in November would be duly installed as president on March 4, 1865. Such a course was "due to the people," Lincoln said, "both on principle and under the Constitution."[67]

Lincoln's commitment to constitutional government cannot be dismissed as empty rhetoric. Throughout the war he supported freedom of speech and freedom of the press. Despite some notable and unfortunate exceptions, anti-Lincoln and anti-Union news organs were left undisturbed.[68] "By all contemporary standards," Hyman has shown, "the 1864 elections were free, and by contemporary standards fair as well."[69] The same was true of the 1862 midterm elections.

Seeing the alternatives, the American people gave Lincoln 55 percent of the popular vote and an overwhelming Electoral College majority of 212–21. Gen. William Tecumseh Sherman's timely capture of Atlanta in September and a spirited and effective Republican campaign, which accused the Democrats of seeking to return to the "hopeless imbecility and rapid progress of national dissolution," turned the tide in the president's favor.

Equally important, perhaps, were two practices that Lincoln had followed throughout his presidency to keep him in close touch with the people. The first, which Lincoln called his "public-opinion baths," were the long hours he spent in the White House listening to any visitor who came to talk with him. "Probably more than any other single agency," historian Richard Carwardine has observed, "they provided the oxygen lacking in the rarified political air of wartime Washington."[70]

The second device was the public letter, which usually took the form of a reply to a letter challenging his leadership. Lincoln caused these exchanges to be widely published in newspapers throughout the country. In keeping with nineteenth-century tradition, he did not campaign. But like earlier presidents, such as James Madison, John Adams, and Thomas Jefferson, Lincoln both observed the convention that proscribed presidential appeals on behalf of their policies and circumvented it. Just as Jefferson had defended his embargo policy in published correspondence, so Lincoln extended this practice to the presidential campaign, broadcasting his arguments to the American people under the pretense of merely responding courteously to an individual correspondent.[71]

The elections of 1864 were characterized by a remarkably spirited, even strident campaign in the midst of military hostilities. Some Democrats charged fraud and corruption when the results were tallied, but McClellan himself granted that Lincoln's claim to a second term was untainted. "For my country's sake I deplore the result," he reflected in a private statement, "but the people have decided with their eyes open."[72] After the election, Lincoln granted that partisan discord "add[ed] not a little" to the strain caused by the war. But the election was necessary: "We cannot have free government without elections; and if rebellion could force us to forgo or postpone a national election, it might fairly claim to have already conquered and ruined us." The free and open campaign, Lincoln concluded, "demonstrated that a people's government can sustain a national election in the midst of a great civil war. Until now, it has not been known to the world that this was a possibility."[73]

These were revealing words. The principal task of Lincoln's presidency had been to demonstrate that republican government could endure even in the midst of a violent national struggle that threatened its survival. As he remarked on one occasion, "It has long been a grave question whether any government, not too strong for the liberties of its people, can be strong enough to maintain its existence in great emergencies."[74] Lincoln's conduct of the Civil War seemed to answer this question in the affirmative. As Randall wrote, "In a legal study of the war the two most significant facts are perhaps these: the wide extent of the war powers; and, in contrast to that, the manner in which the men in authority were nevertheless controlled by the American people's sense of constitutional government."[75]

Although he was not the main speaker at the dedication of the Union cemetery at Gettysburg, Pennsylvania, on November 19, 1863, Abraham Lincoln's short speech there has become one of the most cherished of the nation.

LINCOLN'S LEGACY

Absent the Civil War, Abraham Lincoln's ability, even his desire to lead the nation would have been severely constrained. The Republican Party he repre sented in the 1860 presidential election consisted mostly of former Whigs. Like Lincoln himself, they were dedicated to reversing the executive aggrandizement of the Jacksonians. Indeed, much of what Lincoln accomplished in consolidating presidential power during the Civil War surprised his Republican colleagues in Congress. As described in the next chapter, they acted forcefully to weaken the presidency after he was assassinated in 1865.

Lincoln never abandoned his political principles. Even in war, he did not forsake entirely the Whig view of executive power that he had defended in the 1830s and 1840s. Consistent with this view, Lincoln denied that the president could veto bills merely because he disagreed with them; only legislation that he regarded as unconstitutional was returned to Congress.[76] He deferred almost entirely to Congress on matters unrelated to the war, "contributing little more than his signature" when Republican lawmakers "created a Department of Agriculture, established land-grant colleges, passed the Homestead Act [to encourage western settlement], instituted the income tax, and erected the legislative framework that would lead to the construction of a transcontinental railroad."[77] As Carl Schurz, a postwar Republican reformer, wrote of Lincoln: "With scrupulous care he endeavored, even under the most trying circumstances, to remain strictly within the constitutional limits of his authority; and whenever the boundary became indistinct, or when the dangers of the situation forced him to cross it, he was equally careful to mark his acts as exceptional measures, justifiable only by the imperative necessities of the civil war, so that they might not pass into history as precedents for similar acts in time of peace."[78]

The powers that Lincoln was willing to accumulate as commander in chief during the Civil War freed him to use the executive office energetically. But the end of hostilities led to a counterrevolution of sorts, which showed that Lincoln's stewardship, remarkable as it was, had not expanded presidential power in a way that could survive in peacetime. "By 1875," political scientist Theodore J. Lowi has observed, "you would not know there had been a war or a Lincoln."[79]

Nevertheless, Lincoln and the Civil War left a lasting imprint on American political life. Lincoln's famous first words in the Gettysburg Address, "Four score and seven years ago," exalted the Declaration of Independence—not the Constitution—as the founding document, the source of "a new nation, conceived in Liberty, and dedicated to the proposition that all men are created equal." Making the most of the November 1863 dedication of the national cemetery at the Gettysburg battlefield, the sort of ceremonial occasion that allowed presidents to speak publicly during the nineteenth century, Lincoln invested the national community with a sense of purpose, even sacredness, that transformed the relationship between power and liberty. His indictment of slavery spawned a new, more positive view of liberty, in which government has an affirmative obligation to ensure equality under the law.

Lincoln's celebration of the Declaration was embodied in the Civil War amendments to the Constitution, which not only abolished slavery (the Thirteenth Amendment), but also guaranteed all Americans the "privileges and immunities" of citizenship, "due process," and "equal protection of the law" against encroachment by the states (the Fourteenth Amendment), and promised African Americans the right to vote (the Fifteenth Amendment). These three Civil War amendments changed the course of constitutional development. The first twelve amendments to the Constitution had limited the powers of the national government. Six of the next seven, beginning with these three, expanded its powers.[80]

The immediate consequences of the Civil War amendments were limited. Lincoln's understanding of the equality guaranteed by the Declaration was modest when compared with the economic aspirations of twentieth-century presidents such as Theodore Roosevelt, Franklin D. Roosevelt, and Lyndon B. Johnson. The reforms of the Civil War were tightly bounded by the nation's long-standing commitment to private property, limited government, and administrative decentralization. Lincoln's contribution was to establish that the national government also had an obligation to ensure equal opportunity. The Union's struggle, he told the special session of Congress in July 1861, was to maintain that "form and substance of government, whose leading object is, to elevate the condition of men—to lift artificial weights from all shoulders—to clear the paths of laudable pursuit for all—to afford all, an unfettered start, and a fair chance, in the race of life."[81]

NOTES

1. See, for example, Robert K. Murray and Tim H. Blessing, "The Presidential Performance Study," *Journal of American History* 70 (December 1983): 535–555; Arthur M. Schlesinger Jr., "Rating the U.S. Presidents: Washington to Clinton," *Political Science Quarterly* 112 (Summer 1997): 179–190; and James Lindgren and Steven G. Calabresi, "Ranking the Presidents," *Wall Street Journal*, November 15, 2000. The Lindgren-Calabresi survey, which included law professors and political scientists as well as historians, was the first in which Lincoln was ranked second to Washington.

2. For a critical examination of the view that Lincoln's presidency was one of "constitutional dictatorship," see Herman Belz, *Lincoln and the Constitution: The Dictatorship Question Reconsidered* (Fort Wayne, Ind.: Louis A. Warren Lincoln Library and Museum, 1984).

3. James G. Randall, *Constitutional Problems under Lincoln*, rev. ed. (Urbana: University of Illinois Press, 1951), 514. See also Edward S. Corwin, *The President: Office and Powers, 1787–1957*, 4th ed. (New York: New York University Press, 1957), 23–24.

4. Randall, *Constitutional Problems under Lincoln,* 30–47; and "Lincoln in the Role of Dictator," *South Atlantic Quarterly* 28 (July 1929): 236–252. See also Belz, *Lincoln and the Constitution,* 5–6.

5. J. B. McClure, ed., *Abraham Lincoln's Speeches* (Chicago: Rhodes and McClure, 1891), 21.

6. Ibid., 22.

7. Corwin, *President: Office and Powers,* 451; Wilfred E. Binkley, *President and Congress* (New York: Knopf, 1947), 110.

8. Garry Wills, *Lincoln at Gettysburg: The Words that Remade America* (New York: Simon and Schuster, 1992), 145 (emphasis in original).

9. James M. McPherson, *Abraham Lincoln and the Second American Revolution* (New York: Oxford University Press, 1991), 41; Lincoln to Horace Greeley, August 22, 1862, in *The Collected Works of Abraham Lincoln,* 9 vols., ed. Roy P. Basler (New Brunswick: Rutgers University Press, 1953), 5:388 (emphasis in original).

10. Undated fragment, written in late 1860 or early 1861, in *New Letters and Papers of Lincoln,* ed. Paul M. Angle (Boston: Houghton Mifflin, 1930), 241–242. Lincoln's reference was to Proverbs 25:11: "A word fitly spoken is like apples of gold in pictures of silver."

11. Allan Nevins, *The Emergence of Lincoln: Prologue to Civil War, 1859–1861* (New York: Scribner's, 1950), 233–239.

12. Lincoln to Joshua A. Speed, August 24, 1855, in *The Political Thought of Abraham Lincoln,* ed. Richard N. Current (Indianapolis: Bobbs-Merrill, 1967), 80.

13. McClure, *Abraham Lincoln's Speeches,* 127.

14. Current, *Political Thought of Abraham Lincoln,* 95 (emphasis in original).

15. Matthew Crenson and Benjamin Ginsberg point out that most major party presidential candidates who have lost elections have outpolled Lincoln. Crenson and Ginsberg, *Presidential Power: Unchecked and Unbalanced* (New York: Norton, 2007), 99. John Quincy Adams's victory in 1824 came before the era of widespread popular voting in presidential elections.

16. Basler, *Collected Works of Abraham Lincoln,* 4:191. This was the first of many public references to God that Lincoln made as president-elect and, especially, as president. See William E. Barton, *The Soul of Abraham Lincoln,* ed. Michael Nelson (Urbana: University of Illinois Press, 2005); originally published in New York by George H. Doran Co. [c. 1920].

17. Charles Sumner, *The Promises of the Declaration of Independence: Eulogy on Abraham Lincoln* (Boston: Ticknor and Fields, 1865), 9.

18. Nevins, *Emergence of Lincoln,* 234.

19. David Herbert Donald, *Lincoln* (London: Jonathan Cape, 1995), 236.

20. Doris Kearns Goodwin, *Team of Rivals: The Political Genius of Abraham Lincoln* (New York: Simon and Schuster, 2005).

21. Stephen B. Oates, *With Malice toward None: The Life of Abraham Lincoln* (New York: Harper and Row, 1977), 224. For an excellent discussion of Lincoln's strained relationship with the more established members of his party, see William Lee Miller, *Lincoln's Virtues* (New York: Knopf, 2002), especially chap. 16, showing how President Lincoln overcame their prejudices and earned their enduring respect.

22. Oates, *With Malice toward None,* 218; Douglas L. Wilson, *Lincoln's Sword: The Presidency and the Power of Words* (New York: Knopf, 2006), chap. 3.

23. James D. Richardson, ed., *Messages and Papers of the Presidents,* 20 vols. (New York: Bureau of National Literature, 1897), 7:3206.

24. Ibid., 7:3211 (emphasis in original).

25. Ibid., 7:3210.

26. Ibid., 7:3208.

27. For an account of Lincoln's views on slavery and the Constitution, see Robert K. Faulkner, "Lincoln and the Constitution," in *Revival of Constitutionalism,* ed. James Muller (Lincoln: University of Nebraska Press, 1988).

28. Miller, *Lincoln's Virtues,* 435–440; Phillip Shaw Paludan, *The Presidency of Abraham Lincoln* (Lawrence: University Press of Kansas, 1994), 33.

29. "Abraham Lincoln's Letter to Albert G. Hodges," in *The Evolving Presidency: Landmark Documents, 1787–2010*, 4th ed., ed. Michael Nelson (Washington, D.C.: CQ Press, 2012), 93–94.

30. Randall, *Constitutional Problems under Lincoln*, 51.

31. Corwin, *President: Office and Powers*, 62.

32. *Prize Cases*, 67 U.S. 635 (1863). For a discussion of this case, see Randall, *Constitutional Problems under Lincoln*, 52–59.

33. Richardson, *Messages and Papers of the Presidents*, 7:3225; Wilson, *Lincoln's Sword*, chap. 4.

34. For a discussion of the importance of the legal distinction between an insurrection and a war against an independent nation, see Randall, *Constitutional Problems under Lincoln*, 59–73.

35. "Proclamation of April 15, 1861," in Richardson, *Messages and Papers of the Presidents*, 7:3299.

36. Corwin, *President: Office and Powers*, 145–147.

37. Richardson, *Messages and Papers of the Presidents*, 7:3299.

38. Greeley cited in Mark E. Neely, *The Last Best Hope of Earth: Abraham Lincoln and the Promise of America* (Cambridge: Harvard University Press, 1993), 129.

39. "*Ex parte Milligan*," in Nelson, *Evolving Presidency*, 103–108. For a discussion of this case, see Randall, *Constitutional Problems under Lincoln*, 180–186.

40. "*Ex parte Milligan*," in Nelson, *Evolving Presidency*, 103–108 (emphasis in original).

41. Crenson and Ginsberg, *Presidential Power*, 329.

42. Ibid.

43. Corwin, *President: Office and Powers*, 234.

44. See *Ex parte Vallandigham*, 68 U.S. 243 (1864), which found acceptable the arrest and sentencing of a prominent antiwar agitator, who was detained for a speech that he gave in Mount Vernon, Ohio.

45. Randall, *Constitutional Problems under Lincoln*, 521.

46. Clinton L. Rossiter, *Constitutional Dictatorship: Crisis Government in the Modern Democracies* (Princeton: Princeton University Press, 1948), 239.

47. Belz, *Lincoln and the Constitution*, 24.

48. Randall, *Constitutional Problems under Lincoln*, 91.

49. Allen C. Guelzo, *Lincoln's Emancipation Proclamation: The End of Slavery in America* (New York: Simon and Schuster, 2004).

50. For a discussion of Lincoln's policy of emancipation, see Faulkner, "Lincoln and the Constitution."

51. Kenneth R. Mayer, *With the Stroke of a Pen: Executive Orders and Presidential Power* (Princeton: Princeton University Press, 2001), 34–35.

52. Richardson, *Messages and Papers of the Presidents*, 7:3359.

53. Lincoln to James C. Conkling, August 26, 1863, in Basler, *Collected Works of Abraham Lincoln*, 6:408–409.

54. Cited in McPherson, *Abraham Lincoln and the Second American Revolution*, 34–35.

55. Lincoln to Charles D. Robinson, August 17, 1864, and Lincoln interview with Alexander W. Randall and Joseph T. Mills, August 19, 1864, in Basler, *Collected Works of Abraham Lincoln*, 7:499–500 and 7:506–507, respectively.

56. Current, *Political Thought of Abraham Lincoln*, 88–89 (emphasis in original).

57. McPherson, *Abraham Lincoln and the Second American Revolution*, 86.

58. Ibid.

59. Eric Foner, *The Fiery Trial: Abraham Lincoln and American Slavery* (New York: W. W. Norton, 2010), 312.

60. Paludan, *Presidency of Abraham Lincoln*, 319.

61. "The Gettysburg Address," in Nelson, *Evolving Presidency*, 97–99.

62. Belz, *Lincoln and the Constitution*, 15.

63. "Democratic Platform of 1864," in *History of American Presidential Elections*, 4 vols., ed. Arthur M. Schlesinger Jr. and Fred I. Israel (New York: Chelsea, 1971), 2:1179–80.

64. Harold M. Hyman, "Election of 1864," in ibid., 2:1167. See also Lord Charnwood, *Abraham Lincoln* (Garden City, N.Y.: Garden City Publishing, 1917), 414–415.

65. Quoted in Hyman, "Election of 1864," 1170.

66. Belz, *Lincoln and the Constitution*, 16.

67. John G. Nicolay and John Hay, eds., *Complete Works of Abraham Lincoln*, 12 vols. (Harrogate, Tenn.: Lincoln Memorial University, 1894), 10:244.

68. Randall, *Constitutional Problems under Lincoln*, chap. 9.

69. Hyman, "Election of 1864," 1175.

70. Richard Carwardine, *Lincoln: A Life of Purpose and Power* (New York: Knopf, 2006), 197.

71. Mel Laracey, "Dear America: Public Letters as an Early Form of Presidential Mass Communication," paper presented at the Annual Meeting of the American Political Science Association, September 2009, Toronto, Canada.

72. Hyman, "Election of 1864," 1175.

73. Nicolay and Hay, *Complete Works of Abraham Lincoln*, 10:263–264.

74. Ibid., 10:263.

75. Randall, *Constitutional Problems under Lincoln*, 522.

76. Belz, *Lincoln and the Constitution*, 12. Lincoln took this position in refusing to veto a bill reducing fees paid to the marshal of the District of Columbia; see Basler, *Collected Works of Abraham Lincoln*, 7:414–415.

77. Crenson and Ginsberg, *Presidential Power*, 102.

78. Carl Schurz, "Abraham Lincoln," in *Abraham Lincoln*, ed. Carl Schurz (New York: Chautauqua Press, 1891), 72.

79. Lowi is cited in Michael Les Benedict, "The Constitution of the Lincoln Presidency and the Republican Era," in *The Constitution and the American Presidency*, ed. Martin Fausold and Alan Shank (Albany: State University of New York Press, 1991), 45.

80. McPherson, *Abraham Lincoln and the Second American Revolution*, 137–138.

81. Current, *Political Thought of Abraham Lincoln*, 187–188.

CHAPTER 7

The Reaction against Presidential Power: Andrew Johnson to William McKinley

---

A
ndrew Johnson, who was elected vice president with Abraham Lincoln in 1864, succeeded to the presidency under extraordinarily difficult circumstances on April 15, 1865, the morning after Lincoln was shot by John Wilkes Booth, a Confederate zealot, at Ford's Theater in Washington. The Civil War established the permanence of the Union and emancipated the slaves, but with the end of hostilities in the spring of 1865 came the enormous problems of Reconstruction. How were the Confederate states to rejoin the Union? What would be the status of the emancipated southern slaves or, for that matter, of northern blacks who had never been enslaved but who still were denied the suffrage and some other basic rights in all but a few states?

Lincoln and a majority of the Republicans in Congress agreed that the major objectives of Reconstruction were to destroy slavery and to strip political power from the erstwhile leaders of the Confederacy. They disagreed, however, about how harsh Reconstruction policies needed to be for freedom to take root in soil tainted by slavery. Lincoln wanted to restore the Union as quickly as possible, without imposing draconian terms for readmission on the rebellious states. The Radicals of his party, however, led by Sen. Charles Sumner of Massachusetts and Rep. Thaddeus Stevens of Pennsylvania, believed that high-ranking Confederates should be punished severely for treason, African Americans should be guaranteed the full rights of citizenship, and southern states should not be granted full membership in the Union until they were thoroughly reconstructed and their loyalty was assured.

The conflict within the Republican Party over Reconstruction remained unresolved as the war drew to an end. In 1863 Lincoln had promulgated a program of reunification for the three Confederate states already conquered by the Union army: Arkansas, Louisiana, and Tennessee. According to this program, if even 10 percent of a state's voters took an oath of allegiance to the United States, the state could form a government and elect members of Congress. The Republican-dominated Congress, declaring that Reconstruction was a legislative, not an executive, function, rejected Lincoln's terms as too lenient and refused to seat legislators from any seceding state but Tennessee, which had been the first to fall to Union forces.

Congress's Reconstruction program was the Wade-Davis bill, which disenfranchised all high-ranking Confederates, stipulated that 50 percent of the voters in a rebel state must take a loyalty oath before elections could be held, and made the abolition of slavery a condition for readmission to the Union. Lincoln's pocket veto of this legislation in July 1864, accompanied by a message in which he argued that reunification was an executive function, provoked Republican leaders in Congress to issue the Wade-Davis Manifesto. The manifesto included a bold attack on Lincoln's Reconstruction program and a strong defense of the "paramount" authority of Congress, reminiscent of the Whigs' assaults on Andrew Jackson.[1] Lincoln's landslide reelection in November 1864 took the wind out of the Radical Republicans' sails, but their strength was restored after he was assassinated. As Wilfred E. Binkley has written, "To those who had applauded the furious blast of the Wade-Davis Manifesto against Lincoln only to see its effect nullified by the triumphant re-election of the President it must have now seemed as if fate, through the assassin's bullet, had at last delivered the government into their hands. Their glee was but ill concealed."[2]

The Radicals initially had confidence in Johnson. Until Lincoln appointed him military governor of Tennessee in early 1862, a post he held until he was nominated as Lincoln's running mate in 1864, then-senator Johnson had seemed to be one of them. He had served on the Radical-dominated congressional Joint Committee on the Conduct of the War, which criticized Lincoln's wartime initiatives constantly, often charging that the president had usurped the rightful powers of Congress. His hatred for the southern plantation elite equaled the Radicals' own. Only a few hours after Lincoln died, the Joint Committee paid a visit to Johnson. Its chair, Sen. Benjamin Wade, the prominent Radical cosponsor of the Wade-Davis bill and manifesto, declared, "Johnson we have faith in you. By the gods, there will be no trouble now in running the government!"[3]

The Radicals' faith was short-lived. Johnson despised African Americans even more than he reviled the white gentry; his loyalty was to the South's yeomanry from which he, a tailor before entering politics, and Jackson, his political hero and fellow Tennessean, had sprung. He kept Lincoln's cabinet, spurning the Radicals' advice "to get rid of the last vestige of Lincolnism." At war's end, Johnson chose not to call Congress, which as customary had recessed until December, into special session for the purpose of jointly establishing a postwar plan of Reconstruction.[4] Instead, Johnson implemented his own more lenient Reconstruction policies with a series of executive proclamations in the late spring and summer of 1865. These allowed the South's white workers and small farmers to elect new state governments, which promptly enacted "Black Codes" that stripped the freed slaves of much of their freedom. Congressional Republicans were furious but unable to respond.

Johnson's unilateral actions no doubt were influenced by the success that Lincoln repeatedly had in executing major policy decisions while Congress was in recess, leaving the legislature with little choice but to ratify the late president's *faits accomplis* when it returned to Washington.[5] But Johnson lacked Lincoln's political skill and electoral mandate, as well as the latitude that the general sense of wartime urgency had allowed him. He also lacked Lincoln's concern for the rights of the emancipated slaves. Congressional Republicans moved to establish control over Reconstruction as soon as Congress, which they dominated in the absence of the South, convened in December 1865.

RECONSTRUCTION AND THE ASSAULT ON EXECUTIVE AUTHORITY

Johnson's struggle with Congress was aggravated by the sharp differences of principle that distinguished him from most Republicans. In contrast to Lincoln, who wanted to strengthen the national government's authority to secure legal equality for African Americans, Johnson challenged Reconstruction legislation in the interest of preserving the rights of the states. To be sure, Johnson was a strong defender of the Union. During the secession crisis of 1860–1861, he was the only southern senator not to join the rebels. But in background and belief Johnson was a Jacksonian Democrat who, like Jackson, believed in an indissoluble union and a strong presidency but a weak national government. Although he surrendered his Democratic affiliation to join Lincoln's "National Union" ticket in the 1864 election, Johnson was never comfortable in the Republican Party.[6]

The new president's Jacksonian commitment to states' rights put him at odds with nearly all Republicans, not just the Radicals. Moderate lawmakers repeatedly approached Johnson with strategies designed to build a consensus around modified versions of the president's own policies. But Johnson rejected these efforts. In February 1866, he vetoed a bill, sponsored by the moderate Republican senator Lyman Trumbull of Illinois, to continue the Freedman's Bureau. Created in March 1865, the bureau provided food, clothing, and medical care to the hundreds of thousands of freed slaves uprooted by the war and helped them make the difficult transition to freedom. The head of the bureau, Gen. Oliver O. Howard, was a passionate abolitionist, committed to "the exercise of benevolent functions hitherto always contended against by our leading statesmen."[7] Johnson regarded the bureau as an unconstitutional extension of the national government's authority in peacetime. In vetoing Trumbull's bill, Johnson was challenging not just the Radicals but every Republican in Congress.

The ties between Johnson and the Republican Party were severed irrevocably in March when he vetoed the 1866 Civil Rights Act, which, like the Freedman's Bureau, enjoyed unanimous support from congressional Republicans. This bill, parts of which later were included in the Fourteenth Amendment, declared African Americans to be citizens and bestowed on all persons born in the United States (except American Indians) an equal right to make and enforce contracts, to sue and be witnesses in the courts, to own land and other property, and to enjoy equal protection of the law.

If Johnson had supported the Civil Rights Act, he would have satisfied the North's desire to protect African Americans in the South. Radical Republicans considered any Reconstruction policy that did not impose some degree of black suffrage on the southern states as tantamount to the perpetuation of "an Oligarchy of the skin." "At this moment," Senator Sumner had proclaimed in his eulogy of Lincoln in June 1865, "all turns on the colored suffrage in the rebel states." But even though the late president supported emancipation, he doubted the wisdom of immediately requiring universal male suffrage.[8] Lincoln's position was shared by moderate Republicans, who did not insist on immediate voting rights as long as progress was made toward fulfilling the other rights of African Americans as citizens.

Johnson's veto of the Civil Rights Act united both congressional Republicans and public opinion against him. On April 6, 1866, the Senate voted 33–15 to repass the bill; three days later the House did the same, 122–41. Congress's enactment of the Civil Rights Act over Johnson's veto was a landmark in constitutional development—the first time in history that legislators had overridden a presidential veto on an important issue. The override was equally significant as a political event: Congress, not the president, was now the master of Reconstruction.[9] Soon afterward, when a vacancy occurred on the Supreme Court, Congress voted to abolish the position rather than let Johnson fill it. Anticipating another possible vacancy, it abolished a second position as well, reducing the size of the Court to seven after the next justice died or retired.

Johnson's staunch belief in the inherent racial inferiority of African Americans underlay every aspect of his opposition to a national Reconstruction policy. As a defender of the Union, Johnson supported the abolition of slavery. "This is your country as well as anybody else's," he told a regiment of black soldiers that had gathered to pay him tribute in October 1865. "This country is founded upon the principle of equality."[10] Yet the president sometimes displayed a visceral belief in white supremacy. As a member of Congress in 1844, he had declared his opposition to one bill because "it would place every splay-footed, bandy-shanked, hump-backed, thick-lipped, flat-nosed, woolly-headed, ebon-colored negro in the country upon an equality with the poor white man."[11] As president, his private secretary recorded in 1868, Johnson "has at times exhibited a morbid distress and feeling against negroes."[12] For example, after meeting with Frederick Douglass, Johnson told his secretary, "I know that damned Douglass; he's just like any nigger, and he would sooner cut a white man's throat than not."[13]

Ideology and politics played an important part in molding Johnson's Reconstruction policies. He was convinced that his views on race relations accorded with those of the vast majority of whites. Any attempt to impose civil rights on the South, he believed, would not only be unconstitutional but also would alienate white southerners and, in all likelihood, most people in the North, where only five states in New England, with minuscule minority populations, allowed African Americans to vote. Johnson calculated that leaving the question of racial equality to the states would satisfy everyone but African Americans, whose disenfranchisement meant they scarcely counted politically, and Radical Republicans, whose principles and politics he abhorred.[14]

The midterm elections of 1866 were widely regarded as a referendum on whether Johnson or Congress should control Reconstruction. Congress had just approved the Fourteenth Amendment, which forbade state governments from abridging the "privileges and immunities" of any citizen, from depriving any person of life, liberty, or property "without due process of law," and from denying anyone the "equal protection of the laws." Desperate to build an alternative to the Republican Party, Johnson focused his campaigning on opposition to ratification by the states. In a speaking tour of the North, which he described as a "Swing around the Circle," the president attacked his congressional opponents and championed a National Union movement made up of supporters of his Reconstruction policies.

That summer, the Union "party," a loose and fractious coalition of disgruntled Democrats, conservative Republicans, and white southerners, held a convention. Johnson celebrated the delegates' resolutions, which supported his Reconstruction program, as a second Declaration of Independence and Emancipation Proclamation that would free the country from congressional control of Reconstruction. At the same time, the president used his appointment and removal powers to purge the cabinet and the federal work force of those who did not support the Union party and to replace them with conservative Republicans. Of those cabinet members who were sympathetic to a congressional role in Reconstruction, only Secretary of War Edwin Stanton remained.[15] At the same time, Johnson attacked the heart of the patronage system by replacing almost seventeen hundred Republican postmasters with his own loyalists.

In the election, Johnson's efforts to build an alternative, president-centered political organization failed. Radical Republicans won significant victories across the North. Disgusted when all the southern states reconstructed by presidential proclamation rejected the Fourteenth Amendment after enacting

racially discriminatory Black Codes, the voters routed the president's followers and gave the Radicals firm control of both houses of Congress. With every
southern state except Tennessee still barred by Congress from choosing representatives and senators, all but 53 of the 226 members of the House were
Republicans, as were all but 9 of 54 senators. Particularly damaging to
Johnson was that he had encouraged the southern states to reject the Fourteenth Amendment.[16]

Spurred by the mandate of the 1866 elections, Congress passed a series of
measures in 1867 that deprived Johnson of control over Reconstruction and
stripped his office of its authority to conduct the affairs of the executive
branch. The Military Reconstruction Act replaced the southern state governments that Johnson had approved with military districts led by military
commanders, who were granted almost complete independence from presidential direction.[17] Congress buttressed the commanders' autonomy by tack-
ing riders onto the 1867 army appropriation bill that required the president
and the secretary of war to transmit their orders through General of the Army
Ulysses S. Grant and forbade the president to relieve, suspend, or transfer
Grant without the Senate's consent. This direct challenge to the president's
authority as commander in chief was covertly instigated by Secretary of War
Stanton, who, along with Grant, cooperated with Republican congressional
leaders.

Johnson vetoed the Military Reconstruction Act, charging that it would
create an "absolute despotism" in the South.[18] He also protested the riders that
Congress had attached to the army appropriation bill by claiming that they
were "out of place in an appropriation act" and "deprived the President of his
constitutional functions as Commander-in-Chief of the Army."[19] Congress
ignored the protest and overrode the veto. Then, to prevent Johnson from
reasserting presidential control of Reconstruction, Congress arranged to stay
in session permanently. This action nullified the president's constitutional
privilege to pocket veto legislation that was passed with fewer than ten days
remaining in a session of Congress.[20]

Having stripped Johnson of his ability to influence legislation and govern
the South, Congress proceeded to divest him of control over the personnel of
the executive branch. In March 1867 Congress, overriding Johnson's veto,
passed the Tenure of Office Act, which prohibited the president from firing
any Senate-confirmed official without first obtaining the Senate's approval.
The act reversed the First Congress's decision in 1789 to uphold the president's unilateral authority to remove executive officials. The struggle against
Johnson had reached the point that neither settled precedents nor explicit
constitutional proscriptions would deter Radical Republicans from undermining the presidency for the sake of punishing the president.

By the spring of 1867 Johnson was helpless to block any legislation that
Congress saw fit to pass. His only recourse was to try once again to appeal

directly to the American people. Thomas Jefferson and, especially, Andrew Jackson had sought to establish closer ties between the presidency and the people, but they had worked through their party organization to do so. Lincoln had relied heavily on the Republican Party to mobilize support for the war and his Reconstruction policies.[21] But Johnson had cut his ties to the Democrats by joining Lincoln's ticket in 1864 and alienated Republicans by his conduct as president. When his efforts to build his own political organization failed, the president no longer had a party.

Johnson fancied himself a good orator, but his forceful attacks on Congress were prone to excess, especially when he was fueled by alcohol or goaded by hecklers. On the evening of February 22, 1866, George Washington's birthday, he told a crowd that had marched to the White House to demonstrate its support for his veto of the Civil Rights Act that new rebels had appeared in the country, this time in the North. These rebels, the Radical Republican leaders in Congress, "had assumed nearly all the powers of government" in order to prevent the restoration of the Union. Johnson charged Stevens, the Pennsylvania representative who led the Radicals in the House, and Sumner of Massachusetts, the president's major opponent in the Senate, with being just as traitorous as the leaders of the Confederacy. He even claimed that his opponents' "intention was to incite assassination," adding that "when I am beheaded I want the American people to be the witness."[22]

Johnson's rhetoric backfired. The vast majority of northerners were outraged when they read, or read about, his speeches, most of which were as aggressive as his Washington's Birthday harangue. The public resented his attack on Stevens and Sumner who, whatever their faults, were certainly not traitors.[23] Moreover, the very purpose of Johnson's speeches—to rouse public opinion against Congress as well as in support of his policies—was generally considered illegitimate conduct during the nineteenth century, a form of demagoguery that was beneath the dignity of the presidency. The use of sharp rhetoric by presidents to sway public opinion would become acceptable, even expected, in the twentieth century, but until then partisan presidential speech making was regarded as a violation of unwritten constitutional norms.[24]

Most of Johnson's speeches were delivered during his "Swing around the Circle." The press quickly seized on this expression as an object of derision and a subject for political cartoons. As historian David Miller Dewitt has described the national reaction to Johnson's "swing,"

> His want of dignity . . . , his insensibility to the decorum due to his high office, his eagerness to exchange repartee with any opponent no matter how low, his slovenly modes of speech and his offenses against good taste, unfairly blazoned as they were before the country, disgusted many persons who were half-inclined to his policy; made many of the judicious among his supporters grow lukewarm; forced his warmest supporters to hang their heads for lack of apology; scattered abroad the ugliest scandals about his personal habits and irretrievably hurt his cause.[25]

This illustration of Andrew Johnson's impeachment trial before the Senate appeared on the cover of the March 14, 1868, issue of Harper's Weekly.

THE IMPEACHMENT OF ANDREW JOHNSON

Johnson's politically improper rhetoric strengthened his opponents and served as the basis for one of the eleven articles of impeachment that were brought against him by the House of Representatives on March 2 and 3, 1868. Article X charged that the president had ignored the duties of his office by seeking to impugn Congress. Johnson had delivered "with a loud voice certain intemperate, inflammatory, and scandalous harangues ... amid cries, jeers, and laughter of the multitude then assembled."[26]

The charge of "bad and improper" rhetoric was not the main ground for Johnson's impeachment, however. Many members of Congress doubted that inflammatory speech, however inappropriate, could be construed as an impeachable offense. The *New York Times* echoed these concerns in an editorial, insisting that Johnson's conduct on the stump involved "only questions of taste and opinion—not of law or definable criminality."[27] Yet, because custom placed severe limitations on direct popular leadership by nineteenth-century executives, the charge was not frivolous.[28] "You will find that these denunciations [against Congress] had a deeper meaning than mere opinion," Massachusetts representative Benjamin F. Butler, the leading proponent of Article X, argued during the impeachment trial. "It may be taken as an axiom in the affairs of nations that no usurper has ever seized upon the legislature of his country until he has familiarized the people with the possibility of so doing by vituperating and decrying it."[29]

Johnson's decision in May 1868 to fire Stanton as secretary of war was the principal issue in the impeachment proceedings. In unilaterally firing Stanton, who despite his position in the cabinet was conspiring regularly with the president's enemies in Congress, Johnson appeared to violate the requirement for Senate approval that was established by the Tenure of Office Act.[30] Although Johnson's intention was to have the courts rule on the constitutionality of the law, the House's strictly partisan 128–47 vote to impeach on February 24, 1868 (no Democrat voted in favor, no Republican voted against) meant that the constitutional question would be decided, in effect, by the Senate, not the judiciary.

Johnson's impeachment trial, which lasted six weeks, threatened both his status as president and the constitutional independence of the presidency. The Senate proceedings resembled less a trial to determine if Johnson had committed "high Crimes and Misdemeanors" than a convention of Radical Republicans for the purpose of running Johnson out of office. At the outset of the trial, their chances were good. By author David Stewart's calculation, Johnson could count on only twelve of the nineteen votes he needed to deny his foes the required two-thirds majority for removal: the Senate's nine Democrats plus three Republicans who usually voted with him.[31] He needed to win over at least seven additional Republicans, even as Radical leaders were doing all they could to bring pro-removal public pressure to bear on them. Moderate Republican senators were threatened in the party press and by voters at home.[32]

If Johnson, however poor a president, had been convicted under these circumstances, the power and prestige of the presidency would have been severely damaged. But seven Republican senators who opposed Johnson's policies and leadership but feared that to remove him would destroy the constitutional system of checks and balances stood up to the pressure of party discipline and public opinion, leaving the Radicals one vote shy. (The final tally was 35–19 in favor of removal.) They also were motivated in part by their reluctance to replace Johnson as president with Benjamin Wade, the personally controversial and politically radical president pro tempore of the Senate who was, in the absence of a vice president, next in the line of succession under prevailing law. Meanwhile, moderate senator Lyman Trumbull expressed the belief of those who stood with Johnson that to convict the president would open the door for Congress to use the impeachment power cavalierly in the future:

> no future president will be safe who happens to differ with a majority of the House and two-thirds of the Senate on any measure deemed by them important, particularly if of a political character. Blinded by partisan zeal, with such an example before them, they will not scruple to remove out of the way any obstacle to the accomplishment of their purposes, and what then becomes of the checks and balances of the Constitution, so carefully devised and so vital to its perpetuity?[33]

ULYSSES S. GRANT AND THE ABDICATION OF EXECUTIVE POWER

The Senate's failure to remove Andrew Johnson did not restore to strength either the president or the presidency. The remainder of Johnson's term was spent in a sullen impasse with Congress. Nor did the election of Ulysses S. Grant in 1868 revive the power of the executive. If the American people, made uneasy by Johnson's subordination to Congress, thought they were electing a

Despite a highly successful military career that suggested unusual executive ability, Gen. Ulysses S. Grant was unable to transfer that success from the battlefield to the White House.

forceful political leader in Grant, they were sorely mistaken. Grant's military career justified the belief that he had unusual leadership ability, but his talents did not transfer directly from the battlefield to the White House. Lacking experience in civil administration, Grant had neither the detailed knowledge of the governmental process needed to perform the role of chief executive nor the political experience required to bend other leaders to his purposes.

Grant's shortcomings as a civilian leader were demonstrated almost immediately. The president had let it be known after his election that he opposed the Tenure of Office Act and would not make any but cabinet appointments until Congress repealed it. The House soon complied, but the Senate, still controlled by the Radical Republicans, approved a "compromise" amendment that essentially preserved its role in the removal of executive officials. Grant was so popular and respected at the time of his inauguration on March 4, 1869, that if he had asserted himself in favor of repeal, he probably would have prevailed. Instead, not realizing the implications of his decision, Grant capitulated to the Senate, which prompted Republicans in both houses to join ranks and support the amendment. An advocate of repeal, former secretary of the navy Gideon Welles, expressed the disappointment of those who hoped Grant would restore the stature of the presidency: "The lawyers duped and cowed him. The poor devil has neither the sagacity and obstinacy for which he has credit, if he assents to this compromise, where the Executive surrenders everything and gets nothing."[34]

Grant's strategic error set the tone for his entire two terms as president. He never recovered the prestige and power that he lost in his first showdown with the Republican leaders.[35] Yet his acquiescence to the Senate on the Tenure of Office Act no doubt was influenced by his concept of the presidency. Grant considered himself to be an administrative officer of the legislature, "disposed to accept without question the work of Congress as the authoritative expression of the will of the American people."[36]

Grant's understanding of executive leadership accorded well with that of the Republican leaders in the Senate, who embraced the old Whig principle of legislative supremacy. In Grant, unlike Lincoln or Johnson, congressional

Republicans had a president they could manage. As a result, the Senate was never more powerful than during Grant's tenure. George F. Hoar, a Republican member of the House, described the Senate's attitude toward the president: "The most eminent Senators . . . would have received as a personal affront a private message from the White House expressing a desire that they should adopt any course in the discharge of their legislative duties that they did not approve. If they visited the White House, it was to give, not to receive advice. . . . Each of these stars kept his own orbit and shone in his sphere within which he tolerated no intrusion from the President or from anybody else."[37]

Congress's dominance was apparent in the magnitude of legislative activity. Between 1865 and 1875, an average of forty-eight hundred bills and resolutions were introduced in each two-year Congress, nearly three times as many as during the previous decade. Post–Civil War legislative activity reached its peak when the Forty-second Congress (1871–1873) enacted 1,012 laws and resolutions.[38]

Grant did not abdicate presidential responsibilities entirely in the face of this legislative onslaught. Indeed, he restored to effectiveness the most important power of the nineteenth-century executive: the veto. Johnson had wielded this weapon aggressively, but most of his vetoes were overturned. Grant vetoed ninety-three bills—more than all of his predecessors combined—and only four were overturned.[39] His most important veto killed the 1874 Inflation Bill, which Congress had passed in response to the Panic of 1873, a serious recession caused by a wave of bank failures throughout the country. The bill would have increased the amount of paper money ("greenbacks") in circulation in the hope that a more expansive currency would ease the growing debt crisis among the small farmers of the West. Although Grant was sympathetic to rural hardship (he owned a farm in St. Louis that lost money), he was reluctant to unleash economic forces that might wreck the government's credit and cause a spiral of uncontrolled inflation. Combined with Congress's passage of the Resumption Act at the president's urging in 1875, historian Frank J. Scaturro has argued, Grant's veto of the Inflation Bill made him "the president most responsible for putting the country on the gold standard."[40] The consequence, according to historian Jean Edward Smith, was that "By the end of the century, the American dollar had become the international symbol of financial stability."[41]

For the most part, however, Grant was uninterested in domestic policy. As a career soldier, he was much more concerned about national security issues. In particular, Grant cast an expansionist eye on Central America. In his first message to Congress, he called for the construction of a canal linking the Caribbean to the Pacific. The president also believed the navy needed a large natural harbor in the region. He hoped to follow through on plans initiated by the Johnson administration to purchase Santo Domingo (now known as the Dominican Republic), which is the home of Samana Bay, one of the best naval anchorages in the Caribbean. But the scheme ran into a buzz saw of opposition in the Senate. Charles Sumner, the chair of the Senate Foreign Relations Committee, opposed Grant's expansionist policies, considering them an affront to the egalitarian ideals that had given birth to the Republican Party. Sumner bitterly scorned the attempt to annex Santo Domingo, which he thought would threaten the independence of neighboring Haiti, the only independent black republic in the world. "To the African belongs the equatorial belt," Sumner said, "and he should enjoy it undisturbed."[42] The senator's moral indignation was fueled by personal resentment. Sorely disappointed that Grant had not named him secretary of state, Sumner was determined to control American foreign policy through his committee. In this instance he prevailed: in 1870 the Senate rejected Grant's treaty, under which Santo Domingo eventually would have become an American state.[43]

Grant had blundered badly. As Smith has written, "Little effort was made to cultivate public opinion and the Senate was kept in the dark. That was Grant's error."[44] Nevertheless, the president did not take the rejection of his Caribbean policy lightly. He persuaded Republican leaders in the Senate to strip Sumner of his chairmanship of the Foreign Relations Committee. This measure of revenge did nothing to advance the president's policy toward Santo Domingo; the treaty was voted down again in 1871. But it did enable Grant to obtain Senate ratification the same year of the Treaty of Washington, which settled the country's lingering disputes with Great Britain. The treaty secured payment to the United States for damages inflicted during the Civil War by the *Alabama* and other British-built Confederate naval vessels. Decrying Great Britain for its hypocrisy (the British had claimed to be antislavery while profiting from the sale of blockade runners to the Confederacy), Sumner had called for an uncompromising stance that would demand compensation for the indirect as well as the direct damages the United States had suffered. The ships, he insisted, not only devastated the American merchant fleet but also prolonged the war.

Although Grant shared Sumner's disdain for Great Britain's pose of neutrality during the Civil War, he was anxious to settle the dispute. With Sumner deposed as chair of the Foreign Relations Committee and Simon Cameron of Pennsylvania, a strong Grant supporter, installed in his place, the treaty committing both nations to submit the issue to arbitration passed the Senate easily. The result was a $15.5 million award to the United States and the establishment of an important precedent in international law. This was the first major quarrel between two world powers to be settled by an international panel of arbitrators.[45] Smith has observed that four decades later "The rules governing maritime neutrality laid out in the

Treaty of Washington . . . were formally adopted by all nations at the second Hague Conference in 1907."[46]

Clearly, Grant was a stronger president than most scholars have recognized, especially during his first term. In the face of a white South grown assertive and a northern public grown weary of Reconstruction, he labored vigorously to secure the rights of African Americans in the South, promoting the enactment of the Fifteenth Amendment's bar against racial discrimination in voting and using the army and the Justice Department, newly elevated to cabinet status, to suppress the Ku Klux Klan in the South.[47] He was overwhelmingly reelected in 1872, winning 56 percent of the popular vote, the highest percentage for any presidential candidate between Andrew Jackson in 1828 and Theodore Roosevelt in 1904. But, according to his biographer Geoffrey Perret, "Grant had no grand vision of his own to guide the country." He was a transitional president in a country that was making its own transition from the Civil War era to the Gilded Age, during which the United States was emerging on the world stage as a commercial and military power. As his stance against the Inflation Bill suggested, Grant tended to view this transition favorably. But he offered no program to oversee its course. Instead, Grant's main concern was to keep "the Republican party in the White House as long as possible in order to keep the Democrats out: Republicans saved the Union; Democrats had threatened its destruction."[48]

The Grant-led Republicans were practical politicians who depended on the spoils system to maintain the vigor of their party's organization. Out of a misplaced faith in the sanctity of party loyalty, Grant exposed his administration to patronage abuses and outright peculation. The most dramatic and probably the most damaging scandal of his presidency involved the evasion of taxes on distilleries by the so-called Whiskey Ring, a group of distillers and bottlers who routinely bribed revenue agents to avoid paying taxes on their product. The ring included Gen. John A. McDonald, the collector of internal revenue in St. Louis who colluded with Treasury officials and the president's close friend and secretary, Gen. Orville E. Babcock, to defraud the government of millions of dollars.

One of the most disconcerting aspects of the scandal was Grant's effort to protect Babcock, who was acquitted on the strength of a deposition in his favor from the president. Grant even appointed Babcock as inspector of lighthouses.[49] Still worse, the president repaid Secretary of the Treasury Benjamin H. Bristow's efforts to break the Whiskey Ring and bring its perpetrators, including Babcock, to justice by making clear that Bristow was no longer welcome in the cabinet. Grant, no doubt, was also irritated by Bristow's political ambition. He became convinced that the Treasury secretary had been intriguing against him all along "to ruin his reputation and install Bristow as his successor."[50] Bristow resigned in 1876.

Although Grant's conduct in the Whiskey Ring scandal was unfortunate, he was personally honest and, more important, was concerned about the existing system of public administration. In early 1870 he called for civil service reform, declaring that "the present system [of party patronage] does not secure the best men and often not even fit men, for public place."[51] After receiving the necessary authority from Congress in March, Grant established a board, soon known as the Civil Service Commission, and charged it to devise reformist rules and regulations. George William Curtis, a leader of the national civil service reform movement, was appointed to chair the commission, which also supervised the new competitive examination system for hiring in each department. Thus did one of the most corrupt presidential administrations in history make the first earnest attempt to reform the civil service.

Despite this promising beginning, most of what happened during Grant's second term thwarted the cause of civil service reform. The patronage system had long been dominated by individual members of Congress, and they liked it that way. Sen. Roscoe Conkling of New York, the leader of the so-called Stalwart wing of the Republican Party, led an assault on the new commission. He was supported not only by the leaders of his own party but by patronage-seeking Democrats as well.

The rise of the Stalwarts reveals much about the political ambiance of the post–Civil War era. Like the Radical Republicans, the Stalwarts initially were committed to the fundamental reconstruction of the South. But as the war and its aftermath gradually faded in political significance, defending patronage and maintaining the party organization became the Stalwarts' paramount concern. They were the product of a new political milieu, in which the needs of the party machinery took precedence over principle. As historian Morton Keller has noted, the Stalwarts' emergence as the dominant faction in the Republican Party signified the shift from a "politics of ideology to a politics of organization."[52]

Republicans who opposed the Stalwart-led transformation of their party and supported civil service reform turned in the early 1870s to a third party, the Liberal Republicans. But Liberal Republicanism never flourished at the grass roots. After nominating the celebrated New York newspaper editor Horace Greeley to run (unsuccessfully) against Grant in 1872, Liberal Republicans became anathema to the president and therefore were unable to work cooperatively with him to fend off the congressional attack on the Civil Service Commission. Stalwart Republicans and Democrats assailed the commission's rules as unconstitutional, aristocratic, and fatal to the ascendancy of any party.

Instead of defending his civil service reform program, Grant resigned himself to cooperating with the Stalwarts. He then yielded when Congress refused to allocate funds for the Civil Service Commission in 1874. Proclaiming once more his belief that the legislature was the proper branch to make domestic policy, the president announced in his annual message on December 7, 1874, that if Congress did not pass a civil service reform law before adjourning, he would discontinue the system. Congress adjourned without taking action, and on March 9, 1875, Grant ordered that civil service examining boards throughout the country be disbanded.[53]

THE FIGHT TO RESTORE PRESIDENTIAL POWER

Grant retired from the presidency in 1877, leaving the office he had occupied for eight years at a low ebb. The Senate, its leaders believed, was "secure in its mastery over the executive."[54] Yet Grant's successor, Rutherford B. Hayes, was determined to emancipate his office from congressional domination. During the Hayes administration, the powers of the presidency were defended persistently and effectively for the first time since the Civil War.

THE PRESIDENCY OF RUTHERFORD B. HAYES

Although Hayes eventually reversed more than a decade of executive decline, his administration began in the least auspicious of circumstances. After sixteen years of Republican rule, a Democratic victory seemed certain in the elections of 1876. In fact, Democratic candidate Samuel J. Tilden, who as governor of New York had exposed the efforts of Boss Tweed and various political rings to corrupt the state's canal system, initially appeared to have won the presidential election.[55] But the electoral votes of Oregon and the three southern states that still were under military rule—Florida, Louisiana, and South Carolina—were in doubt. Without them, Tilden had only 184 electoral votes. If Hayes carried all of the disputed states, he would have 185 votes and win the election.

The partisan battle began when all four states sent two sets of electoral votes to Washington to be counted. Congress responded by creating a fifteen-member electoral commission, eight Republicans and seven Democrats, to sort out the matter. At this point, a deal—the so-called Compromise of 1877—apparently was struck between Republican and southern Democratic leaders. In return for the Democrats acquiescing to Hayes's election, the Republicans promised to remove the occupying military forces from the South. Both sides kept their end of the bargain. On March 2, 1877, the electoral commission, by a strict party vote, rejected the Democratic returns from the doubtful states and declared Hayes the winner by a margin of one electoral vote. Hayes, in turn, removed the federal troops from the South, putting an end to virtually all attempts to enforce the Fourteenth Amendment's guarantees of civil rights to every citizen, including the former slaves. Nor, thereafter, was any serious effort made to uphold the Fifteenth Amendment, which since

1870 had affirmed the right of citizens to vote regardless of "race, color, or previous condition of servitude."[56]

Negotiations between Democrats and Republicans that led to the 1877 agreement had stretched over several months. Prompted by the Democrats regaining control of the House in 1874 and the waning power of the military occupation, Grant maintained a "benevolent neutrality" during the last three months of his administration that enabled the so-called Redeemers of South Carolina and Louisiana to take de facto control of the two remaining Republican governments south of the Mason-Dixon Line.[57] Meanwhile, Tilden maintained what Morton Keller has called an "Olympian (or neurotic)" calm during the 1876 election dispute.[58] He spent one critical month during the crisis compiling a history of past electoral counts. When the issue finally was resolved against him, Tilden said he looked forward to private life "with the consciousness that I shall receive from posterity the credit of having been elected to the highest position in the gift of the people without any cares and responsibilities of the office."[59] As Keller concluded, "The retreat from the purposive, ideological politics of the Civil War could not have been more complete."[60]

It is ironic that such an unsavory political bargain brought to power a president who was uncompromisingly dedicated to reforming the patronage-dominated civil service. Hayes had been a reform-oriented governor of Ohio and had written a ringing endorsement of civil service reform in his letter accepting the Republican presidential nomination. The president's appointing power, he declared, too often had passed improperly into the hands of Congress. In his inaugural address, Hayes proclaimed that civil service reform should be "thorough, radical, and complete."[61]

Congress, for its part, was uninterested in reform. By the end of Grant's second term, the influence of individual senators and, to a lesser extent, representatives on executive appointments had become substantial. Hayes first offended Republican Senate leaders by making his cabinet nominations independently, without consulting them, thereby disrupting the Stalwarts' plan to dictate the composition of the cabinet. With his nomination of former Confederate David M. Key as postmaster general, Hayes also aroused their patriotic wrath. The major insult that the president perpetrated on the Senate, however, was his choice of the civil service reformer Carl Schurz to head the Department of the Interior, a jobs-laden agency that members of Congress feared Schurz would use to wage war on patronage.

Even though Hayes's cabinet nominees were a distinguished and qualified group, the offended Senate "oligarchy" took their selection as a challenge. When the president submitted his nominations for confirmation, the entire list was referred to committees for prolonged examination. Hoping that delay would force the president's hand, the Senate did not exempt even Sen. John

Sherman, whom Hayes had nominated as secretary of the Treasury, from this process, violating the custom that fellow senators, especially those as qualified as Sherman, were confirmed without investigation.

For the Senate to delay the confirmation of an entire cabinet was unprecedented and, it turned out, unpopular. The White House was flooded with telegrams and letters urging Hayes to stand firm. The Senate capitulated to public opinion and, voting almost unanimously, confirmed every cabinet nominee. "For the first time since the Civil War," Wilfred Binkley has written, "the Senate had been vanquished on a clear-cut issue between it and the President."[62]

Yet the great battle between Hayes and Congress was still to come. Having installed a cabinet of his own choosing, the president set his sights on the patronage system. "Now for Civil Service Reform," Hayes wrote in his diary on April 22, 1877, seven weeks after taking office.[63] One of his first acts was to appoint independent commissions to investigate the federal customhouses in New York, San Francisco, New Orleans, and several other port cities. These outposts, which were effectively controlled by local party machines, had fallen into outrageous patterns of corruption in the course of collecting federal revenues. Although the commissions' investigations led to reforms in many areas of the country, the customhouse in New York, which collected more than two-thirds of all custom revenues and provided the federal government with about half of its income, continued to serve the party machine. The commission that investigated the New York customhouse found that employees were hired in response to political pressure and were expected to contribute a percentage of their salary to the party. Not surprisingly, incompetence and corruption among customhouse personnel were widespread.

After receiving the report on the New York customhouse, Hayes decided to replace its three highest officials—Collector Chester A. Arthur, Surveyor General George H. Sharpe, and naval officer Alonzo B. Cornell—all of whom were prominent members of New York's Republican organization. The president's intention was impeded, however, when his nominations were referred to the Senate Commerce Committee, chaired by Stalwart Republican leader Roscoe Conkling of New York. Conkling, for whom the customhouse was an important base of political power, invoked the Tenure of Office Act, which had been revised in 1869, and the session of Congress ended without the nominations being confirmed. Under the amended terms of the act, the Senate no longer could overturn a presidential removal. But until a majority of senators voted to approve the president's choice of a successor, the suspended official remained in office. When Hayes's nominations, which were greeted in the Senate with derisive laughter, were not confirmed, Arthur, Sharpe, and Cornell kept their posts. More important, Conkling and the New York Republican machine retained control of the customhouse.

The stubborn Hayes resolved to continue the fight. On December 12, 1877, he recorded in his diary, "In the language of the press, Senator Conkling has won a great victory over the administration. . . . But the end is not yet. I am right and I shall not give up the contest."[64] The rivalry between the president and the senator was personal: Conkling had opposed Hayes's nomination in 1876 and, after the disputed election, openly mocked him as "Rutherfraud."[65] When Congress adjourned in 1878, Hayes again dismissed the three custom-house officials, replaced them temporarily with recess appointments, and in December sent to the Senate his nominations for the positions. Although Conkling was able to delay Senate action for two months, he finally defeated his cause by delivering a bitter speech against the president in which he alienated many senators by reading from the private correspondence of cabinet members.[66] The Senate voted to confirm Hayes's nominees on February 3, 1879.

In his letter of congratulation to Gen. E. A. Merritt, who was Arthur's replacement, Hayes established principles for the complete overhaul of the New York customhouse's personnel system. Besides insisting that Merritt conduct his office "on strictly business principles," the president required the new collector to confine patronage to the narrowest possible bounds. "Let no man be put out merely because he is a friend of the late collector," he wrote, "and no man be put in merely because he is our friend."[67]

Hayes's victory over Conkling came at great political cost. During the almost eighteen months it took to fire Arthur, Sharpe, and Cornell, the president was virtually powerless as the administrative head of the government. Even though Hayes's triumph restored to the executive some of the powers it had lost since Lincoln's assassination, his administration therefore has been remembered mainly for "holding its ground, rather than for developing new frontiers."[68] Still, Hayes was satisfied with the blows he had struck against the senatorial group that for so long had directed the government. A year after winning his battle for control of the New York customhouse, Hayes wrote in his diary, "The end I have chiefly aimed at has been to break down congressional patronage. The contest has been a bitter one. It has exposed me to attack, opposition, misconstruction, and the actual hatred of powerful men. But I have had great success. No member of either house now attempts even to dictate appointments. My sole right to make appointments is now tacitly conceded."[69]

THE PRESIDENCY OF JAMES A. GARFIELD

The struggle between the president and Congress for control of the executive branch did not end with Hayes's defeat of Conkling. In fact, the battles over appointments that had dominated Hayes's term in office were renewed with unexpected ferocity during the first weeks of James A. Garfield's administration.

By the time of the 1880 election, factionalism had come to dominate American political parties. Garfield, who was nominated by the Republican convention on the thirty-sixth ballot, was chosen as a compromise between Conkling's Stalwarts and the moderate wing of the party (the Half-breeds as they were called), led by Sen. James G. Blaine of Maine.[70] The convention further bandaged party wounds by selecting Chester A. Arthur, Conkling's lieutenant and the deposed head of the New York customhouse, as its vice-presidential candidate. The Democrats settled on a compromise presidential nominee of their own, the pallid and unexceptional Civil War general Winfield Scott Hancock of Pennsylvania, in a convention torn by factional disputes. Of the 9,219,467 popular votes cast in the election, Garfield prevailed over Hancock by a razor-thin margin of 9,457. He won the Electoral College by 214–155. As in the 1876 election, the closeness of the contest was not the result of a keen struggle over major issues. Instead, it was the product of two highly organized, competitive national parties, each bringing its supporters to the polls.

Close elections were the norm throughout the post-Reconstruction era, signifying the public's ambivalence about the Republican and Democratic parties. The electorate's unwillingness to support either party or any individual candidate decisively reflected the dominance of a highly mobilized, intensely competitive form of intraparty factionalism in which presidents were frequently ensnared in organizational battles over local interests and spoils.[71]

Garfield seemed well suited to the new game of party politics. Unlike Hayes, the new president was by nature prone to conciliation and compromise. Once in office, he hoped to work cooperatively with both the Stalwart and Half-breed factions of the Gop. Yet against his will, Garfield was soon caught up in severe factional conflicts. In the heat of these intraparty squabbles, he was forced to continue the assault against overly broad assertions of senatorial courtesy that Hayes had begun.[72]

Garfield's attack on the Senate came in response to the Conklingites' attempt to dictate his choice for secretary of the Treasury. Stalwarts demanded that the president appoint Levi P. Morton, a New York banker. Garfield resisted, arguing that Morton's Wall Street connections and extremely conservative economic views made him anathema to western Republicans. His conciliatory offer to name Morton as secretary of the navy and to consider other Stalwart recommendations for the Treasury was scorned. The Stalwarts' answer was unequivocal: Morton must be the Treasury secretary.

Garfield was not so conciliatory as to yield to such an aggressive challenge to executive authority. After generously recognizing the Conkling wing of the New York Republican Party by placing many of its members in federal positions, he insisted on his own choices for the cabinet, selecting William

Windom, a Republican senator from Minnesota, as Treasury secretary. Garfield now realized, as clearly as had Hayes, that the president's constitutional independence "could be preserved only by a bold challenge of the pretensions of the Senate and a duel to the finish with the most militant champion of senatorial courtesy."[73]

Garfield left no doubt of his intention to challenge the Senate when he nominated William H. Robertson as collector of the port of New York. Robertson was Conkling's political enemy in New York and a friend of his major rival in national politics, James G. Blaine. This made Robertson's appointment a more direct challenge to Conkling and to the practice of senatorial courtesy than Hayes had ever issued. As Garfield wrote to his longtime friend B. A. Hinsdale, the president of Hiram College, "This [nomination] brings on the contest at once and will settle the question whether the President is registering clerk of the Senate or the Executive of the United States. . . . Summed up in a single sentence this is the question: shall the principal port of entry in which more than ninety percent of all our customs duties are collected be under the control of the administration or under the local control of the factional senator?"[74]

Conkling marshaled his political machine in an attempt to compel Garfield to withdraw Robertson's nomination. Vice President Arthur participated fully in these maneuvers, despite stiff criticism from the president's supporters and the press. On the evening of April 14, 1881, Arthur eluded reporters and slipped into the White House for a private conversation with Garfield. He urged the president to withdraw Robertson's nomination on the ground that it would badly fracture the Republican Party in New York and consign its candidates to certain defeat. Garfield refused to budge. Afterward, he wrote to Whitelaw Reid of the New York *Tribune,* "Of course I deprecate war, but if it is brought to my door the bringer will find me at home."[75]

When Conkling and his allies in the Senate hatched a plan to outwit the president by confirming all of his nominees except Robertson, Garfield withdrew every other New York appointment. There would be no further nominations, Garfield insisted, until the issue of who controlled the executive branch was settled. The president's bold maneuver left the Senate practically helpless and rallied his supporters. Garfield recorded the triumph in his diary: "The withdrawal of the New York appointments has brought me vigorous responses from many quarters and I think shows that the public do not desire the continuance of boss rule in the Senate."[76]

On May 16, 1881, seeing that Robertson's confirmation was inevitable, Conkling and his fellow New York senator, Thomas C. Platt, resigned, hoping that the state legislature would buttress their political stature in Washington by reelecting them. The legislature refused. After a long struggle, two other men were chosen to represent New York in the Senate.

Garfield's victory was complete. The Senate confirmed Robertson's nomination unanimously, and Conkling never regained public office. The president's triumph ended the long struggle that had begun with Hayes's attempt to reform the New York customhouse and marked a "milestone in the revival of the power and prestige of the White House."[77]Although the influence that senators wield in suggesting candidates for presidential appointments and rejecting objectionable nominees remained substantial, their claim to supersede executive discretion was ended.

CHESTER A. ARTHUR AND THE ENACTMENT OF CIVIL SERVICE REFORM

Garfield did not have time to pursue a comprehensive program of civil service reform. On July 2, 1881, in a Washington railroad station, a deranged lawyer named Charles J. Guiteau shot the president in the back. Guiteau, who had convinced himself that he deserved a prominent presidential appointment and resented Garfield's assault on the Conkling machine, exclaimed upon being arrested, "I am a Stalwart and Arthur is president."[78] When Garfield died after lingering until September 19, Vice President Arthur indeed became the president.

Civil service reformers expected little from the New York Stalwart. Former president Hayes predicted that Conkling, Arthur's old patron, would be "the power behind the throne, superior to the throne."[79] But Garfield's assassination had inflamed public opinion against the spoils system, and Arthur quickly realized that if he did not support civil service reform, he would jeopardize the precariously superior political position enjoyed by the Republican Party since the Civil War. The new president soon laid to rest the worst fears of those who predicted he would "turn the White House into a larger version of the New York Customhouse."[80] Arthur refused Conkling's "outrageous" demand that he fire the Garfield-appointed collector of the New York customhouse, William Robertson, and appoint a loyal Stalwart in his place. He felt "morally bound to continue the policy of the former president."[81] Intent on strengthening his political position in the country, Arthur surprised his critics and expressed support for limited civil service reform in his first annual message to Congress.

Arthur's commitment to reform was strengthened by the results of the 1882 midterm elections, in which the Democrats achieved substantial gains in the House of Representatives. In his second annual message, the president called on Congress to pass the Pendleton Act, which had been introduced in 1881 by George Hunt Pendleton, a Democratic senator from Ohio. The civil service reform bill contained measures, such as competitive examinations for federal jobs and a ban on political assessments, that Arthur originally had opposed. But when Congress passed the act in early 1883, he signed it. The

Pendleton Act was of limited application. Its coverage extended only to employees of the executive branch in Washington and in major customhouses and post offices around the country. The vast majority—all but 14,000 of 131,000 federal officeholders, including many postal workers—were not covered. Indeed, control of the rich supply of remaining patronage jobs would be the primary source of conflict between Congress and Arthur's Democratic successor, Grover Cleveland.

Nevertheless, as Leonard D. White has written, the enactment of civil service reform in 1883 "was a fundamental turning point in the history of the federal administrative system."[82] In addition to the foothold it established for merit hiring and the bar it erected against on-the-job solicitations of campaign funds from federal employees, the Pendleton Act established a bipartisan, three-member Civil Service Commission, appointed by the president and confirmed by the Senate. The commission was vested with two important powers: to control hiring examinations and to investigate whether the new civil service rules were being enforced. Finally, the president was authorized to expand the bounds of civil service coverage by executive order. However limited its initial application, the Pendleton Act laid a solid foundation on which to build the civil service in succeeding decades.[83]

GROVER CLEVELAND'S FIRST TERM

Neither the Republicans' belated support of civil service reform nor their nomination for president of Speaker of the House James G. Blaine, the leader of the moderate, Half-breed faction of the party, could stave off defeat in the 1884 election. The Democratic standard-bearer, Gov. Grover Cleveland of New York, won a narrow victory. He was the first Democrat to be elected president in twenty-eight years.

Cleveland was the preeminent "Bourbon Democrat"—that is, he led his party's conservative wing, which closely shared the Republicans' skeptical, even hostile stance toward the growing aspirations of industrial workers and small farmers for wide-ranging social and economic reform. The Bourbons thought of themselves as staunch adherents of traditional Jeffersonian and Jacksonian principles in the face of the tremendous changes that were taking place in the late nineteenth-century American economy. They championed lower tariffs, hard money, limited government, and personal freedom. Although these principles had once formed the core of a reform tradition, they had taken on a conservative cast in the Gilded Age. In this new era, large factories and powerful corporations were the real beneficiaries of principles whose original purpose was to protect small farmers, workers, and local business owners.

Bourbon Democratic regimes flourished in the South, where politicians representing big businessmen and planters roused the support of many poor whites by waving the flag of white supremacy. But the Bourbons' Jeffersonian and Jacksonian rhetoric appealed to many northern Democrats as well.[84] Cleveland was especially strong among those midwestern and northeastern members of the party whose antipathy to centralized power was joined to a pro-business philosophy. Historian Horace Samuel Merrill has described these conservative Democrats as "protectors of the existing, although accelerating, course of the industrial revolution. They jealously guarded this machinery of material progress against threats from restless farmers and wage earners."[85]

Moderates in every section of the country believed that Cleveland's election heralded the true end of the bitter conflicts generated by the Civil War. Cleveland was eager to prove them correct. As the head of the party that received its greatest support from the South, he appointed many white southerners to high office, including two to his cabinet. Republicans, unwilling to stop waving the "bloody shirt" of northern resentment of southern secession, continued to portray the Democrats as unworthy to control the federal government. Cleveland's vetoes of multiple military pension bills provided the Republican Party with political ammunition that became even more explosive when the president signed an order returning captured Confederate battle flags to the South.[86] Yet Cleveland's victory in 1884 was proof that the post–Civil War political order would not be upset by the election of a Democrat as president. The 1884 campaign and its aftermath confirmed that recent elections were more about federal patronage than national issues. The Democratic victory also indicated that the nation was turning its attention from the legacy of the Civil War toward tariffs, currency, and other economic matters.[87]

Not surprisingly, the 1884 election brought no moratorium in the patronage-centered struggle between the president and Congress to control appointments to the federal government. By winning major victories against the Senate, Hayes and Garfield had restored some measure of prestige to the presidency, which had been badly tarnished during the Johnson and Grant years. It fell to Cleveland to fight the battle over appointments that finally secured the repeal of the Tenure of Office Act.

The battle began when Cleveland attempted to appoint loyal Democrats who, after being out of office for so long, were hungry to partake of the spoils of patronage. The president was no mere spoilsman. As mayor of Buffalo and governor of New York, he had earned a reputation for reform. As president, Cleveland enforced the Pendleton Act and devoted an enormous amount of time to scrutinizing the qualifications of candidates for the many federal positions that were not covered by the new merit-based civil service hiring procedures. His approach yielded a number of outstanding appointments and won him praise from civil service reformers.

Still, fashioning himself a Jacksonian Democrat, Cleveland appreciated the benefits of the patronage system. He wanted to place deserving Democrats in jobs that had long been held by Republicans. Operating under the constraints of the amended Tenure of Office Act, however, the president was only able to suspend, not remove, federal employees from their jobs. He could not replace officials unless the Senate was in session and approved his nominees. The Republican-controlled Senate was loath to cooperate. Of the 643 suspensions (and corresponding appointments) that Cleveland made during the early days of his presidency, the Senate, after being in session for three months, considered only 17 and confirmed only 15.

The larger controversy between the president and the Senate was joined in a battle for control of a single office, the U.S. attorney for Alabama. When Cleveland suspended the incumbent, George M. Duskin, and nominated John D. Burnett to replace him, the Republican chair of the Senate Judiciary Committee, George F. Edmunds of Vermont, decided to subject the nomination to intense and protracted scrutiny. He asked Cleveland's attorney general to send to his committee all papers pertaining not just to Burnett's appointment but also to Duskin's dismissal. Cleveland directed the attorney general to comply with the request for information about Burnett. But, determined to establish once and for all the president's right to remove federal officials without interference from Congress, Cleveland refused to release any information about his decision to suspend Duskin.

Cleveland's refusal stung Senate Republicans, who responded with a resolution condemning the administration for its unwillingness to cooperate. The president, in turn, sent a message to the Capitol defending his actions and accusing legislators of infringing on his constitutional responsibility as chief executive. Of the Republicans' demand for information about his suspension of federal officials, Cleveland wrote: "They assume the right of the Senate to sit in judgment upon the exercise of my exclusive discretion and executive function, for which I am solely responsible to the people from whom I have so lately received the sacred trust of office. My oath to support and defend the Constitution . . . compel[s] me to refuse compliance with these demands."[88]

Cleveland's message to Congress dramatized his conflict with the Senate in a way that attracted national attention. As in other recent battles of this sort, public opinion supported the president. Recognizing that it was beaten, the Senate found a face-saving avenue of retreat. Someone discovered that during the controversy Duskin's term had expired, which made his suspension by the president no longer necessary. Burnett's appointment as U.S. attorney was readily confirmed.

Cleveland's position on appointments was vindicated a few months later when, with overwhelming support from both parties, Congress voted to repeal the Tenure of Office Act. "Thus," wrote Cleveland long after the event, "was an unhappy controversy happily followed by an expurgation of the last pretense of statutory sanction to an encroachment upon constitutional Executive prerogatives, and thus was a time-honored interpretation of the Constitution restored to us."[89]

CONGRESSIONAL GOVERNMENT AND THE PRELUDE TO A MORE ACTIVE PRESIDENCY

During the twelve years that passed between the beginning of the Hayes administration in 1877 and the end of Cleveland's first term in 1889, the post–Civil War decline in the prestige of the presidency came to an end. The Senate's grip on the details of administration, especially the removal power, was loosened by the defeats administered by Hayes, Garfield, and Cleveland. The struggle to rejuvenate executive independence was advanced by the enactment of civil service reform, which began the process of insulating federal appointments from the parochial concerns of party spoilsmen.

These achievements notwithstanding, the presidency remained small in scale and limited in power during the latter decades of the nineteenth century. The president's control of the executive domain was restored, but the domain itself remained highly constricted. Late nineteenth-century presidents had little influence on government expenditures or, apart from appointments, on the policies pursued by the departments and agencies of the executive branch.

In fiscal affairs, the end of the Civil War had marked a transition from emergency presidential control of the amounts and purposes of government spending to renewed efforts by Congress to reassert its authority. In response, Hayes and Cleveland exercised the veto aggressively to ward off Congress's most egregious attempts to use spending bills to impose its will on the executive. In 1879 Hayes successfully vetoed an army appropriation bill that included riders attached by the Democrats prohibiting federal marshals from employing troops or armed civilians in the southern states to keep the peace during congressional elections. In doing so, Hayes established a powerful precedent against appropriation riders that encroach on executive power.[90]

Yet the veto was strictly a defensive measure when it came to fiscal policy. Indeed, until the Budget and Accounting Act was passed in 1921, presidential authority for taxing and spending was "almost, if not entirely, lacking."[91] Presidents, at least in peacetime, were never involved when departments and agencies made their annual spending estimates and seldom were consulted when congressional committees reviewed those estimates. The secretary of the Treasury was merely a compiler of budget requests. The absence of executive leadership in fiscal matters fostered irresponsible and disorderly budgets, made worse by Congress's practice of devolving its decision-making authority for spending to the House and Senate appropriations committees.

The president's ability to provide guidance in the legislative process and to enlist congressional support for an administration program was also limited during the latter part of the nineteenth century. Indeed, no president of this era advanced a theory of executive power that supported presidential leadership of Congress.

Cleveland fiercely defended executive independence but did not believe that the president's legislative responsibilities went beyond recommending measures for Congress to consider. Even on the tariff issue, which had emerged as the central conflict between Democrats and Republicans in the 1880s, the president made little effort to bend Congress to his will. To be sure, Cleveland opposed protectionism. After the Democrats fared poorly in the 1886 midterm elections, he wrote a forceful message that urged Congress, in conformance with Democratic principles, to reduce tariff rates sharply. But having done this much, the president did little more. As historian John A. Garraty has written, "Like a great lethargic bear, Cleveland had bestirred himself ... and shaken the political hive, but then he slumped back into querulous inactivity."[92] His tariff policy was rejected overwhelmingly by Congress, at considerable cost to his political reputation.

THE PRESIDENCY OF BENJAMIN A. HARRISON

The narrow bounds that constrained presidential leadership in the late nineteenth century led political scientist Woodrow Wilson to declare in 1885, the first year of Cleveland's first term, that "unquestionably, the predominant and controlling force, the center and source of all motive and of all regulative power, is Congress."[93] Cleveland did not challenge the principle of legislative supremacy. His successor, Benjamin A. Harrison, enthusiastically embraced it.

Harrison, a Republican senator from Indiana, won a very close election in 1888. Cleveland, by piling up large majorities in the southern states, actually won the national popular vote, but Harrison narrowly carried the large northern states and therefore the Electoral College. This unusual result (not until 2000 did another discrepancy occur between the popular and the electoral vote outcomes) brought to the presidency a man who understood perfectly Congress's desire to control the conduct of government.

Harrison was one of the Senate leaders who had clashed with Cleveland over the president's removal power. A few weeks after the election, he readily accepted the advice of Republican senator John Sherman: "The President should 'touch elbows with Congress.' He should have no policy distinct from his party and that is better represented in Congress than in the Executive." Suggesting that "Cleveland made a cardinal mistake in [seeking to dictate] a tariff policy to Congress," Sherman encouraged the new president to cultivate friendly relations with legislators and to follow rather than try to lead Republicans in the House and Senate.[94]

In spite of Harrison's unquestioned industry and dignified supervision of executive affairs, his tenure marked a retreat in the struggle to revive the status of the presidency. Comparing Harrison and his predecessor, Garraty wrote, "Cleveland had surrendered to the patronage system after a battle; Harrison embraced it from the start. Cleveland squabbled with Congress, and fumbled [in the tariff controversy] toward presidential leadership at least once; Harrison cheerfully submitted to being practically a figurehead."[95]

The absence of presidential leadership and the triumph of congressional supremacy spawned efforts to reorganize the House and the Senate so they could perform their duties more efficiently. Until the 1880s Congress had been primarily a deliberative body. By the end of the nineteenth century, it was a complex and well-disciplined institution that was organized to govern.

In the House, especially, lawmaking increasingly came under the control of the leadership—that is, the Speaker and the heads of the major committees. The Republican Speaker during Harrison's tenure, Thomas B. Reed, imposed rules on the House that greatly streamlined its chaotic proceedings. Confronted with the minority Democrats' use of the "disappearing quorum," in which members sat mute during attendance calls to deny the Speaker the quorum he needed to conduct business, Reed counted the recalcitrants whether they signified their presence or not. In 1891 the Supreme Court sanctioned the transformation of the House into a more disciplined legislative body by declining to rule unconstitutional this and other "Reed rules," such as a ban on filibusters.[96]

Similar changes occurred in the Senate, so much so that James Bryce, a distinguished English observer of American politics, wrote in 1890 that the upper house was "modern, severe, and practical."[97] Forceful leaders, such as Finance Committee chair Nelson Aldrich of Rhode Island and Appropriations Committee chair William B. Allison of Iowa, imposed rules on the Senate that resembled the controls "Czar" Reed had established in the House. As a result, Republicans were able to bring a previously unknown degree of partisan and procedural discipline to the Senate during Harrison's tenure as president.

The Harrison administration, then, was one in which Congress and the party organizations reigned supreme. A burst of important legislation during the first two years of Harrison's term, including the protectionist McKinley Tariff of 1890, marked the rise of party discipline and congressional efficiency.[98] As such, the Harrison years offered a striking example of Whig-style, Congress-centered party government.[99]

Like the Whigs, and in contrast to conservative Democrats such as Cleveland, the Republicans had long wanted to use the federal government to help achieve their economic objectives. The Republican program originally had been formulated to challenge the slave economy of the South. It now was

Grover Cleveland, president from 1885 to 1889, lost the 1888 election but regained the White House in the election of 1892. He is the only president to have served two nonconsecutive terms.

dedicated to advancing industrial capitalism. Expressing support for private property with an ardor shared by the radicals of his party, Lincoln had said in 1863 that "property is the fruit of labor; . . . a positive good in the world. That some should be rich shows that others may become rich, and hence is just encouragement to industry and enterprise."[100] With the end of Reconstruction, the Republicans' dedication to industrial capitalism became their party's central doctrine, embodied not only in protective tariffs but also in banking policies that provided capital for industrial development. The close identification of the Republican Party with business was, on the whole, politically advantageous because a majority of voters supported protective tariffs and publicly financed internal improvements.[101]

Yet developments were under way in the country that soon would render the Whig-Republican model of party government obsolete. Massive social and economic changes were increasing the scale and complexity of American life, producing jarring economic dislocations and intense political conflicts. In the face of change, pressures mounted for a more expansive national government and more systematic administration of public policy. The limited nineteenth-century polity, which could accommodate decentralized party organizations, political patronage, and a dominant Congress, began to give way to a new style of governance that required consistent and forceful presidential leadership. The rise of intensely ideological political conflict in the 1890s, culminating in the presidential election between Democrat William Jennings Bryan and Republican William McKinley in 1896, as well as the growing role of the United States in world affairs, which accelerated with the Spanish-American War of 1898, set the stage for a significant transformation of the presidency.

GROVER CLEVELAND'S SECOND TERM

The effects of the new political order on the presidency first became apparent during the second term of Grover Cleveland, who defeated Harrison in their 1892 rematch. Cleveland owed his political comeback to the failure of the pro-business Republicans to assuage rising public concerns about the economic dislocations caused by corporate industrialization. The Republican-controlled Fifty-first Congress (1889–1891) had passed the Sherman Antitrust Act to reduce the concentration of economic power in massive corporations. Responding to inflationist pressures to increase the money supply, it also enacted the Sherman Silver Purchase Act to expand the coinage of silver. But this Congress proved to be one of the most unpopular in history. In 1890 the Democrats swept the House elections by a huge majority—the prelude, as it turned out, to Cleveland's victory two years later. When Cleveland and the Democrats were themselves blindsided by a severe economic depression in 1893, the Republicans regained control of Congress in the midterm elections of 1894.

The Democrats' political defeat came soon after Cleveland responded to the Panic of 1893 by wielding the powers of the presidency more vigorously than any president since Lincoln. His call of a special session of Congress to secure repeal of the Sherman Silver Purchase Act represented effective leadership in defense of a gold-based currency. Yet this dramatic departure from the hands-off approach to legislation that Cleveland had pursued during his first term cost him the support of his party. He not only alienated inflationist, pro-silver Democrats such as Nebraska representative William Jennings Bryan, but also offended congressional leaders, who resented the president's aggressive new posture on domestic policy.

The Democratic Party's repudiation of Cleveland was reinforced by his intervention in the Pullman strike against the railroads in 1894. Without consulting John P. Altgeld, the Democratic governor of Illinois, Cleveland dispatched troops to Chicago, supposedly to protect federal property and "to remove obstructions to the United States mails," but actually to restore order by ending the strike. This action infuriated Altgeld, who proclaimed in a telegram to Cleveland that "to absolutely ignore a local government in matters of this kind, when the local government is ready to furnish assistance needed, and is amply able to enforce the law, not only insults the people of this State by imputing to them an inability to govern themselves or an unwillingness to enforce the law, but is in violation of a basic principle of our institutions." Unimpressed, Cleveland replied that "in this hour of danger and public distress, discussion may well give way to active efforts on the part of all in authority to restore obedience to law and to protect life and property."[102]

Cleveland's intervention in the Pullman strike elaborated on precedents set by Lincoln during the Civil War by extending the concept of executive emergency powers beyond the bounds of war and domestic insurrection. The president's use of federal troops was all the more significant because he possessed neither explicit statutory authority for his actions nor an invitation to act from state and local officials.[103] Nevertheless, the president's conduct received a strong endorsement from the Supreme Court in the case of *In re Debs*, which upheld the arrest of Eugene V. Debs and other strike leaders for conspiring to obstruct the mails.[104] The Court ruled that the president was authorized to act by the Constitution's charge to "take Care that the Laws be faithfully executed" and therefore to pursue virtually any measure to protect the peace of the United States.[105]

Although conservative Democrats praised Cleveland, laborers and their supporters turned against the president and his party.[106] The rift between Democrats and industrial workers widened in 1896 when the party's national convention nominated Bryan, a rural Nebraskan, for president and fought the campaign mainly on the issue of "free silver"—that is, Bryan's proposal to inflate the currency by basing it on silver as well as gold. Cleveland was surprised and angered by the convention's repudiation of his leadership. He made no effort to hide his satisfaction when the Republicans won the general election on a platform championing the gold standard. Bryan blamed Cleveland's pro-business policies for his defeat, but his farmers-based campaign had failed to offer a viable alternative to them.

Cleveland's conservatism, especially during his second term, severely damaged his party's political popularity. But so did city dwellers' suspicion of Bryan.[107] Ohio governor William McKinley won a solid victory against Bryan by capturing the industrial states of the Northeast and Midwest. Bryan's support came principally from farmers in the South and West. Although the popular vote was close (McKinley garnered 51 percent to Bryan's 47 percent), the Republican won the Electoral College decisively, capturing 271 votes to the Democrat's 176. Because the industrial cities were the fastest-growing part of the country, the heavy losses the Democrats suffered among workers and other urban voters in 1896 precipitated a lasting partisan realignment in favor of the Republicans.[108]

The 1896 election marked an important change in presidential campaigning. Abandoned by many powerful Democrats and yet confident of his oratorical prowess, Bryan became the first candidate for president to tour the country appealing directly for support from the voters. Blessed with a powerful voice and boundless energy, Bryan visited twenty-seven states and gave more than eight hundred speeches. As historian Gil Troy has described Bryan's ground-breaking campaign, "Consuming up to six meals per day, sleeping in snatches, and taking periodic alcohol rubdowns to preserve his strength—though never imbibing—Bryan sang his silvery song. So many people crowded his train that he simply spoke from the rear platform of the last car, and a campaign tradition was born"—the "whistle-stop" campaign through strings of small-town railway stations.[109]

Although McKinley deliberately offered "a safe, traditional, solidly Midwestern contrast to the fire-breathing Bryan," his approach to campaigning was no less innovative.[110] Building on an approach that Harrison had employed on a small scale in 1888, McKinley and his master political strategist, Mark Hanna, mobilized the national Republican Party for a "front porch campaign" in which the candidate greeted delegations of voters at his home in Canton. From mid-June through November, McKinley spoke to more than three hundred crowds totaling 750,000 visitors from thirty states. Although McKinley's front porch speeches were long on platitudes, each event was carefully planned. Shortly before a delegation arrived, a telegram would reach Canton with information about the group's members, political attachments, and home town. By the time the visitors arrived, McKinley was able to greet some of them by name, mention absent family members, and refer to matters of interest in the visitors' communities.[111]

Like Bryan's whistle-stop tour, McKinley's carefully orchestrated front porch campaign foretold the prominence of candidate-centered rather than party-centered campaigns. Some who visited McKinley's home scavenged souvenirs from Canton, including parts of the famous front porch. Others lavished gifts on the Republican candidate, ranging in size from ink stands to bathtubs. "These gifts," Troy notes, "attested to the increased centrality of the candidate and the desire of individuals to cement their bond with him."[112]

THE PRESIDENCY OF WILLIAM MCKINLEY

The dramatic Republican triumph in the 1896 election brought an astute and skillful politician to the White House. McKinley's presidency is often regarded as an uneventful prelude to the vigorous and energetic administration of his successor, Theodore Roosevelt. But, continuing the forceful leadership shown by Cleveland in his second term, McKinley inaugurated important changes in the executive during his first four years. To be sure, McKinley's tenure was highly traditional in some respects. He, like Benjamin Harrison, was a Republican professional who came to the presidency after a long political apprenticeship in Congress. Consequently, McKinley believed that good government could come only through a strong party organization. He also carried into office a deep and abiding respect for congressional primacy.

Unlike Harrison, McKinley did not permit the presidency to decline on his watch. But even though McKinley's legislative leadership was active—indeed, he was the first post–Civil War president to take the political initiative in Washington without arousing the resentment of his party in Congress[113]—it did not advance the cause of presidential power in enduring ways. His style of influence in Congress resembled that of Jefferson, who had quietly used the congressional caucus to enact the Democratic-Republican program. Jefferson's successors were unable to match his legislative influence, thereby demonstrating the limits of congressional government as an instrument for sustained leadership.

The McKinley years were dominated not by legislation, but by war and foreign policy. The president made an enduring mark on the office as commander in chief and as chief diplomat. In 1898 a conflict arose with Spain over the desire of its colony, Cuba, to gain independence. McKinley favored a peaceful resolution, but he ultimately yielded to public opinion, which, aroused by sensationalistic propaganda in the press, strongly favored war. After setting his course in that direction, McKinley exercised a "day by day, and sometimes . . . hour by hour" supervision of the American military effort that laid the foundation for more intense presidential involvement and greater executive control of foreign policy in the future.[114] The hostilities were so brief, the American victory so complete, and, most important, the acquisition of Spanish territory in the Caribbean and Pacific so considerable that no postwar reaction against executive power occurred, as it had after the Civil War. Indeed, Woodrow Wilson admitted in 1900 that his earlier observations about congressional dominance of the presidency were "hopelessly out of date." As Wilson wrote in the preface to the fifteenth printing of his book *Congressional Government*, "Much of the most important change to be noticed is the result of the war with Spain upon the lodgement and exercise of power within our federal system: the greatly increased power and opportunity for constructive statesmanship given the President, by the plunge into international politics and into the administration of distant dependencies, which has been that war's most striking and momentous consequence."[115]

The acquisition of the Philippines and the greater influence over Cuba that accompanied victory in the Spanish-American War broadened the international obligations of the United States in ways that subdued partisan differences. Owning territory in the Pacific also increased the interests of the United States in the Far East. American participation in China during the Boxer uprising of 1900 and the McKinley administration's successful insistence on the Open Door trade policy in Asia reinforced the public's view that the country now occupied a new and prominent position in world affairs.[116] The Spanish-American War was a landmark in the constitutional development of the executive.[117] As McKinley said to his secretary, "I can no longer be called the President of a party; I am now the President of the whole people."[118]

McKinley's tenure marked an important transformation of the presidency. To be sure, his administration gave only a hint of what was soon to come in the way of vigorous presidential leadership. Committed to a limited role for the national government in domestic affairs, McKinley did not offer or endorse a program to deal with trusts, labor, the civil service, or race relations. But with respect to certain policies, especially trade and foreign affairs, McKinley did seek to influence public opinion about bills and treaties before Congress. Most notably, in speeches and written messages he strongly defended America's right to seize the Philippines from the defeated Spanish.[119] Following in the tradition of the nineteenth-century executive, McKinley said of American policy toward the Philippines that "the whole subject is now with Congress, and Congress is the voice, the conscience, and the judgment of the American people."[120] Nevertheless, the rhetorical effort he devoted to his party's position on the annexation was another sign that the presidency was undergoing important changes in its relationship to Congress and public opinion.

Significantly, Congress did not enact legislation to determine the civil rights and political status of America's first colony. Instead, the legislative branch authorized the executive to create a military government in the Philippines, which enabled McKinley, a wartime president, to capitalize on a foreign crisis and its aftermath to expand the powers of the presidency beyond the limits that had constrained his predecessors.[121]

NOTES

1. "The Wade-Davis Manifesto," August 5, 1864, in *History of American Presidential Elections, 1789–1968,* 4 vols., ed. Arthur M. Schlesinger Jr. and Fred L. Israel (New York: Chelsea, 1971), 2:1195–6.

2. Wilfred E. Binkley, *President and Congress* (New York: Knopf, 1947), 128. For a discussion of the Reconstruction controversy that Johnson inherited, see Albert Castel, *The Presidency of Andrew Johnson* (Lawrence: University Press of Kansas, 1979), 17–20.

3. Quoted in Castel, *Presidency of Andrew Johnson,* 20.

4. Nicole Mellow and Jeffrey Tulis, "Andrew Johnson and the Politics of Failure," in *Formative Acts: Reckoning with Agency in American Politics,* ed. Stephen Skowronek and Matthew Glassman (Philadelphia: University of Pennsylvania Press, 2007).

5. Castel, *Presidency of Andrew Johnson,* 31.

6. LaWanda Cox, *Lincoln and Black Freedom* (Columbia: University of South Carolina Press, 1981), 38.

7. Howard cited in Morton Keller, *Affairs of State: Public Life in Late Nineteenth Century America* (Cambridge: Harvard University Press, 1977), 208–209.

8. Charles Sumner, *The Promises of the Declaration of Independence: Eulogy on Abraham Lincoln* (Boston: Ticknor and Fields, 1865), 56; Roy P. Basler, ed., *The Collected Works of Abraham Lincoln,* 9 vols. (New Brunswick: Rutgers University Press, 1953), 8:403–404; and Cox, *Lincoln and Black Freedom,* 38.

9. On the struggle between Johnson and Congress over civil rights legislation, see Castel, *Presidency of Andrew Johnson,* 68–76; and Binkley, *President and Congress,* 134–135.

10. Johnson cited in LaWanda Cox and John H. Cox, *Politics, Principle, and Prejudice: 1865–1866* (New York: Free Press, 1963), 153.

11. Quoted in David O. Stewart, *Impeached: The Trial of President Andrew Johnson and the Fight for Lincoln's Legacy* (New York: Simon and Schuster, 2009), 16.

12. Cox and Cox, *Principles and Prejudice,* 153.

13. Quoted in Jean Edward Smith, *Grant* (New York: Simon and Schuster, 2001), 426.

14. Castel, *Presidency of Andrew Johnson,* 29–30.

15. Mellow and Tulis, "Andrew Johnson and the Politics of Failure;" see also Keith Whittington *Constitutional Construction: Divided Powers and Constitutional Meaning* (Cambridge: Harvard University Press, 1999), 114–115, 125.

16. Binkley, *President and Congress*, 136–137.

17. Of this bill, Albert Castel has written, "This was—and still is—the single most dramatic piece of legislation to emerge from Congress. It placed millions of citizens under military rule in peace time, deprived hundreds of thousands of their political rights, and enfranchised a race which the vast majority of Americans at the time considered unqualified to participate in the government process." Castel, *Presidency of Andrew Johnson*, 108.

18. James D. Richardson, ed., *Messages and Papers of the Presidents*, 20 vols. (Washington, D.C.: Bureau of National Literature, 1911), 5:3700.

19. Ibid., 5:3870.

20. Binkley, *President and Congress*, 138.

21. Eric McKitrick, "Party Politics and the Union and Confederate War Efforts," in *The American Party Systems: Stages of Development*, 2nd ed., ed. William Nisbet Chambers and Walter Dean Burnham (New York: Oxford University Press, 1975); A. James Reichley, *The Life of the Parties: A History of American Political Parties* (New York: Free Press, 1992), 129–134.

22. Castel, *Presidency of Andrew Johnson*, 68–70; and Stewart, *Impeached*, 52.

23. Ibid., 70.

24. For a discussion of how the constitutional and political constraints on popular rhetoric during the nineteenth century contributed to Johnson's problems with Congress, see Jeffrey Tulis, *The Rhetorical Presidency* (Princeton: Princeton University Press, 1987), 87–93.

25. David Miller Dewitt, *The Impeachment and Trial of Andrew Johnson* (Madison: State Historical Society of Wisconsin, 1967), 123–124.

26. "Articles of Impeachment against Andrew Johnson," in *The Evolving Presidency: Landmark Documents, 1787–2010*, 4th ed. ed. Michael Nelson (Washington, D.C.: CQ Press, 2012), 108–118.

27. *New York Times*, March 5, 1868, 4.

28. The "improper rhetoric" charge had strong support in the House, passing by a vote of 87–41. *New York Times*, March 4, 1868, 1.

29. *New York Times*, March 31, 1868, 8.

30. The act actually provided that department heads hold office "for and during the term of the President by whom they were appointed" unless removed by the president with the Senate's approval. Stanton originally had been appointed by President Lincoln.

31. Stewart, *Impeached*, 164.

32. Dewitt, *Impeachment and Trial of Andrew Johnson*, 517–518.

33. Quoted in ibid., 579.

34. Gideon Welles, *Diary of Gideon Welles*, 3 vols. (Boston: Houghton Mifflin, 1911), 3:560.

35. William M. Goldsmith, ed., *Growth of Presidential Power: A Documented History*, 3 vols. (New York: Chelsea, 1974), 2:1102.

36. Binkley, *President and Congress*, 147.

37. George F. Hoar, *Autobiography of Seventy Years*, 2 vols. (New York: Scribner's, 1903), 2:46.

38. Keller, *Affairs of State*, 108.

39. Frank J. Scaturro, *President Grant Reconsidered* (Lanham, Md.: University Press of America, 1998), 60.

40. Ibid.

41. Jean Edward Smith, *Grant* (New York: Simon and Schuster, 2001), 582.

42. Keller, *Affairs of State*, 95.

43. Geoffrey Perret, *Ulysses S. Grant: Soldier and President* (New York: Random House, 1997), 393–400.

44. Smith, *Grant*, 501.

45. Perret, *Ulysses S. Grant*, 409–410; Keller, *Affairs of State*, 96–97.

46. Smith, *Grant*, 512.

47. Ibid., chap. 18. On the ever more difficult challenges Grant faced in Reconstruction, see Nicholas Lemann, *Redemption: The Last Battle of the Civil War* (New York: Farrar, Straus and Giroux, 2006).

48. Perret, *Ulysses S. Grant*, 416.

49. Leonard D. White, *The Republican Era, 1869–1901: A Study in Administrative History* (New York: Macmillan, 1958), 372–376.

50. Perret, *Ulysses S. Grant*, 44. See also Scaturro, *President Grant Reconsidered*, 36–40.

51. President Ulysses S. Grant, "First Statement to Congress on Civil Service Reform," December 5, 1870, in Goldsmith, *Growth of Presidential Power*, 2:986.

52. Keller, *Affairs of State*, 266–268.

53. James D. Richardson, ed., *Messages and Papers of the Presidents*, 20 vols. (New York: Bureau of National Literature, 1897), 9:4254–5; White, *Republican Era*, 281–287.

54. Binkley, *President and Congress*, 161.

55. The scandals that afflicted the federal government during the Grant administration were, as historian Samuel Eliot Morison has written, merely "the summit of a pyramid of corruption in the Northern states." In New York City, William Marcy ("Boss") Tweed built a Democratic machine, known as Tammany Hall, that stole an estimated $100 million from the city treasury. A similar ring, which operated at the state level under the auspices of the Republican Party (but included some Democrats as well), perpetrated systematic fraud in canal construction, with estimated losses to the state of nearly $1 million. Morison, *The Oxford History of the American People*, 3 vols. (New York: New American Library, 1972), 3:36.

56. The Republicans' willingness to end Reconstruction reflected their disillusionment with the program's disorder and corruption. When the Republican governor of Mississippi telegraphed for federal troops to protect black voters from white "rifle clubs" during the state election of 1875, the attorney general rejected his request, declaring that "the whole public are tired out with these annual outbreaks in the South, and the great majority are now ready to condemn any interference on the part of the government. . . . [P]reserve the peace by the forces in your own state, and let the country see that the citizens of Mississippi, who are largely Republican [that is, the black majority], have the courage to *fight* for their rights and to destroy the bloody ruffians who murder the innocent and unoffending freedmen." Edwards Pierrepoint, cited in Richard Nelson Current, *Those Terrible Carpetbaggers* (New York: Oxford University Press, 1988), 321–322 (emphasis in original).

In the so-called Revolution of 1875, white Mississippians drove blacks from the polls and regained control of the state government. Reconstruction therefore was already collapsing before the Compromise of 1877. Hayes's withdrawal of federal troops from the South only accelerated the demise of Radical Republican policies. James M. McPherson, *Abraham Lincoln and the Second American Revolution* (New York: Oxford University Press, 1991), 148.

57. C. Van Woodward, *Reunion and Reaction* (Boston: Little Brown, 1966), 4, 9–10; Michael Holt, *By One Vote: The Disputed Presidential Election of 1876* (Lawrence: University Press of Kansas, 2008), 246–247.

58. Keller, *Affairs of State*, 258.

59. Quoted in ibid.

60. Ibid.

61. Rutherford B. Hayes, "Inaugural Address," March 5, 1877, in Richardson, *Messages and Papers of the Presidents*, 1911 ed., 6:4396; Hayes's Letter of Acceptance (July 8, 1876), in White, *Republican Era*, 287.

62. Binkley, *President and Congress*, 155.

63. Charles Richard Williams, ed., *Diary and Letters of Rutherford B. Hayes*, 5 vols. (Columbus: Ohio State Archeological and Historical Society, 1924), 3:430 (April 22, 1877).

64. Ibid., 3:454 (December 12, 1877).

65. Ari Hoogenboom, *Outlawing the Spoils* (Urbana: University of Illinois Press, 1961), 156.

66. Binkley, *President and Congress,* 157.

67. President Rutherford B. Hayes, "Letter to General E. A. Merritt Defining Criteria for Appointments to the New York Customhouse," February 4, 1879, in Goldsmith, *Growth of Presidential Power,* 2:1112.

68. Ibid., 2:1113.

69. Williams, *Diary and Letters of Rutherford B. Hayes,* 3:612–613 (July 14, 1880).

70. The Stalwarts labeled Blaine's followers "Half-breeds," implying that they were deficient in Republican loyalty. In reality, the partisanship of the Blaine wing, although it paid lip service to civil service reform, was just as strong as that of the Stalwarts.

71. Keller, *Affairs of State,* 266–268.

72. John A. Garraty, *The New Commonwealth, 1877–1890* (New York: Harper and Row, 1968), 268–273.

73. Binkley, *President and Congress,* 158–159, 172; Theodore Clarke Smith, *The Life and Letters of James Abram Garfield,* 2 vols. (New Haven: Yale University Press, 1925), 2:1103–4.

74. Quoted in Smith, *Life and Letters,* 2:1109.

75. Quoted in Thomas C. Reeves, *Gentleman Boss: The Life of Chester Alan Arthur* (New York: Knopf, 1975), 227.

76. Smith, *Life and Letters,* 2:1127.

77. Garraty, *New Commonwealth,* 273; White, *Republican Era,* 34–35; Binkley, *President and Congress,* 159–160.

78. Kenneth D. Ackerman, *Dark Horse: The Surprising Election and Political Murder of President James A. Garfield* (New York: Carroll and Graf, 2003), 348–380.

79. Williams, *Diary and Letters of Rutherford B. Hayes,* 4:23.

80. Garraty, *New Commonwealth,* 276.

81. Ackerman, *Dark Horse,* 435.

82. White, *Republican Era,* 346.

83. Ibid., 393; see also 301–302.

84. Keller, *Affairs of State,* 556–558.

85. Horace Samuel Merrill, *Bourbon Democracy of the Middle West, 1865–1896* (Baton Rouge: Louisiana State University Press, 1953), vii–viii. For a view of Cleveland that disputes the characterization of him as a Bourbon Democrat, see Richard E. Welch Jr., *The Presidencies of Grover Cleveland* (Lawrence: University Press of Kansas, 1988).

86. Matthew Crenson and Benjamin Ginsberg, *Presidential Power: Unchecked and Unbalanced* (New York: Norton, 2007).

87. Garraty, *New Commonwealth,* 287; Keller, *Affairs of State,* 546.

88. President Grover Cleveland, "Message to the Senate on the President's Power of Removal and Suspension," March 1, 1886, in Goldsmith, *Growth of Presidential Power,* 2:1121.

89. Grover Cleveland, *Presidential Problems* (New York: Century, 1904), 76.

90. White, *Republican Era,* 38.

91. Ibid., 66.

92. Garraty, *New Commonwealth,* 295.

93. Woodrow Wilson, *Congressional Government* Boston: Houghton Mifflin, 1885; Meridian Books, 1956), 31.

94. John Sherman, *Recollections of Forty Years in the House, Senate and Cabinet* (Chicago: Werner Company, 1895), 2:1032.

95. Garraty, *New Commonwealth,* 305.

96. Keller, *Affairs of State,* 302–303.

97. James Bryce, *The American Commonwealth,* 2 vols. (London: Macmillan, 1891), 1:115.

98. Keller, *Affairs of State,* 306.

99. Binkley, *President and Congress,* 182.

100. Lincoln cited in Reichley, *Life of the Parties,* 128.

101. Ibid., 155.

102. Gov. John P. Altgeld, "Telegram to President Grover Cleveland on the Use of Federal Troops in Illinois," July 5, 1894; and President Grover Cleveland, "Telegram to Governor John P. Altgeld on the Use of Federal Troops in Illinois," July 6, 1894, in Goldsmith, *Growth of Presidential Powers,* 2:1155 and 2:1157, respectively.

103. Scott C. James, "The Evolution of the Presidency: Between the Promise and the Fear," in *The Executive Branch,* ed. Joel D. Aberbach and Mark Peterson (New York: Oxford University Press, 2005), 16–17.

104. *In re Debs,* 158 U.S. 564 (1895).

105. Edward S. Corwin, *The President: Office and Powers, 1787–1957,* 4th ed. (New York: New York University Press, 1957), 134.

106. J. Rogers Hollingsworth, *The Whirligig of Politics: The Democracy of Cleveland and Bryan* (Chicago: University of Chicago Press, 1963), 24–25.

107. Welch, *Presidencies of Grover Cleveland,* 211–212.

108. Garraty, *New Commonwealth,* 306.

109. Gil Troy, *See How They Ran: The Changing Role of the Presidential Candidate,* rev. and exp. ed. (Cambridge: Harvard University Press, 1996), 104.

110. Ibid., 105–106.

111. Crenson and Ginsberg, *Presidential Power.*

112. Troy, *See How They Ran,* 106.

113. Binkley, *President and Congress,* 189.

114. Lewis L. Gould, *The Presidency of William McKinley* (Lawrence: University Press of Kansas, 1980), 93.

115. Wilson, *Congressional Government,* 22–23.

116. The Open Door policy was announced in September 1899 by Secretary of State John Hay. It asked the major powers that had imperialistic designs on Asia—notably, France, Germany, Great Britain, Italy, Japan, and Russia—to agree to support freedom of trade in the region. Great Britain was the only nation to accept Hay's proposals fully; the others agreed, but with reservations. Hay, however, chose to interpret their replies as acceptances and announced the Open Door policy to the world.

117. Binkley, *President and Congress,* 191.

118. Quoted in Charles S. Olcott, *William McKinley,* 2 vols. (Boston: Houghton Mifflin, 1916), 2:296.

119. Mel Laracey, *Presidents and the People: The Partisan Story of Going Public* (College Station: Texas A&M Press, 2002), 134–138.

120. William McKinley speech in Chariton, Iowa, October 13, 1898, McKinley Papers, Library of Congress, Washington, D.C. See also Tulis, *Rhetorical Presidency,* 87.

121. Lewis L. Gould, *The Modern American Presidency* (Lawrence: University Press of Kansas, 2003), 13.

CHAPTER 8

Progressive Politics and Executive Power: The Presidencies of Theodore Roosevelt, William Howard Taft, and Woodrow Wilson

D uring the last three decades of the nineteenth century, major changes in American society placed greater burdens on the national govern- ment, and particularly on the presidency.[1] The population of the United States doubled between 1870 and 1900. Urbanization and immigra- tion increased at extraordinary rates. These changes were accompanied by a shift in business activity from local, small-scale manufacturing and commerce to large-scale factory production and mammoth national corporations. The technological breakthroughs and the frenzied search for new markets and new sources of capital that were associated with rapid industrialization caused unprecedented economic growth. From 1863 to 1899 the index of manufac- turing production rose by more than 700 percent. But dynamic growth also generated a wide range of problems that seriously challenged the capacity of the American political system to respond.

For one thing, social and political values were being sacrificed in the unchecked pursuit of economic progress and industrial development. The greater concentration of wealth at the turn of the century yielded giant "trusts" that according to reformers constituted uncontrolled and irresponsi- ble bastions of power. These combinations aroused fears that growing corpo- rate influence might jeopardize equality of opportunity for individuals to climb the economic ladder. Moreover, many people believed that the great business interests had captured and corrupted the men and methods of gov- ernment for their own profit.

The first wave of protest against the financial exploitation and political cor- ruption that industrial growth unleashed was the agrarian Populist revolt, which culminated in William Jennings Bryan's failed campaign for the presi- dency in 1896. The Progressive era took shape as populism collapsed as a political movement. Yet it was a period of urban and middle-class protest against many of the same forces of expanding industrialization and unre- strained finance capitalism that had vexed the Populists. Because progressivism represented the fastest-growing segments of the population, it had a major influence on the nation. As Richard Hofstadter has noted, the Progressive movement "enlarged and redirected" agrarian discontent, bringing about industrial reforms and changes in government institutions that "affected in a striking way . . . the whole tone of American political life."[2]

One effect of the progressive transformation was a modified understanding of the responsibilities of the national government. American society had long been committed to individualism and limited government. But as Elihu Root, who served in Theodore Roosevelt's cabinet, argued in an address to the New York Bar Association in 1912:

> The relations between the employer and employed, between the owners of aggregated capital and the units of organized labor, between the small producer, the small trader, the consumer, and the great transporting and manufacturing and distributing agencies, all present new questions for the solution of which the old reliance upon the free action of individual wills appears quite inadequate. And in many directions the intervention of that organized control which we call government seems necessary to produce the same result of justice and right conduct which obtained through the attrition of individuals before the conditions arose.[3]

The Progressive movement helped foster important changes in the presidency. Although the executive office had developed significantly in the hands of strong leaders such as George Washington, Thomas Jefferson, Andrew Jackson, and Abraham Lincoln, most of the roles and powers of the president remained tightly restricted until the twentieth century. "Congressional government" was the prevailing theme of late nineteenth-century politics in America. The presidencies of Grover Cleveland and William McKinley suggested that a more forceful style of presidential leadership might be emerging, but they did not alter fundamentally the longstanding pattern of legislative dominance.

More than anyone else, Theodore Roosevelt changed that pattern. Dedicated to the progressive concept of active, executive-centered government, he advocated and practiced a vigorous form of leadership that broadly extended the reach of presidential influence. In his aggressive pursuit of a policy agenda and, especially, in his active courting of public opinion, TR (the first president to be known by his initials) recast the presidency in both foreign and domestic affairs, charting the path for future presidents, such as Woodrow Wilson and TR's cousin, Franklin D. Roosevelt, to follow.

THEODORE ROOSEVELT AND THE EXPANSION OF EXECUTIVE POWER

On September 6, 1901, President McKinley was shot by an anarchist while attending the Pan-American Exposition in Buffalo, New York. When

McKinley died on September 14, Vice President Roosevelt became president. Soon after, he announced that he would continue McKinley's policies and cabinet, disregarding the warning of friends that by doing so he would seem but a "pale copy" of the late president. "If a man is fit to be President," TR wrote in his autobiography, "he will speedily so impress himself in the office that the policies pursued will be his anyhow, and he will not have to bother as to whether he is changing them or not."[4]

The prospect of Roosevelt impressing himself on the executive office greatly troubled the party politicians who dominated national politics at the beginning of the twentieth century. The conservative leaders of the Republican Party feared that the young president (at forty-two he remains the youngest person ever to assume the office) was not to be trusted. Throughout his political career, including his tenure as governor of New York, Roosevelt had been known as a progressive and impetuous leader who lived uneasily with his party's patronage practices and pro-business policies. During Roosevelt's two terms as governor, he was so troublesome to the state's party regulars that they took pains to remove him from their midst by securing his nomination for vice president in 1900.

"Anything can happen now that that damn cowboy is in the White House," complained Mark Hanna, the chair of the Republican National Committee, when his friend McKinley died. Conservatives now wished that they had heeded the Republican chair who, when presented with the suggestion that Roosevelt be chosen as McKinley's running mate, complained, "Don't you realize that there's only one life between that madman and the White House?"[5]

Roosevelt's plainspoken and unconventional style aside, he was not the "madman" that Hanna feared. TR was no enemy to business or party interests. Like most progressive reformers, he accepted the new industrial order, wanting only to curb its worst excesses through government regulation. Without moderate reform, Roosevelt believed, the connection between citizens and their leaders that was the essence of republican government would be dangerously attenuated. "Sweeping attacks upon all property, upon all men of means, without regard to whether they do well or ill, would sound the death knell of the Republic," he wrote, "and such attacks become inevitable if decent citizens permit rich men whose lives are corrupt and evil to domineer in swollen pride, unchecked and unhindered, over the destinies of the country."[6]

THEODORE ROOSEVELT'S CONCEPT OF PRESIDENTIAL POWER

In both foreign and domestic affairs, Samuel and Dorothy Rosenman have written, "Roosevelt extended executive authority to the furthest limit permitted in peacetime by the Constitution—if not further."[7] Believing that the traditional restraints on presidential power had subjected the American political system to capture by "special interests," Roosevelt proclaimed that the president is "a steward of the people bound actively and affirmatively to do all he could for the people, and not content himself with the negative merit of keeping his talents undamaged in a napkin."[8]

Roosevelt's confidence that the president possessed a special mandate from the people made him a conscious disciple of Andrew Jackson. Unlike Jackson, however, Roosevelt wanted to join popular leadership to a greater sense of national purpose that entailed an unprecedented expansion of the government's responsibility to secure the nation's social and economic welfare. As he explained many years later:

> My belief was that it was not only his [the president's] right but his duty to do any-thing that the needs of the nation demanded unless action was forbidden by the Constitution or by the laws. Under this interpretation of executive power I did and caused to be done many things not previously done by the President and the heads of the departments. I did not usurp power, but I did greatly broaden the use of executive power. In other words, I acted for the public welfare, I acted for the com-mon well-being of all our people, wherever and in whatever manner was necessary, unless prevented by direct constitutional or legislative provision.[9]

In important respects, Roosevelt's exposition of executive power drew on the defense of a broad authority for the president that Alexander Hamilton had articulated in 1793 under the pen name "Pacificus." "The general doctrine of our Constitution," Hamilton argued, "is that the executive power of the nation is vested in the President; subject only to the exceptions and qualifications which are expressed in the instrument."[10] Washington, Jackson, and Lincoln had taken an expansive view of the president's authority in moments of national crisis. Roosevelt was the first chief executive to embrace the Hamiltonian position as the proper recipe for the conduct of government in ordinary times.

TR's acceptance of Hamiltonian principles certainly was not complete. Hamilton supported an energetic executive because he thought that it would curb, not abet, popular influence. In contrast, Roosevelt expressed and embodied the Progressives' aspiration to establish the president as an agent of social and economic reform. He looked with favor on the statesmanship of Lincoln, whose uncompromising defense of the Union served the "high pur-pose" of advancing equality of opportunity. "Men who understand and prac-tice the deep underlying philosophy of the Lincoln school of American political thought," wrote TR, "are necessarily Hamiltonian in their belief in a strong and efficient National Government and Jeffersonian in their belief in the people as the ultimate authority, and in the welfare of the people as the end of government."[11]

Theodore Roosevelt, far left on stand, ushered in the "rhetorical presidency"—the use of popular rhetoric as a principal technique of presidential leadership.

FROM THEORY TO PRACTICE: THE BEGINNING OF THE RHETORICAL PRESIDENCY

Roosevelt's determination to use the presidency to serve the public interest, as he understood it, brought about a number of significant changes in the conduct of the executive office. Arguably, the most important of these changes was to advance the president's role as the leader of public opinion. Roosevelt ushered in the "rhetorical presidency"—that is, the use of popular rhetoric as a principal technique of presidential leadership.[12] TR was an irrepressible, if not always an eloquent, speaker, and is said to have been the first to describe the presidency as a "bully pulpit."[13]

The rise of the rhetorical presidency signified a dramatic transformation of the founding constitutional theory and early history of the presidency. The framers of the Constitution had wanted to proscribe popular presidential leadership. As Andrew Johnson's ill-fated "Swing around the Circle" had confirmed, during the nineteenth century efforts by the president to rouse the public to support him or his policies were considered illegitimate, a form of demagogy that was beneath the dignity of the office. Strong democratic leaders of the nineteenth century, such as Jefferson, Jackson, and Lincoln, had sought to establish closer ties with the people, but they had worked through their party organizations and the press to do so. William McKinley frequently spoke to public audiences on policy matters, but especially in domestic affairs, he took "only small, hesitant steps against the boundaries of the nineteenth century norms and expectations" that discouraged direct popular leadership.[14] Roosevelt's "stewardship" theory of the executive required the president to forge more personal ties with the public. Accordingly, at times TR appealed directly to the people to bring pressure to bear on members of Congress who were reluctant to support his policies.

Much of Roosevelt's legislative program was designed, as TR put it, to "subordinate the big corporation to the public welfare."[15] But the Republican Party in Congress was led by conservatives—notably Nelson Aldrich of Rhode Island and Eugene Hale of Maine in the Senate and Speaker Joseph Cannon of Illinois in the House—who distrusted anything that smacked of progressivism. Roosevelt sided with the "Old Guard" (they also were called the "stand patters") in their support of the gold standard and their recognition of the need, after the Spanish-American War, for a strong American presence in world affairs. Domestic policy was different. As TR later wrote of his relationship with the Republican Old Guard, "Gradually I was forced to abandon the effort to persuade them to come my way, and then I achieved results only by appealing over the heads of the Senate and House leaders to the people, who were the masters of both of us."[16]

Perhaps the most important product of Roosevelt's popular appeals was the Hepburn Act of 1906. The act enhanced the power of the Interstate Commerce Commission (ICC) to regulate railroad shipping rates and enforce its regulations.[17] Previous laws had failed to prevent the largest corporations from receiving better and cheaper rail service than the smaller shippers.[18] Faced with enormous fixed costs—such as the interest they paid on huge bonded debts and the depreciation on their large and expensive equipment—the railroads were able to meet their overhead only by acceding to the demands for price breaks by massive corporations such as Standard Oil Company, Armour Company, and American Sugar Refining Company.

Determined to remedy these conditions, Roosevelt proposed that Congress strengthen the ICC's regulatory power. In his annual message to Congress in December 1904, Roosevelt urged legislators to draft a law that would forbid railroads to provide large shippers with discriminatory rebates and empower the ICC to impose ceilings on railroad rates in order "to keep the highways of commerce open to all on equal terms."[19]

The president's proposal was received favorably by the House of Representatives, which quickly passed railroad rate legislation in early 1905. But the proposal ran into trouble in the Senate, where the conservative Interstate Commerce Committee conducted extensive public hearings, mostly for the purpose of receiving opposing testimony from railroad executives. The committee managed to consume enough time to prevent the Senate from considering the bill before the summer recess.

The railroads' strategy was shrewd. "The House was the only one of the two [congressional] bodies elected directly by the people," one contemporary observer wrote, "and was therefore regarded contemptuously by the railroads and conservatives generally as reflecting the mob; while the Senate, being elected by state legislators, was regarded as a safe city of refuge."[20] Senators were not elected by the people until the Seventeenth Amendment was enacted in 1913.

But Roosevelt was shrewder still. As the Senate hearings proceeded, the president left Washington for a long vacation in the West. Speculation arose that he had given up on rate regulation.[21] In truth, Roosevelt's swing through the Midwest and Southwest in April and May of 1905 turned out to be a campaign trip for the Hepburn bill.

The president fired his first rhetorical blast in Chicago where, speaking before the Iroquois Republican Club on May 10, he called on the federal government to "take an increasing control over corporations." The first step, Roosevelt argued, "should be the adoption of a law conferring upon one executive body the power of increased supervision and regulation of the great corporations engaged primarily in interstate commerce of the railroads." The ICC should have "ironclad" powers to set rates, which could be suspended by the courts only if they proved to be confiscatory.[22] This speech and similar addresses in Dallas, San Antonio, and Denver received extensive and favorable coverage in the press.

Roosevelt's campaign resumed with a speaking tour of the Southwest in the early fall of 1905. The pressure of public opinion eventually overcame Senate resistance to the Hepburn Act. Secretary of War William Howard Taft told his brother that the president of the Rock Island line had admitted to him that senators he had counted on for "allegiance," although privately still opposed to the Hepburn bill, were yielding because the president had so "roused the people that it was impossible for the Senate to stand against the popular demand."[23] After all, the state legislatures that elected the Senate were themselves elected by the people.

When Congress reconvened in 1906, the House once again passed the railroad law quickly, in early February. This time, however, on May 18 the Senate also passed Roosevelt's bill. Only three senators voted against it.

THEODORE ROOSEVELT AND THE PRESS

Roosevelt's remarkable victory in the battle for the Hepburn Act was helped considerably by the press. He was the first president to recognize fully the press's value as a medium to communicate with the people and the first to understand that journalistic support had to be pursued actively and continually. It was TR's good fortune that his presidency coincided with the development of mass-circulation newspapers and popular magazines. At the beginning of the twentieth century, "cheap and rapid manufacture made possible and even necessary a *mass* market beyond the confines of one faction, party, or following." The age of the "party organ" style of journalism was over.[24]

One group of journalists, whom Roosevelt, borrowing from Bunyan's *Pilgrim's Progress,* labeled the "muckrakers," occupied an especially important place in early twentieth-century politics.[25] They wrote mainly for new and low-priced national magazines such as *McClure's,* a fifteen-cent monthly whose influence on public opinion was almost the equal of Roosevelt's. The president's term for these writers evoked their relentless efforts to expose corruption in the relationship between government and business. According to a writer in the August 1905 issue of the *Atlantic Monthly,* "They expose in countless pages the sordid and depressing rottenness of our politics; the hopeless apathy of our good citizens; the remorseless corruption of our great financiers and business men, who are bribing our legislatures, swindling the public with fraudulent stock schemes, adulterating our food, speculating with trust funds, combining in great monopolies to oppress and destroy small competitors and raise prices."[26]

Roosevelt's grasp of the political potential of the new media was especially apparent in his use of the mass-circulation magazines. Despite his concern that the muckrakers, by fixing their gaze exclusively on the "vile and debasing," neglected the achievements of society's constructive elements, he took advantage of their success at bringing to light many of the evils he wanted to attack. Partly by inspiring intimates in the press to write articles, and partly through the force of his own personality and ideas, TR "kept the pages of the popular magazines glowing with support" for his crusades.[27]

Roosevelt also made good use of the bully pulpit and press in the struggle over the Pure Food and Drug Act, which made it unlawful to manufacture adulterated or mislabeled food and drugs, and the Meat Inspection Act, a response to the gruesome conditions of the meat-packing houses, which were depicted in Upton Sinclair's sensational novel *The Jungle.* Like the Hepburn Act, these laws were enacted in 1906. TR's triumph in the matters of rate regulation, food and drug marketing, and meat inspection signaled a change in the executive. The president's most important political relationship soon would be with the people rather than with his party or with Congress. But Roosevelt also believed that to maintain the constitutional system of government, a balance must exist between presidential initiative and congressional deliberation. Accordingly, even as he insisted that the modern president had to assume a more prominent place in public affairs than his nineteenth-century predecessors, TR worked assiduously to win support in Congress by cooperating with Republican leaders in the Senate and the House whenever possible.

In fighting for the Hepburn Act, for example, Roosevelt directed his energies not only to the podium but also, more craftily, to the halls of Congress. He feigned interest in a bill to reduce tariffs and then traded his abandonment of that controversial proposal for congressional support of his more important objective, railroad regulation. In late November 1904 the president sent Speaker Cannon, "that arch priest of protection," a draft of a special message to Congress urging tariff revision. Shortly thereafter, in a "concession" to Cannon, Roosevelt delivered his annual message, in which nothing was said of the tariff. As TR wrote to a friend, "On the interstate commerce business, which I regard as a principle, I shall fight. On the tariff, which I regard as a matter of expediency, I shall endeavor to get the best results I can, but I shall not break with my party."[28]

At the other end of Pennsylvania Avenue, Cannon, who was already on record against regulating the railroads, gave the Hepburn Act a clear track. When conservatives rose to fight the bill, Roosevelt revived the tariff issue until they retreated. Old Guard Republicans regarded high tariffs as the linchpin of their party's program of industrial development. Ultimately, therefore, they acquiesced to TR's desire for railroad regulation to preserve what they regarded as vital: the hallowed protection of American industry from foreign competition.

Thus in leading Congress, Roosevelt artfully deployed the resources of office and person. He succeeded in part because of his remarkable political gifts and his willingness to compromise to attain his major objectives. But the president's commitment to constitutional government, especially his appreciation of Congress, also was significant. Roosevelt ended his speaking tours before Congress took up the Hepburn bill. He did not speak directly to the people on the eve of crucial votes, nor did he attack members of Congress during the debate. As historian John Morton Blum has written, "Roosevelt's impressive ability to work within the structure of government, like his facility in managing the party, depended less on his arresting manner than on his appreciation of the institutions that shaped American political life."[29]

ROOSEVELT AND POLICY LEADERSHIP

Roosevelt's ability to get a considerable part of his program enacted in the absence of a national crisis and in spite of the tepid support—and sometimes the outright resistance—of his party indicated that a new era of presidential leadership had arrived. From now on, government action would be much more likely to bear the president's personal stamp than in the past.

Roosevelt called his program the "Square Deal." Its theme was that the proper function of government is to maintain a "just balance" between management and labor, between producer and consumer, and between extremists on both sides of the political divide.[30] What made TR's proclamation of the

Square Deal important in the development of the modern presidency was that it invoked principles of fairness as he, rather than his party or Congress, understood them. Several of his successors would define their administrations in similar terms: Woodrow Wilson's New Freedom, Franklin D. Roosevelt's New Deal, Harry S. Truman's Fair Deal, John F. Kennedy's New Frontier, Lyndon B. Johnson's Great Society, George W. Bush's Ownership Society. The effort, nonexistent in the nineteenth century but routine after Roosevelt, to attach a catchy phrase to the president's programmatic philosophy was symptomatic of a new style of leadership in which the executive took the lead in formulating public policy.[31]

Significantly, Roosevelt first used the phrase "Square Deal" during the 1904 presidential campaign to describe his vigorous intervention two years before in a nationwide coal strike. Rather than follow the example of Grover Cleveland, who had sent troops to break up the Pullman strike of 1894, Roosevelt called representatives of the coal industry and the miners to the White House to ask both sides to agree, in patriotic regard for the health and welfare of the nation, to accept binding arbitration. John Mitchell, the head of the United Mine Workers, appreciated the recognition that Roosevelt conferred on the union by calling the conference and pledged to cooperate fully with the president.

When coal industry leaders balked at Roosevelt's proposal, even lecturing the president about the folly of "negotiating with the fomenters of anarchy," TR prepared to take more drastic action. If he could not persuade management to accept arbitration voluntarily, he would appoint a settlement board without their consent and arrange for the governor of Pennsylvania to request federal assistance to keep the peace. Roosevelt also intended to have federal troops "seize the mines and run them as a receiver for the government."

By previous constitutional interpretation, dating back to the *Debs* decision in 1894, the president clearly had the authority to send soldiers into a state to ensure that the national government could exercise its authorized powers, such as to deliver the mail. But nowhere did the Constitution even hint at, must less specify, the president's right to seize and operate private property. As it happened, such an action did not prove necessary: an agreement was reached to end the strike in October 1902, and a five-member commission, appointed by the president, arbitrated the points at issue between the miners and the coal industry. Yet Roosevelt's willingness to act exemplified his style as the "steward of the people."[32] Dedicated to expanding the national government to guarantee a "just balance" between rival claimants in society, Roosevelt became the first president in history to recognize the rights of labor in an industrial dispute.[33] As historian George W. Mowry has written, "By both his actions and threats Roosevelt had moved the government away from its traditional position of isolation from such economic struggles. The government, by precedent if not by law, had become a third force and partner in major labor disputes."[34]

Roosevelt also expanded the executive's responsibility to manage the nation's natural resources. Although the practice of setting aside nationally owned timberlands had begun with Benjamin Harrison and was continued by Grover Cleveland, TR was the first president to adopt a comprehensive con-servation program. Hosting the first national conference on conservation, TR lamented the irresponsibility with which Americans had abused the nation's water, forests, and other natural resources. The time had come, he said, to formulate a national philosophy of conservation: "It is the chief material ques-tion that confronts us, second only . . . to the great moral questions."[35] Credit for this policy belongs in part to Roosevelt's young Forest Service director, Gifford Pinchot, who inspired the president to make conservation a leading cause of his administration. TR did so with his usual energy. By appealing to public opinion and by setting aside 43 million acres of national forest from excessive commercial exploitation, Roosevelt made conservation a national movement.[36]

By 1908, however, Congress had blocked further progress in the conserva-tion program. Farmers, grazers, and water power interests in the West, which was home to most woodlands, won legislation to transfer from the president to Congress the authority to establish national forests in several western states. Tensions reached a breaking point when Roosevelt and Pinchot prepared a "midnight forests" proclamation that protected 16 million acres just before the bill went into effect.

Roosevelt's proclamation not only drove a wedge between the executive and legislative branches, but also failed to resolve the dispute about the appro-priate federal role in managing natural resources. Congress exacted a measure of revenge against the president by killing two important conservation com-missions that Roosevelt created in 1908, the National Country Life Commis-sion and the Inland Waterways Commission. Nevertheless, on leaving office TR could claim, with considerable justification, that the movement to protect the nation's natural resources was one of his administration's most important accomplishments.[37]

Roosevelt's use of executive power in the cause of conservation revealed his understanding that the stewardship theory of the presidency empowered him to act without the explicit authority of the Congress, or even in the face of legislative opposition, when he deemed such action to be in the public interest. Although Lincoln's executive orders during the Civil War offer the most pow-erful historical examples of presidential prerogative, TR was the first president to make extensive use of executive orders to advance his domestic policy. He issued 1,091 executive orders during his two terms, rivaling the 1,259 orders issued by all presidents in the previous 111 years.[38] These orders to various executive departments and agencies were issued under the president's legal and constitutional authority, as broadly interpreted by Roosevelt himself.

ROOSEVELT AND CIVIL SERVICE REFORM

Roosevelt sought not only to expand presidential power but also to professionalize administration and thereby prepare the executive branch for its growing responsibilities. He believed that only steady, nonpartisan administration, not the dictates of the bench or the give and take of partisan and sectional politics in Congress, could properly direct the development of the United States as an industrial society.[39]

In Roosevelt's view, an orderly system of administrative control required a career civil service. To this end, the president prevailed on Congress early in his tenure to increase the Civil Service Commission's budget so that it could effectively supervise the hiring of federal employees.[40] He also extended the coverage of the merit system for hiring, promotion, and tenure almost to the limit of the Pendleton Act. By the time TR left office, about 60 percent of the civil service was included in the merit system, even as the federal workforce expanded from 275,000 in 1901 to 365,000 in 1909.

Most important, the Roosevelt administration marked the dividing line between the traditional Jacksonian commitment to party patronage and the modern recognition that nonpolitical administration was a necessary tool of governance. Americans have never carried the idea of a civil service outside politics to the same lengths as the British. But by the end of the Roosevelt presidency, merit had begun to supplant spoils. Presidential leadership, previously dependent on patronage-seeking state and local party machines, now required careful attention to competent administrative management, sometimes to foster economy and efficiency and sometimes to bolster the power of the increasingly active federal government. In the absence of a large, professional White House staff, Roosevelt showed that a president committed to policy innovation could accomplish a great deal by mobilizing the energies of talented civil servants.[41]

THE PRESIDENT AS WORLD LEADER

Roosevelt's innovative and pathbreaking activism in domestic affairs, important as it was, pales by comparison with his conduct of foreign policy. In domestic matters TR led boldly, but mostly in the interest of moderate reform. In foreign affairs, he believed that new conditions dictated a more decisive break with the past, without interference from Congress. Although the president's authority to initiate foreign policy and to negotiate treaties had become settled practice during the nineteenth century, Roosevelt also asserted primacy in the execution of such matters, even when congressional support was lacking.

TR's executive theory had a policy purpose. The acquisition of territories from Spain gave the United States a new position in world affairs after 1898. Roosevelt was determined to build on this position and make the United States a global power. "Whether we desire it or not," the president told Congress on December 3, 1901, in his first annual message, "we must henceforth recognize that we have international duties no less than international rights."[42] Just as many Progressives believed that laissez-faire must give way to a greater sense of national purpose in domestic affairs, they also urged that Americans' nineteenth-century preference for international isolation be abandoned in favor of the country's "manifest destiny." This doctrine proclaimed for the United States a natural right to expand as much as was necessary for freedom and republican government to survive and prosper. Progressives couched the doctrine in ethical terms, arguing that to extend American territory and influence was not imperialism but altruism.

Practical considerations also prompted a more active foreign policy. The expansion of American territory in the Pacific and the Caribbean required a new emphasis on the Pacific basin, a dominant military presence in Central and South America, and an isthmus canal so that naval power could be maneuvered efficiently between the Atlantic and Pacific Oceans.

THE PANAMA CANAL. Roosevelt considered the canal to be especially important. In his first annual message to Congress, he said, "No single great material work which remains to be undertaken on this continent is of such consequence to the American people as the building of a canal across the isthmus connecting North and South America."[43] Panama, the site eventually chosen for this project, belonged to Colombia. But, to Roosevelt's surprise and embarrassment, Colombia was not willing to allow the United States to build the canal on the president's terms. A complicated round of diplomacy and intrigue ensued that revealed some of the most important characteristics of the Roosevelt era in American foreign policy.

On January 22, 1903, Secretary of State John Hay negotiated and signed a treaty with the Colombian minister in Washington, Thomas Herran. Under the Hay-Herran Treaty, the New Panama Canal Company would construct the canal in return for $40 million from the United States, $10 million from Colombia, and an annual subsidy of $250,000. Complete sovereignty in the three-mile canal zone, however, would belong to the United States in perpetuity. These conditions were rejected by the Colombian leader, José Manuel Marroquin, and by the Colombian Senate. The Colombian government proposed several alternative agreements to the United States, all of which would have provided better financial terms for Colombia and recognized its sovereignty in the canal zone.

Instead of negotiating further, Roosevelt applied direct diplomatic pressure to Colombia by threatening to turn to Nicaragua as an alternative site for the canal. When that tactic failed, Roosevelt took what he wanted by force. He gave tacit support to the efforts of investors in the New Panama Canal Company to foment a secessionist revolution in Panama. He also indicated clearly that if a Panamanian revolution was unsuccessful, he would take possession of the isthmus anyway. Standing on the tenuous legal foundation of an 1846 treaty with Colombia in which both countries had agreed to guarantee the right of transit across the isthmus, TR was prepared to recommend to Congress that the United States occupy the canal zone.[44] When Mark Hanna, a leading Republican senator, was informed of this plan, he counseled patience. The president's reply typified his preference for decisive action: "I think it is well worth considering whether we had not better warn those cat-rabbits that great though our patience has been, it can be exhausted. . . . I feel, that we are certainly justified in morals and . . . justified in law, under the treaty of 1846, in interfering summarily and saying that the canal is to be built and that they shall not stop it."[45]

A successful revolution in Panama made it unnecessary for Roosevelt to attack Colombia, but the president did aid the revolution when it broke out on November 3, 1903. He made sure that an American warship, the U.S.S. *Nashville,* was docked in Colón on the eve of the uprising. During the subsequent fighting, the ship prevented Colombian troops from reinforcing their outnumbered brethren in Panama. On November 6, Panama became an independent nation. The United States granted it diplomatic recognition within ninety minutes. Soon after, the Panamanian government signed a treaty to transfer canal rights to the United States in return for the $10 million Roosevelt originally offered to Colombia.

Roosevelt's course of action in the canal zone controversy applied his stewardship theory of the presidency to foreign policy. He was not reluctant to act quickly and independently, even when congressional support was weak and the legal foundation for his maneuvers was uncertain. Roosevelt treated constitutional criticisms of his policy with disdain. "At different stages of the affair," he wrote, "believers in a do-nothing policy denounced me as having 'usurped authority'—which meant, that when nobody else could or would exercise efficient authority, I exercised it."[46]

Roosevelt built the canal, proclaiming some years later that doing so was "by far the most important action that I took in foreign affairs during the time I was President."[47] Still, Colombia felt cheated and outraged and continued to press its claims for justice. Later, over former president Roosevelt's protest, apologies were extended to Colombia by the Wilson and Harding administrations, along with an indemnity award of $25 million. Even then, as William M. Goldsmith has written, "The wounds inflicted in this incident were never really eradicated."[48]

THE ROOSEVELT COROLLARY. The taking of the canal zone signified a new policy toward Latin America that entailed greater presidential power in foreign affairs. The basic plan for a new Caribbean and Latin American policy had been worked out by McKinley and his secretary of state, John Hay. But under Roosevelt, the new policy was greatly extended. It also was given a precision it previously had lacked.[49]

The desire to dominate the Caribbean was buttressed by Roosevelt's concern that many of the independent republics of Central and South America had weak governments with chaotic finances. Venezuela, for example, had borrowed heavily from Europe, and then refused to pay its debt. In December 1902 England, Germany, and Italy undertook to blockade Venezuela in an effort to extract payment. Germany threatened to take possession of certain Venezuelan cities or customhouses. Roosevelt persuaded all the parties to submit their cases to the Hague Court, an international tribunal, but not before he increased the strength of the fleet in the Caribbean and described to the Germans how vulnerable they were to American naval power in the western Atlantic.[50]

Later, when a similar problem developed in Santo Domingo, Roosevelt decided to modify significantly the Monroe Doctrine. After a corrupt dictatorship left Santo Domingo bankrupt and unable to pay its debts, a revolution erupted. In the early winter of 1903, France, Germany, and Italy threatened to intervene. By the end of the year, a German naval squadron was rumored to be sailing across the Atlantic to protect German interests in the Caribbean. Roosevelt, facing an election in 1904, responded cautiously at first. Before long, however, he formulated a policy proclaiming that it was the duty of the United States to intervene in the affairs of Latin American countries whose governments the president judged to have acted wrongly or been rendered impotent by their leaders' mismanagement. The president announced this policy in December 1904 in his annual message to Congress. The Roosevelt Corollary to the Monroe Doctrine, as it became known, was a bold statement of future American conduct toward the debt-ridden, unstable governments of Latin America:

> All that this country desires is to see the neighboring countries stable, orderly and prosperous. . . . If a nation shows that it knows how to act with reasonable efficiency and decency in social and political matters, if it keeps order and pays its obligations, it need fear no interference by the United States. Chronic wrongdoing, or an impotence which results in a general loosening of the ties of civilized society may in America, as elsewhere, ultimately require intervention by some civilized nation, and in the western hemisphere the adherence of the United States to the Monroe Doctrine may force the United States, however reluctantly, in flagrant cases of such wrongdoing or impotence, to the exercise of an international police power.[51]

The Roosevelt Corollary altered the Monroe Doctrine—which had denied to Europeans the right to intervene in the Western Hemisphere—by sanctioning U.S. intervention in Latin American affairs.[52] Less than a month after

Roosevelt announced the new policy, worsening conditions in Santo Domingo spurred him to translate words into action. In early 1905, confronted on one side by a nation that faced bankruptcy and on the other by European powers demanding satisfaction for their accounts, Roosevelt imposed a treaty on Santo Domingo to establish an American financial protectorate over the island. The arrangement required the United States to prevent any European interference with the Dominican customhouses and authorized it to collect the custom revenues. Forty-five percent of the revenue was then turned over to the Dominican government, and 55 percent was deposited in a New York account for the benefit of the creditors.

Roosevelt sent the treaty to the Senate, declaring that to ratify it promptly would forestall more drastic action in the future. But the Senate did not share the president's sense of urgency and failed to vote on the treaty. Democrats and some Republicans believed that diplomacy was an inherently misguided approach to commercial matters. Resentment of the president's unilateral development of a new foreign policy also contributed to the Senate's unwillingness to support him. Roosevelt responded by implementing the Dominican protectorate as an executive agreement, which further antagonized his congressional critics. The executive agreement was two years old before the Senate finally acquiesced and approved the treaty with minor modifications in 1907.

The eventual success of Roosevelt's Caribbean policy strengthened both his personal political position and, ultimately, the institutional status of the presidency in foreign affairs. "The Constitution did not explicitly give me power to bring about the necessary agreement with Santo Domingo," Roosevelt crowed in 1913. "But, the Constitution did not forbid my doing what I did. I put the agreement into effect, and I continued its execution for two years before the Senate acted; and I would have continued it until the end of my term, if necessary, without any action by Congress."[53]

THE RUSSO-JAPANESE WAR. The extent of Roosevelt's departure from nineteenth-century isolationism was revealed by his bold initiatives in Asia, especially his unprecedented intervention in the conflict between Russia and Japan over China in 1905.

After Russia moved troops into China in 1902—an action that, among other things, threatened the Americans' Open Door policy of free trade in China—Japan staged a devastating surprise attack on the Russian fleet anchored at Port Arthur.[54] Because Roosevelt considered Russia the greater imperialist threat in Asia, his sympathies lay with Japan. Indeed, the president fortified the Japanese with secret verbal assurances that the United States would support them if any of the European powers supported Russia. This extraordinary commitment also included an agreement by Japan to recognize American jurisdiction in the Philippines in return for Roosevelt's recognition of Japan's claim to Korea.[55] For the first time, a president committed the United States to possible future military action, as well as to the recognition of one nation's claim on another nation's territory and sovereignty, without consulting the Senate.

Roosevelt's audacious diplomacy ended in triumph. Although the president favored Japan as a counterweight to Russia's designs on China, he feared that too great a Japanese victory might endanger the peace of the entire Pacific region. When fighting in the Russo-Japanese War tilted dramatically in Japan's favor, Roosevelt arranged, without the knowledge of the cabinet, Congress, or even most of the State Department, for Russian and Japanese diplomats to meet in a secret peace conference at Portsmouth, New Hampshire. There the president managed, through what historian George Mowry has called "patient, tactful and brilliant diplomacy," to bring about the Peace of Portsmouth in September 1905. The agreement achieved a balance of power in Asia that satisfied the interests not just of the warring nations but also, because the Open Door policy was preserved, of the United States.[56] For his efforts, TR became the first American to win the Nobel Peace Prize. Roosevelt's policy advanced further in 1907 when, again without consulting Congress or the cabinet, he sent the American naval battle fleet on a cruise around the world, a daring maneuver that roused public support for an expanded navy and demonstrated to the Japanese the intent and ability of the United States to protect its interests in Asia.[57]

Although Roosevelt's approach to international affairs was singularly successful, he did not complete the task of establishing the United States as a global power. His effort to expand both America's role in the world and the president's responsibility in foreign affairs took place without sustained and serious discussion with either the American people or their representatives in Congress. As Goldsmith has written, "Theodore Roosevelt set the stage for the American President to play a world historical role that in many instances successive Presidents were neither capable of nor inclined to follow, nor were the American people prepared to support it."[58]

THE TROUBLED PRESIDENCY OF WILLIAM HOWARD TAFT

Roosevelt was a remarkably popular and influential president. Indeed, had TR decided to stand for another term in 1908, he almost certainly would have been renominated and reelected. "Few informed people in the country," Mowry has written, "seriously doubted the outcome of the election if Roosevelt decided to stand again."[59]

The decision to step down was not easy, but Roosevelt had promised in November 1904 that he would not run four years later. The three-and-a-half years he had served after succeeding to the presidency in 1901 constituted his first term, Roosevelt stated on election night, and the term to which he had just been elected would be his second. Because he considered the custom that limited presidents to two terms to be a wise one, he would not be "a candidate for or accept another nomination."[60]

Roosevelt's decision not to go back on his promise in 1908, even though he clearly was tempted to do so, revealed his commitment to the traditions and institutions of constitutional government. TR believed strongly that the powers of the president needed to be expanded for the benefit, even the survival, of the nation. But he also knew that democracy would be poorly served if too much power were concentrated in one person. "It is not well that the strong executive should be a perpetual executive," he wrote to British historian George Trevelyan.[61] Roosevelt's "act of abnegation," Mowry has claimed, "was among his greatest contributions to his country."[62]

Self-denial, however, did not prevent Roosevelt from selecting William Howard Taft, his secretary of war and closest adviser during the second term, as his successor. Nor did it stop him from "throwing his hat in the ring" in 1912 to challenge Taft's renomination, charging that his friend and fellow Republican had betrayed the progressive principles he was elected to uphold. Indeed, it is fair to say that Taft spent his entire four years as president uncomfortably in the shadow of Theodore Roosevelt.

Taft sincerely intended to carry on the policies of the Roosevelt administration, and he had more success in doing so than Roosevelt gave him credit for. But Taft was disinclined by philosophy and ill-suited by personality, to imitate TR's stewardship of the presidency. As historian Paolo E. Coletta has written, "While under the spell of the dynamic Roosevelt, Taft had appeared to be a progressive cut from the full Roosevelt cloth. With Roosevelt gone he would return to his basic conservative self and thereby earn the odium of the progressives as one who had deserted the cause."[63]

In the wake of Roosevelt's presidency, Taft seemed an anachronism. Although never saying so publicly, Taft disapproved of TR's theory that it is the president's duty "to do anything that the needs of the nation demand, unless such action is forbidden by the Constitution or the law." Taft's philosophy of executive power, like the understanding that had prevailed during most of the nineteenth century, eschewed a broad interpretation of the president's discretionary authority. As he wrote several years after leaving office, "The true view of the executive function . . . is that the President can exercise no power which cannot be reasonably or fairly traced to some specific grant of power or justly implied or included within such express grant as necessary and proper to its exercise. Such specific grant must be either in the Constitution or in an act of Congress passed in pursuance thereof. There is no undefined residuum of power which he can exercise because it seems to be in the public interest."[64]

William Howard Taft, right, who served as Theodore Roosevelt's secretary of war, was elected president in 1908. Although he intended to continue the policies of the Roosevelt administration, he was accused by progressives of betraying their principles.

Because he construed executive power narrowly, Taft denied that being president required him to exercise either popular or policy leadership. He rejected the notion that he bore a special mandate from the people and refused to make any serious effort to court public opinion or the press. One Taft aide, who also had served with Roosevelt, noted the stark contrast between the two presidents in their relations with reporters and editors: "Mr. Roosevelt understood the necessity of guiding the press to suit one's ends; President Taft has no conception of the press as an adjunct to his office."[65]

Taft also rejected the kind of speaking tours TR had used to publicize his programs and bring public pressure to bear on Congress. Such rhetorical efforts as Taft made came at the urging of his aides, and were undertaken with considerable reluctance. "The Taft administration," Elmer Cornwell has noted, "represented a hiatus in the presidential leadership of opinion, if not actually a retrograde step."[66]

TAFT AND CONGRESS

Taft dedicated himself to a legislative program that would institutionalize in law the reforms that Roosevelt's vigorous and independent executive actions had begun. "Mr. Roosevelt's function has been to preach a crusade against certain evils. He has aroused the people to demand reform," Taft wrote on February 23, 1909, just before his inauguration. "It becomes my business to put such reform into legal execution by the suggestion of certain amendments of the statute in the governmental machinery."[67]

One important area in which the direction of reform remained unclear was conservation. Roosevelt aggressively asserted that the president is the steward of the public welfare in protecting the nation's natural resources. But his "midnight forests" proclamation had led to a bitter confrontation with Congress. When TR left office, the dispute about the national government's responsibility to manage natural resources was still unresolved.

In an effort to make conservation policy a matter of settled law, Taft prepared a special message in 1909 that asked Congress to pass a bill to codify

Roosevelt's executive order. As he wrote to the California conservationist William Kent, "We have a government of limited power under the Constitution, and we have got to work out our problems on the basis of law."[68] But Taft's passive view of presidential power shaped his pursuit of the bill in Congress. He had serious misgivings about interfering in the legislative process. "I have no disposition," Taft told Senate majority leader Aldrich, "to exert any other influence than that which it is my function under the Constitution to exercise."[69]

Although Taft's position on conservation prevailed, his broader policy of forbearance in legislative matters cost him dearly, especially during the early days of his presidency. Indeed, his passivity led people to think that he agreed with the conservative Republican leadership in Congress, which caused an irrevocable split to occur between Taft and the Roosevelt administration alumni whom he had allowed to stay in office. TR's fellow conservationist Gifford Pinchot felt that Taft's unwillingness to act in the absence of explicit authority crippled progressive policies. "It was as though a sharp sword had been succeeded by a roll of paper, legal size," Pinchot later wrote.[70]

Taft's modest definition of executive power governed his relations with Congress even on those policies that were closest to his heart. Of all the campaign promises he made in 1908, Taft was probably the most serious about wanting to reduce tariff rates. He considered the Republican Party's longstanding attachment to protectionism unfortunate. Roosevelt had done nothing about tariffs except to use them as a bargaining chip in his fight for the Hepburn Act. Yet Taft stood by passively in 1910 as Congress watered down his proposal to alter the nation's protectionist trade policies. Senate Republicans added more than eight hundred amendments to the strong tariff reform bill that the House passed. Taft simply signed the version that came out of the House-Senate conference committee, even though it closely resembled the Senate bill.[71]

Faced with a similar challenge, Roosevelt almost certainly would have abandoned his party's congressional leadership, worked to build a bipartisan progressive coalition, and, if all else failed, appealed to the people. Taft, however, remained loyal to the Republican organization, even claiming that the Payne-Aldrich tariff, as the final legislation was called, was "really a good bill." Progressive Republicans, most of whom bucked the president and their party's leaders to vote against the measure, disagreed.[72] Taft lost the political initiative and, as Coletta has noted, "the wounds inflicted in the acrid tariff debate never healed."[73]

Public deference to Congress, by itself, did not foreclose the possibility of an impressive legislative record. Jefferson and McKinley had worked quietly within party councils to exercise considerable influence in Congress. But Taft lacked the political skill to provide this kind of leadership. His pre-presidential experience was confined to judicial and administrative offices, leaving him relatively unversed in public and legislative politics.[74]

Taft also suffered from changing political conditions. The Republican Party was more divided than ever between its increasingly stubborn conservative, pro-business majority and its large and growing progressive minority, which was bent on reform. The outbreak of virtual civil war in the GOP began with a progressive revolt in the House of Representatives. Unwilling to tolerate any longer the conservative policies and arbitrary leadership of Speaker Cannon, Republican insurgents led by Rep. George Norris of Nebraska united with Democrats in March 1910 to strip the Speakership of most of its powers. No longer would the Speaker control the members' committee assignments or the strategically important Rules Committee, which set the House's legislative agenda. Even the Speaker's constitutional role as presiding officer was hemmed in by new rules that limited his discretionary authority.

The weakening of the party leadership, long a bulwark of congressional government, ultimately hastened the transfer of power from Congress to the White House that had first become noticeable during Roosevelt's presidency. The same progressive revolt that reduced the Speaker's power in the House also undermined the foundations of party discipline in the Senate, depriving its leaders of their control of legislative deliberations. Power in both houses of Congress devolved to the committees, especially the committee chairs, who became specialized, autonomous barons of legislation.

Unable to obtain reform from a fractious Congress, the American people demanded that the president provide strong leadership in both congressional and party matters. Governor-elect Woodrow Wilson of New Jersey described the situation well when he said on November 5, 1910, "If I were to sum up all the criticisms that have been made of the gentleman who is now President of the United States, I could express them all in this: The American people are disappointed because he has not led them. . . . They clearly long for someone to put the pressure of the opinion of all the people of the United States upon Congress."[75]

Taft, his narrow construction of executive power notwithstanding, was sensitive to the new public demands. Very late in his term, he suggested that the executive and legislative branches be brought closer by giving cabinet members nonvoting seats in Congress. He also endorsed a presidential commission's call for the president to bind the various departments and agencies to a comprehensive budget. Led by a noted authority on public administration, Frederick Cleveland, the Taft-appointed Commission on Economy and Efficiency argued that the absence of presidential leadership in fiscal matters encouraged wasteful and irresponsible spending by the federal government.[76] Leaving budgetary estimates to the departments and agencies also undermined the chief executive's constitutional obligation to oversee the activities of the executive branch. The Cleveland commission argued that the budget "is the only effective means whereby the Executive may get before the country a comprehensive program with respect to which the legislator must assume responsibility either for action or inaction." Embracing the commission's recommendations, Taft submitted the first executive budget in 1913, just before he left office.[77]

Taft's proposals to strengthen the executive were ignored by Congress. But they revealed that even he had come to recognize that Roosevelt's dynamic leadership and the changing character of the country had placed more responsibility in the presidency than during the nineteenth century.

THE ELECTION OF 1910

Ironically, Taft's most dramatic assertion of presidential leadership proved to be his political undoing. In the 1910 congressional primaries, the president tried to purge several progressives from the Republican Party. Taft had criticized Roosevelt for meddling in the legislative process. Yet Taft's intervention in his party's nominating process marked an unprecedented effort by a president to influence congressional support for his legislative program.

Taft had tried first to mediate between the badly divided factions of his party. But the progressives' opposition to the president's legislative program, especially the Payne-Aldrich tariff, provoked him to join the conservatives' effort to influence the 1910 primary elections. Although Taft took no public position in these contests, he distributed government patronage on the basis of loyalty to his administration's program.

Taft's aggressive, albeit surreptitious, intervention in the primaries was manifestly unsuccessful. Not only were almost all of the progressive Republicans whom he opposed renominated, but their reformist allies defeated conservative incumbents in several other primaries. In the wake of these reversals came the great disaster of the November elections. In 1910, for the first time in sixteen years, the Democrats took control of the House of Representatives. Republicans retained a majority in the Senate, but their control was nominal. Progressive Republican senators now held the balance of power between the regular Republicans and the Democrats.

Taft's purge campaign revealed not just the limits of his personal influence, but also the imposing institutional obstacles to party discipline in national politics. To be sure, the decline of the party leadership's influence in Congress required more assertive presidential efforts to bring together the elected branches of the government. But Taft's approach to this problem, the purge campaign, was undertaken in concert with a Republican Old Guard that was steadily losing ground throughout the country. Nor were the American people ready to support an executive assault on their own, locally elected members of Congress.

PROGRESSIVE POLITICS AND THE ELECTIONS OF 1912

After the Republicans lost control of the House in the 1910 elections, it became apparent that Taft probably would not be reelected. The elections weakened the Republican Party. Across the country and in Congress, Democratic progressives were elected, most of them unattached to William Jennings Bryan, the fiery rural Populist who had led the party to defeat in the 1896, 1900, and 1908 presidential campaigns.

Among the newly elected progressive Democrats was Gov. Woodrow Wilson of New Jersey, a former political science professor and president of Princeton University. Two years later, after a long deadlock, the Democratic national convention nominated him for president on the forty-sixth ballot. The nomination was secured when Bryan, in a symbolic passing of the torch, threw his full support to Wilson in hopes of thwarting the Democratic Party's conservative eastern business interests. Although James Beauchamp "Champ" Clark, the moderate progressive Speaker of the House, had won the votes of a majority of delegates (a sure path to obtaining the required two-thirds at every Democratic convention since 1844) on the tenth ballot, his support from controversial northern party bosses like Tammany Hall's Charles Murphy eventually hurt him. Furious that Clark had joined forces with the "reactionary element of the party," Bryan switched his allegiance from the Speaker to Wilson, a critical turning of the tide that led to Wilson's nomination. After failing for two decades to offer a program that addressed the challenges of the Progressive era, the Democrats suddenly found themselves led by an articulate and forward-looking scholar-politician, the only academician ever to be elected president. Wilson's victory in 1912 was just the third by a Democrat since the Civil War. Enough other Democrats were swept into Congress with him to give the party solid majorities in both houses of Congress for the first time in more than fifty years.[78]

The Democratic opportunity might not have arisen had the Republicans remained united in 1912. An intraparty progressive revolt against Taft and the Old Guard first gave rise to an insurgent candidacy by Wisconsin senator Robert La Follette, who challenged the president's bid for renomination. When La Follette failed to draw much support outside the Midwest, Republican progressives turned to Theodore Roosevelt. On February 21, 1912, TR announced, "My hat is in the ring." Bored by four years of political inactivity and persuaded that his candidacy was indispensable to the progressive cause, Roosevelt abandoned his earlier pledge not to run again for president. That he had declined a "third cup of coffee" in 1908 did not mean that he never intended to drink coffee again, Roosevelt said.[79]

In 1912, for the first time, presidential primaries contributed significantly to the selection of delegates to the national party conventions. Celebrating the right of voters rather than party bosses to choose presidential candidates, Roosevelt publicly challenged Taft to contest the Republican nomination by means of a direct primary in every state. Taft and most party regulars had no interest in embracing such a radical change in the nominating process. But because TR was making the direct primary a *cause célèbre,* many northern state legislatures fought fiercely about whether to enact the proposed reform. In the end, Illinois, Maryland, Massachusetts, Ohio, Pennsylvania, and South Dakota adopted the direct primary. When those six states were added to the seven that already held direct primaries, the result was "a sizeable block of normal Republican states from which a popular referendum could be obtained."[80]

Republican primary voters supported TR in these contests. Of the thirteen states that selected convention delegates in primary elections, Roosevelt carried eleven, accumulating 276 delegates to Taft's 46 and La Follette's 36. Roosevelt even won Taft's home state of Ohio by an almost three-to-two margin.[81] But two-thirds of the national convention's 1,078 delegates were still selected at gatherings dominated by regular state party leaders, who much preferred Taft's stolidity to the frenetic progressivism of Roosevelt. In addition, LaFollette's refusal to withdraw from the race denied Roosevelt the votes of some progressive Republican delegates.

When it became clear at the Republican convention that Roosevelt would not be chosen, he and his followers walked out, reconvening in Chicago on August 5 under the banner of the Progressive Party. Announcing that he felt "as strong as a bull moose" (a simile that the new party adopted as its moniker), Roosevelt delivered a stirring "Confession of Faith" in which he called for "strong national regulation" of interstate corporations; social insurance in times of injury, sickness, unemployment, and old age; and constitutional reforms to establish a "pure democracy." TR's vision of democratic government included the universal adoption of the direct primary, government-led industrial planning, an easier method to amend the Constitution, voter initiatives, binding referenda to restore laws that state courts declared unconstitutional, women's suffrage, and limits on the power of courts to issue labor injunctions. Since leaving the White House, he had moved far beyond the Square Deal to what he called the New Nationalism, embracing a vision of government that preserved his original emphasis on regulating rather than breaking up large industrial corporations while adding a plethora of reforms to democratize the political process and a new role for government that in many ways anticipated the welfare state later associated with his cousin Franklin's New Deal. The national government, Roosevelt wrote, "must inevitably sympathize with the men who have nothing but their wages, with the men who are struggling for a decent life, as opposed to men, however honorable, who are merely fighting for larger profits and autocratic control of big business."[82] TR and his fellow Progressives were certain that voters would put aside their long-standing suspicion of centralized administration if they were convinced they held the reins of power.

Although the Progressive Party was more than a personal vehicle for Roosevelt, his control of it was extraordinary. The Progressive campaign advanced a development foretold by the 1896 Bryan-McKinley contest: the coming of presidential elections conducted less by parties than by individual candidates. Roosevelt's speech to the Progressive Party convention was the first in history by a major presidential candidate, and it elicited a fifty-two-minute standing ovation.[83] His closing words—"We stand at Armageddon, and we battle for the Lord"—roused the delegates to an emotional state that could only be subdued by reverential singing of the "Battle Hymn of the Republic."[84]

The 1912 presidential election was a triumph for the progressive movement, but it sent Wilson, not Roosevelt, to the White House. Like Lincoln, Wilson polled much less than a majority of the national popular vote but won the election easily. The final tally awarded 6.3 million popular votes and 435 electoral votes to Wilson, 4.1 million popular votes and 88 electoral votes (the most ever won by a third party presidential candidate, before or since) to Roosevelt, and 3.5 million popular votes and 8 electoral votes to Taft. Eugene V. Debs collected 900,000 popular votes, the highest total ever for a Socialist Party candidate in a presidential election, but no electoral votes. If progressives Wilson and Roosevelt had not been on the ballot, Debs, whose party had recently elected several hundred local officials bearing the Socialist Party label, undoubtedly would have secured a significantly larger vote.

Above all, the 1912 election was a decisive rejection of the Republican Old Guard. Its candidate, the incumbent Taft, carried only Vermont and Utah. The combined popular vote won by Wilson, Roosevelt, and Debs, each an advocate of progressive policies in one form or another, exceeded 75 percent.[85] The results enabled Wilson to reap the benefits of a reform movement that was cresting just as he entered the White House. The new president seized the opportunity not only to advance progressive social and economic policies, but also to extend the restructuring of executive leadership that Roosevelt had begun.

The Democratic Party's platform, expressing a suspicion of executive power reminiscent of its founder, Thomas Jefferson, called for a constitutional amendment to limit presidents to a single term. But Wilson, impressed by the excitement that TR's "Bull Moose" campaign aroused, quickly disavowed this pledge. As he lamented to Rep. A. Mitchell Palmer of Pennsylvania in February 1913, progressive Democrats "are seeking in every way to extend the power of the people, but in the matter of the Presidency, we fear and distrust the people and seek to bind them hand and foot by rigid constitutional provision." Hoping to deflate support for a one-term limit, Wilson resolved to make the executive office more democratic rather than try to diminish its power.[86]

WOODROW WILSON'S THEORY OF EXECUTIVE LEADERSHIP

Wilson had long wanted to reform radically the principles and institutions of American government in order to ameliorate what he regarded as its disconcerting lack of energy and consistency. In 1879, as a twenty-three-year-old student, Wilson published an article calling for major institutional reforms to establish closer ties between the executive and the legislature. At the time, he believed that this connection could be forged best by enhancing the powers of Congress, the dominant branch of government throughout most of the nineteenth century. Wilson urged the United States to adopt a British-style cabinet system that would concentrate power in an executive board responsible to the legislature. Specifically, he proposed that the Constitution be amended "to give the heads of the Executive departments—the members of the Cabinet—seats in Congress, with the privilege of the initiative in legislation and some part in the unbounded privileges now commanded by the Standing Committees."[87] The president, who in Wilson's view had been rendered virtually useless in the aftermath of the Civil War, would become a figurehead like the British monarch.

Although Wilson never abandoned the idea that checks and balances should be replaced by an American version of parliamentary government, his views about the presidency changed dramatically. In the early 1900s, he argued that the best hope for national leadership now lay in a strong executive.[88] Wilson was influenced by the example of Roosevelt, whose vigorous and independent stewardship demonstrated how powerful even a peacetime president could be. Wilson disagreed strongly with TR about certain institutional and policy matters, but he credited him with charting a new path of presidential leadership. "Whatever else we may think or say of Theodore Roosevelt," Wilson said in 1909, "we must admit he was an aggressive leader. He led Congress—he was not driven by Congress. We may not approve of his methods but we must concede that he made Congress follow him."[89]

Roosevelt's success persuaded Wilson that a new theory of constitutional government was needed to justify and make routine the forceful display of presidential leadership. TR had shown that it was not necessary to amend the Constitution to bring about a closer relationship between the elected branches. Instead, the challenge was to exercise the existing powers of the presidency more fully. "His office," Wilson now said of the president, "is anything he has the sagacity and force to make it."[90] Roosevelt had done much to fulfill the promise of the executive, but Wilson believed that he was too inclined to act in defiance of Congress. The radical excesses of Roosevelt's approach to leadership were confirmed for Wilson by the 1912 election, in which TR championed the right of the people to rule without interference by party organizations. For Wilson, responsible democratic government could not be achieved by direct popular rule, which risked demagogy. A better strategy, Wilson argued, would be to break down the barriers between the president and Congress by making the president a strong party leader. The various components of constitutional government would then work in concert, but without violating the principles and institutions that protect the nation from an unhealthy aggrandizement of executive power.[91]

Because the president is uniquely positioned to lead public opinion and his party, Wilson believed that a talented and energetic executive would encourage thoughtful debates in election campaigns and in the councils of government. Unlike members of Congress, who represent states and localities, the president is the only person nominated by an entire party and elected by the entire nation. "The President represents not so much the party's governing efficiency as its controlling ideals and principles," Wilson wrote. "He is not so much part of its organization as its vital link of connection with the thinking nation. He can dominate his party by being spokesman for the real sentiment and purpose of the country, by giving direction to opinion, by giving the country at once the information and the statements of policy which will enable it to form its judgments alike of parties and men."[92]

Wilson's theory of presidential power required a more comprehensive rethinking of the American constitutional order than did Roosevelt's stewardship model. Although he embraced "pure democracy" as the Progressive Party candidate in 1912, as president TR had accepted the constitutional system of checks and balances, seeking only to revive and modify Hamiltonian nationalism so that the government could address the problems of a modern industrial society. Even when he roused the people to bring pressure to bear on Congress, Roosevelt did so in ways meant to preserve the independence of both branches. His deference to traditional constitutional practices was especially clear in domestic matters. TR campaigned for legislation such as the Hepburn Act only as a last resort and always in a manner that showed respect for congressional deliberations.

Wilson agreed with Roosevelt that the president must direct more attention to national problems. But he also believed that executive leadership would be ineffective or even dangerous if not accompanied by a fundamental change in the government's working arrangements. Such a change would unite the constitutionally separated branches of the government.[93] Most significant, the president's role as party leader would be strengthened. Instead of limiting executive power, as it had during much of the nineteenth century, the party system would be modified so that the president could command Congress's support.

WILSON AND PARTY REFORM

As president, Wilson tried to perfect TR's methods of popular leadership and apply them in a way that would establish him as the leader of Congress and the Democratic Party. Wilson was not completely successful in this endeavor, but his two terms in office did bring about major changes in the presidency.

Wilson's desire to strengthen the president's position within party councils led him to examine closely the presidential nominating process, especially the convention system, which Roosevelt and the Progressives had attacked as boss-dominated and unresponsive to the popular will during the 1912 campaign. The advent of the national conventions, which replaced the congressional caucus near the start of the Jacksonian era, had freed the president to some extent from an undue dependence on Congress. But Wilson charged that because the convention system was founded on patronage-based state and local party organizations, it was ill suited to the modern industrial age. Government in the twentieth century required a sense of purpose that could come only from national and programmatic political parties.[94]

Animated by his understanding of the presidency and the parties, Wilson became a supporter of the presidential primary. In his first annual message to Congress, he urged "the prompt enactment of legislation which will provide for primary elections throughout the country at which the voters of the several parties may choose their nominees for the Presidency without the intervention of nominating conventions."[95] The direct primary, which had been advocated by progressive reformers since the turn of the century, was already being used in many state and local elections. Although Wilson's recommendation to establish a national primary made little headway in Congress, its democratic spirit continued to guide reformers, who fought throughout the twentieth century to weaken the grip of traditional party organizations on the presidency.

THE ART OF POPULAR LEADERSHIP

The national primary proposal was but one manifestation of Wilson's desire to increase the authority of the president and, by doing so, to provide the political system with a greater capacity for change. Wilson also avowed the president's obligation, as the voice of the people, to bring public opinion to bear on Congress. Roosevelt had demonstrated the value of this role but, as Wilson biographer Arthur S. Link has written, "Wilson used it to its fullest advantage and made it inevitable that any future president would be powerful only in so far as he established communication with the people and spoke effectively for them."[96]

In contrast to TR, who regarded popular rhetoric as a method to be used infrequently and only in defense of specific pieces of legislation, Wilson believed that an ongoing effort to inspire the American people was the main ingredient of presidential leadership. His effective use of oratory set a new rhetorical standard. Henceforth presidents would be expected to articulate a vision of the future and guide the nation toward fulfilling it. As Wilson announced in his first inaugural address, "We know our task to be no mere task of politics but a task which shall search us through and through, whether we be able to understand our time and the need of our people, whether we be indeed their spokesmen and interpreters, whether we have the pure heart to comprehend and the rectified will to choose our high course of action."[97]

At his best, Wilson was a spellbinding orator. Although some in Wilson's audience may not have grasped the full meaning of his carefully crafted sentences, there was no mistaking their moral import or the conviction of the man who spoke them. Wilson understood the popular aspirations of his day and was able to translate them into words. In doing so, he explicitly defended and, by example, established the legitimacy of public rhetoric as a principal tool of presidential leadership.

In keeping with his desire to be in close touch with the people, Wilson made enduring innovations in the executive's relationship with the press and with Congress. Unlike Roosevelt, Wilson did not trust reporters and was unwilling to cultivate them personally. He was, however, the first president to have press conferences, which he held frequently during his first two years in office. In a sense, Wilson instituted regular press conferences because he distrusted the Fourth Estate. Less gregarious than Roosevelt, and yet certain that frequent contact with reporters was an essential part of his effort to take the people into his confidence, Wilson found formal press conferences to be an effective forum for his relations with journalists.[98]

Nevertheless, Wilson did not rely solely on the press to communicate his views. The president's preferred devices for public leadership were speeches and formal messages. Wilson began his presidency by reviving the practice abandoned by Jefferson, who believed it resembled too closely the British monarch's annual speech from the throne, of appearing before Congress to deliver important messages, including the annual State of the Union address.

The White House's announcement that Wilson would speak on the issue of tariff reform to the two houses of Congress on April 8, 1913, shocked some legislators. Especially concerned were Democrats who revered the Jeffersonian custom. Sen. John Sharp Williams of Mississippi, an original Wilson supporter, led the uprising, concluding that Wilson's speech "would be the only instance of the breach of the perfectly simple, democratic and American custom of messages in writing which Thomas Jefferson instituted."[99] Williams's hope was in vain: Wilson addressed Congress in person frequently, resuming the practice with his first State of the Union address in December 1913. "As he no doubt foresaw," Elmer E. Cornwell Jr. has written, "this forum would so concentrate public attention as to eliminate the likelihood that the newspapers would either slight or distort his message."[100]

WILSON'S RELATIONS WITH CONGRESS

Appearances before Congress also served Wilson's desire to break down the walls that long had divided the executive from the legislature. Although part of his purpose was to guide public opinion, he found it equally important to establish customs and make symbolic gestures that would strengthen the president's ties to Congress. Wilson began his April 8 address to the somewhat tense legislators by speaking directly to the symbolic purpose of his appearance: "I am very glad indeed to have this opportunity to address the two houses directly and to verify for myself the impression that the President of the United States is a person, not a mere department of government hailing Congress from some isolated island of jealous power, sending messages, not speaking naturally with his own voice—that he is a human being trying to cooperate with other human beings in a common service. After this pleasant experience I shall feel quite normal in all our dealings with one another."[101]

Wilson's precedent-shattering speech was well received by most members of Congress. It launched the first successful campaign for serious tariff reduction—a core Democratic goal that had gone unfulfilled in a Republican era—since before the Civil War. Some of his other innovations were also significant, such as his practice of visiting Capitol Hill to meet personally with legislators while Congress deliberated on an important bill. Wilson followed his dramatic April 1913 address by appearing the next day in the president's room of the Senate to confer with the Finance Committee, which was responsible for tariff legislation. No president since Grant had met with members of a congressional committee in the Capitol. Assessing Wilson's revolutionary approach to congressional relations, his close associate Ray Stannard Baker wrote, "These vigorous innovations occasioned an enormous amount of publicity. The country at large was vastly interested, amused, impressed."[102]

Nothing contributed more to Wilson's leadership of Congress than the control he exerted over House and Senate Democrats. The Democrats were at least as divided between conservatives and progressives as the Republicans. Nevertheless, Wilson decided to work with his party in Congress rather than try to govern with a coalition of progressive Democrats and progressive Republicans, as he might have done. He labored assiduously to formulate a comprehensive legislative program and to establish it as the party plan. He even persuaded the House Democratic caucus to adopt a rule that bound its members to support the administration's policies. Similar discipline was obtained in the traditionally more individualistic Senate, where the Democratic caucus declared that important pieces of legislation such as the tariff bill were party measures and that it was the duty of all Democrats to support them.[103]

Owing to his effective leadership, Wilson was able to drive through Congress the major policies of his 1912 electoral platform, which he heralded as the "New Freedom." The catchphrase expressed Wilson's belief that progressivism, properly understood, was deeply rooted in the traditions of the Democratic Party.

Roosevelt's New Nationalism had accepted the evolution of great corporations as both inevitable and, with strict public regulation of corporate activities by a powerful national government, desirable. In contrast, Wilson wanted to free business competition from monopoly and special privilege, making unnecessary the correspondingly dangerous centralization of regulatory power in Washington. "As to monopolies, which Mr. Roosevelt proposes to legalize and welcome," Wilson remarked during the 1912 campaign, "I know that they are so many cars of juggernaut, and I do not look forward with pleasure to the time when the juggernauts are licensed and driven by commissioners of the United States."[104] As the leader of the Democratic Party, Wilson promised tariff reform, an overhaul of the banking and currency system, and a vigorous antitrust program that would "disentangle" the "colossal community of interest" and restore fair competition to the economy.[105]

To the astonishment of Wilson's friends and enemies alike, Congress approved most elements of the New Freedom agenda in 1913 and 1914. The Underwood Tariff Act became law in October 1913. The Federal Reserve Act, which created the Federal Reserve Board and reconstructed the national banking and currency system, followed in late December. Finally, two statutes were passed in 1914, the Clayton Anti-Trust Act and the Federal Trade Commission Act, to strengthen the government's authority to prevent unfair business competition.

Taken as a whole, Wilson's legislative achievements were remarkable. In contrast with TR, Wilson had turned his fractious party into a disciplined body that provided near-unanimous support for each of his most important measures. In doing so, he enacted programs that many Progressives had been demanding for two decades. The president used the occasion of his 1914 State of the Union address to report proudly to Congress, "Our program of legislation with regard to regulation of business is now virtually complete."[106]

But the New Freedom program was soon compromised by Wilson's own administrative practices, which undermined the implementation of the new laws. Before becoming president, Wilson had often declared his support for the merit system of hiring, promoting, and firing federal employees; at the time of his election he was a vice president of the National Civil Service Reform League. As president-elect, Wilson promised to nominate "progressives—and only progressives" to federal jobs. But to the dismay of the president's reformist supporters, old-style patronage practices dominated his appointments.[107] "The pity is," Secretary of the Navy Josephus Daniels wrote many years later, "that Wilson appointed some who wouldn't recognize a Progressive principle if he met it in the road."[108]

Wilson's approach to appointments was governed by his belief, reluctantly arrived at, that to assault the patronage system would be to undermine party unity and ensure the defeat of his legislative program. The pressure from within his party to employ traditional partisan practices was great. The Democrats had been without federal patronage for sixteen years, ever since Grover Cleveland left office in 1897. The problem was brought to the president's attention by Postmaster General Albert S. Burleson, who largely owed his place in the cabinet to his strong ties with Congress. When Wilson told Burleson at the beginning of his presidency that appointments were to be made without the advice of the "professional politicians," the postmaster general urged otherwise:

> Mr. President, if you pursue this policy it means that your administration is going to be a failure. It means the defeat of measures of reform that you have next to your heart. These little offices don't amount to anything. They are inconsequential. It doesn't amount to a damn who is Postmaster at Paducah, Kentucky. But these little offices mean a great deal to senators and representatives in Congress. If it goes out that the President has turned down Representative So-and-so, and Senator So-and-so, it means that member has great trouble at home.[109]

In the end, Wilson was persuaded. His decision to work through the party marked "one of the early decisive turning points in Wilson's presidential career."[110] It underlay his nearly absolute mastery of the Democratic Party, especially its membership in Congress. But Wilson's political approach to appointments weakened the administrative effectiveness of the reform programs he persuaded Congress to enact. Spoilsmen were less able and often less willing to implement the president's New Freedom legislation than officials chosen for their competence and their commitment to progressive principles would have been.

Wilson's New Freedom program also failed to address the problem of racial discrimination. Indeed, the Democratic victory in 1912 brought into the executive branch southerners who strengthened the grip of Jim Crow laws on southern blacks. "The South," a reporter for *Harper's Weekly* observed, "is in the Saddle."[111] As a native Virginian, Wilson supported cabinet members such as Treasury Secretary William McAdoo and Postmaster General Burleson, who solidified racial segregation in the federal workforce, especially in Washington, D.C. To be sure, neither Roosevelt nor Taft had been champions of racial justice. But Wilson and the Democratic Party actively pursued a policy of segregation in the departments and agencies of the federal government.

Although his commitment to reform was limited by his beliefs and his party, Wilson did transform the presidency substantially. The office that only two decades before had seemed so unimpressive to Wilson the political scientist had been elevated by Wilson the president to a position of unrivaled influence in the American political system. As the *New Republic* proclaimed in December 1914, "Under Mr. Wilson the prestige of the presidency has been fully restored. He has not only expressly acknowledged and acted on this obligation of leadership, as did Mr. Roosevelt, but he has sought to embody it in constitutional form . . . [by] establishing regular forms of cooperation and a better understanding between the Presidency and Congress."[112]

WILSON AS WORLD LEADER

From 1901 to 1909 Roosevelt had expanded the president's influence and reduced the effectiveness of Congress in foreign affairs. Wilson did not shirk his office's new responsibilities. In a lecture at Columbia University in 1907, Professor Wilson expressed the understanding of the executive's obligations in foreign affairs that was to govern his conduct as president:

> The president can never again be the mere domestic figure he has been throughout so large a part of our history. The nation has risen to the first rank in power and resources. . . . Our president must always, henceforth, be one of the great powers of the world, whether he act greatly or wisely or not. . . . We have but begun to see the presidential office in this light; but it is the light which will more and more beat upon it, and more and more determine its character and its effect upon the politics of the nation.[113]

Wilson's approach to foreign affairs was just as ambitious as Roosevelt's and somewhat more idealistic. TR's diplomatic initiatives were rooted in a mixture of progressive philosophy and *realpolitik* that sustained his administration's vigorous pursuit of American strategic and economic interests. Wilson and his first secretary of state, William Jennings Bryan, charted a more high-minded course. They assumed somewhat naively, Link has written, "that moral force controlled the relations of peace, that reason would prevail over ignorance and passion in the formation of public opinion, and that men and nations everywhere were automatically progressing toward an orderly and righteous international society."[114] Wilson was determined to pursue an energetic foreign policy. But he resolved to base it more on altruism and less on narrow considerations of the national interest than Roosevelt's foreign policy had been.

CONFLICT WITH MEXICO

Wilson's noble intentions did not prevent, and probably contributed to, his clumsy intervention in Mexico soon after becoming president. The incident was precipitated by his refusal to recognize the government of Victoriano Huerta, who in February 1913 had overthrown and arranged the murder of the Mexican reformist president Francisco I. Madero. The Taft administration delayed granting diplomatic recognition to the Huerta government in hope of obtaining concessions for American business interests in Mexico. Wilson, however, detested "Dollar Diplomacy," as critics called Taft's approach, and sought instead to impose political reforms on Mexico as the price of recognition. "I shall be asked to explain your Mexican policy. Can you tell me what it is?" Sir William Tyrell of the British Foreign Office, who was returning to England in November 1913, asked Wilson. The president replied in his most decisive manner, "I am going to teach the South American Republics to elect good men!" As historian Burton J. Hendrick has noted, "In its attitude, its phrasing, [this statement] held the key to much Wilson history."[115]

Determined to teach nations how to govern themselves, Wilson repudiated the historic presidential practice of recognizing all foreign governments and improvised for Mexico a radical new test for recognition: "constitutional legitimacy." In other words, was the Mexican government adhering to its own constitution, and, beyond that, was it motivated by a sincere desire to eliminate despotism or merely by self-interest and ambition?[116] To Wilson, the test seemed reasonable and honorable. To the Latin Americans, it was meddling.

Wilson achieved a diplomatic victory when he persuaded Great Britain and other European powers to withhold military and economic support from the Huerta regime. But, still not satisfied, he took measures, such as seizing the port of Veracruz in April 1914, to support a counterrevolution instigated by the "constitutionalist" Venustiano Carranza. Then, when the triumphant Carranza chose to brook no advice from the American president, Wilson threw his support to Gen. Francisco "Pancho" Villa, an erstwhile Carranza ally whose defection prolonged Mexico's civil war for an additional three years. Mexicans deeply resented Wilson's clumsy interventions.

The Mexican situation became especially dangerous after another shift in Wilson's diplomatic position. Villa, who proved no more amenable than Carranza or his predecessor to U.S. control, began to extort ever-increasing financial contributions from American-owned companies in Mexico. In Washington, support for Villa gave way to diplomatic recognition of

Woodrow Wilson was more successful promoting his foreign policy agenda during his European tour of December 1918 than he was during his September 1919 tour of the increasingly isolationist United States.

Carranza, provoking Villa to lead raids into Texas. On March 15, 1916, Wilson sent a punitive expedition under the command of Brig. Gen. John J. Pershing in pursuit of Villa. Carranza, greatly alarmed by the size of the American force in Mexico, even though it was hunting his enemy, demanded in an insulting note that Pershing withdraw. Eventually, after military skirmishes and an exchange of ultimatums, Carranza and Wilson worked out an agreement. The president ordered Pershing to return his troops to Texas on January 26, 1917. Carranza, whose stout resistance to the American government had made him a hero to the Mexican people, was elected president on March 11. The United States recognized his government two days later.

The conflict with Mexico demonstrated that Wilson was determined to play a constructive role in world affairs. But his intervention, however well intentioned, did little to undo, and in fact aggravated, the resentment that Roosevelt's less idealistic policies in Central and South America had caused. According to Link, although Wilson helped pave the way for the independence of the Mexican people, he "interfered in the wrong way so often that he embittered Mexican-American relations for many years to come."[117]

Wilson's severest tests in foreign affairs lay ahead, during and after World War I, when, for the first time, the president was required to exercise executive power in conditions of global conflict. In many respects, Wilson's conduct of the war was exemplary. Yet the same stubbornness and idealism that he displayed toward Mexico eventually led to a tragic defeat in his pursuit of a postwar program of lasting peace.

WORLD WAR I: THE PRESIDENCY AND TOTAL WAR

Wilson was narrowly reelected in 1916, the first Democrat to win two consecutive terms since Andrew Jackson more than eighty years earlier. His party's slogan was "He kept us out of war," referring both to war with Mexico and the "Great War" that had been raging in Europe since 1914. On April 6, 1917, five weeks after his second inauguration and in response to a long series of German submarine attacks on American ships, Wilson signed a proclamation that a state of war existed with Germany. Congress voted to declare war four days after hearing the president's moving and eloquent appeal, in which he called on the United States to end its traditional position of neutrality in European conflicts. "It is a fearful thing to lead this great peaceful people into war, into the most terrible and disastrous of all wars," said Wilson. "But, the right is more precious than peace, and we shall fight for . . . a universal dominion of right by such a concert of free peoples as shall bring peace and safety to all nations and make the world itself at last free."[118]

The war to "make the world safe for democracy," as Wilson called it, placed new demands on the powers of the president. Waging a modern "total war" successfully required the mass production of complex weapons.[119] It also entailed the mobilization and, at a great distance from the United States, the deployment of troops on a grand scale. The president became responsible for organizing and controlling the industrial economy and for coordinating the transportation and communication industries so they could meet the requirements of the military commitment.[120] All this was in addition to the traditional duties of the commander in chief.

The need to impose wartime economic and social controls on American society strained the settled procedures of constitutional government to an extent not seen since the Civil War. Perhaps conscious of the postbellum reaction against presidential authority, Wilson sought explicit delegations of authority from Congress whenever possible. But he did not rely on statutory power for everything: when Congress failed to authorize him to arm merchant vessels, Wilson armed them anyway, realizing that he already had the constitutional right to do so as commander in chief. Yet from the start of his presidency Wilson had believed that the full flowering of presidential authority required legislative support even in wartime, when the expansive character of executive power was well established by constitutional doctrine and historical precedents.

Of the many delegations of power to the president that followed Congress's declaration of war, the most striking was the Lever Food and Fuel Control Act of 1917. The Lever Act granted Wilson authority "to regulate by license the importation, manufacture, storage, mining or distribution of necessaries"— in effect, to regulate almost the entire national economy. Because such an expansive grant was without precedent, the Lever Act was assailed by critics as the precursor to dictatorship. To allay such concerns, the Senate added a provision that created a bipartisan committee to oversee the conduct of the war.

Wilson attacked the Senate amendment vehemently. Hoping to kill it in the House-Senate conference committee, he fired off a letter to the bill's House sponsor, Democrat A. F. Lever of South Carolina, protesting that the proposed oversight committee would "amount to nothing less than an assumption on the part of the legislative body of the executive work of the administration." Wilson invoked the "ominous precedent" of the Joint Committee on the Conduct of the War, which Congress had constituted during the Lincoln administration. That committee, he argued, "was the cause of constant and distressing harassment and rendered [Lincoln's] task all but impossible."[121] By standing firm and by convincing congressional leaders like Lever to do the same, Wilson managed to have the amendment removed. The president signed the Lever Act on August 10, 1917, confirming once more his claim to legislative leadership.

The emergency powers that Wilson accrued during World War I were extraordinary. As Edward S. Corwin has noted, the difference between Wilson's and Lincoln's versions of wartime "dictatorship" was of "method," not of "tenderness for customary constitutional restraints."[122] Once Wilson obtained his extraordinary authority from Congress, he stopped accommodating his party's desire for patronage and instead appointed competent managers to handle the details of administration. The ranks of accomplished wartime administrators included Bernard Baruch, who chaired the powerful War Industries Board; Herbert C. Hoover, who served as food administrator; and Secretary of the Treasury William Gibbs McAdoo, who managed the railroads. Similarly, Wilson left the management of military affairs to his European commander, General Pershing. The president intervened only when important political and diplomatic considerations were involved.[123]

Wilson's style of delegating detailed tasks to trusted members of his administration while continuing to chart the overall direction of the war effort suited his approach to government. It was also an understandable adaptation of presidential leadership to the exigencies of modern warfare. By the twentieth century, war had become too massive and complex an undertaking for the president to supervise closely, as Polk and Lincoln had done in the mid-nineteenth century. It was by providing moral leadership to rouse the public and administrative appointments to sustain the country's engagement in total war that Wilson contributed to the development of the president's role as commander in chief.[124]

As historian John Milton Cooper Jr. observes, Wilson also used war-related moral suasion in a progressive domestic cause. Appearing before the Senate on September 30, 1918, with nearly the entire cabinet in tow, Wilson urged senators to add their approval to the women's suffrage amendment to the Constitution already approved by the House. Wilson had been slow to support the right of women to vote, but he gradually came to see the merit of suffragist Carrie Chapman Catt's argument that disenfranchisement "aroused in patriotic women a just suspicion that man and women are not co-workers for world freedom."[125] "We have made partners of women in this war," Wilson told Congress; "shall we admit them only to a partnership of suffering and sacrifice and not to a partnership of privilege and right?" Although the Senate fell two votes short of the required two-thirds when it voted the next day, it approved the amendment the following June.[126] It was ratified by three-fourths of the states fourteen months later, in August 1920.

THE DEFEAT OF THE LEAGUE OF NATIONS

Ironically, Wilson met defeat in his effort to accomplish the task for which he believed his influence and talents were best suited: the building of a lasting structure of peace among nations. One reason Wilson had been cautious in asserting his powers as commander in chief during the war was that he did not want to jeopardize the opportunity to take charge at the peace table. As historian Ernest R. May has argued, "From the first day of the war to the last, all that Wilson sought was a peace that could be secured by the League of Nations, a peace that would make the world safe for democracy."[127]

Wilson's plan for an international peacekeeping organization was the most controversial of the Fourteen Points, the program of peace that he formulated in early 1918. Wilson hoped to persuade the Allies and the Senate to accept this program, which also included lenient terms for the defeated German nation. The president had to compromise on some of his points in the post-war peace negotiations, particularly those pertaining to the conditions to be imposed on Germany. But the League of Nations was included in the Treaty of Versailles, which the major powers signed in June 1919.

Wilson began the battle to ratify the treaty with little doubt that he would prevail. He had displayed throughout his presidency an almost unsurpassed ability to enlist public support for the causes he championed. Yet in the fight for the league he disdained using the methods that had succeeded so well in passing his New Freedom program. In domestic affairs, Wilson collaborated closely with the House and Senate Democratic leadership, but in foreign affairs, he felt constitutionally justified in acting alone. Whatever the president's formal responsibilities and informal obligations as party leader, Wilson believed that the initiative in foreign policy belonged to the executive "without any restriction." Wilson's views on foreign policy making, no less than

Roosevelt's, resembled those expressed by Alexander Hamilton in the 1793 Pacificus letters. Like Hamilton, Wilson believed in the superiority of the executive in matters of diplomacy, claiming "virtually the power to control them absolutely." [128]

The conflict between Wilson and the Senate over the League of Nations was greatly exacerbated by Wilson's expansive understanding of the president's foreign policy prerogatives. The limits of Wilson's political influence first became evident in the 1918 midterm elections, long before the Versailles treaty was signed. No sooner had the Fourteen Points been pronounced and peace negotiations begun than Congress, tiring of Wilson's independent course, began to challenge his conduct of foreign affairs. Former president Roosevelt abetted the opposition by urging the Senate to repudiate the Fourteen Points. On October 24, 1918, TR sent a telegram encouraging Republican leaders to "dictate peace by hammering guns and not chat about peace to the accompaniment of the clicking typewriters." [129]

Flustered by the Republicans' efforts to discredit him on the eve of the midterm elections, Wilson tried to rally the nation in support of his war policy. On the day after Roosevelt's telegram was released, the president made an unusual appeal to the voters: "If you have approved of my leadership and wish me to be your unembarrassed spokesman in affairs at home and abroad, I earnestly beg that you will express yourself unmistakably to that effect by returning a Democratic majority to both the Senate and the House of Representatives." [130]

Wilson's conflation of partisanship with patriotism was a serious political error. He was loudly criticized for suggesting that the Democrats had a monopoly on loyalty. During the war, many Republicans had supported the president and many Democrats had opposed him. In fact, Wilson had begun his effort to secure a sympathetic Congress in the 1918 elections by intervening in the primaries of his own party in the hope of defeating antiadministration Democratic incumbents in five southern states. [131] Although he was successful in Georgia, Mississippi, South Carolina, and Texas, the intraparty purge campaign cast doubt on the president's claim during the general election that he could not prosecute the war successfully without a Democratic majority in both houses of Congress. [132]

Wilson's unwillingness to tolerate opposition reached beyond the halls of Congress. The president established the Committee on Public Information (CPI), led by George Creel, which enlisted seventy-five thousand speakers to persuade the American people that the war was a crusade for freedom and democracy against the Germans, a barbaric people bent on world domination. Most Americans supported the war. But a significant minority opposed it, including many German and Irish Americans, whose ethnic ties disposed them to doubt the cause of the Allied powers, and progressive activists such as the prominent social worker Jane Addams, who feared that American democracy would be corrupted by the necessities and cruelties of total war. The CPI and several self-styled patriotic groups sought to discourage and sometimes repress dissent. People who refused to buy war bonds were often ridiculed, and some were even assaulted. People with German names, scorned as "hyphenate Americans," were prosecuted indiscriminately. Some school boards outlawed the teaching of the German language.

Wilson's progressive principles did not deter this wave of oppression. Indeed, his view that the war was a moral crusade actually inspired intolerance toward those who disagreed. The president signed the Espionage Act of 1917, which imposed fines of up to $10,000 and jail sentences ranging to twenty years for persons convicted of aiding the enemy or obstructing the recruitment of soldiers. Deciding the following year that the act did not forbid enough forms of dissent, Congress passed and Wilson signed the Sedition Act. Under its authority, he authorized the postmaster general to ban from the mails material that seemed treasonable or seditious. The Sedition Act also made "saying anything" to discourage the purchase of war bonds a crime and declared illegal efforts to "utter, print, write, or publish any disloyal, profane, scurrilous, or abusive language" about the government, the Constitution, or the uniforms worn by soldiers and sailors.

The 1918 campaign, occurring as it did in the midst of the war, seemed an inappropriate occasion for the president to appeal to party loyalty. Indeed, his administration's intolerance of dissent denigrated the principles he championed as the foundation of a "new world order." When the Republicans won control of both houses of Congress for the first time during Wilson's presidency, the *New Republic* scolded Wilson for having discouraged public debate on foreign affairs. Americans had "voted in the dark," the editors argued, and remained "wholly unprepared to deal with the new responsibilities to which [the nation] is committed as the consequence of its own acts and the convulsions of the world."[133] Roosevelt declared soon after the election that "our allies and our enemies and Mr. Wilson himself should all understand that Mr. Wilson has no authority whatever to speak for the American people at this time. His leadership has just been emphatically repudiated by them."[134]

The 1918 elections diminished the president's prestige at home and abroad, adding to the difficulties he was to encounter at the postwar peace conference and, especially, with Congress. Although Wilson managed to salvage parts of his program at Versailles, he failed completely in Washington. Senate opposition to the treaty, especially to its provision for the league, was led by an implacable Wilson foe, Massachusetts Republican Henry Cabot Lodge. As a result of the midterm elections, Lodge became chair of the Senate Foreign Relations Committee. Rejecting compromise with the senator, Wilson left Washington on September 3, 1919, on a month-long speaking tour of the

After Woodrow Wilson fell gravely ill in September 1919 while conducting a speaking tour of the country to gain support for the League of Nations, his wife, Edith, shielded him from the daily responsibilities of the presidency. She screened all papers, business, and visitors while he recovered. The full extent of the power she wielded at this time has never been conclusively determined.

western states. He hoped to revive his long-neglected role as public educator and, in doing so, to create, as he had in the past, a popular groundswell that would force the Senate to ratify the treaty.[135]

Instead, Wilson's speaking tour further reduced his influence. It is possible, but not likely, that the campaign would have succeeded had he not suffered a stroke toward the end of the grueling trip that severely weakened him for the remainder of his presidency. But the tide of public opinion had been moving against the president since the 1918 elections.[136] His unsuccessful campaign for the League of Nations offered dramatic evidence that although the presidency had attained considerable prominence since the turn of the century, the office was still constrained by a powerful, if no longer dominant, Congress and by the vagaries of popular opinion. Because of TR and Wilson, Americans no longer considered it inappropriate for the president to try to rouse public support with rhetorical appeals. But nothing guaranteed that every campaign of persuasion would succeed. The 1920 presidential election, which Warren G. Harding, the conservative, anti-league Republican senator from Ohio, won in a landslide, was a major setback for progressivism and for Wilson's theory of presidential power. So, too, soon after election day, was the final Senate defeat of the League of Nations treaty.

NOTES

1. For a useful review of the effect of the Progressive movement on the presidency, see William M. Goldsmith, ed., *The Growth of Presidential Power: A Documented History,* 3 vols. (New York: Chelsea, 1974), 2:1277–1349.

2. Richard Hofstadter, *The Age of Reform: From Bryan to FDR* (New York: Knopf, 1956), 5.

3. Quoted in Samuel Eliot Morison, *The Oxford History of the American People,* 3 vols. (New York: New American Library, 1972), 3:130–131.

4. Theodore Roosevelt, *The Works of Theodore Roosevelt,* 20 vols. (New York: Scribner's, 1926), 20:340.

5. Hanna is quoted in Samuel and Dorothy Rosenman, *Presidential Style: Some Giants and a Pygmy in the White House* (New York: Harper and Row, 1976), 1.

6. Roosevelt, *Works,* 20:450.

7. Rosenman and Rosenman, *Presidential Style,* 123.

8. Roosevelt, *Works,* 20:347.

9. Ibid., 20:347.

10. See "The Pacificus-Helvidius Letters," in *The Evolving Presidency: Landmark Documents, 1787–2010,* 4th ed., ed. Michael Nelson (Washington, D.C.: CQ Press, 2011), 50–58.

11. Roosevelt, *Works,* 20:414. Lincoln's defense of the Union and audacious use of executive power occurred during the stress of a domestic rebellion. His understanding of the national government's powers and of executive prerogative in less dire circumstances was far more circumscribed than Roosevelt's.

12. Elmer E. Cornwell Jr., *Presidential Leadership of Public Opinion* (Bloomington: Indiana University Press, 1965), 9. See also Jeffrey Tulis, *The Rhetorical Presidency* (Princeton: Princeton University Press, 1987), 97–116; and Gerald Gamm and Renée M. Smith, "Presidents, Parties, and the Public: Evolving Patterns of Interaction, 1877–1929," in *Speaking to the People: The Rhetorical Presidency in Historical Perspective,* ed. Richard J. Ellis (Amherst: University of Massachusetts Press, 1998).

13. There is no direct evidence that Roosevelt ever spoke or wrote this term. In fact, the comment "I have got such a bully pulpit" did not become identified with TR until his friend and political ally Lyman Abbott quoted these words in an article he published toward the end of Roosevelt's presidency. See Abbott, "A Review of President Roosevelt's Administration: IV—Its Influence on Patriotism and Public Service," *Outlook,* February 27, 1909, 430. In a 1919 eulogy to Roosevelt at the Century Club in New York City, the publisher George Haven Putnam also recalled the former president speaking these words.

14. Gerald Gamm and Renée M. Smith, "Presidents, Parties, and the Public: Evolving Patterns of Interaction, 1877–1929), in Ellis, ed., *Speaking to the People,* 97.

15. Roosevelt, *Works,* 20:416.

16. Ibid., 20:342.

17. For a discussion of Roosevelt's campaign on behalf of the Hepburn Act, see Tulis, *Rhetorical Presidency,* 97–116; and Cornwell, *Presidential Leadership of Public Opinion,* 24–26.

18. John Morton Blum, *The Republican Roosevelt* (Cambridge: Harvard University Press, 1954), 74–75.

19. Roosevelt, *Works,* 15:225.

20. Mark Sullivan, *Our Times, 1900–1925* (New York: Scribner's, 1939), 3:226.

21. George W. Mowry, *The Era of Theodore Roosevelt, 1900–1912* (New York: Harper, 1958), 201.

22. "Address delivered before the Iroquois Club, at a banquet in Chicago, May 10, 1905," in *The Roosevelt Policy,* 3 vols., ed. William Griffith (New York: Current Literature, 1919), 1:266–273. See also Mowry, *Era of Theodore Roosevelt,* 201.

23. Quoted in Mowry, *Era of Theodore Roosevelt,* 203.

24. Cornwell, *Presidential Leadership of Public Opinion,* 10.

25. Roosevelt derived the term *muckraker* from the description in John Bunyan's *Pilgrim's Progress* of the Man with the Muck-Rake. "Now it is very necessary that we should not flinch from seeing what is vile and debasing," TR said of the journalists who practiced the literature of exposure: "There is filth on the floor, and it must be scraped up with the muck-rake; and there are times and places where this service is the most needed of all the services that can be performed. But the man who never does anything else, who never speaks or thinks or writes save of his feats with the muck-rake, speedily becomes, not a help to society, not an incitement to good, but one of the most potent forces for evil." Address at the laying of the cornerstone of the office building of the House of Representatives, Washington, D.C., April 14, 1906, found in Willis Fletcher Johnson, ed., *Theodore Roosevelt: Addresses and Papers* (New York: Sun Dial Classics, 1908), 311.

26. George W. Alger, "The Literature of Exposure," *Atlantic Monthly,* August 1905, 210.

27. Sullivan, *Our Times*, 3:83–84.

28. Roosevelt quoted in Blum, *Republican Roosevelt*, 81.

29. Ibid., 87. Political scientist Jeffrey Tulis has noted, "Roosevelt abandoned nineteenth century practice, to be sure, but he did so in a way that retained nineteenth century objectives and accommodated that 'nineteenth century' institution, the Senate." Tulis, *Rhetorical Presidency*, 106–107.

30. Roosevelt, *Works*, 20:482; Rosenman and Rosenman, *Presidential Style*, 47.

31. Tulis, *Rhetorical Presidency*, 96.

32. A full account of Roosevelt's activities during the strike appears in a letter he wrote to Gov. Winthrop Murray Crane of Massachusetts, who was a concerned and apprehensive observer. See Roosevelt to Crane, October 22, 1902, in *Letters of Theodore Roosevelt*, 8 vols., ed. Elting Morrison (Cambridge: Harvard University Press, 1951), 3:359–360. In March 1903 the commission granted the miners a 10 percent wage increase and a nine-hour workday. It also recommended a 10 percent increase in the price of coal, more than enough to compensate the industry for the wage increase. The companies were not required to recognize the United Mine Workers, and formal recognition would not be granted for ten years. But the union won an important victory in the court of public opinion, as did the president. For a recent account of the coal strike settlement, see Edmund Morris, *Theodore Rex* (New York: Random House, 2001), 130–137, 150–169.

33. Mowry, *Era of Theodore Roosevelt*, 138; Rosenman and Rosenman, *Presidential Style*, 73.

34. Mowry, *Era of Theodore Roosevelt*, 140.

35. TR cited in ibid., 516. The conference, held in May 1908, included the nation's governors, the cabinet, all nine justices of the Supreme Court, many members of Congress, representatives of sixty-eight professional societies, social activists, and editors and reporters from both technical and popular publications.

36. Douglas Brinkley, *The Wilderness Warrior: Theodore Roosevelt and the Crusade for America* (New York: Harper, 2009).

37. Clayton S. Ellsworth, "Theodore Roosevelt's Country Life Commission," *Agricultural History* 34 (October 1960): 155–172; Theodore Roosevelt to Sydney Brooks, December 28, 1908, in Morrison, *Letters of Theodore Roosevelt*, 6:1444–5, 1446.

38. Kenneth R. Mayer, *With the Stroke of a Pen: Executive Orders and Presidential Power* (Princeton: Princeton University Press, 2001), 51–52, 75.

39. Blum, *Republican Roosevelt*, 105.

40. William H. Harbaugh, "The Constitution of the Theodore Roosevelt Presidency and the Progressive Era," in *The Constitution and the American Presidency*, ed. Martin Fausold and Alan Shank (Albany: State University of New York Press, 1991), 73–76.

41. Peri E. Arnold, *Remaking the Presidency: Roosevelt, Taft, and Wilson, 1901–1916* (Lawrence: University Press of Kansas, 2009), chap. 3.

42. Roosevelt, *Works*, 15:117.

43. Ibid., 15:114.

44. Ibid., 20:510, 549–550.

45. Roosevelt to Marcus Alonzo Hanna, October 5, 1903, in Morrison, *Letters of Theodore Roosevelt*, 3:625.

46. Roosevelt, *Works*, 20:501.

47. Ibid.

48. Goldsmith, *Growth of Presidential Power*, 2:1233.

49. Mowry, *Era of Theodore Roosevelt*, 155.

50. Goldsmith, *Growth of Presidential Power*, 2:1233–4.

51. Roosevelt, *Works*, 15:256–257.

52. Mowry, *Era of Theodore Roosevelt*, 159.

53. Roosevelt, *Works*, 20:490.

54. When Russia violated the Open Door policy by expanding into Manchuria after 1902 Roosevelt wanted to take action, but he did not think that the American people would

support a military intervention in Asia. Therefore, he welcomed Japan's attack on the Russian fleet in Port Arthur.

55. This agreement is described in a confidential memo to Roosevelt from Secretary of War William Howard Taft, July 29, 1905, in Goldsmith, *Growth of Presidential Power,* 2:1246–7. TR responded almost immediately, indicating that the agreement Taft had worked out with the Japanese prime minister, Count Taro Katsura, was "absolutely correct in every respect" and that he confirmed "every word you have said" (telegram from Roosevelt to Taft, July 31, 1905, in Morrison, *Letters of Theodore Roosevelt,* 4:1293). See also Henry F. Pringle, *The Life and Times of William Howard Taft,* 2 vols. (New York: Farrar and Rinehart, 1939), 1:297–299.

56. Mowry, *Era of Theodore Roosevelt,* 185.

57. Roosevelt describes his decision to send the naval fleet around the world in his autobiography. See *Works,* 20:535–546.

58. Goldsmith, *Growth of Presidential Power,* 2:1269.

59. Mowry, *Era of Theodore Roosevelt,* 226.

60. Ibid., 180; Roosevelt, *Works,* 20:378.

61. Roosevelt to Trevelyan, June 19, 1908, Theodore Roosevelt papers, Manuscript Division, Library of Congress, Washington, D.C.

62. Mowry, *Era of Theodore Roosevelt,* 227.

63. Paolo E. Coletta, *The Presidency of William Howard Taft* (Lawrence: University Press of Kansas, 1973), 48.

64. William Howard Taft, *Our Chief Magistrate and His Powers* (New York: Columbia University Press, 1916), 139–140.

65. Archie Butt, *Taft and Roosevelt: The Intimate Letters of Archie Butt* (Garden City, N.Y.: Doubleday, Doran, 1930), 1:30.

66. Cornwell, *Presidential Leadership of Public Opinion,* 27.

67. Taft to W. R. Nelson, February 23, 1909, cited in Coletta, *Presidency of William Howard Taft,* 45–46.

68. Cited in William Henry Harbaugh, *Power and Responsibility: The Life and Times of Theodore Roosevelt* (New York: Farrar Straus and Cudahy, 1961), 384.

69. Cited in Mowry, *Era of Theodore Roosevelt,* 245.

70. Quoted in Harbaugh, *Power and Responsibility,* 384.

71. Mowry, *Era of Theodore Roosevelt,* 246.

72. Ibid., 246.

73. Coletta, *Presidency of William Howard Taft,* 71.

74. Wilfred E. Binkley, *President and Congress* (New York: Knopf, 1947), 200. The only office that Taft ever ran for, except the presidency, was justice of the State Superior Court in Ohio.

75. Quoted in Ray Stannard Baker, *Woodrow Wilson: Life and Times,* 8 vols. (Garden City, N.Y.: Doubleday, Doran, 1931), 3:181.

76. Leonard D. White has written of James K. Polk's earlier coordination of budget appropriations: "The precedent established by Polk disappeared from view, and a new start had to be made many decades later on this aspect of presidential power." White, *The Jacksonians: A Study in Administrative History, 1829–1861* (New York: Macmillan, 1956), 82.

77. Peri E. Arnold, *Making the Managerial Presidency: Comprehensive Reorganization Planning, 1905–1980* (Princeton: Princeton University Press, 1986), 44–45. On Taft's budget proposals, see Goldsmith, *Growth of Presidential Power,* 3:1471–8.

78. In the new Congress, Democrats outnumbered Republicans by 51 to 44 in the Senate and 290 to 127 in the House.

79. Quoted in Edward S. Corwin, *The President: Office and Powers, 1787–1957,* 4th ed. (New York: New York University Press, 1957), 36.

80. George W. Mowry, *Theodore Roosevelt and the Progressive Movement* (Madison: University of Wisconsin Press, 1946), 228.

81. George W. Mowry, "The Election of 1912," in *History of American Presidential Elections, 1789–1968*, 4 vols., ed. Arthur M. Schlesinger Jr. and Fred L. Israel (New York: Chelsea, 1971), 3:2146.

82. Roosevelt, *Works*, 20:471. On the significance of the 1912 election, see Sidney M. Milkis, *Theodore Roosevelt, the Progressive Party, and the Transformation of American Democracy* (Lawrence: University Press of Kansas, 2009).

83. In accepting the Progressive Party's nomination in person, Roosevelt followed the example of previous third party candidates who scorned the traditions of the two major parties. Soon after being nominated by the Populist Party in 1892, James B. Weaver was summoned to address the convention. Weaver did not formally accept the nomination until a month later, however. Fred Emory Haynes, *James Baird Weaver* (Iowa City: State Historical Society of Iowa, 1919), 310–343. Socialist nominee Eugene Debs went a step further. He attended his party's convention in 1904 and proclaimed his acceptance before the delegates. Bernard J. Brommel, *Eugene V. Debs: Spokesman for Labor and Socialism* (Chicago: Charles H. Kerr Publishing, 1978), 79–80; H. Wayne Morgan, *Eugene V. Debs: Socialist for President* (Syracuse: Syracuse University Press, 1962), 67–68. Roosevelt's stature made his acceptance of the Progressive Party convention's 1912 nomination all the more dramatic. "Marking a new departure in the proceedings of national conventions," reported the *San Francisco Examiner*, "the two candidates [Roosevelt and his running mate, California governor Hiram Johnson] were notified of their nominations, and in the midst of deafening cheers they appeared before the delegates to voice their acceptance and to pledge their best efforts in the coming campaign." *San Francisco Examiner*, August 8, 1912, 1. See also John Allen Gable, *The Bull Moose Years: Theodore Roosevelt and the Progressive Party* (Port Washington, N.Y.: Kennikat Press, 1978), 108.

84. Roosevelt, *Works*, 17:219; and Proceedings of the First National Convention of the Progressive Party, August 5, 6, and 7, 1912, Progressive Party Archives, Theodore Roosevelt Collection, Houghton Library, Harvard University. See also Mowry, "Election of 1912," 3:2151–3, 2164. On the Progressive Party and its legacy, see Sidney M. Milkis and Daniel J. Tichenor, " 'Direct Democracy' and Social Justice: The Progressive Party Campaign of 1912," *Studies in American Political Development* 8 (Fall 1994): 282–340.

85. Goldsmith, *Growth of Presidential Power*, 3:1343; Mowry, "Election of 1912," 3:2163–5.

86. Woodrow Wilson to Alexander Mitchell Palmer, February 5, 1913, in *The Papers of Woodrow Wilson*, 69 vols., ed. Arthur S. Link (Princeton: Princeton University Press, 1974), 27:98–102. Palmer, who worked closely with Wilson in his 1912 campaign, was appointed attorney general in 1919.

87. Woodrow Wilson, "Cabinet Government in the United States," *International Review* 7 (August 1879): 146–163.

88. As noted in Chapter 7, Wilson's revised views on presidential power were first expressed in 1900, in the preface to the fifteenth printing of *Congressional Government*. The growing role of the United States in world affairs and other developments, he had come to believe, were likely to place the president at the center of national politics and government. See Woodrow Wilson, *Congressional Government* (Boston: Houghton Mifflin, 1885; New York: Meridian Books, 1956), 19–23. Subsequently, TR's dynamic leadership convinced Wilson that this likelihood had become a reality. Wilson's mature views on presidential leadership and constitutional change are expressed in Woodrow Wilson, *Constitutional Government in the United States* (New York: Columbia University Press, 1908).

89. Quoted in David Lawrence, *The True Story of Woodrow Wilson* (New York: Doran, 1924), 39.

90. Wilson, *Constitutional Government in the United States*, 68–69.

91. Ibid., 71–72.

92. Ibid., 68.

93. Ibid., 68–69. For a comprehensive treatment of Wilson's understanding of constitutional government, see Daniel D. Stid, *The President as Statesman: Woodrow Wilson and the Constitution* (Lawrence: University Press of Kansas, 1998).

94. James Ceaser, *Presidential Selection: Theory and Development* (Princeton: Princeton University Press, 1979), 173.

95. Woodrow Wilson, "First Annual Message," December 2, 1913, in *The State of the Union Messages of the Presidents,* ed. Fred L. Israel (New York: Chelsea, 1966), 2548.

96. Arthur S. Link, *Wilson and the New Freedom* (Princeton: Princeton University Press, 1956), 149.

97. Link, *Papers of Woodrow Wilson,* 27:151. Wilson's contribution to popular leadership in the United States is assessed in Jeffrey Tulis, *The Rhetorical Presidency* (Princeton: Princeton University Press, 1987), 117–144. For an alternative view of Wilson that portrays him as a reluctant reformer, see Terri Bimes and Stephen Skowronek, "Woodrow Wilson's Critique of Popular Leadership: Reassessing the Modern-Traditional Divide in Presidential History," in *Speaking to the People: The Rhetorical Presidency in Historical Perspective,* ed. Richard J. Ellis (Amherst: University of Massachusetts Press, 1998).

98. Elmer E. Cornwell Jr., *Presidential Leadership of Public Opinion* (Bloomington: Indiana University Press, 1965), 32–44.

99. *New York Times,* April 8, 1913, 1.

100. Cornwell, *Presidential Leadership of Public Opinion,* 46.

101. American Presidency Project, "Woodrow Wilson, Address to a Joint Session of Congress on Tariff Reform, April 8th, 1913," http://www.presidency.ucsb.edu/ws/index.php?pid=65368.

102. Ray Stannard Baker, *Woodrow Wilson: Life and Letters,* 8 vols. (London: Heinemann, 1932), 4:109.

103. Arthur S. Link, *Woodrow Wilson and the Progressive Era, 1910–1917* (New York: Harper and Row, 1954), 35.

104. Quoted in ibid., 21.

105. Woodrow Wilson, "Monopoly or Opportunity," in Goldsmith, *Growth of Presidential Power,* 3:1334–42.

106. Link, *Papers of Woodrow Wilson,* 31:415.

107. Paul Van Riper, *History of the United States Civil Service* (Evanston, Ill.: Row, Peterson, 1958), 230; William Dudley Foulke, *Fighting the Spoilsmen* (New York: Putnam's, 1919; New York: Arno Press, 1974), 226–259.

108. Daniels to Franklin D. Roosevelt, December 15, 1932, Ray Stannard Baker Collection, Franklin D. Roosevelt File, Firestone Library, Princeton University.

109. Quoted in Baker, *Woodrow Wilson: Life and Letters,* 4:45.

110. Link, *Wilson and the New Freedom,* 159.

111. Maurice Low, "The South in the Saddle," *Harper's Weekly,* February 8, 1913, 20; Lewis L. Gould, *The Modern American Presidency* (Lawrence: University Press of Kansas, 2003), 48.

112. *New Republic,* December 5, 1914, 11–12.

113. Wilson, *Constitutional Government in the United States,* 78.

114. Link, *Wilson and the New Freedom,* 277.

115. Burton J. Hendrick, *The Life and Letters of Walter J. Page,* 3 vols. (New York: Doubleday, 1922), 1:204–205.

116. Link, *Wilson and the New Freedom,* 350; Sidney Warren, *The President as World Leader* (Philadelphia: Lippincott, 1964), 81.

117. Link, *Woodrow Wilson and the Progressive Era,* 144.

118. Link, *Papers of Woodrow Wilson,* 41:526.

119. The concept of "total war" applied in part to the Civil War. The assault on slavery and the military tactics of Gen. William T. Sherman, who used armed force against the civilian population of the rebel states, demonstrated the effectiveness of a plan of action that would destroy the enemy's economic system and demoralize the civilian population. See John Bennett Walters, "General William T. Sherman and Total War," *Journal of Southern History* 14 (1948): 447–480. In the twentieth century, however, the concept of total war took on a new, more expansive meaning. With the development of the modern state, war

became an instrument of national policy that mobilized the society's entire population and resources for a prolonged conflict. Edward S. Corwin has defined total war as "the politically ordered participation in the war effort of all personal and social forces, the scientific, the mechanical, the commercial, the economic, the moral, the literary, the artistic, and the psychological." Corwin, *Total War and the Constitution* (New York: Knopf, 1947), 24.

120. For a discussion of Wilson's leadership during World War I, see Goldsmith, *Growth of Presidential Power,* 3:1699–1733.

121. Quoted in Baker, *Woodrow Wilson: Life and Letters,* 7:185–186.

122. Corwin, *President: Office and Powers,* 237.

123. Goldsmith, *Growth of Presidential Power,* 3:1705, 1711.

124. Ibid., 3:1706.

125. Carrie Chapman Catt to Woodrow Wilson, September 29, 1918, as cited in Daniel J. Tichenor, "Leaders, Citizenship Movements, and the Politics Rivals Make," in *Formative Acts: American Politics in the Making,* ed. Stephen Skowronek and Matthew Glassman (Philadelphia: University of Pennsylvania Press, 2007), 261.

126. John Milton Cooper Jr., *Woodrow Wilson: A Biography* (New York: Knopf, 2009), 411–414.

127. Ernest R. May, "Wilson (1917–1918)," in *The Ultimate Decision: The President as Commander in Chief,* ed. Ernest R. May (New York: Braziller, 1960), 131.

128. Wilson, *Constitutional Government in the United States,* 77–79. On Wilson's dual conception of the presidency, see Daniel Stid, "Rhetorical Leadership and 'Common Counsel' in the Presidency of Woodrow Wilson," in Ellis, *Speaking to the People.*

129. Warren, *President as World Leader,* 107.

130. Link, *Papers of Woodrow Wilson,* 51:381.

131. *New York Times,* August 12, 1918, sec. 3, 1. Sidney M. Milkis, "Presidents and Party Purges: With Special Emphasis on the Lessons of 1938," in *Presidents and Their Parties: Leadership or Neglect?* ed. Robert Harmel (New York: Praeger, 1984), 154–157.

132. Cooper judges Wilson's intervention in these 1918 Democratic primaries "the only successful party purge by a president in American history." *Woodrow Wilson,* 437.

133. *New Republic,* November 9, 1918, cited in Thomas J. Knock, *To End All Wars: Woodrow Wilson and the Quest for a New World Order* (New York: Oxford University Press, 1992), 186.

134. Quoted in Warren, *President as World Leader,* 108. The Republicans outnumbered the Democrats in the Sixty-sixth Congress by 237 to 191 in the House and 48 to 47 in the Senate.

135. Knock, *To End All Wars,* 260.

136. The failure of Wilson's campaign for the League of Nations was hardly a foregone conclusion. Indeed, before his health failed Wilson was attracting large, enthusiastic crowds, and the opponents of the treaty were sufficiently concerned about his influence to send out Senators William E. Borah of Idaho and Hiram Johnson of California to give the other side of the argument. See Kendrick A. Clements, *The Presidency of Woodrow Wilson* (Lawrence: University Press of Kansas, 1992), 196.

CHAPTER 9

The Triumph of Conservative Republicanism

The election of Warren G. Harding by a huge majority in 1920 marked the end of the Progressive era. Harding won 60 percent of the national popular vote against the Democratic nominee, Ohio governor James M. Cox, who received just 34 percent. The Socialist Party candidate, Eugene V. Debs, won 3.4 percent of the vote, even though he was in jail for urging resistance to the draft in violation of the 1918 wartime Sedition Act. Harding also swept the Electoral College, winning 404 votes to Cox's 127. Harding carried every state outside the South, and he managed to win 40 percent of the popular vote below the Mason-Dixon Line. His victory in Tennessee marked the first time since the end of Reconstruction that one of the eleven states of the Confederacy voted for a Republican for president. The only bright spot for the Democrats in 1920 was the impression made by their thirty-eight-year-old vice-presidential candidate, Franklin D. Roosevelt, a distant cousin of TR and the assistant secretary of the navy under President Woodrow Wilson. Roosevelt's energetic campaign earned him a prominent national reputation and launched a political career that led to his election as governor of New York in 1928 and president in 1932, despite his battle with polio, which began in 1921 and lasted until he died in 1945.

The landslide election that brought Harding to office was fought on the issues of World War I and the League of Nations.[1] But in rejecting the league, so closely identified with Wilson and his aspirations for national and international reform, voters were expressing their desire for quieter times after two decades of far-reaching and fundamental political change. The return to isolation from world affairs, which the repudiation of the league inaugurated, was accompanied at home by a return to a laissez-faire approach to governing— that is, a partial restoration of the wall that had separated government from the economy before the advent of progressivism.

Harding's election could be explained in no small part by his identification with the nation's longing for a moratorium on change. In May 1920 he told the Home Market Club in Boston, "America's present need is not heroics, but healing; not nostrums but normalcy; not revolution but restoration . . . not surgery but serenity."[2]

The word *normalcy,* in particular, attracted immediate and lasting attention, and a "return to normalcy" became the theme of the 1920 Republican presidential campaign.[3] Normalcy captured the temper of the times as it related not just to public policy, but to the presidency as well. Harding capitalized on the popular reaction against what the Republicans called "executive autocracy." Meanwhile, a stricken President Wilson played into the Republicans' hands. Before Congress adjourned in the summer of 1920, it passed an act to repeal sixty wartime laws that had conferred extraordinary powers on the executive. The Repeal Act was approved by the House of Representatives in a 343–3 vote and by the Senate unanimously. Nevertheless, after Congress adjourned Wilson pocket-vetoed the act, thereby retaining his war powers until Congress met again in December 1920. Historian William Starr Myers has noted that in doing so, "President Wilson . . . took one more step which decisively alienated the average American citizen."[4]

The Republicans resumed power in March 1921, militant in their determination to restore Congress and the party organization to their former stature. As the leader of the committee that officially notified Harding of his nomination by the 1920 Republican convention, Sen. Henry Cabot Lodge presented the candidate with something of an ultimatum. Alluding to the transfer of power from Congress to the presidency during the Wilson administration, Lodge reminded Harding that "the makers of the Constitution intended to coordinate the three great elements of government and strove to guard against either usurpation or trespass by one branch at the expense of the other." "In that spirit," the senator added, "*we all know well,* you will enter upon your great responsibility."[5]

Neither Harding nor his two Republican successors, Calvin Coolidge and Herbert C. Hoover, took exception to the sentiment that Lodge expressed. Their understanding of executive power owed more to William Howard Taft than to Theodore Roosevelt. In fact, the twelve-year tenure of these three presidents is generally regarded as the nadir of presidential power in the twentieth century. As in earlier eras of American history, a period of strong executive leadership was followed by passivity and drift.

There was, however, no restoration of congressional government during the 1920s. Transformed social and economic conditions, as well as the precedents that TR and Wilson had established, did not allow for a complete return to the old order. As Elmer E. Cornwell Jr. has observed, "The stature of the [executive] office in the eyes of the public, which had been growing since 1900, and was given powerful impetus during the Wilson years, at least held its own if it did not actually continue to grow after 1920."[6] Even Harding's concept of "normalcy" did not entail turning back the clock entirely.

As he wrote during the campaign, "The common people—the people of whom Lincoln said that God must have loved them, because he made so many of them—have seen themselves lifted to a new level in the social and economic scheme of the world; and our problems of the future will be to maintain them there."[7]

THE HARDING ERA

In his acceptance speech for the Republican presidential nomination, Harding tried to assuage the

President Woodrow Wilson rides with President-elect Warren G. Harding to Harding's inauguration on March 4, 1921. Harding promised a "return to normalcy" after the Progressive Era and the tumultuous war years.

concerns of Lodge and his Senate colleagues. The nominee pledged that, if elected, he would restore "party government as distinguished from personal government, individual, dictatorial, autocratic, or what not."[8] True to his promise as a candidate, President Harding made little effort to lead Congress. His expressed intention was to reign rather than rule. The president would announce his legislative program, which the Constitution directed him to do, but after that, lawmaking would be the work of Congress. On those rare occasions when Harding did take an interest in legislative matters, his actions almost always showed great deference to Congress. Harding's model was William McKinley, whose influence on Capitol Hill was exercised through consultation and compromise with his party's leadership.[9]

But McKinley-style legislative leadership was no longer possible in the 1920s. The congressional revolt of 1910, which dethroned the Speaker, had weakened the bonds of party in the House. Gone were the days when the president and the Speaker could bring together the executive and legislative branches of the government through quiet conversation. The Senate, too, had been affected by an insurgent revolt against strong party leadership. Moreover, the enactment in 1913 of the Seventeenth Amendment, which provided that the people, not the state legislatures, would elect senators, further undermined party discipline in the upper house. The typical senator, one observer wrote in 1922, "came to think more in terms of himself and his reelection, nearly always an impelling motive, and less in terms of party."[10] Wilson's bold methods of party leadership had forged, at least for a time, new connections between the president and Congress. Harding's passivity guaranteed deadlock and confusion.

One consequence of the new president's forbearance was that his program to address the problems of the postwar economy through higher tariffs and lower taxes made little headway in the legislature. Instead, Congress became bogged down in its own disagreements about what to do. Harding's relations with Congress were aggravated by a battle over bonus payments to World War I veterans. While most Republicans in Congress, pressured by the American Legion of Ex-Servicemen, supported cash compensation for war veterans, Harding and Treasury Secretary Andrew Mellon feared that the high cost of these payments threatened their plan for substantial cuts in taxation prior to the 1922 election.[11] An old friend of the president, Malcolm Jennings, wrote him in the late summer of 1921 that effective "congressional action can only follow the establishment of dominant leadership upon your part."[12] Harding began to regret his pledge to defer to Congress. As his policies foundered on Capitol Hill he replied to Jennings, "I find that I can not carry out my pre-election ideals of an Executive keeping himself aloof from Congress."[13]

Yet regret was unaccompanied by reform. Even when, to the astonishment of many, Harding went before Congress on July 12, 1921, to chide the House and, especially, the Senate for inaction on his economic program, he did not follow through with the sort of forceful and painstaking efforts at public or personal persuasion that might have moved his fractious party to action. Harding did not bow down to Congress, but neither did he have the desire or the ability to lead it.[14]

Fresh from its defeat of the League of Nations, Congress was determined to influence foreign affairs during Harding's term. Most significant, the Senate took the initiative to curb the naval arms race that had preoccupied the major powers since the beginning of World War I. The rejection of the Versailles treaty had ensured that the nation's naval buildup would continue after the war. Many public officials, including Harding, believed that attaining naval supremacy was the only alternative to joining the league. Yet an arms race would be expensive, especially because Great Britain and Japan were determined to match the American deployments.

Responding to this dilemma, progressive Republican senator William E. Borah of Idaho attached an amendment to the 1921 naval appropriation bill that called on the president to invite Great Britain and Japan to a naval disarmament conference. Although Harding tried to replace the rider with a weaker resolution, it passed. Harding was not opposed to having a conference, but he thought it would be prudent to build up the American fleet first.

Still, Harding was not one to engage Congress in a bitter and protracted struggle. Bowing to the legislative will, he convened an international disarmament conference in Washington in late 1921 and early 1922. The Washington Naval Disarmament Conference successfully worked out an agreement not only on naval armaments, but also on relations between the major Pacific powers. Partly to avoid the mistakes of his predecessor in the League of Nations fight, Harding allowed Secretary of State Charles Evans Hughes to take the lead in the disarmament treaty negotiations. The president also appointed Henry Cabot Lodge and Oscar W. Underwood, the ranking members of the Senate Foreign Relations Committee, to the American delegation. Harding gave Lodge and Underwood full responsibility for steering the treaties negotiated at the conference through the Senate.[15] Characteristic of Harding's presidency, however, his outstanding foreign policy accomplishment was the result of a Senate initiative, an indication of "how great had been the reaction against the Wilsonian type of executive."[16]

THE HARDING SCANDALS

Harding's presidency began slowly and ended disastrously. By 1923 it was clear that the country was paying a heavy price for his passive leadership and fawning deference to his party's apparatus. The president's pledge to restore normalcy included a revived enthusiasm for patronage appointments. The steady extension of the merit civil service that had begun with the passage of the Pendleton Act in 1883 and continued afterward, especially during Theodore Roosevelt's presidency, went no further in the Harding administration. Wilson had been willing to manipulate the civil service when party patronage proved useful in getting his program through Congress. But Harding was the only twentieth-century president to embrace the spoils system as worthy in its own right. According to Paul Van Riper, "By the middle of the summer of 1921 the spoils efforts of the Republicans began to assume the proportions of a sizable if not full-scale raid."[17]

Nor was Harding himself reluctant to manipulate the remaining unclassified service, which now constituted around one-fourth of the federal workforce. Some of Harding's appointments were excellent, especially his selection of Hoover as secretary of commerce and Hughes as secretary of state. Many others, however, were reminiscent of the Grant era. Collectively, Harding's appointees produced the worst corruption of any administration since the advent of civil service reform.

The first disturbing situation to come to light involved Charles Forbes, the director of the Veterans Bureau. In March 1923 Harding was told that Forbes had been selling items from the government's medical supply base in Perryville, Maryland, to private contractors at suspiciously low prices. He also was making undercover deals for hospital building contracts and site selections. Forbes was forced to resign, and his principal legal adviser, Charles F. Cramer, committed suicide.[18]

When the Veterans Bureau scandal was quickly followed by another in the attorney general's office, Harding became convinced that his administration was deeply tainted with corruption. Fearing for his reputation and for the fortunes of his party, the president reportedly lamented to journalist William Allen White, "My God, this is a hell of a job! I have no trouble with my enemies. I can take care of my enemies all right. But my damn friends, my goddamn friends, White, they're the ones that keep me walking the floor nights."[19]

Despondent and in poor health, Harding decided to escape Washington on a cross-country speaking tour that would culminate in Alaska. In the course of his return trip, he fell ill with ptomaine poisoning, then pneumonia, and died of an embolism in San Francisco on August 2, 1923. Vice President Calvin Coolidge, the former governor of Massachusetts, became president.

Mercifully for Harding, he died a few months before the uncovering of the Teapot Dome scandal, a complicated and subtle plot to defraud the government that was hatched and executed during his presidency. Teapot Dome, one of the most notorious political scandals in American history, originated with the administration's effort to modify, and in some cases reverse, the conservation policies of Roosevelt, Taft, and Wilson.[20] The prime mover in the affair was Harding's secretary of the interior, Albert B. Fall, who wanted to prevent the navy from continuing to withdraw petroleum-rich lands from private development, a practice devised to provide a reliable supply of oil in future naval emergencies. In 1921 Fall, who was a strong advocate of private development, persuaded Secretary of the Navy Edwin Denby to turn over management of the petroleum reserves to the Interior Department. Fall then rapidly implemented a new program to lease the reserves to certain oil companies, which favored him in turn with personal loans and gifts.

Fall probably did not require payoffs to pursue most of his policies; the leasing program meshed with his ideas about resource development.[21] But the secretary's greed got the better of him, thereby exposing his policies to attack from conservationists and their allies in the Senate. An exhaustive Senate investigation chaired by Montana senator Thomas J. Walsh disclosed that Fall had entered into a corrupt bargain with the oil companies of Edward L. Doheny and Harry F. Sinclair, granting them access to some valuable petroleum deposits that President Wilson had reserved for the navy. The Elk Hill, California, oil reserve was leased to Doheny, and the Teapot Dome oil reserve in Wyoming to Sinclair. In return for the leases, Doheny and Sinclair built some pipelines and storage facilities for the navy on the West Coast and at Pearl Harbor in Hawaii. But Fall personally received at least $100,000 from Doheny and $300,000 from Sinclair.

Armed with these facts and other damaging revelations unearthed by the Senate committee, a special commission appointed by President Coolidge initiated criminal prosecutions in early June 1924. Sinclair, Doheny, and Fall, who had resigned as secretary of the interior before the scandal broke, were charged with conspiracy to defraud the government. The trials and legal maneuvering lasted almost six years, after which Fall was sentenced to a year in jail and a $100,000 fine, and Sinclair received a six-month sentence. But Doheny was acquitted, a ridiculous verdict considering that Fall had been convicted of taking a bribe from him. The acquittal provoked George W. Norris, the progressive Republican senator from Nebraska, to remark that it is "very difficult, if not impossible to convict one hundred million dollars."[22]

BUDGET AND ACCOUNTING ACT OF 1921

Harding's public reputation, which remained high while he was alive, suffered tremendously from the scandalous revelations that rocked Washington after he died. But the Harding administration was not without its achievements. During his tenure, the first national budget system was created, enhancing significantly the president's authority to oversee the expenditures of the executive departments and agencies. The Budget and Accounting Act of 1921 carried into effect the major recommendations of the 1913 Commission on Economy and Efficiency created by President Taft.

The budget act required the president to compile an annual, comprehensive executive budget based on estimates of both the government's financial needs and its revenues for the coming fiscal year. The act also established the Bureau of the Budget to help the president exercise the new budget authority. Although formally part of the Treasury Department, the Budget Bureau was meant to serve as a presidential staff agency. Finally, the act created the General Accounting Office as an auditing arm of Congress.

With the passage of the budget act, the president finally obtained legal authority to oversee the allocation of expenditures in the executive branch (in the past each department had sent its annual budget request straight to Congress). In exercising this authority, the president still had to contend with the powerful fiscal committees in Congress, especially the Ways and Means, Finance, and Appropriations Committees, as well as with the executive agency heads, who for so long had dealt directly with legislators. But the president certainly was able to exert greater authority in budgetary matters with the new act than without it. Indeed, Herbert Emmerich, a scholar and civil servant, has judged the budget act to be "the greatest landmark of our administrative history except for the Constitution itself."[23]

Harding was not the first president to advocate a national budget system. Both Taft and Wilson had supported measures to strengthen the president's authority in fiscal affairs. Indeed, the Republican Congress had passed such a measure in 1920, but Wilson vetoed the bill because it restricted the president's power to remove the comptroller general, who is the head of the General Accounting Office. With a Republican administration in office in 1921, Congress passed the bill again, and President Harding, more willing than Wilson to share power with Congress, signed it.[24] Harding and the first director of the budget bureau, the capable Charles G. Dawes, made effective use of the powers that the new law placed in the president's hands. Harding's 1920 call for a return to normalcy had included a pledge to reduce government spending. Dedicated to fulfilling this pledge, Harding, who had gradually become aware of the need to exercise more purposeful leadership of his party, held his cabinet to a stern fiscal program that in 1923 achieved almost $2 billion in savings.[25]

EXPANSION OF THE PRESIDENT'S REMOVAL POWER

Harding also made an indirect contribution to the president's control of administrative affairs by appointing William Howard Taft as chief justice of the United States in 1921. Taft's majority opinion in *Myers v. United States* (1926) gave constitutional sanction to a sweeping interpretation of the president's removal power.[26] Although repeal of the Tenure of Office Act in 1885 had eliminated one obstacle to presidential removal, nothing prevented Congress from deciding to enact a similar statute in the future. Indeed, as the budget act's restriction on the president's power to remove the comptroller general illustrates, Congress continued to limit the president's ability to create new federal offices and to establish the procedures for filling them.

The 1876 statute that was at issue in the *Myers* case required the president to obtain the advice and consent of the Senate before removing a first-class postmaster from office. On January 20, 1920, President Wilson requested the resignation of postmaster Frank S. Myers. When Myers refused to comply, Wilson removed him by order of the postmaster general.

Surprisingly, the legality of Wilson's action was upheld by a Supreme Court whose chief justice had endorsed, even while serving as president, a narrow theory of executive power. Taft's opinion on behalf of a divided Court displayed a boldness rarely seen during his tenure in the White House. He ruled that Wilson's order was valid because the law restricting the president's authority to remove postmasters was unconstitutional. Arguing that the removal power was inherently executive, Taft insisted that the president must be able to control all executive officeholders, not just highly placed ones. "The imperative reasons requiring an unrestricted power to remove the most important of his subordinates in their most important duties," the chief justice explained, "must . . . control the interpretation of the Constitution as to all appointed by him."[27]

The *Myers* decision was the Court's first foray into the long struggle between the president and Congress for possession of the removal power. Issued by a conservative chief justice appointed by a conservative president, *Myers* offered a telling constitutional endorsement of the expanding boundaries of executive authority. The Supreme Court eventually would restrict somewhat the application of Taft's ruling.[28] But the *Myers* decision, on the heels of the Budget and Accounting Act, was additional evidence that, regardless of who was president, the presidency was unlikely to return to its more modest nineteenth-century status.

PUBLIC RELATIONS IN THE HARDING ERA

Although neither Harding nor his successor, the taciturn Coolidge, aspired to be a lawgiver or a tribune of the people in the manner embraced by Roosevelt and Wilson, each found that he could not advance the laissez-faire economic policies he preferred without taking a strong hand in the administration of the executive departments and agencies. Certainly, Harding's promise of economy in government could not have been fulfilled without the expanded fiscal powers granted to the president by the Budget and Accounting Act. Nor could the national government's involvement in domestic affairs have been reduced without public support. In the wake of TR and Wilson, public relations had become a critical ingredient of successful presidential leadership.[29]

Despite its disastrous end, Harding's presidency did manage to add to the arsenal of presidential techniques for leading public opinion. Having served as the editor and publisher of the *Marion Star* in Ohio before entering politics, Harding had a good sense of how the press worked. He developed an intimacy with journalists that greatly benefited both his 1920 presidential campaign and, until the scandals began to break in 1923, his image as president.

Harding fostered good relations with the press through personal courtesies and institutional innovations. During the 1920 campaign, he had a three-room cottage built near his home in Marion to accommodate the press. There, Harding would meet with reporters daily to discuss political developments in frank, off-the-record sessions. He continued to cultivate the journalistic fraternity during the postelection transition period, as he waited to be inaugurated. He was the first president to recognize that the press could be courted in casual as well as formal encounters, even to the extent of playing golf with certain correspondents.[30]

As president, Harding revived the practice of holding regular press conferences, which Wilson had begun but then allowed to taper off after 1915. It was under Harding that the "White House spokesman" ruse came into being to convey information from the administration to the public without directly attributing it to the president. Harding recognized that this veil between himself and newspaper readers gave him room to maneuver. Finally, Harding was the first president to benefit from "photo opportunities." His administration issued identification cards to members of the newly formed White House News Photographers' Association that granted them access to all public and some private events at which the president appeared. Harding himself posed willingly for photographers several times a week.

Harding's innovations in press relations helped to amplify the effects of his warm and engaging personality and win support for his administration's policies. He also decided to retain Wilson's practice of delivering the annual State of the Union message to Congress in person. Outside of Washington, Harding immensely enjoyed speechmaking tours. The mounting burden of the rhetorical presidency led him to appoint the first presidential speech-writer, journalist Judson Welliver.[31]

Although earlier presidents had sometimes relied on friends and political allies to help them prepare speeches, most had written their own. By 1921, however, the growing importance of the executive office and the expanding newspaper coverage of the president were fueling a greater demand for presidential rhetoric. Harding turned to Welliver to compose brief remarks for ceremonial events as well as the final drafts of major addresses. Yet for all the practical advantages, using a speechwriter distanced the president from the words he spoke. Presidents "relinquished some part of the mental discipline of thinking through an issue for themselves and deciding how best to make a case for a particular policy in exchange for the convenience of having packaged speeches readily available."[32]

Harding died on August 2, 1923, well before the American people realized his shortcomings. Dedicated to a concept of party politics and congressional supremacy that no longer seemed practicable, Harding had always found the White House an uncomfortable place. Sensitive to attacks on his leadership, Harding "maintained the unusual and time-consuming habit of writing personal responses to dozens of letters from ordinary citizens, a habit which increased his workload significantly and eventual contributed to undermining his health."[33] Poring over an immense stack of correspondence, Harding reportedly lamented to an aide, "I am not fit for this office and should never have been here."[34]

Harding served barely two years in office, and scholars have numbered him among the least successful presidents. But Harding's death caused an extraordinary outpouring of national emotion.[35] The crowds that came out to view the train carrying his body to Washington were immense. As historian Robert K. Murray has written, "Every town, every city, every hamlet turned out mourning people, standing silently or kneeling by the tracks and on the station platforms."[36]

The public's reaction reflected the growing prominence of the presidency. Because of the relentless journalistic surveillance of the president's activities that began during his administration, the stature of the office did not shrink but, to a surprising degree, continued to expand during the brief Harding era. As Cornwell has written, "More than ever before, thanks to the media and the use made of them on the President's behalf, the presidency was destined to blow up the man to heroic proportions and project this image constantly on the nation's screen."[37]

THE "SILENT" POLITICS OF CALVIN COOLIDGE

Calvin Coolidge was an unlikely heir to the increasingly public presidency. Plain in appearance and so sparing with words that he was dubbed "Silent Cal," Coolidge's public persona was ordinary at a time when the executive office seemed to require persons of heroic demeanor. Yet in spite of his limitations, and perhaps in part because of them, Coolidge was one of the most popular presidents in history.

Coolidge raised inactivity to an art. When it came to exerting his will on matters of public policy, Coolidge felt even less responsibility to act than had Harding. He made little effort to join with Republican leaders in Congress to advance a legislative program. "I have never felt it was my duty," Coolidge wrote in his autobiography, "to attempt to coerce Senators or Representatives, or to take reprisals. The people sent them to Washington. I felt I discharged my duty when I had done the best that I could with them. In this way I avoided almost entirely a personal opposition, which I think was of more value to the country than the attempt to prevail through arousing personal fear."[38]

Restraint in legislative relations comported with Coolidge's general disdain for programmatic initiatives. "The key to an understanding of the presidential career of Calvin Coolidge is to be found in the fact that he had a distaste for legislation," Wilfred Binkley has written.[39] Even more than Harding, Coolidge believed that there were too many federal programs and that the president's energies should be spent administering the government economically and efficiently. One of the few legislative measures that Coolidge promoted vigorously was the Mellon tax reduction plan of 1923, which took its name from Andrew Mellon, the conservative Treasury secretary who served during the Harding and Coolidge administrations.

Aside from bills such as the tax cut that reduced the national government's involvement in the economy, Coolidge maintained a public silence about legislation that would have befitted a nineteenth-century president. Even in the matter of the protocol of the World Court, a treaty that Coolidge sent to the Senate for ratification, he gave neither encouragement nor direction over to Republican senators. Instead, the president spoke barely a word as his supporters fought a valiant but, in the face of the isolationist mood that gripped the nation after World War I, a losing battle.

Despite Coolidge's lack of success with Congress, he forged a strong bond with the American people. "No other president in our day and time," one commentator observed after Coolidge left office, "has had such close, such continuous and such successful relations with the electorate as Calvin Coolidge had."[40] To some degree, Coolidge had the virtue of his defects. His stern Yankee demeanor and businesslike administrative style offered a welcome respite from the scandals of the Harding administration. He also benefited from the apparent prosperity of the postwar economy. The Harding-Coolidge economic program, with its emphasis on unregulated domestic markets and protection from foreign competition, put "business in the saddle."[41] For a time, business seemed up to the task. Throughout the spring of 1924, revelations about the Harding administration's scandals competed for attention on the front pages with news of rising dividends, profits, and sales.[42] Good times seemed to call for a president who was content to sit tight.[43]

Coolidge's enormous popularity was grounded not just in his commitment to business, but also in his ability to express that commitment in words that exalted the governing principles of the era. "The genius of this day was not altogether material," Coolidge said of the ascendant Republican Party's faith in commerce. "It had its spiritual side, deep and significant. . . . Prosperity came to the people that they might have the resources for more of the refinements of life, more for the needs of education and religion, more to minister to the things of the soul. Power came to the nation that it might the better serve its own citizens and bear its share of the burden of civilization." Coolidge inspired the people by persuading them, as he put it in his 1925 inaugural address, that his program reflected "idealism in its most practical form."[44]

Coolidge's shrewd sense of public relations reinforced his popularity. Extraordinarily faithful in discharging what he felt were his obligations to reporters, Coolidge held 520 press conferences during his five years in office, more per month than any other president, even the gregarious Franklin D. Roosevelt. Under Coolidge, the press conference became a Washington institution that future presidents could not abandon.[45] Moreover, efforts to provide for the comfort and convenience of White House correspondents reached new heights during his administration.[46] Not surprisingly, Coolidge's concern for the press corps won him a considerable measure of goodwill in the press.

On rare occasion, the president used his exceedingly cordial relations with reporters to exert legislative leadership. In each of ten press conferences between December 1923 and June 1924, Coolidge urged Congress to enact the Mellon tax reduction plan. But much of Coolidge's public relations effort was designed to sell himself rather than his policies.

Characteristically, while Republican senators, without an encouraging word from the president, fought a losing battle for the World Court treaty, Coolidge used a White House lunch with prominent writers and editors to display the most benign facets of his personality. "Instead of trying to guide Congress and impress his views on party leaders," a Washington correspondent wrote in 1926, "Mr. Coolidge devotes himself to playing the sort of politics he knows how to play, doing the sort of thing he can do—and in which he is far more interested than in the World Court proposal, which was from the start more or less an annoyance to him."[47]

The politics Coolidge "knows how to play" was a politics of personality that embodied his keen understanding of the public's interest in the human side of the presidency. Convinced that news about his personal activities would pave the way for popular acceptance of his more serious pronouncements, the shy Coolidge threw open his private life to unprecedented press scrutiny. One contemporary reporter suggested that "he was probably the most photographed man who ever occupied the White House. It was a joke among photographers that Mr. Coolidge would don any attire or assume any pose that would produce an interesting picture. He was never too busy to be photographed; nor is it recorded that he ever resented any revelation as to his personal habits."[48]

Important as the newspapers were to Coolidge, his most significant contribution to the development of White House communications was his use of the radio. Lacking the "barnstorming ability" of his recent predecessors, Coolidge was blessed with a new mass medium, which he used effectively to enhance his image. "I am very fortunate I came in with the radio," he told Sen. James E. Watson of Indiana. "I can't make an engaging, rousing, or oratorical speech to a crowd, . . . but I have a good radio voice, and now I can get my messages across to them without acquainting them with my lack of oratorical ability."[49] In the same way he courted reporters, Coolidge used the radio less to rouse public support for his policies than to enhance his popularity. If he had not formed a bond with the voters in this way, Coolidge might have failed to be nominated by his party for a full term in 1924.

Coolidge's first significant public appearance as president was his 1923 State of the Union address, which he delivered at the Capitol on December 6. His speech was also the first presidential message to Congress to be broadcast. Coolidge's clear, incisive New England diction and the appealing content of his message apparently made a profound impression on the national radio audience.[50] From then until the Republican convention in June 1924, Coolidge made certain to speak to the American people at least once each month in carefully prepared radio broadcasts. The Coolidge administration also arranged for radio stations to broadcast the 1924 Republican National Convention, marking the first time the American people could listen to the proceedings of the quadrennial party gathering. The president's speech accepting his party's nomination, which, as was the custom until the 1930s, he made several weeks after the convention, was carried live on radio as well.[51]

Coolidge's overwhelming first-ballot nomination marked an important advance, as Coolidge himself recognized, in the emergence of the president as "the sole repository of party responsibility."[52] The conservative Republican senators who had controlled the GOP since 1912 had little regard for

Calvin Coolidge skillfully cultivated the press and generated favorable public opinion with photo sessions such as this March 1925 meeting with members of the Sioux Indian Republican Club.

Coolidge. Unlike Harding, Coolidge was not one of them—his background was in state politics. Yet they had little choice but to support the president's bid for a full term in 1924. As William Allen White wrote in 1925, "The reason why the senatorial group ceased hoping to defeat Coolidge for the Republican nomination was the obvious fact that Coolidge was getting stronger and stronger with the American people."[53] Noting that the radio had in no small measure made this possible, Cornwell wrote: "Here was the first President in history whom more than a tiny fraction of the populace could actually listen to, and whose voice they could come to know at first hand. Small wonder that the man developed a tangible meaning for millions—more so perhaps than any of his predecessors."[54] Coolidge's hold on the voters was demonstrated in the general election when he defeated the Democratic nominee, John W. Davis, by a three-to-one majority in the Electoral College and by nearly two to one in the national popular vote.

HERBERT C. HOOVER AND THE GREAT DEPRESSION

Coolidge demonstrated that the growing power and prominence of the executive office could be used as effectively by a president who wanted only to reign as by one who, like TR and Wilson, wanted to rule.[55] Coolidge was not simply a throwback to the era of Benjamin Harrison and Rutherford B. Hayes. Instead, his tenure suggested that a president with a shrewd sense of politics and public relations could thrive in the new political conditions of the twentieth century, even a president who was philosophically opposed to expanding government programs and executive power.

When Herbert Hoover, capitalizing on Coolidge's popularity, handily defeated Democrat Al Smith in the 1928 election, many expected that Hoover would be an able, even a brilliant national leader. The "Great Engineer," as he was called, brought to the White House a tremendous reputation for accomplishment and public service from his tenure as food administrator during the Wilson administration and as secretary of commerce under Harding and Coolidge. Dedicated to his Republican predecessors' pro-business policies, and confident that knowledgeable and efficient administration in Washington could build a strong foundation for national prosperity, Hoover seemed perfectly qualified to consolidate the gains of the postwar economic recovery.

Yet the same president who entered office amid such great expectations left four years later as the object of scorn and derision. This startling political reversal was caused in part by the Great Depression, the worst economic crisis in the nation's history. The depression struck with full force when the stock market crashed in October 1929, less than seven months after Hoover was inaugurated. But the Hoover administration was in trouble even before the crash.

Much of Hoover's difficulty as president stemmed from the contrast between his desire to bring about important changes in American society and his unwillingness or inability to undertake the tasks of leadership that could have made these changes possible. Like Harding and Coolidge, Hoover subscribed to a political philosophy that confined the national government to the few activities for which it had clear constitutional authority. But Hoover's fear of big government coexisted with his TR- and Wilson-style faith, born of the Progressive era, in the government's ability to improve social and economic conditions.[56]

Early in his presidency, Hoover called a special session of Congress to recommend a significant legislative program. "No president in a hundred years, excepting Woodrow Wilson, had moved his administration so quickly and so extensively into domestic reform," historian Martin L. Fausold has argued.[57] Hoover called for major changes in tariffs, taxes, conservation, and government organization. He urged Congress to develop programs to deal with the nation's already long-standing depression in agriculture.

Hoover also believed that his administration should mobilize industrial and civic organizations to facilitate better economic coordination and enhanced economic opportunities. He was particularly concerned about several flaws in the nation's recent prosperity: the imbalance between high production and low consumption; the weak agricultural sector; the feverish financial speculation, fueled by unsound monetary and lending policies; the poor organization of labor, which allowed a disproportionate share of corporate profits to go to owners and managers; and inefficient practices in the industrial sector. The solutions to these problems, Hoover believed, lay not in expanding the national government, but in using the presidency and the rest of the executive branch to encourage private institutions to develop more equitable and rational economic arrangements. As secretary of commerce, Hoover had worked successfully with trade associations and farm organizations. Now, as president, he hoped to expand these activities. "By his position," Hoover told the Gridiron Club on December 14, 1929, the president "must, within his capacities, give leadership to the development of moral, social, and economic forces outside of government which make for the betterment of our country."[58]

Hoover's philosophy and personality, however, rendered him incapable of providing the brand of leadership he advocated, especially after the stock market crash in October 1929 acrelerated the economy's rapid descent into depression. Sharing Coolidge's respect for the autonomy of the legislature, Hoover did little to lead the special session of Congress that he called in 1929. After leaving office, Hoover explained his reticence: "The weakening of the legislative arm leads to encroachment by the executive upon the legislative and judicial functions, and inevitably that encroachment is upon individual liberty."[59]

Despite the president's lack of assertiveness, his farm bill, at least, was enacted. The Agricultural Market Act created the Federal Farm Board to administer loans so that agricultural cooperatives could help farmers produce and market their crops. Before a bill that was acceptable to Hoover could pass, however, Republican leaders in the Senate had to quell a revolt by party insurgents. Against the president's wishes, western progressives had moved to subsidize farmers who were exporting commodities at prices lower than the domestic rates. After weeks of deadlock, Congress approved the president's version of the agriculture measure, but with little help from Hoover. "There is some very bad leadership from the bottom of 16th Street," complained former secretary of agriculture William M. Jardine, referring to the White House.[60]

Congress was not so accommodating when the issue was tariffs. The president favored a limited revision of the tariff schedules that would aid only stricken farmers. But a Senate resolution to confine tariff revision to the agricultural schedule was defeated by a single vote. Hoover, who in all likelihood could have swung the vote he needed in order to prevail, refused even to try.[61] He then remained silent as Congress, particularly the Senate, proceeded to increase tariffs on nonfarm as well as farm commodities, eventually passing a bill that raised tariffs to their highest levels in history. Hoover signed the protectionist Smoot-Hawley tariff, which he privately characterized as "vicious, extortionate, and obnoxious," in the face of ardent pleas from all parts of the country to veto it.[62] As journalist Walter Lippmann wrote, "The prospect of a controversy with his own party silenced him, and as far as one can judge by his public acts he abdicated all claims to leadership in the tariff battle."[63]

Hoover's refusal to lead the special session of Congress that he called in 1929 tempered the widespread enthusiasm that had greeted his election. Coolidge's reticence had frustrated some people, but it was in keeping with his indifference to programmatic activism. Hoover's passivity, however, seemed inappropriate to his ambitions for the nation. As Fausold has observed, "No activist president in this century has kept his distance from Congress as did Hoover."[64] By the fall of 1929, even Republican congressional leaders were criticizing Hoover's nonpolitical approach to the presidency. The press, not yet willing to dismiss Hoover as a weak executive, was mystified. Assessing the president's aloofness from the special session, one commentator concluded that "a strange paralysis seemed to rest upon Mr. Hoover during the first year after Congress met."[65]

Hoover's "strange paralysis," which caused only concern and confusion during the early days of his presidency, provoked bitter jests and withering scorn after the onslaught of the depression. Dignified silence in the face of congressional interference with his program was one thing, but for the president to remain above the fray when unemployment reached 25 percent of the workforce seemed heartless. Yet Hoover resisted growing public demands that he assume the mantle of legislative leader and prod congress to produce a body of law that would authorize the executive departments and agencies to assume more responsibility for economic coordination and social services. Instead, White House conferences proliferated. Hoover convened a series of economic stabilization conferences in the cabinet room, inviting the leaders of major industries and labor unions to participate. The main purpose of these conferences was to urge industries and workers to act voluntarily to ameliorate the economic crisis. "We could no more legislate ourselves out of a worldwide depression," Hoover insisted, than we could "exorcise a Caribbean hurricane by statutory law."[66]

The president's remote stance became especially disabling after the Republicans lost control of Congress in the 1930 midterm elections. When congressional Democrats refused to cooperate with him, Hoover chose to suffer in silence, bewailing their intransigence in the privacy of his White House study but declining to go over their heads to the people. As he later wrote in his memoirs, "I had felt deeply that no President should undermine the independence of the legislative and judicial branches by seeking to discredit them. The constitutional division of powers is the bastion of our liberties and was not designed as a battleground to display the prowess of presidents."[67]

The struggling president's constitutional principles, which kept him from exerting public leadership, were reinforced by personal qualities that ill suited him for the tasks of legislative, party, and popular leadership as well. Like Grant, Hoover came to the presidency with no background in elected office. His experience had been as a builder and manager of organizations, not as a politician working to forge legislative coalitions or a popular following. He was comfortable dealing with data, which he could marshal to support a course of action.[68] But, as Lippmann wrote, Hoover was "diffident in the presence of the normal irrationality of democracy."[69]

Uncomfortable with politics and politicians, Hoover also proved unable to form close relationships with reporters or to build on Coolidge's pioneering efforts in radio broadcasting. In the history of presidential communications, Hoover's presidency was important mainly in a negative sense. He abandoned the practice resuscitated by Wilson of presidents appearing in person to deliver major speeches before Congress. He fought losing battles to keep both his private life and his behind-the-scenes efforts to influence public policy out of the public's view. His administration "served to make painfully plain," Cornwell has observed, "that no future President could hope to emerge from his White House ordeal unless he was prepared in talent and temperament to cope with and master the demands of an age of mass communications."[70]

That said, Herbert Hoover was hardly the do-nothing president that Franklin Roosevelt and the Democrats made him out to be in the 1932 election. He repeatedly encouraged efforts by various sectors of the economy to pursue more rational and just business practices. With the onset of the depression, he tried even harder to supply the leadership that the public was demanding.

But Hoover was willing to go only so far. Although he called for programs, such as the Reconstruction Finance Corporation (RFC), that would provide federal loans to banks, railroads, and agricultural organizations, he did little to rouse popular support for these programs or to ensure their effective operation. New York representative Fiorello LaGuardia denounced the RFC as "a millionaire's dole." But LaGuardia and others soon recognized the critical precedent it represented. If Hoover granted federal relief to the banks, then how could he continue to refuse support for the unemployed? "Hoover had given up the ground of high principle," historian David M. Kennedy has written. "He now stood ideologically shorn before a storm of demands for unemployment relief."[71]

Hoover grimly resisted these demands, lecturing Congress and the country about preserving the nation's "rugged individualism" and the integrity of the federal budget. Characteristically, he marshaled the entire executive branch to encourage private and local groups to provide the needy with relief from the depression, but refused to offer direct federal aid. Seeking to come to terms with the great drought of 1930 and 1931, Hoover admonished the Red Cross to feed people rather than have the federal government do it. When the Red

Cross balked and Congress demanded that the government act, Hoover still demurred, stating that direct federal assistance was unconstitutional.

By the end of 1931, Hoover was more willing to relax his stalwart defense of rugged individualism. Excoriating budget deficits and the dangers of the dole, he vetoed the Garner-Wagner relief bill on July 11, 1932. Ten days later, however, the president reluctantly accepted a compromise measure, the Relief and Reconstruction Act, which he signed on July 21, a few weeks after Franklin Roosevelt accepted the Democratic nomination. The act authorized the RFC to finance $1.5 billion in "self-liquidating" public works and to loan $300 million to the states for relief. But this concession was too little and came too late, "especially and woefully so," Kennedy notes, "in the politically crucial area of relief."[72]

Hoover put traditional, nineteenth-century American political practices and principles to their greatest test. But his unalterable commitment to preserve these traditions even in the face of national calamity served only to discredit them. In this way, Hoover unwittingly laid the groundwork for a fundamental break with the politics and policies of the past.

THE TWENTIETH AMENDMENT

On February 6, 1933, less than a month before the end of Hoover's term, the Twentieth Amendment became part of the Constitution. It had cleared Congress in March 1932 and was ratified less than two months later by all the states, the first constitutional amendment in history to win unanimous ratification when initially considered.[73] The amendment was written mainly to shorten the time between the election of the president, vice president, and members of Congress and their entry into office. The hiatus for newly elected representatives and senators (unless the president called Congress into special session, as Hoover did in 1929) had been thirteen months: from election day in November until the first Monday in December of the following year, the date established by Article I of the Constitution as the initial meeting time for each new Congress. The delay for presidents and vice presidents had been about four months, from election day until March 4, the inauguration date that was enshrined in a law passed by Congress in 1792.

Sen. George Norris, the main author of the Twentieth Amendment, sought to remedy three major flaws in the traditional arrangement, which he regarded as suited to the age when travel was difficult and time-consuming and the business of the federal government was relatively minor. The first flaw was the biennial lame-duck session of Congress, which typically lasted from the December after the election until the following March and which included many outgoing members of the defeated party. Second, by not having Congress begin its term before the president, existing procedures authorized the lame-duck Congress, not the newly elected one, to choose the president in the event of a deadlock in the Electoral College, as had happened in 1801 and 1825. Third, Norris regarded four months as too long a time for the nation to have, in effect, two presidents: an outgoing incumbent and an incoming president-elect.

To remedy the lame-duck and two-presidents problem, section 1 of the Twentieth Amendment set noon on January 20 as the beginning of the president's and vice president's four-year term and noon on January 3 as the start of the term for members of Congress. Norris used section 3 of the amendment to address two other potential problems in the presidential and vice-presidential selection process. It provided that if a president-elect were to die before the start of the term, the vice president–elect would be inaugurated as president. Section 3 also stated that if, by inauguration day, no presidential candidate had received either a majority of electoral votes or the support of a majority of state delegations in the House, the vice president–elect, chosen by a simple majority vote of the Senate, would act as president until a president was chosen. (The same would be true if a president-elect were found to be unqualified by virtue of age, citizenship, or residency.) Other provisions of the amendment dealt with equally real but remote possibilities: for example, that a vice president–elect might not be chosen, or that either a winning presidential or vice-presidential candidate might die before receiving "elect" status when Congress counted the electoral votes in early January.

As unlikely as some of the situations contemplated by the Twentieth Amendment are, two events that occurred near the time of the amendment's passage testified to its value. From November 1932 to March 1933, in the last of the four-month transitions, the nation endured a long and awkward interregnum between Hoover, the discredited and defeated incumbent president, and Franklin Roosevelt, his successor—all this in the midst of the Great Depression. And on February 15, 1933, nine days after the amendment entered the Constitution, President-elect Roosevelt narrowly escaped an assassination attempt in Miami, Florida.

NOTES

1. Robert P. Saldin, "World War I and the 'System of 1896,'" *The Journal of Politics* 72, no. 3 (July 2010): 825–836.

2. Harding quoted in Robert K. Murray, *The Harding Era: Warren G. Harding and His Administration* (Minneapolis: University of Minnesota Press, 1969), 70.

3. Confusion still exists about how the word *normalcy* originated. The best guess is that Harding meant *normality* but said *normalcy*.

4. William Starr Myers, *The Republican Party: A History* (New York: Century, 1928), 441.

5. Lodge quoted in Andrew Sinclair, *The Available Man: The Life Behind the Masks of Warren Gamaliel Harding* (New York: Macmillan, 1965), 152 (emphasis in original).

6. Elmer E. Cornwell Jr., *Presidential Leadership of Public Opinion* (Bloomington: Indiana University Press, 1965), 60.

7. Warren Harding, "We Need a Newly Consecrated Americanism," *Independent,* October 1920, in *History of American Presidential Elections, 1789–1968,* 4 vols., ed. Arthur M. Schlesinger Jr. and Fred L. Israel (New York: Chelsea, 1971), 3:2437–9. See also *New York Times,* July 21, 1920, 7.

8. Quoted in Wilfred E. Binkley, *President and Congress* (New York: Knopf, 1947), 217.

9. Ibid.

10. George Rothwell Brown, *The Leadership of Congress* (Indianapolis: Bobbs-Merrill, 1922; New York: Arno Press, 1974), 258.

11. Harding vetoed the World War Adjusted Compensation Act in September 1922. Although the House voted to override his rejection of the bonus bill, the Senate, after a bitter struggle, failed to do so by four votes. Historian Niall Palmer argues that this confrontation shattered Harding's hope that the White House and Congress could return to a cooperative working relationship. See Palmer, "The Veterans' Bonus and the Evolving Presidency of Warren G. Harding, *Presidential Studies Quarterly* 38, no. 1 (March 2008): 39–60.

12. Jennings quoted in Murray, *Harding Era,* 314.

13. Ibid., 128.

14. Ibid.

15. Robert F. Martin, "Warren Gamaliel Harding," in *The American Presidents,* ed. Melvin I. Urofsky (New York and London: Garland, 2000), 309–310.

16. Binkley, *President and Congress,* 221. For a discussion of the events that led up to the Washington Naval Disarmament Conference, see Murray, *Harding Era,* 140–166; and Lindsay Rogers, "American Government and Politics: The Second, Third, and Fourth Sessions of the Sixty-Seventh Congress," *American Political Science Review* 18 (February 1924): 91–93.

17. Paul Van Riper, *History of the United States Civil Service* (Evanston, Ill.: Row, Peterson, 1958), 287.

18. Murray, *Harding Era,* 430.

19. William Allen White, *The Autobiography of William Allen White* (New York: Macmillan, 1946), 619.

20. On the events leading up to the Teapot Dome scandal, see J. Leonard Bates, *The Origins of Teapot Dome: Progressives, Parties, and Petroleum, 1909–1921* (Urbana: University of Illinois, 1963), esp. chaps. 13 and 14; and Burt Noggle, "The Origins of the Teapot Dome Investigation," *Mississippi Valley Historical Review* 64 (September 1957): 237–266. See also "The Teapot Dome Resolution," in *The Evolving Presidency: Landmark Documents, 1787–2010,* 4th ed., ed. Michael Nelson (Washington, D.C.: CQ Press, 2012), 135–137.

21. Fall could not be dismissed as merely one of the "grafters" who attached themselves to the Harding administration. He was able to defend, his belief that the public domain should be opened to private development. As he once told a critic, "Every generation from Adam and Eve down has lived better than the generation before. I don't know how they'll do it—maybe they'll use the energy of the sun or the sea waves—but . . . [they] will live better than we do. I stand for opening up every resource." Quoted in Bates, *Origins of Teapot Dome,* 227–228.

22. George W. Norris, *Fighting Liberal: The Autobiography of George W. Norris* (New York: Macmillan, 1945), 233.

23. Herbert Emmerich, *Federal Organization and Administrative Management* (Tuscaloosa: University of Alabama Press, 1971), 40–41. For a discussion of the enactment and early history of the Budget and Accounting Act, see William M. Goldsmith, ed., *The Growth of Presidential Power: A Documented History,* 3 vols. (New York and London: Chelsea, 1974), 3:1478–95; and Peri E. Arnold, *Making the Managerial Presidency: Comprehensive Reorganization Planning, 1905–1980* (Princeton: Princeton University Press, 1986), 53–55.

24. Lindsay Rogers, "American Government and Politics," *American Political Science Review* 14 (November 1920): 659–671. The comptroller general is appointed by the president, with the advice and consent of the Senate, for a fifteen-year nonrenewable term. The president selects a nominee from a list of at least three individuals recommended by an eight-member bipartisan, bicameral commission of congressional leaders. The comptroller general may not be removed by the president, but only by Congress through impeachment or a joint resolution passed by both houses of Congress. Since 1921, there have been only eight comptrollers general, and no formal attempt has ever been made to remove one.

25. Murray, *Harding Era*, 178.

26. *Myers v. United States*, 272 U.S. 53 (1926).

27. Ibid., at 134.

28. See "*Humphrey's Executor v. United States*," in Nelson, *Evolving Presidency*, 151–157. See also chap. 10 in this volume.

29. Cornwell, *Presidential Leadership of Public Opinion*, 62. Much of the following discussion draws on Cornwell's interesting chapter on public relations in the Harding and Coolidge administrations.

30. Ibid., 63.

31. Ibid., 70.

32. Lewis L. Gould, *The Modern American Presidency* (Lawrence: University Press of Kansas, 2003), 63. Welliver gained some posthumous fame after the creation of the Judson Welliver Society, an organization of former White House speechwriters, which was founded by William Safire, a speechwriter for Richard Nixon. On the origins and development of presidential speechwriting, see Robert Schlesinger. *White House Ghosts: Presidents and Their Speechwriters,* Simon and Schuster, 2008; and Michael Nelson, "Speeches, Speechwriting, and the American Presidency," in *The President's Words: Speeches and Speechwriting in the Modern White House,* eds. Michael Nelson and Russell L. Riley (Lawrence: University Press of Kansas, 2010), 1–26.

33. Palmer, "The Veterans' Bonus and the Evolving Presidency of Warren G. Harding," 54.

34. Quoted in Murray, *Harding Era*, 418.

35. Scholars have consistently ranked Harding, along with Ulysses S. Grant and Franklin Pierce, as America's worst presidents. See Jill L. Curry and Irwin L. Morris, "Explaining Presidential Greatness: The Roles of Peace and Prosperity?" *Presidential Studies Quarterly* 40, no. 3 (September 2010): 515–530 (516–517).

36. Murray, *Harding Era*, 452.

37. Cornwell, *Presidential Leadership of Public Opinion*, 73.

38. Calvin Coolidge, *The Autobiography of Calvin Coolidge* (New York: Cosmopolitan, 1929), 232.

39. Binkley, *President and Congress*, 223.

40. William Allen White, *A Puritan in Babylon* (New York: Macmillan, 1938), v.

41. Edward S. Martin, "Shall Business Run the World?" *Harper's Magazine,* February 1925, 381.

42. Murray, *Harding Era*, 505.

43. In sitting tight, however, Coolidge failed to address certain ominous economic signs, such as underconsumption and feverish stock speculation, that foreshadowed the Great Depression. See Robert H. Ferrell, *The Presidency of Calvin Coolidge* (Lawrence: University Press of Kansas, 1998), 186–189.

44. "The Destiny of America," delivered at Memorial Day services, Northampton, Mass., May 30, 1923, in Calvin Coolidge, *The Price of Freedom: Speeches and Addresses* (New York: Scribner's, 1924), 342; and Calvin Coolidge, "Inaugural Address," March 4, 1925, in *Calvin Coolidge, 1872–1933,* ed. Philip R. Moran (Dobbs Ferry, N.Y.: Oceana, 1970), 65.

45. Gould, *Modern American Presidency,* 68.

46. Cornwell, *Presidential Leadership of Public Opinion,* 74–75.

47. T. R. B., "Washington Notes," *New Republic,* February 10, 1926, 326.

48. The reporter quoted is Jay C. Hayden of the *Detroit News,* who covered the White House for sixteen years. Hayden considered Coolidge to be as masterful as Theodore Roosevelt at the "human interest" game, although "the Coolidge process was more subtle." *Literary Digest,* July 25, 1931, 8.

49. Quoted in Cornwell, *Presidential Leadership of Public Opinion,* 90.

50. Ibid., 323.

51. Gould, *Modern American Presidency,* 70.

52. Coolidge, *Autobiography,* 231.

53. William Allen White, *Calvin Coolidge: The Man Who Is President* (New York: Macmillan, 1925), 137.

54. Cornwell, *Presidential Leadership of Public Opinion,* 92.

55. Ibid., 97.

56. Ellis Hawley, "The Constitution of the Hoover and F. Roosevelt Presidency during the Depression Era, 1900–1939," in *The Constitution and the American Presidency,* ed. Martin L. Fausold and Alan Shank (Albany: State University of New York Press, 1991), 89–91.

57. Martin L. Fausold, *The Presidency of Herbert C. Hoover* (Lawrence: University Press of Kansas, 1985), 56.

58. *Public Papers of the Presidents: Herbert Hoover, March 4 to December 31, 1929* (Washington, D.C.: Government Printing Office, 1974), 472.

59. Herbert Hoover, *The Challenge to Liberty* (New York: Scribner's, 1934), 125–126.

60. Quoted in Fausold, *Presidency of Herbert C. Hoover,* 51.

61. Arthur W. MacMahan, "American Government and Politics: First Session of the Seventy-First Congress," *American Political Science Review* 24 (February 1930): 50–56; Binkley, *President and Congress,* 229–230.

62. Robert Allen and Drew Pearson, *Washington Merry-Go-Round* (New York: Horace Liveright, 1931), 66.

63. Walter Lippmann, "The Peculiar Weakness of Mr. Hoover," *Harper's Magazine,* June 1930, 5.

64. Fausold, *Presidency of Herbert C. Hoover,* 49.

65. Quoted in Binkley, *President and Congress,* 229.

66. Hoover quoted in Matthew Crenson and Benjamin Ginsberg, *Presidential Power, Unchecked and Unbalanced* (New York: Norton, 2007), 149.

67. Herbert Hoover, *The Memoirs of Herbert Hoover: The Great Depression, 1929–1941,* 3 vols. (New York: Macmillan, 1952), 3:104.

68. Binkley, *President and Congress,* 227–228.

69. Lippmann, "Peculiar Weakness of Mr. Hoover," 5.

70. Cornwell, *Presidential Leadership of Public Opinion,* 113.

71. David M. Kennedy, *Freedom from Fear: The American People in Depression and War, 1929–1945* (New York: Oxford University Press, 1999), 85.

72. Ibid., 93.

73. David E. Kyvig, *Explicit and Authentic Acts: Amending the U.S. Constitution, 1776–1995* (Lawrence: University Press of Kansas, 1996), 274.

CHAPTER 10

The Consolidation of the Modern Presidency: Franklin D. Roosevelt to Dwight D. Eisenhower

T he 1932 elections marked the beginning of a new political era. The Democratic candidate, Franklin Delano Roosevelt, became the first member of his party since Franklin Pierce in 1852 to be elected president with a majority of the national popular vote. In the Electoral College, Roosevelt scored a 472–59 landslide, carrying forty-two states to six for the incumbent, Herbert C. Hoover. In the new Congress, Democrats outnumbered Republicans by 60 to 35 in the Senate and 310 to 117 in the House. FDR's victory indicated, in the opinion of progressive Republican journalist William Allen White, "a firm desire on the part of the American people to use government as an agency for human welfare."[1]

Roosevelt did not disappoint this desire. He embraced the progressive reformers' commitment to regulate business in the public interest. But he also believed that it was the federal government's responsibility to guarantee the economic security of its people. The new president brought the welfare state to the United States, years after it became a fixture in other Western nations.

The emergence of the welfare state was closely associated with a redefinition of the public's understanding of rights. In the new version of the American social contract offered by FDR, the national government would assume responsibility for providing an adequate standard of living for families and individuals. In his Commonwealth Club address, which he delivered during the 1932 campaign, Roosevelt declared that the task of modern government was "to assist the development of an economic declaration of rights, an economic constitutional order." He argued that the traditional American emphasis on individual self-reliance must give way to a new understanding of individualism in which the government acts as a regulating and sustaining agency, guaranteeing to each person protection from the worst uncertainties of the marketplace.[2]

Roosevelt's commitment to build a welfare state required a stronger presidency. As he put it, "The day of enlightened administration has come."[3] This concept of presidential responsibility informed his extraordinary leadership in expanding the federal government to meet the demands of a severe domestic crisis, the Great Depression, and then an international one, World War II. The modern presidency became an enduring fixture of the American political system during Roosevelt's long tenure in the White House.

What is the modern presidency?[4] Many of the most important characteristics of the executive date from the Constitutional Convention and the earliest days of the Republic. During the nineteenth century, too, significant presidential patterns and practices took shape. What marked the twentieth-century transformation of the executive was the emergence of the president, rather than Congress or political parties, as the leading instrument of popular rule, "the steward of the public welfare."

Acting on this modern concept of presidential power, Theodore Roosevelt and Woodrow Wilson inaugurated the practices that strengthened the president as popular and legislative leader. It then fell to Franklin Roosevelt to consolidate, or institutionalize, the changes in the executive office that were initiated during the Progressive era. After Roosevelt's long tenure, this new understanding of executive responsibilities would lead even conservative Republican presidents to wield the powers of the office in the manner of their liberal forebears.

FRANKLIN D. ROOSEVELT AND THE MODERN PRESIDENCY

So great an impression did Franklin Roosevelt make on the American political system that surveys of historians nearly always rank him alongside Abraham Lincoln and George Washington as one of the greatest presidents in history.[5] Above all, FDR's high rating owes to his efforts to lead the American people through the Great Depression. Roosevelt came to office in the fourth year of a world economic crisis whose persistence raised grave doubts about the viability of republican government. British historian Arnold J. Toynbee observed that 1931 was distinguished from previous years by one outstanding feature: "In 1931, men and women all over the world were seriously contemplating and frankly discussing the possibility that the Western system of society might break down and cease to exist."[6]

Americans had reason to share these doubts. As Roosevelt prepared to take the oath of office on March 4, 1933, the ranks of the unemployed numbered fifteen million, about one-third of the workforce. In thirty-two states, every bank had been closed by state government edict. On the morning of FDR's inauguration, the New York Stock Exchange closed its doors. Merle Thorpe, the editor of *Nation's Business*, wrote ominously, "Fear, bordering on panic, loss of faith in everything, our fellowman, our institutions, private and government. Worst of all, no faith in ourselves, or the future."[7]

In this atmosphere of national despair, Roosevelt's arrival in Washington was greeted with hope. Everyone who watched and waited, wrote *New York Times* columnist Arthur Krock, was "ready to be enthusiastic over any display of leadership" and eager to be convinced that the new president would exhibit the kind of bold and energetic initiative that the American people had demanded but not received from Hoover.[8]

Unlike his predecessor, Roosevelt was admirably suited to lead by virtue of personality and background. Hoover was aloof and uncomfortable with the demands of the presidency, but FDR believed that he belonged in the office. "The essence of Roosevelt's Presidency," political scientist Clinton Rossiter has written, "was his airy eagerness to meet the age head on."[9] His confidence stemmed from the combination of a privileged, albeit challenging, upbringing in Hyde Park, New York, and an admirable political education as state senator, assistant secretary of the navy in the Wilson administration, vice-presidential candidate in 1920, and two-term governor of New York, then the largest state in the Union.

Roosevelt's faith in his own abilities was accompanied by a willingness to experiment, which he displayed throughout his presidency. The nation became aware of FDR's innovating spirit when, shattering precedent, he hired a small plane to take him to the 1932 Democratic national convention in Chicago to accept his party's nomination for president. In the past, major party nominees had stayed away from the convention, waiting for official notification that they had been nominated.[10] But Roosevelt wanted to demonstrate dramatically that his physical disability (he had lost the use of his legs a year after the 1920 campaign when he was stricken with poliomyelitis) would not hinder him as a candidate or as the president. "The convention rose enthusiastically to the voyageur of the skies" marveled one reporter, "and accepted his method of travel and the fact that he endured its rigors so well as a proof of his venturesome spirit and fine physical equipment for the office of the President of the United States."[11]

Roosevelt also wanted to show his party and the nation that he would not hesitate to break traditions if they stood in the way of his vision of progress. "I have started out on the tasks that lie ahead by breaking the absurd traditions that the candidate should remain in professed ignorance of what has happened for weeks until he is formally notified of that event many weeks later," Roosevelt told the convention on July 2, 1932. "Let it also be symbolic that in so doing I broke traditions. Let it be from now on the task of our party to break foolish traditions."[12]

On inauguration day, March 4, 1933, the cheers that greeted Roosevelt as the car carrying President Hoover and the president-elect approached the Capitol seemed to convey "a tone of understanding," the *New York Times* reported, "that the motor bore not only two men, not only a Democrat elected to succeed a Republican whom he had defeated, but two antagonistic philosophies of government. . . . In the greeting there appeared to be a note of jubilation that the day had come when the new philosophy was to replace the rejected theories of the old."[13]

No such jubilation was evident in Roosevelt's demeanor that day. The president delivered a solemn, compelling inaugural address that spelled out in clear and uncompromising language both his disdain for the age-old practices he thought should be abandoned and his intention to act boldly to deal with the crisis at hand. Laying the blame for the depression squarely on the laissez-faire economic doctrines and halting leadership of his conservative Republican predecessors, Roosevelt summoned the nation to a higher purpose: "The money changers have fled from their high seats in the temple of our civilization. We may now restore that temple to ancient truths. The measure of that restoration lies in the extent to which we apply social values more noble than mere monetary profit."[14]

Just as boldly, the new president stated his determination to lead the nation and its government:

> It is to be hoped that the normal balance of Executive and legislative authority may be wholly adequate to meet the unprecedented task before us. . . . But in the event that Congress shall fail to take [action] . . . and in the event that the national emergency is still critical, I shall not evade the clear course of duty that will then confront me. I shall ask the Congress for one remaining instrument to meet the crisis—broad executive power to wage a war against the emergency, as great as the power that would be given to me if we were in fact invaded by a foreign foe.[15]

Roosevelt lost no time translating intentions into action. On March 5, one day after taking the oath of office, he issued the "Bank Holiday Proclamation," which suspended "the heavy and unwarranted withdrawals of gold and currency from our banking institutions" in the states where banks remained open. The bank edict, an unprecedented exercise of executive power in peacetime, declared that from March 6 to March 9, banks in the United States must suspend all transactions.[16]

During the final days of the Hoover administration, Secretary of Commerce Ogden Mills had urged the outgoing president to call a bank holiday, arguing that legal authority to do so could be found in the Trading with the Enemy Act of 1917. But Hoover was reluctant to act on his own initiative, especially after his attorney general questioned whether a wartime measure could be applied to a peacetime situation, no matter how grave. Hoover might have been willing to close the banks if the president-elect had offered public support, but Roosevelt refused to assume responsibility for any action before becoming president. Once sworn in, however, FDR did not hesitate to use the full powers of his office to address the national emergency. He felt no reluctance about attacking the banking crisis with a World War I measure. On the same day that he declared the bank holiday, Roosevelt issued another executive order calling Congress into special session. Four days later, on March 9, he introduced the Emergency Banking Bill, which marshaled the full resources of the Federal Reserve Board to support the faltering banks and thereby restore the people's confidence in the banking system. The bill was the first to be passed during the extraordinary "One Hundred Days" (from noon on March 9, to 1:00 a.m. on June 15, 1933), when Congress passed a relentless succession of Roosevelt-sponsored laws. Remarkably, the bank bill was enacted in less than eight hours. Forty-five minutes later, with photographers recording the scene, Roosevelt signed it into law.

FDR promptly announced that he would speak directly to the people on Sunday evening, March 12, to explain in a radio address what he had done about the banks and why he had done it. This was the first of his "fireside chats," which were a revolutionary advance in presidential use of the mass media.[17] Calvin Coolidge and, less successfully, Hoover had spoken on the radio, but only to broadcast fixed, formal pronouncements. FDR's chats sounded relaxed, creating the illusion that the president was dropping by his listeners' homes to tell them what he was doing in Washington and why he was doing it. The purpose was less to pronounce policy or rouse citizens to action than to develop an intimate bond with the people and shape their opinions.

Of all the fireside chats that Roosevelt gave (he delivered two or three each year), none was more successful than the first. Both FDR's comfortable radio style and the phrasing of his message were ideally suited to his purpose of reassurance. "We had a bad banking situation," he said. "Some of our bankers had shown themselves either incompetent or dishonest in handling people's funds." Yet most bankers worked hard and well, Roosevelt pointed out, and, besides, the task at hand was not to lay blame for the crisis, but to end it: "It was the government's job to straighten out the situation and do it as quickly as possible. And the job is being performed. . . . Confidence and courage are the essentials of success in carrying out our plan. You people must have faith; you must not be stampeded by rumors or guesses. Let us unite in banishing fear. We have provided the machinery to restore our financial system; it is up to you to support it and make it work."[18]

The bank bill and the fireside chat ended the banking crisis: there were no runs on the banks when they reopened on Monday morning, March 13. On the contrary, deposits far exceeded withdrawals as hoarded currency poured back into the vaults. A few days later, the New York Stock Exchange, closed since March 4, opened with the greatest single-day rise in memory. "Capitalism was saved in eight days," Roosevelt's aide Raymond Moley declared dramatically.[19]

Similar adulation was expressed not just by FDR's friends but also by his opponents. An "incredible change has come over the face of things here in the United States in a single week," editorialized the *Wall Street Journal*, because "the new administration in Washington has superbly risen to the occasion." To be sure, the *Journal* warned, only "a good beginning had been made" and "incalculable tasks" remained. But "there are times when a beginning is nearly everything."[20]

The first two weeks of Roosevelt's presidency lifted the spirit of the country. Clearly, the new president had forged a vital link between the government and the people. White House clerks who were accustomed to opening a thousand pieces of mail per day during peak periods found themselves snowed under by the 460,000 letters that greeted FDR's inauguration. As William Hopkins, who worked in the White House correspondence section, remembered, "The mail started coming in by the truckloads. They couldn't even get the envelopes open."[21]

THE NEW DEAL

The early days of the Roosevelt administration brought the presidency into its own as the nation's primary source of popular and legislative leadership. A close bond developed between FDR and most Americans during the struggle to end the depression. The advent of the welfare state, which entailed a massive transfer of the burden to help those in need from the states and the private sector to the national government, created new responsibilities for the president. Roosevelt initiated this transfer, carefully preparing the nation for the revolutionary departures in public policy that took place during the 1930s.

The centerpiece of Roosevelt's program was the Social Security Act, which created a comprehensive federal system of old age and unemployment insurance. Selling social security was no easy task. On June 19, 1934, remarking on the unusual American commitment to individual self-reliance, Sen. Hugo Black of Alabama wrote to a member of the Roosevelt administration: "The public in our country has little conception of the possibilities of social insurance. . . . [T]here are few people in this country who realize such systems of social insurance have been adopted in most of the civilized countries in the world."[22]

Fourteen months after Black's letter, the Social Security Act of 1935 sailed through Congress and was ceremoniously signed into law by the president. In the interim, FDR had nurtured public opinion carefully. He saw his task as one of civic education, teaching the American people that social insurance was consistent with, not alien to, their values. The president was confident that if he taught the people well, they would pass the lessons on to their representatives in Congress.

In filling his role as teacher, Roosevelt argued that the development of a national industrial society made it impossible for most individuals to achieve financial security within the familiar bonds of family and neighborhood. Instead, the complexities of great cities and of organized industry required that the federal government help people secure their welfare in time of need. To bring this lesson home, in a fireside chat on June 28, 1934, Roosevelt included a folksy yet effective illustration: the remodeling of the White House's West Wing, which he likened to the adoption of social security. After describing the wiring and plumbing and the modern means of keeping offices cool in the hot Washington summer that were being installed, Roosevelt noted, "It is this combination of the old and new that marks orderly peaceful progress, not only in building buildings, but in building government itself. . . . All that we do seeks to fulfill the historic traditions of the American people."[23]

Roosevelt's leadership on this issue involved, as one presidential scholar has written, "a careful process of grafting social security onto the stalk of traditional American values."[24] By the end of this process, the president had moved the nation beyond the traditional idea that rights embody only guarantees against government oppression to a new understanding, articulated in his Commonwealth Club address, that government must also ensure the right to economic security. He credited Abraham Lincoln for transfusing "with new meaning the concepts of our constitutional fathers" and for assuring "a Government having for its broad purpose the promotion of life, liberty, and happiness of all the people."[25] Lincoln had praised the Declaration of Independence for giving birth to a positive understanding of liberty, in which government's "leading object" was "to afford all, an unfettered start, and a fair chance in the race of life." Roosevelt now argued that the time had come to adopt, at least in spirit, a new Declaration, a new idea of rights which acknowledged that "necessitous men are not free men."[26] It was just such an understanding that Roosevelt had in mind when, at the 1932 Democratic convention, he pledged himself to "a new deal for the American people."[27]

The 1935 Social Security Act included old age insurance, unemployment insurance, and Aid to Families with Dependent Children (AFDC), popularly known as welfare. By European standards, the social security program was quite limited. Because old age insurance did not cover domestic and hotel workers, teachers, and nurses, it excluded most African Americans and women from its benefits. Furthermore, it did not include any support for health care, and its levels of welfare spending were low. The welfare and unemployment provisions also left considerable discretion and funding responsibility to the states, which dealt out payments unevenly. Nevertheless, social security marked a watershed in the national government's assumption of the responsibility to protect individuals from the uncertainties of the market. Its components, especially old age pensions, grew over the years, so that social security became the largest of all federal programs.

Significantly, the need for voters to ratify the New Deal agenda, with its embodiment of a new individualism, was the principal message of Roosevelt's first reelection bid in 1936. The Democratic Party's platform for that campaign, drafted by Roosevelt, was written as a pastiche of the Declaration of Independence. The platform claimed with respect to the Social Security Act, "We hold this truth to be self-evident—that the test of representative government is its ability to promote the safety and happiness of the people. . . . On the foundation of the Social Security Act we are determined to erect a structure of economic security for all our people."[28]

The New Deal was a series of legislative acts, executive orders, and presidential proclamations that sought not only to secure individual security but also to remedy the broader economic problems that underlay the Great Depression. During Roosevelt's tenure as president, not only was social security established to aid the aged, the unemployed, the disabled, and widows with dependent children, but work projects were financed by the greatest peacetime appropriation in history. In addition, for the first time the national government fostered unionization. When Roosevelt became president, almost no factory workers belonged to a labor union. Within a few years, industrial unionism was firmly established, largely because of the National Labor Relations Act (the Wagner Act) of 1935, which empowered the government to enter factories and conduct elections so that workers could freely decide whether to join a union.

Finally, Roosevelt demanded that business recognize the superior authority of the federal government. Like his cousin Theodore, he fashioned himself a conservative reformer who sought not to oppose private enterprise but to strengthen it by curbing business's most abusive practices and by ameliorating the most extreme conditions of economic hardship. FDR was opposed in this effort by an unreconstructed segment of the American business community, which denied to the federal government any right to regulate commercial activity. As the president complained in a letter to Harvard law professor Felix Frankfurter in February 1937, "It is the same old story of those who have property to fail to realize that I am the best friend the profit system ever had, even though I add my denunciation of unconscionable profits."[29]

Roosevelt's resentment of his critics in business was intense. "These economic royalists complain that we seek to overthrow the institutions of America," he told a roaring crowd at the 1936 Democratic convention. "What they really complain of is that we seek to take away their power." The time had come, Roosevelt insisted, "to overthrow this kind of power." The New Deal regulatory program greatly extended the responsibility of the federal government, especially the president, to guarantee "equal opportunity in the market place" to the average citizen.[30] Describing a range of Roosevelt-sponsored regulatory laws, such as the Securities and Exchange Act and the Public Utility Holding Company Act, historian William E. Leuchtenburg wrote: "Although the New Deal always operated within a capitalist framework, Roosevelt insisted that there was a national interest that it was the duty of the President to represent and, when the situation called for it, to impose."[31]

Not every major innovation in public policy during the 1930s originated in the White House. Some New Deal programs, such as the Tennessee Valley Authority, had long been on the public agenda, lacking only the impetus of a national crisis and a presidential endorsement.[32] Other parts of what Roosevelt called the new "economic constitutional order," such as the Wagner Act, redounded to the president's political benefit even though he supported them only haltingly. That FDR was hailed for the efforts of New York senator Robert F. Wagner and others signified the American people's growing tendency to think of the president as the government.

The 1936 election ensured that the important political changes of Roosevelt's first term would endure. In 1932 his victory had been more a rejection of Hoover than an endorsement of FDR and his party. The 1936 election, however, was a sweeping confirmation of his leadership and of the New Deal. FDR won 60 percent of the popular vote—the largest majority yet obtained by a presidential candidate—and carried every state but Maine and Vermont.[33] The election also strengthened the Democratic hold on Congress, marking the Democrats' emergence as the nation's new majority party.

INSTITUTIONALIZATION OF THE MODERN PRESIDENCY

As Americans' regard for the presidency as the government's preeminent source of moral leadership, legislative guidance, and policy innovation grew, pressures mounted to increase the size and professionalism of the president's staff. A modest office since the time of its creation, the presidency developed after the 1930s into a full-blown institution.

Roosevelt hastened this development when he named three of the country's foremost scholars of public administration—Louis Brownlow, Charles E. Merriam, and Luther Gulick—to the newly formed President's Committee on Administrative Management. Concluding that "the President needs help," the Brownlow Committee, as it came to be called, proposed the creation of the Executive Office of the President (EOP). The EOP would include the Bureau of the Budget, which had been housed in the Treasury Department since its birth in 1921, and a new White House Office, to be staffed by loyal and energetic presidential aides whose importance would be constrained by their "passion for anonymity." In contrast to the cabinet departments and independent agencies, which were extensively influenced by Congress, the EOP was designed as a presidential institution, responsible for tasks closely linked to the president's priorities and staffed by individuals who shared the president's political and policy objectives.[34] Most of those named by the president to fill important positions in the EOP did not require Senate confirmation.

The Brownlow Committee also sought to enhance the president's control of the expanding activities of the executive branch. By 1937 the Roosevelt administration was confronting a bewildering array of new and sometimes autonomous government agencies whose number and independence offended the president's vision of a unified and energetic executive. Roosevelt, in fact, remarked shortly after the 1936 election that administrative management was the least successful aspect of his first term and professed relief that the Republicans had not concentrated their fire on this weakness during the campaign.[35] The Brownlow Committee called for an overhaul of the executive branch, recommending that all of the more than one hundred agencies then in existence be integrated into twelve major departments, each controlled by the president. Thus would "the national will be expressed not merely in a brief, exultant moment of electoral decision, but in a persistent, determined, competent day-by-day administration of what the nation has decided to do."[36]

Roosevelt wholeheartedly supported the Brownlow Committee's recommendations. Congress, for its part, had little quarrel with the new EOP. But the proposal embedded in the 1937 executive reorganization bill to overhaul the departments and agencies sparked one of the most intense controversies of FDR's presidency. His two-year battle for comprehensive administrative reform wrote a new chapter in the long-standing struggle between the president and Congress for control of administration.

What gave the battle special intensity was that it occurred just as administration was becoming an important arena of public policy. As Gulick reported approvingly, the expansion of welfare and regulatory programs during the New Deal meant that the complex responsibilities of government increasingly were set forth in loosely written statutes, each little more than "a declaration of war [on a problem], so that the essence of the program is in reality in the gradual unfolding of the plan in actual administration."[37] The struggle between the president and Congress for control of the departments and agencies was no longer a simple squabble over patronage and power. The right to shape the direction and character of American society was also at stake.

When Congress finally did enact the Executive Reorganization Act of 1939, it granted the president new administrative powers, but fewer than he wanted. It placed a two-year limit on FDR's authority to reorganize the bureaucracy and exempted twenty-one important government agencies. Nevertheless, Roosevelt's implementation of the 1939 statute by Executive Order 8248 effected many of the Brownlow Committee's recommendations. The order created the Executive Office of the President and moved several existing agencies under its umbrella. In addition to the White House Office and the refurbished and strengthened Bureau of the Budget, which was transferred from the Treasury Department, the new EOP included the National Resources Planning Board, a long-term planning agency. The transplanted Budget Bureau began to acquire much greater powers, eventually assuming responsibility to oversee the formation of the president's domestic program.

Because the creation of the EOP enhanced the capacity of the president to manage the expanding activities of the executive branch, it was an "epoch making event in the history of American institutions," wrote Gulick, and "perhaps the most important single step in the institutionalization of the presidency."[38] Most significant, the 1939 reforms hastened the development of the "administrative presidency," in which domestic policy is shaped on the president's behalf through executive orders, rule making by executive departments and agencies, and policy implementation.[39] To be sure, the absence of detail in Article II of the Constitution had always left the door open for independent presidential action, but the institutionalization of the presidency established an organizational apparatus that presidents and their appointees could use to short-circuit the separation of powers, accelerating the transfer of authority from Congress to the executive.

CONSTITUTIONAL CRISIS

The New Deal provoked a serious constitutional crisis toward the end of FDR's first term. Roosevelt argued that the modern presidency, like the welfare state, was in keeping with sound constitutional principles. "The only thing that has been happening," he told the nation in a fireside chat on May 7, 1933, "has been to designate the President as the agency to carry out certain of the purposes of Congress. This was constitutional and in keeping with past American traditions."[40] Opponents of the New Deal strenuously disagreed. "As they saw it," historian Ellis Hawley has written, "the balance and separation of powers established by the Constitution were being destroyed by a power-seeking presidency gathering into itself the power that should be exercised by Congress and the states."[41]

The ranks of New Deal critics included not just Roosevelt's enemies in Congress and business, but also a majority of the Supreme Court. In 1935 and 1936 the Court struck down several important pieces of New Deal legislation, and many legal commentators expected that the Social Security Act and Wagner Act would be the next to fall. Roosevelt, whose second-term inauguration was the first to be held on January 20 under the new Twentieth Amendment, responded on February 5, 1937, with the most controversial action of his presidency, the "Court-packing" bill. The bill provided that for every justice who failed to retire within six months of reaching the age of seventy, the president must appoint a new justice. Six of the nine justices were already seventy or older, which meant that Roosevelt would be able to enlarge the Court to fifteen members by making new appointments. Presumably, these new justices would overcome the Court's resistance to the New Deal.

Although some earlier strong presidents—notably Thomas Jefferson, Andrew Jackson, and Abraham Lincoln—had fought with the Supreme Court, the intensity of the response to FDR's Court plan was unprecedented. Day after day for the next several months, stories about the Court-packing conflict rated banner headlines in the nation's newspapers. The controversy sparked debates in every corner of the country: in Beaumont, Texas, a movie audience cheered rival arguments about the Court bill when they were shown on the screen.[42]

Roosevelt's plan sought to eliminate the final constitutional barrier to a vast expansion of government activity, thereby ratifying the president's power to direct the affairs of state. Significantly, the two Supreme Court decisions that enraged FDR the most were *Humphrey's Executor v. United States* and *Schechter Poultry Corp. v. United States,* both of which imposed constraints on the president's personal authority.[43] The decisions were handed down on May 27, 1935, soon known to New Dealers as "Black Monday." In different ways, each decision threatened to derail the institutional changes that Roosevelt believed were necessary to solve the underlying problems of the depression.

The decision in *Humphrey's Executor* denied the president the right to remove appointees from the independent regulatory commissions, a legal power that Roosevelt and his advisers thought had been established by tradition and affirmed by precedent in *Myers v. United States* nine years earlier.[44] The *Schechter* ruling was a direct challenge to the modern administrative state. It declared that the discretionary authority Congress had granted, at Roosevelt's request, to the National Recovery Administration, the leading economic agency of the early New Deal, was an unconstitutional delegation of legislative power to the executive.

Although the Court-packing bill failed in Congress, Roosevelt claimed that in losing the battle he had won the war. The Court never again struck down a New Deal law. In fact, since 1937 the Supreme Court has not invalidated any significant federal statute to regulate the economy, nor has the Court judged any law (with the exception of the Line Item Veto Act of 1996) to be an unconstitutional delegation of congressional authority to the president.[45] Most of the judicial barriers to presidential power have fallen.

But the bitter fight over Court-packing cost the president dearly. Although the 1936 election had given the Democrats roughly three-fourths majorities in both the House and the Senate, the Court issue effectively brought Roosevelt's mastery of Congress and his party to an end. Moreover, it served as a lightning rod for the New Deal's opponents, spurring a resurgence of congressional independence and the formation of a bipartisan "conservative coalition." The new alliance of Republicans and southern Democrats blocked nearly every presidential reform initiative from 1937 until the mid-1960s.

Roosevelt's first response to the ideological fissure in Congress was to try to unseat entrenched conservative Democrats in the 1938 midterm elections. He intervened in one gubernatorial primary and several congressional primaries in a bold effort to replace recalcitrant Democrats with candidates who were "100 percent New Dealers." Although William Howard Taft and Woodrow Wilson also had tried to rid their parties of uncooperative members, Roosevelt's campaign was conducted on an unprecedented scale and, unlike the previous efforts, bypassed the regular party organization. The extent to which his action was regarded as a shocking departure from the norm was indicated by the label—"the purge"—that the press gave it. The term evoked Adolf Hitler's attempt to weed out dissenters from the German Nazi Party and Joseph Stalin's elimination of suspected opponents from the Soviet Communist Party.

The purge campaign failed, and all but two of the incumbent Democrats whom Roosevelt opposed were renominated. Widely condemned as an assault

Franklin Roosevelt, center, made several trips overseas to confer with Allied leaders about military strategy and the post–World War II world. In February 1945 Roosevelt conferred at Yalta with Winston Churchill, left, and Joseph Stalin, right.

on the constitutional system of checks and balances, the president's actions galvanized the political opposition, contributing to the heavy losses the Democrats sustained in the 1938 midterm elections. Indeed, the purge campaign, like the Court bill, strengthened the anti–New Deal conservative coalition. Peter Gerry, a conservative Democratic senator from Rhode Island, wrote to North Carolina senator Josiah Bailey, a fellow conservative Democrat, in September 1938: "The victories of [conservative Democrats] have had even a greater effect than I had hoped for. They show that Roosevelt cannot control Senators for he does not have the weight with voters in his party that the New Dealers thought he possessed."[46] Since FDR's unhappy experience in 1938, presidents generally have shied away from open intervention in House and Senate primaries.[47] Nevertheless, even though the purge failed, it initiated changes in the Democratic party that would eventually lead to the transformation of American politics.[48]

FOREIGN POLICY

The economic crisis that dominated Roosevelt's first two terms was displaced in the late 1930s by the approach and then the outbreak of World War II. Even before the United States declared war one day after the Japanese attack on Pearl Harbor on December 7, 1941, the growing American involvement in the conflicts in Europe and Asia intensified the concentration of power in the national government, its administrative apparatus, and the president. Significantly, it was the international crisis that allowed Roosevelt to stand for reelection in 1940. His victory made him the only president in history to break the two-term tradition. In 1944, during the latter stages of the war, FDR won a fourth term. Only his death in April 1945 cut short his protracted reign.[49]

In 1937 Roosevelt began to confront the isolationist mood that had dominated the country since the end of World War I.[50] Speaking in Chicago, he strongly attacked the aggression of Germany and Japan, whose armies had recently invaded the demilitarized Rhineland and China, respectively. "The peace, the freedom and the security of ninety percent of the population of the world is being jeopardized by the remaining ten percent who are threatening a breakdown of all international order and law," said Roosevelt. "Surely the ninety percent who want to live in peace under law and in accordance with moral standards that have received almost universal acceptance through the centuries, can and must find some way to make their will prevail."[51]

Although the immediate reaction to the president's speech was favorable, a severe backlash soon set in, demonstrating clearly that neither Congress nor the American people were prepared to intervene in Europe or Asia. To some extent, the clash between interventionists and isolationists became a clash between the president and Congress over which branch would control foreign policy, just as it had in the final months of the Wilson administration. But

Roosevelt was more willing than Wilson to act on his own, often with little warrant in statute or precedent. Ironically, his efforts were fortified by the same Court that had been such an obstacle to his domestic program.

On December 21, 1936, in *United States v. Curtiss-Wright Export Corp.*, the Supreme Court upheld a 1934 law that authorized the president to place an embargo on the sale of American-made weapons to countries engaged in armed conflict. The law had been passed with the so-called Chaco war between Bolivia and Paraguay in mind, and Roosevelt quickly forbade the sale of arms to both countries. Weapons merchants challenged the measure as an unlawful delegation of legislative authority to the president. A federal district court agreed. But in a somewhat surprising opinion written by conservative justice George Sutherland, a near-unanimous Supreme Court laid down a sweeping doctrine of presidential supremacy in foreign policy.

The Court held that the president's constitutional powers in domestic and foreign affairs are fundamentally different. "The broad statement that the federal government can exercise no power except those specifically stated in the Constitution, and such implied powers as are necessary and proper to carry into effect the enumerated powers," Justice Sutherland wrote, "is categorically true only in respect to internal affairs." In foreign affairs, the actions of the president as the government's "sole organ" in international relations depend neither on a specific grant of power from the Constitution nor on authorization from Congress. Because executive authority in foreign policy is "plenary and exclusive," the president enjoys a freedom from statutory restriction that "would not be admissible were domestic affairs alone involved."[52]

The *Curtiss-Wright* case established as constitutional doctrine the sweeping defense of the president's authority in foreign affairs that Alexander Hamilton, writing as "Pacificus," had offered in 1793 to defend President Washington's Neutrality Proclamation. Along with *United States v. Belmont* (1937), which justified the president's right to circumvent the treaty process by negotiating binding executive agreements with the leaders of other countries, *Curtiss-Wright* made it virtually impossible to challenge Roosevelt's increasingly internationalist policies on constitutional grounds.[53]

Relying on his broad, Court-sanctioned understanding of presidential authority, Roosevelt concluded a controversial agreement with Great Britain in 1940. The deal, which paved the way for the United States to send fifty naval destroyers to help Great Britain in its desperate battle with Nazi Germany, marked a departure from the official American policy of neutrality. In contrast, Roosevelt's Lend Lease program to aid Great Britain required congressional action because it involved an initial appropriation of about $7 billion. The debate over Lend Lease and its eventual enactment by Congress produced the sort of broad, albeit rough, consensus within the government that Roosevelt had not been able to achieve through unilateral executive action. Before Lend Lease, "the most Americans would commit themselves to was aid to the democracies short of war," historian David M. Kennedy has written. Now Roosevelt had "edged them closer to a commitment to aid the democracies even at the risk of war."[54]

Once under way, World War II greatly accelerated the flow of power from Congress and the courts to the president, allowing Roosevelt to assert an inherent executive prerogative more boldly than he could have before Japan's attack on Pearl Harbor. Under conditions of total war, Roosevelt believed, the president is authorized not only to direct military operations abroad but also to manage economic and social affairs at home. In a bold— critics said brazen—expression of his theory of presidential power, Roosevelt insisted that an effective program of wage and price controls be created. "I ask the Congress," FDR said in his Labor Day message of September 7, 1942, "to take . . . action by the first of October. Inaction on your part by that date will leave me with an inescapable responsibility to the people of this country to see to it that the war effort is no longer imperiled by threat of economic chaos." If Congress did not act, Roosevelt warned, "I shall accept the responsibility and I will act."[55] Congress enacted the economic controls that the president demanded, and Roosevelt never had to follow through on his threat.

The Supreme Court's acquiescence to presidential power also peaked during World War II.[56] In *Yakus v. United States* (1944) the justices upheld the wage and price controls that Roosevelt issued to implement the authority he secured from Congress in 1942. In justifying these regulatory controls, which relied on the vaguest of legislative standards, the Court all but abandoned the nondelegation principle announced in its 1935 *Schechter* decision.[57] In *Ex parte Quirin,* the Court sanctioned Roosevelt's use of a military tribunal to try eight Germans who came to America to commit acts of sabotage. After the Germans were captured in June 1942, Roosevelt convened a secret tribunal on July 2, which sentenced the eight men to death. The president later commuted the death sentences of the two prisoners who confessed and assisted in capturing the others. The remaining six were executed on August 8 in Washington.

The Court issued the *Quirin* decision on July 31, 1942, but did not release its full opinion until October 29. Writing for the Court, Chief Justice Harlan Fiske Stone distinguished *Quirin* from the Civil War era case of *Ex parte Milligan* because Milligan, the defendant in that case, was not "part of or associated with the armed forces of the enemy." Moreover, Stone wrote, the conditions of modern warfare made more likely and insidious the acts of sabotage on American soil that justified military commissions:

Modern warfare is directed at the destruction of enemy war supplies and the imple-
ments of their production and transportation, quite as much as at the armed forces.
. . . The law of war cannot rightly treat those agents of enemy armies who enter our
territory, armed with explosives intended for the destruction of war industries and
supplies, as any the less belligerent enemies than are agents similarly entering for the
purpose of destroying fortified places or our Armed Forces. By passing our boundaries for such purposes without uniform or other emblem signifying their belligerent status, or by discarding that means of identification after entry, such enemies
become unlawful belligerents subject to trial and punishment.[58]

Although the public strongly supported the Roosevelt administration's
treatment of Nazi saboteurs, a large part of the academic and legal community
argued that *Quirin* set a dangerous precedent. Indeed, because of the harsh
criticism leveled at Roosevelt's military tribunals order, the White House
modified it when a second set of saboteurs was captured in 1944. The legacy
of Roosevelt's use of military tribunals and the *Quirin* decision took on new
relevance after the September 11, 2001, terrorist attacks on New York and
Washington. President George W. Bush's authorization of military tribunals to
try those who helped the terrorists attack the United States closely mimicked
the language of Roosevelt's 1942 executive order on the *Quirin* saboteurs.[59]

The Court's most controversial decision during World War II was
Korematsu v. United States (1944), in which a majority of justices condoned
the Roosevelt administration's use of a racial classification to imprison many
Japanese Americans.[60] On February 8, 1942, Roosevelt signed an executive
order authorizing the removal of one hundred thousand American citizens of
Japanese descent from their homes on the West Coast to isolated, desolate
relocation camps. These citizens had committed no crime, and, although FDR
justified his order on grounds of "military necessity," he offered no real
evidence to demonstrate that they posed a security risk. Indeed, to prove their
American patriotism, many of the young men who were sent to the camps
enlisted in the American armed forces and served with distinction.

This affront to American ideals of justice was not FDR's idea. It originated
with California politicians, most notably state attorney general Earl Warren,
who later served as chief justice of the United States. The politicians were
reacting to the widespread fears that arose in the wake of Japan's sneak attack
on Pearl Harbor and the racism that falsely equated Japanese Americans with
Japanese nationals. Some members of the administration opposed the internment order but, like FDR, they were preoccupied with winning the war and
were unwilling to go out of their way to help such politically vulnerable victims. One such victim, Fred Korematsu, was a twenty-three-year-old Ameri-
can-born citizen who had a good job, an Italian-American fiancée, and no
wish to leave either one. After his arrest for violating the military's evacuation
order, Korematsu authorized the American Civil Liberties Union to use his
case as a test of the internment policy.

Clearly uneasy about the *Korematsu* case, the Court acknowledged that "all legal restrictions which curtail the civil rights of a single racial group are immediately suspect." Nevertheless, Justice Hugo Black's majority opinion concluded that military necessity provided sufficient grounds to believe that the internment of Japanese American citizens was justified. "[W]hen under conditions of modern warfare our shores are threatened by hostile forces," Black wrote, "the power to protect must be commensurate with the threatened danger." In dissent, Justice Robert Jackson argued that such extreme judicial deference to executive power in wartime posed a dire threat to constitutional rights: "[O]nce a judicial opinion rationalizes . . . an order to show that it conforms to the Constitution, or rather rationalizes the Constitution to show that the Constitution sanctions such an order, the Court for all time has validated the principle of racial discrimination in criminal procedure and of transplanting American citizens. The principle then lies about like a loaded weapon ready for the hand of any authority that can bring forward a plausible claim of an urgent need."[61]

In the decades since *Korematsu*, no racially restrictive law has ever passed the constitutional test of military necessity endorsed by the Supreme Court in that case. In truth, soon after the war ended in 1945 the Court's ruling came to be regarded as a judicial travesty. In 1948 Congress provided $37 million in reparations for the victims of Japanese internment. In another burst of conscience forty years later, Congress awarded $20,000 to each surviving detainee. In 1998 President Bill Clinton awarded the nation's highest civilian honor, the Presidential Medal of Freedom, to Fred Korematsu.[62] Yet these official acts of atonement never completely erased the deeply troubling failure of Congress and the Supreme Court to strike a constitutional balance that gave the president enough authority to make the nation safe while preventing serious abuses of individual freedom.

YALTA AND THE COLD WAR

The national security state continued to grow when World War II gave way to a new international struggle, which became known as the cold war. The historic summit in February 1945 at Yalta, a Soviet port on the Crimean Peninsula, set the stage for this struggle. The leaders of the "Big Three" wartime allies—Joseph Stalin of the Soviet Union, Winston Churchill of Great Britain, and Roosevelt—came to the conference hoping not just to develop a strategy to end World War II, but also to reach an agreement on the shape of the postwar world.

Roosevelt's principal objective at Yalta was to create the sort of structure for cooperation among the major powers that the victorious nations had failed to achieve after World War I. He attached special significance to the voting procedures and membership rules that would govern the United Nations (UN), the new international organization approved in outline form at Dumbarton Oaks, in Washington, in the fall of 1944. Stalin, fearing that the United States and Great Britain would combine to relegate the Soviet Union to permanent minority status, held out for a single nation veto in the UN Security Council, the body charged with principal responsibility for maintaining international peace. Roosevelt and Churchill acceded to Stalin's demand, ensuring that no action could be imposed on a major power without its consent.[63]

The UN agreement was forged in the midst of intense wrangling about the future of Eastern Europe, especially Poland. The Red Army had already overrun Bulgaria, Hungary, and Romania and had advanced through eastern Germany to within miles of Berlin. Stalin was determined to translate his hard-won military advantage into permanent political gain. Anxious to bring Stalin into the war against Japan, Roosevelt had neither the will nor the way to challenge Soviet domination of Eastern Europe. But, joined by Churchill, he wanted political cover for his acquiescence to Russian hegemony. The result at Yalta was the Declaration on Liberated Europe. The declaration pledged the signatories "to arrange and conduct free elections" in the liberated nations of Eastern Europe to create governments that were "broadly representative of all elements." But this pledge proved hollow. As Roosevelt's chief of staff, Adm. William Leahy, said when he saw the draft, "Mr. President, this is so elastic that the Russians can stretch it all the way from Yalta to Washington without ever technically breaking it."[64]

After Yalta, instead of implementing the agreed-on procedure to form a new democratic government in Poland, the Russians installed a pro-Soviet regime. Churchill advocated a forceful response, but Roosevelt urged the British prime minister to "minimize the general Soviet problem as much as possible." FDR agreed with Churchill that the United States and Great Britain "must be firm," but he remained committed to diplomacy. In the president's view, the prospects for peace based on cooperation among the victors depended on the success of the UN. Although the single-veto voting procedure established for the Security Council threatened to hamstring the new organization, Roosevelt hoped that Yalta had at least established a framework for continued negotiation.[65]

Because the Yalta agreements were purely executive, the president did not send them to Congress for debate and ratification. They proved to be highly controversial. Critics alleged that Roosevelt, sick and mentally enfeebled, had conceded too much to Stalin, betraying Poland and delivering Eastern Europe into Soviet hands. These charges, David Kennedy has concluded, are "vastly overdrawn."[66] Roosevelt was unquestionably ill at Yalta. But he conceded little there that he had not signaled his willingness to concede at an earlier conference in Tehran, when he was in full command of his faculties. Arguments that Roosevelt was too soft in accepting Stalin's demands ignore the military situation on the ground, which gave the president few options. While the Soviets were completing their victory drive in Eastern Europe, the Americans and British were still recovering from the terrible Battle of the Bulge in which they had fought to regain critical ground against a massive German counterattack in Belgium and France. Roosevelt's military advisers also were pushing him to secure a firm Soviet commitment to enter the war against Japan as soon as possible, and the president had no reason to count on the atomic bomb being ready in time.[67] "I didn't say the result was good," Roosevelt conceded to an associate, "I said it was the best I could do."[68]

THE MODERN PRESIDENCY SUSTAINED: HARRY S. TRUMAN AND DWIGHT D. EISENHOWER

Franklin Roosevelt dominated American political life for more than twelve years. His long tenure raised serious concerns about the dangers of concentrating too much power in the executive. After he died in 1945, conservative political leaders stood poised to modify the constitutional and political changes that had greatly enhanced presidential power since 1933. But FDR had transformed politics in the United States permanently. Under his tutelage, Americans now expected the federal government to remain active in domestic and global affairs and the president to take the lead within the constitutional framework of government. The presidency's place in the political system was therefore settled but uneasy.

TRUMAN AND THE ROOSEVELT INHERITANCE

When the Senate adjourned at about five o'clock on April 12, 1945, Vice President Harry S. Truman made his way to the office of House Speaker Sam Rayburn to join his friends for an afternoon round of bourbon and water. No sooner had his drink been poured than the vice president received a telephone call from White House press secretary Steve Early, who told him to come to the executive mansion as soon as possible. When Truman arrived, Eleanor Roosevelt put her arm around his shoulders and said softly, "Harry, the president is dead." After a moment of shock, Truman recovered sufficiently to ask, "Is there anything I can do for you?" She replied, "Is there anything we can do for you? For you're the one in trouble now."[69]

Eleanor Roosevelt was not the only one who felt that Truman was in trouble. With the country still at war, it seemed incomprehensible that anyone, let alone this "little man" from Missouri, as some of Truman's contemporaries disdainfully called him, could take Roosevelt's place as president of the United States. "For a time he walked," journalist William S. White wrote, "as completely as the smallest laborer who had been a 'Roosevelt man,' in the long shadow of the dead President."[70]

Truman eventually was able to emerge from FDR's shadow, but not because he had much ability to rouse the public. In this respect, the contrast between Truman and Roosevelt was striking. "Truman possessed little or no charisma, struggled with an ego more fragile than most observers have understood, and had extreme distaste for the need to manipulate others," historian Alonzo L. Hamby has written.[71] A poor speaker who was awkward in the presence of reporters and microphones, Truman suffered persistently low popularity. His public approval rating was less than 50 percent during most of his tenure, including his final three years as president.[72]

In other respects, however, Truman was a solid successor to Roosevelt. He believed deeply in the changes the New Deal had wrought in American society. Well aware of his personal limitations, he also recognized that the legacy of FDR called for active and ongoing presidential leadership. Indeed, Truman likened being president to "riding a tiger. You have to keep on riding or be swallowed."[73]

THE FAIR DEAL. When Truman assumed the presidency, some predicted that this supremely practical politician, who had been placed on the ticket as the Democratic nominee for vice president in 1944 mainly to appease the party's southern and big-city leaders, would readily adapt to the more conservative mood that befell the country during the twilight of the war. A close Roosevelt associate, Samuel Rosenman, informed the new president that his "conservative friends," particularly some of his former colleagues on Capitol Hill, believed that Truman was "going to be quite a shock to those who followed Roosevelt—that the New Deal [was] as good as dead."[74]

Truman's twenty-one-point message to Congress on September 6, 1945, made clear that he would not be to Roosevelt what Harding had been to Wilson. The message, which introduced the president's "Fair Deal" agenda, marked the moment when Truman felt he finally assumed the executive office in his own right. "This legislative program," he wrote in his memoirs, "was a reminder to the Democratic party, to the country, and to the Congress that progress in government lies along the road to sound reform in our private enterprise system and that progressive democracy has to continue to keep pace with changing conditions."[75]

The Fair Deal was Truman's attempt to codify Roosevelt's vision of a postwar economic order. "We have accepted," Roosevelt had proclaimed in his 1944 State of the Union address, "a Second Bill of Rights under which a new basis of security and prosperity can be established for all—regardless of station, race, or creed."[76] To fulfill Roosevelt's vision, Truman argued, the federal government must guarantee everyone a useful and remunerative job, adequate medical care, a decent home, and a good education.

The program that Truman presented to Congress in 1945 was an appeal, as he put it, "to make the attainment of those rights the essence of post-war

economic life."[77] He called for the extension of social security to more workers, a higher minimum wage, national health insurance, urban development,
and full employment. But Congress approved few of Truman's twenty-one
points, and the results of the 1946 congressional elections appeared to represent the public's dramatic rejection of the Fair Deal. The Republicans
campaigned on the theme that the country had "had enough" of Roosevelt-
Truman–style liberalism. For the first time in sixteen years, the Democrats
no longer controlled Congress.

But Truman marshaled all of the resources accrued by his office during
Roosevelt's tenure to prove otherwise. In the aftermath of the 1946 elections,
he fought every attempt by the Republican Eightieth Congress to dismantle
the New Deal. Truman cast more than two hundred vetoes during his presidency, mostly on matters of tax and labor policy. The conservative coalition of
Republicans and southern Democrats, the same alliance that had plagued
FDR during his second term, often overrode these vetoes. But as political scientist Fred I. Greenstein has noted, Truman's forceful defiance in the face of
overwhelming legislative opposition "accustomed all but the most conservative national political actors to look at the president as the main framer of the
agenda for political debate—even when much of the debate involved castiga-
tion of his proposals."[78]

Truman's most significant veto was of the Taft-Hartley Act, which was
widely regarded as an attack on labor unions.[79] On June 20, 1947, Truman
sent a stinging veto message to Congress asserting that the bill "would reverse
the basic direction of our national labor policy." That evening he went on the
radio to declare, "We do not need—and we do not want—legislation which
will take fundamental rights away from our working people."[80] Although
Truman's Taft-Hartley veto was overridden by Congress, organized labor
lined up solidly behind him. The veto also earned him praise from middle-
class liberals, most of whom supported the unions. Truman "has given
American liberalism the fighting chance that it seemed to have lost with the
death of Roosevelt," the *Nation* editorialized.[81]

Shrewdly taking the political initiative, Truman turned the 1948 presidential election into a referendum on the New Deal. When he surprised nearly
everyone by winning a come-from-behind victory against his Republican
opponent, Gov. Thomas E. Dewey of New York, Truman stepped at least partially out of FDR's shadow. The president had saved the New Deal and revived
the Democratic coalition, and the assertiveness he displayed in his battles with
Congress confirmed the preeminence of the modern executive in legislative
affairs.

Although Truman never was able to shatter the stalemate in domestic
policy that endured throughout his presidency, he could claim some successes.
His social security, minimum wage, and public housing proposals were

enacted during the Eighty-first Congress, which, as a result of the 1948 elections, was again controlled by the Democrats. More important, the Truman administration was remarkably successful in assembling a bipartisan congressional coalition to support the president's policy toward the Soviet Union. In the weeks preceding his death, FDR had begun to take a more jaundiced view of Stalin. But it was left to Truman to formulate the American response to Soviet aggression in Eastern Europe.

Appearing before a joint session of Congress on March 12, 1947, Truman requested military aid for the endangered governments of Greece and Turkey. Unlike his most recent Democratic predecessors, Wilson and FDR, Truman was not responding to an obvious military threat, such as the Germans' unrestricted submarine warfare in 1917 or the Nazi conquest of Western Europe in 1940. Both of these events had led to war, which the president desperately wanted to avoid in the nuclear age. Instead, Truman articulated a policy of containment, promising to keep the Soviet empire from extending its borders.[82] Although maintaining a strong nuclear arsenal, stationing American troops in Europe and Asia, and supplying arms to vulnerable regimes would help to deter Soviet imperialism, Truman argued, the most effective way to assist threatened nations was with economic and financial aid. "The seeds of totalitarianism," he said, "are nurtured by misery and want." Proclaiming a policy that reporters quickly dubbed the Truman Doctrine, the president declared "that it must be the policy of the United States to support free peoples who are resisting attempted subjugation by armed minorities or by outside pressures."[83]

To win support for his containment policy, Truman had to overcome resistance in both political parties. The most vociferous opposition came from liberal Democrats led by former vice president Henry Wallace. Speaking at enthusiastic rallies around the country, Wallace appealed to those on the left who continued to think of the Soviet Union as a wartime ally rather than a hostile power. Republican opponents of the Truman Doctrine were led by Ohio senator Robert A. Taft, whose staunch defense of isolationism and fiscal restraint had earned him the title of "Mr. Republican." Seizing the political center, the strategic high ground of American politics, Truman eventually prevailed over the forces of appeasement and isolation.[84] Internationalist Republicans and Democrats in Congress united to authorize the Truman Doctrine to contain communist expansion, the Marshall Plan to rebuild Europe economically, and the North Atlantic Treaty Organization (NATO) to defend the West against Soviet aggression.

THE MARSHALL PLAN. The creation of the Marshall Plan was especially remarkable: it was enacted in 1948 by a Republican-controlled Congress, at the behest of a Democratic president, during an election year.[85] In part, Truman owed his success in implementing the plan to the escalating threat posed by the Soviet Union. In February 1948 Soviet-backed communists seized power in Czechoslovakia, eliminating the last independent democracy in Eastern Europe and consolidating Soviet control of the region.

Equally important, however, was Truman's deft statesmanship. Recognizing the enormous prestige of Secretary of State George C. Marshall, who had served with distinction as the army's chief of staff during World War II, Truman dismissed White House aide Clark M. Clifford's suggestion that the plan bear the president's name. Not only had Marshall's commencement address at Harvard University in June 1947 given prominence to the idea of helping to rebuild Europe, but also Truman knew that the widely venerated general would do a much better job of selling the measure than he could.[86] Assisted by Marshall, the president adroitly cultivated bipartisan support, working effectively with Senate Foreign Relations Committee chair Arthur H. Vandenberg of Michigan, who assumed the critical and delicate role of mediator between the administration and congressional Republicans. Vandenberg expected advance consultation from the administration, and he received it in frequent meetings with the president and secretary of state. In addition, when Vandenberg requested that a "nonpartisan" business leader, Studebaker Corporation president Paul Hoffman, head the agency created to direct the Marshall Plan, Truman appointed Hoffman despite his initial preference for someone else.[87]

CIVIL RIGHTS. Frustrated by his limited success with Congress in domestic matters, Truman resolved to stake out a substantial sphere for independent presidential action concerning civil rights. In doing so, he became the first president to enlist the powers of the modern office in the cause of racial justice. On December 5, 1946, Truman established by executive order the President's Committee on Civil Rights (PCCR), which was authorized "to determine whether and in what respect current law enforcement measures and the authority and means possessed by Federal, State, and local governments may be strengthened and improved to safeguard the civil rights of the people."[88] Truman was no zealot for minority rights but, more than most elected officials of his day, he was determined to do something about racial segregation.

Although African Americans first became an important part of the Democratic coalition in 1936, Roosevelt's New Deal did little to address directly the injustices of southern Jim Crow–style segregation. But World War II and its aftermath spurred Truman to come to terms with the "Negro Question." During the war, more than a million African Americans migrated to large northern and western states, such as Michigan and California, that were rich in electoral votes. In addition, the cold war prompted the Truman administration to recognize that discrimination against Americans of color damaged the United States as it vied with the Soviet Union for influence in Africa, Asia, and Latin America. Finally, although Truman was a border state politician with close ties to southern legislators and strong sympathy for the region they represented, he believed that the president was obligated to uphold the fundamental rights of all Americans. Truman found it especially intolerable that outrageous discriminatory acts were inflicted on black men in uniform, to whom he felt the country owed a great debt of gratitude.[89]

Truman's bold initiative in launching a national investigation of racial injustice reopened critical issues that generally had been ignored in Washington since the end of Reconstruction. "No political act since the Compromise of 1877," biographer Taylor Branch has argued, "so profoundly influenced race relations; in a sense it was a repeal of 1877."[90] To be sure, conservative southern Democrats in Congress blocked Truman's civil rights proposals. But when legislators failed to approve the bill he recommended after receiving the PCCR's report, Truman did what he could on his own authority as chief executive. In July 1948, during the presidential campaign, Truman issued two executive orders. One drew on the president's power as commander in chief to decree that "there should be equality of treatment and opportunity in the Armed Services without regard to race, color, religion or national origin." Although the order did not explicitly condemn racial segregation, Truman established a committee headed by Solicitor General Charles Fahey that set the stage for the integration of the armed forces. Truman's other executive order forbade racial and ethnic discrimination in the federal civil service and established a Fair Employment Board to monitor hiring. This order was designed to uproot the discriminatory federal employment practices planted by the Wilson administration.

Truman's civil rights orders risked alienating southern white Democrats— the "Solid South" that constituted his party's traditional bastion of electoral strength. Indeed, after the 1948 Democratic convention adopted a civil rights plank, South Carolina governor Strom Thurmond and his white supremacist allies bolted to form a third party that seriously threatened Truman's chances for winning the election. Running as the States' Rights Party, or "Dixiecrat," nominee, Thurmond carried the four Deep South states of Alabama, Louisiana, Mississippi, and South Carolina. Although losing these states cost Truman only thirty-nine electoral votes, his civil rights agenda had opened a fissure in the Democratic Party that eventually spurred major defections of southern white voters to the Republican Party. Not wishing to aggravate the cleavage he had opened in his party, Truman de-emphasized civil rights after his triumphant 1948 election. But his civil rights initiatives and his use of executive power to advance them had significant consequences for both African Americans and the modern presidency. As historian John Hope Franklin stated in a 1968 address, "The crucial turning point in viewing the problem of race as a national problem occurred when the executive branch of the federal government began actively to assume a major role."[91]

EXECUTIVE ACTION AND FOREIGN AFFAIRS. As bold and controversial as his civil rights measures were, Truman's most daring and politically costly independent initiatives came in the realm of international security. These included his 1945 decision to use atomic weapons against Japan to bring an end to World War II and his decision in 1950 to commit American troops to combat in Korea. The Korean intervention, which followed communist North Korea's invasion of South Korea, was another important extension of the president's powers as commander in chief. For the first time, American troops waged a full-scale war without a congressional declaration.

In part, Truman's intervention in Korea was a logical consequence of the postwar emergence of the United States as a superpower, actively and constantly engaged in international affairs. In 1945 the Senate overwhelmingly ratified the charter that established the United Nations, and Congress passed the United Nations Participation Act, which made the United States subject to certain UN decisions. Truman invoked this act as the primary legal justification for his deployment of troops in Korea. Once the UN Security Council decided to help South Korea, the president argued, he had no choice but to respond under Articles 39 and 42 of the UN Charter.

But Truman also defended his actions in Korea by claiming to have a sweeping executive power to deploy the armed forces of the United States without consulting Congress. To be sure, Truman was able to cite precedents from the administrations of earlier commanders in chief. But all of these precedents involved limited interventions to suppress piracy or to protect American citizens who were endangered by foreign disorders. Truman's real rationale was that the cold war against communism and the president's new responsibilities as the leader of the free world greatly diminished Congress's role in foreign policy. As he said in March 1951, "The congressional power to declare war has fallen into abeyance because wars are no longer declared in advance."[92]

The powers of the modern presidency still had their limits, however, even in foreign policy. Truman paid dearly in the coin of public and congressional criticism as the war in Korea dragged on. Most important, his claim that the Korean conflict endowed the president with emergency economic powers was rebuffed by the Supreme Court after he seized control of the nation's steel mills in 1952. For fear of alienating the unions, Truman had refused to apply the Taft-Hartley Act, which authorized the president to impose an eighty-day cooling-off period on labor and management in an industrial dispute in order to postpone a strike. Instead, on April 8 he ordered Secretary of Commerce Charles Sawyer to take control of the steel mills. Truman argued that a "work stoppage would immediately jeopardize and imperil our national defense."

Less than two months later, the Court, in *Youngstown Sheet and Tube Co. v. Sawyer,* disabused the president of his belief that in a national emergency he could do anything that the Constitution or Congress had not explicitly forbidden.[93] Justice Hugo Black declared in his majority opinion that Truman must return the mills to their owners because his seizure order was a de facto statute that preempted Congress's lawmaking power:

> In the framework of our Constitution, the President's power to see that the laws are faithfully executed refutes the idea that he is to be a lawmaker. The Constitution limits his functions in the lawmaking process to the recommending of laws he thinks wise and the vetoing of laws he thinks bad. And the Constitution is neither silent nor equivocal about who shall make laws which the President is to execute. The first section of the first article says that "All legislative powers herein granted shall be vested in a Congress of the United States."[94]

The Court's decision surprised many people. Truman could cite numerous precedents of presidents intervening militarily in labor disputes. Theodore Roosevelt had threatened to seize and run the mines during the anthracite coal strike of 1902 if mediation failed.[95] Franklin Roosevelt seized the North American Aviation Plant at Inglewood, California, on June 9, 1941, six months before Pearl Harbor, arguing that his power to act derived from the "aggregate" of the Constitution and the laws.[96] Not since 1866 had the Supreme Court ruled against a president in the exercise of prerogative power, and in that case, *Ex parte Milligan,* the Court declared that Lincoln's use of military tribunals during the Civil War was invalid only after the war was over.[97] Small wonder, then, that Truman believed his action would be upheld, especially because the Court was stacked with his and Roosevelt's appointees.[98]

In truth, the Court's decision did not severely circumscribe the president's powers as commander in chief. Only Justices Black and William O. Douglas questioned whether the president had emergency powers. The opinions of the four other justices in the six-member majority applied strictly to the case at hand, emphasizing that Congress had explicitly rejected presidential seizure as a method of settling industrial disputes when it passed the Taft-Hartley Act. Justice Robert Jackson's concurring opinion offered a test for the Court to use when weighing presidential powers against congressional action. Whenever the president acts "pursuant to an express or implied authorization of Congress," Jackson argued, "his authority is at its maximum, for it includes all that he possesses in his own right plus all that Congress can delegate." The most difficult cases involve presidential actions taken "in absence of either a congressional grant or denial of authority." Where the law is silent, Jackson acknowledged, there is "a zone of twilight" in which the president and Congress have "concurrent authority." In this grey area, the test of constitutionality depends on the circumstance: "the imperatives of events and contemporary imponderables rather than on abstract theories of law." Truman's actions in the steel dispute, however, disavowed a law properly passed by Congress, clearly exceeding the limits of presidential authority:

When the president takes measures incompatible with the expressed or implied will of Congress, his power is at its lowest ebb, for then he can rely only upon his own constitutional powers minus any constitutional powers of Congress in the matter. Courts can sustain exclusive Presidential control in such a case only by disabling the Congress from acting upon the subject. Presidential claim to a power at once so conclusive and preclusive must be scrutinized with caution, for what is at stake is the equilibrium established by our constitutional system.[99]

Youngstown was "an important foundation," historian Maeva Marcus has written, "for the reaffirmation of the proposition that the President is not above the law."[100] Truman's defeat in the steel crisis meant that he and his successors would have to exercise the expanded powers of the presidency more carefully. The Court, however, did not strike a crippling blow to the president's powers as commander in chief. Indeed, the justices might have sustained Truman's seizure of the steel mills if Congress had not passed the Taft-Hartley Act, which provided the president with other ways to keep the mills running.

TRUMAN AND THE MODERN PRESIDENCY. Truman's tenure as president reaffirmed the modern presidency. He demonstrated that a president without extraordinary political gifts or popularity could achieve important objectives, define the terms of national political debate, and control at least the main lines of domestic and foreign policy. In part, Truman succeeded because he was operating in the new political environment of big government. The welfare state at home and international leadership abroad inevitably concentrated major responsibilities in the White House.

But Truman also made an independent contribution to the development of the presidency by formalizing and expanding it as an institution. Although Franklin Roosevelt had created the Executive Office of the President, FDR's own staff was loosely structured, reflecting his penchant for improvised, ad hoc arrangements. Truman, in contrast, was a systematic administrator. During his presidency, responsibilities within the White House Office were defined clearly. Truman also used the Bureau of the Budget more extensively than Roosevelt, relying on it heavily in performing his executive and legislative duties. Truman assigned responsibility to the Budget Bureau to clear and coordinate all legislative requests that originated within the federal departments and to draft White House–sponsored legislation and executive orders.[101] As a result, he developed an advisory process in which most policies came to him only for decision, not, as with FDR, for development.

Congress helped Truman to institutionalize the presidency, sometimes unintentionally. Congressionally initiated statutes established the Council of Economic Advisers (CEA) in 1946 and the National Security Council (NSC) in 1947 to help the president formulate fiscal and foreign policy, respectively. Although many legislators had hoped that the CEA and NSC would serve as checks on the president's autonomy in economic and security matters by making the president consult with other, Senate-confirmed officials, Truman effectively domesticated the councils—that is, he made them part of the president's team.

In addition to establishing the NSC, the National Security Act created two other executive bodies that strengthened the president's capacity to influence world affairs. One was the Central Intelligence Agency (CIA), a powerful new tool of American foreign policy in the cold war era. Although Truman feared he might be creating a "Gestapo"-style secret police, unification of the government's previously far-flung intelligence activities appealed to his desire for centralization and clear lines of responsibility.

The other new agency was the Department of Defense, which housed under one roof the previously separate branches of the armed forces. By the end of World War II, most members of Congress were convinced that the chaotic, antagonistic bureaucracies responsible for the national defense needed to be consolidated. Truman, characteristically, favored any effort to make administration more orderly. The 1947 statute created the National Military Establishment, headed by a secretary of defense, who was charged with coordinating the operations of the army, navy, marines, and air force. This task proved to be herculean; indeed, it eventually helped drive the first secretary, James Forrestal, to nervous collapse and suicide. In 1949 Congress enacted amendments proposed by Forrestal and Truman to strengthen the authority of the secretary and replace the National Military Establishment with a full-blown Department of Defense. To further centralize military planning, the 1949 amendments also created the position of chairman of the Joint Chiefs of Staff (JCS) to denote the officer who would serve as the principal military adviser to the defense secretary and the president. These changes did not eliminate interservice rivalries, but the new cabinet-level department, along with the NSC and CIA, greatly increased the resources available to the president in directing foreign and military policy.[102]

Truman's effort to strengthen the institutional presidency received surprising help from former president Herbert Hoover. The Republican-controlled Eightieth Congress had appointed Hoover to head the Commission on the Organization of the Executive Branch of the Government. The task of the commission, as Republican leaders understood it, was to lay the groundwork for an assault on New Deal programs and to circumscribe the executive by foreclosing the possibility of another personalized, FDR-style administration. Yet Hoover, who as president had grappled with the problems of running the executive branch, saw the need to fortify the presidency.[103]

After much study, the Hoover Commission submitted a report very similar to the one the Brownlow Committee had written in 1937 to support FDR's program of administrative reform. The president still needed help, the Hoover

Commission argued, especially to supervise the far-flung activities of the enlarged executive branch. Its recommendations formed the basis of the 1949 Reorganization Act and authorized Truman, who enthusiastically embraced the commission's report, to make important changes in many of the departments, agencies, and independent regulatory commissions.

Especially significant was Truman's Reorganization Plan No. 8, which he issued in 1950. Truman included provisions in the plan that eroded the regulatory commissions' autonomy from presidential influence and thereby reduced the effect of the Court's ruling in *Humphrey's Executor v. United States* that the president may not fire a commissioner. Under the reorganization plan, the chairs of the regulatory commissions would be "appointed by the president and serve at his pleasure." The chairs, in turn, were granted considerable authority to oversee the daily business of their commissions and to appoint and supervise commission staff. Consequently, presidents were better able to give direction to regulatory agencies than in the past.[104]

Hoover's endorsement of executive reorganization suggested that a bipartisan consensus had formed in support of the modern presidency. Republicans had "historically been against Presidents," one Truman aide noted, but Hoover's interest in the problems of administrative management offered Republican support for "the kind of Chief Executive office that will have enough authority and the right kind of organization to do the most difficult jobs."[105]

THE TWENTY-SECOND AMENDMENT

One of the political aftershocks of the New Deal and Fair Deal was the Twenty-second Amendment, which was proposed by the Republican-dominated Eightieth Congress in 1947 and ratified by the states in 1951. The amendment prohibits any person from being elected president more than two times. It also limits vice presidents who succeed to the presidency to one elected term if they have served more than half of a departed president's four-year term. (If they have served half or less than half of a term, they may be elected twice, for a maximum tenure of ten years.) Although the amendment specifically exempted the incumbent Truman from its coverage, it was a posthumous slap at Franklin Roosevelt, who had challenged the two-term tradition by being elected president four times.

THE TWO-TERM TRADITION. The source of the two-term tradition was Thomas Jefferson, who was the first president to argue that no one should serve more than eight years as chief executive. Responding on December 10, 1807, to a letter from the Vermont state legislature asking him to run for a third term (six other states sent similar letters), Jefferson replied, "If some termination of the services of the Chief Magistrate be not fixed by the

Constitution, or supplied by practice, his office, nominally four years, will in fact become for life, and history shows how easily that degenerates into an inheritance." To strengthen his argument for a two-term limit, Jefferson invoked "the sound precedent set by an illustrious predecessor," George Washington.[106]

Jefferson's invocation of Washington was historically inaccurate. Washington had left the presidency after two terms but, as he explained in his Farewell Address, he did so not as a matter of principle but because he thought the country needed to learn that the Constitution would work even if he were not president. More personally, he longed for "the shade of retirement."[107] Even so, Jefferson's defense of a two-term limit took root quickly in presidential politics. Indeed, the Whig Party and many Democrats soon argued for a one-term limit. Of the first thirty presidents (Washington to Hoover), twenty served one term or less, and none served more than two terms.

In the late nineteenth and early twentieth centuries, the issue of a third term arose only occasionally. Ulysses S. Grant (in 1876) and Woodrow Wilson (in 1920) would have liked to serve another four years, but they were too unpopular at the end of their second terms even to be renominated by their parties. In 1908 Theodore Roosevelt declined a certain renomination and, considering his great popularity, a probable reelection, calling the two-term limit a "wise custom." Four years later, however, he ran for president again, first as an unsuccessful contender for the Republican nomination, then as a third party candidate.

The two-term tradition was broken by Franklin Roosevelt in 1940. In 1937 Roosevelt had declared that his "great ambition on January 20, 1941," was to "turn over this desk and chair in the White House" to a successor. But in 1939 World War II broke out in Europe, with little prospect that the United States would be able to remain above the fray. Waiting until the Democratic convention in July 1940, Roosevelt finally signaled his willingness to be renominated. The delegates jubilantly approved, knowing that FDR offered the party its best chance for victory.

Public opinion polls had shown that voters were deeply divided about the propriety of Roosevelt's candidacy, and Republicans took up the cry "No Third Term!" on behalf of their nominee, business leader Wendell Willkie. Democrats rejoined that in perilous times the country would be foolish to "change horses in midstream." Roosevelt won the election, but by a much narrower popular vote margin than in 1936—five million votes, down from eleven million. In 1944, with the United States and its allies nearing victory in World War II, Roosevelt won another term by three million votes. Ill at the time of his fourth election, he died less than three months after the inauguration.

THE AMENDMENT PASSES. Congress had never been fully satisfied with the original Constitution's provision for unrestricted presidential reeligibility. From 1789 to 1947, 270 resolutions to limit the president's tenure were introduced in the House and Senate.[108] But the Roosevelt years added a partisan dimension to this long-standing concern. In 1932 the Republicans, who had formed the nation's majority party since 1860, were driven from power by Roosevelt's New Deal Democratic coalition. Conservative Democrats, mostly southerners, lost control of their party to liberals and northerners.

In the midterm elections of 1946, Republicans regained a majority of both houses of Congress. On February 6, 1947, less than five weeks after the opening of the Eightieth Congress, the House passed a strict two-term amendment to the Constitution by a vote of 285–121. Republicans supported the amendment unanimously (238–0). Democrats opposed it 47–121, with three-fourths of the Democratic yea votes coming from southerners. Freshman representative John F. Kennedy of Massachusetts, whose father, Ambassador Joseph P. Kennedy, had fallen out with Roosevelt, was one of only two northeastern Democrats to support the amendment. Five weeks later, on March 12, the Senate passed by a vote of 59–23 a slightly different version of the amendment. It allowed a successor president who had served one full term and half or less of another to seek an additional term. Republican senators, like their House colleagues, were unanimous in support (46–0); Democrats opposed the amendment by a vote of 13 (9 of them southerners) to 23. The differences between the two houses' versions were ironed out in favor of the Senate. Final congressional passage took place on March 24, 1947.

Debate on the Twenty-second Amendment painted a highly partisan issue with a thin coat of constitutional philosophy. Republicans contended that a two-term limit would protect Americans against the threat of an overly personalized presidency. Republican representative Karl Mundt of South Dakota less cautiously proclaimed that the amendment "grows directly out of the unfortunate experience we had in this country in 1940 and again in 1944." Democrats such as Rep. Estes Kefauver of Tennessee argued that the people, "by a mere majority vote, have the opportunity of deciding every four years whether they want to terminate the services of the President if he stands for reelection."[109] Little, if any, consideration was given to the reasoning behind the Constitutional Convention's carefully considered decision to place no restrictions on presidential reeligibility.

After it was proposed by Congress, the Twenty-second Amendment received a mixed response from the states. Only one other amendment to the Constitution has taken longer to ratify than the three years, eleven months, required for the two-term limit.[110] Eighteen state legislatures— exactly half the needed number—approved the amendment in 1947, all of

Despite numerous precedents for executive intervention in labor disputes, President Harry Truman's seizure of steel mills during the Korean War was widely denounced. The Supreme Court ruled the action illegal.

them in predominantly Republican states. Afterward, ratification proceeded slowly, with most victories coming in the conservative Democratic South.[111] Approval from the required three-fourths of the states was attained on February 27, 1951. Had the amendment not exempted Truman from its coverage, it might have foundered on the shoals of overt (instead of merely implicit) partisanship.

DWIGHT D. EISENHOWER: THE RELUCTANT MODERN PRESIDENT

Like the Hoover Commission, and in contrast to the Twenty-second Amendment, the presidency of Dwight Eisenhower fostered bipartisan acceptance of the modern presidency.[112] But Eisenhower's contribution was reluctant. Although the first Republican president in twenty years had no intention of trying to dismantle the Roosevelt Revolution, he came to the White House in 1953 with a different understanding of the executive office than Roosevelt, as well as with different aspirations for the federal role in American society.

Eisenhower had served as supreme Allied commander in Europe, a position to which FDR appointed him, and was the most celebrated of the World War II generals. "Ike," as he was known to the nation and the world, brought to the presidency a soldier's sense of duty. He was determined not to lead the federal government into new and untried activities but instead to restore a sense of national calm after the controversial and frenetic activism of the Roosevelt and Truman years. "Eisenhower has been a sort of Roosevelt in reverse," Richard Neustadt wrote in 1960. "Roosevelt was a politician seeking personal power; Eisenhower . . . came to crown a reputation not make one. He wanted to be arbiter, not master. His love was not for power but for duty."[113]

Eisenhower's concern for duty initially inclined him to accept the argument of some Republicans that balance should be restored to the relationship between the president and Congress. Ike was not a strong partisan; in fact, some Democrats had tried to draft him to run for president in 1948, only to discover that he considered it so much his soldierly duty to remain above politics that he never had voted. But Eisenhower did accept the prevailing Republican doctrine that the proper relationship between Congress and the president had been upset by his immediate Democratic predecessors, FDR and Truman. Eisenhower even decided not to submit a legislative program to Congress in 1953.

Some Americans regarded Eisenhower's constant professions of respect for Congress as refreshing evidence that the hallowed traditions of legislative government were being restored. Others, however, especially in the press, looked disdainfully on what one observer called Eisenhower's "civic textbook concept of the three branches of the federal government."[114] Reporters insisted on grading Ike at the end of his first hundred days, and he did not fare well. In an article published in May 1953, Washington correspondent Joseph C. Harsch observed, "The memory of Franklin Roosevelt's voracious seizure and joyous exercise of presidential power twenty years earlier contributes to a companion illusion of a man who slipped into the White House by the back door on January 20, 1953, and hasn't yet found his way to the President's desk."[115]

THE HIDDEN HAND. Appearances to the contrary, Eisenhower did not passively watch history unfold. He exercised power with much more relish and shrewdness than his contemporaries realized. Ike's was a "hidden-hand" presidency, as Fred Greenstein has called it, in which the president exercises power behind the scenes while presenting the public with an image of detachment from Washington's political machinations.[116] Eisenhower's approach to leadership was designed to free him from an inherent difficulty of the modern presidency. On the one hand, the president is expected to be a chief of state who stands above politics, upholds the Constitution, and lends dignity to the national government—a kind of latter-day George Washington. On the other hand, the president must be a chief of government in the style of Thomas Jefferson and Andrew Jackson—that is, an engine of change who gets things done by leading his party and Congress in pursuit of a program. Ultimately, Eisenhower believed, the dignity and influence of the office were lost when the president not only led politically but also appeared to lead politically, as he thought Truman had done.

Ike's solution to the dilemma of modern executive leadership was not to abdicate responsibility for policy. Although he was a domestic conservative who had no desire to innovate programmatically except in modest, incremental ways, Eisenhower believed that the New Deal was an established part of modern American government. When his conservative brother Edgar criticized him privately for carrying on FDR's liberal policies, the president replied bluntly: "Should any political party attempt to abolish social security, unemployment insurance and eliminate labor laws and farm programs, you should not hear of that party again in our political history."[117] As historian Oscar Handlin wrote soon after Ike left office, "Eisenhower made palatable to most Republicans the social welfare legislation of the preceding two decades. In the 1950s, the New Deal ceased to be an active political issue and became an accepted part of the American past. No other figure could have achieved that transformation."[118] Most significantly, Eisenhower managed to get an expansion of social security through a Republican-controlled Congress. The law extended benefits to many parts of society that FDR's compromised bill had failed to cover: hotel workers, laundry workers, all agricultural workers, and state and local government employees.

In foreign policy, too, Eisenhower carried on most of the policies of his two Democratic predecessors. Unlike many Republicans, Ike had long shared the internationalist perspective of FDR and Truman. He was contemptuous of Republicans—notably Senate leader Robert Taft, his main rival for the party's presidential nomination in 1952—who wanted the United States to withdraw into isolation from world affairs.[119] Eisenhower decided to run for president, some said, not because he enjoyed politics, but because he felt a duty to lead the internationalist wing of the Republican Party and to preserve the postwar foreign policy that he, as the first commander of the North Atlantic Treaty Organization, had helped to create.[120] "Observers sensed," William Leuchtenburg has noted, "that even when Eisenhower did not acknowledge that he was FDR's legatee, he had the same internationalist aspirations."[121]

Eisenhower realized that because of the New Deal legacy and the emergence of the United States as the leader of the free world it was no longer possible for the president simply to preside. The task instead, as he understood it, was to lead without seeming to lead, to remain quietly and persistently involved in political affairs while maintaining the public face of the genial national hero.

The most instructive example of Eisenhower's hidden-hand approach to government was his handling of Sen. Joseph McCarthy. Since 1950 the nation had been traumatized by the Wisconsin Republican. McCarthy had taken a real problem—communist infiltration of the federal government during the 1930s and 1940s—and made it seem bigger and more frightening than it was through wild exaggeration and reckless slander. Eisenhower refused to publicly attack McCarthy, who chaired the Senate Committee on Government Operations and its subcommittee on investigations, even though he regarded the senator's "red-baiting" as demagogy of the worst sort. The president's critics claimed that by not upbraiding McCarthy, Eisenhower abetted the senator in unjustly ruining many lives and careers. But Eisenhower's public silence did not bespeak timidity or tacit approval. Rather, he feared that to take on McCarthy publicly would undermine the dignity of the presidency and the unity of the Republican Party, thereby jeopardizing his chances of pursuing an internationalist foreign policy. "I will not," Eisenhower told his brother Milton, "get into a pissing contest with that skunk."[122]

Working closely with his press secretary, James Hagerty, the president instead used the media and his congressional allies to undermine McCarthy's political effectiveness.[123] Through Hagerty, Eisenhower helped to manage the congressional hearings that culminated in McCarthy's censure by the Senate in December 1954. In addition, Eisenhower and Vice President Richard Nixon condemned in general terms the kinds of actions in which McCarthy engaged without condemning the senator by name. The public would not turn against McCarthy, Ike was convinced, until it was persuaded that the values and institutions the senator was attacking needed to be defended.

Eisenhower's most notable reproof came when McCarthy's adherents around the country purged libraries of politically controversial books and harassed educators. "Don't join the book burners," the president told an audience at Dartmouth College. "Don't think you are going to conceal faults by concealing evidence that they ever existed. . . . How will we defeat communism unless we know what it is?" The right of the people to express ideas, he said, is "unquestioned, or it isn't American."[124] A few months later, Eisenhower proclaimed that teachers were loyal citizens who enjoyed "true freedom of thought, untrammeled by political fashion or expediency."[125] Although the president named no names in his speeches and press conferences, he said in response to a reporter's question that McCarthy's Senate investigations threatened the values that it claimed to be defending.[126]

As his handling of McCarthy illustrates, Eisenhower did not reject the modern presidency. Rather, he tried to manage its responsibilities in a way that suited his own strengths and political objectives. Despite criticism in the press, Eisenhower remained extraordinarily popular with the American people. Calvin Coolidge had shown that presidential leadership of public opinion need not be confined to efforts at reform or innovation. Eisenhower's popularity similarly indicated that the public sometimes appreciates quiet leadership to preserve the status quo. "Among the qualities that the American government must exhibit is dignity," Eisenhower wrote in a 1960 letter to Henry Luce, the publisher of *Time* and *Life* magazines. "In turn, the principal governmental spokesman must strive to display it."[127]

EISENHOWER'S LEGACY. Eisenhower was criticized in his time by presidential scholars for the work he left undone. "No president in history," wrote Clinton Rossiter, "was ever more powerfully armed to persuade the minds of men and face up to the inevitable and then failed more poignantly to use his power."[128] To be sure, the foundations of the welfare state and of America's international obligations were sustained during Eisenhower's tenure and, in some instances, were extended. Social security was expanded and new regional security alliances such as the Southeast Asia Treaty Organization (SEATO) were formed, with the United States at their center. But to most liberals, Eisenhower, for all his popularity, failed as president by not rousing the country to redress its problems of civil rights and education.

Critics charged, in particular, that Eisenhower's approach to civil rights revealed a troubling deficiency in his understanding of presidential responsibility. In 1954 the Supreme Court decision in *Brown v. Board of Education of Topeka* struck down state laws that mandated racially segregated public schools. The Truman administration had supported the plaintiffs in this case, submitting a thirty-two-page brief that proved useful to the justices.[129] By uniting the executive and judiciary in the struggle against racial discrimination, the Court's unanimous ruling in *Brown* raised the hopes of civil rights reformers that segregation had finally been routed.[130] But Eisenhower dampened these hopes by refusing to say whether he approved or disapproved of the decision. His equivocation helped to set the stage for the ugly racial incident that occurred in Little Rock, Arkansas.

In September 1957 the Democratic governor of Arkansas, Orval Faubus, mobilized his state's National Guard unit in an effort to thwart a federal court order to begin desegregating Little Rock's all-white Central High School. Eisenhower tried to stay out of the controversy, initially conducting only a single, inconclusive meeting with Faubus at the president's summer home in Newport, Rhode Island, on September 14. Upon returning to Arkansas, Faubus, who believed that Eisenhower was indifferent to the situation in his state, defied the president's private request to instruct the Arkansas National Guard to enforce the court order. Instead, Faubus withdrew the guard from around the school. On September 23, nine African American students were turned away from Central High School by a howling, hate-filled mob of segregationists from Arkansas and other states. Faubus continued to inflame the onrushing crisis with defiant rhetoric.

Eisenhower was still reluctant to interfere in Little Rock, believing that to use federal troops to enforce desegregation might cause the violence to spread. But when neither state nor local authorities dispersed the mob, the president could no longer avoid responsibility. If he had failed to act in the face of Arkansas's defiance of the court order, Eisenhower would have yielded to every segregationist governor the right to break the law. The unfortunate consequence of delay was that when Eisenhower did act, he was forced to deploy massive military power domestically. On September 24 a contingent of army paratroopers was dispatched to Little Rock. The next day, Americans saw shocking front-page photographs of troops wielding bayonets in an American city.

Many have found it difficult to understand Eisenhower's conduct in the Little Rock crisis. To his credit, however, he eventually did act firmly, and in doing so he established a precedent that would make it difficult for future presidents to deny the federal interest in the nation's schools and in race relations, which until then had been regarded as essentially state and local matters.[131] Faced with violent resistance to integration of the University of Mississippi in 1961, President Kennedy dispatched soldiers to restore order and help enforce the law.

Eisenhower also contributed to the institutionalization of the modern presidency. Drawing on his long experience with military staffs, the president enlarged and formally organized the White House Office. This is not to say that Eisenhower arranged the White House along military lines, as many Washington observers concluded. Instead, the respect for careful organization that Ike developed as an army general predisposed him to take seriously the recommendations of the Brownlow and Hoover Commissions that a clearer and more formal line of command and communications be established between the White House and the executive departments and agencies.[132] The line Eisenhower established ran from the president through his chief of staff to the rest of the president's team and back again. Former New Hampshire governor Sherman Adams, who was the first White House chief of staff, worked zealously to free the president from the everyday demands of the White House and executive branch.[133]

Eisenhower also created the first White House office of legislative liaison. The liaison office was headed by Maj. Gen. Wilton B. "Jerry" Persons, a retired army officer who had handled Eisenhower's congressional relations when he served as the army's chief of staff and, after World War II, as NATO commander. The task of the liaison office was to promote the president's policies on Capitol Hill.

Although Eisenhower offered no legislative program to Congress during his first year, pressure from several quarters soon forced him to become more involved in legislative matters. Having talked of "restoring the balance" between the branches, Eisenhower quickly realized that even a moderately conservative president who wants mostly to curb policy innovation must ensure that his views are presented effectively to Congress. A presidential program accompanied the State of the Union message in January 1954, and Eisenhower and his legislative liaison office worked to enact it. During his eight years as president, Ike became increasingly involved in legislative issues, such as the successful efforts to create the federal interstate highway system and to launch a space program. He even managed to work well with a Congress that, after the 1954 midterm elections, was controlled by the Democrats.

Eisenhower's "special triumph" in congressional relations was to hold down defense spending.[134] The former military commander wanted to avoid an arms race with the Soviet Union, fearing that a military buildup would trigger uncontrollable inflation and eventually bankrupt the United States without providing additional security. During his second term, Democrats in

Congress, led by Sen. John F. Kennedy, criticized the president for putting a balanced budget ahead of the national defense. But Eisenhower, confident of his own military judgment, was unmoved. Inheriting a $50 billion annual defense budget from Truman, he reduced it to $40 billion.

The importance of controlling defense spending was the principal theme of Eisenhower's 1961 farewell address, the first of its kind to be delivered on television. The president did not downplay the threat of communism, which he said "commands our whole attention, absorbs our whole being." At the same time, Eisenhower warned the country "to guard against the acquisition of unwarranted influence, whether sought or not, by the military-industrial complex." The conjunction of an immense military establishment and a large arms industry held "the potential for the disastrous rise of misplaced power." The task of statesmanship, the president insisted, was not to rouse the people to make the "emotional and transitory sacrifice of crisis," but rather to constrain the national security state through "the proper meshing of the huge industrial and military machinery of defense with our peaceful methods and goals, so that security and liberty may prosper together."[135]

After a doubtful start, then, Eisenhower upheld the modern presidency. His defense of the twentieth-century executive was never more apparent than in his efforts to defeat the Bricker Amendment, which proposed changing the Constitution to curtail the president's authority to conduct the nation's foreign policy. By the terms of the amendment, executive agreements with other nations would take effect only if they were approved by Congress and did not conflict with state laws. As historian Elmo Richardson has noted, "The idea was, of course, a belated response to Franklin Roosevelt's personal diplomacy."[136] The amendment's author, Republican senator John Bricker of Ohio, and its adherents in Congress endorsed isolationist sentiments that Eisenhower believed would threaten the future of the Republican Party and, ultimately, the United States.

In the Senate, mostly because of the president's personal influence, the Bricker Amendment fell one vote shy of passage. The close division indicated that many Americans still believed that the modern chief executive's power in foreign affairs was excessive. It was the reluctant modern president, "Dwight D. Eisenhower—nobody else," an embittered Senator Bricker claimed, who preserved the executive's right to make international agreements unilaterally.[137]

NOTES

1. White quoted in Stefan Lorant, *The Presidency: A Pictorial History of Presidential Elections from Washington to Truman* (New York: Macmillan, 1957), 594.

2. Franklin D. Roosevelt, *Public Papers and Addresses,* 13 vols., ed. Samuel J. Rosenman (New York: Random House, 1938–1950), 1:751–752.

3. Ibid., 1:752.

4. Many political scientists, most notably Fred I. Greenstein, consider Franklin Roosevelt to be the first "modern" president. See Greenstein, "Introduction: Toward a Modern Presidency," in *Leadership in the Modern Presidency*, ed. Fred I. Greenstein (Cambridge: Harvard University Press, 1988). As Jeffrey K. Tulis argues, however, many of the characteristics of the executive that Greenstein identifies as distinctly modern, such as legislative leadership, found practical expression in the nineteenth century, if not earlier. Tulis, *The Rhetorical Presidency* (Princeton: Princeton University Press, 1987), esp. chap. 1. Stephen Skowronek provides the most systematic challenge to the traditional-modern divide. He offers a cyclical theory of presidential power that downplays the transformation of the executive office during the twentieth century. Skowronek, *The Politics Presidents Make: Leadership from John Adams to Bill Clinton* (Cambridge: Harvard University Press, 1997).

5. See, for example, Robert K. Murray and Tim H. Blessing, "The Presidential Performance Study: A Progress Report," *Journal of American History* 70 (December 1983): 542; and Arthur M. Schlesinger Jr., "Rating the Presidents: Washington to Clinton," *Political Science Quarterly* 112 (Summer 1997): 179–190. These polls ranked FDR as the second greatest president in history, surpassed only by Abraham Lincoln. A 2005 poll conducted by the *Wall Street Journal*, with James Lindgren of Northwestern Law School and the Federalist Society, in which the editors adjusted the results to give Democratic- and Republican-leaning scholars equal weight, rated Roosevelt third, behind George Washington and Abraham Lincoln, http://www.opinionjournal.com/extra/?id=110007243. On the consistent ranking of FDR as one of America's greatest presidents, see Jill L. Curry and Irwin L. Morris. "Explaining Presidential Greatness: The Roles of Peace and Prosperity?" *Presidential Studies Quarterly* 40, no. 3 (September, 2010): 515–530.

6. Arnold J. Toynbee, *Survey of International Affairs, 1931* (London: Oxford University Press, 1932), 1.

7. Thorpe quoted in Robert M. Collins, *The Business Response to Keynes* (New York: Columbia University Press, 1981), 28.

8. *New York Times*, March 4, 1933, 1.

9. Clinton Rossiter, *The American Presidency*, 2nd ed. (New York: Harcourt, Brace and World, 1960), 145.

10. After bolting from the Republican Party in 1912, Theodore Roosevelt appeared before the gathering in Chicago that launched the Bull Moose campaign. FDR was the first nominee to address a regular national convention.

11. *New York Times*, July 3, 1932, 1.

12. Roosevelt, *Public Papers and Addresses*, 1:647–648.

13. *New York Times*, March 5, 1933, 3.

14. "Franklin D. Roosevelt's First Inaugural Address," in *The Evolving Presidency: Landmark Documents, 1787–2010*, 4th ed., ed. Michael Nelson (Washington, D.C.: CQ Press, 2012), 146–151.

15. Ibid.

16. Ibid.

17. The term *fireside chat* was first used by Robert Trout of the Columbia Broadcasting System's Washington station, who introduced FDR on the occasion of his first radio address. At ten o'clock on the evening of March 12, 1933, Trout told sixty million people, seated before twenty million radios, that "the President wants to come into your home and sit at your fireside for a little fireside chat." Kenneth S. Davis, *FDR: The New Deal Years, 1933–1937* (New York: Random House, 1986), 60.

18. Roosevelt, *Public Papers and Addresses*, 2:65.

19. Raymond Moley, *After Seven Years* (New York: Harper and Brothers, 1939), 155.

20. *Wall Street Journal*, March 13, 1933, in Frank Freidel, *FDR: Launching the New Deal* (Boston: Little, Brown, 1973), 236.

21. Hopkins is quoted in Fred I. Greenstein, "Nine Presidents in Search of a Modern Presidency," in Greenstein, *Leadership in the Modern Presidency*, 299. See also James T. Patterson, "The Rise of Presidential Power before World War I," *Law and Contemporary*

Problems 40 (Spring 1976): 53–57; and Louis Brownlow, *The President and the Presidency* (Chicago: Public Administration Service, 1949), 69–71.

22. Black to James Farley, June 19, 1934, box 34, folder "Roosevelt, Franklin D., 1934," James Farley Papers, Manuscripts Division, Library of Congress, Washington, D.C.

23. Roosevelt, *Public Papers and Addresses*, 3:317–318.

24. Elmer E. Cornwell Jr., *Presidential Leadership of Public Opinion* (Bloomington: Indiana University Press, 1965), 131.

25. Franklin D. Roosevelt, " 'A Tribute to Abraham Lincoln,' to Be Read on His Birthday," January 25, 1936, *Public Papers and Addresses*, 5:68.

26. Ibid., 5:233.

27. Ibid., 1:659.

28. "Democratic Platform of 1936," in *National Party Platforms*, ed. Donald Bruce Johnson (Urbana: University of Illinois Press, 1978), 360. Evidence of FDR's dominant role in drafting the platform can be found in the President's Secretary file 143, folder "Democratic Platform," Franklin D. Roosevelt Papers, Franklin D. Roosevelt Library, Hyde Park, N.Y.

29. Roosevelt to Frankfurter, February 9, 1937, Felix Frankfurter Papers, microfilm reel 60, Manuscripts Department, Library of Congress, Washington, D.C.

30. Roosevelt, *Public Papers and Addresses*, 5:234.

31. William E. Leuchtenburg, "Franklin D. Roosevelt: The First Modern President," in Greenstein, *Leadership in the Modern Presidency*, 27.

32. Greenstein, "Nine Presidents," 299. Congress created the Tennessee Valley Authority (TVA) in May 1933. The agency was authorized to sell electric power to states, counties, and municipalities; it also was empowered to construct dams on the Tennessee River. The TVA is widely regarded as one of the most successful New Deal programs, contributing greatly to flood control and to the dissemination of electric power throughout the southeastern United States.

33. The magnitude of FDR's popular vote victory has been exceeded only by Lyndon B. Johnson's triumph over Barry Goldwater in 1964.

34. Matthew Dickinson, "The Executive Office of the President: The Paradox of Politicization," in *The Executive Branch*, ed. Joel D. Aberbach and Mark A. Peterson (New York: Oxford University Press, 2005).

35. Louis Brownlow, *A Passion for Anonymity* (Chicago: University of Chicago Press, 1958), 392.

36. *Report of the President's Committee on Administrative Management* (Washington, D.C.: Government Printing Office, 1937), 53. See also "Report of the Brownlow Committee," in Nelson, *Evolving Presidency*, 168–173.

37. Luther Gulick, "Politics, Administration, and the New Deal," *Annals* 169 (September 1933): 64.

38. Gulick quoted in Rossiter, *American Presidency*, 129.

39. The term *administrative presidency* is drawn from Richard Nathan's book on the use of administrative strategies by modern presidents to pursue their policy objectives. See Richard Nathan, *The Administrative Presidency* (New York: Wiley, 1983).

40. Roosevelt, *Public Papers and Addresses*, 2:161.

41. Ellis Hawley, "The Constitution of the Hoover and F. Roosevelt Presidency during the Depression Era, 1900–1939," in *The Constitution and the American Presidency*, ed. Martin L. Fausold and Alan Shank (Albany: State University of New York Press, 1991), 94.

42. William E. Leuchtenburg, "Franklin D. Roosevelt's Supreme Court 'Packing' Plan," in *Essays on the New Deal*, ed. Harold M. Hollingsworth and William F. Holmes (Austin: University of Texas Press, 1969), 76–77. See also Michael Nelson, "The President and the Court: Reinterpreting the Court-Packing Episode of 1937," *Political Science Quarterly* 103 (Summer 1988): 267–293; and Jeff Shesol, *Supreme Power: Franklin Roosevelt vs. the Supreme Court* (New York: W. W. Norton, 2010).

43. *Humphrey's Executor v. United States*, 295 U.S. 602 (1935); *Schechter Poultry Corp. v. United States*, 295 U.S. 495 (1935).

44. See the discussion of *Myers* in Chapter 8 in this volume.

45. Leuchtenburg, "Franklin D. Roosevelt's Supreme Court 'Packing' Plan," 115. On the line-item veto, see *"Clinton v. City of New York,"* in Nelson, *Evolving Presidency,* 273–278.

46. Gerry to Bailey, n.d., Josiah William Bailey Papers, Senatorial Series, Political National Papers, box 476, folder "September to October, 1938," Manuscripts Division, William R. Perkins Library, Duke University, Durham, N.C.

47. For a detailed account of the 1938 purge campaign, see Sidney M. Milkis, "Presidents and Party Purges: With Special Emphasis on the Lessons of 1938," in *Presidents and Their Parties: Leadership or Neglect?* ed. Robert Harmel (New York: Praeger, 1984).

48. Susan Dunn, *Roosevelt's Purge: How Roosevelt Fought to Change the Democratic Party* (Cambridge: Belknap Press of Harvard University Press, 2010).

49. Because no other Democrat seemed capable of carrying forward the New Deal principles, many progressives began working for Roosevelt's renomination at the end of 1938. It was the foreign policy crisis, however, that finally persuaded Roosevelt to stand for reelection in 1940.

50. Hawley, "Constitution of the Hoover and F. Roosevelt Presidency," 99–100.

51. Roosevelt, *Public Papers and Addresses,* 6:410.

52. *United States v. Curtiss-Wright Export Corp.,* 299 U.S. 304 (1936).

53. *United States v. Belmont,* 301 U.S. 324 (1937). On Hamilton, see Chapter 3 in this volume.

54. David M. Kennedy, *Freedom from Fear: The American People in Depression and War, 1929–1945* (New York: Oxford University Press, 1999), 474.

55. *Congressional Record,* 77th Cong., 2nd sess., 1942, 7044.

56. R. Shep Melnick, "The Courts, Jurisprudence, and the Executive Branch," in Aberbach and Peterson, *Executive Branch,* 458.

57. *Yakus v. United States,* 321 U.S. 414 (1944).

58. *Ex parte Quirin,* 317 U.S. 1 (1942).

59. Andrew Rudalevige, *The New Imperial Presidency: Renewing Presidential Power after Watergate* (Ann Arbor: University of Michigan Press, 2005), 230.

60. *Korematsu v. United States,* 323 U.S. 214 (1944).

61. Id. at 245–246.

62. Kennedy, *Freedom from Fear,* 756–759.

63. George McJimsey, *The Presidency of Franklin Delano Roosevelt* (Lawrence: University Press of Kansas, 2000), 277–278. The five nations that could veto any proposal before the Security Council were the United States, Soviet Union, Great Britain, France, and China.

64. Leahy quoted in Kennedy, *Freedom from Fear,* 802. The discussion of Yalta owes much to Kennedy's examination of this conference. See especially chap. 22.

65. McJimsey, *Presidency of Franklin Delano Roosevelt,* 281–282.

66. Kennedy, *Freedom from Fear,* 807. For a recent critique of Roosevelt's foreign policy, see Seyom Brown, "Idealism, Realpolitik, or Domestic Politics," in *The New Deal and the Triumph of Liberalism,* ed. Sidney M. Milkis and Jerome Mileur (Amherst: University of Massachusetts Press, 2002).

67. Brown, "Idealism, Realpolitik, or Domestic Politics," 306–307.

68. Roosevelt quoted in Kennedy, *Freedom from Fear,* 807.

69. Harry Truman, *Memoirs,* 2 vols. (Garden City, N.Y.: Doubleday, 1955), 1:4–5; William E. Leuchtenburg, *In the Shadow of FDR: From Harry Truman to Ronald Reagan,* rev. ed. (Ithaca: Cornell University Press, 1985), 1.

70. William S. White, "The Memoirs of Harry S. Truman," *New Republic,* November 7, 1955, 16.

71. Alonzo L. Hamby, "Harry S. Truman: Insecurity and Responsibility," in Greenstein, *Leadership in the Modern Presidency,* 42.

72. Ibid., 42–43.

73. Quoted in Larry Berman, *The New American Presidency* (Boston: Little, Brown, 1987), 212.

74. Truman, *Memoirs,* 1:483.

75. Ibid., 1:485–486.

76. Roosevelt, *Public Papers and Addresses,* 13:41.

77. Harry S. Truman, *Public Papers of the Presidents of the United States: Harry S. Truman,* 14 vols. (Washington, D.C.: Government Printing Office, 1961–1966), 1:279.

78. Greenstein, "Nine Presidents," 306.

79. The Taft-Hartley Act outlawed the closed shop, made unions liable for damages caused by breaches of contract, enabled the president to declare an eighty-day cooling-off period before a strike, forbade unions to make political contributions or to exact excessive dues, and required elected union officials to take an oath that they were not communists.

80. Truman, *Public Papers of the Presidents,* 3:289, 299.

81. *Nation,* June 28, 1947, 755.

82. Alonzo L. Hamby, *Man of the People: A Life of Harry S. Truman* (New York: Oxford University Press, 1995), 387.

83. Truman, *Public Papers of the President,* 3:178–179.

84. Hamby, *Man of the People,* 393.

85. Richard Neustadt, *Presidential Power and the Modern Presidents: The Politics of Leadership from Roosevelt to Reagan,* 4th ed. (New York: Free Press, 1990), 40. The first edition of this book was published in 1960 by Wiley.

86. Hamby, *Man of the People,* 395.

87. Neustadt, *Presidential Power and the Modern Presidents,* 45.

88. President Harry S. Truman, "Executive Order 9308 Establishing the President's Committee on Civil Rights," December 5, 1946, in *Growth of Presidential Power: A Documented History,* 3 vols., ed. William M. Goldsmith (New York: Chelsea, 1974), 3:1568–9.

89. William E. Leuchtenburg, *The White House Looks South: Franklin Roosevelt, Harry S. Truman, and Lyndon B. Johnson* (Baton Rouge: Louisiana State University Press, 2005), 147–225.

90. Branch quoted in ibid., 367. In the Compromise of 1877, Republicans gained the presidency and Democrats secured the withdrawal of federal troops from the South.

91. John Hope Franklin, "Civil Rights and the Truman Administration," Public Address at the University of Chicago, April 5, 1968, in *Conference of Scholars on the Truman Administration and Human Rights,* ed. Donald McCoy, Richard T. Reutten, and J. R. Fuchs (Independence, Mo.: Harry S Truman Library Institute, 1968), 134. On the presidents' use of executive orders to promote civil rights, see Kenneth R. Mayer, *With the Stroke of a Pen: Executive Orders and Presidential Power* (Princeton: Princeton University Press, 2001), chap. 6.

92. Truman, *Public Papers of the President,* 11:176.

93. *Youngstown Sheet and Tube Co. v. Sawyer,* 343 U.S. 579 (1952).

94. Id. at 587.

95. See Chapter 8 in this volume.

96. Richard M. Pious, *The American Presidency* (New York: Basic Books, 1979), 66; Edward S. Corwin, *The President: Office and Powers, 1787–1957,* 4th ed. (New York: New York University Press, 1957), 408–410.

97. Pious, *American Presidency,* 67; see also Chapter 6 in this volume.

98. On Roosevelt's Court appointees, see Noah Feldman, *Scorpions: The Battles and Triumphs of FDR's Great Supreme Court Justices* (New York: Twelve, 2010).

99. *Youngstown Sheet and Tube Co. v. Sawyer,* at 637; Pious, *American Presidency,* 64–69.

100. Maeva Marcus, *Truman and the Steel Seizure Case: The Limits of Presidential Power* (New York: Columbia University Press, 1977), 248.

101. Greenstein, "Nine Presidents," 304.

102. Hamby, *Man of the People,* 309–311. With the enactment of the Goldwater-Nichols Act in 1986, the president's authority over the military was further strengthened. It authorized the president rather than the Joint Chiefs of Staff to select the JCS chair.

103. Peri E. Arnold, *Making the Managerial Presidency: Comprehensive Reorganization Planning, 1905–1980* (Princeton: Princeton University Press, 1986), 127.

104. Martha Derthick and Paul J. Quirk, *The Politics of Deregulation* (Washington, D.C.: Brookings, 1985), 61–74.

105. Truman's budget director James Webb, as quoted in Arnold, *Making the Managerial Presidency,* 142.

106. "Thomas Jefferson's Letter to the Vermont Legislature," in Nelson, *Evolving Presidency,* 73–75.

107. Indeed, Washington wrote in a 1788 letter that "I differ widely myself from Mr. Jefferson . . . as to the expediency of rotation in that department [the presidency]." Corwin, *President,* 333.

108. Paul G. Willis and George L. Willis, "The Politics of the Twenty-Second Amendment," *Western Political Quarterly* 5 (September 1952): 469.

109. Ibid., 470.

110. The Twenty-seventh Amendment, which restricts Congress's ability to raise its members' salaries, was ratified in 1992, a record 203 years after Congress proposed it in 1789.

111. Every Truman-sponsored civil rights initiative prompted a few more southern legislatures to ratify. David E. Kyvig, *Explicit and Authentic Acts: Amending the U.S. Constitution, 1776–1995* (Lawrence: University Press of Kansas, 1996), 332–333.

112. The second Hoover Commission was created by Congress in 1953. Republican leaders in the House and Senate hoped that this time the commission would not be sidetracked from its mission to reduce the size of the government. These hopes were realized. Although the first Hoover Commission had become interested primarily in improving the administrative management of the executive branch, the second concentrated on issues of policy and function. At the heart of the second commission's recommendations was the idea that many of the Roosevelt-era programs and agencies had been counterproductive. But the commission's conservative ideological approach guaranteed that it would have little influence on the Eisenhower administration, which accepted most of the changes brought by the New Deal. See Arnold, *Making the Managerial Presidency,* 166–227.

113. Neustadt, *Presidential Power and the Modern Presidents,* 139.

114. Marquis Childs, *Eisenhower: Captive Hero* (New York: Harcourt, Brace, 1958), 179.

115. Joseph C. Harsch, "Eisenhower's First Hundred Days," *Reporter,* May 12, 1953, 9.

116. Fred I. Greenstein, *The Hidden-Hand Presidency: Eisenhower as Leader* (New York: Basic Books, 1982).

117. Dwight David Eisenhower to Edgar Newton Eisenhower, November 8, 1954, http://www.eisenhowermemorial.org/presidential-papers/first-term/documents/1147.cfm.

118. Oscar Handlin, "The Eisenhower Administration: A Self-Portrait," *Atlantic Monthly,* November 1963, 68.

119. Elmo Richardson, *The Presidency of Dwight D. Eisenhower* (Lawrence: University Press of Kansas, 1979), 14.

120. Erwin C. Hargrove, *The Power of the Modern Presidency* (Philadelphia: Temple University Press, 1974), 60.

121. Leuchtenburg, In the Shadow of FDR, 48.

122. Eisenhower quoted in Stephen E. Ambrose, "The Eisenhower Revival," in *Rethinking the Presidency,* ed. Thomas E. Cronin (Boston: Little, Brown, 1982), 107.

123. Greenstein, *Hidden-Hand Presidency,* chap. 5.

124. "Remarks at Dartmouth College Commencement Exercises," Hanover, N.H., June 14, 1953, *Public Papers of the Presidents of the United States: Dwight D. Eisenhower, 1953* (Washington, D.C.: Government Printing Office, 1960), 415.

125. "Address at the Sixth National Assembly of the United Church of Women," Atlantic City, October 6, 1953, *Public Papers of the Presidents of the United States: Dwight D. Eisenhower, 1953,* 639.

126. Richardson, *Presidency of Dwight D. Eisenhower*, 55.

127. Quoted in Fred I. Greenstein, "Dwight D. Eisenhower: Leadership Theorist in the White House," in Greenstein, *Leadership in the Modern Presidency*, 104–105.

128. Rossiter, *American Presidency*, 163.

129. Leuchtenburg, *White House Looks South*, 219.

130. *Brown v. Board of Education of Topeka*, 347 U.S. 483 (1954).

131. Goldsmith, Growth of Presidential Power, 3:1619. See also "Dwight D. Eisenhower's Little Rock Executive Order," in Nelson, *Evolving Presidency*, 183–186.

132. Philip G. Henderson, *Managing the Presidency: The Eisenhower Legacy—From Kennedy to Reagan* (Boulder: Westview Press, 1988), 17–24.

133. Greenstein, "Nine Presidents," 307–311.

134. Ambrose, "Eisenhower Revival," 108.

135. Eisenhower, *Public Papers of the Presidents, 1960–1961*, 1038–9.

136. Richardson, *Presidency of Dwight D. Eisenhower*, 51.

137. Bricker quoted in Gary W. Reichard, *The Reaffirmation of Republicanism: Eisenhower and the Eighty-Third Congress* (Knoxville: University of Tennessee Press, 1975), 67.

CHAPTER 11

Personalizing the Presidency:
John F. Kennedy to Jimmy Carter

I n his influential book *Presidential Power*, first published in 1960, political scientist Richard E. Neustadt, a former aide in the Truman White House, declared that "the same conditions that promote [the modern president's] leadership in form preclude a guarantee of leadership in fact."[1] Neustadt's study reaffirmed Woodrow Wilson's argument at the beginning of the twentieth century that the president is responsible for leading the United States to a higher level of political discourse and national action. But Neustadt cautioned that at midcentury this obligation fell upon the president with no assurance of "an influence commensurate with services performed." In fact, the modern president could count only on being a "clerk" whose help would be demanded but not always reciprocated by others.[2]

Neustadt's solution to the dilemma of the modern presidency was for each president to struggle to overcome the political obstacles that fetter the office. It was the president's job to resurrect the aggressive and skillful style of leadership that Franklin D. Roosevelt had displayed, so that congressional leaders, cabinet officers, party officials, and others would "feel obliged" to do what the president "wants done."[3] Neustadt regarded the relatively restrained approach to the office that Dwight D. Eisenhower had taken as a sure path to political stagnation.

John F. Kennedy read Neustadt's book—indeed, some pundits believed at the time that it was the blueprint for the vigorous style of leadership that animated his presidency. But, as Fred I. Greenstein has noted, *Presidential Power* mostly clarified and defended the theory of good presidential leadership that already was current—namely, "that of an informal, Rooseveltian conduct of the presidency that contrasted with current perceptions of Eisenhower's operating manner."[4] Not surprisingly, then, the effort to expand the powers of the modern executive characterized not only the Kennedy administration, but also the administrations of his two successors, Lyndon B. Johnson and Richard Nixon.

In the early 1970s serious doubts arose about how compatible unrestrained executive power was with the public interest. Developments during the Johnson and, especially, the Nixon era kindled the belief that a return to the traditional separation of powers was needed to restore constitutional government to its proper moorings. Nixon's successors, Gerald R. Ford and Jimmy Carter, inherited a much-tarnished and somewhat diminished office.

JOHN F. KENNEDY AND THE RISE OF THE "PERSONAL PRESIDENCY"

Kennedy was elected president in 1960 to "get this country moving again" by lifting the United States out of the complacency that seemed to have settled on it during the Eisenhower years. The combination of a sluggish economy, simmering racial problems, and the Soviet threat had created doubts about the nation's future that led a slim plurality of the voters back to the Democratic Party. In addition, the still-popular Eisenhower, who disapproved of the Twenty-second Amendment, was forbidden to run again—an ironic consequence of the Republican-inspired two-term constitutional limit.[5]

Running against Vice President Richard Nixon, Kennedy campaigned on a theme of change, tying that theme to the presidency itself. The United States could no longer afford a president, he declared, "who is praised primarily for what he did not do, the disasters he prevented, the bills he vetoed—a President wishing his subordinates would produce more missiles or build more schools." Instead, Kennedy insisted, the nation "needs a Chief Executive who is the vital center of action in our whole scheme of government." The president must be "willing and able to summon his national constituency to its finest hour—to alert the people to our dangers and our opportunities—to demand of them the sacrifices that will be necessary."[6]

On November 22, 1963, less than three years after he took the oath as president, Kennedy was assassinated by Lee Harvey Oswald in Dallas, Texas. His death traumatized the nation. All of the presidents who died in office had been deeply mourned, but only Abraham Lincoln's death evoked as profound a sense of unfulfilled promise as Kennedy's. Forty-three years old at the time of his inauguration, Kennedy was the youngest person ever elected as president. The striking down of such a vital, attractive leader in the prime of life, leaving behind his stoic young widow and two small children, left Americans with an extraordinary sense of personal loss.[7] Yet despite his truncated term, or perhaps because of it, Kennedy enjoys a lasting place in American culture. Much like the warrior Achilles in ancient Greece, Kennedy is "part not of history but of myth."[8]

Long after his assassination, national surveys continued to show that Americans regarded Kennedy as the finest of the modern presidents. Remarkably, Kennedy edged out FDR in a 1987 Harris poll as the "best" president in domestic affairs, a result that measured the outsized Kennedy mystique more than the modest Kennedy record.[9] Kennedy's popularity persisted not only because of his tragic death, but also because of certain qualities that he displayed as president. "Beyond question," historian Carl M. Brauer has written, "Kennedy was inspirational in a way that few presidents have been."[10] Franklin Roosevelt's great achievement as a moral leader was to bring the United States through the dark days of the Great Depression and World War II. In a like manner, Kennedy sought to inspire the nation to meet the challenges of the postwar era. Roosevelt's New Deal, Kennedy said in his acceptance speech at the 1960 Democratic convention, had "promised security and succor to those in need." But more prosperous times called for a New Frontier that was "not a set of promises" but "a set of challenges." The New Frontier "sums up not what I intend to offer the American people, but what I intend to ask of them," he declared. "It appeals to their pride, not their pocketbook—it holds out the promise of more sacrifice instead of security."[11]

Kennedy's inaugural address, the most important speech of his presidency, placed this challenge before the nation. Uplifting and optimistic in tone, it articulated a vision that greatly augmented the fragile basis of support he had received from the extremely close election (Kennedy's margin of victory was only 120,000 popular votes out of the nearly 69 million cast). Both liberals and conservatives found something to applaud in the new president's celebration of sacrifice and mission. The best-remembered passages from the address emphasized these themes:

> In the long history of the world, only a few generations have been granted the role of defending freedom in its hours of maximum danger. I do not shrink from this responsibility—I welcome it. I do not believe that any of us would exchange places with any other people or any other generation. The energy, the faith, the devotion which we bring to this endeavor will light our country and those who serve it—and the glow from that fire can truly light the world.

> And so, my fellow Americans: ask not what your country can do for you—ask what you can do for your country.[12]

Kennedy's call for personal sacrifice and national glory resonated with the historical experience of postwar America. The giftedness, or charisma, of the young president matched America's feeling that it could solve the world's problems and break through the ancient barriers that previously had limited humankind—even, as Kennedy pledged, "landing a man on the moon and returning him safely to the earth."[13]

THE FIRST TELEVISION PRESIDENT

It was not just Kennedy's words that stirred the public, but also the vibrant and reassuring image he conveyed when delivering them. His administration marked a revolutionary advance in the use of television in politics. Although Eisenhower was the first president to appear on television regularly, "it was under and because of Kennedy that television became an essential determinant—probably the essential determinant—of a president's ability to lead the nation."[14] As political scientist Bruce Miroff has written, throughout his presidency Kennedy and other members of his administration staged widely publicized "spectacles," or message-laden symbolic displays, that "projected youth, vigor, and novelty, that recast the [presidency] itself as a headquarters for intelligence and masterful will."[15]

Kennedy's televised speeches were but one element of his strategy of public communication. After his inauguration, the president went before the cameras only nine times to deliver a prepared address. Convinced that viewers would tire quickly of formal speech making, he relied instead on the press conference as his principal forum for reaching the public. Kennedy was the first president to allow press conferences to be televised without restriction, recognizing that live broadcasts of his give and take with reporters would be a superb means of addressing the nation. Eisenhower's press conferences had been televised, but they were taped and the White House retained the right to edit them for broadcast. Ike's press secretary, James C. Hagerty, believed that live television was dangerous because the president might misspeak on a sensitive matter, jeopardizing national security. But Kennedy, who had benefited greatly from his televised debates with Nixon in 1960, regarded television as an ally.

Previous presidents, especially FDR, had used press conferences to encourage reporters to convey their messages to the American people. But the live, televised press conference relegated reporters to the role of supporting actors. Under Kennedy's auspices, the press conference became the functional equivalent of the fireside chat. It gave the president a relatively informal and personal way to reach the public directly, over the heads of Congress and the proprietors of the media.

The public saw and heard more of Kennedy through press conferences than in any other way. Yet he held only sixty-four of them, fewer per month than Roosevelt, Truman, or Eisenhower. "He realized the dangers as well as the possibilities of television," historian James N. Giglio has written. "Overexposure became his major concern."[16]

Kennedy's adept and well-timed television appearances made a positive impression on the American people. Opinion surveys revealed a 91 percent public approval rating of his performance in press conferences. The keys to his success were careful preparation and an ability to appear relaxed and in command before the cameras.[17] Kennedy's pleasing personality, quick wit, and impressive knowledge of government set a standard that his successors have struggled to meet.[18]

THE PERSONAL PRESIDENCY

Woodrow Wilson believed that the "extraordinary isolation" of the presidency, if used effectively, allowed the president both to inspire and to benefit from public opinion. Wilson himself, and later FDR, did much to advance the president's relationship with the people. But with Kennedy and the advent of television, what political scientist Theodore J. Lowi has called the "personal presidency" came into its own.[19]

Kennedy's effective use of television was part of his personalization of the office. His presidential campaign and his governing style also established significant precedents.

All of Kennedy's campaigns for office, including his run for the presidency, were highly personal undertakings. Indeed, they were managed by members of his family, usually his brother Robert. The success of Kennedy's organization, the "Kennedy Machine" as it was called, diminished the importance of the regular party organization. In winning the Democratic nomination for president in 1960, Kennedy outmaneuvered most of the established leaders of the party, whose initial attitude toward his candidacy had been skeptical, if not hostile, mostly because no Roman Catholic had ever been elected president. To thwart them, he went outside normal party channels, using political amateurs to round up votes in the state primaries and, after succeeding in that arena, virtually forcing the convention to accept him as its nominee. Kennedy's triumph changed presidential politics. Henceforth, campaigns for president would be directed by the candidates' personal advisers and strategists. Coordination and liaison with the party would be of secondary importance.[20]

The Kennedy organization also made its mark on the government. Kennedy appointed most members of his campaign staff to similar positions in the White House Office, which further contributed to the personalization of the presidency. To reinforce this development, Kennedy concentrated more responsibility for policymaking in the White House than was the practice in past administrations. The once-anonymous staff, now assigned to oversee the activities of the departments and agencies, began to develop into a government unto itself. For example, Kennedy's assistant for national security, McGeorge Bundy, carried out many duties traditionally reserved for the secretary of state.[21] According to Robert F. Kennedy, JFK "felt at the end that the ten or twelve people in the White House who worked under his direction with Mac Bundy . . . really performed all the functions of the State Department."[22] Operations that were too big to be run out of the White House Office, such as the Peace Corps, were housed in independent agencies, where they would be free of standard bureaucratic routine. As political scientists Matthew Crenson and Benjamin Ginsberg have written, "the Kennedy administration foreshadowed a new anti-bureaucratic consensus" that would enable each president to more readily put his stamp on the executive branch, but at the risk of sacrificing valuable political experience and policy expertise.[23]

THE KENNEDY LEGACY

Although Kennedy was very popular during his brief stay in the White House, many aspects of his presidency were unsuccessful. His administration was responsible for the disastrous invasion of Cuba on April 17, 1961, by a brigade of fourteen hundred exiles from the communist regime of Fidel Castro. The rebels were crushed three days after landing in Zapata Swamp at Cuba's Bay of Pigs. Their failure to overthrow Castro was a humiliating defeat for Kennedy, who had been in office less than one hundred days.

The Bay of Pigs was not Kennedy's final attempt to overthrow Castro. The president's militant anticommunism and strong animus against Cuba's ruler led to a series of failed plots to assassinate him. "Although the defenders of the president have asserted that these schemes went forward without his knowledge," presidential historian Lewis L. Gould has written, "it is clear that John and Robert Kennedy created a climate in the White House where such covert ventures received implicit sanction at the highest levels." Moreover, reliance on covert action advanced the dangerous creed that on matters of national security presidents could work outside the law to accomplish their foreign policy objectives.[24]

Kennedy also can be faulted for accelerating the deployment of nuclear missiles to fulfill a campaign promise to close the "missile gap" with the Soviet Union. The nuclear buildup was carried out even though an intelligence analysis conducted soon after Kennedy took office revealed that the missile gap was a myth. In truth, Soviet missile development lagged far behind that of the United States. Yet once the Soviets responded to Kennedy's buildup with a buildup of their own, the United States was forced into a spiraling arms race.[25]

Finally, the Kennedy administration initiated the ill-fated American involvement in Vietnam. Intense pressure to intervene in Southeast Asia had been brought to bear on President Eisenhower by the military when the French colonial government collapsed in July 1954. But Eisenhower had decided to stay out of the region, certain that victory on the battlefield was impossible. Kennedy also doubted the wisdom of direct involvement in Vietnam, but he sent more than sixteen thousand military advisers to assist the South Vietnamese army in counterinsurgency warfare. He later encouraged a military coup against the government of Ngo Dinh Diem in Saigon. Diem's death profoundly destabilized South Vietnam. In the view of Kennedy's successor, Lyndon Johnson, it also obligated the United States to support any subsequent regime. "Though [Kennedy] privately thought the United States 'overcommitted' in Southeast Asia," Arthur M. Schlesinger Jr., a historian who served on Kennedy's staff, has written, "he permitted the commitment to grow. It was the fatal error of his presidency."[26]

Yet Kennedy did not lack for significant accomplishments as president. During the Cuban missile crisis, in particular, he led brilliantly under the most difficult circumstances. For several days in October 1962 after the United States discovered Soviet missiles in Cuba, the world was poised on the brink of a nuclear war. Kennedy and Soviet premier Nikita Khrushchev engaged in what

Secretary of State Dean Rusk later called an "eyeball to eyeball" confrontation. The impasse was resolved only when, in response to an American naval quarantine of Cuba, the Soviets agreed to dismantle their newly installed missiles. In return, the United States pledged not to attack Cuba. Kennedy also assured Khrushchev privately that he would remove American nuclear missiles from Turkey, which shared a border with the Soviet Union. Throughout the crisis, Kennedy combined firmness with restraint, a course that allowed Khrushchev to yield to the president's demands without being publicly humiliated. As Carl Brauer has written of Kennedy's conduct, "He looked at things from the Soviet side, compromised on secondary issues, did not play politics, and when he succeeded in getting the missiles removed, did not gloat or boast."[27]

Kennedy's triumph in the missile crisis demonstrated that he had matured considerably since the Bay of Pigs fiasco. His growth in office also was apparent when he took steps to make another such crisis less likely. Speaking at American University on June 10, 1963, Kennedy called for a nuclear test ban treaty that would reduce tensions with the Soviets. Both the United States and the Soviet Union, he argued, had a mutual interest in halting the arms race and seeking an eventual end to the cold war: "For in the final analysis, our most basic common link is that we all inhabit this small planet. We all breathe the same air. We all cherish our children's future. And we are all mortal. . . . Let us reexamine our attitude toward the cold war, remembering that we are not engaged in a debate, seeking to pile up debating points."[28]

On August 5, 1963, the United States and the Soviet Union signed a nuclear test ban treaty, their first bilateral arms control agreement. The treaty was only a small step forward (it did not ban underground tests, for example), but it did lay the groundwork for more substantial progress in the future.

For supporters of the president, the missile crisis triumph and the test ban treaty were signs of developing greatness. But Kennedy's destiny, as journalist Theodore H. White observed, was to be "cut off at the promise, not after the performance."[29] One of the most frequent criticisms of Kennedy, both when he was president and after his death, was that he pledged much more in the way of domestic reform than he delivered. In particular, JFK was faulted for his failures as a legislative leader. His New Frontier program embodied the high expectations he had articulated in his inaugural address. In advocating medical insurance for the elderly (Medicare) and federal aid to education, Kennedy sought to extend the accomplishments of Roosevelt and Truman, his most recent Democratic predecessors. In other ways, however, he sought to reshape his party's liberal tradition by offering initiatives, such as the Peace Corps and civil rights legislation, that reflected the themes of national service and social justice he had injected into the 1960 presidential campaign. Some of Kennedy's legislative initiatives, including the Peace Corps, became law. But most of his important bills were spurned by Congress.[30]

Kennedy's relations with legislators were extraordinarily difficult throughout his abbreviated presidency. The Democrats had a 65–35 majority in the Senate and a 263–174 advantage in the House. But twenty-one of the Democratic senators and ninety-nine of the Democratic representatives were southerners, and most of them voted with the Republicans against Kennedy's liberal agenda.

Kennedy's precarious position in Congress was revealed within days of his becoming president. The administration, with Speaker Sam Rayburn's support, moved to take control of the House Rules Committee, the conservative coalition's principal legislative stronghold. In the previous Congress, the Rules Committee, which had the power to prevent legislation from reaching the floor for debate, had eight Democratic and four Republican members. But two of the Democrats were southern conservatives, who joined with Republicans to block reform legislation. At the outset of the Kennedy administration, Rayburn proposed adding three new members, two of them administration loyalists, to the committee, which would provide an 8–7 majority for most of Kennedy's bills. Yet even with the new president's open and active support and with Rayburn drawing on his considerable store of influence and goodwill, the administration won the House vote to expand the committee by only a narrow majority, 217–212. As Kennedy told one of his aides, the outcome was not so much a show of strength as a measure of "what we are up against."[31]

Kennedy's troubles in persuading Congress to enact his domestic program were not just a matter of stubborn legislative resistance to change. Although he was superb at planning and running a presidential campaign, Kennedy was just as bored and impatient with congressional politics during his presidency as he had been while serving in the House for six years and the Senate for eight years. "The very qualities of appearance, style and cast of mind that won [Kennedy] the admiration of the intellectual and diplomatic worlds somehow marked him as an outsider in his dealings with the Congress," noted James Reston.[32]

Kennedy was far from indifferent to the legislative process, however. The one area where he expanded on the staff organization of the Eisenhower administration was in congressional relations. Under Lawrence O'Brien, the Office of Congressional Relations was joined to a network of legislative liaison specialists in the executive agencies and departments that greatly increased its effective force of operations and visibility on Capitol Hill. Yet some members of Congress complained that Kennedy's Congressional relations staff was too visible and lacked respect for the legislative process. By late 1963 the president's program was in deep trouble.[33] Several measures that Kennedy sought, particularly Medicare, federal aid to education, and civil rights, remained in legislative limbo at the time of his death.

Before he went to Dallas on November 22, 1963, JFK was looking forward to the 1964 election, which he hoped would bring enough new liberal Democrats into Congress to move the New Frontier forward. He also talked privately about a postelection military withdrawal from Vietnam. It is impossible to know whether Kennedy would have accomplished his domestic goals and avoided the travail of Vietnam if he had lived, but the inability to deliver on promises has been a recurring problem of the modern presidency.

Partly because of Kennedy, the evolution of the executive gave rise to a more powerful, prominent, and yet politically isolated president. Indeed, the modern presidency was transformed into an elaborate and far-reaching institution with considerable autonomous power. At the same time, however, most modern presidents have distanced themselves from their party and Congress, making it more difficult to satisfy public demands by enacting lasting reforms. Kennedy did not create most of these conditions. But his legacy to his successors was a significant personalization of the presidency that greatly accentuated its separation from the other centers of political power in the United States.

During Kennedy's one thousand days in office, the great promise of the personal presidency was widely celebrated. But developments within a few years of his death—the escalation of the Vietnam War and the divisions it opened in American society, the growing tendency of both liberals and conservatives to distrust government, and the popular disillusionment with presidential power—revealed the less desirable consequences of the Kennedy administration's innovations.

LYNDON B. JOHNSON AND PRESIDENTIAL GOVERNMENT

The tragedy in Dallas placed the presidency in the hands of Lyndon Johnson, a Texan whom Kennedy had selected as his vice-presidential running mate in 1960 to balance the ticket geographically. LBJ's effective campaigning in the South, especially in Texas and Louisiana, was crucial to the Democrats' narrow victory against Nixon. Before becoming vice president, Johnson was known as a consummate political operator in the Senate, where as majority leader he exercised enormous influence during the Eisenhower years.[34] It remained to be seen, however, whether the quintessential legislative insider could adapt successfully to the requirements of the presidency.

Johnson's challenges as a successor president were compounded by the bitterness that many liberals felt about a southern power broker taking the place of their fallen leader. Johnson himself observed that African Americans, especially, whose hopes for equality and justice had been raised by Kennedy,

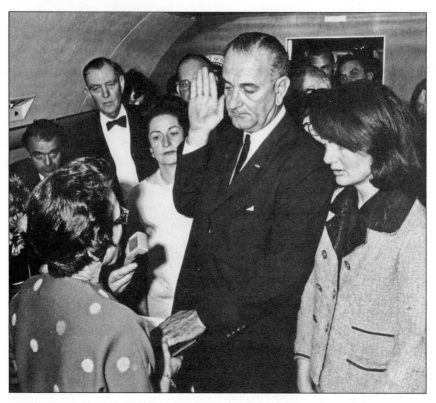

On November 22, 1963, Lyndon Johnson took the presidential oath of office aboard Air Force One *from federal district judge Sarah T. Hughes. Jacqueline Kennedy is on Johnson's left.*

were disconcerted to awake "one morning to discover that their future was in the hands of a President born in the South."[35] After all, it was southern Democrats in Congress who had blocked Kennedy's civil rights legislation. From the moment Johnson became president, the press stressed that he was the first southerner in a century to occupy the White House—"the first since another southerner named Johnson had taken power, also as the result of an assassination."[36]

Despite these obstacles, Johnson quickly grasped the reins of power. Indeed, he did more than reassure the nation and build confidence in his leadership. "In the wake of Kennedy's assassination," Jeffrey K. Tulis has written, "Lyndon Johnson was able to turn the country's grief into a commitment to a moral crusade."[37] Johnson's crusade extended beyond completing the New Frontier. As William E. Leuchtenburg has observed, "He aimed instead to be 'the greatest of them all, the whole bunch of them.' And to be the greatest president in history, he needed not to match Roosevelt's performance but to surpass it."[38]

In many ways, Johnson was inadequate to the demands of the modern presidency, especially as a public educator. Unlike other twentieth- and twenty-first-century presidents who wanted to remake the nation, LBJ neglected, even scorned, the bully pulpit. Yet Johnson profoundly influenced the modern presidency in other ways. He more than maintained the power and independence of the executive office. Regrettably, however, his failings brought into serious question, for the first time since the 1930s, the widespread assumption that the national interest is served whenever the president dominates the affairs of state.

THE GREAT SOCIETY

Johnson defined as his first task the enactment of Kennedy's New Frontier, including civil rights, a tax cut, and Medicare. He succeeded: Congress passed all of these controversial measures in short order. Especially noteworthy was the Civil Rights Act of 1964. When Kennedy died, the bill was bogged down in the Senate. But, invoking the memory of the fallen leader and bringing to bear his own extraordinary skill and experience in legislative politics, Johnson prevailed.

The new president's greatest strength as majority leader of the Senate had been personal persuasion, a talent he now used to convince the Senate Republican leader, Everett Dirksen, to endorse the bill and enlist moderate Republicans in the cause. But this support came with a price. Dirksen insisted on legislative compromises that limited the power of the new Equal Employment Opportunity Commission (EEOC) and authorized the Justice Department to bring suits only against businesses that had a clear "pattern and practice" of discrimination.[39] These compromises assuaged moderate Republicans' distaste for overlapping bureaucracies and excessive litigation, as well as their desire to protect northern and western businesses from intrusive federal agencies. Still, the principal objective of the civil rights bill—eliminating entrenched segregation in the South—was preserved.

The bipartisan alliance forged by Johnson and Dirksen sounded the death knell for the conservative coalition against civil rights. For the first time, the Senate voted cloture against a southern filibuster designed to thwart a civil rights bill and did so by a substantial 71–29 majority. Once the filibuster was ended, Congress passed the bill quickly, and Johnson signed it on July 2, 1964.[40]

The passage of the Civil Rights Act of 1964 signaled a dramatic reinvigoration of the president's preeminence as legislative leader. Even more important, the act enlisted the president and several executive agencies in the ongoing effort to ban racial discrimination. It empowered the federal bureaucracy—especially the Department of Justice, the Department of Health, Education and Welfare, and the newly formed EEOC—to assist the courts by creating parallel enforcement mechanisms for civil rights. These mechanisms proved to be effective; and in four years the Johnson administration accomplished more desegregation in southern schools than the courts had in the previous fourteen.[41]

Johnson's successful battle for civil rights dazzled the liberals in his party. Presidential scholar and self-professed Kennedy loyalist James MacGregor Burns wrote, "What will baffle the historian . . . will be how the complete Senate man moved so surely into the presidency and began to employ from the start the levers of presidential influence."[42] But the civil rights bill was only the beginning. "Many people felt we should rest after the victory of the 1964 Civil Rights Act, take it easy on Congress, and leave some breathing space for the bureaucracy and nation," wrote Johnson in his memoir. "But, there was no time to rest."[43]

Johnson's desire to move beyond Kennedy's New Frontier agenda toward what he called the "Great Society" made him impatient to push on. The 1964 elections, in which he and the Democrats won a resounding victory over the Republicans and their candidate, the archconservative senator Barry Goldwater of Arizona, provided the opportunity to do so. The election gave LBJ the most convincing popular mandate in history—more decisive, even, than FDR's triumph in 1936. Johnson won more than 60 percent of the national popular vote, and the Democrats gained thirty-seven seats in the House and one in the Senate, which secured two-thirds majorities for them in both houses of Congress.

Johnson gave the signature speech of his presidency on May 22, 1964, in a commencement address at the University of Michigan. His bold vision treated the reform aspirations of the past only as a point of departure:

> The Great Society rests on abundance and liberty for all. It demands an end of poverty and racial justice, to which we are totally committed in our time. But this is just the beginning. . . .
>
> The Great Society is a place where every child can find knowledge to enrich his mind and to enlarge his talents. It is a place where leisure is a welcome chance to build and reflect, not a feared cause of boredom and restlessness. It is a place where the city of man serves not only the needs of the body and the demands of commerce but the desire for beauty and the hunger of community.[44]

Johnson's vision gave rise to a legislative program of extraordinary breadth, which he placed before the Eighty-ninth Congress when it convened in January 1965. Congress responded enthusiastically. "No [Congress] since Reconstruction," Theodore White observed, "or perhaps since Roosevelt's seventy-third Congress of 1933–34, did more to reorder the nation."[45] In 1965 alone, Congress passed eighty of Johnson's legislative proposals, denying him only three. The new laws included important policy departures such as Medicaid, the Voting Rights Act, the Older Americans Act, the Elementary and Secondary Education Act, the War on Poverty, the Air Pollution Control Act, and legislation to create the Department of Transportation and the Department of Housing and Urban Development.

JOHNSON AND THE INSTITUTION OF THE PRESIDENCY

Johnson's domination of the political process had enduring effects on the presidency, some of which extended developments that had begun with Kennedy. Acting on his legislative ambitions, Kennedy had designed a free-wheeling process of policy innovation that departed from the existing practice of letting domestic proposals move methodically through the departments and agencies and then undergo screening and clarification in the Bureau of the Budget. Johnson went much further. More and more, policies began to be invented by the White House staff, which was committed to moving quickly on the president's agenda. At the same time, career officials in the departments and agencies and professional policy analysts in the Budget Bureau became less influential.

Joseph Califano, the chief White House aide for domestic affairs, supervised the creation of dozens of task forces composed of government officials and prominent academics. These task forces were charged with formulating innovative proposals in virtually every area of domestic policy, including poverty, environmental quality, urban planning, and aid to education. The Johnson administration took great care to immunize the task forces against political pressure, even keeping their proceedings secret. Moreover, task force members were told not to worry about whether their recommendations would be acceptable to Congress or to party leaders.[46]

Several task force proposals became law; indeed, they formed the heart of the Great Society agenda. Almost as important, however, was the revolutionary character of the process itself. By placing policy development under White House supervision, free from traditional institutional restraints, the task force approach avoided what Johnson and his advisers regarded as the bureaucratic timidity and conservatism of the existing departments and agencies. Califano's group was the precursor of the Domestic Council, which was established by Johnson's successor, Richard Nixon, and of the domestic policy staffs that have been a part of every subsequent administration.[47] As James Gaither, an assistant to Califano, observed, "I regard the change [in legislative program development] as one of the most significant institutional changes of the presidency. . . . It reflected the president's . . . belief that the traditional processes were not producing the kind of innovative and imaginative new approaches that were necessary to deal with the very significant problems that were facing the country."[48]

The early years of the Johnson administration marked the historical height of "presidential government." The White House and the Executive Office of the President had been increasingly active in formulating programs since the administration of Franklin Roosevelt. Under Johnson, however, political and policy responsibility was concentrated in the presidency to an unprecedented extent. Major domestic policy innovations were conceived in the White House, hastened through Congress by the extraordinary legislative skill of the president and his sophisticated congressional liaison team, and administered by new or refurbished executive agencies that had been designed to respond to the president's directives. Finally, Johnson established a personal governing coalition that reached beyond his party. As columnist David Broder wrote in 1966, more than was true of any of his predecessors, LBJ's leadership and program depended "for its success largely on the skill, negotiating ability, and maneuvering of the president."[49]

Soon, however, Johnson overextended himself. Ironically, the personalization of his presidency contributed to its undoing. Although LBJ was a gifted washington insider, he could not rouse the American people in the ways required by the office he had helped to re-create. As his aide Harry MacPherson noted, Johnson was incapable of "rising above the dirt of 'political governing,' so that he could inspire the nation."[50] His best words and teachings were laws and policies, but he was unable to cultivate the broad, stable base of popular support that his domestic agenda required in enter to be implemented effectively. Even Johnson realized that his most serious weakness as president was "a general inability to stimulate, inspire, and unite all the public in the country."[51]

Since its inception under Theodore Roosevelt and Woodrow Wilson, the modern presidency has been grounded in a theory of executive power that enjoins the president to be both the shaper and the instrument of the popular will. Johnson, however, was inclined to ignore the normal tasks of public leadership in his pursuit of policies and programs that he hoped would serve the nation's long-term interests. LBJ's "gargantuan aspirations" actually magnified the political burdens of the modern executive. His obvious domination of the legislative process ensured that he, not Congress, would be blamed if the Great Society programs failed. And fail many of them did, the victims of hasty packaging and unrealistic goals.[52]

THE FALL OF LYNDON JOHNSON

The war in Vietnam clearly demonstrated both Johnson's shortcomings and the more troubling aspects of presidential government. In 1965 the president concluded that only by committing a large contingent of American forces to combat could he prevent a communist takeover in South Vietnam. Johnson's extraordinary ability to build a governing coalition in Washington helped to sustain the Americanization of the war. With little resistance from either Congress or, in the beginning, the public, the troop commitment rose from 23,000 at the end of 1964 to 181,000 a year later, 389,000 a year after that, and 500,000 by the end of 1967.

The war in Southeast Asia became, in an unprecedented way, the president's war. Harry S. Truman had at least been able to claim that the United States was "carrying out an obligation for the United Nations" when he sent troops to fight in Korea. But in Vietnam, Richard M. Pious has noted, "no treaty obligations or other commitments required the United States to intervene."[53] Nor did Congress declare war. It passed only the Gulf of Tonkin Resolution, which was rushed through both houses at Johnson's request on August 7, 1964, after the communists allegedly attacked two American naval destroyers off the coast of North Vietnam. The resolution stated that Congress "approves and supports the determination of the President, as Commander-in-Chief, to take all necessary measures to repel any armed attack against the forces of the United States and to prevent further aggression."[54] Johnson, who believed that Truman had erred politically by not asking Congress to support the Korean War, was anxious to have a legislative endorsement.

But the Gulf of Tonkin Resolution was hardly "the functional equivalent of a declaration of war," as Under Secretary of State Nicholas Katzenbach claimed at a Senate hearing in 1967.[55] Johnson believed that the resolution could help to protect his political flank, but that he already had all the constitutional authority he needed to deploy troops to Vietnam. In March 1966 the State Department's legal adviser wrote, "There can be no question in present circumstances of the President's authority to commit U.S. forces to the defense of South Vietnam. The grant of authority to the President in Article 2 of the Constitution extends to the actions of the United States currently undertaken in Vietnam." Johnson embraced this position at a news conference on August 18, 1967. Speaking of the Gulf of Tonkin Resolution, he said, "We stated then and we repeat now, we did not think the resolution was necessary to do what we did and what we're doing. But we thought it was desirable and we thought if we were going to ask them [Congress] to stay the whole route and if we expected them to be there on the landing we ought to ask them to be there on the take off."[56]

By early 1968, however, the military situation in Vietnam had deteriorated, and Johnson's political consensus at home had crumbled. The last president not to seek reelection after only five years in office had been Calvin Coolidge. On March 31 Johnson astonished the nation and the world by announcing, "I shall not seek, and I will not accept, the nomination of my party for another term as your President." But Johnson never lost his faith in the extraordinary powers of the presidency. Nor, even under the stress of war, did he ever give up his dream of the Great Society. Indeed, Johnson's insistence on trying to have "guns and butter"—the Vietnam War and the Great Society—subjected the economy to inflationary strains that were aggravated by his reluctance to ask Congress to enact a tax increase.

THE TWENTY-FIFTH AMENDMENT

One enduring legacy of the Kennedy-Johnson years was the Twenty-fifth Amendment, proposed by Congress in 1965 and ratified by the states in 1967. The main purpose of the amendment was to provide for two separate but related situations: presidential disabilities and vacancies in the vice presidency.

The need for a reform like the Twenty-fifth Amendment had long been apparent. As with the death, resignation, or impeachment of the president, the original Constitution stated in Article II, section 1: "in Case of the . . . Inability [of the president] to discharge the Powers and Duties of the said Office, the Same shall devolve on the Vice President." The Constitution gave no guidance about what a disability was, how the vice president was to step in should the need arise, or even whether the vice president was to become president or merely assume the powers and duties of the office until the president recovered (did "the Same" refer to "the Powers and Duties" or to "the said Office"?).[57] During the long disabilities of Presidents James A. Garfield and Woodrow Wilson, the problems raised by the Constitution's vagueness became obvious.[58]

Vice-presidential vacancies were another frequent historical occurrence. The vice presidency becomes vacant when the president dies, resigns, or is impeached and removed, or when the vice president dies, resigns, or is impeached and removed. Such circumstances left the nation without a vice president on sixteen occasions between 1789 and 1963: seven times because the vice president died, eight times because the president died, and once because the vice president resigned.[59] By the merest chance, a double vacancy in the presidency and vice presidency never occurred.

Public and congressional concern about the problems of presidential disability and vice-presidential vacancy was minor and episodic through most of American history. Concern usually rose for a brief period while a president was disabled and then waned when the crisis passed. From 1945 to 1963, however, a combination of events placed these problems high on the nation's constitutional agenda.

The invention and spread of nuclear weapons and intercontinental ballistic missiles after 1945 heightened public concern that an able president always be available to wield the powers of the office in the event of a sudden Soviet attack. Then, in rapid succession, President Eisenhower suffered a series of temporarily disabling illnesses—a heart attack in 1955, an ileitis attack and operation in 1956, and a stroke in 1957. Kennedy's assassination in 1963 left the nation with a president, Lyndon Johnson, who had a history of heart trouble and whose legally designated successors under the Presidential Succession Act of 1947 were an old and ailing Speaker of the House, John W. McCormack, and, as Senate president pro tempore, an even older and frailer Carl Hayden.

In December 1963, less than a month after Kennedy was assassinated, Birch Bayh, a Democratic senator from Indiana and the chair of the Senate Judiciary Committee's Subcommittee on Constitutional Amendments, announced that he would hold hearings in early 1964 to consider constitutional remedies to the disability and vacancy problems. Coordinating his efforts with those of a special committee of the American Bar Association, Bayh drafted the proposal that formed the basis for the Senate subcommittee's hearings and, with minor modifications, soon entered the Constitution as the Twenty-fifth Amendment.

The Senate approved the amendment on September 29, 1964, by a vote of 65–0. The House did not act in 1964, possibly because to propose an amendment to fill vice-presidential vacancies would be perceived as a slap at Speaker McCormack, who was still first in line to succeed President Johnson. In 1965, however, just months after the election of Hubert H. Humphrey as Johnson's vice president, the House joined the Senate, which had reaffirmed its support of the amendment by a 72–0 vote on February 19, and on April 13 voted its approval, 368–29.

PRESIDENTIAL DISABILITIES

From the beginning, most congressional concerns about the Twenty-fifth Amendment involved its disability provisions. As drafted by Bayh and enacted by Congress, three situations were covered by sections 3 and 4 of the amendment. In the first, the president is "unable to discharge the powers and duties of his office" and recognizes this condition—say, before or after undergoing surgery. A simple letter from the president to the Speaker of the House and the president pro tempore of the Senate is all it takes to make the vice president the acting president. A subsequent presidential letter declaring that the disability is ended restores the president's powers.

In the second situation, the president is disabled but, perhaps having suddenly lost consciousness, is unable to say so. Should this happen, either the vice president or the head of an executive department may call a meeting of the vice president and cabinet to discuss the situation. If both the vice president and a majority of the heads of the departments declare the president disabled, the vice president becomes acting president—again, until the president writes to the leaders of Congress to announce an end to the disability.

The third situation covered by the disability portions of the amendment is the most troubling. It involves instances, such as questionable mental health or severe physical impairment, in which the president's ability to fulfill the office is in doubt—the president claims to be able, but the vice president and the cabinet disagree. The amendment provides that if this happens, the vice president becomes acting president until Congress can resolve the matter. Congress would have a maximum of three weeks to decide whether the president is disabled, with a two-thirds vote of both the House and the Senate needed to overturn the president's judgment. But because the Twenty-fifth Amendment only transfers power to the vice president for as long as the presidential disability lasts, a subsequent claim of restored health by the president would set the whole process in motion again.

Some critics of the Bayh proposal argued that it vested too much power in the executive branch to make disability determinations. An alternative proposal was to create a disability commission that included members of all three branches, perhaps joined by some physicians. Bayh defended his proposal by saying that any move to strip power from the president by officials outside the administration risked violating the constitutional separation of powers. In the end, both to satisfy the critics and to preclude the possibility that a president might fire some or all department heads in order to forestall a disability declaration, the amendment authorized Congress, at its discretion, to substitute another body for the cabinet.

Although the Twenty-fifth Amendment created an elaborate set of procedures for disability determinations, it included no definition of *disability*. It is clear from the congressional debate that disability is not to be equated with incompetence, laziness, unpopularity, or impeachable conduct. As to what disability is, Congress thought that any definition it might write into the Constitution in 1965 would be rendered obsolete by changes in medical science.

VICE-PRESIDENTIAL VACANCIES

By the mid-1960s members of Congress generally agreed that the vice president should be replaced when the office becomes vacant, both to increase the likelihood of a smooth succession to the presidency, if needed, by a member of the president's party and to ensure that the presidential disability provisions of the amendment will always have a vice president on hand to execute them. Bayh proposed that the president nominate a new vice president when a vacancy occurs and that a majority of both houses of Congress, voting separately, decide whether to confirm the nomination. His proposal prevailed and became section 2 of the Twenty-fifth Amendment, but not before consideration was given to having Congress or the Electoral College from the previous election choose the vice president. Proposals to impose a time limit on Congress to either vote on a president's nominee for vice president or forfeit its right to reject the nomination were also considered and rejected.

No serious opposition to the Twenty-fifth Amendment arose during the ratification process. The required approval of thirty-eight states was attained on February 10, 1967, barely a year and a half after Congress proposed the amendment. Little did any of those involved in its passage realize that during the next seven years an extraordinary series of events would cause the vice presidency to become vacant twice.

THE PRESIDENCY OF RICHARD NIXON

The legacy of the Johnson years for the presidency was mixed: more governing authority but less political influence. Soon after LBJ left the White House, one of his assistants, George E. Reedy, wrote, "We may well be witnessing the first lengthening shadows that will become the twilight of the presidency."[60] The failure in Vietnam had fostered cynicism about the merits of presidential policies, opposition to the unilateral use of presidential power, and a greater inclination in the news media to challenge the wisdom of presidential proposals and the veracity of presidential statements.[61] Yet much was still demanded of presidents. They remained at the center of citizens' ever-growing expectations of government.

THE 1968 ELECTION: PARTY REFORM AND DIVIDED GOVERNMENT

The 1968 elections dramatically displayed the political disarray in which Johnson left the country. Vice President Humphrey, the Democratic nominee for president, led a bitterly divided party. Its convention in Chicago was ravaged by controversy, both within the hall and in the streets, where antiwar demonstrators clashed violently with the Chicago police. Without contesting a single primary, Humphrey was nominated by his party's state and local leaders, who still controlled a majority of the delegates and who preferred him to the antiwar candidate, Sen. Eugene McCarthy. Humphrey's more powerful opponent, Sen. Robert F. Kennedy, had been assassinated on June 4, the night of his triumph in the California primary.

Politically, Humphrey was damaged goods. As Johnson's vice president, he found it difficult to distance himself from "Johnson's war." Unwilling to embrace the war yet unable to make a clean break, he looked weak. Humphrey was rejected not only by the antiwar wing of his party but also by conservative Democratic voters, many of whom looked with favor on the third party candidacy of George C. Wallace, the segregationist governor of Alabama.

Humphrey's controversial nomination and the failure of his general election campaign against the Republican candidate, former vice president Richard Nixon, gave rise to important institutional reforms. The rules of the Democratic Party were revised in 1971 by the party-appointed McGovern-Fraser

Commission in an effort to make presidential nominating conventions more representative of the party's rank and file.[62] In response to the new rules, most states shifted from selecting delegates in closed councils of party regulars to electing them in direct primaries or open caucuses. Although the Democrats initiated these changes, many were codified in state laws that affected the Republican Party almost as much.

The declining influence of the traditional party organizations was apparent not only in the new nominating rules, but also in the perceptions and habits of voters. Beginning with the 1968 election, voters exhibited a greater tendency to split their tickets—that is, to divide their votes between the parties. Although ticket splitting began to decline in the 1980s, it continued to express strong ambivalence about the Democratic and Republican parties.

The chief result of split-ticket voting and public alienation from the two-party system was divided government, in which the president's party does not control Congress. Divided government not only had a profound effect on the course of the Nixon administration, but also exacerbated the problems of modern presidential governance that had become so obvious during the Johnson years. Despite the Democratic disarray in 1968, Nixon did not win a decisive mandate to govern. The Democrats retained clear control of both houses of Congress, making Nixon the first new president since Zachary Taylor in 1848 to be elected without a majority for his party in either the House or the Senate.

Congress was not the only rival for power that Nixon faced. Because the country had elected only one other Republican president since 1932, the departments and agencies of the executive branch included a large preponderance of Democrats. Most of them were protected by civil service procedures, which had been extended "upward, outward and downward" since the New Deal to encompass almost the entire federal workforce. Moreover, as Paul Van Riper has observed, because patronage since the 1930s had been "a sort of intellectual and ideological patronage rather than the more traditional partisan type," the domestic and diplomatic bureaucracy had been infused with a strong liberal bias.[63] Eisenhower had faced pockets of bureaucratic resistance, but the magnitude of the opposition was much more threatening to a conservative Republican president whose party did not control either house of Congress.

In his memoirs, Nixon explained in colorful terms that one of his administration's most important tasks was to place its stamp on the federal bureaucracy as rapidly as possible: "I urged the new Cabinet members to move quickly to replace holdover bureaucrats with people who believed in what we were trying to do. I warned that if we did not act quickly, they would become captives of the bureaucracy they were trying to change. . . . 'If we don't get rid of those people, they will either sabotage us from within, or they'll just sit back on their well-paid asses and wait for the next election to bring back their old bosses.'"[64]

All the more galling to the Nixon White House was the ease with which the president's own appointees to head the departments and agencies were co-opted by civil servants, who managed to enlist them as allies against many of the administration's policies. Nixon's White House domestic policy adviser, John Ehrlichman, remarked at a press briefing in late 1972 that after administration officials were appointed and had their pictures taken with the president, "we only see them at the annual White House Christmas Party; they go off and marry the natives."[65]

THE NEW FEDERALISM

The first Republican president of the New Deal era, Dwight Eisenhower, often spoke of "restoring the balance" between the branches by returning authority from the president to Congress. To be sure, Eisenhower eventually accepted the responsibilities of the modern executive, especially as he came to realize that even politically moderate presidents have to exert strong leadership if they want to limit the expansion of the federal government's activities. But Eisenhower was a reluctant modern president. His "hidden-hand" approach emphasized both flexible accommodation to the New Deal and respect for the other institutions of American government.

Nixon, in contrast, aggressively sought to expand presidential power. At the time he took office, aspects of the New Deal approach to the modern welfare state were being seriously questioned, even by liberals. The new intellectual and political climate seemed to present an opportunity to change domestic policy significantly. Moreover, unlike Eisenhower, who was cautious almost to a fault, Nixon was a self-described "chance taker."[66] His entire political career was punctuated by personal crises and bold responses. "It is therefore not surprising," historian Joan Hoff-Wilson has written, "that as president he rationalized many of his foreign and domestic initiatives as crises (or at least intolerable impasses) that could be resolved only by dramatic and sometimes drastic measures."[67]

Nixon made a more determined effort than Eisenhower to use the presidency as a lever for a broadly conservative domestic policy. Indeed, he was the first Republican president since Theodore Roosevelt to embrace an expansive understanding of executive authority. But in contrast to TR, who was also the first chief executive of either party to regard the president as the steward of the public welfare, Nixon sought to recast the office as the agent of the growing skepticism about social reform.

Even Nixon, however, was not rigidly opposed to the welfare state.[68] The main purpose of his major domestic policy initiative, the New Federalism, was to sort out the responsibilities of governance so that national problems would be handled by the national government and problems more amenable to decentralized solutions would be handled by state and local authorities. Welfare, which Nixon believed required a national set of standards, was an example of the former. Job training, which he thought would benefit from a more flexible approach, typified the latter.

Nixon also pursued a liberal civil rights program that made affirmative action—the practice of granting preferences in employment, contracting, and education on the basis of race or gender—a national policy. It was during the Johnson presidency that civil rights programs had first shifted from color blindness to affirmative action. Johnson issued Executive Order 11246, which both authorized the secretary of labor to require compliance reports on hiring practices from government contractors and mandated that these contractors make serious efforts to recruit minority applicants. The order also created the Office of Federal Contract Compliance to oversee administration of the new policy. Under Nixon, the potential power of Executive Order 11246 was fully exploited. Nixon's labor secretary, George Shultz, issued a directive called the Philadelphia Plan, which required local construction companies and unions to adopt "specific goals and timetables" for hiring minorities. A second implementing order extended the first one to federal contractors of all kinds and stipulated that they had to recruit workforces that reflected the racial makeup of the applicant pools in their local areas. The Nixon administration aggressively pursued affirmative action not only in contract compliance but also, through Executive Order 11478, in hiring for the federal civil service. In doing so, political scientist Kenneth R. Mayer has written, Nixon created "the modern structure of affirmative action that has repeatedly been upheld [by the courts] as a valid exercise of the president's executive authority."[69]

Nixon's New Federalism was conservative mainly in its challenge to the New Deal presumption that social problems are always addressed most effectively at the national level. This challenge was enough, however, to provoke powerful opposition in the Democratic Congress and, especially, in the departments and agencies of the executive branch, which would have lost power to the states and localities if the New Federalism had been enacted.[70]

Nixon's commitment to selective decentralization in the federal system went hand in hand with his paramount desire to centralize power in the White House. Like Andrew Jackson, he was convinced that the federal government and its special interests had grown so powerful that only a strong president could "reverse the flow of power and resources from the states and communities to Washington."[71] Leonard Garment, a member of the president's legal staff, observed that "the central paradox of the Nixon administration was that in order to reduce federal power, it was first necessary to increase presidential power." Or, as Nixon himself said, "Bringing power to the White House was necessary to dishit out."[72]

Nixon's aggrandizement of presidential power extended to foreign policy. Certainly, it was in his political interest to end the war in Vietnam as soon as possible. "I am not going to end up like LBJ," Nixon said, "holed up in the White House afraid to show my face on the street. I'm going to stop that war. Fast."[73]

But Nixon was no more successful than Johnson in obtaining what he called "peace with honor"—that is, a way to bring American troops home without losing South Vietnam to the communists.[74] The "honor" component of this goal was of primary importance to Nixon. He and his national security adviser, Henry Kissinger, believed that unless they could extricate the United States from the war in a manner that demonstrated resoluteness of purpose and certainty of action, they would lose respect abroad from friends and foes alike. "Ending the war honorably," Kissinger argued, "is essential for the peace of the world. Any other solution may unloose forces that would complicate the prospects of international order."[75]

Vietnam consumed Nixon's first term, from January 20, 1969, until the war was concluded, at least formally, on January 27, 1973. During these four years, Nixon actually escalated the American involvement by secretly bombing North Vietnamese military enclaves in Cambodia, a neighboring neutral country. When bombing failed to do the job, Nixon told the nation on April 30, 1970, that he was sending troops to invade Cambodia—a militarily futile venture that provoked massive antiwar demonstrations around the country and an uncommonly hostile reaction from Congress.

Nixon's policies in Vietnam not only reinforced his aggressive use of presidential power, but also made it more controversial. Like Truman and Johnson, Nixon believed that in time of war the president may assume extraordinary powers. But he was to find, as Truman and Johnson did before him and George W. Bush did afterward, that public acceptance of a claim of sweeping executive power does not redound automatically to a president who prosecutes an unpopular, undeclared war.

Nixon's determination to expand the boundaries of presidential power in the face of growing political resistance encouraged him to pursue his domestic and foreign policies by executive fiat. In doing so, he effected significant changes in the organization and conduct of the presidency. But he also planted the seeds of his own disgrace and resignation in 1974.[76]

Nixon's "administrative presidency" was born of his inability to persuade Congress to enact the New Federalism. Although Nixon took a legislative approach to reform during his first two years as president, most of his proposals bogged down on Capitol Hill. In response, he shifted to a strategy to achieve his objectives through administrative action. As scholar-practitioner Richard P. Nathan has noted, "Nixon came to the conclusion sometime in 1971 that in many areas of government, particularly domestic affairs, *operations is policy.* Many day-to-day management tasks for domestic programs—for example, regulation writing, grant approval, and budget apportionment—are substantive and therefore involve policy."[77]

The first phase of Nixon's administrative strategy was to expand and reorganize the Executive Office of the President (EOP) so that it could preempt the traditional responsibilities of the departments and agencies. Nixon doubled the staff of the White House Office from 292 under Johnson to 583 by the end of his first term. With size came power. Nixon loyalists in the White House and in the other agencies of the EOP not only formulated policy, as in the Johnson administration, but also tried to carry out policy.

In foreign affairs, Kissinger created the first completely White House–dominated system of policymaking. Starting with Kennedy, the president's national security adviser had assumed a greater share of the responsibilities of the State Department. But Nixon and Kissinger built a foreign policy staff of unprecedented scale and influence. So marginal was the State Department that Secretary William Rogers was not even told in advance of the administration's most important diplomatic initiative, the opening to China. Nixon visited China in February 1972 after nearly a quarter-century of fierce hostility between the United States and the communist Chinese government that had taken power in 1949.[78]

The staff of the newly formed Domestic Council, headed by Ehrlichman, took charge of domestic policymaking. In addition, Nixon reorganized and expanded the Bureau of the Budget to strengthen the president's influence in domestic affairs. On July 1, 1970, by executive order, the Budget Bureau became the Office of Management and Budget (OMB), with a new supervisory layer of presidentially appointed assistant directors for policy inserted between the OMB director and the office's senior civil servants. Consequently, the budget office not only assumed additional responsibility for administrative management but also became more responsive to the president.

By itself, the swelling of the EOP, both the president's own White House–based staff and the OMB, did not bring about full presidential control of public policy. Recalcitrant bureaucrats and their allies in Congress were still able to resist many of Nixon's efforts to seize the levers of administrative power. Two weeks before the 1968 election, former president Eisenhower had written that he hoped for a victory so sweeping that it would give Nixon "a strong, clear mandate" and a Republican Congress. Eisenhower noted that such a victory would help Nixon to "change the ingrained power structure of the federal government (the heritage of the years of Democratic rule), placing more responsibility at state and local levels."[79] Not only did Nixon's razor-thin victory in 1968 fail to bring in a Republican Congress but, befitting his four-year-long emphasis on an autonomous presidency, even his landslide reelection in 1972 did little to help his party. The Republicans failed to make inroads in the House, the Senate, or the state legislatures.

Still lacking the support he needed from Congress to become an effective legislative leader, Nixon resolved to carry the administrative presidency a step further during his second term. In 1973 he undertook an extensive reorganization plan designed to re-create the bureaucracy in his own image. The president moved proven loyalists into the departments and agencies and then consolidated leadership of the bureaucracy into a "supercabinet" of four secretaries whose job was to implement all of the administration's policies. One of these "supersecretaries" was Kissinger, who became secretary of state while retaining his position as the assistant to the president for national security affairs. As such, Kissinger became responsible, in a formal as well as an informal sense, for foreign policy, second only to Nixon himself.

AN IMPERIAL PRESIDENCY?

Nixon's attempt to extend the bounds of presidential authority and, by so doing, to achieve his political and policy objectives unilaterally has been widely regarded as an unprecedented usurpation of power and, ultimately, the cause of the Watergate scandal, which forced him to resign from office in 1974. It was, to be sure, both the improprieties of the president's personal reelection organization, the Committee to Re-elect the President (CREEP to its critics)—particularly its attempt to bug telephones in the offices of the Democratic National Committee—and the subsequent efforts by the president and his aides to cover up the planning of the break-in that brought down the Nixon administration.

But Nixon's version of the administrative presidency was not entirely new. In important respects, it was a logical extension of the evolving modern office. The reelection committee's complete autonomy from the regular Republican organization during Nixon's campaign for a second term was merely the culmination of the recent history of presidential preemption of the traditional responsibilities of the national party committees. As for the post-reelection phase of Nixon's administrative reform strategy, in which the president concentrated managerial authority in the hands of a few White House aides and cabinet secretaries, it simply extended recent presidents' practice of reconstructing the executive branch as a more formidable instrument of presidential government. The irony is that the strategy of pursuing policy goals through administrative action, which had been invented mainly by Roosevelt, Johnson, and other Democrats, was considered especially suitable by a Republican president who faced a Congress and a bureaucracy that were determined to preserve those Democratic presidents' programs.

After witnessing the indiscretions of the Johnson and Nixon years, historian Arthur M. Schlesinger Jr., until then an eloquent defender of strong presidential leadership, wrote in 1973, "In the last years presidential primacy, so indispensable to the political order, has turned into presidential supremacy. The constitutional presidency—as events so apparently disparate as the Indochina War and the Watergate affair showed—has become the imperial presidency and threatens to be the revolutionary presidency."[80]

In truth, as Nixon learned to his regret, the federal government could not be remade by executive fiat. The modern presidency was never truly imperial; its power depended on agreement by Congress, the bureaucracy, and the courts that responsibilities should be delegated to the executive. By the time Johnson left office, the political environment had become less supportive of strong presidential leadership. Nixon only strengthened opposition to the unilateral use of executive power by further attenuating the bonds that tied the president to Congress and the party system.

More than anything else, perhaps, Nixon's bitter relations with Congress were the source of his downfall. His early inability to win support on Capitol Hill for his New Federalism proposals and his conduct of the war led him to construe the powers of his office much too broadly, which only aggravated the relationship. Nixon's use of his power as commander in chief to bomb Cambodia in 1969 and invade it in 1970 provoked a major public and legislative protest. So too did his sweeping application of the president's traditional right to impound—that is, not spend—funds that had been appropriated by Congress. Nixon defended his challenge to Congress's power of the purse as inherent in his own power as chief executive. Although Caspar Weinberger, Nixon's deputy budget director, conceded in a 1971 appearance before a Senate panel that Congress had the power to *appropriate*, he insisted that it "did not follow from this . . . that the *expenditure* of government funds involved an exclusively legislative function." A law passed by Congress to appropriate funds, Weinberger asserted, was "permissive and not mandatory in nature."[81]

Unlike several of his predecessors, Nixon did not impound funds to achieve economy and efficiency. Instead, he was attempting to contravene the policies of the Democratic Congress by undoing the legislative process. His assault on the Office of Economic Opportunity (OEO), the agency responsible for leading the War on Poverty and a symbol of the Great Society, was undertaken to challenge Congress for the right to govern. Congress had appropriated funds to continue the OEO, but Nixon had the agency's acting director, Howard Phillips, issue orders to dismantle it. Nixon also refused to nominate Phillips as the permanent OEO director because he knew the nomination would be rejected by the Senate.[82] Former vice president Humphrey, who was elected to the Senate in 1970, charged that the Nixon administration's assault on the OEO amounted to a "policy impoundment"—that is, the modification or even elimination of a program authorized by Congress.[83]

But Watergate or no Watergate, a war still would have occurred between Nixon and Congress. Both sides had geared up for a constitutional struggle before anything was known about the Watergate affair. Indeed, Congress's willingness to take the extraordinary step of removing the president in 1974 was in part a response to Nixon's repeated efforts to circumvent the legislative process.[84]

WATERGATE AND ITS LEGACY

The unsavory events that forced Nixon to resign as president on August 9, 1974, created a political atmosphere so sour with disgust and disillusionment that it threatened the civility and public trust on which any government depends.[85] The break-in at the Democratic National Committee was carried out by five members of a secret White House investigating unit (the so-called plumbers), which originally had been formed to plug the leaks to reporters that had compromised the Nixon administration's policy in Vietnam. In 1972, however, the plumbers' activities were extended to "campaign intelligence" relating to Nixon's bid for reelection. On June 17, the five men who were trying to bug the Democrats' telephones were caught and arrested in the party's national headquarters at the Watergate Hotel in Washington.

"At its simple, most tangible level," political scientist A. James Reichley has observed, "Watergate was nothing more than dirty politics. A gang of office-holders, unsure of their chances of winning the next election, set out through illegal means to shift the odds in their favor."[86] Such behavior, however deplorable, was hardly unprecedented.

What made the Watergate scandal more than a "third rate burglary"—the characterization offered by Nixon's press secretary, Ron Ziegler—was its close association with the modern presidency. The malicious activities sanctioned by Nixon and some of his associates accelerated the existing trend toward presidential isolation. For years, presidents had been encouraged to try to run the government from the White House and to vest their political fortunes in a small circle of loyalists.

The planning of the break-in and other acts of political sabotage, in which Attorney General John Mitchell and several White House aides participated, and the various efforts by the president and others to interfere with the FBI's investigation and the Justice Department's prosecution of the case after the Watergate burglars were arrested, involved a logical, although perverse, abuse of the expanded powers of the modern presidency. Many of these powers had originated in wartime, and, not surprisingly, one of the Nixon administration's first lines of defense was to avow its concern for national security in a perilous world. Nixon even justified his decision to fire Archibald Cox, the special Watergate prosecutor who had issued a subpoena to force the president to release certain secret White House tape recordings, by arguing that to acquiesce to Cox's aggressive investigation would make the president appear weak in the eyes of Soviet Communist Party chief Leonid Brezhnev and other foreign leaders.[87]

The president invoked an absolute executive privilege in carrying out the "Saturday night massacre," as the firing of Cox on October 20, 1973, came to be called. Nixon also claimed executive privilege in response to the demands of the Senate select investigating committee, the Watergate grand jury, and the House Judiciary Committee. To be sure, presidents had always invoked executive privilege. Historically, the claim that the president's confidential discussions and papers are exempt from examination by the other branches of government had been constitutionally less controversial than, for example, the extent of the president's removal power. But Nixon was the first president to argue that executive privilege has no limits. In doing so, he conflated legitimate national security interests with his own political interest in staying in power.

The firing of Cox aroused a firestorm of protest, forcing Nixon to appoint a new special prosecutor, Leon Jaworski, and to give him the same powers that Cox had wielded, including specific authorization to go to court to contest the president's effort to withhold any evidence that the prosecutor sought. On April 16, 1974, Jaworski asked that Nixon be subpoenaed to produce tapes and documents relating to sixty-four White House conversations, which the special prosecutor believed he needed in order to try seven associates of the president who had been indicted by the Watergate grand jury for conspiracy to defraud the United States and obstruct justice. Jaworski also expected that the White House tapes would establish whether Nixon was part of the original Watergate conspiracy, the post–break-in cover-up, or both.

The controversy that was created by Jaworski's motion and Nixon's refusal to comply was ultimately settled by the Supreme Court. In *United States v. Nixon,* the Court rejected Nixon's claim to an absolute executive privilege and, specifically, to the exclusive right to determine when the privilege was properly invoked. The Court's unanimous decision, issued on July 24, 1974, and written by Chief Justice Warren Burger, a Nixon appointee, stated that "to read the Art[icle] II powers of the President as providing an absolute privilege as against a subpoena essential to enforcement of criminal statutes . . . would upset the constitutional balance of 'a workable government.'"[88]

The Court agreed with Nixon that some form of executive privilege is "fundamental to the operation of government and inextricably rooted in the separation of powers under the Constitution."[89] (This decision was the first in which the justices formally upheld any version of the privilege.) But the Court brushed aside Nixon's argument that executive privilege may be invoked even in criminal proceedings that involve no issues of national security. It endorsed, instead, Justice Robert Jackson's argument in *Youngstown Sheet and Tube Company v. Sawyer* (1952) that presidential claims must be balanced against the powers and duties of Congress and the courts. The *Youngstown* precedent led Chief Justice Burger to conclude that "when the ground for asserting privilege as to subpoenaed materials sought for use in a criminal trial is based only on the generalized interest in confidentiality, it cannot prevail over the fundamental demands of due process of law in the fair administration of criminal justice. The generalized assertion of privilege must yield to the demonstrated specific need for evidence in a pending criminal trial."[90]

Nixon's presidency came to an end shortly after the House Judiciary Committee, acting on the heels of the Court's decision in the tapes case, voted on August 4, to impeach him. The president's chances of surviving a Senate trial were dealt a further blow when he admitted that among the tapes he had been ordered to surrender were some that clearly implicated him in the Watergate cover-up. Even the president's Republican supporters on the Judiciary Committee conceded that he had virtually confessed to obstruction of justice.[91] All of them announced that they would vote for impeachment on the House floor.

On August 8, in a speech to the nation, Nixon announced his decision to resign the next day. "Throughout the long and difficult period of Watergate, I have felt it was my duty to persevere; to make every possible effort to complete my term of office to which you elected me," he said. "In the past few days, however, it has become evident to me that I no longer have a strong enough political base in the Congress to justify continuing that effort."[92] Thus, as Alonzo L. Hamby has written, Nixon's tenure as president "ended in personal disaster. Worse, he left the presidency itself an object of suspicion and scorn, awaiting a new Roosevelt or Eisenhower to restore its standing and provide a demoralized public with a sense of movement and purpose that could come only from the occupant of the White House."[93]

The Watergate scandal provoked Congress to pass a multitude of new laws to curb the powers of the presidency. More significant, Watergate shattered the recent consensus in American politics—already undermined by the controversies of the Johnson administration and Nixon's earlier claims to unilateral executive authority—that strong presidential leadership embodies the public interest. When asked in 1959 whether the president or Congress should have "the most say in government," a representative sample of Americans favored the president by 61 percent to 17 percent. A similar survey in 1977 indicated a striking reversal: 58 percent believed that Congress should have the most say. Only 26 percent supported presidential primacy.[94]

One important law that Congress passed to restrict the unilateral exercise of presidential power was the Congressional Budget and Impoundment Control Act of 1974, which required the president to obtain Congress's approval before impounding any funds. The act established budget committees in the House and the Senate to coordinate and strengthen the legislature's involvement in fiscal policymaking, and it created the Congressional Budget Office, a legislative staff agency that would make available to Congress the same sort of fiscal expertise that the OMB provided to the executive branch. In a separate bill, Congress modified the OMB. After fifty-three years as a purely presidential agency, the OMB's director and deputy directors were made subject to Senate confirmation.[95]

Congress also reasserted its influence in foreign affairs. The Case Act, which it passed in 1972 to curb the growing presidential tendency to engage in personal diplomacy, required that all executive agreements with foreign governments be reported to Congress. The War Powers Resolution, which Congress enacted over Nixon's veto in 1973, was intended to prevent another Vietnam—that is, any prolonged period of presidential war making without formal authorization from Congress. The resolution required the president to consult with Congress "in every possible instance" before committing troops to combat and to submit a report to the legislature within forty-eight hours of doing so. After sixty days, the troops were to be removed unless Congress voted either to declare war or to authorize their continued deployment.[96]

In and of themselves, these laws did not restrict the modern presidency severely. Presidents have honored the War Powers Resolution more in the breach than the observance. But their enactment expressed Congress's determination to reestablish itself as an equal, if not the dominant, partner in governing the nation. In effect, congressional procedures were reformed to produce a more aggressive legislature. Decentralized since its rebellion against Speaker Joseph Cannon in the early twentieth century, Congress became even more so. Some of the power of the standing committees devolved to the subcommittees, whose numbers, staff, and autonomy grew rapidly. The rise of subcommittee government posed a severe challenge to the modern president's preeminence in legislative and administrative affairs. As political scientist R. Shep Melnick has written, "Using subcommittee resources, members initiated new programs and revised old ones, challenging the president for the title of 'Chief Legislator.' No longer would Congress respond to calls for action by passing vague legislation telling the executive to do something. Now Congress was writing detailed statutes which not infrequently deviated from the president's program. Subcommittees were also using oversight hearings to make sure that administrators paid heed not just to the letter of legislation, but to its spirit as well."[97]

Under the Twenty-fifth Amendment, Gerald Ford was nominated as vice president by Richard Nixon after the resignation of Spiro T. Agnew. A year later Ford became the first president to succeed to the presidency because his predecessor resigned and the first never to have been elected to the office of president or vice president.

GERALD R. FORD AND THE POST-WATERGATE ERA

Vice President Gerald Ford succeeded to the presidency on August 9, 1974. He inherited some of the most difficult circumstances faced by any president. Ford had never run for national or even statewide office; his electoral experience was confined to Michigan's Fifth Congressional District. He was representing this district in the House, which he served as Republican leader, when, on October 10, 1973, Vice President Spiro T. Agnew was forced to resign in response to the revelation that he had been taking bribes ever since he was the county executive of Baltimore County, Maryland.[98] Charged to do so by the recently enacted Twenty-fifth Amendment, Nixon nominated Ford to replace Agnew.[99] The new vice president took office on December 6, after being confirmed by both houses of Congress. When the Watergate scandal forced Nixon to resign, Ford became the first, and so far the only, president never to have been elected either as president or as vice president.

Ford was a unique president in one other respect. Never before had a vice president succeeded to the presidency because his predecessor resigned. That Nixon left office in disgrace made the start of Ford's tenure especially inauspicious. Not only did Ford lack an electoral mandate, but also he became president when the country was still deeply scarred and divided by the Vietnam War, when respect for the presidency was greatly diminished, and when the nation's economy and foreign relations were in disarray. Reflecting on this period, Kissinger later recalled, "The Presidency was in shambles."[100]

Combining symbolic actions with changes in public policy and leadership style, Ford made an earnest effort to restore integrity to the presidency and to purge the nation of its preoccupation with Watergate.[101] One of his first decisions was to nominate Nelson A. Rockefeller, the long-respected former governor of New York, for vice president. He also removed many of the trappings of the so-called imperial presidency. Within weeks Ford reduced the White House staff by 10 percent, from 540 to 485. On a lighter note, on certain occasions the Marine band was instructed to replace "Hail to the Chief" with the University of Michigan's fight song. And the living quarters in the White House became officially "the residence" rather than "the mansion."

Symbolic changes were accompanied by new policies and a new presidential style. After three days in office, Ford accepted the recommendation of a Senate resolution that he convene a White House "summit" on the economy. The Conference on Inflation, which included business and labor leaders and a bipartisan group of economists, and other events, such as numerous meetings between the new president and groups of governors, mayors, and county officials, were all part of Ford's attempt to open the doors of the White House.

Perhaps Ford's most dramatic gesture to heal the nation's wounds was his plan of amnesty for the fifty thousand draft evaders and deserters from the Vietnam War. The president offered not an unconditional pardon, but a program in which those who wanted amnesty could earn it. Ford announced the program on August 19, 1974, the eleventh day of his presidency, before the most challenging of audiences, the annual convention of the Veterans of Foreign Wars in Chicago. "This decision," a Ford aide has written, "was not preceded by full or elaborate deliberations. His decision appears to have been driven not only by compassion but also by its symbolic value in helping to put the recent past behind the nation."[102]

Ford's innovations in symbolism, style, and policy initially earned his administration considerable goodwill. His self-effacing manner seemed less to diminish the presidency than to endow it with an endearing folksiness. The press responded with favorable accounts and images of the new president toasting his own English muffins in the morning and taking a healthy swim at the end of the day. During his first week in office, Ford received a 71 percent approval rating in the Gallup poll. Only 3 percent of Americans disapproved of his performance.[103]

Almost overnight, however, Ford's standing with the public and the press crumbled. On September 8, only four weeks after he became president, Ford announced that he was granting Nixon "a full, free and absolute pardon."[104]

As with the Vietnam amnesty program, Ford wanted to lay to rest the nation's recent unhappy past. Instead, sprung as it was on an unprepared public that wanted to see Nixon indicted and convicted, if not jailed, the pardon turned Ford into Watergate's final victim. As political scientist Roger Porter, a member of the Ford administration, has noted, "For many Americans, this single act overwhelmed the aura of openness, accessibility, and candor that he had so successfully begun to establish."[105] By the end of September, Ford's approval rating had dropped to 50 percent.[106] The press's early celebration of his unpretentious personal style gave way to an unleashing of scorn and ridicule. The president was now caricatured as a clumsy, slow-witted bumbler at best and at worst, a craven politician who had secretly traded the promise of a pardon for Nixon's resignation.

Few joined the most cynical of Ford's critics in challenging his personal integrity. Despite the outcry over the Nixon pardon, the new president's plain, forthright manner did much, as his successor Jimmy Carter said in his 1977 inaugural address, "to heal our land."[107] But Ford was unable to restore the power of the modern presidency. The limits of his influence were revealed most clearly by his inability to work his will with an aggressive and sometimes hostile Democratic Congress. The 1974 congressional elections, which swelled the already substantial Democratic majority by fifty-two seats in the House and four in the Senate, made the task of legislative leadership still more difficult.

Ford did not wilt in the face of partisan opposition. He even had some success with Congress in reducing corporate regulations and cutting taxes. But, for the most part, Ford's influence was greatest when it was negative. He cast sixty-six vetoes, mostly against spending bills, during his twenty-nine months in office and was overridden only twelve times. As such, the Ford administration was more like the energetic late nineteenth-century executive than the modern presidency. "The strength of Congress consists in the right to pass statutes; the strength of the President in his right to veto them," British scholar James Bryce had observed in 1890.[108]

Ford's difficulties with Congress did not stop at the water's edge. As in domestic policy, Congress was unwilling to let the Ford administration have its way in foreign affairs, the area in which presidents traditionally have operated from their strongest legal and political position. Ford was determined not to diminish the foreign policy powers of his office despite the Vietnam legacy and the War Powers Resolution. He did not consult Congress in May 1975 when he sent troops to recover the merchant ship *Mayaguez* and its crew after they were seized by Cambodia. But Congress refused to respond to some of Ford's most urgent proposals: his request for emergency assistance for the disintegrating government of South Vietnam, his plea to lift an embargo on American aid to Turkey, and his plan to help the anti-Marxist guerrillas in

Angola. More than anything, it was the lack of congressional support in foreign affairs that caused Ford to complain in March 1976 that "there had been a swing of the 'historic pendulum' toward Congress, raising the possibility of a disruptive erosion of the president's ability to govern."[109]

Ford's own ability to govern was also weakened by the reformed presidential nominating process. He had barely settled into the presidency when his administration was forced to shift its attention from the politics of governing to the politics of election. Although Ford had hoped to win his party's nomination for president in 1976 by staying on the job in Washington, he had to campaign furiously to stave off defeat. The new primaries-based, media-driven nominating process enabled Ronald Reagan, the conservative former governor of California, to mount a strong challenge to the incumbent president within his own party. Reagan did not defeat Ford, but he came close, earning nearly half the ballots at the Republican national convention and complicating the president's task of winning the fall election. Ford's victory at the convention was Pyrrhic. Incumbent presidents who face tough fights for their party's nomination almost always lose the general election.

Ford was no exception. When he lost to former Georgia governor Jimmy Carter, a man whom he viewed as "an outsider with little more going for him than a winning smile," Ford felt he had every reason to believe that the presidency was slipping into receivership.[110] Carter's four years as president did little to convince observers that he was wrong.

A PRESIDENT NAMED JIMMY

James Earl Carter—he preferred "Jimmy"—embodied the extremes of promise and disappointment to which the contemporary executive office is prone. His elevation to the White House was a remarkable personal triumph, as was his initial popularity as president. Yet so far did Carter fall politically that, as Greenstein has noted, "at the time he left office his reputation had nowhere to go but up."[111]

A one-term governor who was virtually unknown outside of Georgia before he ran for president, Carter won the 1976 Democratic nomination with little support from his party's leaders. His campaign demonstrated how readily, under the new rules that governed the nominating process, a political outsider could win a presidential nomination by parlaying early primary victories in a few small states into a national convention majority. After the election, hoping to solidify his personal relationship with the people, Carter went farther than Ford in trying to eliminate imperial trappings from the presidency, sometimes carrying his own luggage as a candidate and as president. At his inauguration, the new president and his family stepped from their black limousine and walked the mile from the Capitol to the White House.

Yet Carter's informality, which had appealed to many voters during the campaign, worked to his detriment once he became president. As with Ford, it did not take long for the White House press corps to begin treating the president's unpretentious manner as an expression of his modest talents. Carter's early attempt to deliver the televised equivalent of a fireside chat, for example, is remembered less for its content (it was about energy policy) than for the unfavorable reviews his appearance in a cardigan sweater received. In part, this reaction indicated, as the House Speaker Thomas P. "Tip" O'Neill observed, "that most people prefer a little pomp in their presidents."[112] More fundamentally, it reinforced the suspicion that Carter lacked what it takes to lead the Washington community.

Unlike Eisenhower and most other presidents, Carter failed to recognize that presidential authority requires a certain measure of ceremony. He eventually came to understand this, albeit too late. "In reducing the imperial presidency," Carter wrote in his memoirs, "I overreacted at first. We began to receive many complaints that I had gone too far in cutting back the pomp and ceremony, so after a few months I authorized the band to play 'Hail to the Chief' on special occasions. I found it to be impressive and enjoyed it."[113]

But Carter's problems went beyond style and symbolism. Before the end of his first year as president, it became obvious that he was having a terrible time with Congress. Nixon and Ford had experienced similar problems, but they confronted a legislature that was controlled by the opposition party. Carter's Congress was two-thirds Democratic. His presidency revealed that the tensions between the White House and Congress were not simply an artifact of divided government. Presidents and legislators had become, in effect, independent political entrepreneurs, each establishing their own constituencies. As a result, the two branches were even less likely than in the past to regard each other as partners in the shared endeavor of promoting the party program. "I learned the hard way," Carter wrote, "that there was no party loyalty or discipline when a complicated or controversial issue was at stake—none. Each legislator had to be wooed and won individually. It was every member for himself, and the devil take the hindmost!"[114]

Arguably, Carter contributed to the disarray he protested. He had run for president by building a personal electoral constituency. Having won, he saw no need to court Congress. As political scientist Larry Berman has written, "Carter believed that as an outsider his greatest advantage was that he could 'dance with the lady he came to the dance with.' He believed that the mere threat of going to the people would make Speaker Tip O'Neill or Senate Finance Committee Chairman Russell Long quiver."[115]

Carter's failures with Congress may also be attributed in part to the inexperience of his staff, which consisted mainly of "the provincial veterans of his campaign team."[116] But the Georgia loyalists' lack of schooling in the ways of

Washington was less problematic than their arrogance toward Congress as an institution. Assessing Carter's ineffective legislative liaison office, Speaker O'Neill complained, "Frank Moore, a former public relations man from Georgia, was the [director of] congressional liaison, but he didn't know beans about Congress. On the other hand you don't have to be a legislative genius to figure out that Pennsylvania Avenue is a two-way street, and that members of Congress are entitled to certain basic courtesies. As Speaker, I didn't always have time to return my phone calls, either. But at least I made sure that somebody on my staff got back to the callers."[117]

Carter learned from his mistakes, and after his first year in office he established better relations with Congress. The president's record with the Ninety-fifth Congress was, in fact, quite respectable. In 1978, at Carter's urging, the Senate ratified the controversial Panama Canal treaties, which gradually turned control of the canal over to Panama. Congress enacted airline deregulation, civil service reform, and natural gas pricing legislation, and eliminated some of the most egregious pork barrel public works projects from the budget.

Carter's performance as chief legislator benefited from his effective White House Office of Public Liaison (OPL). Nixon had created the OPL in 1970 as an organizational home within the White House staff for the growing number of aides assigned to cultivate support from various constituency groups. Carter expanded and formalized the OPL's activities. By the time he left office in 1981, special staff members were assigned not only to traditional constituencies such as African Americans, labor, and business, but also to consumers, women, the elderly, Jews, Latinos, white ethnic Catholics, Vietnam veterans, and gays.[118] Headed by Anne Wexler, Carter's OPL represented a significant contribution to the institutional presidency, making it possible for a president who lacks great rhetorical ability to form linkages with the public. As political scientist Erwin C. Hargrove has written, "The Wexler office compensated for Carter's limitations as a presidential persuader by institutionalizing the persuasion function . . . by bringing groups of citizens to the White House for briefings by the president and others on current legislative issues."[119]

In addition to his occasional legislative achievements, Carter scored a personal diplomatic triumph with the September 17, 1978, signing of the Camp David Accords by Egyptian president Anwar Sadat and Israeli prime minister Menachem Begin. Frustrated with the difficulty of persuading Begin and Sadat to negotiate solutions to the conflicts that had made their countries enemies, Carter boldly invited both leaders to the presidential retreat at Camp David. Carter's unwavering determination to reach an agreement and his keen mind for detail, which he displayed throughout the thirteen days of diplomacy between the two Middle Eastern leaders, were crucial in bringing about the first rapprochement between Israel and an Arab nation.[120] But, despite the accomplishments of his last three years in office, Carter never recovered fully from the confusion and ineptness of his early days as president. His poor start colored his relations with Congress, the press, and the public for the rest of his term.

Much of Carter's problem was that his outsider's approach to the presidency required the kind of effective popular leadership that would enable him to appeal to the people over the heads of legislators and lobbyists. Yet rousing the American people was not Carter's strong suit.[121] He was an effective campaigner in 1976, presenting himself to the voters as a moral, trustworthy leader and a competent manager at a time of widespread disillusionment with dishonesty and inefficiency in Washington. But, in addition to his modest speaking abilities, Carter lacked a unifying vision that would enable him to lead the nation in a particular direction. Having offered, during his first few months in office, a bewildering array of legislative proposals on energy, welfare, education, urban decay, and much more, Carter failed to provide any integrating themes that the public or his party could use to make sense of these measures. "I came to think," wrote his speechwriter James Fallows, "that Carter believes fifty things, but no one thing."[122]

The incoherence of Carter's early domestic program embodied the indecisive approach to politics and policy that permeated his entire presidency. Politically, Carter wanted to move the Democratic Party to the center so that it could compete more effectively in an era when New Deal and Great Society liberalism appeared to be losing support among the voters. He said often and earnestly that he intended to reduce government waste, run the bureaucracy efficiently, and balance the budget. In practice, however, Carter's approach to his party was usually aloof, occasionally accommodating, but never purposeful.

In matters of public policy, the White House staff embodied the president's desire to be fiercely independent and a scourge to traditional Democratic approaches. But when it came to the cabinet, most of his appointees were liberal Washington insiders, such as Joseph Califano (Health, Education and Welfare), Cyrus Vance (State), and Patricia Roberts Harris (Housing and Urban Development). Carter also appointed aggressive liberal advocates to many regulatory agencies, including Michael Pertschuk (Federal Trade Commission) and Joan Claybrook (National Highway Traffic Safety Administration). Not surprisingly, they proceeded to convert their strong commitment to social and economic regulation into government policy. Carter's appointments gave the collective impression that he was an irresolute leader who was eager to accommodate the loudest factions of his party.

Jimmy Carter brought together Egyptian president Anwar Sadat and Israeli prime minister Menachem Begin at Camp David in September 1978. Their signing of the Camp David Accords was a historic moment in the arduous process of bringing peace to the Middle East.

Even when some of Carter's proposals were enacted, the public seldom believed he deserved the credit. Yet, perversely, during the latter part of Carter's presidency, when he was overcome by setbacks that really were beyond his control—notably the wildly inflationary OPEC oil price increases that led to gasoline shortages and Iran's seizure of more than fifty American hostages—he was roundly blamed. Any president, no matter how gifted, would have had trouble dealing with these problems. But Carter's style of leadership brought down on him the full brunt of adversity. His tendency to personalize problems of state was especially damaging during the hostage crisis, which lasted 444 days, from November 4, 1979, until the final day of his presidency, January 20, 1981, when the hostages were at last released. "As the problem failed to go away," Hargrove has noted, "Carter became a prisoner in the White House, and the initial public favor that he had received by personalizing the issue turned sour."[123]

The consuming crises of Carter's presidency did not prevent him from fending off a serious challenge from Massachusetts senator Edward M. Kennedy for the 1980 Democratic nomination. Indeed, during the crucial early primaries of January and February, Carter benefited from the surge in popularity that any president receives at the onset of a national crisis. But Carter entered the fall campaign burdened, as Ford had been in 1976, by a divided party, as well as by a public image as a weak and indecisive leader that only grew as the hostage crisis dragged on inconclusively. He was trounced by Ronald Reagan in the general election, the first time that a president had been defeated for reelection since Herbert Hoover lost to Franklin Roosevelt in 1932.

NOTES

1. Richard E. Neustadt, *Presidential Power and the Modern Presidents: The Politics of Leadership from Roosevelt to Reagan,* 4th ed. (New York: Free Press, 1990), 8. For an appreciative assessment of *Presidential Power,* see Michael Nelson, "Neustadt's 'Presidential Power' at 50," *Chronicle of Higher Education,* April 2, 2010, B6-8.

2. Neustadt, *Presidential Power*, 8.

3. Ibid., 9.

4. Fred I. Greenstein, "Nine Presidents in Search of a Modern Presidency," in *Leadership in the Modern Presidency*, ed. Fred I. Greenstein (Cambridge: Harvard University Press, 1988), 314.

5. John Eisenhower, the president's son and deputy chief of staff, reported that Eisenhower would have run again. Michael R. Beschloss, *Mayday: Eisenhower, Khrushchev, and the U-2 Affair* (New York: Harper and Row, 1986), 3.

6. John F. Kennedy, speech to the National Press Club, Washington, D.C., January 14, 1960, in *"Let the Word Go Forth": The Speeches, Statements and Writings of John F. Kennedy*, ed. Theodore C. Sorensen (New York: Delacorte, 1988), 17–23.

7. Jacqueline Kennedy planted in the public mind the Camelot mythology that has grown up around her husband's legend. Summoning the highly regarded journalist Theodore White to Hyannis Port a few days after JFK's funeral, the grieving widow said that she did not want her husband's enemies to shape the history of his short administration. Instead, she did some shaping of her own, relating how she and the president had enjoyed listening to the music from the popular Broadway show *Camelot* in the evenings before they went to sleep. Jack's favorite line, she told White, defined his tragic presidency: "Don't let it be forgot, that once there was a spot, for one brief shining moment that was known as Camelot." Barbara A. Perry, "John Fitzgerald Kennedy," in *The American Presidents,* ed. Melvin I. Urofsky (New York: Garland, 2000), 395.

8. William E. Leuchtenburg, *In the Shadow of FDR: From Harry Truman to Ronald Reagan*, rev. ed. (Ithaca: Cornell University Press, 1985), 119. See also Michael Nelson, "Kennedy and Achilles: A Classical Approach to Political Science," *PS: Political Science and Politics* 29 (September 1996): 505–510.

9. Cited in Larry Berman, *The New American Presidency* (Boston: Little, Brown, 1987), 237.

10. Carl M. Brauer, "John F. Kennedy: The Endurance of Inspirational Leadership," in Greenstein, *Leadership in the Modern Presidency,* 109.

11. John F. Kennedy, "Acceptance of Presidential Nomination," Democratic National Convention, Los Angeles, California, July 15, 1960, in Sorensen, *"Let the Word Go Forth,"* 101.

12. "John F. Kennedy's Inaugural Address," in *The Evolving Presidency:* Landmark *Documents, 1787–2010,* 4th ed., ed. Michael Nelson (Washington, D.C.: CQ Press, 2012), 187–191. See also James N. Giglio, *The Presidency of John F. Kennedy* (Lawrence: University Press of Kansas, 1991), 2728.

13. For a more complete discussion of the Kennedy myth in popular culture, see Nelson, "Kennedy and Achilles."

14. Brauer, "John F. Kennedy," 119.

15. Bruce Miroff, "The Presidency and the Public: Leadership as Spectacle," in *The Presidency and the Political System,* 5th ed., ed. Michael Nelson (Washington, D.C.: CQ Press, 1998), 305.

16. Giglio, *Presidency of John F. Kennedy,* 261.

17. Kennedy's preparation for press conferences involved his press secretary, Pierre Salinger, and cabinet members, who anticipated the questions that reporters would ask, gathered background information, and prepped the president in briefing sessions. Salinger occasionally prompted friendly reporters to ask certain questions, hinting that the president would have something important to say in response. On Kennedy's relationship with the press, see ibid., 255–275.

18. Brauer, "John F. Kennedy," 118.

19. Theodore J. Lowi, *The Personal President: Power Invested, Promise Unfulfilled* (Ithaca: Cornell University Press, 1985).

20. Ibid., 75–76; Harold F. Bass, "The President and the National Party Organization," in *Presidents and Their Parties: Leadership or Neglect?* ed. Robert Harmel (New York:

Praeger, 1984), 62; David Broder, *The Party's Over: The Failure of Politics in America* (New York: Harper and Row, 1972), 18–26.

21. Greenstein, "Nine Presidents," 325–326.

22. Quoted in Brauer, "John F. Kennedy," 131.

23. Matthew Crenson and Benjamin Ginsberg, *Presidential Power: Unchecked and Unbalanced* (New York: W. W. Norton, 2007), 188.

24. Lewis L. Gould, *The Modern American Presidency* (Lawrence: University Press of Kansas, 2003), 133.

25. Desmond Ball, *Politics and Force Levels: The Strategic Missile Program of the Kennedy Administration* (Berkeley: University of California Press, 1980), esp. chap. 11.

26. Arthur M. Schlesinger Jr., *The Cycles of American History* (Boston: Houghton-Mifflin, 1986), 414.

27. Brauer, "John F. Kennedy," 132. Recent findings, based on tapes of the president's meetings with the Executive Committee of the National Security Council (ExComm), the group he convened to manage the Cuban missile crisis, support the proposition that this was Kennedy's finest hour. See Ernest R. May and Philip D. Zelikow, eds., *The Kennedy Tapes: Inside the White House during the Cuban Missile Crisis* (Cambridge: Harvard University Press, 1997), 663–701.

28. *Public Papers of the Presidents of the United States: John F. Kennedy, 1963* (Washington, D.C.: Government Printing Office, 1964), 462.

29. Theodore H. White, *In Search of History: A Personal Adventure* (New York: Harper and Row, 1978), 518.

30. On Kennedy's New Frontier program, see Giglio, *Presidency of John F. Kennedy,* 97–121.

31. Broder, *Party's Over,* 31; James L. Sundquist, *The Decline and Resurgence of Congress* (Washington, D.C.: Brookings, 1981), 373–374.

32. Reston, "What Was Killed," 126.

33. Crenson and Ginsberg, *Presidential Power,* 189–190.

34. Robert A. Caro, *Master of the Senate: The Years of Lyndon Johnson* (New York: Random House, 2002); Rowland Evans and Robert Novak, *Lyndon B. Johnson: The Exercise of Power* (New York: New American Library, 1966).

35. Lyndon Baines Johnson, *The Vantage Point: Perspectives on the Presidency, 1963–1969* (New York: Holt, Rinehart, and Winston, 1971), 18.

36. William E. Leuchtenburg, *The White House Looks South: Franklin D. Roosevelt, Harry S. Truman, and Lyndon B. Johnson* (Baton Rouge: Louisiana State University Press, 2005), 297.

37. Jeffrey K. Tulis, *The Rhetorical Presidency* (Princeton: Princeton University Press, 1987), 162.

38. Leuchtenburg, *In the Shadow of FDR,* 142.

39. At Dirksen's insistence, the EEOC, which was charged in the administration's bill with preventing racial and sexual discriminatory practices in employment, was stripped of its authority to file suit in the courts. The commission had the power to recommend litigation, but only the Justice Department had the power to initiate a suit. The Justice Department, in turn, could file suits only under conditions in which obvious discriminatory practices, notably Jim Crow laws in the South, prevailed. On Dirksen's relationship with Johnson and the role that the Republican Senate leader played in enacting civil rights legislation, see Byron C. Hulsey, *Everett C. Dirksen and His Presidents: How a Senate Giant Shaped American Politics* (Lawrence: University Press of Kansas, 2000), 183–204.

40. LBJ describes the legislative maneuvering that led to the enactment of the 1964 civil rights bill in his memoirs; see Johnson, *Vantage Point,* 159–160.

41. R. Shep Melnick, "The Courts, Congress, and Programmatic Rights," in *Remaking American Politics,* ed. Richard A. Harris and Sidney M. Milkis (Boulder: Westview Press, 1989), 192–195. In 1954 in *Brown v. Board of Education of Topeka,* the Supreme Court had declared segregated public schools to be unconstitutional.

42. James MacGregor Burns, "Confessions of a Kennedy Man," in *To Heal and to Build: The Programs of President Lyndon B. Johnson,* ed. James MacGregor Burns (New York: McGraw Hill, 1968), 417.

43. Johnson, *Vantage Point,* 160.

44. "Lyndon B. Johnson's Great Society Speech," in Nelson, *Evolving Presidency,* 199–203.

45. Theodore White, *America in Search of Itself: The Making of the President, 1956–1980* (New York: Harper and Row, 1982), 124.

46. William E. Leuchtenburg, "The Genesis of the Great Society," *Reporter,* April 21, 1966, 38.

47. Greenstein, "Nine Presidents," 329. See also Michael Nelson, "Domestic Policy, Domestic Policy Advisers, and the American Presidency," in *Governing at Home: The White House and Domestic Policy Making,* eds. Michael Nelson and Russell L. Riley (Lawrence: University Press of Kansas, 2011), 1–23.

48. James Gaither, *Oral History,* interviewed by Dorothy Pierce (Tape 1: November 19, 1968, 24; Tape 4: January 17, 1969, 1–2), Lyndon Baines Johnson Library, Austin, Texas.

49. David Broder, "Consensus Politics: End of an Experiment," *Atlantic Monthly,* October 1966, 62.

50. Sidney M. Milkis, interview with Harry MacPherson, July 30, 1985.

51. *CBS Cronkite Interview with Lyndon Johnson,* no. 1, December 27, 1969, "Why I Chose Not to Run," 5, Lyndon Baines Johnson Library, Austin, Texas.

52. Tulis, *Rhetorical Presidency,* 172.

53. Richard M. Pious, *The American Presidency* (New York: Basic Books, 1979), 399.

54. "Lyndon B. Johnson's Gulf of Tonkin Message," in Nelson, *Evolving Presidency,* 203–207.

55. Senate Foreign Relations Committee, "National Commitments," Senate Report 797, 90th Cong., 1st sess., 1967, 19–22.

56. Quoted in ibid., 21–22.

57. The right of the vice president to succeed to the office, not just assume the powers, of the presidency, also is treated in the amendment. In 1841 John Tyler had asserted the vice president's right to full succession when he succeeded William Henry Harrison, which set the precedent for future successions. Section 1 of the Twenty-fifth Amendment simply wrote this precedent into the Constitution: "In case of the removal of the President from office or of his death or resignation, the Vice President shall become President."

58. Garfield lay dying for eighty days after he was shot in 1881. His cabinet met to discuss the situation, but concluded that if Vice President Chester A. Arthur were to invoke paragraph 6, he would legally become president, thus barring Garfield from resuming the office should he recover. Woodrow Wilson's cabinet and many members of Congress were more disposed to transfer power temporarily to Vice President Thomas R. Marshall during Wilson's long disability in 1919 and 1920, but the Constitution's lack of guidance stayed their hands. When Secretary of State Robert Lansing raised the possibility with Joseph Tumulty, Wilson's secretary, Tumulty replied, "You may rest assured that while Woodrow Wilson is lying in the White House on the broad of his back I will not be a party to ousting him." Marshall confided to his secretary, "I am not going to seize the place and then have Wilson—recovered—come around and say, 'Get off, you usurper.'" John D. Feerick, *The Twenty-fifth Amendment* (New York: Fordham University Press, 1976), 9; Irving G. Williams, *The Rise of the Vice Presidency* (Washington, D.C.: Public Affairs Press, 1956), 112–114. Although Garfield's and Wilson's disabilities were unusual for their length, nearly one in three presidents has been disabled for at least a brief period of his term. In addition to Garfield and Wilson, James Madison, William Henry Harrison, Chester A. Arthur, Grover Cleveland, William McKinley, Warren G. Harding, Franklin D. Roosevelt, Dwight D. Eisenhower, John F. Kennedy, and Ronald Reagan were temporarily disabled. Feerick, *Twenty-fifth Amendment,* chap. 1. Historian Robert Dallek argues that the problem of presidential fitness is so serious that the provisions of the Twenty-Fifth Amendment provide inadequate

protection against it. He proposes that a panel of independent experts be established to advise the public on whether a candidate is healthy enough to serve as president. If the public does not follow the panel's lead, but the experts prove to be more foresighted than the public, the people should be able to recall a president. Dallek prescribes a constitutional amendment allowing voters to remove a president in a referendum. Robert Dallek, "Presidential Fitness and Presidential Lies: The Historical Record and a Proposal for Reform," *Presidential Studies Quarterly* 40, no. 1 (March 2010), 14:9–22.

59.   The seven vice presidents who died in office were George Clinton, Elbridge Gerry, William R. King, Henry Wilson, Thomas A. Hendricks, Garret A. Hobart, and James S. Sherman. The eight presidents who died in office were William Henry Harrison, Zachary Taylor, Abraham Lincoln, James A. Garfield, William L. McKinley, Warren G. Harding, Franklin D. Roosevelt, and John F. Kennedy. The vice president who resigned was John C. Calhoun.

60.   George E. Reedy, *The Twilight of the Presidency* (New York: New American Library, 1970), xv.

61.   Greenstein, "Nine Presidents," 330.

62.   "The McGovern-Fraser Commission Report," in Nelson, *Evolving Presidency,* 210–216.

63.   Paul Van Riper, *History of the United States Civil Service* (Evanston, Ill.: Row, Peterson, 1958), 327.

64.   Richard Nixon, *RN: The Memoirs of Richard Nixon* (New York: Grosset and Dunlap, 1978), 352.

65.   Quoted in Richard P. Nathan, *The Administrative Presidency* (New York: Wiley, 1983), 30.

66.   Stewart Alsop, "Mystery of Richard Nixon," *Saturday Evening Post,* July 12, 1958, 28.

67.   Joan Hoff-Wilson, "Richard M. Nixon: The Corporate Presidency," in Greenstein, *Leadership in the Modern Presidency,* 165.

68.   "The President as Potentate," *American Prospect,* November 5, 2001, 42–46.

69.   Kenneth R. Mayer, *With the Stroke of a Pen: Executive Orders and Presidential Power* (Princeton: Princeton University Press, 2001), 204.

70.   Nathan, *Administrative Presidency,* 27.

71.   "Annual Message to Congress on the State of the Union," January 22, 1971, *Public Papers of the Presidents of the United States: Richard Nixon, 1971* (Washington, D.C.: Government Printing Office, 1972), 53. See also A. James Reichley, *Conservatives in an Age of Change: The Nixon and Ford Administrations* (Washington, D.C.: Brookings, 1985), 257–259.

72.   Garment quoted in Reichley, *Conservatives in an Age of Change,* 259. Nixon quoted in Hoff-Wilson, "Richard M. Nixon," 177.

73.   Quoted in George C. Herring, *America's Longest War: The United States and Vietnam* (New York: Wiley, 1979), 219.

74.   Larry Berman, *No Peace, No Honor: Nixon, Kissinger, and Betrayal in Vietnam* (New York: Free Press, 2001).

75.   Henry A. Kissinger, "The Viet Nam Negotiations," *Foreign Affairs* 47 (January 1969): 234. For a dissenting view on the need to secure "peace with honor" lest the international standing of the United States be diminished, see Robert Dallek, *Nixon and Kissinger: Partners in Power* (New York: HarperCollins, 2007).

76.   Hoff-Wilson, "Richard M. Nixon," 165.

77.   Nathan, *Administrative Presidency,* 45 (emphasis in original).

78.   Greenstein, "Nine Presidents," 332; "Richard Nixon's China Trip Announcement," in Nelson, *Evolving Presidency,* 207–210. For a balanced account of Nixon's "administrative presidency," see Nathan, *Administrative Presidency,* 43–56; on Kissinger's NSC, see John D. Leecacos, "Kissinger's Apparat," *Foreign Policy* 5 (Winter 1971-1972): 3–27; on the China trip, see Margaret Macmillan, *Nixon and Mao: The Week that Changed the World* (New York: Random House, 2007).

79. Eisenhower quoted in Stephen E. Ambrose, *Eisenhower: The President* (New York: Simon and Schuster, 1984), 673.

80. Arthur M. Schlesinger Jr., *The Imperial Presidency* (New York: Popular Library, 1973), 10.

81. Weinberger cited in Andrew Rudalevige, *The New Imperial Presidency* (Ann Arbor: University of Michigan Press, 2005), 89 (emphasis in original).

82. Berman, *New American Presidency,* 263.

83. Humphrey cited in Rudalevige, *New Imperial Presidency,* 90.

84. Greenstein, "Nine Presidents," 334; Stephen E. Ambrose, *Nixon: Ruin and Recovery, 1973–1990,* vol. 3 (New York: Simon and Schuster, 1991), 59–80.

85. This section draws on the insights of Reichley, *Conservatives in an Age of Change,* 250–261.

86. Ibid., 250.

87. Ibid., 259.

88. *United States v. Nixon,* 418 U.S. 683 (1974), at 707, 712.

89. Id. at 708.

90. Id. at 713.

91. William M. Goldsmith, ed., *The Growth of Presidential Power: A Documented History,* 3 vols. (New York: Chelsea, 1974), 3:2274; Pious, *American Presidency,* 75–78. See also "The 'Smoking Gun' Watergate Tapes," in *The Evolving Presidency: Addresses, Cases, Essays, Letters, Reports, Resolutions, Transcripts, and Other Landmark Documents, 1787–2004,* 2nd ed., ed. Michael Nelson (Washington, D.C.: CQ Press, 2004), 201–207.

92. Richard M. Nixon, "Resignation Address," August 8, 1974, in Goldsmith, *Growth of Presidential Power,* 3:2275.

93. Alonzo L. Hamby, *Liberalism and Its Challengers: From FDR to Bush,* 2nd ed. (New York: Oxford University Press, 1992), 338.

94. These surveys are discussed in James MacGregor Burns, J. W. Peltason, and Thomas Cronin, *Government by the People,* 11th ed. (Englewood Cliffs, N.J.: Prentice Hall, 1981), 359.

95. Greenstein, "Nine Presidents," 335.

96. "The War Powers Resolution," in Nelson, *Evolving Presidency,* 4th ed., 216–222.

97. R. Shep Melnick, "The Politics of Partnership," *Public Administration Review* 45 (November 1985): 655.

98. Jules Witcover, *Very Strange Bedfellows: The Short and Unhappy Marriage of Richard Nixon and Spiro Agnew* (New York: Public Affairs, 2007).

99. In the absence of the Twenty-fifth Amendment, Agnew's resignation would have left Carl W. Albert, the Democratic Speaker of the House, next in the line of succession, immensely complicating the Nixon removal process.

100. Kissinger quoted in Roger Porter, "Gerald Ford: A Healing Presidency," in Greenstein, *Leadership in the Modern Presidency,* 199.

101. These changes are discussed in ibid., 206–213.

102. Ibid., 208.

103. Berman, *New American Presidency,* 293–294.

104. "Gerald Ford's Pardon of Richard Nixon," in Nelson, *Evolving Presidency,* 4th ed., 234–238.

105. Porter, "Gerald Ford," 208–209.

106. Michael Nelson, ed., *Congressional Quarterly's Guide to the Presidency,* 2nd ed. (Washington, D.C.: Congressional Quarterly, 1996), 2:1757.

107. "Inaugural Address of President Jimmy Carter," January 20, 1977, *Public Papers of the Presidents of the United States: Jimmy Carter, 1977* (Washington, D.C.: Government Printing Office, 1977), 1:1.

108. James Bryce, *The American Commonwealth,* 2 vols. (London: Macmillan, 1891), 1:221.

109. Ford quoted in Philip Shabecoff, "Presidency Is Found Weaker under Ford," *New York Times,* March 28, 1976, 1.

110. Gerald R. Ford, *A Time to Heal* (New York: Harper and Row, 1979), 378.

111. Greenstein, "Nine Presidents," 340.

112. Tip O'Neill, with William Novak, *Man of the House* (New York: St. Martin's Press, 1987), 376.

113. Jimmy Carter, *Keeping Faith: Memoirs of a President* (New York: Bantam Books, 1982), 27.

114. Ibid., 80.

115. Berman, *New American Presidency*, 315.

116. Greenstein, "Nine Presidents," 339.

117. O'Neill, *Man of the House*, 369. See also John A. Farrell, *Tip O'Neill and the Democratic Century* (Boston: Little, Brown, 2001).

118. John P. Burke, "The Institutional Presidency," in Nelson, *Presidency and the Political System*, 419.

119. Erwin C. Hargrove, "Jimmy Carter: The Politics of Public Goods," in Greenstein, *Leadership in the Modern Presidency*, 251.

120. William B. Quandt, *Camp David: Peacemaking and Politics* (Washington, D.C.: Brookings, 1986).

121. Hargrove, "Jimmy Carter," 233.

122. James Fallows, "The Passionless Presidency," *Atlantic Monthly*, May 1979, 42.

123. Hargrove, "Jimmy Carter," 254.

CHAPTER 12

A Restoration of Presidential Power?
Ronald Reagan and George H. W. Bush

In 1980 Richard E. Neustadt wrote, "Watching President Carter in early 1979 sparked the question, is the Presidency possible?"[1] It seemed during the final days of the Carter administration that the presidency no longer worked, that presidents had become frustrated beyond hope by a weakened party system, hostile news media, a congeries of powerful special interest groups, an intransigent bureaucracy, an aggressive Congress, assertive courts, and a demoralized public. Of the five presidents who held office from 1961 to 1980, none completed two terms.

"Among the consequences of Reagan's election to the presidency," Jeffrey K. Tulis wrote in 1987, "was the rewriting of textbooks on American government." No longer could one claim that fragmented and demoralized political conditions inevitably "would frustrate the efforts of any president to accomplish substantial policy objectives, to maintain popularity, and to avoid blame for activities beyond his control."[2] In contrast to Gerald R. Ford and Jimmy Carter, Reagan successfully advanced an ambitious legislative program in 1981 and 1982. He was renominated by his party without opposition and reelected handily in 1984. From the beginning of his first term until the damaging revelations of the Iran-contra affair in 1986, Reagan and his associates convinced most Americans that a strong, effective, popular leader had restored the presidency to preeminence in the political system. Rebounding from Iran-contra, he retired from the White House as the most popular president since John F. Kennedy.

THE REAGAN REVOLUTION

Reagan's political success prompted considerable speculation that the 1980 election, like the election of 1932, had launched a partisan realignment in American politics. Although the New Deal Democratic coalition had been unraveling since the 1960s, Reagan was the first president since William McKinley in 1896 to envision an enduring conservative Republican majority. Richard Nixon, Ford, and Carter were relatively conservative presidents, and each of them challenged certain policies of the New Deal and the Great Society. But they generally accommodated themselves to liberalism, seeking mainly to curb its excesses and to administer its programs more economically. Reagan, in contrast, had been outspoken in his conservatism for many years, prompting some pundits to dub his landslide victory in 1980 the "Reagan Revolution."

In truth, Reagan's victory was somewhat ambiguous. In the three-way race between Reagan, Carter, and a former Republican, Rep. John Anderson of Illinois, Reagan won by a landslide in the Electoral College, sweeping forty-four states with 489 electoral votes. Yet his 51 percent of the popular vote was only a three-percentage-point increase over Ford's tally as the Republican nominee in 1976. The results of the congressional elections were more impressive. For the first time since 1952, the Republicans won a majority in the Senate, and several prominent liberal Democrats were defeated. The ranks of House Republicans rose by thirty-three seats, although the Democrats retained clear control of the lower chamber.

Reagan's ability to transform his ambiguous electoral victory into concrete legislative achievements testified to his considerable rhetorical gifts. Critics dismissed his ability to communicate effectively as a former actor's trick of the trade—the talent to learn and deliver his lines on camera. But Reagan's supporters maintained that there was logic and substance to his message. In their view he was not the "Great Communicator" but the "Great Rhetorician" who, like Woodrow Wilson, the two Roosevelts, and Kennedy before him, articulated a vision that inspired the nation.[3]

Reagan's message as candidate and as president was but a variation on the theme that he had been enunciating ever since he gave a nationally televised address on behalf of the Republican Party on October 27, 1964. "The Speech," as conservative admirers called it, had a single theme: centrally administered government weakens a free people. A strong national state had so perverted the concept of liberty in the United States, Reagan argued, that "natural unalienable rights" had come to be regarded as a "dispensation of government," stripping the people of their self-reliance and capacity for self-rule. "The real destroyer of the liberties of the people," Reagan warned, "is he who spreads among them bounties, donations, and benefits."[4] Seventeen years later, in his inaugural address—the first by a president in more than fifty years to appeal for limited government—Reagan sounded the same theme: "In this present crisis, government is not the solution to our problem; government is the problem. From time to time we've been tempted to believe that society has become too complex to be managed by self-rule, that government by an elite group is superior to government for, by, and of the people. Well, if no one among us is capable of governing himself, then who among us has the capacity to govern someone else? All of us together—in and out of government— must bear the burden."[5]

Reagan's rhetoric challenged the fundamental principles of the New Deal. The important thing, political scientist Hugh Heclo has argued, is not that Reagan "said anything fundamentally new," but rather that in the political context created by the New Deal and Great Society, "Reagan continued to uphold something old."[6] Yet Reagan issued his challenge to the welfare state in terms that paid homage to Franklin Roosevelt. Indeed, Reagan made an extraordinary effort to associate himself with the New Deal president. In 1980 he referred to FDR so frequently in his acceptance speech to the Republican national convention that the *New York Times* titled its lead editorial the next day "Franklin Delano Reagan."[7]

Quoting Roosevelt did not mean that Reagan had "moved toward the center," as the *Times* editorial claimed. Rather, William E. Leuchtenburg has observed, Reagan "exploited Roosevelt for conservative ends." He concluded his address by calling on the delegates to fulfill the promise that FDR made in his own acceptance speech to the Democratic convention in July 1932: "to eliminate unnecessary functions of government." Reagan's invocation of Roosevelt, then, was designed in part to dramatize the failures and false promises of the New Deal and to highlight what Reagan had been proclaiming for two decades: government had become too big and too remote from the people.[8]

But Reagan's identification with Roosevelt also reflected his desire to lead as FDR had led, fully exploiting the powers of the modern presidency to move the United States toward a new "rendezvous with destiny." Nixon had seen the possibility of using his office to lead the country away from the New Deal, but not as clearly as Reagan saw it. As for public policy, Reagan's agenda was less reminiscent of Nixon than of an earlier and less pragmatic defender of limited government—Calvin Coolidge. Reagan's public addresses, like Coolidge's, conveyed the president's commitment to limited government in moral terms, as a righteous cause that served humankind at home and abroad.[9]

Reagan's inclination to state his governing philosophy in exalted language shone forth most clearly in his March 8, 1983, speech to the National Association of Evangelicals. After expressing disdain for the Soviet Union's "evil empire" as another "sad, bizarre, chapter in human history," Reagan concluded,

I believe ... the source of our strength in the quest for human freedom is not material, but spiritual. And because it knows no limitation, it must terrify and ultimately triumph over those who would enslave their fellow man. For in the words of Isaiah: "He giveth power to the faint; and to them that have no might He increased strength. ... But they that wait upon the Lord shall renew their strength; they shall mount up with wings as eagles; they shall run, and not be weary. ... "

Yes, change your world. One of our Founding Fathers, Thomas Paine, said, "We have it within our power to begin the world over again." We can do it, doing together what no one church could do by itself.[10]

Although critics accused former actor Ronald Reagan of making insubstantial speeches that glossed over the issues, others called him the "Great Rhetorician," pointing to his ability to inspire the nation with his ideas.

Reagan's privately stated approach to the cold war with the Soviet Union was simple: "We win. They lose."[11] Diplomatic historian John Lewis Gaddis has argued that far from being naïve, Reagan "could see beyond complexity to simplicity." According to Gaddis, although "theorists of international relations insisted that . . . Soviet-American bipolarity would last as far into the future as anyone could see," Reagan saw something different: an economically backward Soviet Union that would topple if pushed. He dramatically accelerated the arms race, straining the Soviet economy to the breaking point, and then delivered the coup de grâce by vowing to develop the Strategic Defense Initiative, his dream of a high-tech anti-missile shield over the United States. "The reaction, in the Kremlin, approached panic" because the Soviets knew they lacked both the money and the computer technology to keep up.[12] Driven past their breaking point, the Soviet empire and then the Soviet Union itself dissolved shortly after Reagan left office.

Reagan's political opponents, who were far less optimistic about his policies than he was, found the president's rhetoric to be merely bright packaging on a harshly conservative public philosophy. But Reagan's words and the political vision they expressed stirred many Americans' deeply rooted and widely shared political values. The simplicity of his message, the dignity of his public demeanor, even his limited faith in government, captivated the popular imagination.

REAGAN AND CONGRESS

Reagan's rhetoric was matched by his skill as a legislative leader. Unlike the Carter administration, one scholar has observed, the Reagan administration "hit the ground running." Reagan's aides carefully studied Carter's errors and crafted a first-year strategy that would succeed in just those ways that Carter had failed. In contrast to Carter's bewildering array of early legislative proposals, Reagan concentrated on two themes: shrinking the welfare state and expanding the military.[13] His administration embodied these themes in the three bold proposals on which he had based his election campaign: a large income tax cut, a significant reduction in domestic spending, and an enormous increase in spending on national defense.

Reagan's clear sense of direction was not his only point of contrast with Carter. Like Carter, Reagan had campaigned for president by running against the ills of Washington. But, once elected, Reagan recognized that it no longer made sense to continue to attack the Washington community. He lavished attention on members of Congress, frequently visiting Capitol Hill for meetings or telephoning members of the House and Senate on the eve of important votes. "We had to lasso him to keep him off the Hill," one close aide recalled about the president's first year.[14]

Reagan's personal relations with Congress were buttressed by a strong Executive Office of the President (EOP). In contrast to Carter, who had relied on the parochial veterans of his presidential campaign to organize and operate his staff, Reagan's White House Office and the Office of Management and Budget (the two main units of the EOP) included not just personal loyalists, but also skilled veterans from earlier Republican administrations. Reagan's able and experienced staff compensated for the president's own lack of interest in the details of public policy. Even his political opponents were impressed. "All in all, the Reagan team in 1981 was probably the best run political operation unit I've ever seen," Speaker of the House Thomas P. "Tip" O'Neill, a Democrat, noted in his memoirs. "I didn't like their mean-spirited philosophy, but they knew where they were going and they knew how to get there."[15]

The president's enormous popular appeal, his willingness to lobby Congress for his programs, and the political skill of his staff enabled the Reagan administration to mount a legislative campaign in 1981 that rivaled the early breakthroughs of Wilson's New Freedom, FDR's New Deal, and Johnson's Great Society. Reagan persuaded Congress to approve a dramatic departure in fiscal policy: more than $35 billion in domestic program reductions; a multi-year package of nearly $750 billion in tax cuts; and a three-year, 27 percent increase in defense spending. "In slightly more than six months," journalist Hedrick Smith wrote in 1982, Reagan "had achieved more than political Washington had dreamed possible on the day of his inauguration."[16]

Reagan's first year as president seemed to restore the executive's preeminence as chief legislator. Both by courting members of Congress assiduously and by going over their heads to the people when necessary, Reagan worked his will on the legislative process, despite the Democratic majority in the House. In doing so, he actually turned the Congressional Budget and Impoundment Control Act, which Congress had enacted in 1974 to strengthen its own hand in fiscal policy, on its head.

Reagan's OMB director, David Stockman, discovered a way that the administration could use one provision of the budget act—the "reconciliation" process, which Congress had created to coordinate its budget-making activities more effectively—to bind the legislature to the president's program. Reconciliation authorized the House and Senate budget committees to bring together every proposed change in the budget in a single bill. The House Appropriations Committee belatedly described in a 1982 report how this approach played into the hands of the president: "It is much easier for the Executive Branch to gain support for its program when it is packaged in one bill rather than pursuing each and every authorization and appropriation measure to insure compliance with the Executive's program. This device tends to aid the Executive Branch in gaining additional control over budget matters and to circumvent the will of Congress."[17]

After a televised speech to Congress on April 28, 1981, made all the more dramatic by his rapid recovery from a would-be assassin's near-fatal gunshot wound on March 30, Reagan won a substantial legislative victory on a comprehensive budget resolution. The resolution incorporated every element of his economic policy: greater spending on defense, less spending on domestic programs, and a huge tax cut. The president's appearance on Capitol Hill produced what House Republican leader Robert Michel described as "the kind of reception that makes a few of the waverers feel, 'Gosh, how can I buck that?'"[18] Yet Reagan directed his speech beyond the mostly Democratic Congress to the television audience at home. The House majority leader, Jim Wright of Texas, was among those who lamented Reagan's budget victory as a dramatic setback in Congress's post-Watergate struggle to regain its independence. He complained bitterly that the administration was trying to "dictate every last scintilla, every last phrase" of legislation.[19] Even worse from Wright's standpoint, the president succeeded.

But Reagan's hastily conceived economic package suffered from some of the same defects as the Great Society. As Tulis has written, "Like Johnson's, this public policy was prepared hastily in the executive branch, and like the War on Poverty, the nation's legislature played no substantive role in planning the program."[20] The substantial tax cuts exceeded by far the reductions in domestic spending and were accompanied by large increases in defense spending. Conservatives such as New York representative Jack Kemp had argued that the tax cut would not increase the budget deficit. They were persuaded by "supply-side" economists such as Arthur Laffer and Paul Craig Roberts that a large tax cut would stimulate productivity so much that rising tax revenues would balance the budget by 1984. Inflation would fall, the supply-siders maintained, along with interest rates. Private savings, in turn, would increase because investors' fears of inflation would be allayed.[21] Yet, as OMB director Stockman privately admitted at the time, "None of us really understand what's going on with all these numbers."[22] Some of the supply-siders' predictions came true: the economy eventually boomed and, with strong support from Federal Reserve Board chair Paul Volcker, inflation dropped steeply. Other predictions proved inaccurate. In particular, tax receipts did not grow enough to prevent the Reagan administration from running the largest annual budget deficits in history. The national debt grew from $1 trillion in 1981 to $3 trillion in 1989.

Yet the unintended consequences of Reagan's fiscal program did not affect the president's standing with the public. Even when he faced political adversity, as he did during the severe economic recession of 1982, Reagan remained confident, vowing to "stay the course." Unlike Johnson, he seldom agonized over his own or his office's legitimacy. As Fred I. Greenstein has written, "Several of the modern presidents bore their responsibilities like crosses. Others, including Reagan for most of his presidency, were able to maintain control of the national political agenda, in part by concrete accomplishments, but also by exuding confidence and self-assurance."[23]

REAGAN AS PARTY LEADER

Reagan's hopes that his principles would animate a national political realignment never flagged, even after the Democrats rebounded in the 1982 congressional elections. His own reelection in 1984, in which he won 59 percent of the popular vote and all but thirteen electoral votes, convinced the president that events were moving his way. In a speech to the National Conservative Political Action Conference in March 1985, Reagan claimed that the triumphs of 1980 and 1984 had laid the foundation for a new conservative political orthodoxy that would endure well beyond his administration: "The tide of history is moving irresistibly in our direction. Why? Because the other side is virtually bankrupt of ideas. It has nothing more to say, nothing to add to the debate. It has spent its intellectual capital—such as it was—and it did its deeds."[24]

Reagan's efforts to inaugurate a new political era benefited from, and in turn helped to galvanize, a renewal of party politics. The nearly century-long development of the modern presidency had helped to foster a serious decline in the traditional, decentralized, patronage-based political parties. Yet during the late 1970s and 1980s, a new form of party politics began to emerge. The erosion of old-style partisan organizations allowed a more national and issues-oriented party system to take shape, forging new bonds between presidents and their parties.

The Republican Party, in particular, developed a strong institutional apparatus, which displayed unprecedented strength at the national level during the 1980s.[25] Because the reconstituted party system was associated less with political patronage than with issues, ideology, and sophisticated fund-raising techniques, it did not pose as much of an obstacle to the personal and programmatic ambitions of presidents as the traditional system had. Indeed, by 1984 the Republicans had become a solidly conservative party, made over in Reagan's image.

Significantly, it was Reagan who broke with the practice of the modern presidency and identified his presidency closely with his party. The president worked hard to strengthen the Republicans' organizational and popular base, surprising his own White House political director with his "total readiness" to raise funds and make speeches for the party and its candidates.[26] Even after the 1984 election, in which the Reagan campaign generally went its own way, Sen. Robert J. Dole said, "Nixon thought he could build a conservative majority that was above party, and Ford tried to strengthen the traditional Republican party. Reagan is trying to expand the Republican party to include a majority."[27]

The Reagan experience suggests how the relationship between modern presidents and the modern parties can be mutually beneficial. Republican support solidified Reagan's personal popularity and laid the political foundation for his program in Congress. In turn, the president served his fellow Republicans by strengthening their fund-raising efforts and encouraging voters to extend their loyalties not just to him but to his party. Surveys taken after the 1984 election revealed that the Republicans had attained virtual parity with the Democrats among voters for the first time since the 1940s.[28]

The 1980s marked a watershed of renewed and strengthened ties between presidents and the party system. Unwilling to fall permanently behind the Republicans, the Democrats also became a more centralized and programmatic party, with an ideological center that was decidedly liberal. The combined effect of the New Deal, the Great Society, and the conservative Republican response, was to sharply reduce the presence of traditional southern Democrats in Congress, emancipating the party from the conservative ball and chain that long had hobbled its forward liberal march. In the Seventy-fifth Congress (1937–1939), which balked at Franklin Roosevelt's "Court-packing" plan, the thirteen southern states (the Old Confederacy, plus Kentucky and Oklahoma) had held 120 House seats, of which 117 were in Democratic hands. In the 100th Congress, near the end of the Reagan era, those same states had 124 seats. But only 85 of them were Democratic; nearly a third had migrated to the Republican side of the aisle. Meanwhile, the 1965 Voting Rights Act had substantially increased the number of African American voters in the South, transforming the behavior of southern Democrats in Congress in a liberal direction. "It was the sign of the times in 1983," journalist Alan Ehrenhalt wrote in 1987, "when Southern Democrats [in Congress] voted 78–12 in favor of the holiday honoring the Rev. Martin Luther King."[29]

REAGAN AND THE ADMINISTRATIVE PRESIDENCY

Despite the transformation of the party system, the Reagan Revolution was hardly the dawn of a new era in which the president was subordinate to his party. Reagan never converted his personal popularity into Republican control of Congress. In fact, the Reagan administration seldom presented its programs in strongly partisan terms that would give the voters a compelling reason to endorse a Republican realignment or a fundamental reshaping of liberal programs. Because Reagan's successful campaign in 1984 relied on fuzzy, feel-good themes such as "It's morning again in America" rather than on sharply defined issue stands that would clarify the voters' choice between Democratic and Republican views of the future, the Democrats had no trouble maintaining their strong majority in the House of Representatives. Two years later, they recaptured the Senate. The White House worked closely with the Republican National Committee and Republican candidates, but it avoided a forthright partisan message. As Rep. Vin Weber, a Minnesota Republican, complained in 1986, "The focus was on . . . the same feel good empty rhetoric that dominated the 1984 race."[30]

The failure to bring about a full-scale Republican realignment circumscribed the achievements of the Reagan administration. Nevertheless, Reagan accomplished a great deal as president. Although his 1981 tax and budget victories did not dismantle the welfare state, they did set the stage for a significant reordering of priorities in Washington. The enormous budget deficits that the tax cuts and defense buildup created limited the Democratic Congress's ability to enact new spending programs. In fact, during Reagan's first six years as president, Congress did not create a single major program. In 1986 the Reagan-sponsored Tax Reform Act further reduced congressional hopes of raising more revenue by lowering the income tax rates and eliminating many of the exemptions, deductions, and preferences that traditionally had made it politically possible to increase those rates.

The budget deficit and the overhaul of the tax system placed the Democratic Party in a serious bind. As former vice president Walter F. Mondale, the Democratic presidential nominee in 1984, lamented, "Reagan has practiced the politics of subtraction. He knows the public wants to spend money on the old folks, protecting the environment and aiding education. And he's figured out the only way to stop it is to deny the revenues. No matter how powerful the argument the Democrats make for the use of government to serve some purpose, the answer must be no."[31] Conservatives gleefully called this strategy "starve the beast."

The Reagan administration did spend money, however: it oversaw the largest peacetime military buildup in history. The president also demonstrated that it was politically possible, despite the lingering trauma of Vietnam, to deploy troops abroad. In 1983, disregarding the War Powers Resolution, Reagan reasserted the president's powers as commander in chief by invading the Caribbean island of Grenada and deposing its communist government. In 1986 he ordered that Libya be bombed in retaliation for a terrorist attack in West Berlin that took the lives of two Americans soldiers. In both of these episodes, the duration of the military involvement was brief, casualties were few, and victory was assured. Consequently, public and congressional support for the president was high.

Still, Reagan suffered reversals on some important matters. After 1982 Congress refused to cut domestic spending any further. It also required the administration to slow the pace of its rearmament program and restricted the president's ability to aid the anti-Marxist contra rebels in Nicaragua.

In the face of mounting legislative opposition, the Reagan White House resorted to some of the same tactics of "institutional combat" that Nixon and his staff had employed.[32] To support the Nicaraguan contras, it secretly built an alternative intelligence network within the staff of the National Security Council (NSC). This covert network conducted operations that Congress either had refused to approve (such as continued military aid to the contras) or almost certainly would not have countenanced if Reagan had ever asked it to (such as the sale of weapons to Iran). Its efforts exposed the administration to severe political risks and, eventually, to a damaging scandal, the Iran-contra affair. In November 1986 the nation learned that with Reagan's approval the United States had sold weapons to Iran and that, with or without the president's knowledge, some of the proceeds had been used by Marine colonel Oliver North and other NSC staff members to assist the contras.

Public reaction to revelations of the Iran-contra affair in November 1986 was swift and dramatic. Reagan's approval rating fell from 67 percent to 46 percent in one month. The Iranian arms sales, which apparently had been undertaken to secure the release of seven Americans who were being held hostage by terrorists in Beirut, Lebanon, were not illegal. But they ran directly counter to the administration's hard-line antiterrorism policies. The diversion of funds to the Nicaraguan rebels clearly violated the Boland Amendment, a 1985 congressional ban on aid to the contras.

Responding to strong political pressure from Congress, the news media, and the American people, the president appointed former Texas Republican senator John Tower to chair a bipartisan review board. The Tower Commission roundly criticized Reagan's management style in its 1987 report, even suggesting that the president was blithely out of touch with his own administration, a figurehead who reigned at the mercy of his staff. But the Iran-contra affair was not simply a matter of the president being asleep on his watch. It also revealed the Reagan administration's determination to carry out its foreign policy without interference from Congress or anyone else.

Although the president may not have known about the diversion of funds to the contras, the news should not have surprised him. The so-called Reagan Doctrine committed the United States to support insurrections throughout the world against third world Marxist states, such as Nicaragua, Angola, and Afghanistan. Reagan also made it clear to his national security adviser, Robert C. McFarlane, and to McFarlane's successor, John M. Poindexter, that he wanted them to keep the contra resistance alive "body and soul."[33] As the minority (that is, the Republican-written) report of the congressional committee that investigated the Iran-contra affair concluded, "President Reagan gave his subordinates strong, clear and consistent guidance about the basic thrust of the policies he wanted them to pursue toward Nicaragua. There is some question and dispute about *precisely* the level at which he chose to follow the operational details. There is no doubt, however, . . . [that] the President set the U.S. policy toward Nicaragua, with few if any ambiguities, and then left subordinates more or less free to implement it." [34]

Many, if not most, of the Republican senators and representatives who signed the minority report supported Reagan's efforts to aid the contras: "Our *only* regret is that the administration was not open enough with Congress about what it was doing." Reagan's long-term efforts to build support for his policies would have been enhanced, they argued, if he had confronted Congress directly by vetoing the Boland Amendment and taking his case to the American people. [35]

The Reagan administration's strategy of circumventing rather than publicly confronting Congress testified to both the continuing limits on presidential party leadership and the ineffectiveness of the statutory restraints that Congress had imposed on the presidency in foreign affairs since the Vietnam War and the Watergate scandal. The prospects for a new spirit of cooperation and discipline within a revamped party system dissolved in Reagan's pursuit of policy through the deployment of the "administrative presidency." According to Richard M. Pious, "Iran-Contra was not due to a weak and uninvolved president mismanaging the national-security decision-making process," as the Tower Commission claimed. Rather, it was symptomatic of the restoration of presidential prerogative in foreign policy—the excesses of what Pious calls the "National Security Constitution." [36]

Reagan's use of the administrative presidency in foreign policy was hardly an aberration. As a matter of course, when the president and his advisers confronted legislative resistance on any issue, foreign or domestic, they chose administrative avenues to advance their goals unilaterally. Indeed, often they did not even try to modify the statutory basis of a liberal program, turning instead to executive discretion as a first resort.

Of the modern presidents who preceded him, Reagan was the most administratively ambitious. Not only was policymaking concentrated in the White House staff and other units of the EOP, but also care was taken to plant Reagan loyalists in the departments and agencies to ride herd on civil servants and carry forth the president's policies. As political scientist Bert A. Rockman has noted, "It was the Nixon Presidency, particularly in its aborted second term, that became celebrated for its deployment [of the administrative presidency], but the Reagan Presidency intended to perfect the strategy and to do that from the beginning." [37]

Reagan's most controversial administrative action targeted Social Security.[38] Without consulting even Republican members of Congress, in May 1981 the president proposed deep and immediate cuts in benefits for early retirees—that is, persons between the ages of sixty-two and sixty-four who chose to retire with reduced benefits rather than wait for full benefits at the normal retirement age of sixty-five. The administration also proposed to eliminate a statutory provision that guaranteed retirees a minimum benefit. The attempt to cut Social Security payments sparked a furious reaction in Congress. Members of both parties repudiated the administration overwhelmingly, with the Senate voting 96–0 against the cut in early retirement benefits and the House voting 405–13 against the proposal to eliminate the guarantee of minimum benefits. Although Congress's opposition was bipartisan, Speaker O'Neill turned the Reagan administration's mistake into a campaign issue that Democrats successfully exploited in the 1982 midterm elections and for years to come.

OMB director David Stockman, the leading proponent of the president's Social Security proposals, conceded that the punishing defeat in Congress marked the end of the effort to arrest the growth of Social Security. "The centerpiece of the American welfare state had now been overwhelmingly ratified and affirmed in the white heat of political confrontation," he wrote after leaving office.[39] Nevertheless, the defeat did not discourage Reagan appointees in the Social Security Administration (SSA) from trying to cut Social Security through administrative action. Claiming authority from a 1980 law that mandated a review of the disability program, they engaged in a large-scale effort to purge the rolls of those whom they considered ineligible. Between 1981 and 1984 the SSA informed nearly a half-million people that they no longer qualified for disability benefits.

Congressional Democrats maintained that the Reagan administration's action violated the intent of the 1980 legislation by reviewing cases with budget savings, not administrative reform, as the real goal. Federal courts overturned the agency's rulings against more than two hundred thousand claimants and interpreted the disability statute to require the SSA to prove that a recipient's medical condition had improved before it could cut off benefits. The SSA, under Reagan's appointees, refused to accept this ruling, arguing that the statute itself made no mention of a "medical improvement standard."

Although the SSA restored benefits to the specific individuals who had won in court, it refused to change its general policy to conform to the predominant judicial interpretation of the law. In response, some judges threatened the agency with contempt of court. After a two-year struggle to resolve the dispute, Congress passed the Disability Benefits Reform Act of 1984, which enshrined the medical improvement standard in law. The protracted battle over disability insurance testified dramatically to the Reagan administration's fervent commitment to challenge the social welfare policies of the past, with or without authorization from Congress or the courts.[40]

In the area of social regulation, the Reagan administration's efforts to weaken environmental, consumer, and civil rights enforcement were also pursued through administrative action rather than legislative change. Reagan's Executive Orders 12291 and 12498 mandated a comprehensive review of proposed agency regulations by the OMB. Reagan also appointed a Task Force on Regulatory Relief, headed by Vice President George H. W. Bush, to apply cost-benefit analysis to existing rules. The task force's review included a reconsideration of the "midnight rules" issued in the last days of the Carter administration. On January 29, 1981, Reagan imposed a sixty-day freeze on these regulations, and ultimately rejected many of them.[41]

In sum, Reagan advanced the development of the administrative presidency by resuming the decades-long trend toward concentrating power in the White House that had been suspended briefly in the aftermath of the Vietnam War and Watergate scandal. He also confirmed for conservatives that centralizing power in the presidency was essential to carrying out their objectives. As Greenstein has written, "Nixon and Reagan had the courage to act on what once were the convictions of liberals, taking it for granted that the president should use whatever power he can muster, including power to administer programs, to shape policy."[42]

Except for the Iran-contra affair, reliance on the administrative presidency did not appear to affect Reagan's strong ties to the public. After the televised Iran-contra congressional hearings concluded in the summer of 1987, Reagan recaptured a large measure of public approval. By the end of the year, with the signing in Washington of the Intermediate-range Nuclear Forces (INF) Treaty with the Soviet Union, Reagan had fully reclaimed the political high ground. During his first term, Reagan had endured unrelenting criticism from liberals for his decision to deploy intermediate-range Pershing missiles in West Germany as a deterrent to the Soviet nuclear presence. The INF Treaty, which eliminated American and Soviet intermediate-range nuclear missiles from Europe, vindicated Reagan's hard-line stance against his critics at home and the Soviets abroad, enshrining him as a peacemaker on the great stage of East-West relations.[43] Throughout 1988 Reagan's approval rating improved steadily, eventually reaching 63 percent.

Underlying Reagan's political resilience was his ability to make his program the new foundation of national political discourse. As political scientist Walter Dean Burnham wrote in 1989, "Ronald Reagan was the most ideological President, and the leader of the most ideological administration, in modern American history."[44] To a remarkable extent, Reagan demonstrated that a firm ideological purpose could substitute for long hours, exhaustive attention to detail, and a dominant political party. Lacking a firm ideological purpose,

Nixon's version of the administrative presidency was little more than a strategy to make the government dance to his tune. For Reagan, Rockman has noted, "the administrative presidency was a mechanism to ensure responsiveness to a political agenda that Reagan, and certainly his followers, hoped would outlast his own tenure in office."[45] Reagan's rhetoric defined the agenda of his presidency. His reconstruction of the executive branch was a principal instrument through which his rhetoric gained force.

Yet for all of his popularity, and despite his policy successes at home and abroad, Reagan did not become the "Roosevelt of the Right." "The one goal that consistently eluded him, and the one that Roosevelt achieved," Alonzo L. Hamby has written, "was that of an enduring political realignment in the form of a broad coalition of interest groups loosely held together by an ideology."[46]

The importance of presidential politics and administration in the Reagan presidency may actually have reduced the prospects for a Republican realignment. Journalist Sidney Blumenthal has argued that Reagan "did not reinvent the Republican party so much as transcend it. His primary political instrument was the conservative movement, which inhabited the party out of convenience."[47] Blumenthal's observation is only partly correct. Reagan's commitment to strengthening the GOP was sincere and, in many respects, effective. Nevertheless, his administration's devotion to certain tenets of conservative ideology led it to rely on unilateral executive action in ways that ultimately compromised the president's support for his party. "Too many of those around [the president] seem to have a sense of party that begins and ends in the Oval Office," Secretary of Labor William Brock lamented in 1987. "Too many really don't understand what it means to link the White House to a party in a way that creates an alliance between the presidency, the House, and the Senate, or between the national party and officials at the state and local level."[48] Brock's criticism was echoed by many Republican officials as the Reagan years drew to a close.

To some extent, at least, Republican leaders were justified in blaming Reagan's personalistic style of leadership for his failure to convert his popularity into Republican control of the entire government. From a broader historical perspective, however, Reagan's emphasis on presidential politics was a logical response to the New Deal and its consolidation of the modern presidency. Although Roosevelt's leadership was the principal ingredient in a full-scale Democratic realignment, it aimed to establish the president rather than the party as the steward of the public welfare. The New Deal, like its successor in the 1960s, the Great Society, was less a partisan program than an exercise in expanding the president's power. It was not surprising, then, that the challenge to liberal policies that culminated in the elevation of Reagan to the White House in 1980 produced a conservative administrative presidency, which further slowed the revival of partisan politics.[49]

REAGAN'S LEGACY AND THE ACCESSION OF
GEORGE H. W. BUSH

Reagan's politically successful tenure notwithstanding, the modern presidency of the 1980s did not command the political system, as it had during the early years of the Johnson administration. Instead, the executive was challenged forcefully by a modern Congress that had developed its own tools of influence. For example, members of Congress, acting in partnership with the courts, bureaucratic agencies, interest groups, and the media, were able to modify the Reagan administration's program of regulatory relief for corporations and other private institutions.

The embarrassing revelations of the Iran-contra affair also proved helpful to the Democratic Congress in opposing the Reagan administration during its final two years, although more in matters of personnel and policy than of politics. Among other things, the president was compelled to appoint a national security adviser, a director of the Central Intelligence Agency, and a White House chief of staff who were acceptable to Congress. In the realm of policy, the president was unable to advance his conservative agenda. Indeed, he found it possible to take only those initiatives—most notably nuclear arms reduction with the Soviet Union—that coincided with the agenda of the liberal opposition.[50]

A REAGAN COURT?

Reagan's effect on the federal judiciary is perhaps the best example of both the force and the limitations of the Reagan Revolution. During the 1960s and 1970s, the courts had joined with liberal members of Congress and interest groups to broaden legal rules and procedures in ways that served the interests of African Americans, feminists, environmentalists, and other Democratic constituencies. The Reagan administration worked hard to disrupt this alliance.[51] By the end of Reagan's second term, he had appointed enough conservative judges to move the federal courts considerably to the right.

In keeping with its effort to transform the terms of national political discourse, the Reagan administration "hoped to foster an intellectual revolution on the bench and enhance the influence of conservative principles on American jurisprudence."[52] Prominent conservative legal scholars, such as Ralph K. Winter and Robert H. Bork of Yale University and Richard Posner of the University of Chicago, were appointed to the federal appeals courts. In 1986, when Chief Justice Warren Burger announced his retirement from the Supreme Court, Reagan promoted Justice William H. Rehnquist to chief justice and replaced him with Judge Antonin Scalia, who joined Reagan's earlier appointee, Sandra Day O'Connor. Rehnquist and Scalia strongly supported the administration's legal agenda; indeed, they had indirectly helped to shape it.

The administration based many of its positions on separation of powers, federalism, and the competing claims of majority rule and minority rights on Rehnquist's and Scalia's legal writings and judicial opinions.[53]

Reagan's campaign to reconstitute the federal judiciary reached its limit in 1987, when he nominated Judge Bork to the Supreme Court. Bork was perhaps the most prominent conservative legal scholar in the country, a brilliant and outspoken critic of the liberals' recent procedural and programmatic judicial innovations. His appointment almost certainly would have tilted a closely divided Court decisively to the right on controversial issues such as abortion, affirmative action, and the death penalty.[54]

The controversy that greeted Bork's nomination was extraordinary. The public debate that ensued was without parallel in the history of judicial nominations for its partisanship and vitriol. The debate was stoked in part by extensive media and direct-mail campaigns by liberal and conservative interest groups. Equally incendiary were the Senate confirmation hearings, which were broadcast on national television. In five days of questioning before the mostly Democratic Judiciary Committee, Bork abandoned the practice of previous controversial nominees, such as Louis Brandeis in 1916, of letting their records speak for them. Instead, as political scientist David M. O'Brien has noted, "Bork sought to explain, clarify, and amend his twenty-five year record as a Yale Law School professor, as a solicitor general, and as a judge. That broke with tradition and gave the appearance of a public relations campaign."[55]

In a resounding defeat for the Reagan administration, Bork became the twenty-eighth Supreme Court nominee in American history—but only the fourth in the twentieth century—to fail to be confirmed by the Senate. No previous nominee had been battered as badly as Bork during his nearly thirty hours of testimony before the Judiciary Committee. The vote to reject him was 58–42, the widest margin of disapproval in the history of Supreme Court nominations.

In part, Bork's rejection testified to the widespread public resistance to the Reagan administration's social agenda. Although most voters supported cutting taxes and strengthening the nation's defenses, the administration's plan to restore "traditional" American values by retreating from liberal policies on civil rights, abortion, and prayer in the public schools was much more controversial. The breadth of the opposition to Reagan's social agenda was apparent in the vote against Bork, which included thirteen southern Democratic senators and six moderate Republicans.

Bork's rejection also testified to the heightened level of conflict over judicial nominations that has marked the era of divided government, which was ushered in by the elections of 1968. From 1900 to 1968, a period in which the same party usually controlled both the presidency and the Senate, the president's nominees were almost always confirmed; the approval rate was forty-two of forty-five, or 93 percent. Since then, however, institutional combat—usually between a Republican executive and a Democratic legislature—and the expanding policy activism of the judiciary have combined to overtly politicize the judicial appointment process.[56]

Still, the eight years of judicial appointments by Reagan left behind an important and enduring legacy. A minor, although highly publicized, postscript to the Bork nomination was Reagan's next nominee, federal appeals court judge Douglas H. Ginsburg. A young protégé of Bork, Ginsburg was forced to withdraw amid revelations that he had smoked marijuana not only as a student, but also as a law professor. Eventually, the administration nominated a moderate conservative jurist who was acceptable to the Senate, Judge Anthony M. Kennedy.

Because Reagan was the first two-term president since Dwight D. Eisenhower, he was able to select 78 appeals court judges and 290 district court judges, nearly one-half of the entire federal judiciary. In making these appointments, Reagan successfully modified the tradition that lower-court judgeships are mostly a matter of senatorial patronage. He strengthened the president's control over judicial selection by requiring prospective nominees to demonstrate their conservative credentials. In doing so, Reagan ensured that the federal courts, although not prepared to roll back the national government's responsibilities or reverse the civil rights revolution of the 1960s and 1970s, would issue more conservative rulings than in the past.[57]

IMMIGRATION AND NATURALIZATION SERVICE V. CHADHA

The most important Supreme Court decision affecting the presidency during the Reagan years was *Immigration and Naturalization Service v. Chadha,* also known as the legislative veto case.[58] In the half-century since FDR's New Deal expanded the scope of federal activity, Congress increasingly had dealt with complex problems of public policy by writing laws in broad language and granting the executive branch wide discretion on how to implement them. To prevent federal agencies or even the president from exercising this discretion in ways that legislators disapproved, Congress also included in many laws a provision that enabled it to pass judgment on what the executive did. This provision, known as the legislative veto, permitted Congress to overturn an executive regulation or action within a prescribed length of time, often ninety days. The veto requirement ranged in difficulty from a concurrent resolution of both the House and the Senate to an objection by a single designated committee in either house. In all cases, legislative vetoes were final: the president, who can veto ordinary bills passed by Congress, had no power to overturn a legislative veto. From 1932 to 1982 the legislative veto was written into more than 250 laws, including the War Powers Resolution.

On June 23, 1983, the Supreme Court ruled 7–2 that the legislative veto was unconstitutional. The case originated in 1974 when Jagdish Rai Chadha, a Kenyan student who had overstayed his visa, received permission from the INS to remain in the United States. Relying on the legislative veto provision of the Immigration and Naturalization Act of 1952, the House voted in 1975 to deport Chadha. He then sued, challenging the constitutional basis of the House action.

Writing for a majority of justices, Chief Justice Burger argued that the legislative veto violated the Constitution's separation of powers, in particular the "presentment clause" of Article I, section 7, which says that binding actions by Congress must be presented to the president for signature or veto. "The Constitution sought to divide the delegated powers of the new federal government into three defined categories, legislative, executive, and judicial," Burger wrote, "to assure, as nearly as possible, that each Branch of government would confine itself to its assigned responsibility." In a blistering dissent, Justice Byron R. White complained that having allowed the legislature to delegate substantial authority to the executive ever since the legal controversy over the New Deal, the Court was foolish to deny Congress its best tool for overseeing how that authority was exercised.

The *Chadha* decision turned out to be a less decisive victory for the presidency than it seemed at the time. Since the Court's ruling, Congress has continued to pass laws that contain legislative veto provisions, most of which require the executive to obtain the approval of the House and Senate appropriations committees. Indeed, more legislative vetoes have been enacted since the *Chadha* decision than were passed prior to it. Furthermore, various de facto legislative vetoes have been implemented through informal agreements between Congress and the executive. The 1996 Contract with America Advancement Act, which restricted the payment of public benefits to substance abusers, included a "report and wait" provision that requires an executive agency to submit a report to each house of Congress on any significant rule it issues. For these "major rules," the statute grants Congress a minimum of sixty days to review the measure, during which time it may pass a joint disapproval resolution rejecting it. Although some critics have argued that the availability of "report and wait" provisions and other devices that allow Congress to scrutinize executive action has rendered *Chadha* largely irrelevant, congressional oversight has decreased significantly since the mid-1970s. Any congressional vote to reject an executive rule under the Contract with America Advancement Act must be signed by the president to take effect. More broadly, Andrew Rudalevige has written,

After two popular terms as president, Ronald Reagan passed leadership of the "Reagan Revolution" to the newly inaugurated President George H. W. Bush.

"vigorous [congressional committee] hearings on matters of policy have dropped off sharply."[59]

THE 1988 ELECTION AND THE CONTINUATION OF DIVIDED GOVERNMENT

Reagan did not transform either Washington or national politics completely. But he did strengthen the Republican beachhead in the federal government, solidifying his party's recent dominance of the presidency and providing more and better opportunities for conservatives to attain positions of influence. At the same time, Reagan's two terms witnessed an intensification of the struggle between the executive and the legislature.

The era of divided government that began in 1968 has been marked not just by differences between the president and Congress about public policy, but also by each branch's harsh assaults on the other. Republican efforts to enhance the unilateral powers of the executive and to circumvent legislative restrictions on presidential conduct have been matched by Democratic initiatives to burden the executive with smothering oversight by congressional committees and statutory limits on presidential power.

A major, if not the main, forum for partisan conflict during the Reagan years was a series of investigations in which the Democrats and the Republicans sought to discredit one another. From the early 1970s to the mid-1980s the number of indictments brought by federal prosecutors against national, state, and local officials increased tenfold. These indictments involved more than a dozen members of Congress, several federal judges, and a substantial number of high-ranking executive officials. As political scientist Morris P. Fiorina has noted, "Divided government encourages a full airing of any and all misdeeds, real and imagined."[60]

To be sure, the heightened legal scrutiny of public officials was in part a response to the Watergate scandal. To prevent another Nixon-style "Saturday night massacre" of a special prosecutor, Congress passed the Ethics in Government Act of 1978, which provided for the appointment of independent counsels to investigate allegations of criminal activity by executive officials. Not surprisingly, divided government encouraged the exploitation of the act for partisan purposes. In the 1980s congressional Democrats found themselves in a position to demand criminal investigations and possible jail sentences for their Republican opponents in the executive branch. When Bill Clinton became president in 1993, congressional Republicans turned the tables with a vengeance. As partisan disagreements were transformed into criminal charges, disgrace and imprisonment joined electoral defeat as the risks of political combat.[61] Moreover, investigations under the new ethics statute tended to deflect attention from legitimate constitutional and policy debates and to focus the attention of Congress, the news media, and citizens on scandals.

Institutional polarization and divided government did not end with Reagan's retirement in 1989. On November 8, 1988, when the voters elected a Republican president, George H. W. Bush, and a Democratic Congress, it was the fifth time in the previous six presidential elections that they had divided control of the government between the parties. In contrast, when Eisenhower took the oath of office for the second time in 1957, he was the first president since Grover Cleveland in 1885 to begin a term with even one house of Congress controlled by the opposition party.

Vice President Bush's easy victory over his Democratic opponent, Massachusetts governor Michael Dukakis, was in one sense a triumph for Reagan. Bush won the support of almost 80 percent of the voters, who said they approved of Reagan's performance as president.[62] Like Andrew Jackson, who in 1836 had aided Martin Van Buren, the last incumbent vice president to be elected president, Reagan proved to be unusually helpful to his vice president, both in his popularity and in his active support during the campaign.[63]

Yet Bush's triumph was limited. Never before had a new president—elected by a 426–111 electoral vote landslide, no less—had to endure the other party gaining ground on election day in the House, the Senate, the state governorships, and the state legislatures.[64] Never before had the voters given a newly elected president fewer fellow partisans in Congress than they gave Bush.

Never had the constitutional system of "separated institutions sharing powers" been characterized by such clear partisan segmentation.

Divided government was nothing new at the time Bush became president. Of his four most recent predecessors, only Carter had served with a Congress controlled by the president's party. But the intensity of the division between the parties had grown, aggravating the differences between the branches. When Nixon and Ford were in the White House, the majority of Democrats in Congress were liberals, but a significant minority were southern conservatives who often supported the Republican president. Similarly, although most congressional Republicans in this era were conservatives, several were northeastern or Pacific Coast liberals who often voted with the Democrats. By the time Bush became president, southern voters had replaced almost all of their conservative Democrats in Congress with Republicans and northeastern voters had replaced the vast majority of liberal Republicans with Democrats.[65] Since the time of Bush's election, divided government has meant that Congress is controlled not just by the opposite party from the president, but by an ideologically united opposition party.

THE BUSH PRESIDENCY

The story of the Bush presidency is briefly, if oversimply, told: triumph in foreign affairs, failure in domestic policy. Unfortunately for Bush, in November 1992 the voters cared more about the latter than they did about the former. In his bid for reelection, the president was soundly defeated by Bill Clinton, the Democratic governor of Arkansas.

FOREIGN AFFAIRS

By experience and interest, George Bush was strongly oriented toward foreign policy. Although international affairs had not been a prominent theme of his election campaign in 1988, it was in a sense the theme of his career. Before becoming president, Bush had served as the American ambassador to the United Nations, the emissary to China, and the director of the Central Intelligence Agency. In the diplomatic arena, Bush was the most widely traveled vice president in history. Through these positions, he had cultivated a wide personal acquaintance with world leaders. As president, Bush spent hours at a time touching base with his fellow presidents and prime ministers by telephone. He also chose strong foreign policy advisers: former Reagan chief of staff and secretary of the Treasury James A. Baker III as secretary of state, former Ford chief of staff Richard B. Cheney as secretary of defense, former air force general Brent Scowcroft as national security adviser (a position he had held in the Ford administration), and former Reagan national security adviser and army general Colin Powell as chairman of the Joint

Chiefs of Staff.[66] Once they were selected, Bush forged his advisers into a cohesive team.

Bush's accomplishments in foreign policy nearly spanned the globe. He inherited two simmering problems in Latin America from the Reagan administration: one in Nicaragua and the other in Panama. In 1989 Bush was able to work out an agreement with Democratic congressional leaders on Nicaragua, the most acrimonious issue that had divided Reagan from Congress. Although Bush and Secretary of State Baker were contra supporters, they understood that Congress could not be persuaded to approve new military assistance to the anticommunist Nicaraguan rebels. Determined to find a bipartisan solution that would end the long and enervating interbranch conflict over contra aid, Baker and congressional leaders struck a deal to provide $4.5 million a month in nonlethal assistance to the contras for a limited period. The administration then roused sufficient pressure from Europe, the Soviet Union, Latin America, and Democratic members of Congress to persuade the Marxist Sandinista government of Nicaragua to conduct a fair election in February 1990. To Bush's delight, the Sandinistas lost.

Bush acted militarily rather than diplomatically to accomplish his main objective in Panama, which was to remove from power the anti-American dictator, Gen. Manuel Noriega. In Bush's view, Noriega's offenses were legion: election fraud, money laundering, clandestine arms trading, and drug trafficking. (The Panamanian leader had been indicted on the latter charge by a U.S. federal grand jury in 1988.) Matters came to a head when Noriega annulled the results of a presidential election. On December 15, 1989, the Panamanian legislature accorded him "maximum leader" status in a self-declared "state of war" with the United States. Five days later, Bush responded by sending twelve thousand troops to the Canal Zone to join the twelve thousand already stationed there to capture Noriega and return him to American soil to stand trial. Guillermo Endara, the winner of the annulled election, was sworn in as president. Operation Just Cause, as Bush named the Panama invasion, was not only the largest American military effort since Vietnam, but also was considerably more successful.

In Europe, Bush oversaw the collapse of the Soviet empire and, soon after, of the Soviet Union itself. He was encouraging but not intrusive in 1989 and 1990 when first Poland, then East Germany, and then the other Soviet-dominated governments of Eastern Europe collapsed, followed in 1991 by the dissolution of the Soviet Union. Critics variously charged that the president was either too reticent in publicly celebrating communism's fall or too willing to interfere in other countries' affairs. In truth, Bush adroitly avoided both extremes. A more assertive policy may well have provoked a defensive, even military, response from the Soviets. A less supportive one could have turned the newly free and democratic governments of Eastern Europe against the

United States. Meanwhile, Bush responded to the fall of communism with substantial but not draconian reductions in defense spending.

In the Middle East, Bush's major accomplishment was to assemble a large and diverse multinational coalition to support and finance his Operation Desert Shield campaign against Iraq and its brutal leader, Saddam Hussein. The campaign, which culminated in 1991 in the Persian Gulf War, began within hours of Iraq's military occupation of Kuwait, a neighboring oil-rich state, on August 1, 1990. Working the phone, Bush rallied the leaders of the Soviet Union, China, Japan, Europe, and several Arab nations in support of his strategy of diplomatic, economic, and military pressure on Iraq. He also dispatched nearly half a million American soldiers to Saudi Arabia and persuaded the other members of the coalition to pay $54 billion of the operation's $61 billion final cost.

When Hussein remained adamant in his refusal to withdraw from Kuwait, Bush won strong approval from the United Nations on November 29, 1990, and narrow approval from Congress on January 12, 1991, to drive Iraq from Kuwait if it did not leave voluntarily by January 15. After the deadline came and went, Operation Desert Shield became Operation Desert Storm. On January 16 American and other allied bombers began a thirty-eight-day air campaign to cripple Iraq's military and communications infrastructure. On February 23 the ground invasion was launched, and in four days the allies' military offensive drove the Iraqi forces out of Kuwait and severely weakened Saddam Hussein's capacity to threaten neighboring nations and dominate the world's petroleum market. Nevertheless, Hussein remained in power, much to Bush's surprise and disappointment. The president had expected that military defeat would lead to Hussein's overthrow by the Iraqis themselves.

Substantively and politically, the victory over Iraq was the high point of the Bush presidency—it was all downhill from there. The patriotic fervor aroused by the Gulf War served only to conceal fundamental differences about foreign policy between the president and Congress that foreshadowed a renewal of institutional conflict. The January 1991 vote that authorized Bush to use troops against Iraq had revealed a legislature deeply divided along partisan lines. Not since the War of 1812 had Congress so narrowly approved the use of military force. Although Republicans lined up solidly in favor of the president (42–2 in the Senate and 165–3 in the House), Democrats voted against authorizing military action by large margins: 45–10 in the Senate and 179–86 in the House. After the vote, the Bush administration issued a statement denying that the president needed legislative approval to implement the UN resolution authorizing force against Iraq. Viewing this conflict between Bush and Congress as another episode of the "National Security Constitution," Richard Pious criticized the administration's statement as the most recent example of "presidents . . . playing a shell game, claiming to act according to law yet dispensing with statutory law at their convenience in national security matters."[67]

Although he was not able to transcend partisan differences over foreign policy, Bush displayed a deft and steady hand in this arena throughout his four years as president. After losing the 1992 election, he was the most active lame-duck president in history. In December 1992 and January 1993 Bush dispatched twenty-five thousand American troops to restore social order and bring humanitarian relief to the starvation-plagued, warlord-dominated African nation of Somalia. He signed the North American Free Trade Agreement (NAFTA) with Canada and Mexico, eased restrictions on American trade with Vietnam, ordered the aerial bombing of some sections of Iraq to enforce compliance with the agreement that ended the Gulf War, and signed with Russian president Boris Yeltsin a second Strategic Arms Reduction Treaty (START II), which promised to reduce the number of nuclear warheads in the American and former Soviet arsenals from nearly twenty-four thousand to no more than sixty-five hundred. Finally, Bush outraged congressional Democrats by pardoning former secretary of defense Caspar Weinberger and five other high Reagan administration officials for any crimes they may have committed during the Iran-contra affair.

Bush's pardons represented a Republican protest against the independent counsel law. The president and his advisers were furious that Iran-contra special prosecutor Lawrence Walsh had handed down his indictment of Weinberger and the other officials just four days before the 1992 election. Moreover, Walsh's announcement charged not only that Weinberger had lied when he denied taking extensive notes during Reagan administration meetings about ransoming hostages from Lebanon, but also that as Reagan's vice president, Bush was involved in at least one of those meetings. Bush had claimed that he was not "in the loop" when the arms-for-hostages deal was discussed.[68] The president and his supporters cried foul, claiming that Walsh had engaged in improper politicking.

Bush offered no defense of his role in the Iran-contra affair. But in his postelection announcement of the pardon, he criticized the Ethics in Government Act, especially its independent counsel provisions, for "a profoundly troubling development in the political and legal climate of our country: the criminalization of policy differences." Reflecting on nearly two decades of institutional combat, the president proposed that these differences be "addressed in the political arena, without the Damocles sword of criminality hanging over the heads of some combatants. . . . [T]he proper forum is the voting booth, not the courtroom."[69]

Although congressional Democrats and the press attacked Bush for pardoning the Reagan administration officials and criticizing the Ethics in

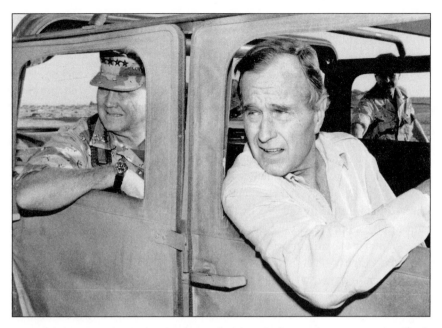

In November 1990 President Bush and Gen. Norman Schwarzkopf reviewed U.S. troops stationed in the Persian Gulf region. Three months later the United Sates led a coalition of twenty-eight nations to victory over Iraq in Kuwait.

Government Act, Bush had offered the first effective defense by a president against independent prosecutions. "Walsh had become the issue by the end" of the controversy, political scientist Katy Harriger has observed, "in large measure . . . through the effective creation of doubt by his targets about his methods and motives." Most important, the Iran-contra investigation precipitated a raging debate about the Ethics in Government Act. As Harriger concluded, "The real question is whether something designed to promote public confidence is in fact undermining it."[70] This question would become all the more important during the presidency of Bush's successor, Bill Clinton.

DOMESTIC AFFAIRS

In his 1988 presidential campaign, Bush had portrayed himself as the true heir to Reagan in domestic policy, albeit a "kinder and gentler" version of the conservative president, as he put it in his acceptance speech to the Republican national convention. Bush's "Read my lips: no new taxes" campaign pledge was joined to a promise to be the "education president" and the "environmental president." Bush carried the theme of consolidation past the election. His inaugural address not only thanked Reagan "for the wonderful things that you have done for America," but also was laden with repeated invocations of words such as *continuity, continuance,* and *continuum.* In April 1989 Bush reaffirmed his status as Reagan's heir by telling reporters, "We didn't come in here throwing the rascals out." His chief of staff, former New Hampshire governor John Sununu, described the Bush administration as a "friendly take-over" of its predecessor.[71]

In contrast to Reagan, however, Bush gave almost all of his attention as president to his constitutional roles as chief diplomat and commander in chief. International triumphs and crises aside, domestic policy, not foreign policy, usually drives the electoral process.[72] National security and foreign policy had been Republican strong suits in recent elections and had helped to attract some erstwhile opponents—the so-called Reagan Democrats—to the party. By 1992, however, the collapse of the Soviet empire had removed the threat of communism and greatly lessened concerns about national security and foreign policy.[73] On election day only 8 percent of the voters said that foreign policy was an important consideration in their choice of a presidential candidate. Eighty-seven percent of this small group voted for Bush, but many more voters resented what they regarded as his concentration on the world's problems at the expense of their own, especially the economic recession that began in 1990.[74] To be sure, Bush could have done things differently. Riding high politically after the triumph of Operation Desert Storm in March 1991 (his approval rating reached 89 percent), Bush had enjoyed a rare opportunity to try to mobilize Congress in support of a domestic legislative agenda. But he had no such agenda. As Sununu told a conservative audience in November 1990, "There's not a single piece of legislation that needs to be passed in the next two years for this president. In fact, if Congress wants to come together, adjourn, and leave, it's all right with us."[75]

To the extent that Bush did deal with domestic affairs, he was generally unsuccessful. His main challenge, coming after Reagan, was to smooth out the rough edges of his predecessor's generally successful economic policies, especially the huge budget deficits. But Bush failed in this effort. In September 1990 he abandoned his "no new taxes" pledge in return for congressional Democrats' agreement to reduce federal spending over a five-year period and to enact a budgetary reform, dubbed PAYGO, that required all increases in direct spending or revenue decreases to be offset by other spending decreases or revenue increases. Announcing the budget deal at the White House, Bush proclaimed, "It is balanced, it is fair, and in my view, it is what the United States of America needs." A month later, inundated by criticism from conservative, anti-tax Republicans and from voters who were outraged that he had violated his main campaign promise, Bush told reporters that the agreement made him "gag," a sentiment that he maintained through the end of the 1992 election campaign.[76]

Meanwhile, the deficit continued to rise. The accumulated shortfalls of Bush's four years as president added another trillion dollars to the national debt. The reason for the growing deficits was that, although inflation remained low and the Federal Reserve Board had pushed down interest rates, the economy was suffering in other ways that had strong budgetary side effects. Real economic growth averaged about 1 percent per year during the Bush administration, the lowest rate in any four-year period since the Great Depression. In response, Americans' real per capita income fell, unemployment rose to 7.8 percent, and more businesses failed than during any administration since the Hoover years. Because of the weak economy, tax revenues decreased even as government expenditures increased to meet the rising demand for unemployment insurance, food stamps, and other forms of public assistance.

Bush's record was at best mixed in his other domestic challenge: to soften the hard edges of Reagan's conservative approach to the environment and civil rights, which had been unpopular even when Reagan was president.[77] Bush acted to remedy this neglect by signing the Clean Air Act of 1990 and the Civil Rights Act of 1991. But in each case, his commitment to reform was less than total. The Civil Rights Act became law only after a long and acrimonious battle with Congress over the issue of racial quotas. The Clean Air Act was soon undermined by the Council on Competitiveness, a regulatory review board chaired by Vice President Dan Quayle that served as business's court of last resort in the Bush administration.

Bush's failures in domestic policy were failures of purpose and interest, not of political skill. The president wooed members of Congress and reporters with an endless series of White House visits, games of golf and horseshoes, personal notes, and other favors and courtesies. Such encounters, along with scores of formal and informal news conferences, helped Bush, who was a poor speechmaker, to get his message out to the American people. Partly as a result of these efforts, he was able to persuade Congress to sustain all but one of his vetoes. Bush's 98 percent success rate (only one of forty-six vetoes was overridden) was unprecedentedly high for a president facing a Congress controlled by the other party.[78]

Bush also shepherded two Supreme Court nominations through the Democratic Senate without losing any, something Reagan had been unable to do. This was no easy task. New Hampshire judge David Souter (1990) was controversial because of his alleged lack of appropriate experience, and federal appeals court judge Clarence Thomas (1991), a black conservative, was charged with sexual harassment by a former employee, Anita Hill, in a series of televised public hearings. In addition, Bush named 37 federal appeals court judges and 148 federal district court judges during his presidency. All of them won Senate approval.

Although the White House boasted of securing a conservative majority on the Supreme Court, Souter turned out to be much more liberal than Bush expected and the fierce battle waged over the Thomas nomination left the nation uneasy. The Senate confirmed Thomas by a margin of 52–48, the closest Supreme Court vote in more than a century and one that reflected the same sort of bitter partisan division that had characterized the Bork hearings. Thomas was spared Bork's fate by the votes he received from eleven Democratic senators, most of them southerners, whose support was encouraged by the strong base that the judge, a Georgia native, cultivated among southern blacks.

The heightened level of conflict over the judiciary in the era of divided government extended to legislative battles about court rulings, such as the one that led Congress to pass the 1991 Civil Rights Act. The act, championed by congressional Democrats, nullified nine previous Supreme Court rulings in order to shift the burden of proof in antidiscrimination lawsuits from employees to employers. Bush had vetoed a similar bill in 1990, arguing that it would lead to hiring quotas for minorities and women. But in the wake of the explosive Thomas hearings, he decided to sign the modified version of the bill that Congress passed in 1991. At the same time, Bush issued a "signing statement"—that is, a written statement by the president interpreting the law being signed—that offered a narrower construction of the act than Democratic members of Congress had intended when they passed it.[79]

Bush's signing statement for the Civil Rights Act of 1991 was the most controversial use of a tactic that he sometimes employed during his presidency to shape legislation. As Bush described this practice in an address delivered at Princeton University, "[On] many occasions during my presidency, I have stated that statutory provisions violating the Constitution have no binding legal force."[80] Such signing statements declared certain features of congressional statutes null and void by executive fiat. Previous presidents had used signing statements, and the Reagan administration was the first to deploy these actions as part of a comprehensive plan to strengthen the administrative presidency.[81] But Bush issued more of them, and with greater consequences, than his predecessors. In doing so, he significantly expanded a method by which the president could avoid directly confronting Congress with a veto, yet still pursue his legislative objectives. "Taken overall," a former general counsel of the House of Representatives has written, "the 1989–1992 outpouring of signing statements that purposed to strike down or revise new laws staked a major presidential claim to personal power."[82]

It soon became clear that institutional conflict between Bush and the Democratic Congress would not be confined to legislation and nominations. As the 1992 elections approached in the midst of a serious recession, the Bush administration turned its attention to "liberating the economy" from new government regulations spawned by legislation on the environment, consumer protection, and discrimination against the disabled.[83] The Council on Competitiveness assumed increasing importance in executive deliberations, putting regulatory agencies on notice that the administration expected them to justify the cost to business and consumers of existing and proposed regulations. One liberal interest group complained that the president was "waging war" on his own agencies.[84]

Bush ran against the Democratic Congress as well as his opponent, Bill Clinton, in 1992. In the end, however, the Democrats not only captured the presidency, but also retained control of both houses of Congress, temporarily ending twelve years of divided rule in American government. In his 1989 inaugural address, Bush had urged that harsh ideological and partisan conflict give way to a new spirit of cooperation. Yet serious substantive disagreements between the president and Congress defied Bush's efforts to make "the old bipartisanship new again." Some political analysts had regarded divided partisan control of the presidency and Congress as the healthy consequence of the voters' desire to mute the ideological polarization that characterizes modern party politics. But the Bush years dramatically revealed how thoroughly divided government obscures political responsibility and mires the president and Congress in petty, virulent clashes that undermine respect for the nation's political institutions. Clinton's victory, then, represented more than a rejection of the incumbent president. It also expressed the voters' hope that the institutional combat they had witnessed during the era of divided government would abate.

NOTES

1. Richard E. Neustadt, *Presidential Power and the Modern Presidents: The Politics of Leadership from Roosevelt to Reagan,* 4th ed. (New York: Free Press, 1990), 230.

2. Jeffrey K. Tulis, *The Rhetorical Presidency* (Princeton: Princeton University Press, 1987), 189.

3. On Reagan's use of rhetoric, see William Ker Muir Jr., *The Bully Pulpit: The Presidential Leadership of Ronald Reagan* (San Francisco: Institute for Contemporary Studies, 1992); and Hugh Heclo, "Ronald Reagan and the American Public Philosophy," in *The Reagan Presidency: Pragmatic Conservatism and Its Legacies,* eds. Elliot Brownlee and Hugh Davis Graham (Lawrence: University Press of Kansas, 2003). Heclo argues that Reagan "is among that handful of American politicians, and a much smaller group of Presidents, who have conducted their careers primarily as a struggle about ideas" (18).

4. Ronald Reagan, "A Time for Choosing," October 27, 1964, in *Ronald Reagan Talks to America,* ed. Richard M. Scaife (Old Greenwich, Conn.: Devin Adair, 1983), 4–5. See also Muir, *Bully Pulpit,* 175–176.

5. "Ronald Reagan's First Inaugural Address," in *The Evolving Presidency: Landmark Documents, 1787–2010,* ed. Michael Nelson (Washington, D.C.: CQ Press, 2012), 253–259.

6. Heclo, "Ronald Reagan and the American Public Philosophy," 23.

7. *New York Times,* July 20, 1980, E20.

8. William E. Leuchtenburg, *In the Shadow of FDR: From Harry Truman to Ronald Reagan,* rev. ed. (Ithaca: Cornell University Press, 1985), 210. See also Alonzo L. Hamby, *Liberalism and Its Challengers: From F. D. R. to Bush,* 2nd ed. (New York: Oxford University Press, 1992), chap. 8.

9. One of Reagan's speechwriters claimed that Calvin Coolidge—not FDR—was the president who most affected Reagan during both his early years and his presidency. In crafting Reagan's addresses, speechwriters often studied those of Coolidge. Rep. Dana Rohrabacher, R-Calif., former speechwriter to President Reagan, interview by Sidney M. Milkis, July 31, 1989.

10. *Public Papers of the Presidents of the United States: Ronald Reagan, 1983* (Washington, D.C.: Government Printing Office, 1984), 1:364. See also Muir, *Bully Pulpit,* 74–78.

11. Richard Reeves, *President Reagan: The Triumph of Imagination* (New York: Simon and Schuster, 2006), xiv.

12. John Lewis Gaddis, *The Cold War: A New History* (New York: Penguin, 2006), 217, 196.

13. Marc Landy and Martin A. Levin, "The Hedgehog and the Fox," *Brandeis Review* 7 (Fall 1987): 17–19.

14. Charles O. Jones, "Ronald Reagan and the U.S. Congress," in *The Reagan Legacy,* ed. Charles O. Jones (Chatham, N.J.: Chatham House, 1988), 37.

15. Tip O'Neill, with William Novak, *Man of the House* (New York: St. Martin's Press, 1987), 410, 413.

16. Hedrick Smith, "The President as Coalition Builder: Reagan's First Year," in *Rethinking the Presidency,* ed. Thomas E. Cronin (Boston: Little, Brown, 1982), 274.

17. House of Representatives, Committee on Appropriations, *Views and Estimates on the Budget Proposed for Fiscal Year 1983,* 97th Cong., 2nd sess., 1982, 12.

18. Quoted in Smith, "President as Coalition Builder," 278.

19. Quoted in Samuel Kernell, *Going Public: New Strategies of Presidential Leadership* (Washington, D.C.: CQ Press, 1986), 118.

20. Tulis, *Rhetorical Presidency,* 197.

21. James P. Pfiffner, *The President and Economic Policy* (Philadelphia: Institute for the Study of Human Issues, 1986), 122.

22. Quoted in William Greider, *The Education of David Stockman and Other Americans* (New York: Dutton, 1982), 33. See also David Stockman, *The Triumph of Politics: Why the Reagan Revolution Failed* (New York: Harper and Row, 1986), 79–99.

23. Fred I. Greenstein, "Nine Presidents in Search of a Modern Presidency," in *Leadership in the Modern Presidency,* ed. Fred I. Greenstein (Cambridge: Harvard University Press, 1988), 345.

24. "Remarks of the President to the 12th Annual Conservative Political Action Conference," Sheraton-Washington Hotel, Washington, D.C., March 1, 1985 (mimeographed copy provided to the authors by the White House).

25. On the transformation of party politics, see A. James Reichley, "The Rise of National Parties," in *The New Direction in American Politics,* ed. John E. Chubb and Paul E. Peterson (Washington, D.C.: Brookings, 1985). By the end of the 1980s, Reichley was much less hopeful that the emerging national parties were well suited to perform the historic partisan function of mobilizing public support for political values and governmental policies. See his richly detailed study, *The Life of the Parties: A History of American Political Parties* (New York: Free Press, 1992), esp. chaps. 18–21.

26. David S. Broder, "A Party Leader Who Works at It," *Boston Globe,* October 21, 1985, 14; Mitchell Daniels, assistant to the president for political and governmental affairs, interview by Sidney M. Milkis, June 5, 1986.

27. Dole quoted in Reichley, "Rise of National Parties," 176.

28. Earl Black and Merle Black, *Divided America: The Ferocious Power Struggle in American Politics* (New York: Simon and Schuster, 2007).

29. Alan Ehrenhalt, "Changing South Perils Conservative Coalition," *Congressional Quarterly Weekly Report,* August 1, 1987, 1704.

30. Vin Weber, interview by Sidney M. Milkis, July 28, 1987.

31. James M. Perry and David Shribman, "Reagan Era Restored Faith in Government until Recent Slippage," *Wall Street Journal,* November 30, 1987, 1, 13. See also William

Schneider, "The Political Legacy of the Reagan Years," in *The Reagan Legacy,* ed. Sidney Blumenthal and Thomas Byrne Edsall (New York: Pantheon Books, 1988); and Walter Dean Burnham, "The Reagan Heritage," in *The Election of 1988: Report and Interpretations,* ed. Gerald M. Pomper (Chatham, N.J.: Chatham House, 1989).

32. Benjamin Ginsberg and Martin Shefter, *Politics by Other Means: Politicians, Prosecutors, and the Press from Watergate to Whitewater,* rev. and updated ed. (New York: Norton, 1999), esp. chap. 5.

33. *Final Report of the Independent Counsel for Iran/Contra Matters,* vol. 1: *Investigations and Prosecutions,* Lawrence E. Walsh, Independent Counsel, Washington, D.C., August 4, 1993, esp. chap. 27.

34. *Report of the Congressional Committees Investigating the Iran-Contra Affair,* with supplemental minority and additional views, H. Doc. 100-433, S. Doc. 100-216, 100th Cong., 1st sess., November 13, 1987, 501 (emphasis in original). See also Lou Cannon's biography of Reagan, which covers the Iran-contra episode in great detail. Cannon reports that

> Reagan, who knew little about how any federal program operated and was largely uninterested in matters of process, may not have known specifically that proceeds from the Iran arms sales were being placed into accounts for the contras. . . . But what Reagan certainly knew and consistently conveyed to his subordinates was that the contras needed far more help than Congress was willing to give them. Because of this knowledge and belief, Reagan encouraged Americans and friendly foreign leaders to help the contra cause. Oliver North may have gone beyond his instructions, but he was carrying out missions that Reagan wanted accomplished, both in his efforts to free the hostages and to help the Nicaraguan rebels. It is no wonder that Reagan considered North a national hero.

> Cannon, *President Reagan: The Role of a Lifetime* (New York: Simon and Schuster, 1991), 718.

35. *Report of the Congressional Committees Investigating the Iran-Contra Affair,* 515 (emphasis in original). The division among those who served on the House and Senate select committees was highly partisan, but not completely so. Three Republican senators signed the majority document, which was far more condemning of the administration's actions: Warren Rudman of New Hampshire; William Cohen of Maine; and Paul Tribble of Virginia. The House committee divided strictly along party lines.

36. Richard M. Pious, "Prerogative Power and the Reagan Presidency: A Review Essay," *Political Science Quarterly* 106 (Fall 1991): 499–510.

37. Bert A. Rockman, "The Style and Organization of the Reagan Presidency," in Jones, *Reagan Legacy,* 10.

38. On the Reagan administration's efforts to reform Social Security, see Martha Derthick and Steven M. Teles, "Riding the Third Rail: Social Security," in Brownlee and Graham, *The Reagan Presidency.*

39. Stockman, *Triumph of Politics,* 193.

40. Pamela Fessler, "Disability Measure Wins Unanimous Approval," *Congressional Quarterly Weekly Report,* September 22, 1984, 2332–4. For a comprehensive discussion of the running battle between the Reagan administration and the federal courts over statutory interpretation, see R. Shep Melnick, *Between the Lines: Interpreting Welfare Rights* (Washington, D.C.: Brookings, 1994).

41. Richard A. Harris and Sidney M. Milkis, *The Politics of Regulatory Change: A Tale of Two Agencies,* 2nd ed. (New York: Oxford University Press, 1996). The "midnight rules" were issued by the Carter administration between December 29, 1980, and January 23, 1981. The strong disagreement in regulatory philosophy between Carter's appointees and the incoming conservative Republican administration intensified the traditional last-minute attempt by departing officials to push through favored policies. Carter's regulators essentially

cleared their desks of all rules pending at the end of 1980, producing more than two hundred new regulations in both proposed and final form. The rules, which represented a wide range of social causes for which Reagan and his regulatory task force had little sympathy, fell largely within the purview of the Environmental Protection Agency and the Occupational Safety and Health Administration. See Edward Paul Fuchs, *Presidents, Management, and Regulation* (Englewood Cliffs, N.J.: Prentice Hall, 1988), 85–90.

42. Greenstein, "Nine Presidents," 345.

43. I. M. Destler, "Reagan and the World: An Awesome Stubbornness," in Jones, *Reagan Legacy,* 249–253.

44. Burnham, "Reagan Heritage," 1.

45. Rockman, "Style and Organization of the Reagan Presidency," 11.

46. Hamby, *Liberalism and Its Challengers,* 385.

47. Sidney Blumenthal, *The Rise of the Counterestablishment: From Conservative Ideology to Political Power* (New York: Times Books, 1986), 9.

48. William Brock, secretary, Department of Labor, interview by Sidney M. Milkis, August 12, 1987.

49. On the New Deal and its legacy for the presidency and party system, see Sidney M. Milkis, *The President and the Parties: The Transformation of the American Party System since the New Deal* (New York: Oxford University Press, 1993).

50. Ginsberg and Shefter, *Politics by Other Means,* 148.

51. R. Shep Melnick, "The Courts, Congress, and Programmatic Rights," in *Remaking American Politics,* ed. Richard A. Harris and Sidney M. Milkis (Boulder: Westview Press, 1989). See also Mark Silverstein and Benjamin Ginsberg, "The Supreme Court and the New Politics of Judicial Power," *Political Science Quarterly* 102 (Fall 1987): 371–388.

52. Ginsberg and Shefter, *Politics by Other Means,* 154–156.

53. David M. O'Brien, "The Reagan Judges: His Most Enduring Legacy?" in Jones, *Reagan Legacy,* 86–87.

54. Ibid., 90.

55. Ibid., 91.

56. For a discussion of the politics of judicial appointments under the conditions of divided rule, see Michael Nelson, "Constitutional Aspects of the Elections," in *The Elections of 1988,* ed. Michael Nelson (Washington, D.C.: CQ Press, 1989), 201–205.

57. David A. Yalof, "The Presidency and the Judiciary," in *The Presidency and the Political System,* 8th ed., ed. Michael Nelson (Washington, D.C.: CQ Press, 2006), 481–507.

58. "Immigration and Naturalization Service v. Chadha," in Nelson, *Evolving Presidency,* 259–269.

59. Andrew Rudalevige, *The New Imperial Presidency: Renewing Presidential Power After Watergate* (Ann Arbor: University of Michigan Press, 2005), 178.

60. Morris P. Fiorina, *Congress: Keystone of the Washington Establishment,* 2nd ed. (New Haven: Yale University Press, 1989), 164, n. 27; Ginsberg and Shefter, *Politics by Other Means,* 23–46; Nelson, "Constitutional Aspects of the Elections," 201. For an excellent account of the cultural and institutional bases of scandal in U.S. politics, see Suzanne Garment, *Scandal: The Culture of Mistrust in American Politics* (New York: Random House, 1991).

61. Linda Greenhouse, "Ethics in Government: The Price of Good Intentions," *New York Times,* February 1, 1998, sec. 1, 5; Cass Sunstein, "Unchecked, Unbalanced: The Independent Counsel Act," *American Prospect* (May-June 1998): 20–27.

62. Nelson, "Constitutional Aspects of the Elections," 192.

63. Ibid., 191–192.

64. The Democrats gained two seats in the House, one in the Senate, one governorship, and more than a dozen seats in the state legislatures.

65. Keith T. Poole and Howard Rosenthal, *Congress: A Political History of Roll Call Voting* (New York: Oxford University Press, 1997).

66. Cheney was not Bush's first choice as secretary of defense; it was former Texas Republican senator John Tower. But in a partisan display characteristic of the divided

government era, the Senate rejected Tower's nomination, the first time in history that a newly elected president's cabinet nominee had not been confirmed. Ironically, the Senate rejected Tower on the recommendation of the committee he formerly had headed—Armed Services.

67. Pious, "Prerogative Power and the Reagan Presidency," 510, n. 27.

68. Irvin Molotsky, "Bush Aides Urging Weinberger Pardon in Iran-Arms Affair," *New York Times,* November 7, 1992, 1; "Prosecutor in Iran-Contra Rebukes Dole," *New York Times,* November 11, 1992, D2; "Inquiry into Iran-Contra Prosecutor Is Asked," *New York Times,* November 12, 1992, A21.

69. "Text of President Bush's Statement on the Pardon of Weinberger and Others," *New York Times,* December 25, 1992, A22.

70. Harriger quoted in Greenhouse, "Ethics in Government: The Price of Good Intentions."

71. Quoted in Michael Duffy and Dan Goodgame, *Marching in Place: The Status Quo Presidency of George Bush* (New York: Simon and Schuster, 1992), 19.

72. Stephen Hess and Michael Nelson, "Foreign Policy: Dominance and Decisiveness in Presidential Elections," in *The Elections of 1984,* ed. Michael Nelson (Washington, D.C.: CQ Press, 1985), 129–154.

73. James Ceaser and Andrew Busch, *Upside Down and Inside Out: The 1992 Elections and American Politics* (Lanham, Md.: Rowman and Littlefield, 1993), 15.

74. Laurence I. Barrett, "A New Coalition for the 1990s," *Time,* November 16, 1992, 47–48.

75. Duffy and Goodgame, *Marching in Place,* 70–71, 283.

76. Ibid., 83, 285.

77. Erwin C. Hargrove and Michael Nelson, "The Presidency: Reagan and the Cycle of Politics and Policy," in Nelson, *Elections of 1984,* 201–202.

78. Congress's one successful veto override came on October 5, 1992, on a bill to reregulate cable television.

79. The Civil Rights Act of 1991 restored the legal standard established by the Supreme Court's ruling in *Griggs v. Duke Power Company,* 401 U.S. 424 (1971), which held employers responsible for justifying employment practices that were avowedly race- and gender-neutral but in practice had an "adverse impact" on women and minorities. The 1989 ruling in *Wards Cove Packing Co. v. Atonio,* 490 U.S. 642 (1989), had shifted the burden, declaring that workers had to show that companies had no legitimate need for the challenged practices. The new legislation instructed the courts to follow the standard of *Griggs* and eight related rulings prior to *Ward's Cove.* Bush agreed to sign the 1991 act, but he proclaimed in his signing statement that documents introduced by Senate Republican leader Robert Dole, which offered a narrow interpretation of the statute, would "be treated as authoritative guidance by all officials in the executive branch with respect to the law of disparate impact as well as other matters covered in the document." Joan Biskupic, "Bush Signs Anti-Job Bias Bill amid Furor over Preferences," *Congressional Quarterly Weekly Report,* November 23, 1991, 3463.

80. Christopher S. Kelley, " A Matter of Direction: the Reagan Administration, the Signing Statement, and the 1986 Westlaw Decision," *William and Mary Bill of Rights Journal* 16, issue 1 (2007): 283–306

81. Bush quoted in Charles Tiefer, *The Semi-Sovereign Presidency: The Bush Administration's Strategy for Governing without Congress* (Boulder: Westview Press, 1994), 3.

82. Ibid.

83. Jonathan Rauch, "The Regulatory President," *National Journal,* November 30, 1991, 2902–6.

84. OMB Watch, "President Bush's Regulatory Moratorium," *OMB Watch Alert,* January 24, 1992.

CHAPTER 13

Bill Clinton and the Modern Presidency

F
rom the beginning, Bill Clinton's presidency was marked by an unusual number of "firsts." With his electoral victory in 1992, he became the first Democrat to be elected president in sixteen years. Reelection in 1996 made him the first Democrat to win a second term since Franklin D. Roosevelt. The 1996 presidential election was also the first in history in which a Democratic candidate was able to surmount a Republican victory in the accompanying congressional elections. In policy terms, Clinton became the first president to balance the federal budget since fiscal year 1969.

The Clinton presidency was also marked by some less desirable firsts, at least from the standpoint of the president and his supporters. Clinton was the first two-term president since Woodrow Wilson to win with less than a majority of the popular vote in both of his elections and the only twentieth-century president to gain the office twice with fewer than four hundred electoral votes. By the end of his first hundred days in office, Clinton had a lower public approval rating than any other newly elected president in the history of polling. Finally, he was the first Democratic president to serve more than two years with a Republican Congress.

From January 1998, when the president's sexual relationship with White House intern Monica Lewinsky was revealed, until February 1999, when the Senate voted to acquit him of impeachment charges, Clinton navigated uncharted political waters. He was plagued all year by press and prosecutorial investigations into his relationship with Lewinsky and his efforts to conceal that relationship from the courts. In December 1998 Clinton became the first elected president in history to be impeached by the House of Representatives (Andrew Johnson, the only other impeached president, had succeeded to the office when Abraham Lincoln died). Yet in the November midterm elections, for the first time since 1822, the party of a second-term president gained seats in Congress.

President Clinton's dramatic ups and downs can be attributed both to his qualities as a leader and to the political times in which he served. In some ways, volatility was the story of Clinton's political life. As governor of Arkansas and as president, Clinton's first two years in office were desperately unsuccessful.

410

In other ways, the fluctuations of Clinton's fortunes mirrored the instability of American politics in an era of divided government, strong partisan loyalties in Congress and among Republican and Democratic activists, and widespread public distrust of the political process. Clinton's extraordinary political dexterity often served him well at a time when most Americans tended to resist the programmatic and ideological ambitions of both major parties.

THE ELECTION OF 1992

The 1992 presidential election that brought Clinton to power was no ordinary affair. Perhaps the most remarkable feature of the campaign was the precipitous decline in President George H. W. Bush's political fortunes throughout the year. So formidable was Bush's standing in the polls in 1991 that his reelection, and a fourth consecutive Republican victory, appeared all but inevitable. Bush's post–Gulf War popularity, however, masked the country's profound uneasiness about his seeming indifference to domestic affairs. Moreover, his successful foreign policy exploits suppressed only temporarily tensions within the Republican Party, largely centered on cultural and social issues such as abortion and immigration, which had come to the fore with the end of the cold war.

Bush's experience was a painful reminder of the modern executive's extraordinary isolation.[1] Over the years, the presidency had been freed from the constraints of party, only to be subjected instead to a volatile political environment. The twentieth-century evolution of the office had taught Americans that the president was to serve as their tribune, the embodiment of the popular will. Yet Bush was ill suited to the tasks of public leadership. "When the weight of the [modern office] is put upon a figure as flimsy as George Bush," conservative columnist George F. Will complained, "the presidency buckles."[2]

Bush's 38 percent of the national popular vote in 1992 was the lowest received by an incumbent president since William Howard Taft finished third in 1912. Like Taft, whose bid for reelection was plagued by the presence in the race of Theodore Roosevelt, the former Republican president, Bush was beset by a strong third party candidate, the self-made Texas billionaire H. Ross Perot. In fact, Perot's 19 percent of the popular vote posed the most serious electoral challenge to the two-party system since Roosevelt's Progressive Party campaign.

The comparison between TR and Perot is instructive. Roosevelt's candidacy foretold not only the emergence of an active and expansive national government, but also of presidential elections conducted less by party organizations than by candidates and their personal advisers. Roosevelt and his Democratic rival in the 1912 election, Woodrow Wilson, offered a new concept of political leadership that regarded the president, rather than the party or Congress, as the leading agent of representative government in the United States. The public's acceptance of that concept triggered, in turn, a new dynamic, later enhanced by Franklin D. Roosevelt's approach to leadership and by the emergence of the broadcast media, that subordinated the collective responsibility of the political party to the president's leadership of public opinion. Ronald Reagan's presidency revealed that even conservative chief executives now considered it legitimate, even essential, to rouse the public in the support of their programs.

The Perot campaign underscored just how much presidential politics had been emancipated from the constraints of party. Perot had never held public office of any kind, and his campaign, dominated by thirty-minute "infomercials" and hour-long appearances on talk shows, set a new standard for direct, plebiscitary appeals to the voters without even the pretense of a party campaign. (He added the pretense four years later, running in 1996 as the nominee of the Reform Party, his own short-lived creation.) Turning aside pleas to form a genuine third party from those who were interested in renewing the party system, Perot held no primary elections or nominating convention to launch his candidacy. Instead, he called his supporters to arms on the popular CNN talk show *Larry King Live*.[3] To be sure, Perot's success as an independent candidate was not based merely on a personal following; his campaign aroused supporters who strongly identified with his commitment to fiscal responsibility, campaign finance reform, economic nationalism, and a restrained foreign policy. Indeed, the Perot constituency continued to influence elections and party alignments through the 2004 election.[4] Nevertheless, the plebiscitary style of Perot's leadership raised serious questions about how his personal standing and issue positions could ever become an enduring feature of American politics.

A change in the structure of the media during the 1980s abetted Perot's circumvention of party politics in 1992. With the advent of cable television and the proliferation of political talk shows, candidates had unprecedented opportunities to address the voters directly. These shows served as Perot's early primaries and caucuses. His ratings victories in cable appearances sparked invitations to appear on *Good Morning America* and *Today,* which in one instance gave him two hours to answer viewers' questions.[5] In the end, however, the American people invested their hopes for constructive change more cautiously, in the possibility that Clinton represented a new form of Democratic politics that would cure the ills brought on by the ideological and institutional conflicts of the 1970s and 1980s. Clinton dedicated his campaign to principles and politics that he claimed "transcended" the left-right debate that had immobilized the nation during those two decades. For the central themes of his presidential campaign, Clinton drew on ideas developed by the

Democratic Leadership Council (DLC), a moderate group within the Democratic Party. (He had served as one of the group's leaders in the mid-1980s). As Clinton declared frequently during the 1992 campaign, these ideas represented a new philosophy of government that would "honor middle class values, restore public trust, create a new sense of community, and make America work again." He heralded a "New Covenant" that in the name of "opportunity, responsibility, and community" would seek to constrain the public demands for economic entitlements that had been unleashed by the New Deal.

The essence of Clinton's message was that the long-standing liberal commitment to guarantee economic welfare through entitlement programs such as Social Security, Medicare, Medicaid, and Aid to Families with Dependent Children had gone too far. The main objective of the New Covenant was to correct the tendency of Americans to celebrate individual rights and government entitlements unreservedly, without acknowledging the responsibilities citizens have to each other and to their country. An admirer of John F. Kennedy, Clinton based his philosophy of government on Kennedy's call for a renewed dedication to national community and service, as exemplified by the Peace Corps.

Clinton's New Democratic message appeared to work. To be sure, his 43 percent share of the popular vote was hardly a mandate. Indeed, it was roughly

The 1992 campaign was revolutionary in the way candidates used nontraditional media to attract votes. Bill Clinton reached out to young adult voters when he answered questions on the MTV program Choose or Lose.

the same percentage that losing Democratic candidates had received in the previous three elections. But support for Clinton was broad, and his margin of victory over Bush was impressive. Clinton won a 370–168 Electoral College majority by sweeping thirty-two states, many of which had not voted for a Democrat since 1964. In the congressional elections, the Democrats preserved their majorities in both the House and Senate.

THE FIRST YEAR OF THE CLINTON PRESIDENCY

Clinton's first one hundred days as president "diminished public expectations," the *Washington Post* reported, "that he—or anyone else—can do much to turn around a country that seven out of ten voters think is going in the wrong direction."[6] Hoping to be a dominating president in the tradition of FDR, LBJ, and Reagan, Clinton was targeted with the same sort of ridicule that had plagued his most recent Democratic predecessor, Jimmy Carter. Like Carter, Clinton was a former governor of a southern state whom many believed was in over his head. As Walter Dean Burnham observed during the summer of 1993, "There has been no successful transition yet from the very small and parochial world of Little Rock to Big Time Washington."[7]

The White House press corps, the most hostile faced by any president since Nixon, amplified Clinton's weaknesses. Because the proliferation of television talk shows and local news programs allowed the new president to speak directly to the American people, Washington correspondents often felt left out of the picture. Indeed, Clinton held only one White House press conference during his first three months as president.[8] Frustrated by their diminishing influence, White House correspondents eagerly pounced on the administration's gaffes. News accounts of serious White House lapses in judgment, ranging from a much-maligned $200 onboard haircut as *Air Force One* was parked at the Los Angeles airport to the trashing of Clinton's first two choices for attorney general, Zoë Baird and Kimba Wood, for employing illegal immigrants as nannies, left the country incredulous.[9]

The transition from governor to president had already become rocky when Clinton assembled a White House staff headed by close associates from Arkansas (such as Chief of Staff Thomas F. "Mack" McClarty) who appeared to be unprepared for the complexity and toughness of Washington politics. Clinton did name some impressive figures to the cabinet, including Sen. Lloyd Bentsen of Texas as secretary of the Treasury, Wisconsin representative Les Aspin as secretary of defense, and former Arizona governor Bruce Babbitt as secretary of the interior. But he was limited in his choices by the scarcity of Democrats with executive experience in Washington. Shut out of the White House since 1981, the party had been in no position to groom skilled administrators. Even Aspin and Bentsen, accomplished lawmakers, were not fully prepared for the challenges of running a major executive department.[10] The larger problem, however, was Clinton's governing style. He centered political and policy decisions in the White House staff. The staff, in turn, manifested the virtues and flaws of the president, who, to a much greater extent than his recent Republican predecessors, assumed the daily burden of detailed decision making.[11]

Indeed, most of Clinton's early political difficulties originated with the president himself. Clinton seemed desperate to please all sides, a leadership flaw that was magnified by a Democratic Party fashioned from a demanding constellation of sometimes competing interest groups.[12] During the campaign, Clinton had professed to be a New Democrat who would challenge these groups and ignore their demands for more entitlement programs. But the president's commitment to controlling government spending and recasting the welfare state was obscured during the first hundred days by his traditional liberal actions. For example, no sooner had Clinton been inaugurated than he announced his intention to issue an executive order to lift the longstanding ban on gays and lesbians in the military. This policy could be carried out instantly—"with the stroke of a pen," Clinton believed—leaving him free, as he had promised during his quest for the presidency, to focus "like a laser" on the economy.

It was unrealistic to expect, however, that such a divisive social issue could be resolved at that time by executive order. To be sure, the development of the administrative presidency had given presidents more power to conduct domestic policy by executive fiat. But, as Reagan and Bush had discovered, the use of this power often provoked powerful opposition from Congress, interest groups, and the bureaucracy. Intense resistance by the respected head of the Joint Chiefs of Staff, Gen. Colin Powell, and the influential Democratic chair of the Senate Armed Services Committee, Sam Nunn of Georgia, forced Clinton to defer his executive order on gays and lesbians for six months while he sought a compromise solution. The president's retreat then aroused the ire of gay and lesbian activists, who had given him strong financial and organizational support in the election.[13] In the end, Clinton and the Congress settled on a compromise—the "Don't Ask, Don't Tell" policy—that banned gays from serving openly in the military.

In his frustration, the president announced that he was "frankly appalled" at how much time he was spending on enervating social issues. Even more distressing, his plan to invest new federal funds in the economy foundered on the rock of the budget deficit. Citing the $350 billion deficit he had inherited from the Bush administration, Clinton withdrew his promise of a middle class tax cut. He proposed instead to cut $500 billion from the deficit in five years through additional taxes and a shift away from the spending priorities pursued during the Reagan and Bush years. In his first budget, Clinton proposed to transfer funds from the Defense Department to an array of traditional Democratic social programs. He called for a large expansion of federal tax credits for low-income working families with children, at a cost to the Treasury of $27 billion; an extra $13.8 billion for the Head Start program; and $3.6 billion for the Supplemental Food Program for Women, Infants, and Children.

Clinton's plan, even though it promised to reduce the deficit, did not clearly distinguish him from conventional "tax-and-spend" Democrats, a charge that congressional Republicans leveled at the president with alacrity. Meanwhile, the Republicans marched in lockstep opposition to Clinton's economic program, especially his $16 billion short-term stimulus package, which he offered as a hedge against the economic contraction that might result from shrinking the budget deficit. The Republican leader in the Senate, Robert J. Dole, regularly resorted to the filibuster as a tool of partisan opposition.[14] His army of forty-three Republican senators was too small to enact legislation, but it was more than adequate to thwart Clinton on the stimulus bill and most other measures. Except in budgetary matters, imposing cloture on a Senate filibuster requires sixty votes.

The Republican strategy was unprecedented. Historically, the filibuster had been employed by Senate mavericks or regional minorities to obstruct party leaders.[15] That the Republican leadership orchestrated filibusters to ensnare the president testified to the bitter partisanship that lingered from the Reagan-Bush era, as well as to Clinton's failure during the early days of his presidency to move the country beyond the interbranch conflicts spawned by divided government. Moderate Democrats, including Clinton's allies in the DLC, argued that the president would have been less vulnerable to the Republicans' obstructionist tactics if he had governed more clearly as a New Democrat. Instead, the tax increases and liberal social policies that Clinton supported enabled Republicans to tar him as a conventional liberal whose commitment to reform had expired at the end of his presidential campaign.[16]

Clinton's acquiescence to traditional liberal causes was in some ways understandable. It was a logical response to the modern institutional separation between presidents and their parties. The centrist wing of the Democratic Party that Clinton represented was a minority wing. The majority of Democratic activists and members of Congress still preferred entitlements to opportunities and regulation to responsibility.[17] Only the unpopularity of some traditional liberal groups and the modern emphasis on candidate-centered presidential campaigns had made Clinton's nomination and election possible. The media-driven caucuses and primaries that determine party nominations enabled him, like Carter in 1976, to seize the Democratic mantle as a political outsider. But they offered the new president no means to transform his party when he took office. To bring about the centrist agenda he advocated during the election, Clinton would have had to risk a brutal confrontation with the major powers in the Democratic Party. Such a battle might have left him no less isolated than Carter.

Although the early Clinton presidency was a period of profound political frustration, the president won some important victories. In June 1993 the Senate and House narrowly passed modified versions of his $500 billion deficit reduction plan. In August Clinton successfully forged a budget deal in a congressional conference committee without any support from Republican legislators, who voted unanimously against the plan. The House adopted the conference report by 218–216, and the Senate approved it 50–50, with Vice President Al Gore casting the deciding vote. Clinton won this narrow, bruising victory only after promising moderate Democrats that he would offer another package of spending cuts in the fall.[18]

The Clinton administration linked the prospects for achieving new savings to its "reinventing government" (REGO) program. This initiative was originally championed by journalist David Osborne and former city manager Ted Gabler, who argued that the failure of traditional bureaucracies to solve basic social and economic problems demonstrated the need for an alternative to standard, centralized administration.[19] A prominent feature of Clinton's New Democrat agenda, REGO was the centerpiece of the National Performance Review (NPR), which Clinton asked Gore to chair. The vice president's report, issued with much fanfare in September 1993, offered a set of proposals that Gore claimed would save $108 billion in five years by trimming 252,000 jobs from the federal civil service, overhauling federal procurement laws, updating the government's information systems, eliminating a few programs and subsidies, and cutting bureaucratic red tape. Beyond budgetary savings, the report called for "a new customer service contract with the American people, a new guarantee of effective, efficient, and responsive government."[20] Critics dismissed the promise of government reinvention as hollow rhetoric, and Congress failed to enact some of Gore's most important recommendations. Nevertheless, as Donald F. Kettl, a prominent scholar of the American bureaucracy, has written, the NPR accomplished far more than critics anticipated: "It energized employees, . . . attracted citizens, . . . drew media attention to government management, . . . and made the point that management matters."[21]

In November 1993 Clinton achieved a more important first-year victory, winning the battle to pass the North American Free Trade Agreement (NAFTA) with Canada and Mexico, which his Republican predecessor had negotiated. This time he knew that a partisan approach would not work. Indeed, Democratic support for free trade was so weak that Clinton had to rely on winning more Republican than Democratic votes in Congress. Reviving his identity as a political outsider, the president launched a successful campaign for the treaty by reaching beyond Congress to the American people.

The turning point in the struggle came when the administration challenged Ross Perot, the leading opponent of NAFTA, to debate Vice President Gore on *Larry King Live*. Gore's forceful and optimistic defense of open markets went down well with the large television audience, securing enough popular support to persuade Congress to approve the trade agreement.[22]

NAFTA was one of the few foreign policy issues in which Clinton initially took much interest. "No president in the last fifty years has tried to do what Bill Clinton has done in foreign policy," observed presidential historian Michael Bechloss, "which is essentially to keep it away from the Oval Office as much as possible."[23] Nevertheless, when Clinton took office, he found the international arena brimming with actual and potential crises that demanded his attention. Among other things, he faced a challenge from Saddam Hussein, whose assassination plot against former president Bush provoked Clinton in June 1993 to order air strikes against an Iraqi intelligence installation. Saber rattling by the Iraqi leader would be a recurring irritant throughout the Clinton presidency.

The administration faced its most troubling foreign policy predicament in Somalia, where Clinton allowed American troops deployed for humanitarian purposes at the end of the Bush administration to become part of a dangerous and controversial United Nations peacekeeping mission. Operating under the authority of Security Council resolutions that ordered the capture of warlord Mohammed Aidid, the mostly American UN forces became the target of attacks in which soldiers were wounded, captured, or killed. In October, despite strong pressure from Congress to withdraw from Somalia, Clinton sent reinforcements. Finally, with Congress threatening to cut off funding for the mission by February 1, 1994, two months earlier than the president intended, the Clinton administration agreed to limit its mission to protecting American forces and securing supply lines for relief aid.[24] Somalia appeared to underscore Clinton's lack of surefootedness in international affairs.

THE 1994 ELECTIONS AND THE RESTORATION OF DIVIDED GOVERNMENT

After the successful fight for NAFTA in November 1993, hopes rose among Democratic moderates that Clinton had begun the task of dedicating his party to the New Democrat principles and policies he espoused during the 1992 campaign, such as personal responsibility through welfare reform. But the Clinton administration's next major legislative battle was for its health care program, which promised to "guarantee all Americans a comprehensive package of benefits over the course of an entire lifetime." The formulation of this program marked the apotheosis of New Deal administrative politics. It was designed behind closed doors by the 630 members of the Task Force on

National Health Reform, which was headed by the first lady, Hillary Rodham Clinton. The program would create a government entitlement, funded by a new payroll tax on workers and businesses and administered by a massively complex bureaucratic apparatus.[25] As such, it was hardly the leaner, more efficient government envisioned in Clinton's National Performance Review. With its complexity (the bill was 1,342 pages long), cost (an estimated $50 billion–$100 billion per year), and obtrusive bureaucracy, the Clinton proposal was an easy target for Republicans.[26]

Although the administration hoped to forge bipartisan cooperation in Congress and a broad consensus among the voters, the possibilities for comprehensive reform hinged on settling differences about the appropriate role of government that had divided the parties and the country for six decades. This task proved impossible. Health care reform died in 1994 when a compromise measure, negotiated by Senate Democratic leader George Mitchell of Maine and Republican senator John Chafee of Rhode Island, failed to win enough Republican support to break a threatened filibuster.[27] In the end, Clinton enraged conservatives by proposing such an ambitious program and dismayed liberals by failing to enact it. The defeat of the president's health plan reminded voters that he had not lived up to his campaign promise to overcome the bitter partisan battles of the Reagan and Bush years.

Clinton and his party paid dearly in the 1994 midterm elections, not just for the failure of health care reform, but also for the success of his 1993 deficit reduction plan. As political scientist Gary C. Jacobson has shown, the public's long-standing desire for a balanced budget has always been tempered by its opposition to the reductions in government spending and the increases in federal taxes that balancing the budget usually requires.[28]

The Republicans gained fifty-two seats in the House and eight in the Senate, taking control of Congress for the first time in forty-two years. They achieved their victory in a campaign that was unusually ideological and partisan. The charged atmosphere of the election owed much to the efforts of House Republican leader Newt Gingrich of Georgia. Gingrich persuaded more than three hundred of his party's House candidates to sign a Republican "Contract with America," which promised to restore limited government by eliminating federal programs, reducing regulatory burdens, and cutting taxes. Clinton's attacks on the contract during the campaign seemed to backfire, serving only to abet the Republicans in their effort to highlight the president's failure to transform the Democratic Party and mute partisan division in Washington.

Disenchantment with Clinton was especially strong in the South, where Republicans registered some of their greatest gains. White southerners had begun rebelling against the Democratic Party in presidential elections with the Dixiecrat revolt of 1948. More recently, Reagan had expanded the

Republicans' appeal by taking conservative positions on taxes, national defense, and social issues. In 1980 Reagan won ten of the eleven former Confederate states against Jimmy Carter, a Georgian. Clinton managed to win only four in 1992.

What distinguished the 1994 elections is that a large majority of southern whites supported Republican candidates in congressional and state elections. Previously, southern Democrats had been able to insulate themselves from those aspects of the national party that whites found unappealing. But Clinton's first two years as president eroded that insulation. "Clinton had earned praise as one of the brightest, most agile governors in his region," journalists Dan Balz and Ronald Brownstein wrote after the 1994 elections, "but, as President his policies, from his advocacy of ending discrimination against homosexuals in the military to his economic and health care programs that stressed big government activism, often seemed like a stick in the eye of his native South."[29] Starting with the 1994 elections, southern Republicans commanded a majority of the region's governorships, a majority of seats in the Senate, and a majority of seats in the House.

The dramatic Republican triumph in 1994 led political pundits to suggest that Clinton was, for all intents and purposes, a lame-duck president. Indeed, as Gingrich seized control of the legislative initiative during the early months of the 104th Congress, Clinton was left to assert plaintively, "The president is relevant here."

THE COMEBACK PRESIDENT

The seeds of Clinton's reelection in 1996 were sown in the disastrous elections of 1994. This was an ironic but not altogether surprising result: in 1946, 1954, and 1986 the party that took away control of one or both houses of Congress from the president's party proceeded to overreach politically and open the door for a presidential comeback. Clinton's initial response to the conservative Republican triumph in 1994 was conciliatory, even contrite. "I think what [the voters] told us was, 'Look, two years ago we made one change, now we made another change.'"[30] Hoping to revive the impression created during the 1992 campaign that he represented a fresh approach to government, Clinton resurrected his New Covenant message of "opportunity, responsibility, and community." In translating this message into action, Clinton embraced campaign adviser Dick Morris's goals of "triangulation" in policy and, in presidential style, a more dignified, statesmanlike demeanor.

TRIANGULATION, OR THE "THIRD WAY"

Morris persuaded Clinton that it was important not only to stake out a position in the political center, but also to find new issues that would allow him to

Fresh from the triumph of his budget battle with the Republican Congress, President Bill Clinton, center, enters the House chamber to deliver his 1996 State of the Union address.

rise above the conventional left-right political spectrum and offer a "third way." The baseline of the new political triangle would be occupied at its opposite ends by liberal Democrats and conservative Republicans, with Clinton hovering at a point above and between them. As Morris urged Clinton to embrace, and thereby neutralize, Republican issues such as crime, taxes, welfare, and the budget, the president displayed a renewed commitment to middle class concerns. "I had discovered the middle class in [my] presidential campaign," Clinton said, "and forsaken them as president."[31]

Clinton's adoption of the triangulation strategy clearly accounts for his approach to the defining controversy of his third year as president: the battle with the 104th Congress over the fiscal year 1996 budget. Fresh from their triumph in the midterm elections, the Gingrich-led Republicans went beyond the promises of the Contract with America by committing themselves to cut taxes and domestic spending dramatically. Congressional Democrats opposed them on both counts, aiming most of their fire at the proposed spending reductions. In mid-1995 Clinton angered these Democrats by boldly embracing the Republicans' goal of a balanced budget. But he also infuriated the Republicans by insisting that Democratic programs such as Medicare, Medicaid, educational funding, and environmental enforcement be left substantially unaltered. The public, roused by the millions of dollars in pro-administration television ads financed by the Democratic National Committee, supported the president. When the Republicans tried to impose their own budget on Clinton, he refused to yield. The president then persuaded the voters that not he, but Gingrich, Dole, and the Republican Congress, were responsible for the two federal government shutdowns that began in late 1995 in the absence of a budget agreement.

When Congress returned to Washington in January 1996 for the second session of the 104th Congress, it was not to Gingrich's agenda of reducing government but rather to the measured tones of Clinton's State of the Union address. The president, having outmaneuvered the Republican Congress the previous year, now co-opted its most popular theme, declaring that "the era of big government is over."[32] This line was not a mere rhetorical flourish. The National Performance Review's second annual report, issued in September 1995, suggested that the REGO-spawned budgetary savings and personnel cutbacks promised by Vice President Gore two years earlier would actually be achieved.[33] More significant, Clinton withstood furious criticism from liberal members of his party and in August signed the Welfare Reform Act of 1996, which replaced a sixty-year-old entitlement to cash payments for low-income mothers and their dependent children with temporary assistance and a strict work requirement.[34] Clinton conceded that the act was flawed, cutting too deeply into nutritional programs for the working poor and unfairly denying support to legal immigrants. Nevertheless, by forcing welfare recipients to take jobs, the new act advanced a fundamental principle that Clinton had championed in the 1992 campaign: "recreating the Nation's social bargain with the poor."[35]

ACTING PRESIDENTIAL

Hoping to strengthen his credentials as an effective, independent executive, Clinton began to present himself to the voters as statesmanlike, rather than partisan or political. After the April 19, 1995, bombing of the Oklahoma City federal building by domestic terrorist Timothy McVeigh, the president had his first opportunity since the 1994 elections to do so. His effort was successful. As one observer recorded, in the aftermath of the traumatic bombing Clinton "exhibited the take-charge determination as well as the on-key rhetoric that Americans expect of their president in times of trouble."[36]

Clinton's presidential surefootedness in Oklahoma City was not an isolated event. Political scientist Paul Light has pointed out that presidents typically undergo a "cycle of increasing effectiveness" that comes with experience in office.[37] Adhering to the pattern of his long tenure as governor of Arkansas, Clinton put his on-the-job training to good use. The White House staff, hastily thrown together late in the transition period that followed the 1992 election and equally chaotic during the first two years of his presidency, began to function more effectively after he appointed longtime Washington insider

Leon Panetta as chief of staff and Michael McCurry as press secretary while keeping the best of the Arkansans, notably deputy White House counsel Bruce Lindsey.[38] Meanwhile, Clinton learned how to deal with a professional, independent-minded Republican Congress after many years of working with the part-time, Democrat-dominated legislature of his state. His deportment mirrored his growth. Out went his much-photographed (and much-ridiculed) jogging shorts, public confession of his preference for "boxers" over "briefs," and diffident salutes on formal military occasions. In came (after sessions spent studying videotapes of Reagan) a straight, shoulders-back posture and, with some coaching, crisp salutes.

In foreign policy, the president gained confidence as commander in chief when he discovered during the final two years of his first term that the American people respected him for having the courage to make unpopular decisions that extended American assistance to Bosnia, Haiti, and Mexico. In November 1995, after Clinton overruled public opinion and strong congressional opposition by sending twenty thousand troops to a peacekeeping mission in Bosnia, the voters' approval of his handling of foreign policy went up. Privately, he likened the phenomenon to "telling your children to go to the dentist—they don't want to go, but they know you're right."[39]

Clinton initially was reluctant to intervene in the Balkans, but the plight of the Bosnian Muslims, who were being victimized by Serbian leader Slobodan Milosevic's "ethnic cleansing" (that is, exile or extermination) schemes, and pressure from America's European allies eventually persuaded the president to deploy military forces to the region. His resolve to uphold American responsibilities in the world, coming on the heels of his confrontation with Congress over the budget, appeared to belie his reputation as a waffler who lacked a clear set of principles. The president really was, as Clinton had insisted in the aftermath of the 1994 elections, "relevant."

THE ELECTIONS OF 1996

Clinton's strategy of triangulation and acting presidential was clearly evident in his 1996 general election campaign. The president held firmly to the centrist ground he staked out after the 1994 midterm elections, campaigning on the same New Democratic themes that had served him well in 1992. In dozens of appearances around the country, Clinton argued that he and Gore represented a proven, moderate alternative to the extremism of Gingrich and the 104th Congress. He pointed with pride to the economic progress that had flowed from the initially unpopular tax increases and spending reductions of his first term: four consecutive years of low inflation, a sharp drop in the unemployment rate, steady economic growth, and a reduction in the annual budget deficit from $290 billion the year he became president to $106 billion in the fourth year of his term. He celebrated the first-term enactment of laws such as welfare reform and the service-based AmeriCorps program, along with his successful defense of "Medicare, Medicaid, education, and the environment" against alleged assaults by Republican budget cutters. Finally, to buttress his stature as a unifying rather than a partisan leader, Clinton struck appealing presidential poses for the television cameras, signing environmental legislation at the Grand Canyon and presiding over an emergency Arab-Israeli summit conference at the White House.

Still, Clinton's discussion of the future during the campaign was hardly the stuff of which mandates are made. Standing under banners that proclaimed "Building America's Bridge to the 21st Century," Clinton repeatedly offered empty "bridge" rhetoric to the voters in lieu of substantive discussion of his plans for a second term. By one count, he used the word an average nine times per speech.[40]

In addition, even when his lead in the polls stretched to fifteen points, Clinton resisted tying his campaign to the fortunes of congressional Democrats. The president's remarkable political comeback in 1995 had been fueled by "soft money" donations supposedly designated for Democratic Party–building activities and therefore not limited by federal campaign finance laws.[41] But these donations were used instead to mount television advertising campaigns, such as the media blast at the Republican Congress during the 1995 budget battle, that championed the president's independence from partisan squabbles. Determined to win a clear majority of the national popular vote and wary of alienating voters who might resist giving him too cooperative a Congress, Clinton seldom endorsed the election of a Democratic House and Senate. He did not raise money for his party's congressional candidates until late in the campaign. Media exposure during the campaign's final days of the administration's legally questionable fund-raising methods helped to push Clinton's share of the popular vote below 50 percent as well as undermining the Democrats' effort to retake the House.[42]

Bland as it was, Clinton's campaign was visionary when compared with that of his Republican opponent, Robert Dole.[43] The seventy-three-year-old Senate veteran, who in three previous runs for national office had never displayed strong gifts as a campaigner, showed little improvement in 1996. Without a strategy, Dole lurched from tactic to tactic. In one speech, inadvertently underscoring his campaign's lack of a theme, Dole proclaimed, "It all boils down to one word. Trust. . . . That's what the election is all about. Trust." He then added, "It's about leadership. It's about family. It's about business. It's about the next century."[44] In an attempt to escape the petty and virulent conflicts of the 104th Congress, Dole resigned his position as majority leader at the beginning of the campaign, and then left the Senate altogether in June. But Dole was never able to shed his image as a Washington insider. Departing from carefully crafted speech texts, he often lapsed into staccato bursts of legislative shorthand that Washington insiders understood but that left most voters baffled.

Only Ross Perot could claim the mantle of outsider in 1996, but his quirky personality did not wear well the second time around. "When we ask people to use one word to describe him," reported the pollster Andrew Kohut, "the words are just awful—'rich,' 'crazy,' 'idiot,' 'egotistical.'"[45] Nevertheless, Perot's campaign drew considerable support, demonstrating once again the vulnerability of the ideologically polarized two-party system to a centrist attack, however eccentric. Indeed, Perot's resilience confirmed the place of significant independent candidates in the electoral landscape. Four of the eight presidential elections between 1968 and 1996 featured such candidates: the 1968 election in which George C. Wallace received 14 percent of the popular vote and forty-six electoral votes; the 1980 election in which John B. Anderson received 7 percent of the popular vote; and the elections of 1992 and 1996 in which Ross Perot won 19 percent and 8 percent, respectively. During this period, independent candidates received an average of 7.5 percent of the popular vote per election, which was five times higher than the 1.5 percent such candidates averaged in the eight preceding elections from 1936 to 1964.

The persistence of independent candidates in contemporary political life testified to the declining role of late twentieth-century parties in cultivating loyalties and organizing elections. In some ways, Clinton openly imitated Perot's personalistic politics. Triangulation was conceived as a campaign strategy that would portray the president as an outsider who disdained the petty and mean-spirited skirmishes that had entangled both major parties since the late 1960s. On election day, Clinton won 49 percent of the popular vote to Dole's 41 percent and 379 electoral votes to Dole's 159. Although the president's reelection strategy, supported by a strong economy, was effective, the candidate-centered campaign that Clinton conducted denied him any chance to win a mandate based on a change-oriented policy agenda and long congressional coattails. In fact, the Democrats lost two seats in the Senate, which nearly outweighed their modest gain of nine seats in the House.

More ominously, in 1996 only 49 percent of the eligible electorate voted, the lowest turnout since 1924, when many women, newly enfranchised by the Nineteenth Amendment, were unfamiliar with voting and many states had registration laws that discriminated against African Americans. Just as strong party attachments increase voters' psychological involvement in politics and make the act of voting seem meaningful, so do weak attachments tend to distance voters from politics and undermine their sense of political efficacy. With the rise of candidate-centered campaigns, fewer Americans saw a connection between what they said on election day and what the government did afterward.

President Bill Clinton, left, is emphatic in denying he had an affair with White House intern Monica Lewinsky. His main adversary, independent counsel Kenneth Starr, right, regarded the president's lies about the Lewinsky affair as impeachable conduct.

BALANCED BUDGETS, IMPEACHMENT POLITICS, AND THE LIMITS OF THE THIRD WAY

Clinton staked his success as president on forging a third way between Republican conservatism and Democratic liberalism.[46] His gift for compromise was displayed in May 1997, when he and Republican congressional leaders agreed on a plan to balance the budget by 2002. Arguably, this deal was struck on Republican terms. The most dramatic measures in the budget—the first tax cut in sixteen years, the largest Medicare savings ever enacted into law, and five-year constraints on discretionary spending—shifted national priorities in a decidedly conservative direction.[47]

Nevertheless, Clinton exacted some important concessions from the Republicans, enough to enable him to persuade a majority of Democrats in Congress to support the plan. Most significant, the 1997 Balanced Budget Act smoothed the rough edges of the Welfare Reform Act of 1996. It provided substantial additional funding for immigrant benefits and a bit more for food stamps. It also included $16 billion for the new federally funded and administered State Children's Health Insurance Program for low-income working families who were not eligible for Medicaid. These concessions, along with earlier increases Clinton had won in the earned-income tax credit for the working poor, allowed him to claim that he had fulfilled his promise to negotiate a new social contract with people who were trying hard to work their way out of poverty.[48]

To be sure, the budget agreement between the White House and the Republican-controlled Congress was possible only because of a revenue windfall caused by the robust economy, which enabled Clinton and Republican leaders to avoid the kinds of hard choices over program cuts and taxes that had animated the bitter struggles of the Bush presidency and Clinton's first term.[49] Even so, the rapprochement, which in fiscal year 1998 brought about the first balanced budget in three decades, testifies to the ability of modern presidents to advance principles and pursue policies that defy the sharp cleavages of the national party system.

The Clinton administration and Republicans in Congress also collaborated to enact the 1999 Gramm-Leach-Bliley Act, which repealed the Glass-Steagall Act, a law passed during the early days of the New Deal to establish a fire wall between banking and speculation. Gramm-Leach-Bliley removed this barrier by allowing banks to merge with insurance companies and investment houses. The restraint on banks' financial activity had come to be viewed as an impediment to economic growth since the 1980s, and there were several attempts to remove it during the Reagan and Bush presidencies. The view of Clinton and his secretary of the Treasury, Lawrence Summers, that "new" Democratic principles called for a "modernization" of financial markets appealed to a Republican-controlled Congress anxious to free markets. The act passed with overwhelming bipartisan support and was signed by the president in December 1999. Sen. Byron Dorgan, a Democrat from North Dakota, who stood against the tide of free market ambrosia of the late 1990s, warned that the law would create banks that were "too big to fail" and fuel irresponsible speculation that threaten savings and investments. Dismissed as a Cassandra, would Dorgan, one of only eight senators who voted against Gramm-Leach-Bliley, was vindicated ten years later when undisciplined banks and investment houses brought the American economy to the brink of collapse.[50]

For better or worse, bipartisan agreements between Clinton and the Republicans were the exception. Bitter and polarized partisan politics remained the rule. Just as Reagan and Bush were plagued by independent counsels who investigated alleged abuses in their administrations, so too were Clinton and members of his cabinet subjected to intense legal scrutiny. Republicans had long opposed reauthorization of the 1978 Ethics in Government Act, which provided for the appointment of independent counsels. But their resistance to Democratic efforts to reauthorize the statute came to an end in 1993, when the president and first lady were accused of shady financial dealings in an Arkansas real estate investment known as Whitewater during the 1980s. Before Clinton became president, the activities pursued by a chief executive prior to taking office were rarely the subject of controversy or even

serious inquiry. But partisan rancor in Washington fueled Republicans' eagerness to repay the Democrats for their attacks on the Reagan and Bush presidencies by subjecting the Clintons to unprecedented congressional and legal
scrutiny. Although no clear evidence of impropriety was found in the Whitewater investigation, critics raised enough disturbing questions to justify calls
for an independent counsel appointed under the statute that Democrats so
often had used, and Republicans protested against, in the past.[51]

In January 1998 independent counsel Kenneth W. Starr was authorized to
expand the scope of the Whitewater inquiry to pursue allegations that the
president had lied under oath about an affair with a twenty-one-year-old
White House intern, Monica Lewinsky, and that Clinton and his friend Vernon Jordan had encouraged her to do the same. The Clinton administration's
response was to accuse Starr, a prominent Republican, and his supporters in
Congress of orchestrating a blatantly partisan campaign to bring down the
president. Clinton's rapid counterattack proved effective in the court of public
opinion. The president's approval rating remained high, as voters continued
to focus on his record of "peace, prosperity, and moderation."[52]

Reluctant to cooperate with Starr's investigation, Clinton made broad
claims of executive privilege that were, as the *New York Times* observed,
"freighted with echoes of Watergate and President Nixon's efforts to keep
his White House tapes secret."[53] The president's assertion of an executive
privilege to keep aides Sidney Blumenthal and Bruce Lindsey, as well as
Secret Service agents, from testifying before the grand jury convened by
Starr was rebuffed by a federal district court judge, and the White House
eventually abandoned the effort. But Clinton continued to press a claim of
lawyer-client privilege in an effort to limit the questioning of Lindsey, his
closest confidant.

Congressional Democrats were slow to rally to Clinton's defense. Most
Democratic legislators, still smarting from the president's seeming indifference
to their programmatic commitments and desire to regain control of Congress,
initially were silent as the Republicans sought to exploit his peccadilloes.[54]
Clinton's uneasy relationship with his party in Congress also threatened his
legislative program. For example, the great majority of House Democrats
refused to give the president fast-track authority to negotiate international
trade agreements, a power that previous Democratic Congresses had readily
conferred on Republican presidents Ford, Reagan, and Bush.

Democrats also challenged the line-item veto, a power that the Republican
Congress granted to the president in a 1996 act in the hope that a Republican
would be wielding it after the election. The new law was passed with Clinton's
strong support over widespread Democratic opposition. It empowered the
president to cancel any new spending projects, narrowly targeted tax breaks,
and entitlement programs within five days of signing a money bill, subject to

override by a two-thirds vote of both the House and the Senate. Clinton used the line-item veto to cancel twenty-eight provisions in eleven laws, ranging from $15,000 for a new police training center in Arab, Alabama, to $30 million for an air force program to intercept an asteroid in space.

Within days of the Line Item Veto Act of 1996 taking effect, Sen. Robert Byrd of West Virginia and several other congressional Democrats sued to overturn it as a violation of the constitutional provision that allows the president to veto only a "bill." The Supreme Court dismissed their case in 1997, ruling that Byrd and his colleagues lacked standing to sue because they had not suffered any direct injury from the line-item veto. On June 25, 1998, however, in *Clinton v. City of New York,* a six-justice majority declared the act unconstitutional in response to lawsuits filed by New York City, which objected to Clinton's veto of a tax break tied to the Medicaid program, and by the Snake River (Idaho) Potato Growers, who had lost a capital gains tax advantage for farmers' cooperatives. Relying on the presentment clause of Article I, section 7 (every bill "shall be presented to the President of the United States" for either approval or veto), Justice John Paul Stevens wrote that line-item vetoes are "the functional equivalent of partial repeal of acts of Congress," even though "there is no provision in the Constitution that authorizes the president to enact, amend, or to repeal statutes."[55] Fifteen years earlier, the Court had relied heavily on the same constitutional clause in *Immigration and Naturalization Service v. Chadha,* when it declared unconstitutional Congress's long-standing use of the legislative veto to second-guess the executive branch after delegating it authority to make discretionary decisions about how laws should be implemented.

With the decline of Clinton's personal stature and the historical pattern of substantial losses for the parties of second-term presidents at midterm, nearly every political expert predicted that the Republicans would emerge from the 1998 elections with a tighter grip on Congress and, consequently, on the president's political fate.[56] But the Republicans had been preoccupied by the Lewinsky scandal for the entire year and lacked an appealing campaign message. They were unable to increase their 55–45 margin in the Senate and lost five seats in the House, leaving them with a slim 223–211 majority. Clinton, the first Democrat since FDR to be reelected to a second term, also became the first president since Roosevelt to see his party gain seats in a midterm election. Bitterly disappointed by the results, the Republicans fell into soul-searching and recriminations. Ironically, it was the hero of their 1994 ascent to power, Speaker Newt Gingrich, whose political fate was sealed by the elections. Soon after the results were tallied, Gingrich announced that he was resigning not only his leadership position but also his seat in Congress. Ironically, Gingrich's fall from grace was abetted by his admission during the impeachment hearings that he, too, had engaged in an extramarital affair.

The 1998 elections seemed likely to take the steam out of the House impeachment inquiry. But as the president gathered with friends and aides to celebrate what appeared to be another remarkable political comeback, the Republicans prepared to move forward with impeachment. A centrist, poll-driven politician, Clinton underestimated the willingness of congressional Republicans to defy the survey-tested will of the people.[57] In truth, the hands of Republican legislators were tied. Their core constituencies—the Republican primary voters and, especially, the conservative party activists who control congressional nominations—strongly favored impeachment.[58]

In December 1998, after nearly a year of dramatic and tawdry politics, Clinton was impeached on separate counts of perjury and obstruction of justice by a bitterly divided House of Representatives. The House voted virtually along party lines to recommend that the Senate remove the president from office. Article I, the perjury count, was approved by a vote of 226–206, with Republicans providing all but five of the aye votes and Democrats providing all but five of the nays. The 221–212 vote in favor of Article II, which charged Clinton with obstruction of justice, was almost as partisan. Only five Democrats voted for the article, and only thirteen Republicans voted against it.[59]

But even impeachment did not undermine Clinton's popular support. After a five-week Senate trial, the president's accusers failed to gain a simple majority, much less the constitutionally mandated two-thirds, to support either charge against him. On February 12, 1999, the Senate rejected the perjury article, 55–45, with ten Republicans joining all forty-five Democrats to vote against conviction. Just six minutes later, with five Republicans breaking ranks, the Senate split 50–50 on the article accusing the president of obstruction of justice. Clinton's job was safe.

The most obvious casualty of the impeachment controversy was the Ethics in Government Act, which Congress did not reauthorize when it lapsed in the summer of 1999. Less obvious was the effect of the impeachment debacle on the modern presidency. To be an effective deterrent of executive abuse, Alexander Hamilton wrote in *Federalist* No. 65, impeachment should be used only to investigate a serious "violation of some public trust." Although sharp partisanship was evident in the impeachment inquiries concerning Andrew Johnson and Richard Nixon, both of these cases involved contests over important constitutional questions. In contrast, as historian Lewis L. Gould has argued, the Clinton impeachment failed to rise above raw and disruptive partisan combat: "Either the Republicans in 1998 and 1999 were serious and lacked sufficient acumen to achieve their goals, or they were playing games with the Constitution for temporary political advantage. Either way, they discredited impeachment as part of the constitutional system of checks and balances."[60]

Although he was acquitted by the Senate and remained popular with the public, Clinton's problems with the Republican Congress continued. Virtually every item on his legislative agenda—each of them politically appealing in its own right—failed to be enacted, including campaign finance reform, tobacco regulation, school construction, a minimum wage increase, and a patient's bill of rights. But the perception that Clinton was an enfeebled president, thwarted at every turn by fierce Republican opposition and unsteady Democratic support, was belied by his aggressive use of the administrative presidency during all six years that the Republicans controlled Congress. Beginning in 1995 the president issued a blizzard of executive orders, regulations, proclamations, and other decrees on matters such as tobacco regulation and environmental protection to achieve his goals, with or without the blessing of Congress.[61]

Clinton also upheld Lyndon Johnson's Executive Order 11246, which mandates affirmative action targets for federal contractors, against a frontal assault by the courts. In *Adarand Constructors, Inc. v. Pena* (1995) the Supreme Court overturned a program that paid contractors a bonus of up to 10 percent for each subcontract awarded to "socially or economically disadvantaged"—that is, minority-owned—firms.[62] Ruling that all racial preferences are constitutionally suspect, this opinion was the first in which the Court rejected a contracting set-aside program. In the face of judicial scrutiny and mounting political opposition to Executive Order 11246 (all the leading contenders for the 1996 Republican presidential nomination promised to rescind it if elected), the Clinton administration eliminated seventeen set-aside programs, but preserved the affirmative action employment practices it had imposed on government contractors. In May 1998 Clinton issued Executive Order 13087, which for the first time prohibited federal agencies from discriminating in employment on the basis of sexual orientation. Although Republican legislators and conservative religious groups denounced Clinton for creating a new protected class of people eligible for affirmative action benefits, Congress did not act. As it had throughout the twentieth century, Congress proved unable, or unwilling, to reverse executive orders through legislation.[63]

Late in his second term, Clinton also defied congressional opposition to the use of military force in the Balkans. This time it was in Kosovo, a province of Serbia, where Slobodan Milosevic's ruthless and repressive domination of the majority Muslim population revived the terrible spectre of ethnic cleansing. Although the House defeated a resolution in May 1999 endorsing the administration's bombing campaign in Kosovo, Clinton's persistence eventually forced Milosevic to accept a peace settlement. Once criticized for his lack of experience and interest in military affairs, Clinton now readily embraced the president's authority as commander in chief.[64]

Still, any moral authority Clinton may have had at the beginning of his administration to establish a new covenant of rights and responsibilities between citizens and their government was severely undermined by the public's distaste for his personal conduct. The virulent partisanship that characterized the impeachment process forced Clinton to seek refuge once again among his fellow Democrats in Congress, thereby short-circuiting his plans to pursue entitlement reform as the capstone of his presidency.[65] In the wake of the impeachment debacle, Clinton positioned himself as the champion of the status quo when it came to Social Security and Medicare, urging Congress to invest a significant share of the mounting budget surplus in these traditional liberal programs.[66]

Meanwhile, Clinton's efforts to avoid litigation and impeachment led to a series of court decisions that weakened the authority of the presidency. On May 27, 1997, in *Clinton v. Jones,* the Supreme Court unanimously rejected the president's claim of immunity against a sexual harassment lawsuit brought by Paula Corbin Jones, a former Arkansas state employee.[67] The ruling established that even sitting presidents are subject to civil suits. It also set the stage for the sworn depositions by Lewinsky and Clinton in Jones's case that provoked the independent counsel to charge the president with perjury and obstruction of justice. Moreover, Starr's investigation established legal precedents by securing appeals court rulings that neither the president's Secret Service agents nor the government lawyers he consulted could refuse to testify in a criminal investigation by invoking executive privilege.[68] The main effect of Clinton's efforts to forestall investigations of his conduct as governor and president was to corrode the constitutional safeguards of presidential immunity and executive privilege.

Shorn of these protections, Clinton's successors were encouraged to conduct their personal lives in a manner that would not lead to public embarrassment. But with the rise of a plebiscitary form of presidential leadership, presidents became politically less accountable than in the past. As with Clinton's third way, his president-centric alternative not just to the opposition party but to his own, modern presidents encourage citizens to invest their support in an individual leader for a time, subject to quick abandonment if they become dissatisfied with the leader's style or performance. By relying on personal charm and organization to promote his policies, and by subordinating the collective welfare of his party to his own political ambitions, Clinton may have further weakened civic life in the United States. All previous realignments in American political history required extraordinary party leadership, in which reform presidents played a principal role in forming a new party or remaking an existing one.[69] But developments since the Progressive era—the direct primary, the expansion of national administrative power, and the rise of the mass media—have encouraged presidents such as Clinton to seek office and govern as the heads of organizations they create in their own image.

NOTES

1. The term *extraordinary isolation* is Woodrow Wilson's. See Wilson, *Constitutional Government in the United States* (New York: Columbia University Press, 1908), 69.

2. George F. Will, "The Veep and the Blatherskite," *Newsweek*, June 29, 1992, 72.

3. See, for example, Theodore J. Lowi, "The Party Crasher," *New York Times Magazine*, August 23, 1992, 28, 33.

4. Ronald B. Rapoport and Walter J. Stone, *Three's a Crowd: The Dynamic of Third Parties, Ross Perot, and Republican Resurgence* (Ann Arbor: University of Michigan Press, 2007).

5. James Ceaser and Andrew Busch, *Upside Down and Inside Out: The 1992 Elections and American Politics* (Lanham, Md.: Rowman and Littlefield, 1993), 105. See also Philip Meyer, "The Media Reformation: Giving the Agenda Back to the People," in *The Elections of 1992*, ed. Michael Nelson (Washington, D.C.: CQ Press, 1993), 89–98.

6. Dan Balz and David Broder, "President Clinton's First One Hundred Days," *Washington Post*, April 29, 1993, A1. The first one hundred days of an administration are an early benchmark of presidential performance that Franklin Roosevelt inadvertently bequeathed to his successors.

7. Walter Dean Burnham, "On the Shoals, Nearing the Rocks," *American Prospect*, 14 (Summer 1993): 10–11.

8. Sidney Blumenthal, "The Syndicated Presidency," *New Yorker*, April 5, 1993, 42–47.

9. Kimba Wood was never actually nominated as attorney general. Burned once by his hasty pick of Zoë Baird, Clinton awaited the results of a full background check before announcing his near-certain choice of Wood, a New York federal judge. When it was disclosed that Wood, like Baird, had hired an illegal immigrant to babysit her children, a jittery White House pushed her to withdraw.

10. Lewis L. Gould, *The Modern American Presidency* (Lawrence: University Press of Kansas, 2003), 218.

11. "From what one can tell," presidential scholar Joel D. Aberbach has written, "real responsibility for most [of the early political and policy difficulties] lies primarily in the White House [and White House staff] . . . , not in the agencies or their appointed or career personnel." Aberbach, "The Federal Executive under Clinton," in *The Clinton Presidency: First Appraisals*, ed. Colin Campbell and Bert A. Rockman (Chatham, N.J.: Chatham House, 1996), 176. See also Burt Solomon, "A One-Man Band," *National Journal*, April 24, 1993, 970–974.

12. James W. Cicconi, a former member of the Reagan and Bush White Houses, cited in Burt Solomon, "Musical Chairs in the West Wing May Bring Order from Cacophony," *National Journal*, June 26, 1993, 1661.

13. Thomas L. Friedman, "Ready or Not, Clinton Is Rattling the Country," *New York Times*, January 31, 1993, sec. 4, 1.

14. George Hager and David S. McCloud, "Test for Divided Democrats: Forge a Budget Battle," *Congressional Quarterly Weekly Report*, June 26, 1993, 1631–5.

15. Alan Brinkley, "The 43% President," *New York Times Magazine*, July 4, 1993, 22.

16. Will Marshall, president, Progressive Policy Institute, interview by Sidney M. Milkis, May 20, 1997. See also Sidney Blumenthal, "Bob Dole's First Strike," *New Yorker*, May 3, 1993, 40–46.

17. As an official of the Democratic National Committee acknowledged, there were serious "institutional" difficulties in reconciling Clinton's New Democratic principles with the "base" of the party. The leading financial contributors and core voters of the party were more liberal than the president, making it difficult for the administration to provide clear moral leadership. Personal interview, not for attribution, by Sidney M. Milkis, July 11, 1997.

18. Douglas Jehl, "Rejoicing Is Muted for the President in Budget Victory," *New York Times*, August 8, 1993, 1, 23; David Shribman, "Budget Win a Hollow Win for President,"

Boston Globe, August 8, 1993. See also Paul J. Quirk and Joseph Hinchcliffe, "Domestic Policy: The Trials of a Centrist Democrat," in Campbell and Rockman, *Clinton Presidency,* 272–274.

19. David Osborne and Ted Gabler, *Reinventing Government: How the Entrepreneurial Spirit Is Transforming the Public Sector* (Reading, Mass.: Addison-Wesley, 1992).

20. Al Gore, *Creating a Government that Works Better and Costs Less,* Report of the National Performance Review, September 7, 1993 (Washington, D.C.: Government Printing Office, 1993).

21. Donald F. Kettl, *Reinventing Government? Appraising the National Performance Review* (Washington, D.C.: Brookings, 1994), ix. See also Joel D. Aberbach, "A Reinvented Government, or the Same Old Government?" in *The Clinton Legacy,* ed. Colin Campbell and Bert A. Rockman (New York: Chatham House, 2000); and Jonathan D. Breul and John M. Kamensky, "Federal Government Reform: Lessons from Clinton's 'Reinventing Government' and Bush's 'Management Agenda' Initiatives," *Public Administration Review* 68 (November/December 2008): 1009–26.

22. David Shribman, "A New Brand of D.C. Politics," *Boston Globe,* November 18, 1993, 15; Gwen Ifill, "56 Long Days of Coordinated Persuasion," *New York Times,* November 19, 1993, A27. See also Barbara Sinclair, "Trying to Govern in a Negative Era," in Campbell and Rockman, *Clinton Presidency,* 109–111.

23. CNN transcripts, July 5, 1993.

24. Clifford Krause, "White House Reaches a Deal with Byrd on Role in Somalia," *New York Times,* October 15, 1993, A12.

25. These details were included in Clinton's address to Congress on the health care plan and reported in *Congressional Quarterly Weekly Report,* September 25, 1993, 2582–6. See also Robin Toner, "Alliance to Buy Health Care: Bureaucrat or Public Servant," *New York Times,* December 5, 1993, 1, 38.

26. For a fuller account of the health care reform battle, see Haynes Johnson and David S. Broder, *The System: The American Way of Politics at the Breaking Point* (Boston: Little, Brown, 1996); and Theda Skocpol, *Boomerang: Clinton's Health Security Effort and the Turn against Government* (New York: Norton, 1996).

27. Adam Clymer, "National Health Program, President's Greatest Goal, Declared Dead in Congress," *New York Times,* September 27, 1994, A1, B10. For a sound and interesting case study of the Clinton health care program, see Cathie Jo Martin, "Mandating Social Change within Corporate America" (paper presented at the annual meeting of the American Political Science Association, New York September 1–4, 1994). Martin's study shows that health care reform became the victim of a battle between "radically different world views about the state and corporation in modern society."

28. Gary C. Jacobson, "Deficit Cutting Politics and Congressional Elections," *Political Science Quarterly* 108 (Fall 1993): 375–402; Jacobson, "The 1994 House Elections in Perspective," in *Midterm: The Elections of 1994 in Context,* ed. Philip A. Klinkner (Boulder: Westview Press, 1996), 1–20.

29. Dan Balz and Ronald Brownstein, *Storming the Gates: Protest Politics and the Republican Revival* (New York: Little Brown, 1996), 207.

30. Bob Woodward, *The Choice* (New York: Simon and Schuster, 1996), 23.

31. Ibid., 25.

32. "Bill Clinton's Third State of the Union Address," in *The Evolving Presidency: Landmark Documents, 1787–2010,* 4th ed., ed. Michael Nelson (Washington, D.C.: CQ Press, 2012), 269–273.

33. Al Gore, *Commonsense Government* (New York: Random House, 1995), 7.

34. The replaced program was Aid to Families with Dependent Children.

35. William Jefferson Clinton, "Remarks on Signing the Personal Responsibility and Opportunity Reconciliation Act," *Weekly Compilation of Presidential Documents,* August 22, 1996, 1484–9. Political scientists Joe Soss and Sanford Schram argue that welfare reform did not change the public's negative view of "welfare"; nor did it redound to the benefit of

the Democratic Party. See Soss and Schram, "A Public Transformed" Welfare Reform as Policy Feedback," *American Political Science Review* 101, no. 1 (February 2007): 111–127.

36. "Victory March," *Newsweek,* November 18, 1996, 48.

37. Paul Light, *The President's Agenda: Domestic Policy Choice from Kennedy to Reagan* (Baltimore: Johns Hopkins University Press, 1991), 37.

38. Howard Kurtz, *Spin Cycle: Inside the Clinton Propaganda Machine* (New York: Free Press, 1998).

39. Woodward, *Choice,* 368.

40. "A Bridge Too Far," *New York Times,* October 16, 1996.

41. Anthony Corrado, "Financing the 1996 Elections," in *The Election of 1996,* ed. Gerald Pomper (Chatham, N.J.: Chatham House, 1997). "Soft money" had its home in the 1979 amendments to the campaign finance legislation of 1974 as part of a broader effort to strengthen national party organizations. By 1992 both Democrats and Republicans had come to depend on it to finance the expensive media campaigns that dominated national elections. As such, the parties violated the spirit of the 1979 amendments, which were meant to increase party spending on traditional grassroots boosterism and get-out-the-vote drives rather than mass media campaigns. More to the point, the institutional separation between the president and the parties allowed, even encouraged, the exploitation of these funds by presidential candidates. See Beth Donovan, "Much-Maligned 'Soft Money' Is Precious to Both Parties," *National Journal,* May 15, 1993, 1195–1200. The Bipartisan Campaign Finance Reform Act of 2002 prohibited national parties from raising and spending "soft money."

42. Michael Nelson, "The Election: Turbulence and Tranquility in Contemporary American Politics," in *The Elections of 1996,* ed. Michael Nelson (Washington, D.C.: CQ Press, 1997), 52; Gary C. Jacobson, "The 105th Congress: Unprecedented and Unsurprising," in Nelson, *The Elections of 1996,* 161.

43. Almost one in five voters identified a "vision for the future" as the most important quality driving their presidential vote; Clinton received 77 percent of their votes. See James W. Ceaser and Andrew E. Busch, *Losing to Win: The 1996 Elections and American Politics* (Lanham, Md.: Rowman and Littlefield, 1997), 166.

44. "Dole, in 3-Prong Effort, Seeks to Add Spark to His Campaign," *New York Times,* September 11, 1996.

45. "The Third Dimension," transcript of segment on *The Newshour with Jim Lehrer,* August 19, 1996.

46. Clinton's "third way" politics is placed in historical perspective and carefully analyzed in Stephen Skowronek, *The Politics Presidents Make: Leadership from John Adams to Bill Clinton* (Cambridge: Harvard University Press, 1999), 447–464.

47. Daniel J. Palazzolo, *Done Deal? The Politics of the 1997 Budget Agreement* (Chatham, N.J.: Chatham House, 1999), 189.

48. R. Kent Weaver, "Ending Welfare as We Know It," in *The Social Divide: Political Parties and the Future of Activist Government,* ed. Margaret Weir (Washington, D.C.: Brookings, 1998), 397.

49. Richard Stevenson, "After Year of Wrangling, Accord Is Reached on Plan to Balance the Budget by 2002," *New York Times,* May 3, 1997, 1.

50. "Glass-Steagall Act: The Senators and Economists Who Got it Right," June 11, 2009, *Huffington Post,* http://www.huffingtonpost.com/2009/05/11/glass-steagall-act-the-se_n_201557.html.

51. Gould, *Modern American Presidency,* 225–226.

52. John R. Zaller, "Monica Lewinsky's Contribution to Political Science," *PS: Political Science and Politics* 31 (June 1998): 182–189.

53. John M. Broder, "In Aide's Claim, Echoes of Watergate," *New York Times,* May 12, 1998.

54. Adam Clymer, "Under Attack, Clinton Gets No Cover from His Party," *New York Times,* March 16, 1997, 1; Jeffrey L. Katz and Dan Carney, "Clinton's Latest, Worst Troubles

Put His Whole Agenda on Hold," *Congressional Quarterly Weekly Report,* January 24, 1998, 164–165; Richard L. Berke, "Republicans End Silence on Troubles of President," *New York Times,* March 1, 1998, 20; Peter Baker, *The Breach: Inside the Impeachment and Trial of William Jefferson Clinton* (New York: Scribner's, 2000).

55. *"Clinton v. City of New York,"* in Nelson, *Evolving Presidency,* 273–278.

56. Janny Scott, "Talking Heads Post-Mortem: All Wrong, All the Time," *New York Times,* November 8, 1998, A22.

57. Richard L. Berke, John M. Broder, and Don Van Natta Jr., "How Republican Determination Upset Clinton's Backing at the Polls," *New York Times,* December 28, 1998.

58. Gary C. Jacobson, *The Politics of Congressional Elections,* 5th ed. (New York: Longman, 2000), 258–259.

59. Two other proposed articles were defeated in the House: one dealing with perjury by 205–229 and the other dealing with abuse of power by 148–285. Only the latter vote, which included eighty-one Republican nays, was anything close to bipartisan.

60. Gould, *Modern American Presidency,* 230.

61. Robert Pear, "The Presidential Pen Is Still Mighty," *New York Times,* June 28, 1998.

62. *Adarand Constructors, Inc. v. Pena,* 515 U.S. 200 (1995).

63. Kenneth R. Mayer, *With the Stroke of a Pen: Executive Orders and Presidential Power* (Princeton: Princeton University Press, 2001), 210–215.

64. Emily O. Goldman and Larry Berman, "Engaging the World: First Impressions of the Clinton Foreign Policy Legacy," in Campbell and Rockman, *Clinton Legacy,* 246–249; Paul Starobin, "The Liberal Hawk Soars," *National Journal,* May 14, 1999.

65. Will Marshall, president, Progressive Policy Institute, interview by Sidney M. Milkis, June 14, 1999.

66. David E. Rosenbaum, "Surplus a Salve for Clinton and Congress," *New York Times,* June 29, 1999.

67. *Clinton v. Jones,* 520 U.S. 681 (1997).

68. See *In re: Sealed Case,* No. 98-3069 (United States Court of Appeals), July 7, 1998; and *In re: Bruce Lindsey (Grand Jury Testimony),* No. 98-3060 (United States Court of Appeals), July 27, 1998. On how Clinton's legal battles set precedents that limited the institutional prerogatives of the presidency, see David M. O'Brien, "Judicial Legacies: The Clinton Presidency and the Courts," in Campbell and Rockman, *Clinton Legacy.*

69. On this point, see Marc Landy and Sidney M. Milkis, *Presidential Greatness* (Lawrence: University Press of Kansas, 2000).

CHAPTER 14

George W. Bush and
Unilateral Presidential Power

B y the close of the Clinton era, the Republicans controlled both houses
of Congress and occupied the governorships of nine of the ten largest
states, all except California. Realizing that to defeat Vice President
Al Gore, the Democratic nominee for president in 2000, they would have to
find a politically moderate candidate, the large-state Republican governors
united behind a colleague, Gov. George W. Bush of Texas. The governors' display of solidarity was evidence that even though candidate-centered politics
had supplanted party-centered politics since the waning of the New Deal, it
was still possible, at least for Republicans, to put the party's political well-
being first. The governors rallied behind Bush in part because he came from
the largest Republican state and shared his father's name. In securing the
nomination, Bush also benefited from being close to the leaders of the GOP's
strongly conservative congressional wing, especially House leaders Richard K.
Armey and Tom DeLay, both Texans.

Bush's most serious challenge came from a fellow moderate who, like
George H. W. Bush but not George W. Bush, was a war hero: Sen. John
McCain of Arizona. Campaigning with the energy, spontaneity, and nationalist fervor of a latter-day Theodore Roosevelt, McCain garnered enough votes
from independents in New Hampshire to win the primary and jeopardize
Bush's nomination. Bush survived the challenge by moving to the right, especially on the social issues so important to Christian conservatives. He soundly
defeated McCain in the decisive South Carolina primary.

Neither Bush's pre-presidential experience nor the themes he stressed in his
campaign gave any hint that he would be able to deal with a foreign policy
crisis if one should arise. Like three of his four most recent predecessors—
Jimmy Carter, Ronald Reagan, and Bill Clinton—Bush was a former state
governor with no experience in Washington. Like them, too, he was elected on
an almost purely domestic platform. Unlike Carter, Reagan, and Clinton,
however, Bush assembled a widely admired team of foreign policy profession-
als to staff his administration. Nearly all of them were experienced hands from

other recent Republican administrations. The senior Bush's secretary of defense, Richard B. Cheney, became George W. Bush's vice president. Colin Powell, who had served as Reagan's national security adviser and then as chairman of the Joint Chiefs of Staff, returned to government as secretary of state. Condoleezza Rice, previously a National Security Council staff member, became the president's national security adviser. For secretary of defense, Bush chose Donald H. Rumsfeld, who had held the same position under Gerald R. Ford.

After terrorists attacked the World Trade Center and the Pentagon on September 11, 2001, Bush declared, "This is what my presidency is about."[1] To be sure, his presidency was about other things as well, some of them significant as policy and some as politics. In the end, however, the fate of the Bush presidency hinged less on his decision to launch the war on terrorism against the al Qaeda network and the Taliban regime that protected it in Afghanistan than on his subsequent decision to extend the war to Iraq. Bush's resolute leadership in the wake of the September 11 attacks earned him and his party considerable political success, culminating in a narrow but decisive reelection victory in 2004. By 2006, however, the growing unpopularity of the war in Iraq and other policy failures had thrown the Bush administration into political free fall. In 2008 Bush was a political albatross around the neck of the Republican candidate bidding to succeed him, Senator McCain.

The Democrats' strong comeback in the 2006 midterm elections, in which they regained control of Congress for the first time in twelve years, and the victory of their presidential nominee in 2008, Sen. Barack Obama of Illinois, badly compromised Bush's first-term political achievements. More broadly, the successes and failures of the Bush presidency raised once again a familiar dilemma: how can the country maintain an executive that is strong enough to meet imposing challenges at home and abroad but not so strong as to defy accountability to Congress and the public? Although this dilemma is as old as the Republic, Bush's extraordinary reliance on the unilateral powers of the presidency, some of them widely disputed, raised it in an especially extreme form.[2]

THE 2000 ELECTION

At the September 2000 meeting of the American Political Science Association, seven renowned scholars forecast the outcome of the November presidential election using models that incorporated measures of economic growth and public approval of the incumbent president. They unanimously predicted that Gore would defeat Bush by a margin of 6 percent to 20 percent of the national popular vote.[3] For four years the economy had grown at an annual rate of at least 4 percent, and President Clinton's job approval rating had stayed above

60 percent, the highest and most consistent ratings for a second-term president in the history of polling. In addition, unemployment had fallen during every year of Clinton's two-term presidency, eventually dropping below 4 percent; the average annual rate of inflation during the Clinton years was the lowest since the early 1960s; and the enormous budget deficits that Clinton inherited from his predecessor had become substantial budget surpluses.

Obviously, the political scientists' predictions were wrong: the election was extremely close, and in the end Gore lost. Telling the voters in his acceptance speech at the Democratic national convention that "I stand here tonight as my own man" was a politically appropriate response to the candidate-centered nature of modern presidential politics, which places a premium on distinguishing oneself from one's party and predecessors.[4] But rejecting Clinton's repeated offers to campaign for him, which party leaders pleaded with Gore to accept, was not.[5] Even worse, instead of emphasizing the national prosperity that had marked the Clinton-Gore years, Gore ran a populist-style, "people, not the powerful" campaign, better suited for a candidate challenging an incumbent in economic hard times than for a vice president seeking to extend his party's control of the presidency in good times. Gore's strongest political advantage in 2000 was his ability to ask the voters: if eight years of Democratic rule has produced peace and prosperity, why elect a Republican? Yet in the three nationally televised debates with Bush, Gore never mentioned Clinton. "We might have blown it," a Gore aide said near the end of the campaign. "We didn't remind people of how well off they are."[6]

Surprisingly, the debates were another reason for Gore's defeat. Gore carried into the campaign a reputation as an aggressive, experienced, and skillful debater, a reputation that Bush did not have.[7] Yet in the first debate, Gore lost ground by treating his opponent in an unattractively disdainful way, often speaking condescendingly when it was his turn and then sighing and grimacing while Bush spoke. Chastened by the adverse public response, Gore was deferential to the point of seeming obsequious during the second debate. He hit his stride in the third debate, but the inconsistency of his manner from one debate to the next fed voters' doubts about who Gore really was. Bush did not dominate any of the debates, but voters saw the same Bush in all three. Having entered the debates trailing Gore by five percentage points in the polls, Bush came out of them with a five-point lead.

Third party politics also worked to Gore's disadvantage. The Reform Party, formed by H. Ross Perot in 1996, seemed likely to draw voters from the Republican nominee, but it self-destructed in 2000 after conservative political commentator Pat Buchanan captured its nomination. Buchanan shared some core Reform positions, especially strong opposition to free trade, but he spoke more frequently on social and cultural issues that divided the party such as abortion, affirmative action, and gay rights. Buchanan's nomination at the

Reform convention provoked Perot to endorse Bush. On election day, Buchanan received less than 1 percent of the national popular vote.

Ralph Nader, the longtime consumer activist and Green Party nominee, ran a much stronger campaign than Buchanan, winning 3 percent of the national popular vote. Because many of Nader's votes came at Gore's expense, Gore had to campaign harder to carry northern progressive states such as Minnesota and Oregon than he would have had Nader not been on the ballot. In Florida, Nader received 97,419 votes, many more than Gore needed to win the state, its twenty-five electoral votes, and the presidency. Nationally, the exit poll indicated that Nader supporters preferred Gore to Bush by 47 percent to 21 percent.[8]

In the end, both Bush and Gore presented themselves to the voters as pragmatic centrists. For all Gore's efforts to separate himself from Clinton by adopting a populist theme, the actual policy positions he took during the campaign gave no indication that he contemplated a significant departure from Clinton's "third way" Democratic course. Bush fashioned an appeal based on "compassionate conservatism." Instead of being reflexively antigovernment in the Reagan tradition, he emphasized the need for a federal role in ameliorating poverty and improving education.[9] Although both Gore and Bush had been anointed by their parties' leaders, each ran independently of his party and sought a strategic center between Democratic liberalism and Republican conservatism.

The 2000 election ended in a virtual tie, with the deadlock ultimately resolved by the Supreme Court. In the end, the Bush versus Gore election campaign was less decisive than the *Bush v. Gore* Supreme Court case. In many of its features, the protracted, bitter legal dispute that lasted for five weeks after the voters cast their ballots resembled the institutional clashes that had dominated the final third of the twentieth century, culminating in the Clinton impeachment. These clashes raised doubts about whether a nation that historically resolved most of its political conflicts through the electoral process had grown accustomed to institutional combat instead.[10]

BUSH V. GORE

The "postelection election" of 2000 began in the predawn hours of Wednesday, November 8, when the television networks, which earlier had declared Bush the winner on the basis of his projected victory in Florida, decided that Florida was actually too close to call. Gore dispatched a team of lawyers to Tallahassee to investigate charges by local Democrats that they had been cheated out of their votes. Claiming that voting machines had failed to count all of his ballots and therefore had thwarted the will of the people, Gore called for a hand count in four counties that had voted strongly Democratic and were controlled by Democratic election commissions. The core of Gore's legal challenge, which was supported by Florida's Democrat-dominated supreme court, was that a hand count would show the true intent of the voters and, in all likelihood, overcome Bush's minuscule lead, which had shrunk from a reported 1,784 votes on election night to 327 votes after a statewide machine recount was conducted a few days later.

Bush's lawyers appealed to the U.S. Supreme Court to stop the hand count ordered by the state supreme court in the four disputed counties. They argued that the Florida court's decision violated both the Constitution's provision that the state legislature must determine how a state's electors will be chosen and the 1887 Electoral Count Act's requirement, passed in the wake of the disputed 1876 Hayes-Tilden election, that electors must be chosen according to state laws enacted in advance of the election. Bush's lawyers also claimed that the recount violated the equal protection clause of the Fourteenth Amendment because no uniform standard would govern the recounting of votes in the state's different counties.

Even as the lawyers from both sides chased each other from courtroom to courtroom, Bush pressed advantages that he alone enjoyed. Florida secretary of state Katherine Harris, who under state law was charged to certify the results of the election and oversee any recounts that took place, had cochaired the state's Bush campaign. The state legislature, which arguably had the power under the Electoral Count Act to appoint a slate of electors if all other approaches failed, was heavily Republican. The governor of Florida was Bush's brother. As governor, Jeb Bush was charged by the Electoral Count Act to officially notify the National Archives in Washington which slate of electors his state had chosen.[11] Republican presidents had appointed seven of the nine justices of the U.S. Supreme Court, which on December 9 agreed to the Bush legal team's request to resolve the controversy. Bush also benefited from the simple passage of time. Because the Electoral Count Act required that states decide by December 12 which candidate's slate of electors had been chosen, any recounts presumably would have to be completed by then.

Discerning the intent of voters who had imperfectly marked their ballots was the subject of the Supreme Court decision. A seven-justice majority decreed that the counting process ordered by the Florida Supreme Court, which required a manual count of every "under-vote" (that is, every ballot for which a machine had failed to register a vote for president), was unconstitutional. By failing to establish a uniform standard that every county in the state would use to judge the voters' intention, the Florida court had violated the Fourteenth Amendment's requirement that states safeguard the right of individuals to the "equal protection of the laws."

The Court divided more closely and bitterly in the second, decisive part of its ruling. In a 5–4 vote, the Court found that the Florida court had also

After being sworn in as the forty-third president of the United States, George W. Bush sings the national anthem with former president Bill Clinton and former vice president Al Gore on inauguration day, January 20, 2001.

violated the Constitution by over-ruling the state legislature, which had indicated its intention to take advantage of an Electoral Count Act provision that insulates a state's electors from challenge as long as they are certified by December 12. Because any recount would frustrate the constitutional prerogative of the state legislature to determine how electors are chosen, the Court decreed, "we reverse the judgment of the Supreme Court of Florida ordering the recount to proceed." [12] The Supreme Court issued its decision on the evening of December 12, leaving Florida no time to recount the votes even if identical procedures for doing so could be implemented in every county.

Gore conceded the election the next day. But his surrender did not take place without considerable protest. Gore's supporters were emboldened by Justice John Paul Stevens's dissenting opinion, in which he decried the Court's majority for emphasizing Florida's need to certify its electoral votes by December 12 rather than enforcing the state's obligation to determine the intention of its voters. "Although we may never know with complete certainty the identity of the winner of this year's Presidential election," Stevens wrote, "the identity of the loser is perfectly clear. It is the Nation's confidence in the judge as an impartial guardian of the rule of law." [13]

THE EARLY MONTHS OF THE BUSH PRESIDENCY

Bush began his presidency in 2001 with the Republicans in control of Congress, although by the narrowest of margins. The Republican majority in the House was 222–211, the same as before the election. A four-seat Democratic gain in the Senate elections created a 50–50 division between the parties, with Vice President Cheney able to break any ties in the Republicans' favor. Like Clinton at the beginning of his administration, Bush chose to cooperate with his party's strongly ideological leaders in Congress. His decision to emphasize traditional conservative issues such as tax cuts, regulatory relief, energy production, and missile defense risked alienating moderate Republicans, a small but pivotal group in the closely divided House and Senate.

Bush reaped both the benefits and the costs of this early strategy of partisan conservatism. The president persuaded Congress to enact the leading conservative plank in his 2000 platform, a $1.3 trillion tax cut. But the Republicans lost control of the Senate in May 2001 when Sen. James M. Jeffords of Vermont announced that he was changing his allegiance from the Republican to the Democratic caucus.[14] Within days, every Senate committee and subcommittee chairmanship was transferred to Democratic hands.

Facing the prospect of ongoing partisan obstruction in the Senate, the Bush administration intensified its efforts to consolidate authority within the White House. The president assigned his political adviser, Karl Rove, to take the lead in recruiting candidates and devising Republican campaign strategies for the 2002 state and congressional elections. In doing so, Bush undercut the authority of the Republican National Committee chair, Gov. James S. Gilmore III of Virginia. Politics was joined to policy when, midway through 2001, Rove began repositioning the president as a centrist, nontraditional Republican. By the end of his first summer in office, Bush had begun to stress educational reform and "faith-based" social services, not taxes and national defense.[15]

Bush's revival of his campaign theme of compassionate conservatism, White House aides argued, embodied conservative values but not conservative opposition to an active federal government.[16] "The invisible hand works many miracles," Bush had said in July 1999. "But it cannot touch the human heart. . . . We are a nation of rugged individuals. But we are also the country of the second chance—tied together by bonds of friendship and community and solidarity."

In part, Bush proposed to fulfill the moral commitment he endorsed with policies that supported nonprofit groups working outside of government. In doing so, he called for changes in federal and state regulations that would allow churches and other faith-based organizations to play a larger role in providing government-funded social services to the poor, the addicted, the illiterate, and others in need of help. But Bush also wanted the federal government to play an important part in securing the general welfare. Although conservatives had once sought to eliminate the Department of Education, Bush proposed the No Child Left Behind Act, which charged the department to make public schools more accountable by linking federal aid to national standards and measurements of student learning.

For as long as the president continued to emphasize it, compassionate conservatism promised to soften the harsh antigovernment edge of the Republican Party. It also gave the president a platform from which to act independently of his party. Because programs such as faith-based initiatives and educational reform were not major priorities within Republican councils, Bush advanced several of his objectives through bipartisan cooperation or executive orders.[17]

The No Child Left Behind Act in particular seemed less a use of government to secure Republican principles than an uneasy compromise between liberals' demand for more spending and conservatives' insistence on standards.[18] Bush trumpeted his alliance with the Democratic Party's leading liberal icon, Sen. Edward M. Kennedy of Massachusetts, when signing the bill in January 2002. One year later, Bush persuaded both parties in Congress to adopt PEPFAR—the President's Emergency Plan for AIDS Relief—a five-year, $15 billion plan to combat AIDS in Africa.[19]

No less than Clinton's third way, Bush's compassionate conservatism promised to transcend the long-standing contest in American politics between rights-based claims to entitlement programs and the virtues of individual responsibility. His first prime-time address to the nation on a specific issue, stem cell research, represented another effort to satisfy both sides. Many religious conservatives viewed stem cell research using human embryos as a form of abortion that violates the rights of the unborn. But most Americans opposed closing the door to stem cell research, valuing its promise of scientific progress toward curing diseases.

Bush's August 9 address tried but failed to bridge the two sides of the debate. In a solution that the president characterized as "careful and prayerful," but which detractors dismissed as clumsy and calculating, the president announced that federal grants could be used to conduct studies on stem cells that already had been harvested from embryos left over at fertility clinics. But he prohibited the national government from supporting research that involved the creation or destruction of any new embryos.

Bush's attempt to resolve the stem cell controversy highlighted the tension between the modern presidency and constitutional democracy. The president's policy came in the form of an executive order, which granted authority to oversee stem cell research to the newly created President's Council on Bioethics. But the controversy could not be ended by fiat. It resurfaced in the 2004 presidential election and again in Congress's decision in 2006 to pass a bill lifting the restrictions that Bush had placed on federally funded embryonic stem cell research. Bush's veto of this bill, the first veto of his presidency, ended the legislative challenge at the expense of fueling a political one. Democrats kept the issue alive in the 2006 midterm elections, in which they took control of both houses of Congress from the Republicans. If public debate over stem cells was truly required, Democrats argued, why should the issue be resolved by appointed experts rather than by elected officials in Congress? By delegating the issue to an administrative board, Bush had confirmed an important legacy of the modern presidency: a more active and better-equipped national government, but one that often eschews legislative deliberation.[20] The fragility of this approach was revealed in February 2009, when the Democratic Congress overturned Bush's executive order by passing a bill to broadly fund stem cell research, and Obama, the newly elected Democratic president, signed it into law.

SEPTEMBER 11 AND THE WAR ON TERRORISM

Bush's agenda changed dramatically when the United States was struck by terrorists from the al Qaeda network on September 11, 2001. In the aftermath of the first attack on the American continent since the War of 1812, and the deadliest in the nation's history, the country rallied behind the president. Polls showed a remarkable and almost immediate jump in public support for Bush, from 51 percent approval of the job he was doing as president to 90 percent approval within days of the attacks. A strong public and congressional consensus quickly formed in support of his initial military response against al Qaeda and the Taliban regime in Afghanistan that harbored the terrorist network's leaders.[21]

Hardly a critical word was heard when the Bush administration created the White House–based Office of Homeland Security, imposed tighter restrictions on airport security, and embraced deficit spending to help the economy and fight the war in Afghanistan. Bush justified the war on terrorism in words reminiscent of Franklin D. Roosevelt's promise of greater security and Winston Churchill's call for resoluteness in the face of an evil foe. "Freedom and fear are at war," Bush told a joint session of Congress in a televised address on September 20. "The advance of human freedom—the great achievement of our time and great hope of every time—now depends on us. . . . We will not tire, we will not falter, and we will not fail."[22]

Bush's response to the September 11 attacks was both a continuation of and a departure from the progressive internationalist tradition that has dominated the modern presidency since Theodore Roosevelt and Woodrow Wilson. Like a true progressive, Bush emphasized that the war on terrorism was both an effort to protect American lives and property and a crusade to advance liberty and democracy. But he also made clear that the United States would set its own course, welcoming consultation and assistance from other nations but refusing to be deterred by the misgivings of even its closest allies. Wilson trumpeted the need for a League of Nations to enforce a lasting peace. FDR invested considerable diplomatic and political capital in working with the wartime allies to found the United Nations. Bush's father gathered a broad international coalition to prosecute the Persian Gulf War of 1991. But Bush did not wait for a massive allied force to form before invading Afghanistan in October 2001. The war was fought and the Taliban overthrown by American special forces and Central Intelligence Agency operatives working in close coordination with Afghanistan's Northern Alliance.

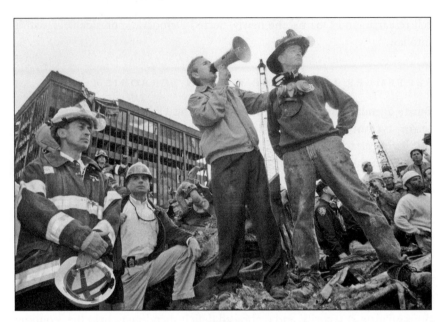

President George W. Bush addresses a crowd of firefighters, rescue workers, and volunteers at Ground Zero—the 16-acre plot where the 110-story World Trade Center towers once stood—three days after two hijacked planes struck the buildings on September 11, 2001.

The war on terrorism created a political dilemma for the Democrats. Although Bush's public approval ratings declined from their 90 percent peak, the decline was gradual, and his conduct of the presidency was still supported by 68 percent of Americans in November 2002.[23] For as long as Bush remained popular, Democratic officeholders could not oppose his policies without appearing unpatriotic. But they were most in tune with Wilsonian progressivism on the very matter that Bush was least so: international cooperation. Democrats treasured close ties with the West European allies and were strongly committed to respecting and working through international bodies, especially the United Nations.

AN EXPANDED PRESIDENCY

As Bush prepared the nation for new responsibilities at home and abroad, presidential scholars and public officials revived warnings, dormant since the Nixon years, about what political scientist Andrew Rudalevige called "the new imperial presidency."[24] Already executive-centered in its approach to politics and policy, the Bush White House became even more insulated from Congress and the Republican Party as it planned and fought the multifront war on terrorism. Democratic and Republican legislators complained when

White House Homeland Security director Tom Ridge refused to testify before Congress. The administration claimed that Ridge's office was a presidential agency whose director and staff were exempt from congressional grilling.

Similarly, bipartisan criticism of Attorney General John Ashcroft emerged when the administration unilaterally instituted measures to crack down on terrorism at home, including military tribunals to try suspected foreign terrorists.[25] According to an executive order issued by President Bush on November 13, 2001, "unlawful enemy combatants" would be brought to trial not in a civil court but in a military tribunal and with no right of appeal. Although some American citizens were later designated as enemy combatants, the order targeted noncitizens whom the president determined to be present or former members of al Qaeda; to have "engaged in, aided or abetted, or conspired to commit acts of international terrorism or acts in preparation thereof" that would have "adverse effects" on the "United States, its citizens, national security, foreign policy, or economy"; or to have "knowingly harbored" someone who had. The executive order defended the president's power to establish military tribunals without congressional authorization by invoking Franklin Roosevelt's 1942 proclamation about the *Quirin* saboteurs. But, as critics pointed out, FDR's order was drafted retrospectively to apply to a specific case, not prospectively to apply to any individuals the president might decide were enemies of the United States.[26]

For a time, these complaints paled against the aura of political invincibility that Bush enjoyed after September 11. But the roots of Congress's resentment of executive slights ran deep. Beginning in spring 2002, Bush administration officials openly pursued the possibility of a war in Iraq aimed at removing Iraqi dictator Saddam Hussein from power. In October 2002, at the president's request, Congress passed a resolution authorizing him to use military force against Iraq "as he determines to be necessary." In doing so, legislators sustained Bush's revival of the cold war–era belief that any overriding cause—the containment of communism then, the war against terrorism now—justifies the expansive use of presidential power around the globe.

The Bush administration's decision to seek a congressional endorsement of its policy toward Iraq was an exception to its rule of unilateral executive action, but only a partial one. Bush made clear that he would not be bound by an adverse vote. The president's broader determination to fight the war on terrorism outside the bounds of conventional legal constraints was a constant source of tension between the White House and Congress. Indeed, congressional resistance became bipartisan during Bush's second term. By late 2005, buttressed by revelations that the administration had used the highly secret National Security Agency to monitor suspicious domestic communications without judicial review or consultation with Congress, legislators began to fight back. In addition to their concern about the president's policy of creating military tribunals to try enemy combatants and his use of surveillance to monitor overseas phone calls, they objected to the administration's broad rules permitting tough interrogations of suspected terrorists.

In particular, a series of memos from the Central Intelligence Agency's general counsel and the Justice Department's Office of Legal Counsel claimed for the CIA wide powers of imprisonment and interrogation that in some cases overrode the Geneva Conventions, the international code that has governed the treatment of prisoners and civilians during wartime and postwar occupations for more than half a century. Because terrorists were not fighting on behalf of an established state or in uniform, the Bush administration argued, they were not covered by the international law of war. The president approved a permissive set of rules governing interrogations, which allowed the CIA to establish detention centers in secret overseas locations. Suspected terrorists were subjected to severe interrogation techniques, including "water-boarding," in which a bound prisoner is brought to the brink of drowning.

In the face of vigorous White House opposition, Congress, led by Senator McCain, himself a victim of torture as a prisoner of war in Vietnam, passed the Detainee Treatment Act of 2005. Bush signed the bill, which prohibited interrogation techniques that involve "cruel, inhuman, or degrading treatment or punishment." But the president appended a statement to his signature, objecting to some of the new law's provisions and explicitly reserving the right to interpret them "in a manner consistent with the constitutional authority of the President to supervise the unitary executive branch and as Commander in Chief." The phrase "unitary executive branch" referred to the Bush administration's theory, popular in certain conservative legal circles, that neither Congress nor the courts may restrict the president's authority to command employees and agencies of the executive branch.[27] Following, indeed wildly exceeding, the practice of his three most recent predecessors—Ronald Reagan, George H. W. Bush, and Bill Clinton—Bush used signing statements to declare that he would not enforce about twelve hundred provisions of laws as he signed them, about twice as many as all previous presidents combined.[28] In each case, Bush's purpose was to insulate executive power from legislative and judicial direction, especially in matters pertaining to national and homeland security.[29]

The president's defense of a largely unchecked unitary executive was challenged in the Supreme Court. On June 29, 2006, the Court's ruling in *Hamdan v. Rumsfeld* strongly limited the president's power to create military tribunals for and employ aggressive interrogation techniques against suspected terrorists imprisoned at the U.S. naval base in Guantánamo Bay, Cuba.[30] Brushing aside the administration's pleas not to second-guess the commander in chief during wartime, a five-justice majority ruled that the tribunals were neither authorized by federal law nor justified by military necessity and that they violated the Geneva Conventions. Consequently, the Court ordered, no military tribunal could try either Salam Ahmed Hamdan, a former aide to al Qaeda leader Osama bin Laden, or anyone else unless the president did one of two things that he had steadfastly refused to do: operate the tribunals by the established laws governing regular military courts martial or ask Congress for specific permission to proceed differently.

Responding to *Hamdan,* Bush had little choice but to press for legislation endorsing his approach to terrorists. His efforts to persuade Congress to narrowly define American obligations under the Geneva Conventions met strong resistance in the Senate. Three respected Republicans—John McCain, Lindsay Graham of South Carolina, and John Warner of Virginia, the chair of the Armed Services Committee—rejected the administration's approach not only as unbefitting a free nation but also as an invitation to other countries to abuse any American soldiers they might hold as prisoners. Anxious to resolve this dispute before the 2006 elections, Bush and the dissident Republicans reached a compromise in September 2006. The White House yielded its desire to secure congressional approval for a constricted interpretation of Article 3 of the Geneva Conventions, which requires humane treatment of detainees and prohibits "violence to life and person," including "outrages upon personal dignity." In return, Congress delegated to the president the dominant role in deciding which interrogation methods are permitted by Article 3. The Military Commissions Act, which Bush signed into law on October 18, 2006, also authorized the use of military tribunals and eliminated habeas corpus jurisdiction for any "enemy combatant" held in American custody. Although the Supreme Court ruled in *Boumediene v. Bush* (2008) that enemy combatants have a constitutional right to file petitions for habeas corpus in federal court, it left intact the remainder of the Military Commissions Act.[31]

The war on terrorism affirmed the preeminence of the modern presidency in other ways as well. The new responsibilities that the war thrust on the executive led Bush, at the urging of many members of Congress, to pursue major institutional reforms of the executive branch. In June 2002 he called for the creation of a Department of Homeland Security, outlining the most ambitious reorganization of the federal government since the 1940s. Likening his plan to the 1947 National Security Act, which authorized President Harry S. Truman to create the National Security Council and the Department of Defense, Bush asked Congress to create "a single, permanent department with an overriding and urgent mission: securing the homeland of America, and protecting the American people."[32]

Bush had initially resisted forming another government department.[33] The small Office of Homeland Security that he created by executive order in the frantic days after September 11 was part of the White House staff and was headed by Ridge, who enjoyed a close personal relationship with the president. The administration changed course, however, when faced with criticism about whether it had done everything possible to prevent the September 11 attacks and taken adequate measures to forestall similar acts in the future. Ridge's office, critics claimed, lacked authority over the budgets and activities of the many executive agencies whose actions he was responsible for coordinating.

Once Bush was persuaded to transform the homeland security office into a full-scale homeland security department, he urged Congress to enact legislation moving twenty-two executive agencies and 170,000 federal employees, including the Customs Service, Secret Service, Immigration and Naturalization Service, and Federal Emergency Management Agency, into the new department.[34] Congressional Democrats and Republicans looked favorably on Bush's proposal, in part because Congress has more authority over a department than over a White House office. The president's plan promised to end the protracted struggle (Concerning) whether Ridge was obligated to testify before Congress about his budget and programs. As the head of a department, he clearly was accountable to the legislature. At the same time, the creation of the department signified that homeland security had become an ongoing responsibility of the national government.

Bush and Congress also gave the executive branch new responsibilities for regulating the economy. In the early 2000s the collapse of Enron, a huge energy trading corporation, and WorldCom, a leading telecommunications company, amid revelations of fraudulent accounting practices and unethical boardroom scheming, caused the stock market and consumer confidence to plummet. As a pro-business conservative, Bush lacked the credibility on regulatory issues that he enjoyed on homeland security and the war on terrorism. But facing criticism from members of his party who feared that business scandals would hurt Republicans in the 2002 midterm elections, Bush rushed to take charge of efforts, already well advanced in Congress, to reform corporate behavior. Sounding more like TR than Ronald Reagan, the president gave a tough speech on Wall Street in July 2002, proclaiming that America's "greatest economic need is higher ethical standards—standards enforced by strict laws and upheld by responsible business leaders." A few weeks later, Bush signed the Sarbanes-Oxley Act, celebrating it as "the most far-reaching reform of American business practices since the time of Franklin Delano Roosevelt." Among other provisions, the act strengthened the Securities and Exchange Commission, which had been created as part of FDR's New Deal, and formed a Public Accounting and Oversight Board "to enforce professional standards, ethics, and competence for the accounting profession."[35] Effective as Sarbanes-Oxley was in preventing Enron-style disasters, however, it did nothing to forestall the ruinous speculation in mortgage-backed securities and other exotic financial instruments that triggered a massive meltdown of the nation's financial system in late summer 2008, sending the country to the brink of depression for the first time since the 1930s.

BUSH AND THE REPUBLICAN PARTY

For much of the history of the modern presidency, executive power has tended to undermine the major political parties. The forging of direct ties between the White House and the public, combined with aggressive executive administration, has tended to subordinate party loyalty to the personal and programmatic ambitions of the president. From the outset, Bush's presidency was different. After winning the 2000 election, he and political adviser Karl Rove became strongly committed to making the Republican Party an enduring governing majority. As such, the Bush presidency shows how a strongly partisan president can try to use the expanded powers of the office for party-building purposes.

With steadfast support from Republican leaders in Congress, Bush exploited his party's ideology and organization to advance a conservative, executive centered administrative state. A similar effort had begun during the Reagan administration, but Bush trumped Reagan in his commitment to "big government conservatism."[36] The most dramatic example of this approach was Bush's foreign policy, especially the controversial Bush Doctrine of preventive war against terrorist states or states that harbor terrorists. "If we wait for threats to materialize," the president declared in a June 1, 2002, graduation address at the United States Military Academy at West Point, "we will have waited too long." Because "the war on terrorism will not be won on the defensive," he added, "we must take the battle to the enemy, disrupt his plans, and confront the worst threats before they emerge." Referring to "unbalanced dictators with weapons of mass destruction," Bush left little doubt that he intended to use his new prevention doctrine to justify a war against Saddam Hussein's regime in Iraq.[37]

Bush-style big government conservatism extended to domestic policy as well. Rather than try to curtail New Deal and Great Society entitlement programs, as President Reagan and the Gingrich-led 104th Congress had tried to do, Bush sought to recast these programs in conservative form. His goal was to cement ties between the Republican Party and groups that embrace generally conservative values but whose members rely on government help. Bush's faith-based social services initiative was, in part, a response to religious organizations' belief that they had been unfairly disadvantaged in obtaining federal funds to help the poor, uneducated, and addicted. With his commitment to the No Child Left Behind education reform, Bush sought to mobilize conservatives to make public schools better by making them more demanding. Finally, in an effort to win support from senior citizens, in 2003 Bush secured congressional enactment of an extremely costly prescription drug program for the elderly as a part of Medicare.

Even Bush's most spectacular domestic policy failure, his doomed effort at the start of the second term to reform Social Security, reflected his commitment to deploy the federal government for conservative objectives. Unlike Reagan, Bush proposed not to cut Social Security benefits but to privatize them by allowing workers to divert some of their Social Security payroll taxes into personal retirement accounts. This reform, the president claimed, would yield beneficiaries a better rate of return on their contributions and would recast the core New Deal entitlement program so that individuals would assume greater responsibility to plan for their own retirement. The federal government would still force people to save, restrict the investment choices they could make, and regulate the pace at which they could withdraw their money in retirement.[38] Bush campaigned around the country for his plan, but it went nowhere in Congress. Like Clinton's equally sweeping proposal to reform health care in 1993 and 1994, Social Security reform foundered on the shoals of partisan opposition and the public's reluctance to change a system that most felt worked reasonably well.

The Bush administration's party-building activities complemented its agenda of big government conservatism. The president's active recruitment of Republican candidates and diligent fundraising considerably strengthened the national party organization. His public displays of religious faith and use of strong moral language solidified the Republican loyalties of religious conservatives. Large tax cuts in 2001 and 2003 were equally appealing to the party's economic conservatives. During Bush's first term, these efforts yielded handsome political returns.

Risking the bipartisan support he accrued in the aftermath of September 11, Bush threw himself into the 2002 midterm elections earlier and more energetically than any president in history. Bush and Rove recruited strong Republican challengers to face incumbent Democratic senators, even to the point of intervening in state party politics to do so. The president spoke at sixty-seven fundraising events that raised a record $141 million in campaign contributions for the GOP and its candidates. Throughout the fall, he campaigned ardently for his party's nominees.

The results of the elections vindicated Bush's decision to become actively involved in the campaign. The Republicans gained two seats in the Senate, moving them from minority to majority status, while increasing their majority in the House of Representatives. Political analysts were quick to describe the historic nature of the Republican victory. It marked the first time in more than a century that the president's party had regained control of the Senate in a midterm election. It was the first election since 1934—and the first ever for a Republican president—in which the president's party gained seats in both houses of Congress midway through the first term. Analysts were quick to credit Bush with his party's success.

Yet Bush and Rove could not take all the credit for the Republican gains. Since the late 1970s the Republican Party had been developing into a formidable national organization in which the Republican National Committee, rather than the state and local organizations, was the principal sponsor of party-building activities. For a time, this top-down approach to party revitalization risked becoming too centralized and too dependent on television advertising to perform the parties' traditional role of mobilizing voters. Convinced that it had been out-organized on the ground by the Democrats in 2000, Republicans developed a massive grassroots voter mobilization operation for Bush's reelection campaign in 2004. Unlike the Democrats, who since the New Deal had relied on auxiliary groups such as labor unions to get out the vote, the GOP created its own national organization to mobilize supporters.[39] Indeed, one could argue that the Republicans built the first national party machine in American history—an elaborate network of campaign volunteers concentrated in the sixteen most competitive states. The Republican organization was crucial to Bush's narrow but decisive victory against the Democratic nominee, Sen. John Kerry of Massachusetts: 51 percent to 48 percent in the popular vote and 286 to 251 in the Electoral College.[40]

In the arena of presidential party building, Bush surpassed Reagan, whose popularity never translated into Republican majorities in both houses of Congress. In 2004 Bush became the first incumbent since Franklin Roosevelt to win a second term while his party was gaining seats in the House and Senate. Bush's four most recently reelected predecessors—Dwight D. Eisenhower in 1956, Richard Nixon in 1972, Ronald Reagan in 1984, and Bill Clinton in 1996—won by much larger margins than he did. But theirs were "lonely landslides" in which the president did well but his party suffered in the congressional elections.[41]

In fact, the 2004 campaign may have marked a milestone in the development of united, ideologically distinctive political parties. The new party system had already strengthened partisan discipline in Congress, and it had been a valuable source of campaign funds and other services for candidates. But it had failed to stir the passions and allegiance of the American people, as attested by the declining voter turnout from the 1960s to 2000. In contrast, the 2004 campaign was passionate, polarized, and participatory. Significantly, both the Republicans' grassroots organizations and the get-out-the-vote campaign of Americans Coming Together (ACT), the group that assumed principal responsibility for Kerry's voter mobilization effort, were organized outside the regular state and local party organizations.[42] Both campaigns sought to recruit new grassroots activists to serve as local leaders in a national party offensive. Voter turnout rose from 51 percent in 2000 to 55 percent in 2004, allowing Bush to win 11.5 million more popular votes in 2004 than he had in his first victory, the largest increase ever for a president from one election to the next.[43] Beyond its immediate effectiveness in securing Bush's reelection, then, the Republicans' White House–inspired mobilization effort in 2004 provided a plausible blueprint for a revitalized party politics that draws more people into the political process and renews the linkages between citizens and their elected officials.

Although Bush's leadership of the Republican Party marked the most systematic effort by a modern president to create a strong national party, the prospect of parties holding the modern presidency accountable was never great. As Rove has argued, the national parties that have emerged since the 1980s are "of great importance in the tactical and mechanical aspects of electing a president." But they are "less important in developing a political and policy strategy for the White House." In effect, parties serve as a critical "means to the president's end."

Not surprisingly, the Bush reelection campaign sought to frame the voters' choice in 2004 as between two individuals, not between the Republican and Democratic platforms. Voters were urged to focus on the candidates' character and temperament. In the lingering aftermath of the September 11 attacks, Republicans wanted Americans to ask themselves which candidate would do a better job of waging the war on terrorism. As Matthew Dowd, the Bush campaign's top strategist, suggested, "People want someone they can count on in tough times, and [after September 11] Bush filled this paternalistic role."[45] The Kerry campaign, for its part, emphasized the senator's intelligence and strength of character. A central theme of the 2004 Democratic national convention was Kerry's military service in Vietnam. He accepted the nomination with a salute and an emphatic announcement that he was "reporting for duty!" The convention focused on presenting Kerry as the candidate who displayed the "strength required of a leader in post–9-11 America."[46]

Kerry's electoral chances suffered when Republicans characterized his erratic support for the war in Iraq as "flip-flopping," which appeared to defy his campaign's emphasis on the candidate's strength of character. Like many Democrats in Congress, Kerry justified his vote for the Iraq War resolution in 2002 by claiming that he was merely voting to authorize the president to decide whether to go to war. Kerry maintained throughout the campaign that he would have cast the same vote even after seeing how frustrating the situation had become in Iraq. After all, he said, "I believe it's the right authority for the president to have."[47] Kerry's acceptance of executive aggrandizement badly hamstrung his effort to challenge Bush on the central issue of the 2004 election. Ultimately, as Dowd acknowledged, "both parties' organizing force has focused on President Bush—the Republicans in defense of his leadership; the Democrats in opposition—hostility—to it."[48]

The 2006 midterm election confirmed this tendency toward president-centered partisan voting, even in a nonpresidential year. The Democrats based their victorious campaign on opposition to a president who, although increasingly unpopular because of the war in Iraq and the ineffective federal response to the devastation wrought in New Orleans by Hurricane Katrina in August 2005, would not be on the ballot in 2008.[49] In the aftermath of the election, attitudes toward Bush and the parties remained closely interwoven, both in Congress and the country. An April 2007 *New York Times*/CBS News poll found that Bush's approval rating among all voters was 32 percent, but among Republicans it was more than twice as high—66 percent.[50] That same month, in a crucial vote on funding for the Iraq war, House and Senate Republicans voted 195–2 and 45–2, respectively, against a bill that tied the appropriation to a schedule for military withdrawal, while House and Senate Democrats voted 216–13 and 49–0, respectively, in favor of the bill.[51] When Bush vetoed the legislation, Republican loyalists in Congress united to prevent the Democrats from attaining the two-thirds majority needed to override the veto.

Early in his second term, President George W. Bush appointed two justices to the Supreme Court. Bush looks on as his first appointee, Chief Justice John Roberts, administers the oath of office to his second appointee, Justice Samuel Alito.

COURTS AND PARTIES

Since the end of the Lyndon Johnson administration, presidents and the Senate have been engaged in acrimonious battles over nominations to the Supreme Court and appellate judgeships. But partisan rancor reached new heights during the Bush presidency. In the wake of the Republicans' victory in 2004, Senate majority leader Bill Frist of Tennessee, with encouragement from Bush, considered employing what came to be called the "nuclear option"— that is, having Vice President Cheney rule filibusters against judicial nominations out of order so that judges could be voted on and confirmed by a simple majority of senators. The polarizing struggle over the filibuster was resolved in May 2005 when a bipartisan group of Senate moderates—dubbed the Gang of 14—agreed to oppose both the nuclear option and filibusters except under "extraordinary circumstances."

Just how long this uneasy truce would last remained uncertain. The retirement of Justice Sandra Day O'Connor and the death of Chief Justice William H. Rehnquist in the fall of 2005 gave Bush the opportunity to make two Supreme Court appointments and thereby move the Court in a conservative direction.[52] The White House, the Senate, and activists on both the left and right immediately prepared to renew their partisan combat over judicial nominations.

Ironically, the main conflict that ensued was not between Democrats and Republicans but between the president and conservatives in his own party. Bush's first nominee, appellate court judge John G. Roberts Jr., did not generate much opposition. Roberts had a conservative record as a member of the Reagan administration's Justice Department and, as a federal judge, he had not left a long enough paper trail for liberals to attack. Equally important, Roberts was nominated to replace the conservative Rehnquist. The prospect of appointing one conservative, especially someone who showed great poise and charm during his Senate confirmation hearings, in place of another did not arouse fierce partisan fervor.

Bush's choice to replace Justice O'Connor, who for a decade had cast the swing vote between liberals and conservatives on many critical Supreme Court decisions, drew much greater scrutiny. When the president announced that he was nominating his White House counsel, Harriet Miers, to the seat, conservative Republicans responded angrily. Miers had been a respected lawyer in Texas, the president's personal attorney, and a legal adviser during Bush's two gubernatorial campaigns—but not much else. Republican activists were outraged that the president passed over proven conservative jurists in favor of a nominee with no record as a constitutional thinker. Bush, for his part, assumed that the Republican base he had cultivated so assiduously for five years would support anyone he chose. He assured Senate Republicans and conservative activists that Miers was an evangelical Christian who as a justice would uphold traditional family values. But judicial politics had become too polarized for conservatives to accept an unknown quantity on anyone's say-so, even the president's. After weeks of acrimony, Bush withdrew Miers's nomination and substituted Samuel A. Alito, who like Roberts had been a proven conservative in the Reagan administration and was an appellate judge.

The epic battle many pundits predicted over the Alito nomination never materialized. Memos that Alito had written in the 1980s expressing conservative positions on abortion and affirmative action did arouse liberal ire when they came to light. But Alito's modest demeanor before the Senate Judiciary Committee, his strong professional reputation as a judge, and his pledge to uphold the law rather than promote conservative doctrine made it difficult for Senate Democrats to portray him as extreme enough to justify a filibuster. Alito's confirmation was assured when the Gang of 14 met shortly before the Senate vote and unanimously decided that the "extraordinary circumstances" stipulation of their 2005 agreement did not apply in this case. Absent a filibuster, Alito was confirmed on a nearly party-line vote of 58–42.

As Republicans celebrated and Democrats lamented the consolidation of a narrow conservative majority on the Supreme Court, liberals conceded that their only hope of influencing judicial politics was to start winning congressional and presidential elections. The first of these hopes was realized in 2006. The Democrats' aggressive and well-organized national campaign secured a congressional majority capable of blocking any conservative judicial nominations Bush might make during his final two years in office. No additional Supreme Court vacancies occurred while Bush was president, and his remaining appellate court nominees were either judicial moderates or remained unconfirmed. In addition, in 2007 congressional Democrats went after Attorney General Alberto Gonzales with a vengeance when it turned out that the Bush administration had fired eight U.S. attorneys for being insufficiently partisan. Although U.S. attorneys serve four-year terms "at the pleasure of the president," their role in the judicial process gave Democrats reason to argue that the Bush administration was subverting the nonpartisan enforcement of the law.

Partisan rancor also marked public reactions to the post–midterm elections report of the bipartisan Iraq Study Group, cochaired by Republican James A. Baker III, a former secretary of state, and Democrat Lee Hamilton, a former chair of the House Foreign Affairs Committee. Baker, Hamilton, and their widely respected colleagues in the study group had tried to find a compromise between the Bush administration, intent on staying the course in Iraq, and Democratic congressional leaders who wanted to withdraw

American troops from the conflict. But neither side was interested in compromise. Bush labeled the report, which called for a gradual reduction in America's military presence, a plan for surrender, while liberals criticized it for not proposing a firm timetable for withdrawal.

As unpopular as Bush was in early 2007, he was not devoid of power. That Democrats had won the midterm elections by promising to end the war in Iraq meant nothing to a president whose willingness to resort to unilateral executive action had characterized his entire administration. The day after the election Bush fired Secretary of Defense Rumsfeld, signaling his desire for a new strategy for success in the war. He found such a strategy in the counterinsurgency approach championed by Gen. David Petraeus, who argued that American forces could bring stability to Iraq only by protecting the Iraqi people in the neighborhoods where they lived. Far from requiring fewer troops, this new strategy required more. Relying on his authority as commander in chief, Bush sent an additional twenty thousand soldiers to Iraq—the so-called "surge." Congressional Democrats sputtered but acquiesced, pinning their hopes on the election of a new Democratic president in 2008 who, using his or her own unilateral authority, would bring the American involvement in Iraq to a speedy conclusion.

NOTES

1. Bob Woodward, *Bush at War* (New York: Simon and Schuster, 2002), 102.

2. Starting with Richard Nixon, Republican success in presidential elections fostered an embrace of presidential power among conservatives, who during the Democratic administrations of Franklin D. Roosevelt and Harry S. Truman had been harshly critical. Liberal Democrats followed a reverse trajectory. See Julian E. Zelizer, "How Conservatives Learned to Stop Worrying and Love Presidential Power," in *The Presidency of George W. Bush*, ed. Julian Zelizer (Princeton: Princeton University Press, 2010), chap. 2.

3. Robert G. Kaiser, "Academics Say It's Elementary: Gore Wins," *Washington Post*, August 31, 2000. "It's not even going to be close," said Michael Lewis-Beck of the University of Iowa as early as May. Robert G. Kaiser, "Is This Any Way to Pick a Winner?" *Washington Post*, May 26, 2000.

4. Thomas M. DeFrank, "I'm My Own Man, Says Al," *New York Daily News*, August 18, 2000.

5. David S. Broder, "Gore's Clinton Problem," *Washington Post National Weekly Edition*, October 30, 2000, 4.

6. "What a Long, Strange Trip," *Newsweek*, November 20, 2000, 126.

7. James Fallows, "An Acquired Taste," *Atlantic Monthly*, July 2000, 33–53.

8. Thirty percent said they would not have voted at all. Peter Slevin, "A Defiant Nader Stands Up to Criticism," *Washington Post*, November 9, 2000.

9. James W. Ceaser and Andrew Busch, *The Perfect Tie: The True Story of the Presidential Election* (Lanham, Md.: Rowman and Littlefield, 2001), 37–46. See also Wilson Carey McWilliams, "The Meaning of the Election," in *The Election of 2000*, ed. Gerald Pomper (New York: Chatham House, 2000), 179–185.

10. Michael Nelson, "The Postelection Election: Politics by Other Means," in Nelson, *Elections of 2000*, ed. Michael Nelson (Washington, D.C.: CQ Press, 2001), 211–224.

11. Ibid., 220–221.

12. "*Bush v. Gore*," in *The Evolving Presidency: Landmark Documents, 1787–2010*, 4th ed., ed. Michael Nelson (Washington, D.C.: CQ Press, 2012), 283–290.

13. Ibid., Justice Stevens, with whom Justice Ginsberg and Justice Breyer join, dissenting, at 5, 7.

14. Tish Durkin, "The Scene: The Jeffords Defection and the Risk of Snap Judgments," *National Journal*, May 26, 2001.

15. Fred Barnes, "The Impresario: Karl Rove, Orchestrator of the Bush White House," *Weekly Standard*, August 20, 2001; Carl M. Cannon and Alexis Simendinger, "The Evolution of Karl Rove," *National Journal*, April 27, 2002, 1210–6.

16. Karl Rove, interview by Sidney M. Milkis, November 15, 2001. Michael Gerson, Bush's principal speechwriter, noted that the president's rhetoric did not try to "split the difference" between liberalism and conservatism. Rather, Bush's speeches sought to convey how "activist government could be used for conservative ends." Michael Gerson, interview by Sidney M. Milkis, November 15, 2001.

17. On January 29, 2001, Bush created a faith-based office and charged it to "eliminate unnecessary legislative, regulatory, and other bureaucratic barriers that impede faith-based and other community efforts to solve social problems." Executive Order 13199, Establishment of Faith-Based and Community Initiatives. He also ordered the Departments of Labor, Education, Health and Human Services, and Housing and Urban Development, as well as the attorney general's office, to establish Centers for Faith-Based and Community Initiatives within their departments. These centers were to perform internal audits, identifying barriers to the participation of faith-based organizations in providing social services and to devise plans to remove these barriers. Executive Order 13198, Agency Responsibilities with Respect to Faith-Based and Community Initiatives, January 29, 2001. The education bill involved a compromise between the White House, which wanted accountability, and liberal Democrats in the Senate, such as Edward M. Kennedy, who wanted greater spending. The president referred to his rapprochement with Kennedy in his 2002 State of the Union address, joking about how the folks back in the Crawford, Texas, Coffee House would be shocked when they heard him praise the Senate's leading liberal. Bush and his advisers viewed education as the issue that would distinguish him from other conservative Republicans. George W. Bush, "State of the Union Address," January 29, 2002, http://www.whitehouse.gov; Rove interview.

18. David S. Broder, "Long Road to Reform: Negotiators Force Education Legislation," *Washington Post*, December 17, 2001.

19. For a thoughtful treatment of compassionate conservatism in the Bush presidency, see Kevin M. Kruse, "Compassionate Conservatism: Religion in the Age of George W. Bush," in Zelizer, *Presidency of George W. Bush*, chap. 10.

20. "President Names Members of Bioethics Council, Statement by the Press Secretary," January 16, 2002, http://www.whitehouse.gov.

21. Richard Morin, "He Has the Public's Approval," *Washington Post National Weekly Edition*, September 24–30, 2001, 8. See also Marc J. Hetherington and Michael Nelson, "Anatomy of a Rally Effect: George W. Bush and the War on Terrorism," *PS: Political Science and Politics* 36 (January 2003): 37–42.

22. "George W. Bush's War on Terrorism Address," in Nelson, *Evolving Presidency*, 290–298.

23. Hetherington and Nelson, "Anatomy of a Rally Effect."

24. Andrew Rudalevige, *The New Imperial Presidency: Renewing Presidential Power after Watergate* (Ann Arbor: University of Michigan Press, 2005). See also Matthew Crenson and Benjamin Ginsberg, *Presidential Power: Unchecked and Unbalanced* (New York: Norton, 2007).

25. David Nather and Jill Barshay, "Hill Warning: Respect Level from White House Too Low," *CQ Weekly*, March 9, 2002.

26. Rudalevige, *New Imperial Presidency*, 229–231.

27. For a discussion of the unitary executive that places it in historical perspective, see Stephen Skowronek, "Conservative Insurgency: A Developmental Perspective on the Unitary Executive," *Harvard Law Review* 122 (June 2009): 2070–2103.

28. "George W. Bush's Signing Statement for the Defense Supplemental Appropriations Act," in Nelson, *Evolving Presidency*, 304–308. See also Crenson and Ginsberg, *Presidential Power*, 190–202. Reagan used signing statements to challenge 71 provisions of new laws, and Clinton did so 105 times. Each president served eight years.

29. Thomas Mann and Norman Ornstein, "The Threat of Bush's Signing Statements," *San Diego Union-Tribune,* July 7, 2006.

30. *Hamdan v. Rumsfeld,* 548 U.S. 557 (2006).

31. Michael A. Fletcher, "Bush Signs Terrorism Measure," *Washington Post,* October 18, 2006; *Boumediene v. Bush,* 553 U.S. 723 (2008).

32. George W. Bush, "Address to the Nation," June 6, 2002, http://www.whitehouse.gov.

33. Michael Nelson, "George W. Bush and Congress: The Electoral Connection," in *Considering the Bush Presidency,* ed. Gary L. Gregg II and Mark J. Rozell (New York: Oxford University Press, 2004), 141–159.

34. Mike Allen and Bill Miller, "Bush Seeks Security Department; Cabinet-Level Agency Would Coordinate Anti-Terrorism Effort," *Washington Post,* June 6, 2002.

35. George W. Bush, "Executive Order, Establishing the Corporate Fraud Task Force," July 9, 2002, http://www.whitehouse.gov; Bush, "Statement, Signing the Corporate Corruption Bill," July 30, 2002, http://www.whitehouse.gov.

36. Michael Nelson, "Ronald Reagan, George W. Bush, and GOPtimism," *Chronicle Review,* March 17, 2006, B13–15.

37. "The Bush Doctrine," in Nelson, *Evolving Presidency,* 298–304.

38. Stephen Mufson, "FDR's Deal in Bush's Terms," *Washington Post,* February 20, 2005.

39. The Democratic strategy was increasingly less effective, however, as union membership declined from about 40 percent of the workforce in 1950 to about 20 percent in 1980 and 13 percent in 2004. Michael Nelson, "George W. Bush, Majority President," in *The Elections of 2004,* ed. Michael Nelson (Washington: CQ Press, 2005), 1–17.

40. Matthew Dowd, political strategist for the Bush-Cheney campaign, interview by Sidney M. Milkis, July 8, 2004. See also Matt Bai, "The Multilevel Marketing of the President," *New York Times Magazine,* April 25, 2004, 43.

41. Nelson, "George W. Bush, Majority President."

42. The tendency of the Democratic Party to rely on auxiliary organizations such as labor unions was reinforced by the enactment of the Bipartisan Campaign Finance Reform Act in 2002, which proscribed party organizations, but not independent issue groups, from raising and spending "soft" money. The "527 groups," named for the section of the tax code that regulates them, were formed outside of the regular party organization, in part to circumvent campaign finance regulations. No less important, however, was the view of some leaders of the 527 organizations that the Democratic National Committee and state parties were not capable of mobilizing the base support of liberal causes. Personal interview with ACT official, not for attribution, by Sidney M. Milkis, August 19, 2005. These groups formed an alliance to build an impressive media and ground campaign to match the efforts of the Republican Party.

43. Paul R. Abramson, John H. Aldrich, and David W. Rohde, *Change and Continuity in the 2004 and 2006 Elections* (Washington, D.C.: CQ Press, 2007), 85.

44. Karl Rove, interview by Sidney M. Milkis, November 15, 2001.

45. Matthew Dowd, interview by Sidney M. Milkis, July 20, 2005.

46. Tad Devine, political strategist, John Kerry-John Edwards '04, interview by Sidney M. Milkis, July 2004.

47. Comment by John Kerry on CNN's *Inside Politics,* August 9, 2004.

48. Matthew Dowd, interview by Sidney M. Milkis, July 26, 2004.

49. The 2006 elections are discussed in Abramson, Aldrich, and Rohde, *Change and Continuity,* and in Larry J. Sabato, *The Sixth Year Itch: The Rise and Fall of the George W. Bush Presidency* (New York: Longman, 2007).

50. Janet Elder, "For Most Bush Voters, No Regrets after 2 Years," *New York Times,* May 2, 2007.

51. CNN.com, "Senate Passes Iraq Withdrawal Bill; Veto Threat Looms," April 26, 2007, http://www.cnn.com/2007/POLITICS/04/26/congress.iraq/index.html.

52. See Jan Crawford Greenburg, *Supreme Conflict: The Inside Story of the Struggle for Control of the United States Supreme Court* (New York: Penguin Press, 2007).

CHAPTER 15

Barack Obama and the Dilemma of Modern Presidential Leadership

D
emocratic senator Barack Obama of Illinois offered voters "Change
We Can Believe In" during the 2008 presidential campaign. But his
extraordinary two-year quest for the White House left unclear what
kind of change he proposed. In substantial part, Obama ran an idealistic campaign that sought to reprise the modern president's role as a leader governing
independently of political party. An African American candidate who promised to transcend the country's seemingly intractable racial divide, Obama
also pledged to overcome the raw partisanship that polarized the Washington
community during the Clinton and Bush administrations. To be sure, Obama
provoked considerable opposition from conservatives, who dismissed him as
a doctrinaire liberal posing as a statesman eager to lift the nation out of the
muck of partisan rancor. His candidacy was also heavily criticized by his
major rival for the Democratic nomination, Sen. Hillary Rodham Clinton of
New York, the former first lady, who, as the first strong woman contender for
president, also had a legitimate claim to the progressive mantle. To a remarkable degree, however, Obama outshone Clinton in inspiring the voters.
Although the nomination contest between them was very close, the feelings
Clinton evoked paled in comparison to the sentiment aroused by Obama that
he represented "a new kind of politics" that would move the country beyond
the angry divisions of the previous two decades.

Yet the hopes Obama raised for a "postpartisan era" disguised the partisan
practices animating his quest for the White House, which employed some of
the same tactics that already had redefined twenty-first century American
politics.[1] Launching his campaign in early 2007, with George W. Bush's political fortunes in free fall, Obama naturally sought to distinguish himself from
the incumbent. If Bush was "a divider, not a uniter," Obama would seek to
transcend partisan divisions in the name of national unity. Yet the lessons of
Bush's first five years in office, in which the president racked up numerous
impressive victories with a strongly partisan approach to campaigning and
governing, could not be easily dismissed. Because of the gains the Democrats

462

made in the 2006 and 2008 elections, Obama enjoyed large—and largely sup-portive—congressional majorities when he became president in January 2009. Regional realignments since the 1960s had greatly reduced the influence of conservative southerners—the "ball and chain that had hobbled liberalism's forward march"—within the Democratic Party.[2] Consequently, Democrats were no longer the fragile and ideologically disparate group they had been in 1977 when Carter assumed office, or even in 1993 when Clinton became president. Rather, they were a remarkably cohesive left-of-center party that was very responsive to Obama's legislative program.[3]

Many of Obama's campaign promises—such as major government invest-ments in health care, education, the environment, and alternative energy—expressed long-standing Democratic commitments. Furthermore, Obama and his advisers saw enormous potential in the national party politics that Bush had practiced; indeed, the Obama campaign's organizational efforts were modeled on the techniques that Republicans pioneered in 2004. Eschew-ing the Democrats' traditional reliance on organized labor and other con-stituency groups to mobilize the party faithful, Obama built a powerful, centralized grassroots organization linked to the national party. His victory in the election advanced an executive-centered party system that relied on the president to pronounce party doctrine, raise campaign funds, mobilize grass-roots support, recruit candidates, and campaign on behalf of his partisan brethren.

After becoming president, Obama continued to walk the fine line between the postpartisan approach that appealed to many of his young idealistic fol-lowers and the partisan politics practiced with aplomb by his Republican predecessor (and favored by many Democratic activists). The president's legislative strategy tacked between bipartisan efforts to reach out to Repub-lican members of Congress and partisan appeals designed to shore up support from Democrats. At the organizational level, Obama established his grassroots campaign "machine" as an essential, but partially independent, component of the Democratic National Committee, modifying its name from Obama for America to Organizing for America (OFA). The president exhibited a willingness to work collaboratively on legislative issues with Con-gress, especially Democratic leaders in the House of Representatives and Senate, and an enthusiasm for the independence afforded by the modern administrative presidency. In attempting this difficult balancing act, how-ever, Obama risked looking weak or indecisive. The results of the 2010 mid-term elections, in which the Republicans regained control of the House and reduced the Democrats' majority in the Senate, cast serious doubt on his ability to effectively strike a balance between sharp partisanship and nonpar-tisan administration.

THE 2008 ELECTIONS

From the beginning, 2008 promised to be one of the most wide-open presidential contests in all of American history. For the first time since 1928, there was neither a sitting president seeking reelection nor a sitting vice president seeking to become president. Moreover, the two leading candidates for the Democratic nomination were a woman and an African American. Never before had a major political party nominated anyone other than a white male for president. Adding to the stakes of the election were the critical international and domestic challenges the country faced: combat troops in Iraq and Afghanistan and a severe recession at home, the worst economic crisis since the Great Depression.

That the 2008 campaign aroused such interest and participation can also be attributed to Obama's insurgent campaign, which combined Internet-based recruitment of volunteers, the use of data files to target potential supporters, and old-fashioned door-to-door canvassing to upset the heavily favored Clinton in the nomination contest and to defeat the highly respected Republican nominee, Sen. John McCain of Arizona, in the general election. Obama's campaign strategy elaborated on the organizational tactics that had worked successfully for Bush and the Republicans in 2002 and, especially, in 2004. The remarkable effectiveness of Obama's fund-raising operation, which drew heavily on Internet-solicited donations, further reflected lessons learned from the Bush campaign. Especially adept at soliciting small contributions, Obama became the first major party candidate for president to refuse public funds for the general election.

Obama's impressive grassroots organization was the institutional manifestation of his transformative message; in contrast, Clinton and McCain offered the voters experience in a year when they were looking for change. In 2002 Obama, then a state senator, had criticized the Iraq war while Clinton was voting for the congressional resolution authorizing military action. Clinton hoped to deflect attention from this controversial part of her record by arguing that she was the more qualified candidate to assume the burdens of office in a dangerous, uncertain world. But basing her campaign on experience weakened Clinton's claim to be a transformative candidate in her own right.[4] Similarly, the general election pitted the youthful Illinois senator against a seventy-two-year-old Republican who would have been the oldest person ever to assume the presidency. McCain's steadfast support for the Iraq war, joined to his comment during the height of the fall 2008 financial crisis that "the fundamentals of our economy are strong," inclined independent voters to associate his candidacy with the unpopular policies of the Bush administration.

Obama's victory was hardly inevitable: many pundits doubted that an African American could ever be elected president, let alone a candidate of such limited experience in government who bore such an exotic sounding name. Yet Obama and his running mate, Sen. Joseph Biden of Delaware, were triumphant. Winning 53 percent of the national popular vote, Obama became the first Democrat since Lyndon B. Johnson in 1964 to win a decisive majority from the electorate. In securing two-thirds of the electoral votes (365 to McCain's 173), Obama held all twenty states won by John Kerry in 2004 and added nine states that Bush had captured, including three in the South: Florida, North Carolina, and Virginia. Like the formidable Bush-Cheney machine in 2004, the Obama-Biden organization relied in part on the regular party apparatus. Howard Dean, chair of the Democratic National Committee (DNC), had decided in 2006 to strengthen Democratic organizations throughout the country, an approach that state and local party leaders credited with abetting the party's impressive victories in the midterm elections and in 2008.[5] While Obama was winning the presidency, Democrats won twenty-one additional seats in the House and eight in the Senate. These victories, coming on top of major Democratic gains in 2006, appeared to have "effectively reversed the verdict of 1994, leaving the partisan balance in Congress as solidly Democratic as it was before that year's Republican takeover."[6]

IDEOLOGY, PARTISAN POLITICS, AND THE DEMOCRATIC PARTY

The historic nature of Obama's victory in 2008 prompted speculation that he might become a transformative president like Jefferson, Jackson, Lincoln, and FDR. Obama's considerable political gifts and ambition further encouraged analogies to America's most consequential presidents. Obama claimed a particular kinship with Lincoln. He launched his campaign in Springfield, Illinois; took the oath of office with his hand on the same Bible that Lincoln used in 1861; and, in Lincoln-like fashion, celebrated the Declaration of Independence as the lodestar of equality. But Obama's style of governing and the programs he advanced during his first two years in office revealed that his ambition more closely resembled that of the most important progressive leaders of the twentieth century—TR, Wilson, and, especially, FDR—who celebrated a new understanding of liberty that relied less on natural rights and individual self-reliance than on a more expansive, collective sense of freedom at home and abroad. FDR and his New Deal political allies committed themselves, rhetorically and programmatically, to two new rights—freedom from want, embodied by the welfare state, and freedom from fear, embodied by the national security state—to supplement the traditional freedoms of speech and religion. This new sense of entitlement went hand-in-hand with the development of the modern executive establishment, which gave important form to these new commitments. TR memorably described the modern president as the "steward of the public welfare." This role, which FDR embraced so fully, and not any notion of being the second great emancipator, was what most appealed to Obama.

From the start of his administration, Obama channeled FDR and the New Deal. He asked scholars to prepare memos on Roosevelt's first hundred days; pursued "bold, persistent experimentation" during the early days of his administration in the form of a massive $814 billion economic stimulus package; and trumpeted an ambitious long-term program of structural reform, which he dubbed the "New Foundation." First announced in an address at Georgetown University on April 14, 2009, and echoed in subsequent speeches, most notably, the president's first State of the Union message, on January 27, 2010, Obama's New Foundation proposed to build a regulatory framework for the economy; to transform access to higher education into an entitlement; to harness renewable energy that reduces climate change and creates new jobs; and, most important, to achieve major health care reform, the signature program of Obama's first two years in office.[7]

Steeped in the progressive tradition, Obama tended to reject in principle partisan solutions to domestic and international problems. Indeed, *The Audacity of Hope*, his unofficial entrée into presidential politics, opens with a sharp criticism of the partisanship practiced by "Republicans and Democrats" (the title of the book's first chapter).[8] In part, Obama's call for the country to move beyond Democratic liberalism and Republican conservatism was grounded in the view—central to the creation of the modern presidency—that strident partisan conflict prevents the government from effectively addressing the nation's problems. As he explained in 2008, the "partisan battles of the 1990s and 2000s" had left both parties exhausted, unable to articulate solutions to the pressing challenges posed by rising health care costs, a floundering public education system, and unsustainable consumption of Fossil Fuels. Obama also expressed concern that partisan rancor was driving ordinary Americans away from politics and eroding their faith in the nation's democratic institutions. Discussing the politicization of patriotism during the war on terrorism, he lamented that "the question of who is—or is not—a patriot all too often poisons our political debates, in ways that divide us rather than bringing us together."[9]

Against the harsh partisanship and disillusionment of contemporary politics, Obama promised to restore the luster of progressive leadership. Echoing the postpartisan hopes of previous reform leaders, he offered a consensual approach to politics grounded in the wisdom of "the whole people." To make his appeal for unity resonate widely, Obama reached out to "Independents and Republicans who've lost their faith in their Washington leaders but want to believe again—who desperately want something new."[10] Obama's promise to transcend party remained a staple of his rhetoric. "On this day," he declared

Obama's "Hope" poster in the 2008 election expressed his theme of transcending the strong partisan polarization dividing red states from blue states.

in his inaugural address, "we come to proclaim an end to the petty grievances and false promises, the recriminations and worn-out dogmas that for far too long have strangled our politics . . . in the words of Scripture, the time has come to set aside childish things."[11] The new president repeatedly vowed to work with Republicans on pressing issues.

The stubborn racial and ethnic divisions that have shaped America's past caused many previous calls to the "whole people" to ring hollow, or even to appear mischievous.[12] But Obama promised to forge a new multiracial coalition that would free the steward of the public welfare from these old limitations.[13] The child of a white mother from Kansas and a black father from Kenya, a man of color raised in Hawaii and Indonesia, and a community organizer schooled in Chicago politics, Obama seemed perfectly poised to rise above, as no previous modern president had, the racial, ethnic, religious, and economic differences that divide the country. He also inspired hope that he could transcend the divisions between "red" America and "blue" America. Shepard Fairey's stylized lithograph, "Hope," which Obama and his followers adapted as their official campaign poster, framed Obama's face in red and blue to demonstrate, Fairey said, how he would overcome the differences between Republican and Democratic politics in America.[14]

Although Obama's renunciation of party squabbles resonated with many Americans, it occasionally frustrated Democratic activists, who argued that the president should train his rhetorical fire on Republican failures rather than on the "partisan culture in Washington." Some commentators took these complaints as evidence that Obama was wholly inattentive to the demands of party leadership.[15] But Obama's paeans to unity were accompanied by efforts to establish sharp divisions between the "failed" policies of "the previous administration" and his own approach, which drew extensively on mainstream Democratic ideas and proposals.[16] Indeed, in his campaign speeches Obama repeatedly castigated the "worn dogma that says we should give more to those at the top and hope that their good fortune trickles down to the hardworking many." Moving beyond this barely veiled critique of Reagan Republicanism, Obama ticked off failures of the Bush administration in words that could have been used by any Democratic candidate. "For eight long years," he exclaimed in typical lament, "our President sacrificed investments in health care, and education, and energy, and infrastructure on the altar of tax breaks for big corporations and wealthy CEOs—trillions of dollars in giveaways that proved neither compassionate nor conservative."[17] One of Obama's most effective criticisms of McCain was that the Republican nominee's celebrated status as a political maverick thinly veiled a doctrinaire partisan who supported Bush's flawed approach to governing.

Just as candidate Obama criticized Bush on ostensibly nonpartisan grounds while deploying conventional Democratic rhetoric, so did he seek to recast Democratic priorities as nonpartisan causes. "If this election is about whether or not to end this war, or pass universal health care, or make more college affordable," he said, "it won't just be a Democratic victory; it will be an American victory."[18] But the tension between Obama's postpartisan rhetoric and his commitment to traditional Democratic priorities became more jarring when he confronted the realities of governing. The artful joining of pragmatism and partisanship gave way to awkward vacillation amid fierce battles over the major issues that dominated his first year as president: economic stimulus, the budget, financial reform, and, most of all, health care reform. True to his promise to transcend partisan divisions, Obama repeatedly sought to attract support for his initiatives from Republican legislators, thereby frustrating liberal Democrats who feared that he was conceding too much. But Obama's fundamentally Democratic policies were anathema to all but a few members of the staunchly conservative Republican caucus, who were inclined to resist what they viewed as a liberal agenda garbed in the cloak of postpartisanship. Consequently, even as Obama scored major legislative victories, his simultaneous efforts to transcend party and rally the Democratic base led many independent voters to question his leadership, bringing about a steady decline in his public approval ratings from the high sixties to the mid-forties.

THE NEW FOUNDATION AND PARTISAN RANCOR

The limits of Obama's pragmatism were first exposed in his attempt to respond to the worsening economic crisis. He regarded his stimulus package as an extension of the Bush administration's Troubled Asset Relief Program (TARP), which was impressively nonpartisan. Indeed, candidate Obama had joined the deliberations on the bank bailout during Bush's final days in office and had lent critical support to the struggle to persuade a reluctant Democratic Congress to pass it. Yet as president, Obama failed to set the terms of his party's response to the economic emergency or to invest it with bipartisan legitimacy.[19] Democrats and many liberal activists urged him to support a massive economic stimulus bill that would spend more than a trillion dollars to create jobs and rebuild the nation's infrastructure. Although the president's plan was impressive in scope and relied on "traditionally liberal notions of using government spending to spur growth," it was not as large as many liberals had hoped, and it included $300 billion in tax breaks designed to appeal to Republican legislators.[20] This approach dismayed many Democrats without eliciting enthusiasm from Republicans.[21] The stimulus bill, formally titled the American Recovery and Reinvestment Act, passed without a single Republican vote in the House.[22] In the Senate, Democratic leaders cut a deal with moderate Republican senators to reduce the bill's price tag, but only three Republicans voted for it.[23] The tension between Obama's postpartisan and partisan approaches was on full display in his response to these developments: he conceded that the Recovery Act was "not a perfect bill," but readily signed it into law in February 2009.[24]

Struggles over the federal budget showed that Obama's efforts to reconcile partisanship with a nonpartisan leadership style were gradually giving way to the realities of party polarization. The administration's proposed $3.6 trillion budget for fiscal year 2010 called for major investments in health care, education, and alternative energy; a cap and trade scheme for curbing greenhouse gas emissions; a tax cut for middle class families; and a significant increase in taxes on the wealthy, leading some analysts to compare it with Lyndon Johnson's Great Society program.[25] Obama embraced this comparison, declaring in early March 2009: "I came to provide the sweeping change that this country demanded when it went to the polls in November. That is the change this budget starts to make."[26] Republicans charged the administration with profligacy and waste.[27] Facing growing criticism of his proposal in Congress and rising public concern about the federal deficit, the president rallied congressional Democrats by reminding them that "we're all in this together" and that "if we don't pass the budget, it will empower those [Republican] critics who don't want to see anything getting done."[28] Obama's partisan approach contributed to a partisan outcome. In April 2009 Congress passed the budget with most of its major spending priorities intact, but without a single Republican vote in either the House or Senate.

Still, even as Democrats celebrated a major victory on the budget, Obama reached out to moderates and Republicans by calling for $17 billion in cuts as well as for "PAYGO" (pay-as-you-go) legislation that would force Congress to offset tax cuts and spending increases with equivalent tax increases and spending cuts.[29] As the American economy continued to sputter in early 2010—and as massive budget deficits destabilized West European nations such as Iceland, Ireland, Greece, Portugal, and Spain—the president's uneasiness over the budget deficit increased, much to the chagrin of liberal Democrats in Congress.[30] Although the president proposed to increase spending on health care and education in the 2011 fiscal year, he also called for a three-year freeze on other discretionary domestic spending.[31] Furthermore, when members of Congress failed to agree to the creation of a national commission to explore ways of addressing the deficit, Obama created one on his own in February 2010, telling commissioners that "everything has to be on the table" in the effort to reduce the deficit.[32] Obama's budgetary politics mirrored his approach to the stimulus, combining appeals across the political aisle with more partisan approaches.

The Obama administration's shifting strategy on the budget was inexorably linked to the politics of health care, which had crucial implications for the government's long-term fiscal situation.[33] The epic battle over reform of the nation's health care system brought the tension between postpartisanship and partisanship into sharp relief. Health care for all Americans had been the Democrats' holy grail since the Roosevelt administration, and Obama's determination to be the "last president" to have to address the issue spoke to liberal Democrats' hopes for a fundamental break from the patchwork, employment-based system of insurance that left millions of Americans without health care. Liberals saw Obama's expressed support for a public health care option that would compete with private providers as the emblem of his commitment to sweeping reform. Appealing to deficit hawks in both parties, however, Obama also vowed to support only those proposals that did not add to the national debt. From the start, the president walked a tightrope between satisfying his party's liberal base and reaching out to centrist Democrats, independents, and moderate Republicans.

As health care legislation wended its way through Congress, Obama continued to tack between conciliatory and partisan leadership strategies. He shifted position to support a proposal offered by McCain during the 2008 campaign but opposed by many liberal Democrats and union members that would help pay for reform by limiting the tax exemption for employer-provided health benefits.[34] The issue of whether federal funds should support health plans covering abortion found Obama siding with centrists over liberals: in the end, he agreed to issue an executive order that would block federal funding for abortions.[35] Most important, as resistance to reform among Republicans and centrist Democrats intensified in the waning months of 2009, Obama gradually retreated from the public option in a bid to consolidate support among moderates in both parties.[36] These moves—especially the president's abandonment of the public option—enraged many Democratic activists, leading liberal icon (and former DNC chair) Howard Dean to urge congressional Democrats to kill the legislation.[37]

Even as he tacked to the center on some provisions, however, Obama used partisan strategies to help move the legislative process forward, especially when it became apparent that virtually every congressional Republican would oppose health reform legislation. As early as April 2009, Obama pressed Democrats not to foreswear use of the budget reconciliation process to secure victory in the Senate. Budget reconciliation would allow passage of the bill with fifty-one votes instead of the sixty needed to overcome a filibuster.[38] The president also made numerous appearances at rallies and town hall meetings to whip up support among Democrats, and he leveraged OFA, his former grassroots campaign organization, to pressure members of Congress to enact comprehensive health care reform.[39] By midyear Obama, convinced that Republicans were going to vote overwhelmingly against any health reform bill, unleashed administration officials to pepper their public statements with criticisms of Republican intransigence and delay.[40]

As the debate over reform dragged into the early months of 2010—with Republicans having unanimously opposed versions of the health care bill in both houses of Congress—the president intensified his rhetorical assault. In his 2010 State of the Union address, Obama spoke directly to congressional Republicans, arguing, "If the Republican leadership is going to insist that 60 votes in the Senate are required to do any business at all in this town—a supermajority—then the responsibility to govern is now yours as well. Just saying no to everything may be good short-term politics, but it's not leadership." As he upped the rhetorical ante, the president also engaged in a series of political maneuvers to put the GOP on the spot. A ballyhooed bipartisan "health care summit" in February 2010 was less an effort to hear Republican alternatives for reform than to dramatize Republican intransigence.[41] Scheduled in the wake of the January 20 special election in Massachusetts, which sent Republican Scott Brown to the Senate and reduced the Democratic ranks to fifty-nine, the televised proceedings showed Obama engaged in a high-stakes game of political poker. By calling the GOP's hand, he hoped to prepare the public for a purely Democratic bill.

The final push for health care reform featured Obama at a series of campaign-style rallies in Missouri, Ohio, Pennsylvania, and Virginia, where the impassioned president taunted Republicans for failing to take responsibility

President Barack Obama appeals for Republican support of his health care reform bill at a February 25, 2010, health care "summit."

for expanding coverage and reducing health care costs. As Obama pointedly noted in a March 8, 2010, speech at Arcadia University in Glenside, Pennsylvania, "I got all my Republican colleagues out there saying, well, no, no, no, we want to focus on things like cost. You had ten years. What happened? What were you doing?"[42]

In the immediate aftermath of Obama's multistate swing, health care reform was passed into law through a two-step process that obviated a Republican filibuster. The House passed the Senate version of the bill, and the Senate subsequently used the budget reconciliation process to remove provisions odious to House Democrats. No Republican voted for the legislation in either chamber. Although the Republicans' unwillingness to compromise gave eloquent testimony to their partisan approach to legislating, Obama's leadership revealed a partisan streak of its own. The *New York Times* concluded that "in the course of this debate, Mr. Obama has lost something. . . . Gone is the promise on which he rode to victory less than a year and a half ago—the promise of a 'postpartisan' Washington in which rationality and calm discourse replaced partisan bickering."[43] Shaped by a polarized party system, the signal legislative achievement of the president's first two years became the only major entitlement program ever to become law without a single Republican vote.

New-style partisan politics also framed the debate over, and the eventual passage of, the Wall Street Reform and Consumer Protection Act, which was enacted soon after the health care bill. Informally called Dodd-Frank after the Democrats who steered it through Congress, Sen. Christopher Dodd of Connecticut and Rep. Barney Frank of Massachusetts, the financial reform law created a new consumer protection agency within the Federal Reserve Board and gave the government power to regulate large banks and investment houses. Dodd-Frank was in the tradition of the Glass-Steagall Act, enacted during the early days of the New Deal, which, until its repeal in 1998, had separated savings banks from Wall Street investment firms. Cast against the sins exposed by the unregulated securities market that both Republicans and Democrats had supported until the economic implosion of fall 2008, the act sought to protect borrowers against abuses by mortgage and credit card lenders; to more closely regulate large banks and financial firms that were "too big to fail"; and to limit abuses of activities such as proprietary trading, hedge funds, and private equity holdings.[44] As with health reform, Obama sought to sell financial reform as a critical ingredient of the New Foundation and, as with health care, Dodd-Frank passed along sharply divided partisan lines (only six congressional Republicans voted for it) and failed to win the president much credit with the public. Once again, the programmatically ambitious president found it difficult to navigate a political environment characterized by bitter division in Washington and a citizenry that remained alienated from the capital's partisan rancor.

OBAMA, PARTISANSHIP, AND THE WAR ON TERRORISM

Obama's difficulty navigating a middle way in foreign policy offers perhaps the most striking example of how the responsibilities of the modern presidency clash with the contemporary party system. Obama inherited international commitments that pulled him away from his party's liberal base. The war on terrorism—and especially the war in Iraq—had deeply divided Americans along partisan lines during Bush's presidency.[45] Obama rose to national prominence in part because of his steadfast opposition to the Iraq war, which energized Democratic activists dissatisfied with Senator Clinton's early hawkishness. If elected, candidate Obama promised, he would "begin the phased redeployment of combat troops . . . needed for long-term success in Iraq and the security interests of the United States."[46] He also appealed to the Democratic base by pledging to close the Guantánamo Bay prison for detainees in the war on terrorism and to end the Bush administration's policy permitting torture of enemy combatants, both of which were extremely unpopular among liberals. Promising a departure from his predecessor's combative diplomatic style, which many Democrats viewed as counterproductive, Obama pledged that in general his administration would pursue a more multilateral foreign policy, as well as engage in high-level talks with antagonists such as Iran.[47]

Even though he pleased Democrats with his campaign promises concerning Iraq, Guantánamo, and torture, not all of Obama's positions appealed to liberal activists. In fact, as a candidate he took a hawkish stance on Afghanistan, pledging to order strikes against targets in Pakistan if he received actionable intelligence that terrorists were seeking refuge within that nation's borders. "We must refocus our efforts on Afghanistan and Pakistan—the central front in our war against al Qaeda—so that we are confronting terrorists where their roots run deepest," Obama wrote in 2007 in a major article in *Foreign Affairs.*[48]

After becoming president, Obama continued to steer between policies that satisfied liberal Democrats and policies that sustained the basic commitments of the national security state. In his first days in office, Obama banned the use of torture in interrogations and began efforts to close the Guantánamo Bay prison.[49] More notably, in a February 2009 announcement eagerly anticipated by Democratic critics of the war in Iraq, Obama ordered a major drawdown of forces, declaring that "our combat mission in Iraq will end" in August 2010.[50] He also made important symbolic efforts to revamp America's image in the international community, especially in the Muslim world. The president's June 2009 address at Cairo University marked a significant rhetorical departure from Bush's "with us or against us" approach. Obama vowed to "seek a new beginning between the United States and Muslims around the world, one based on mutual interest and mutual respect, and one based upon the truth that America and Islam are not exclusive and need not be in competition."[51]

At the same time, the president embraced significant aspects of Bush's war on terrorism. Obama retained important Bush-era military and foreign policy advisers, including Secretary of Defense Robert Gates, marking the first time a defense secretary had been carried over from one administration to the next; Joint Chiefs of Staff chair Mike Mullen; Gen. David Petraeus; Gen. Douglas Lute, the White House coordinator for Afghanistan and Pakistan; and Nick Rasmussen, the National Security Council is senior director for terrorism.[52] Obama also appointed his chief Democratic rival, Hillary Clinton, as secretary of state. These appointments presaged critical policy decisions that disappointed civil libertarians and Democratic activists. The Obama administration essentially continued the Bush administration's practice of holding enemy combatants without trial in military prisons, as well as its policy of trying at least some of these figures in military courts.[53] The president expanded the use of Predator drones to assassinate suspected terrorists, including American citizens, residing in Afghanistan, Pakistan, and Yemen. Although the administration promised to end "extraordinary renditions" of terrorist suspects to nations likely to torture them, "it has not ruled out this process in general," according to international relations scholar Michael Desch, "and appears to have adopted the same less stringent criteria employed by the Bush administration to gauge the likelihood that another country will employ torture."[54]

Perhaps the most significant Bush policy that Obama adopted was the military "surge." Embracing the same strategy that Bush deployed in Iraq during the final two years of his presidency, Obama announced in a December 2009 speech at West Point that he would send an additional thirty thousand American troops to back the beleaguered Afghan government.[55] Although the president also promised to begin drawing down American forces from Afghanistan in 2011, the slow pace of subsequent military progress imperiled this timetable.[56] Obama's approach to the Afghan war infuriated Democrats who thought that he would order an expedited schedule of withdrawal from the embattled nation. Indeed, in July 2010, 153 House Democrats, including Speaker Nancy Pelosi, voted to require the president to establish an even clearer timetable for withdrawal; it was defeated primarily on the strength of Republican votes.[57] Later that month, the House passed a $59 billion spending bill to continue financing the war in Afghanistan on a 308–114 vote, but because 102 Democrats voted against the bill, the 148 Democrats who supported it had to rely on 160 Republican votes.[58]

In sum, the president's statecraft—his persistent efforts to balance postpartisan and partisan themes—brought him significant policy victories without changing the broader, politically polarized environment. Indeed, the public came to view the president in starkly partisan terms. By July 2010, 78 percent of Democrats approved of Obama's performance as president, but only 11 percent of Republicans.[59] Rather than transcend partisanship, Obama's presidency reinforced, and perhaps intensified, the partisan rancor that roiled the country.

OBAMA AND THE ADMINISTRATIVE PRESIDENCY

The emergence of an executive-centered party system seriously challenges the argument that the administrative presidency has diminished collective partisan responsibility. Born of the Progressive and New Deal eras, the liberal administrative state sheltered programs like Social Security and Medicare from the vagaries of party politics and public opinion. But the expansion of programmatic liberalism in the 1960s and 1970s fractured the political order, ultimately encouraging Republican presidents to use administrative power for conservative ends. Ronald Reagan and George W. Bush, especially, sought to exploit executive administration to achieve objectives they could not achieve legislatively. In the short term, these two Republican presidents were able to strengthen the GOP by servicing the demands of important party constituencies and advancing the party's ideological goals. In the long run, however, their aggressive administrative actions mired them in constitutional controversies and policy disputes. By retreating to the politics of executive administration, Reagan and Bush implicitly admitted that their ambitions exceeded what could plausibly be achieved through legislation.

Unlike Reagan and Bush, Obama chose to work closely in his party Congress, leaving the details of important bills to Democratic leaders and committee chairs. But Obama did not neglect the administrative presidency; indeed, he sought to accomplish several controversial objectives through executive means. In organizing the White House Office, Obama appointed a number of policy "czars" with broad authority to "cut through—or leapfrog— the traditional bureaucracy" in matters of national security, climate change, economic policy, health care, housing, and education.[60] On taking office, the president reversed a number of important domestic and foreign policies with a stroke of the pen, issuing executive orders that reversed orders previously signed by Bush.[61]

As was the case with Reagan and Bush, many of these administrative actions appealed to important party constituencies. Obama signed several executive orders reversing Bush policies opposed by organized labor, and he rescinded a Bush order denying funds to international family planning groups that provide abortion-related services.[62] In a move that elicited approval from environmentalists, Obama issued an order raising fuel efficiency standards on all cars and light trucks built after 2011.[63] Following through on a prominent campaign pledge, he ordered the closing of the Guantánamo Bay prison by January 2010, but closure efforts stalled when Congress resisted any relocation of detainees to prisons within the United States.

Not all of Obama's early executive orders promoted traditional Democratic causes. Some were meant to reinforce the postpartisan image he cultivated as a candidate. Obama issued orders expanding the reach of Bush's Office of Faith-Based Initiatives, angering liberal Democrats who argued that funding faith-based programs violates the separation of church and state and subsidizes organizations that discriminate in their hiring practices.[64] On the controversial issue of stem cell research, Obama countermanded Bush's prohibition on federal funding for research on new cell lines but stopped short of supporting work on all new lines, as Democratic activists hoped. Instead, he limited government-sponsored research to cells taken from unused fertility clinic embryos.[65] Obama's order creating a commission to study the deficit met with ambivalence among liberal Democrats, who feared that the panel's recommendation might include cuts to New Deal and Great Society entitlement programs.[66]

More broadly, Obama vigorously asserted presidential authority to direct the executive branch, even in contravention of laws passed by Congress. Although candidate Obama sharply criticized Bush's use of signing statements to invalidate parts of congressional legislation, President Obama embraced the practice, provoking mounting criticism from lawmakers of both parties.[67] In March 2009 he used a signing statement to reserve the president's right to bypass provisions blocking the reallocation of funds among programs without prior approval from Congress.[68] In July, after a signing statement that voided a provision of a law expanding assistance to the International Monetary Fund and World Bank was rebuked on a bipartisan 429–2 House vote, Obama agreed to limit his use of such statements. But he did not abandon his self-proclaimed right to shelve congressional acts. Rather than openly challenge legal provisions with which it disagrees, the administration declared that it might quietly ignore them, using opinions from the Office of Legal Counsel to guide its efforts.[69]

More than any other feature of his presidency, Obama's administrative politics expressed his commitment to resuscitate the progressive belief that "agencies staffed by experts schooled in social and natural science and employing the scientific method in their decision making, could rise above partisanship and interest groups."[70] Reagan and Bush had sought to weaken regulatory agencies formed during the major reform periods of the twentieth century, including the Environmental Protection Agency, the Food and Drug Administration, the Occupational and Safety Administration, and the Securities and Exchange Commission. In contrast, Obama intended to revive professional regulators' "bureaucratic autonomy."[71]

Obama began by appointing Cass Sunstein, a prominent liberal pragmatist, as head of the Office of Information and Regulatory Affairs (OIRA). Republican presidents had created OIRA to champion cost-benefit analyses proscribing regulatory enforcement. Sunstein quickly injected progressive principles into the agency's regulatory review process, fostering more aggressive enforcement that extended environmental standards into the controversial area of climate change.[72] No less important than these administrative changes were the major regulatory statutes enacted during the first two years of the Obama presidency. The health care bill and the Dodd-Frank act greatly enhanced the role of the executive branch in the enormously important health care and financial sectors of the economy, thereby laying the foundation for a new regulatory era.

The Obama administration's unsteady response to the BP oil disaster, caused by an explosion on the Deepwater Horizon oil rig in the Gulf of Mexico in April 2010, revealed the high risks attending administrative politics. To be sure, the oil spill presented technical challenges that would have strained the capacities of any administration. But the episode was especially troubling for a president who had promised to restore professionalism to executive management. It quickly became apparent that federal regulatory agencies, especially the Minerals Management Service (MMS), had applied lax standards to BP's deepwater drilling operation prior to the disaster, despite BP's shoddy environmental record.[73] In Obama's defense, he had inherited an enfeebled regulatory regime from his predecessors and had planned to target MMS for reform. But reform had lagged while the administration's commitment to offshore drilling expanded.[74]

After the Gulf explosion, federal agencies were hesitant to take charge, instead waiting for BP to resolve the crisis.[75] When the government finally got involved, its actions did little to reassure the public. The federal cleanup response was plagued by inadequate preparation, lack of supplies, and poor coordination with state, local, and private efforts.[76] In an aggressive attempt to prevent a replay of the BP disaster, the president ordered a six-month moratorium on deepwater drilling; but the order was soon rescinded by a federal judge, who found it too sweeping. Although Obama imposed another moratorium that sought to meet the federal court's objection to the first, it was riddled with loopholes that allowed several kinds of drilling to continue.[77]

The Obama administration did secure important victories during the cleanup efforts, including a pledge from BP to spend $20 billion compensating individuals harmed by the disaster. Nevertheless, even after the oil flow was finally staunched in mid-July, the effects of the debacle on the president and his party were severe. As pollster Steve Lombardo argued, "The oil leak has become a symbol of voters' frustrations with government. The spill crystallized the problem for voters—'Government can't do anything right.'"[78] With the Democrats already facing a difficult midterm election, the BP disaster undermined a crucial source of potential electoral support for their candidates: public confidence in the president's ability to manage crises.

THE 2010 MIDTERM ELECTIONS

The BP disaster—Obama's Katrina, as some pundits dubbed it—exacerbated the voters' discontent with the stubborn persistence of poor economic conditions. The huge stimulus package did little to reduce unemployment, which increased during Obama's first two years in office from 7 percent to nearly 10 percent. The administration claimed that the economic crisis would have been much worse without the emergency measures he and congressional Democrats had taken, but such counterfactuals are seldom politically persuasive. The 2010 midterm elections, as the president acknowledged, resulted in a "shellacking" for his party. The Republicans gained sixty-three seats in the House to reclaim control of the lower chamber—the worst defeat for a president's party in an off-year election since 1938. In the Senate, the GOP added six seats, leaving Obama and the Democrats without the filibuster proof three-fifths majority needed to enact controversial legislation.

As has been the case since the emergence of the executive-centered party system, the midterm elections were a referendum on the president. The 54 percent of voters who disapproved of Obama's performance voted 85 percent to 11 percent for House Republican candidates. The elections also showed the disconnection between the polarized party system and the more moderate American public. Only 43 percent of voters had a favorable opinion of the Democratic Party, and the Republican Party fared even worse: 41 percent.[79]

BARACK OBAMA, THE MODERN PRESIDENCY, AND AMERICAN DEMOCRACY

As Theodore Roosevelt's description of the modern presidency trumpeted, the "steward of the public welfare" is supposed to strengthen American democracy. But the question remains whether the executive of a vast bureaucratic state can truly be the direct representative of the people. In 1990 political scientist Robert Dahl spoke for a host of critics when he argued that in reality the modern presidency is a "pseudo-democratic institution."[80] This concern has only heightened in recent years with the gradual erosion of the constraints on executive prerogative that Congress enacted after Watergate and accentuated, scholars and pundits fear, by a seemingly permanent war on terrorism and the worst economic crisis since the Great Depression.

In the nineteenth century, highly mobilized, highly localized political parties emerged to restrain presidential aggrandizement and keep the presidency "safe for democracy." But this decentralized party state cramped the development of a national government that could ameliorate injustices at home and dangerous imperialism abroad. The modern party system, in contrast, encounters an executive-centered bureaucratic state that was well-suited to tackle economic insecurity, racial, segregation, and totalitarianism, but lacks adequate means to foster common deliberation and public judgment, the pillars of a vital civic culture.

Perhaps the reinvigorated national parties that have arisen during the past quarter-century will reconnect the modern presidency to America's democratic tradition. Improving on the innovative techniques developed by the Bush-Cheney campaign in 2004, Obama developed a "reciprocal top-down and bottom-up campaign strategy" that mobilized followers to "realize their collective strength."[81] For all the controversy attending it, the health care battle, fueled by lively, sometime vitriolic town meetings throughout the country, revealed that the recrudescence of partisanship has renewed interest in politics. Pitting Obama's OFA against the new grassroots conservative Tea

Party movement, the health care battle showed, as one Democratic congressional staffer observed, that "the age of apathy is over, and that's a good thing."[82] Yet the president paid dearly in the coin of public opinion when he chose to work hand-in-glove with congressional Democratic leaders Harry Reid and Nancy Pelosi. Although he achieved an impressive legislative record by collaborating with his partisan brethren in Congress, Obama gave the appearance of sustaining, even strengthening the harsh inside-the-Beltway politics his 2008 campaign had promised to transcend. In the end, he was caught on the horns of the dilemma of modern presidential leadership: "the core tension between an assertive ideological base and a considerably more centrist American electorate."[83]

Still, a substantial part of Obama's original political appeal was his determination to transcend traditional partisan and ideological divisions and establish a more consensual form of politics grounded in the authority of "We, the People." During the lame-duck session of Congress that followed the 2010 elections, he appeared to regain his political standing as a unifier by striking a deal with Republican leaders that extended the Bush era tax cuts, which he had denounced during the 2008 campaign, in exchange for extending unemployment benefits. His public approval rating soon rose above 50 percent.

Even after the beating he took in the midterm elections, then, Obama's supporters hoped, and his opponents feared, that he might yet restore the luster of the modern presidency by reviving the progressive ideal of "enlightened administration." Yet success might exact costs on the political system. Although sometimes joined to enduring programmatic achievement, such leadership can deteriorate into a plebiscitary form of politics. As historian Sean Wilentz warned in 2008, "What is troubling about the [Obama] campaign is that it's gone beyond hope and change to redemption. He is posing as a figure who is the one person who will redeem our politics. And what I fear is, that ends up promising more from politics than politics can deliver."[84] Only time will tell whether Obama's progressive leadership proves to be effective statecraft that enshrines his charisma in enduring reform and a new Democratic majority or marks instead the latest stage in the development of an executive that subordinates party building to the cult of personality.

Recent events suggest that executive aggrandizement will continue to complicate efforts to realize the democratic potential of the new party system. The rise of the modern presidency has placed a premium on candidate-centered campaigns and organization. More important, the contemporary office summons individuals whose ambition is best served by establishing an electoral coalition and method of governing outside of party politics. The rise of the modern presidency therefore encourages each president to exploit the full splendor of the executive office at the expense of public debate and resolution, which best takes place in Congress and the state legislatures. Such encouragement can only be incited further by the Democrats' declining political fortunes, which threaten to isolate Obama from Congress, as well as by a seemingly permanent war on terrorism, which he vowed to continue. Like Reagan and Bush, Obama may be tempted to retreat to the politics of administration to accomplish major policy objectives, raising questions of constitutional propriety and undermining the political legitimacy of his actions. Ultimately, Americans should not depend on presidents to resist temptation on their own. The burden of the twenty-first century is to hold the modern presidency to account by restraining well-meaning but dangerous ambition that weakens the fabric of American constitutional government.

NOTES

1. Obama never uttered this phrase and denied in his second State of the Union message that he expected his election to "usher in . . . some post-partisan era." "Remarks of the President in State of Union Address," January 27, 2010, www.whitehouse.gov. But other than change, the message that resonated most in his campaign was his promise to gather a coalition of Democrats, Republicans, and independents behind an agenda of sweeping change. See Jonathan Weisman, "GOP Doubts, Fears 'Post-Partisan' Obama," *Washington Post*, January 7, 2008; and Richard Cohen, "State of the Union: Obama Plays Grown Up," *Washington Post*, January 27, 2010.

2. The "ball and chain" reference comes from Thomas Stokes, *Chip Off My Shoulder* (Princeton: Princeton University Press, 1940), 503. On the regional realignments that have transformed the party system, see Nicole Mellow, *The State of Disunion: Regional Sources of Modern American Partisanship* (Baltimore: Johns Hopkins University Press, 2008).

3. Even the so-called "Blue Dogs"—moderate Democrats who mostly hail from southern and border states—are not nearly as powerful or obstreperous as were the Southern Democrats who plagued past Democrat presidents. Rhodes Cook, "Not Your Father's Democratic Congress," *Larry Sabato's Crystal Ball*, February 19, 2009, www.centerforpolitics.org.

4. Michael Nelson, "The Setting: Diversifying the Presidential Talent Pool," in *The Elections of 2008*, ed. Michael Nelson (Washington, D.C.: CQ Press, 2009).

5. Elaine Kamarck, "Assessing Dean's Fifty-State Strategy in the 2006 Midterm Elections," *Forum* 4, no. 3 (2006), www.bepress.com/forum/vol4/iss3/art5; and Ari Berman, "The Dean Legacy," *The Nation*, February 28, 2008.

6. Gary C. Jacobson, "Congress: the Second Democratic Wave," in Nelson, *The Elections of 2008*, 100.

7. Barack Obama, Remarks on the Economy, Georgetown University, April 14, 2009, http://www.whitehouse.gov/the-press-office/remarks-president-economy-georgetown-university.

8. Barack Obama, *The Audacity of Hope* (New York: Vintage Books, 2006), 51–52.

9. Barack Obama, "The America We Love," Independence, Missouri, June 30, 2008.

10. Barack Obama, "Our Moment is Now," Des Moines, Iowa, December 27, 2007; Barack Obama, "The Past Versus the Future," Denver, Colorado, January 30, 2008.

11. Barack Obama, "Inaugural Address," January 20, 2009.

12. Desmond King and Rogers Smith, "Racial Orders in American Political Development," in *Race and American Political Development*, ed. Joseph Lowndes, Julie Nvkov, and Dorian T. Warren (New York: Routledge, 2008).

13. Philip A. Klinkner and Thomas Schaller, "LBJ's Revenge: The 2008 Election and the Rise of the Great Society Coalition, *Forum* 6, issue 4, article 9 (2008).

14. Joseph Lowndes, "Barack Obama, the Body Politic, and the Contest Over American National Identity," presentation for American Studies Association, November 2009.

15. Matt Bai, "Democrat in Chief?" *New York Times Magazine,* June 7, 2010.

16. Interview with Gov. Tim Kaine, Director, Democratic National Committee, August 9, 2010.

17. Barack Obama, "Change that Works for You," Raleigh, North Carolina, June 9, 2008.

18. Barack Obama, "A Change We Can Believe In," Spartanburg, South Carolina, November 3, 2007.

19. Morton Keller, *The Unbearable Heaviness of Governing: The Obama Administration in Historical Perspective* (Stanford, Calif.: Hoover Institution Press, 2010), 11.

20. Peter Baker and David Herszenhorn, "Senate Allies Fault Obama on Stimulus," *New York Times,* January 9, 2009.

21. Carl Hulse, "Obama Team Makes Early Efforts to Show Willingness to Reach Out to Republicans," *New York Times,* January 20, 2009; Jackie Calmes and Carl Hulse, "Obama, Visiting G.O.P. Lawmakers, Is Open to Some Compromises on Stimulus," *New York Times,* January 28, 2009.

22. Jackie Calmes, "House Passes Stimulus Plan with No G.O.P. Votes," *New York Times,* January 29, 2009.

23. Sheryl Gay Stolberg and Helene Cooper, "Obama Makes Case as Stimulus Bill Clears Hurdle," *New York Times,* February 10, 2009.

24. Sheryl Gay Stolberg, "Signing Stimulus, Obama Doesn't Rule Out More," *New York Times,* February 18, 2009.

25. David Sanger, "'Great Society' Plan for the Middle Class," *New York Times,* February 28, 2009.

26. Quoted in Peter Baker, "Obama Calls His Budget Sweeping, Needed Change," *New York Times,* March 1, 2009.

27. Carl Hulse, "Republicans Split on Need to Offer Rival for Budget," *New York Times,* March 14, 2009.

28. Quoted in Carl Hulse, "Obama Goes to Lawmakers on Budget," *New York Times,* March 31, 2009.

29. Jackie Calmes, "Obama Will Propose $17 Billion in Budget Cuts," *New York Times,* May 7, 2009; Sheryl Gay Stolberg, "President Emphasizes Discipline in Budgets," *New York Times,* April 26, 2009; Sheryl Gay Stolberg, "Obama Aims to Revive 'Pay As You Go,'" *New York Times,* June 10, 2009.

30. Matt Bai, "For Democrats, Debt Debate and Familiar Ring of Disunity," *New York Times,* July 7, 2010.

31. Susan Milligan and Alan Wirzbicki, "Budget Reflects Dire Realities, Obama Says," *Boston Globe,* February 2, 2010.

32. Quoted in Jackie Calmes, "Obama Tells Debt Commission 'Everything Has to Be on the Table,'" *New York Times,* April 27, 2010.

33. Sheryl Gay Stolberg, "Obama Says Health Plan Won't Add to Deficit," *New York Times,* July 18, 2009.

34. John Harwood, "Bipartisan Health Bill is Possible, Leaders Say," *New York Times,* June 8, 2009; David Herszenhorn, "Democrats Divide over a Proposal to Tax Health Benefits," *New York Times,* July 9, 2009.

35. "Executive Order Ensuring Enforcement of Abortion Restrictions in the Patient Protection and Affordable Care Act," March 24, 2010.

36. See, for example, Robert Pear and David Herszenhorn, "House Democrats End Impasse on Health Bill," *New York Times,* July 30, 2009; David Kirkpatrick, "Obama is Taking an Active Role in Talks on Health Care Plan," *New York Times,* August 13, 2009; Sheryl Gay Stolberg, "'Public Option' in Health Plan May be Dropped," *New York Times,*

August 17, 2009; Peter Baker, "Compromising on Two Issues, Obama Gets Partial Wins," *New York Times,* December 20, 2009.

37. Adam Nagourney, "Debate Shows Obama Plays by Washington's Rules," *New York Times,* December 26, 2009.

38. Carl Hulse, "Obama Tactic Shields Health Care Bill from a Filibuster," *New York Times,* April 25, 2009.

39. Quoted in Christina Bellantoni, "Transcript: OFA's Mitch Stewart and Jeremy Bird Speak to TPMDC," Talking Points Memo, November 11, 2009. For details on OFA's role in the health reform debate, see Ari Melber, "Year One of Organizing for America: The Permanent Field Campaign in a Digital Age," *techPresident Special Report,* January 2010, www.techpresident.com/ofayear1.

40. Carl Hulse and Jeff Zeleny, "Democrats Seem Set to Go It Alone on a Health Bill," *New York Times,* August 19, 2009.

41. Carrie Budoff Brown and Patrick O'Connor, "No High Hopes for Health Care Summit," *Politico,* February 9, 2010; Carrie Budoff Brown and Glenn Thrush, "Pelosi Steeled W. H. for Health Push," *Politico,* March 20, 2010.

42. Barack Obama, "Remarks by the President on Health Insurance Reform," Arcadia University, Glenside, Pennsylvania, March 8, 2010.

43. David Sanger, "Big Win for Obama, But at What Cost?" *New York Times,* March 21, 2010.

44. Keller, *The Unbearable Heaviness of Governing,* 63–64.

45. Gary Jacobson, *A Divider, Not a Uniter: George W. Bush and the American People* (Longman, 2007).

46. Quote is from Barack Obama, "My Plan for Iraq," *New York Times,* July 14, 2008. On the relationship between Obama's antiwar stance and his popularity among Democrats, see Gary Jacobson, "George W. Bush, the Iraq War, and the Election of Barack Obama," *Presidential Studies Quarterly* 40(2010): 212.

47. Peter Baker, "Obama's War Over Terror," *New York Times Magazine,* January 17, 2010.

48. Barack Obama, "Renewing American Leadership," *Foreign Affairs,* July/August 2007, 9.

49. Scott Wilson, "The Making of a Wartime Commander in Chief," *Washington Post,* January 19, 2010; Charlie Savage, "Closing Guantánamo Fades as a Priority," *New York Times,* June 25, 2010.

50. "President Obama Said Friday He Plans to Withdraw Most U.S. Troops from Iraq by the End of August 2010," *CNN.com,* February 23, 2009.

51. Barack Obama, "Remarks by the President on a New Beginning," Cairo University, Cairo, Egypt, June 4, 2009.

52. Peter Baker, "Obama's War Over Terror," *New York Times Magazine,* January 17, 2010.

53. Charlie Savage, "No Terror Evidence Against Some Detainees," *New York Times,* May 28, 2010.

54. Michael C. Desch, "The More Things Change, the More They Stay the Same: The Liberal Tradition and Obama's Counterterrorism Policy," *PS: Political Science and Politics* 43 (2010): 426.

55. Barack Obama, "Remarks by the President in Address to the Nation on the Way Forward in Afghanistan and Pakistan," United States Military Academy, West Point, New York, December 2009.

56. Peter Baker and Mark Landler, "Setbacks Cloud U.S. Plans to Get Out of Afghanistan," *New York Times,* June 14, 2010; Peter Baker, "With Shift in Afghanistan, Talk Turns to Exit," *New York Times,* June 28, 2010.

57. David Sanger, "Afghan Deadline is Cutting Two Ways," *New York Times,* July 21, 2010.

58. Elisabeth Bumiller and Carl Hulse, "House Approves Money for Wars, but Rift Deepens," *New York Times,* July 27, 2010.

59. For summaries of poll trends on Obama's job approval ratings, see Pollster.com: http://www.pollster.com/polls/us/jobapproval-obama-dems.php; and http://www.pollster.com/polls/us/jobapproval-obama-reps.php.

60. Michael D. Shear and Ceci Connolly, "Obama Assembles Powerful West Wing," *Washington Post,* January 8, 2009.

61. Sheryl Gay Stolberg, "Great Limits Come with Great Power, Ex-Candidate Finds," *New York Times,* January 25, 2009.

62. David Stout, "Obama Moves to Reverse Bush's Labor Policies," *New York Times,* January 31, 2009; Andrea Stone, "Abortion Foes Find New Climate: Obama Repeats Commitment to Right to Choose," *USA Today,* January 23, 2009.

63. Suzanne Goldenberg, "Obama Presses for Tougher Controls on US Car Emissions," *The Guardian,* January 27, 2009.

64. Michelle Boorstein and Kimberly Kindy, "Faith-Based Office to Expand its Reach," *Washington Post,* February 6, 2009; Carrie Johnson, "Obama Cautious on Faith-Based Initiatives," *Washington Post,* September 15, 2009.

65. Ceci Connolly, "Compromise Rules Issued on Embryonic Stem Cells," *Washington Post,* April 18, 2009.

66. Jackie Calmes, "Obama, on Own, to Set Up Panel on Nation's Debt," *New York Times,* January 27, 2010.

67. Charlie Savage, "Obama's Embrace of Bush Tactic Criticized by Lawmakers from Both Parties," *New York Times,* August 9, 2009.

68. Charlie Savage, "Obama Says He Can Ignore Some Parts of Spending Bill," *New York Times,* March 12, 2009.

69. Charlie Savage, "Obama Takes New Route to Opposing Parts of Laws," *New York Times,* January 9, 2010.

70. John B. Judis, "The Quiet Revolution," *New Republic,* February 1, 2001, www.tnr.com.

71. Daniel Carpenter, *The Forging of Bureaucratic Autonomy: Regulations, Networks, and Policy Innovations in Executive Agencies, 1862–1928* (Princeton: Princeton University Press, 2001).

72. Benjamin Wallace-Wells, "Cass Sunstein Wants to Nudge Us," *New York Times Magazine,* May 16, 2010; David A. Fahrenthold and Juliet Eilperin, "EPA Left to Pick Up Climate Change Where Congress Dropped Debate," *Washington Post,* August 4, 2010.

73. Ian Urbina, "U.S. Said to Allow Drilling Without Needed Permits," *New York Times,* May 14, 2010.

74. John Broder and Michael Luo, "Reforms Slow to Arrive at Drilling Agency," *New York Times,* May 30, 2010.

75. Campbell Robertson and Eric Lipton, "U.S. Missed Chances to Act on Oil Spill," *New York Times,* May 1, 2010.

76. Campbell Robertson, "Efforts to Repel Oil Spill are Described as Chaotic," *New York Times,* June 14, 2010.

77. Julian Zelizer, "It's Obama's White House, but it's Still Bush's World," *Washington Post,* August 15, 2010.

78. Steve Lombardo, "Will Plugging the Gulf Leak Save the Democrats' Ship in November?" *Pollster.com,* July 16, 2010, http://www.pollster.com/blogs/will_plugging_the_gulf_leak_sa.php.

79. Gary Langer, "2010 Elections Exit Poll Analysis: The Political Price of Economic Pain," *ABC News,* November 3, 2010, http://abcnews.go.com/Politics/2010-midterms-political-price-economic-pain/story?id=12041739.

80. Robert Dahl, "The Myth of the Presidential Mandate," *Political Science Quarterly* 105 (1990): 355–372.

81. Hugh Heclo, "The Once and Future Chief Executive: Prophesy versus Prediction," remarks delivered at the 4th Annual Symposium in Honor of Ronald Reagan, "The Future of the American Presidency," Regent University, Virginia Beach, Virginia, February 6, 2009.

82. Personal interview with Democratic congressional staff member, July 19, 2010.

83. Keller, *The Unbearable Heaviness of Governing*," 148.

84. Quoted in Kate Zernike, "The Charisma Mandate," *New York Times*, February 17, 2008. Wilentz felt that his criticism of Obama's charismatic leadership was vindicated by the 2010 shellacking. See Sean Wilentz, "Live by the Movement, Die by the Movement, *New Republic*, November 9, 2010.

CHAPTER 16

The Vice Presidency

lmost since its creation, the vice presidency has been an easy and frequent target of political humor. Benjamin Franklin quipped that the
vice president should be addressed as "Your Superfluous Excellency."
Mr. Dooley, the invented character of writer Finley Peter Dunne, described the
office as "not a crime exactly. Ye can't be sint to jail f'r it, but it's kind iv a
disgrace. It's like writin' anonymous letters." George and Ira Gershwin's 1931
musical, *Of Thee I Sing,* featured a fictitious vice president whose name
(which no one in the play could remember) was Alexander Throttlebottom.
Vice President Throttlebottom spent most of his time feeding pigeons in a
park and unsuccessfully trying to find two people willing to serve as references
so he could get a library card.

Even some vice presidents have poked fun at the office. Thomas R. Marshall,
who was Woodrow Wilson's vice president for two terms, said that the vice
president is like "a man in a cataleptic fit; he cannot speak; he cannot move; he
suffers no pain; he is perfectly conscious of all that goes on, but has no part in
it." Marshall also told the story of two brothers: "One ran away to sea; the other
was elected vice president. And nothing was heard of either of them again."
John Nance Garner was a fairly active vice president during the first two terms
of Franklin D. Roosevelt's administration, but his pithy assessment of the office
(at least the G-rated version of what he said) is probably the most frequently
quoted of all: "The vice presidency isn't worth a pitcher of warm spit."[1]

Many a truth about the vice presidency has been spoken in jest. In terms of
constitutional authority, the office was born weak and has not grown much
stronger. But lost in all the laughter is an appreciation of the importance—
ongoing for more than a century and accelerating in recent decades—of the
position that the vice president occupies in the American political system.

The vice presidency is most significant when, cocoon-like, it empties itself
to provide a successor to the presidency. "I am vice president," said John
Adams, the first person to hold the office. "In this I am nothing, but I may be
everything."[2] Nine vice presidents, about one-fifth of those who have served
in the office, became president when the incumbent chief executive died or
resigned: John Tyler, Millard Fillmore, Andrew Johnson, Chester A. Arthur,

Theodore Roosevelt, Calvin Coolidge, Harry S. Truman, Lyndon B. Johnson, and Gerald R. Ford. Collectively, these successor presidents led the nation for forty-two years.

Besides its long-standing role as presidential successor, the vice presidency has become an important electoral springboard to the presidency. Seven of the eleven most recent vice presidents prior to Joseph Biden were later nominated for president in their own right: Richard Nixon, Lyndon Johnson, Hubert H. Humphrey, Gerald Ford, Walter F. Mondale, George H. W. Bush, and Al Gore. In all four of the elections from 1960 to 2000 in which the president did not or could not run for reelection, the incumbent party nominated the vice president as its presidential candidate. Richard B. Cheney, who became George W. Bush's vice president in 2001, was the rare modern vice president to take office with no intention of seeking the presidency. In addition to Cheney's history of heart problems, his preference for operating outside the limelight accounts for his lack of political ambition.

Finally, recent changes in the vice presidency have given substance to the office, especially because presidents have come to regard their vice presidents as valuable, wide-ranging senior advisers. Modern vice presidents have a lot more to do than, as Vice President Marshall joked, "to ring the White House bell every morning and ask what is the state of health of the president."[3]

The vice presidency, then, both as successor and springboard to the presidency and as an institution in its own right, has become an important office. But its history is a problematic one, and not all of the problems have been solved. The history of the vice presidency may be organized usefully into four main periods: the founding period, the nineteenth century, the first half of the twentieth century, and the modern era.

THE FOUNDING PERIOD

The vice presidency was invented late in the Constitutional Convention, not because the delegates saw any need for such an office, but rather as a means to perfect the arrangements they had made for presidential election and succession and, to some degree, for leadership of the Senate (see Chapter 2). The original Constitution provided that the vice presidency would be awarded to the person who received the second-highest number of electoral votes for president. If two or more candidates finished in a second-place tie in the presidential election, the Senate would choose among them.

The only ongoing responsibility the framers of the Constitution assigned to the vice president was to preside over the Senate, casting tie-breaking votes. The vice president's more important duty was to stand by as successor to the president in the event of the president's death, impeachment, resignation, or "inability to discharge the Powers and Duties" of the office. But the Constitution was vague about whether the vice president was to assume the office of president or only its powers and duties under these circumstances, as well as about whether the succession was to last until the end of the departed president's four-year term or only until a special election could be held to choose a new president. The Constitution also left the word *inability* undefined and provided no procedure for the vice president to take power in the event the president became disabled. Finally, by giving the vice president both legislative and executive responsibilities, the Constitution deprived the office of solid moorings in either Congress or the presidency.

Although the vice presidency solved several constitutional design problems related to the presidency and the Senate, it was plagued from birth by problems of its own. First, the office's hybrid status was bound to arouse suspicion in legislative councils because it is partly executive and in executive councils because it is partly legislative. Second, the vice president's single ongoing responsibility, to preside over the Senate, is not very important. Third, the poorly defined successor role has been an inevitable source of confusion and, at times, of tension between the president and the vice president. The fabled "heartbeat away" that separates the vice president from the presidency is, after all, the president's. Finally, more than any other institution of the new government, the vice presidency required the realization of the framers' hope that political parties would not develop. The office would seem less a brilliant than a rash improvisation of the Constitutional Convention if it were occupied as a matter of course by the president's leading partisan foe.

Midway through John Adams's tenure as vice president, he lamented to his wife, Abigail, that "my country has in its wisdom contrived for me the most insignificant office that ever the invention of man contrived or his imagination conceived."[4] Little did Adams realize that during the period he served the vice presidency was at an early peak of influence. Because the Senate was small and still relatively unorganized, Adams was able to cast twenty-nine tie-breaking votes (still the record), guide the upper house's agenda, and intervene in debate. Adams also was respected and sometimes consulted on diplomatic and other matters by President George Washington, who invited him to meet with the cabinet in the president's absence. Moreover, having won the vice presidency by receiving the second-largest number of electoral votes for president in 1789 and 1792, it is not surprising that Adams was elected president in 1796 after Washington left office.

Adams's election as president was different from Washington's, however. The framers' hopes notwithstanding, two political parties, the Federalists and the Democratic-Republicans, emerged during the Washington administration. The result in 1796 was the election of Adams, the Federalist, as president, and Thomas Jefferson, the Democratic-Republicans' presidential nominee, as vice president. Adams tried to lure Jefferson into an active role in the administration by urging him to undertake a diplomatic mission to France, but Jefferson, eager to build his own party and win the presidency from Adams, would have no part of it. He justified his refusal by claiming that, constitutionally, the vice presidency is a legislative office. By Jefferson's own testimony, that was the end of his dealings with President Adams, except on formal occasions. He did make a mark as Senate president by writing a book, *Manual of Parliamentary Practice*. Although the Senate never formally adopted it, the book became the upper house's working procedural guide. But most of Jefferson's congressional activities involved behind-the-scenes opposition to Adams and the Federalists.

Dissatisfied with the divided partisan result of the 1796 election, in 1800 each party nominated a complete ticket and instructed its electors to cast their two votes for its presidential and vice-presidential candidates. The intention was that both candidates would be elected; the result was that neither was. After the electors voted as instructed, Jefferson and his vice-presidential running mate, Aaron Burr of New York, ended up with an equal number of votes—for president. The House of Representatives was required to choose between them. It eventually elected Jefferson, but not before Federalist mischief makers kept the outcome uncertain through thirty-six ballots.

One result of the election of 1800 was the Burr vice presidency, which was marked by bad relations between Burr and Jefferson (they were personally incompatible and represented different factions of the party) and by various misdeeds, including a duel in which Burr shot and killed former Treasury secretary Alexander Hamilton. Another result was the widespread realization that something had to be done about the Electoral College so that it could accommodate the emergence of party competition. Vice-presidential selection was the problem. An obvious solution was to require electors to vote separately for president and vice president.

In opposing the proposal for a separate ballot, some members of Congress argued that it would create a worse problem than it solved. Because "the vice president will not stand on such high ground in the method proposed as he does in the present mode of a double ballot [for president]," predicted Rep. Samuel Taggart of Massachusetts, the nation could expect that "great care will not be taken in the selection of a character to fill that office." Sen. William Plumer of New Hampshire warned that such care as was taken would be "to procure votes for the president."[5] Taggart and Plumer, who were leaders of the rapidly declining Federalist Party, also shared the widespread Federalist belief that finishing second in presidential elections offered their party its only hope of securing even a toehold in the executive branch.[6] In truth, as the nomination of Burr indicated, the parties had already begun to degrade the vice presidency into a device for geographically balancing the ticket in the election.

In 1804 a constitutional amendment was introduced in Congress to abolish the vice presidency rather than continue it in a form diminished from its original status as the position awarded to the second-most-qualified person to be president. But the amendment failed by a vote of 12–19 in the Senate and 27–85 in the House. Instead, a different constitutional amendment was enacted. The Twelfth Amendment provides that electors, rather than voting for two persons as president, "shall name in their ballots the person voted for as President, and in distinct ballots the person voted for as Vice President." It also stipulates that if no one receives a majority of electoral votes for vice president, then "from the two highest numbers on the list, the Senate shall choose the Vice President; a quorum for the purpose shall consist of two-thirds of the whole number of Senators, and a majority of the whole number shall be necessary to a choice." The Twelfth Amendment's final provision extends the Constitution's original age, citizenship, and residency qualifications for president to the vice president.

THE VICE PRESIDENCY IN THE NINETEENTH CENTURY

The development of political parties and the enactment of the Twelfth Amendment sent the constitutionally weak vice presidency into a tailspin that lasted until the end of the nineteenth century. Party leaders, not presidential candidates (who usually were not even present at national nominating conventions and who, if present, were expected to be seen and not heard), chose the nominees for vice president, which did not foster trust or respect between the president and the vice president once in office. Aggravating the tension were the main criteria that party leaders applied to vice-presidential selection. One criterion was that the nominee placate the region or faction of the party that had been most dissatisfied with the presidential nomination, which led to numerous New York-Virginia, North-South, Stalwart-Progressive, and hard money-soft money pairings. Another criterion was that the nominee be able to carry a swing state in the general election where the presidential candidate was not sufficiently popular. This tactic failed more than it succeeded: only 45 percent of presidential candidates in the nineteenth century carried their vice-presidential running mate's home state.[7]

In addition to fostering tension within the government, ticket balancing placed such a stigma on the vice presidency that many political leaders were unwilling to accept a nomination. Daniel Webster, declining the vice-presidential place on the Whig Party ticket in 1848, said, "I do not propose to be buried until I am dead."[8] Those who were nominated and elected found that fresh political problems four years after their nomination invariably led party leaders to balance the ticket differently: no first-term vice president in the nineteenth century was nominated for a second term by a party convention. Nor, after Vice President Martin Van Buren in 1836, was any nineteenth-century vice president elected or even nominated for president.

Finally, the vice president's role as Senate president (which most vice presidents, following Jefferson's lead and for want of other duties, spent considerable time performing) became more ceremonial during the nineteenth century as the Senate took greater charge of its own affairs. John C. Calhoun, who served from 1825 to 1832, was the last vice president whom the Senate allowed to appoint its committees.

Not surprisingly, the nineteenth-century vice presidents make up a virtual rogues' gallery of personal and political failures. Because the office was so unappealing, many of the politicians who could be enticed to run for vice president were old or in bad health. George Clinton of New York, the first vice president elected under the Twelfth Amendment, was both: "an old man who is too feeble to aspire to the presidency."[9] Clinton was the first of six nineteenth-century vice presidents to die in office, all of natural causes. He was followed by Elbridge Gerry, William R. King (who took his oath of office in Cuba where he was receiving treatment for tuberculosis and where he died a month later), Henry Wilson, Thomas A. Hendricks, and Garret A. Hobart. Some vice presidents became embroiled in financial scandals. Daniel D. Tompkins was charged with keeping inadequate financial records while serving as governor of New York during the War of 1812. Schuyler Colfax and Henry Wilson were implicated in the Crédit Mobilier stock scandal of the 1870s.

Other vice presidents fell prey to personal weaknesses or political jealousies. Tompkins and Andrew Johnson were heavy drinkers; Johnson's first vice-presidential address to the Senate impressed listeners, including President Abraham Lincoln, as a drunken harangue. Van Buren's vice president, Richard M. Johnson, kept a series of slave mistresses, educating the children of one but selling another when she lost interest in him.[10] George Clinton, John C. Calhoun, and Chester A. Arthur each publicly expressed his dislike for the president with whom he served. Clinton refused to attend President James Madison's inauguration and openly attacked the administration's foreign and domestic policies. Calhoun alienated two presidents, John Quincy Adams and Andrew Jackson, by using his position as Senate president to subvert their policies and appointments; he then resigned in 1832 to accept South Carolina's election as senator. Arthur attacked President James A. Garfield over a patronage quarrel. "Garfield has not been square, nor honorable, nor truthful . . . ," he told the *New York Herald*. "It's a hard thing to say of a president of the United States, but it's only the truth."[11]

The history of the nineteenth-century vice presidency is not entirely bleak. A certain measure of comity existed between a few presidents and vice presidents, notably Jackson and Van Buren, James K. Polk and George M.

Dallas, Abraham Lincoln and Hannibal Hamlin, Rutherford B. Hayes and William A. Wheeler, and William McKinley and Garret Hobart. But even in these administrations the vice president was not invited to cabinet meetings or entrusted with important tasks. What strengthened most of the relationships was the president's respect for the vice president's advice, which was sought informally, and the vice president's effectiveness as an advocate of the administration's policies in the Senate.

In one area of constitutional responsibility—presidential succession—the vice presidency took a giant step forward in the nineteenth century. The succession question did not arise until 1841, when William Henry Harrison became the first president to die in office. The language of the Constitution provided little guidance about whether the vice president, John Tyler, was to become president for the remainder of Harrison's term or acting president until a special election could be held. All the delegates to the Constitutional Convention were dead, and the most complete record of the convention, which could have helped to clarify the delegates' intentions, was not readily available. (As described in Chapter 2, they had wanted a special election to occur.) In this uncertain situation, Tyler's claim to both the presidency and the balance of Harrison's term was accepted grudgingly, setting a precedent that the next successor president, Millard Fillmore, was able to follow without controversy. Vice President Fillmore succeeded to the presidency in 1850, after President Zachary Taylor died.

But even this bright spot in the early history of the vice presidency was tarnished. Because Tyler and Harrison came from different wings of the Whig Party, Tyler's presidency was marred by debilitating disagreements with Whig leaders in Congress and in the late president's cabinet. All but one of the cabinet members resigned within five months. Fillmore and the two other nineteenth-century successor presidents, Johnson and Arthur, encountered similar problems. They too had been chosen to run for vice president because they represented a faction of the party different from the presidential nominee, and each of them lost all or most of the cabinet members he inherited within two (Fillmore) to six months (Arthur). Johnson's problems were even more dire. He was impeached by the House and came within one vote of being removed from office by the Senate. Indeed, of the four vice presidents who succeeded to the presidency in the nineteenth century, none is considered a successful president. In the most thorough round of historians' rankings, Johnson was rated a failure in the presidency, Tyler and Fillmore as below average, and Arthur as average.[12] Nor were any of the nineteenth-century successor presidents nominated to run for a full term in their own right.

Unresolved issues of succession and disability also vexed the vice presidency during the nineteenth century. Taken together, six vice-presidential deaths, one vice-presidential resignation, and four presidential deaths left the nation without a vice president during eleven of the century's twenty-five presidential terms. President Taylor's death in July 1850 and Vice President King's in April 1853 meant that, with the exception of the month that King spent in Cuba after taking the oath of office there in March 1853, there was no vice president for seven consecutive years. Fortunately, no president has ever died while the vice presidency was vacant.

The issue of vice-presidential responsibility in periods of presidential disability also remained unresolved. Five nineteenth-century presidents were disabled for measurable lengths of time.[13] In 1881, during the eighty days that President Garfield lay wounded before dying from an assassin's bullet, Vice President Arthur stood by helplessly, unwilling to act and thereby risk being accused of coveting the presidency.

Perhaps the unkindest epitaph for the nineteenth-century vice presidency was written by political scientist Woodrow Wilson in his 1885 book *Congressional Government*. After spending less than a page on the vice presidency (in the chapter on "The Senate," not the chapter on "The Executive"), Wilson concluded that "the chief embarrassment in discussing this office is that in explaining how little there is to be said about it one has evidently said all there is to say."[14]

THEODORE ROOSEVELT TO HARRY S. TRUMAN

The rise of mass-circulation magazines and newspaper wire services, a new style of active presidential campaigning, and alterations in the vice-presidential nominating process enhanced the status of the vice presidency during the first half of the twentieth century. In 1900 the Republican nominee, Theodore Roosevelt, became the first vice-presidential candidate (and, other than William Jennings Bryan, the Democratic nominee for president in 1896, the first member of a national party ticket) to campaign vigorously across the country. While President William McKinley waged a sedate reelection campaign, Roosevelt gave 673 speeches to three million listeners in twenty-four states.

The national reputation that Roosevelt gained through travel and the media stood him in good stead when he succeeded to the presidency after McKinley was assassinated in 1901. Roosevelt was able to reverse the earlier pattern of successor presidents and establish a new one: unlike Tyler, Fillmore, Andrew Johnson, and Arthur, Roosevelt was nominated by his party to run for a full term as president in 1904. TR's nomination set the precedent for Coolidge in 1924, Truman in 1948, Lyndon Johnson in 1964, and Ford in 1976. His success also helps to explain another new pattern that contrasts sharply with nineteenth-century practice. Starting with James S. Sherman in 1912, ten of the eleven elected vice presidents who wanted a second term have been nominated for reelection.[15]

In addition to the political precedents he established, Roosevelt helped to lay the intellectual groundwork for enhancing the vice presidency as an institution. In an 1896 article, he argued that the president and vice president should share the same "views and principles" and that the vice president "should always be . . . consulted by the president on every great party question. It would be very well if he were given a seat in the Cabinet . . . a vote [in the Senate], on ordinary occasions, and perchance on occasion a voice in the debates."[16]

That said, Roosevelt was unable as vice president and unwilling as president to practice what he preached about the vice presidency. Party leaders imposed the vice-presidential nomination of Charles W. Fairbanks on Roosevelt in 1904 (TR was from the progressive wing of the Republican Party, Fairbanks from the Old Guard) in the same way they had forced Roosevelt's own nomination as vice president on McKinley in 1900, and for the same reason: to balance the ticket. Neither McKinley nor Roosevelt liked or trusted his vice president, much less assigned him responsibilities. In fact, TR often repeated the humorist Dunne's response when Roosevelt said he was thinking of going down in a submarine: "Well, you really shouldn't do it—unless you take Fairbanks with you."[17]

Still, the enhanced political status of the vice presidency soon began to make it a more attractive office to some able and experienced political leaders, including Charles G. Dawes, who had served in three administrations and shared in the 1925 Nobel Peace Prize; Charles Curtis, the Senate majority leader; and Garner, the Speaker of the House. With somewhat more talent to offer, a few vice presidents were given new responsibilities by the presidents they served. John Adams had been the last vice president to meet with the cabinet, but when President Wilson went to Europe in 1918 to negotiate the treaty that ended World War I, he asked Vice President Marshall to preside in his absence. Wilson's successor, Warren G. Harding, invited Vice President Coolidge to meet with the cabinet as a matter of course, as has every president since Franklin Roosevelt.[18]

FDR, like Theodore Roosevelt, had run for vice president before becoming president (he lost in 1920) and written an article to urge that the responsibilities of the vice presidency be expanded. In the article, Roosevelt had identified four useful roles that the vice president could perform: cabinet member, presidential adviser, liaison to Congress, and policymaker in areas "that do not belong in the province" of any particular department or agency.[19]

As president, Roosevelt initially had so much respect for Garner that, even though the conservative Texan's nomination had been imposed on him at the 1932 Democratic convention, FDR relied on him during the first term as "a combination presiding officer, cabinet officer, personal counselor, legislative tactician, Cassandra, and sounding board."[20] Most significant, Garner served as an important liaison between Roosevelt and Congress. It was Garner's suggestion that led to the practice, which presidents continue to follow, of meeting regularly with congressional leaders. Garner also undertook a goodwill mission abroad at Roosevelt's behest, another innovation that virtually all administrations have continued.

During their second term, Roosevelt and Garner had a falling-out over the president's plan to pack the Supreme Court, his support for organized labor, and other liberal policies. Garner even challenged Roosevelt for the party's 1940 presidential nomination. The rupture between the president and the vice president set the stage for an important modification of the vice-presidential selection process that was designed to foster greater harmony between presidents and vice presidents. In 1936, at Roosevelt's insistence, the Democrats had already abolished their two-thirds rule for presidential nominations, which meant that candidates for president no longer had to engage in as much political horse trading as they used to with the vice presidency and other administration posts to win at the convention. (The party also abolished the two-thirds rule for vice-presidential nominations, reducing the degree of consensus needed for that decision as well.) In 1940 Roosevelt completed his coup by seizing the party leaders' traditional power to determine nominations for vice president and making it his own. Roosevelt's tactic was simple: he threatened that unless the convention chose Secretary of Agriculture Henry A. Wallace for vice president (which it was loath to do), he would refuse the Democratic nomination for president.

Unlike Garner and many of his other predecessors, Wallace had never been a member of Congress, and while serving as vice president he spent little time on Capitol Hill. But he did become the only vice president to be appointed to head a government agency. In July 1941 Roosevelt named Wallace to chair the new Economic Defense Board, a three-thousand-member wartime preparation agency. After World War II was declared in December, it was renamed the Board of Economic Warfare and assigned major procurement responsibilities. Unfortunately, the powers and duties of Wallace's agency overlapped with those of several cabinet departments, notably State and Commerce. These overlaps generated interagency conflicts about jurisdiction and policy that weakened the war effort and undermined Wallace's authority. But because the vice president is a constitutionally independent officer whom the president cannot command or remove, at least not in the usual sense, Roosevelt felt compelled to abolish the warfare board, leaving Wallace embarrassed and devoid of function. In the end, what initially had seemed to be a new birth of vice-presidential power turned out to be false labor. No president since Roosevelt has asked the vice president to head an executive agency.

Nevertheless, the steadily growing involvement of the vice president in executive branch activities persisted under Wallace. The vice president continued to sit with the cabinet, advise the president, and travel abroad as an administration emissary. Wallace's lack of involvement with Congress reflected another emerging characteristic of the twentieth-century vice presidency: the atrophy of the office's role as president of the Senate. In some ways, the first development explains the second. To the extent that vice presidents became more involved with the president, they had less time to spend on the floor of the Senate and less ability to win its members' trust. But changes in the Senate also help to account for the decline of the vice president's constitutional responsibilities in that institution. The admission of new states increased the size of the Senate and made tie votes statistically less probable. The Senate also became more institutionalized, developing its own body of rules and procedural precedents, which the president of the Senate was expected merely to announce on the advice of the parliamentarian.

Advances in the visibility, stature, and extraconstitutional responsibilities of the vice presidency may help to explain the office's improved performance of its main constitutional duty: to provide an able successor to the presidency. Historians have rated two of the five twentieth-century successor presidents (Theodore Roosevelt and Truman) as near-great, one as above average (Lyndon Johnson), and only one (Coolidge) as below average.[21]

For all its progress, however, the vice presidency at midcentury remained a fundamentally weak office. Its constitutional status was substantially unaltered, although the Twentieth Amendment (1933) did establish the full successorship of the vice president–elect in the event of the president-elect's death. Ticket balancing to unite the party and increase its appeal on election day continued to dominate the selection of vice-presidential candidates. All the ambiguities of the vice president's rights and duties in times of presidential disability were still unresolved, as dramatized by the passive role that Marshall felt compelled to play (for fear of being branded a usurper) during the prolonged illness of Woodrow Wilson. And tension continued to mark some presidential–vice-presidential pairings, although less frequently after FDR won for presidential candidates the right to choose their running mates.

Even the glimmerings of enhanced vice-presidential influence sometimes seemed to be no more than that. When Roosevelt ran for a fourth term in 1944, he replaced the unpopular Wallace with Sen. Harry Truman of Missouri. On inauguration day in 1945, the president's health was declining, and World War II was coming to a close. Yet Truman later was to say that in his eighty-two days as vice president, "I don't think I saw Roosevelt but twice . . . except at cabinet meetings."[22] Truman was at most only dimly aware of the existence of the atomic bomb, the Allies' plans for the postwar world, and the serious deterioration of the president's health. In this woeful state of unpreparedness,

On April 12, 1945, Vice President Harry Truman took the presidential oath of office as his wife and daughter looked on. Later that day he told a friend, "I feel like I have been struck by a bolt of lightning."

Truman succeeded to the presidency and its full range of powers and duties when Roosevelt died on April 12. He told a friend later that day, "I feel like I have been struck by a bolt of lightning."[23]

THE MODERN VICE PRESIDENCY

Truman's lack of preparation to succeed to the presidency in 1945, along with the subsequent development of an ongoing cold war between the United States and the Soviet Union and the proliferation of intercontinental ballistic missiles armed with nuclear warheads, heightened public concern that the vice president be a leader who is ready and able to step into the presidency at a moment's notice. (Historically, six of nine presidential successions have occurred during the vice president's first eight months in office.[24]) This concern has had important consequences for the selection, activities, succession and disability, and political status of the vice presidency.

SELECTION

To meet the new public expectations about vice-presidential competence, most modern presidential candidates have paid considerable attention to experience, ability, and political compatibility in selecting their running mates. Winning votes on election day is still as much the goal as in the days of old-style ticket balancing. But presidential nominees realize that voters now care more about competence and loyalty—a vice-presidential candidate's ability to succeed to the presidency ably and to carry on the departed president's policies faithfully—than they do about having all regions of the country or factions of the party represented on the ticket.[25] This realization helped create the climate for a more influential vice presidency. As legal scholar Joel K. Goldstein has shown, the president is most likely to assign responsibilities to the vice president when the two are personally and politically compatible and when the president believes that the vice president has talents the administration needs.[26] Because of the new selection criteria, these conditions have been met in almost every recent administration.

Little is left to chance in modern vice-presidential selection, at least when the presidential nominating contest is settled well in advance of the convention, as has been typical since 1952. Jimmy Carter set a precedent in 1976 when he conducted a careful, organized preconvention search for a running mate. Aides compiled and scrutinized a list of four hundred Democratic officeholders, and then winnowed it down to seven finalists who were investigated and ultimately interviewed by Carter. Carter leaked the list of finalists to the news media, both to gauge public reaction to them and to ensure that any scandalous or embarrassing behavior would be revealed before he made his choice rather than afterward. In the end, Carter tapped Sen. Walter F. Mondale of Minnesota at the convention. Carter's model of vice-presidential selection caught on to such an extent that it is now standard operating procedure for presidential candidates.[27]

The fruits of the new emphasis on loyalty and competence and the new care invested in the selection process are evident in the roster of postwar vice-presidential nominees. The modern era has been marked by an almost complete absence of ideologically opposed running mates, and those vice-presidential candidates who have differed on the issues with the head of the ticket have hastened to gloss over past disagreements and deny that any exist in the present. The record on competence is even more compelling. From 1948 to 2008 numerous vice-presidential candidates were the more experienced members of the ticket in high government office. These candidates include John Sparkman in 1952, Estes Kefauver in 1956, Lyndon Johnson and Henry Cabot Lodge in 1960, Walter Mondale in 1976, George H. W. Bush in 1980, Lloyd Bentsen in 1988, Al Gore in 1992, Richard Cheney in 2000, and Joseph Biden in 2008.[28] As a six-term senator from Delaware, Biden brought more experience in high office to his party's ticket than any previous vice president, offsetting presidential nominee Barack Obama's relatively thin resumé as a less-than-one-term senator. "We needed a running mate . . . who brought some gray hair and years of experience here in Washington," said David Axelrod, Obama's chief political consultant.[29]

To be sure, nothing guarantees that reasoned, responsible vice-presidential nominees will be chosen in every presidential election. Politicians do not always see their interests clearly. Richard Nixon, the Republican presidential nominee in 1968, was too clever by half when, acting on the theory that a relatively unknown running mate would have few enemies and cost the ticket few votes, he chose Maryland governor Spiro T. Agnew as his candidate for vice president.[30] In 1984 many observers thought Mondale seemed too eager to placate feminist groups within the Democratic Party when he selected Geraldine A. Ferraro, a three-term member of the House of Representatives with no notable foreign affairs experience, as his running mate. Similarly, George McGovern may have been overly concerned about satisfying organized labor when he picked Missouri senator Thomas Eagleton in 1972. It was revealed soon after Eagleton's nomination that he had concealed from McGovern the electroshock therapy he had undergone for a nervous break-down, which led to his being dropped from the ticket.

John McCain's selection of first-term Alaska governor Sarah Palin as his running mate in 2008 was another product of constituency pressures, albeit indirectly. McCain's first choice was Sen. Joseph Lieberman of Connecticut, a close friend who had been the Democratic vice-presidential candidate in 2000. When Republican activists objected that awarding a place on the GOP ticket to a pro-choice Democrat would severely divide the party, McCain hastily looked for a different way of reinforcing his "maverick" image with a different kind of nontraditional choice. He tapped Palin, a woman with a reputation as a political outsider even in her own state.[31]

What seems certain, however, is that the presidential candidate who pays insufficient attention to competence and loyalty in choosing the vice-presidential nominee will suffer for it in the election. The news media will run critical stories, the other party will air harsh commercials, and the now-traditional vice-presidential debate, which is nationally televised in prime time, may reveal the nominee as an unworthy presidential successor.[32] Vice-presidential candidates dominate the campaign news during at least two periods: when their names are announced and during the week bracketing the vice-presidential debate. A candidate for president who chooses an unimpressive running mate not only forfeits an opportunity to gain positive news coverage but also invites its opposite.[33]

In the 1988 election Bush's selection of the inarticulate Quayle may have reduced his margin of victory in the popular vote by as much as four to eight percentage points.[34] In contrast, Clinton's choice of Gore in 1992 successfully defied all the conventions of ticket balancing. Like Clinton, Gore was a southerner, a Baptist, a moderate, and a baby boomer whose intelligence and ability appealed to many voters.[35] In July 1992 a *Time*-CNN poll found that when asked, "Who do you think is more qualified to be president—Quayle or

Gore?"—63 percent of respondents said Gore, and 21 percent named the incumbent vice president, Quayle.[36]

To screen potential running mates in 2000, George W. Bush established a vetting process headed by Cheney, a veteran Washington politician with experience in the House of Representatives, in the corporate world, and in several Republican administrations, including prominent service as President Ford's chief of staff and as secretary of defense under Bush's father. Bush accepted Cheney's criteria for an ideal nominee—someone with experience in the White House, Congress, the private sector, and as head of an executive department—and ended up choosing one of the very few people who met these criteria: Cheney himself.[37] The selection was surprising in one way because most of the speculation had centered on Bush's fellow big-state Republican governors, such as Tom Ridge of Pennsylvania and John Engler of Michigan. But in a more important way, Bush's selection of Cheney was not surprising at all. Governors who have been nominated for president—FDR in 1932, Alfred M. Landon in 1936, Thomas E. Dewey in 1944, Adlai Stevenson in 1952 and 1956, Carter in 1976, Reagan in 1980, Dukakis in 1988, Clinton in 1992, and Bush himself in 2000—almost always have chosen veteran Washington figures for vice president.[38] They have done so to reassure the voters that their own inexperience in national government, especially in foreign policy, will be offset by the vice president's experience. Bush underlined this virtue of the Cheney nomination by declaring that he had chosen him less to help win the election than to help him govern "as a valuable partner"—a shrewd tactic for helping Bush win the election.[39]

Gore, persuaded of Warren Christopher's skill at screening potential Democratic running mates by the former secretary of state's work for Clinton in 1992 (which had led to Gore's own selection), enlisted Christopher to help in 2000. Between February and July, Christopher and Gore whittled a list of about forty names down to four, all of them senators: John Edwards of North Carolina, Bob Kerrey of Nebraska, John F. Kerry of Massachusetts, and Lieberman of Connecticut, who was added to the list at Gore's insistence. Gore wanted to make a bold choice that would help to establish him in the voters' minds as a leader in his own right, not just as President Clinton's loyal lieutenant. When the time came, no one doubted the boldness of Gore's decision to choose Lieberman, a deeply religious Jew who had publicly criticized Clinton's behavior during the Monica Lewinsky affair as "immoral."

In the end, Bush's selection of Cheney and Gore's of Lieberman helped their tickets in offsetting ways. In the election day exit poll, 72 percent of all voters said that Lieberman's religion would make him neither a better nor a worse vice president, and of the remaining 28 percent, twice as many thought it would make him a better one. Asked whom they would prefer as vice president, 46 percent of voters said Lieberman and 48 percent said Cheney, a statistical wash. Cheney's main contribution to Bush was indirect. His extensive experience in foreign affairs helps to explain why a majority of the voters who regarded foreign policy as the most important issue in the election supported Bush, even though Bush's background in this area was considerably weaker than Gore's.[40]

In 2004 Democratic presidential candidate John Kerry chose his chief rival for the nomination, Sen. John Edwards, as his vice-presidential running mate. Kerry's choice of someone he had just defeated was not unusual: eight of the twenty vice-presidential nominees from 1960 to 2004 had already run for president at least once. But Kerry and Edwards often seemed uncomfortable together in joint appearances, and, remarkably, the Kerry campaign made no effort to carry Edwards's home state of North Carolina. Four years later, Obama selected Biden, who had been one of his opponents in the 2008 Democratic nominating contest. Obama's choice of the experienced Biden did him far more good than McCain's selection of the inexperienced Palin. Voters who worried about McCain's age (at seventy-two he was bidding to become the oldest person ever elected president) were especially alarmed at Palin's lack of knowledge about foreign affairs. Exit polls showed that although 66 percent thought Biden was "qualified to be president if necessary," only 38 percent thought that Palin was.[41]

A concern for competence and loyalty in the vice presidency characterized the solution Congress invented in the 1960s to a recurring problem made urgent by the challenges of the postwar era: vice-presidential vacancies. The Twenty-fifth Amendment, ratified in 1967, established a procedure for selecting vice presidents in unusual circumstances. Before then, the vice presidency had been vacant for parts of sixteen administrations, leaving the president with no constitutionally designated successor.[42] The new amendment stated that "whenever there is a vacancy in the office of the Vice President, the President shall nominate a Vice President who shall take office upon confirmation by a majority vote of both Houses of Congress," voting separately. This procedure came in handy, albeit in circumstances its authors scarcely had imagined, twice within a few years. In 1973 Vice President Agnew resigned as part of a plea bargain to reduce bribery charges and was replaced by Ford. In 1974 Ford became president after President Nixon resigned to avert impeachment proceedings, and Ford appointed former New York governor Nelson A. Rockefeller to fill the vacated vice presidency.

ACTIVITIES

Modern presidents try to reassure the nation that the vice president is prepared to succeed to the presidency at a moment's notice by keeping their vice presidents informed about most matters of state. As President Dwight D. Eisenhower remarked at a news conference: "Even if Mr. Nixon and I were not good friends, I would still have him in every important conference of government, so that if the grim reaper would find it time to remove me from the scene, he is ready to step in without any interruption."[43] In 1949, at President Truman's request, the vice president was made a statutory member of the National Security Council.[44] Vice presidents also receive full national security briefings on a regular basis.

As a further means of public reassurance, most presidents now encourage their vice presidents to stay active in prominent ways. Since FDR began the practice with Garner, presidents have sent their vice presidents abroad with growing frequency on a variety of diplomatic missions, ranging from simple expressions of American goodwill to actual negotiations. Vice presidents since Garner also have sat regularly with the cabinet and have served, to some degree, as a legislative liaison between the president and Congress. In that capacity, they count votes on Capitol Hill, lobby discreetly, and listen to complaints and suggestions.

Alben W. Barkley, who served as vice president in the second Truman administration, elevated the ceremonial duties of the office to center stage. Some of these, such as crowning beauty queens (a Barkley favorite), have been inconsequential. Others, such as college commencement addresses and appearances at events that symbolize administration goals, need not be. Nixon, serving a president who did not enjoy partisan politics, carved out new vice-presidential roles that were as insignificant as chair of a minor study commission and as important as chief public advocate of the administration's policies, leadership, and party. The advocacy role exposed the vice president to a wide range of politically important audiences, including interest groups, party activists, journalists, and the general public.

During the 1960s and 1970s vice presidents began to accumulate greater institutional resources to help them fulfill their more extensive duties. Lyndon Johnson, who served with President Kennedy, gained for the vice presidency an impressive suite of offices in the Executive Office Building, adjacent to the White House. Agnew won a line item in the executive budget. The result was to free vice presidents from their earlier dependence on Congress for office space and operating funds.

Even more significant institutional gains were registered by Ford and Rockefeller, the two vice presidents who were appointed under the Twenty-fifth Amendment and whose agreements to serve were urgently needed, for political reasons, by their presidents. Ford, who feared becoming too dependent on a president who might well be removed from office, persuaded Nixon to increase dramatically his budget for hiring staff. The new personnel included support staff for press relations, speech writing, scheduling, and administration (which meant that vice presidents no longer had to depend on the often-preoccupied White House staff for these functions); policy staff (enabling vice presidents to develop useful ideas and advice on matters of presidential concern); and political staff (to help vice presidents protect their interests and further their ambitions). Rockefeller secured a weekly place on the president's calendar for a private meeting. He also enhanced the perquisites of the vice presidency—everything from a better airplane to serve as *Air Force Two* to an official residence (the Admiral's House at the Naval Observatory) and a redesigned seal for the office. The old seal had shown an eagle at rest; the new one displayed a wingspread eagle with a claw full of arrows and a starburst at its head.[45]

The vice presidency came into full flower during Mondale's tenure in the Carter administration. As Carter's running mate in 1976, Mondale participated in the first nationally televised debate between the vice-presidential candidates. His most tangible contribution to the institution during his term as vice president was the authorization he won to attend all presidential meetings, receive full access to the flow of papers to and from the president, and occupy an office in the West Wing of the White House.[46] Most important, perhaps, Mondale demonstrated that the vice president could serve the president (who, as noted above, had selected him with unprecedented care) as a valued adviser on virtually all matters of politics and public policy. Most vice presidents in the modern era had been consulted by their presidents on at least some important matters—Johnson on space issues, Humphrey on civil rights, Rockefeller on domestic policy. But no vice president had ever attained Mondale's status as a wide-ranging senior adviser to the president.

As vice president to President Reagan, George H. W. Bush was heir to all the institutional gains in roles and resources made by his recent predecessors. Although he did not enter office enjoying the same close relationship with Reagan that Mondale had with Carter, Bush worked hard and for the most part successfully to win the president's confidence. When Bush became president, he fostered an even stronger relationship with Quayle, whom he appointed to chair the new White House Council on Competitiveness, a de facto board of regulatory review that was empowered to overturn regulations issuing from the federal bureaucracy.[47]

From the beginning, Clinton's relationship with Gore rivaled Carter's with Mondale for trust and responsibility. Until strains developed when Gore ran for president in 2000, their relationship exceeded any previous one between a president and a vice president. Gore became one of the administration's star players in September 1993 when he issued the fat-trimming "reinventing government" report of the National Performance Review. Two months later, he soundly defeated administration critic H. Ross Perot in a widely watched, nationally televised debate about the proposed North American Free Trade Agreement.

In addition to handling specific assignments, Gore was one of the three or four people whose advice Clinton sought on virtually every important matter of presidential politics and policy. On one occasion in 1993, when Clinton was immobilized with doubt about how to proceed with his economic program in Congress, he asked Gore, "What can I do?" Gore replied, with considerable exasperation, "You can get with the goddamn program!" After a pause, Clinton said, "Okay."[48] According to veteran Washington reporter Elizabeth Drew, "Gore was in large measure responsible for the boldness of Clinton's economic program."[49] In 1998 a Clinton adviser listed several "areas where Al Gore makes the decisions—and the president rubberstamps[:] . . . science, technology, NASA, telecommunications, the environment, family leave, tobacco, nuclear dealings with the Russians, media violence, the Internet, privacy issues, and, of course, reinventing government."[50]

Especially during his first term, Richard Cheney's responsibilities in the administration of George W. Bush surpassed those of any vice president in history, including Mondale and Gore.[51] One reporter described Cheney's role as "war minister, über diplomat, political adviser and consigliere to President Bush."[52] Another writer noted that Cheney's voice was the final one Bush wanted to hear before making an important decision. "What does Dick think?" the president routinely asked.[53] Historian Douglas Brinkley described Cheney as "the vortex in the White House on foreign policy making. Everything comes through him."[54]

Cheney's influence was felt even before he took office, when Bush asked him to direct the transition from election to inauguration, the only time a vice president has been assigned this task. In the spring of 2001 Cheney was charged with developing the administration's energy policy initiative. After the September 11, 2001, terrorist attacks on New York City's World Trade Center and the Pentagon, Cheney was Bush's primary adviser in formulating the war against the Taliban regime in Afghanistan, which was harboring the al Qaeda terrorists responsible for the attacks. His role in the war to topple the Saddam Hussein regime in Iraq, which was launched in 2003, was much more controversial. Cheney relentlessly pressed the case, in speeches and in private administration councils, that Saddam had stockpiled weapons of mass destruction and was cooperating with al Qaeda. Although Saddam was easily defeated by American and allied forces, neither of these justifications for the war proved valid. Still worse, anti-American insurgents in Iraq waged guerilla warfare against the occupying forces for several years, undermining public approval at home and abroad of Bush's performance as president as well as of Cheney's as vice president.[55]

Cheney spent nearly all of his time working with Bush, but in at least one instance he revived the vice president's long dormant role as an influential president of the Senate. As evidence of just how attenuated the role had become, when Vice President Agnew wandered onto the Senate floor in 1969 to ask Idaho senator Len Jordan, a fellow Republican, if the administration could count on his vote for a tax bill, Jordan barked, "You had it until now." The outraged senator then formulated the "Jordan Rule": "When the vice president lobbies on the Senate floor for a bill, vote the other way."[56] Rockefeller made a similar misstep, with similar consequences, in 1975. But in 2005, when Senate Democrats threatened to filibuster some of Bush's appellate court nominations, Cheney made clear that as Senate president he would rule that filibusters of judicial appointments could be ended by a simple majority vote rather than the customary three-fifths majority. The vice president was acting at the request of Senate Republicans, however; he was not acting on his own.

The combination of power and unpopularity made Cheney a target in the 2008 election. "Vice President Cheney has been the most dangerous vice president we've had probably in American history," charged Biden in the vice-presidential debate, and Palin did not rise to defend him. Biden insisted that his primary job as vice president would be to advise the president and then to accept and defend his decisions. "Every major decision he'll be making, I'll be sitting in the room to give my best advice," Biden told the national television audience.[57] In practice, Obama handed Biden a series of specific assignments during his first two years as vice president: chairing a middle class task force, overseeing spending on projects designed to stimulate the economy, lobbying

Jimmy Carter, right, regarded his vice president, Walter Mondale, as a valued adviser on virtually all matters of politics and public policy, a status no earlier vice president had attained. Mondale also was authorized to attend all presidential meetings and was allowed full access to the flow of papers to and from the president.

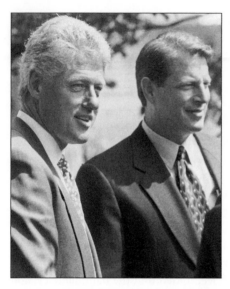

From the beginning, President Bill Clinton, left, relied heavily on Vice President Al Gore for advice and support.

Vice President Richard Cheney, shown here with President George W. Bush, represents what many believe to be the most hands-on, active second-in-command since the start of the presidency.

on Capitol Hill, visiting foreign capitals, winding down the war in Iraq, and campaigning for Democratic candidates in the 2010 midterm elections. But none of these responsibilities detracted from Biden's primary role as a wide-ranging senior adviser whom the president prized for speaking his mind. During Obama's lengthy review of American policy in Afghanistan, Biden was a forceful and effective "house skeptic" about further military involvement. "He's got wisdom, he's got experience, he's blunt, and he's loyal," said Obama—"all the qualities you could ask for in a governing partner and in a vice president."[58]

Every vice president realizes that the extent to which the new activities of the office translate into real influence still depends in large part on the president's perception of the vice president's ability, energy, and, perhaps most important, loyalty. Because of the new vice-presidential selection criteria, this perception is more likely to be favorable today than at any time in the nation's history. And, because of the institutionalization of numerous roles and resources in the vice presidency, the vice president has a greater opportunity than ever to exert real influence on the president.

SUCCESSION AND DISABILITY

In addition to creating a procedure to fill vice-presidential vacancies, the Twenty-fifth Amendment accomplished two other purposes that, taken together, expressed "a new constitutional vision" of the vice presidency as "an important institution in American government."[59] One was to state explicitly the right of the vice president to assume the presidency and serve for the remainder of the departed president's term if the president dies, resigns, or is impeached and removed. In this respect, the amendment was a formality that conferred constitutional sanction on the tradition that Tyler established after President Harrison died in 1841. The other was to create a set of procedures to handle situations of presidential disability. As discussed in Chapter 11, the amendment provided constitutional methods both for the president to name the vice president as acting president during a time of disability and for the vice president and a majority of the heads of the departments to make that decision if the president is unable to do so. The amendment even created a procedure to be followed if the vice president and the cabinet believe the president to be disabled and the president disagrees. The vice president would become acting president, but the president would be restored to power within twenty-one days unless declared disabled by two-thirds of both the House and the Senate.

Only a few clear instances of presidential disability have arisen since the Twenty-fifth Amendment was passed.[60] The first occurred when Reagan was shot on March 30, 1981. Some thought was given, then and in the days afterward, to naming Vice President Bush as acting president. But White House aides discouraged any such action for fear that to do so would make Reagan appear weak and would confuse the nation and foreign governments.[61]

Criticism of the administration's failure to act in 1981 shaped its preparation for the second instance of presidential disability, Reagan's scheduled cancer surgery on July 13, 1985. This time Reagan did relinquish his powers and duties to Bush before going under anesthesia. Curiously, he did not explicitly invoke the Twenty-fifth Amendment in doing so, saying instead that he was not convinced that the amendment was meant to apply to "such brief and temporary periods of incapacity" as his surgery. Still, a precedent was established, raising expectations that the Twenty-fifth Amendment would work as intended in future administrations. This precedent was followed in 2002 and 2007 when George W. Bush cited the amendment in transferring authority to Cheney just before being anesthetized for a surgical procedure. Although the vice president was not called on to do anything during his few hours as acting president, Bush explained to the press, "We're at war and I just want to be super-cautious."[62]

POLITICAL STATUS

The vice president enjoys a curious political status. Until George H. W. Bush's victory in 1988, no incumbent vice president had been elected president since 1836, when Van Buren was chosen. Yet, in a marked departure from previous political history, the vice presidency has become the most effective stepping stone to a major-party presidential nomination in the postwar era. Of the modern vice presidents, Nixon, Humphrey, Mondale, Bush, and Gore were nominated directly for president, and Truman, Johnson, and Ford were nominated for a full term after succeeding to the presidency. Agnew and Rockefeller did not actively seek a presidential nomination, and Cheney made clear from the start that he would not be a candidate. Biden, who will be seventy-four in 2016, has eschewed any presidential ambitions, albeit less definitively than Cheney.

What accounts for the recent ascendancy of the vice presidency in the politics of presidential nominations? First, the two-term limit that was imposed on the president by the Twenty-second Amendment in 1951 made it possible for the vice president to step forward as a presidential candidate during the president's second term without alienating the president, as Nixon (1960), Bush (1988), and Gore (2000) did. This effect of the amendment was wholly unanticipated when it was enacted. Second, the roles that Vice President Nixon developed, with Eisenhower's encouragement, as party builder (campaigning during election years, raising funds between elections) and as public advocate of the administration and its policies uniquely situate the vice president to win friends among the party activists who influence presidential nominations. Finally, the recent growth in vice-presidential activities has made the vice presidency a more prestigious office and therefore a more plausible stepping stone to the presidency. Even the trappings of the office—the airplane, official residence, seal, Secret Service contingent, and West Wing office—testify to its prestige.[63]

Perhaps more important, in their efforts to assure the nation that they are fulfilling their responsibility to prepare for a possible emergency succession, presidents make public claims, inflated or otherwise, about the participation of the vice president in the administration. The typical modern vice president can argue plausibly, as Mondale frequently did, that the vice presidency "may be the best training of all" for the presidency. "I'm privy to all the same secret information as the president," Mondale said. "I have unlimited access to the president. I'm usually with him when all the central decisions are being made. I've been through several of those crises that a president inevitably confronts, and I see how they work. I've been through the budget process. I've been through the diplomatic ventures. I've been through a host of congressional fights as seen from the presidential perspective."[64]

Yet vice presidents who are nominated by their party for president carry certain disadvantages into the fall campaign that are as surely grounded in the office as the advantages they bring to the nominating contest.[65] Indeed, some of the activities of the modern vice presidency that are most appealing to the party activists who influence nominations may repel members of the broader electorate that decides the general election. Days and nights spent fertilizing the party's grass roots with fervent, sometimes slashing political rhetoric can alienate voters who look to the presidency for leadership that unites rather than divides. Gore's blurt to a 1998 postimpeachment rally of Democratic House members that Clinton "will be regarded in the history books as one of our greatest presidents" doubtless roused the spirits of his fellow partisans, but it seemed wildly excessive to almost everyone else.[66]

Certain institutional qualities of the modern vice presidency also handicap the vice president who becomes a presidential candidate. Vice presidents must work hard to gain a share of the credit for the successes of the administration, but they can count on being attacked by the other party's presidential nominee for all of the administration's shortcomings. Such attacks allow no effective response. A vice president who tries to stand apart from the administration may alienate the president and cause voters to wonder why the criticisms were not voiced earlier, when they might have made a difference. Gore did himself no good when he spent the evening of his official announcement for president telling the *20/20* television audience that Clinton's behavior in the Monica Lewinsky affair was "inexcusable."[67]

The vice president's difficulties are only compounded when it comes to matters of public policy. For example, every time during the 2000 campaign that Gore identified a problem he wanted to solve as president, George W. Bush would chastise him for not already persuading Clinton to solve it. During their first debate, when Gore mentioned his proposal to extend prescription drug benefits to seniors, Bush replied, "Four years ago they campaigned on getting prescription drug benefits for seniors. And now they're campaigning on getting prescription drug benefits for seniors. It seems like they can't get it done."[68]

Vice presidents can always say that loyalty to the president forecloses public disagreement, but that course is no less perilous. The public that values loyalty in a vice president values other qualities in a potential president. Strength, independence, and vision are what most voters look for—the very qualities that vice presidents almost never have an opportunity to display.[69] Polls that through much of the election year showed Gore trailing Bush in the category of leadership were less about the candidates than about the vice presidency. So was the election day exit poll showing that voters who regarded strong leadership as the personal quality they wanted most in a president supported Bush by 64 percent to 34 percent.[70]

Although the political handicaps that vice presidents carry into the general election campaign are formidable, they need not be insurmountable. As with all things vice-presidential, much depends on their relationship with the presidents they serve. One of the main reasons that sitting vice presidents Nixon and Humphrey lost is that their presidents were so unhelpful. When a reporter asked Eisenhower to name a single "major idea of [Nixon's] you had adopted" as president, he replied, "If you give me a week, I might think of one."[71] Johnson treated Humphrey spitefully as soon as it became clear that the 1968 Democratic convention was not going to draft the president for another term, despite his earlier withdrawal from the race.

In contrast, more than a century earlier Van Buren benefited enormously from his association with President Andrew Jackson, who regarded his vice president's election to the presidency as validation of the transformation he had wrought in American politics and government. Reagan was equally committed to Bush's success in 1988, putting ego aside to praise the vice president's contributions to what the president began calling the "Reagan-Bush administration." Reagan's popularity was of even greater benefit to Bush, who won the votes of 80 percent of those who approved of Reagan's performance as president.[72]

Although Clinton said in 2000 that he wished he could run for a third term (and identified Gore only as "the next best thing"),[73] he shared Jackson's and Reagan's belief that his legacy was closely tied to his vice president's political success. Gore, however, chose to distance himself from the popular Clinton, rejecting the president's repeated offers to campaign for him, which party leaders urged Gore to accept.[74] Instead of emphasizing the national prosperity that had marked the Clinton-Gore years, Gore ran a populist-style campaign more appropriate for a candidate challenging an incumbent in economic hard times than for a vice president seeking to extend his party's control of the presidency in good times. In the three nationally televised debates with Bush, Gore never mentioned Clinton.

To be sure, vice presidents are not destined to lose presidential elections any more than they are destined to win presidential nominations. Before Bush was elected in 1988, Nixon in 1960 and Humphrey in 1968 each came within two percentage points of victory. In 2000 Gore won the national popular vote and came very close in the Electoral College. But the electoral tensions that vice presidents face as presidential candidates inhere in the office. As President Eisenhower once observed, "To promise and pledge *new* effort, *new* programs, and *new* ideas without appearing to criticize the current party and administration—that is indeed an exercise in tightrope walking."[75]

CONCLUSION

In matters of selection, activities, succession and disability, and political status, the vice presidency has come a long way, especially since 1945. But the curious electoral history of the vice presidency is a reminder that for all its progress as an institution, some weaknesses of the office endure. Although new selection criteria make the nomination of vice-presidential candidates who are qualified to be president more likely, the examples of Agnew in 1968,

Eagleton in 1972, Ferraro in 1984, and Quayle in 1988 indicate that older patterns of choice are not yet extinct.

The new selection criteria may foster greater harmony in office between the president and the vice president, but they do not guarantee it. Perhaps it is not surprising that Johnson and Nixon, the two modern presidents who inflicted the greatest pain on their vice presidents, were once vice presidents themselves.[76]

Finally, although vice presidents enjoy more resources, responsibilities, and influence than ever before, they do so mainly at the sufferance of the president. The price of power for a vice president can be high—unflagging loyalty, sublimation of one's own views and ambitions, and willingness to answer to the president's beck and call. But, in view of the inherent constitutional weakness of the office, no other path to influence exists.

NOTES

1. These familiar quotations about the vice presidency may be found in Michael Dorman, *The Second Man: The Changing Role of the Vice Presidency* (New York: Delacorte Press, 1968), 6–7.

2. Quoted in Paul C. Light, *Vice-Presidential Power: Advice and Influence in the White House* (Baltimore: Johns Hopkins University Press, 1984), 13.

3. Thomas R. Marshall, *Recollections* (Indianapolis: Bobbs-Merrill, 1925), 368.

4. Quoted in David McCullough, *John Adams* (New York: Simon and Schuster, 2001), 447.

5. Quoted in Joel K. Goldstein, *The Modern American Vice Presidency* (Princeton: Princeton University Press, 1982).

6. David E. Kyvig, *Explicit and Authentic Acts: Amending the U.S. Constitution, 1776–1995* (Lawrence: University Press of Kansas, 1996), 116.

7. Jody C. Baumgartner, *The American Vice Presidency Reconsidered* (Westport, Conn.: Praeger, 2006), 19.

8. Quoted in Thomas E. Cronin, "Rethinking the Vice Presidency," in *Rethinking the Vice Presidency,* ed. Thomas E. Cronin (Boston: Little, Brown, 1982), 326. Rather than being buried, Webster would have succeeded to the presidency when Zachary Taylor died in 1850.

9. Matthew Crenson and Benjamin Ginsberg, *Presidential Power: Unchecked and Unbalanced* (New York: Norton, 2007), 66.

10. Johnson was the protagonist in two other unique events in the history of the vice presidency. In the election of 1836, Virginia's Democratic electors refused to vote for Johnson because they objected to his interracial sexual extravagances. This situation left Johnson one vote short of the required electoral vote majority, so the Senate elected him by 33–16. Four years later, Johnson refused to withdraw as a candidate for the Democratic nomination for vice president, dividing the party convention to such an extent that it selected no vice-presidential candidate at all. The Democrats lost the election.

11. Quoted in Irving G. Williams, *The Rise of the Vice Presidency* (Washington, D.C.: Public Affairs Press, 1956), 66.

12. Robert K. Murray and Tim H. Blessing, "The Presidential Performance Study: A Progress Report," *Journal of American History* 70 (December 1983): 535–555. The same ratings prevailed in an October 2000 survey of historians, political scientists, and law professors. James Lindgren and Steven G. Calabresi, "Ranking the Presidents," *Wall Street Journal,* November 15, 2000. See also "C-Span 2009 Historians' Presidential Leadership Survey," http://www.c-span.org/PresidentialSurvey/Overall-Ranking.aspx.

13. The five nineteenth-century presidents who were disabled for a measurable period of time were Madison, William Henry Harrison, Arthur, Garfield, and Grover Cleveland. John D. Feerick, *The Twenty-fifth Amendment* (New York: Fordham University Press, 1976), chap. 1.

14. Woodrow Wilson, *Congressional Government* (New York: Meridian Books, 1956), 162.

15. The exception was Henry A. Wallace in 1944. For a detailed historical perspective on the growing political security of vice presidents, see George S. Sirgiovanni, "Dumping the Vice President: A Historical Overview and Analysis," *Presidential Studies Quarterly* 24 (Fall 1994): 765–782.

16. Theodore Roosevelt, "The Three Vice-Presidential Candidates and What They Represent," *Review of Reviews,* September 1896, 289.

17. Quoted in Williams, *Rise of the Vice Presidency,* 89.

18. Marshall's decision to accept Wilson's invitation to meet with the cabinet was made with some misgivings. Although he once had described the president as "my commander-in-chief" whose "orders would be obeyed," Marshall believed that, constitutionally, the vice president, as president of the Senate, was a "member of the legislative branch," ill-suited to executive responsibilities. He told the cabinet he wanted it clearly understood that he was present only "informally and personally" and would "preside in an unofficial and informal way." Before his inauguration in 1925, Vice President Dawes said publicly that he would not accept an invitation from President Coolidge to meet with the cabinet, if, as seemed likely, one were forthcoming. "The cabinet and those who sit with it should always do so at the discretion and inclination of the president . . . ," Dawes told reporters, overlooking the possibility that Coolidge might wish to exercise his discretion to have the vice president present. "No precedent should be established which creates a different and arbitrary method of selection." Williams, *Rise of the Vice Presidency,* 108–110, 134.

19. Franklin D. Roosevelt, "Can the Vice President Be Useful?" *Saturday Evening Post,* October 6, 1920, 8.

20. Williams, *Rise of the Vice Presidency,* 158–159.

21. Murray and Blessing, "Presidential Performance Study," 535–555. An October 2000 survey of presidential scholars obtained the same results, except that Coolidge was ranked average instead of below average. Lindgren and Calabresi, "Ranking the Presidents." For more recent confirmation of these judgments, see "C-Span 2009 Historians' Presidential Leaderships Survey."

22. Quoted in Williams, *Rise of the Vice Presidency,* 219.

23. Quoted in Robert J. Donovan, *Conflict and Crisis: The Presidency of Harry S. Truman, 1945–1948* (New York: Norton, 1977), 15.

24. All but the successions of Millard Fillmore, Calvin Coolidge, and Lyndon Johnson.

25. Since 1940 ticket balancing has been of little explanatory value in accounting for vice-presidential nominations. Lee Sigelman and Paul J. Wahlbeck, "The 'Veepstakes': Strategic Choice in Presidential Running Mate Selection," *American Political Science Review* 91 (December 1997): 862.

26. Goldstein, *Modern American Vice Presidency,* 147–148.

27. Michael Nelson, "Choosing the Vice President," *PS: Political Science and Politics* 21 (Fall 1988): 858–868; Nelson, "The Elections: Turbulence and Tranquility in Contemporary American Politics," in *The Elections of 1996,* ed. Michael Nelson (Washington, D.C.: CQ Press, 1997), 66–70.

28. Goldstein, *Modern American Vice Presidency,* 85; updated by the authors.

29. Quoted in Jules Witcover, *Joe Biden: A Life of Trial and Redemption* (New York: HarperCollins, 2010), 413.

30. Jules Witcover, *Very Strange Bedfellows: The Short and Unhappy Marriage of Richard Nixon and Spiro Agnew* (New York: Public Affairs, 2007).

31. See Dan Balz and Haynes Johnson, *The Battle for America 2008* (New York: Viking, 2009), chap. 26; and John Heileman and Mark Halperin, *Game Change: Obama and the*

Clintons, McCain and Palin, and the Race of a Lifetime (New York: HarperCollins, 2010), chap. 20.

32. The debates appear to have at least a short-term effect on voter intentions. Thomas M. Holbrook, "The Behavioral Consequences of Vice-Presidential Debates," *American Politics Quarterly* 22 (October 1994): 469–482.

33. Baumgartner, *American Vice Presidency Reconsidered,* chap. 5.

34. Michael Nelson, "Constitutional Aspects of the Elections," in *The Elections of 1988,* ed. Michael Nelson (Washington, D.C.: CQ Press, 1989), 190. For a more general treatment, see Martin P. Wattenberg, "The Role of Vice Presidential Candidate Ratings in Presidential Voting Behavior," *American Politics Quarterly* 23 (October 1995): 504–514.

35. Michael Nelson, "The Presidency: Clinton and the Cycle of Politics and Policy," in *The Elections of 1992,* ed. Michael Nelson (Washington, D.C.: CQ Press, 1993), 125–132.

36. *National Journal,* August 8, 1992, 1862.

37. Bob Woodward, *State of Denial: Bush at War, Part III* (New York: Simon and Schuster, 2006), xiii.

38. In 1948 Dewey chose a fellow governor, Earl Warren of California, as his running mate. The ticket lost.

39. David Von Drehle, "First, Do No Harm," *Washington Post National Weekly Edition,* July 31, 2000, 9.

40. Michael Nelson, "The Election: Ordinary Politics, Extraordinary Outcome," in *The Elections of 2000,* ed. Michael Nelson (Washington, D.C.: CQ Press, 2001), 72–75.

41. "Exit Polls," http://www.cnn.com/ELECTION/2008/results/polls/#val=USP00p4.

42. Vice-presidential vacancies occurred seven times because the vice president died, once because the vice president resigned, and eight times because the president died.

43. *Public Papers of the Presidents* (Washington, D.C.: Government Printing Office, 1957), 132.

44. The only other task assigned to the vice president by law is to serve on the Board of Regents of the Smithsonian Institution.

45. Rockefeller also headed the White House Domestic Council, an assignment that ended in failure, as did Henry Wallace's. Michael Nelson, "Nelson A. Rockefeller and the American Vice Presidency," in *Gerald R. Ford and the Politics of Post-Watergate America,* vol. 1, ed. Bernard J. Firestone and Alexej Ugrinsky (Westport, Conn.: Greenwood Press, 1993), 139–160.

46. "Walter F. Mondale's Memo to Jimmy Carter on the Role of the Vice President," in *The Evolving Presidency: Landmark Documents, 1787—2010,* ed. Michael Nelson (Washington, D.C.: CQ Press, 2012). 238–246.

47. Fred Barnes, "Danny Gets His Gun," *New Republic,* June 26, 1989, 10–11; Bob Woodward and David S. Broder, *The Man Who Would Be President: Dan Quayle* (New York: Simon and Schuster, 1992).

48. Bob Woodward, *The Agenda: Inside the Clinton White House* (New York: Simon and Schuster, 1994), 281.

49. Elizabeth Drew, *On the Edge: The Clinton Presidency* (New York: Simon and Schuster, 1994), 228.

50. Richard L. Berke, "The Gore Guide to the Future," *New York Times Magazine,* February 22, 1998, 47. For additional evidence of Gore's influence, see Joseph A. Pika, "The Vice Presidency: New Opportunities, Old Constraints," in *The Presidency and the Political System,* 5th ed., ed. Michael Nelson (Washington, D.C.: CQ Press, 1998), 547–559.

51. On the Cheney vice presidency, see Michael Nelson, "Richard Cheney and the Power of the Modern Vice Presidency," in *Ambition and Division: Legacies of the George W. Bush Presidency,* ed. Steven E. Schier (Pittsburgh: University of Pittsburgh Press, 2009), 172–189; and Barton Gellman, *Angler: The Cheney Vice Presidency* (New York: Penguin, 2008.

52. Eric Schmitt, "The Vice President: Out Front or Low Profile, Cheney Keeps Powerful Role," *New York Times,* October 7, 2001.

53. Susan Page, "Cheney Takes 'Backseat' in a Strong Way," *USA Today*, November 16, 2001.

54. Brinkley quoted in Barbara Slavin, "Cheney Rewrites Role in Foreign Policy," *USA Today*, July 29, 2002.

55. Cheney's influence in the Bush administration and especially his role in the war on Iraq are chronicled in Bob Woodward, *Bush at War* (New York: Simon and Schuster, 2002); Woodward, *Plan of Attack* (New York: Simon and Schuster, 2004); and Woodward, *State of Denial*.

56. Baumgartner, *American Vice Presidency Reconsidered*, 116.

57. "Transcript: The Vice Presidential Debate," *New York Times*, October 2, 2008.

58. Witcover, *Joe Biden*, 477. Biden's role in the Afghanistan review is discussed in Bob Woodward, *Obama's War* (New York: Simon and Schuster, 2010).

59. Joel K. Goldstein, "The New Constitutional Vice Presidency," *Wake Forest Law Review* 30 (Fall 1995): 526.

60. Reportedly, some White House aides regarded Reagan as mentally incapable in 1987. See Jane Mayer and Doyle McManus, *Landslide: The Unmaking of a President, 1984–1988* (Boston: Houghton Mifflin, 1988), vii–xi.

61. Lawrence I. Barrett, *Gambling with History: Ronald Reagan in the White House* (Garden City, N.Y.: Doubleday, 1983), chap. 7. See also Del Question Wilber, *Rawhile Down: The Near Assassination of Ronald Reagan* (New York: Henry Holt, 2011), esp. chaps. 12–13.

62. The White House, Office of the Press Secretary, "Remarks by the President upon Departure for Camp David," June 28, 2002.

63. As Vice President Ford remarked in 1974, "I am now surrounded by a clutch of Secret Service agents, reporters and cameramen, and assorted well-wishers. When I travel I am greeted by bands playing 'Hail Columbia' and introduced to audiences with great solemnity instead of just as 'my good friend, Jerry Ford.' " Quoted in Light, *Vice-Presidential Power*, 10.

64. Quoted in Cronin, "Rethinking the Vice Presidency," 338.

65. The following discussion is drawn from Nelson, "The Election," 55–92; and Michael Nelson, "The Curse of the Vice Presidency," *American Prospect*, July 31, 2000, 20–24.

66. Bill Turque, *Inventing Al Gore* (Boston: Houghton Mifflin, 2000), 356.

67. Ibid., 361.

68. "Transcript of Debate between Vice President Gore and Governor Bush," *New York Times*, October 4, 2000.

69. Michael Nelson, "Evaluating the Presidency," in *The Presidency and the Political System*, 7th ed., ed. Michael Nelson (Washington, D.C.: CQ Press, 2002).

70. Nelson, "The Election."

71. Jules Witcover, *Crapshoot: Rolling the Dice for the Vice Presidency* (New York: Crown, 1992), 138.

72. Nelson, "Constitutional Aspects of the Elections," 190.

73. David E. Sanger, "After 'Next Best Thing,' Clinton Carefully Praises Gore," *New York Times*, November 4, 2000.

74. David S. Broder, "Gore's Clinton Problem," *Washington Post National Weekly Edition*, October 30, 2000, 4.

75. Dwight D. Eisenhower, *Waging Peace* (Garden City, N.Y.: Doubleday, 1965), 596.

76. Paul Light calls this the "abused child syndrome." Light, *Vice-Presidential Power*, 108.

Appendix

Constitution of the United States   517

U.S. Presidents and Vice Presidents   536

Summary of Presidential Elections, 1789–2004   539

Constitution of the United States

We the People of the United States, in Order to form a more perfect Union, establish Justice, insure domestic Tranquility, provide for the common defence, promote the general Welfare, and secure the Blessings of Liberty to ourselves and our Posterity, do ordain and establish this Constitution for the United States of America.

ARTICLE I

Section 1. All legislative Powers herein granted shall be vested in a Congress of the United States, which shall consist of a Senate and House of Representatives.

Section 2. The House of Representatives shall be composed of Members chosen every second Year by the People of the several States, and the Electors in each State shall have the Qualifications requisite for Electors of the most numerous Branch of the State Legislature.

No Person shall be a Representative who shall not have attained to the age of twenty five Years, and been seven Years a Citizen of the United States, and who shall not, when elected, be an Inhabitant of that State in which he shall be chosen.

[Representatives and direct Taxes shall be apportioned among the several States which may be included within this Union, according to their respective Numbers, which shall be determined by adding to the whole Number of free Persons, including those bound to Service for a Term of Years, and excluding Indians not taxed, three fifths of all other Persons.][1] The actual Enumeration shall be made within three Years after the first Meeting of the Congress of the United States, and within every subsequent Term of ten Years, in such Manner as they shall by Law direct. The Number of Representatives shall not exceed one for every thirty Thousand, but each State shall have at Least one Representative; and until such enumeration shall be made, the State of New Hampshire shall be entitled to chuse three, Massachusetts eight, Rhode-Island and Providence Plantations one, Connecticut five, New-York six, New Jersey four, Pennsylvania eight, Delaware one, Maryland six, Virginia ten, North Carolina five, South Carolina five, and Georgia three.

When vacancies happen in the Representation from any State, the Executive Authority thereof shall issue Writs of Election to fill such Vacancies.

The House of Representatives shall chuse their Speaker and other Officers; and shall have the sole Power of Impeachment.

Section 3. The Senate of the United States shall be composed of two Senators from each State, [chosen by the Legislature thereof,]² for six Years; and each Senator shall have one Vote.

Immediately after they shall be assembled in Consequence of the first Election, they shall be divided as equally as may be into three Classes. The Seats of the Senators of the first Class shall be vacated at the Expiration of the second Year, of the second Class at the Expiration of the fourth Year, and of the third Class at the Expiration of the sixth Year, so that one third may be chosen every second Year; [and if Vacancies happen by Resignation, or otherwise, during the Recess of the Legislature of any State, the Executive thereof may make temporary Appointments until the next Meeting of the Legislature, which shall then fill such Vacancies.]³

No Person shall be a Senator who shall not have attained to the Age of thirty Years, and been nine Years a Citizen of the United States, and who shall not, when elected, be an Inhabitant of that State for which he shall be chosen.

The Vice President of the United States shall be President of the Senate, but shall have no Vote, unless they be equally divided.

The Senate shall chuse their other Officers, and also a President pro tempore, in the Absence of the Vice President, or when he shall exercise the Office of President of the United States.

The Senate shall have the sole Power to try all Impeachments. When sitting for that Purpose, they shall be on Oath or Affirmation. When the President of the United States is tried, the Chief Justice shall preside: And no Person shall be convicted without the Concurrence of two thirds of the Members present.

Judgment in Cases of Impeachment shall not extend further than to removal from Office, and disqualification to hold and enjoy any Office of honor, Trust or Profit under the United States: but the Party convicted shall nevertheless be liable and subject to Indictment, Trial, Judgment and Punishment, according to Law.

Section 4. The Times, Places and Manner of holding Elections for Senators and Representatives, shall be prescribed in each State by the Legislature thereof; but the Congress may at any time by Law make or alter such Regulations, except as to the Places of chusing Senators.

The Congress shall assemble at least once in every Year, and such Meeting shall [be on the first Monday in December],⁴ unless they shall by Law appoint a different Day.

Section 5. Each House shall be the Judge of the Elections, Returns and Qualifications of its own Members, and a Majority of each shall constitute a Quorum to do Business; but a smaller Number may adjourn from day to day, and may be authorized to compel the Attendance of absent Members, in such Manner, and under such Penalties as each House may provide.

Each House may determine the Rules of its Proceedings, punish its Members for disorderly Behaviour, and, with the Concurrence of two thirds, expel a Member.

Each House shall keep a Journal of its Proceedings, and from time to time publish the same, excepting such Parts as may in their Judgment require Secrecy; and the Yeas and Nays of the Members of either House on any question shall, at the Desire of one fifth of those Present, be entered on the Journal.

Neither House, during the Session of Congress, shall, without the Consent of the other, adjourn for more than three days, nor to any other Place than that in which the two Houses shall be sitting.

Section 6. The Senators and Representatives shall receive a Compensation for their Services, to be ascertained by Law, and paid out of the Treasury of the United States. They shall in all Cases, except Treason, Felony and Breach of the Peace, be privileged from Arrest during their Attendance at the Session of their respective Houses, and in going to and returning from the same; and for any Speech or Debate in either House, they shall not be questioned in any other Place.

No Senator or Representative shall, during the Time for which he was elected, be appointed to any civil Office under the Authority of the United States, which shall have been created, or the Emoluments whereof shall have been encreased during such time; and no Person holding any Office under the United States, shall be a Member of either House during his Continuance in Office.

Section 7. All Bills for raising Revenue shall originate in the House of Representatives; but the Senate may propose or concur with Amendments as on other Bills.

Every Bill which shall have passed the House of Representatives and the Senate, shall, before it become a Law, be presented to the President of the United States; If he approve he shall sign it, but if not he shall return it, with his Objections to that House in which it shall have originated, who shall enter the Objections at large on their Journal, and proceed to reconsider it. If after such Reconsideration two thirds of that House shall agree to pass the Bill, it shall be sent, together with the Objections, to the other House, by which it shall likewise be reconsidered, and if approved by two thirds of that House, it shall become a Law. But in all such Cases the Votes of both Houses shall be determined by yeas and Nays, and the Names of the Persons voting for and against the Bill shall be entered on the Journal of each House respectively. If any Bill shall not be returned by the President within ten Days (Sundays excepted) after it shall have been presented to him, the Same shall be a Law, in like Manner as if he had signed it, unless the Congress by their Adjournment prevent its Return, in which Case it shall not be a Law.

Every Order, Resolution, or Vote to which the Concurrence of the Senate and House of Representatives may be necessary (except on a question of

Adjournment) shall be presented to the President of the United States; and before the Same shall take Effect, shall be approved by him, or being disapproved by him, shall be repassed by two thirds of the Senate and House of Representatives, according to the Rules and Limitations prescribed in the Case of a Bill.

Section 8. The Congress shall have Power To lay and collect Taxes, Duties, Imposts and Excises, to pay the Debts and provide for the common Defence and general Welfare of the United States; but all Duties, Imposts and Excises shall be uniform throughout the United States;

To borrow Money on the credit of the United States;

To regulate Commerce with foreign Nations, and among the several States, and with the Indian Tribes;

To establish an uniform Rule of Naturalization, and uniform Laws on the subject of Bankruptcies throughout the United States;

To coin Money, regulate the Value thereof, and of foreign Coin, and fix the Standard of Weights and Measures;

To provide for the Punishment of counterfeiting the Securities and current Coin of the United States;

To establish Post Offices and post Roads;

To promote the Progress of Science and useful Arts, by securing for limited Times to Authors and Inventors the exclusive Right to their respective Writings and Discoveries;

To constitute Tribunals inferior to the supreme Court;

To define and punish Piracies and Felonies committed on the high Seas, and Offences against the Law of Nations;

To declare War, grant Letters of Marque and Reprisal, and make Rules concerning Captures on Land and Water;

To raise and support Armies, but no Appropriation of Money to that Use shall be for a longer Term than two Years;

To provide and maintain a Navy;

To make Rules for the Government and Regulation of the land and naval Forces;

To provide for calling forth the Militia to execute the Laws of the Union, suppress Insurrections and repel Invasions;

To provide for organizing, arming, and disciplining, the Militia, and for governing such Part of them as may be employed in the Service of the United States, reserving to the States respectively, the Appointment of the Officers, and the Authority of training the Militia according to the discipline prescribed by Congress;

To exercise exclusive Legislation in all Cases whatsoever, over such District (not exceeding ten Miles square) as may, by Cession of particular States, and the Acceptance of Congress, become the Seat of the Government of the United

States, and to exercise like Authority over all Places purchased by the Consent of the Legislature of the State in which the Same shall be, for the Erection of Forts, Magazines, Arsenals, dock-Yards, and other needful Buildings;—And

To make all Laws which shall be necessary and proper for carrying into Execution the foregoing Powers, and all other Powers vested by this Constitution in the Government of the United States, or in any Department or Officer thereof.

Section 9. The Migration or Importation of such Persons as any of the States now existing shall think proper to admit, shall not be prohibited by the Congress prior to the Year one thousand eight hundred and eight, but a Tax or duty may be imposed on such Importation, not exceeding ten dollars for each Person.

The Privilege of the Writ of Habeas Corpus shall not be suspended, unless when in Cases of Rebellion or Invasion the public Safety may require it.

No Bill of Attainder or ex post facto Law shall be passed.

No Capitation, or other direct, Tax shall be laid, unless in Proportion to the Census or Enumeration herein before directed to be taken.[5]

No Tax or Duty shall be laid on Articles exported from any State.

No Preference shall be given by any Regulation of Commerce or Revenue to the Ports of one State over those of another; nor shall Vessels bound to, or from, one State, be obliged to enter, clear, or pay Duties in another.

No Money shall be drawn from the Treasury, but in Consequence of Appropriations made by Law; and a regular Statement and Account of the Receipts and Expenditures of all public Money shall be published from time to time.

No Title of Nobility shall be granted by the United States: And no Person holding any Office of Profit or Trust under them, shall, without the Consent of the Congress, accept of any present, Emolument, Office, or Title, of any kind whatever, from any King, Prince, or foreign State.

Section 10. No State shall enter into any Treaty, Alliance, or Confederation; grant Letters of Marque and Reprisal; coin Money; emit Bills of Credit; make any Thing but gold and silver Coin a Tender in Payment of Debts; pass any Bill of Attainder, ex post facto Law, or Law impairing the Obligation of Contracts, or grant any Title of Nobility.

No State shall, without the Consent of the Congress, lay any Imposts or Duties on Imports or Exports, except what may be absolutely necessary for executing its inspection Laws: and the net Produce of all Duties and Imposts, laid by any State on Imports or Exports, shall be for the Use of the Treasury of the United States; and all such Laws shall be subject to the Revision and Controul of the Congress.

No State shall, without the Consent of Congress, lay any Duty of Tonnage, keep Troops, or Ships of War in time of Peace, enter into any Agreement or Compact with another State, or with a foreign Power, or engage in War, unless actually invaded, or in such imminent Danger as will not admit of delay.

ARTICLE II

Section 1. The executive Power shall be vested in a President of the United States of America. He shall hold his Office during the Term of four Years, and, together with the Vice President, chosen for the same Term, be elected, as follows:

Each State shall appoint, in such Manner as the Legislature thereof may direct, a Number of Electors, equal to the whole Number of Senators and Representatives to which the State may be entitled in the Congress: but no Senator or Representative, or Person holding an Office of Trust or Profit under the United States, shall be appointed an Elector.

[The Electors shall meet in their respective States, and vote by Ballot for two Persons, of whom one at least shall not be an Inhabitant of the same State with themselves. And they shall make a List of all the Persons voted for, and of the Number of Votes for each; which List they shall sign and certify, and transmit sealed to the Seat of the Government of the United States, directed to the President of the Senate. The President of the Senate shall, in the Presence of the Senate and House of Representatives, open all the Certificates, and the Votes shall then be counted. The Person having the greatest Number of Votes shall be the President, if such Number be a Majority of the whole Number of Electors appointed; and if there be more than one who have such Majority, and have an equal Number of Votes, then the House of Representatives shall immediately chuse by Ballot one of them for President; and if no Person have a Majority, then from the five highest on the list the said House shall in like Manner chuse the President. But in chusing the President, the Votes shall be taken by States, the Representation from each State having one Vote; A quorum for this Purpose shall consist of a Member or Members from two thirds of the States, and a Majority of all the States shall be necessary to a Choice. In every Case, after the Choice of the President, the Person having the greatest Number of Votes of the Electors shall be the Vice President. But if there should remain two or more who have equal Votes, the Senate shall chuse from them by Ballot the Vice President.][6]

The Congress may determine the Time of chusing the Electors, and the Day on which they shall give their Votes; which Day shall be the same throughout the United States.

No Person except a natural born Citizen, or a Citizen of the United States, at the time of the Adoption of this Constitution, shall be eligible to the Office of President; neither shall any Person be eligible to that Office who shall not have attained to the Age of thirty five Years, and been fourteen Years a Resident within the United States.

In Case of the Removal of the President from Office, or of his Death, Resignation, or Inability to discharge the Powers and Duties of the said Office,[7] the Same shall devolve on the Vice President, and the Congress may by Law provide for the Case of Removal, Death, Resignation or Inability, both of the President and Vice President, declaring what Officer shall then act as President, and such Officer shall act accordingly, until the Disability be removed, or a President shall be elected.

The President shall, at stated Times, receive for his Services, a Compensation, which shall neither be encreased nor diminished during the Period for which he shall have been elected, and he shall not receive within that Period any other Emolument from the United States, or any of them.

Before he enter on the Execution of his Office, he shall take the following Oath or Affirmation:—"I do solemnly swear (or affirm) that I will faithfully execute the Office of President of the United States, and will to the best of my Ability, preserve, protect and defend the Constitution of the United States."

Section 2. The President shall be Commander in Chief of the Army and Navy of the United States, and of the Militia of the several States, when called into the actual Service of the United States; he may require the Opinion, in writing, of the principal Officer in each of the executive Departments, upon any Subject relating to the Duties of their respective Offices, and he shall have Power to grant Reprieves and Pardons for Offences against the United States, except in Cases of Impeachment.

He shall have Power, by and with the Advice and Consent of the Senate, to make Treaties, provided two thirds of the Senators present concur; and he shall nominate, and by and with the Advice and Consent of the Senate, shall appoint Ambassadors, other public Ministers and Consuls, Judges of the supreme Court, and all other Officers of the United States, whose Appointments are not herein otherwise provided for, and which shall be established by Law: but the Congress may by Law vest the Appointment of such inferior Officers, as they think proper, in the President alone, in the Courts of Law, or in the Heads of Departments.

The President shall have Power to fill up all Vacancies that may happen during the Recess of the Senate, by granting Commissions which shall expire at the End of their next Session.

Section 3. He shall from time to time give to the Congress Information of the State of the Union, and recommend to their Consideration such Measures as he shall judge necessary and expedient; he may, on extraordinary Occasions, convene both Houses, or either of them, and in Case of Disagreement between them, with Respect to the Time of Adjournment, he may adjourn them to such Time as he shall think proper; he shall receive Ambassadors and other public Ministers; he shall take Care that the Laws be faithfully executed, and shall Commission all the Officers of the United States.

Section 4. The President, Vice President and all civil Officers of the United States, shall be removed from Office on Impeachment for, and Conviction of, Treason, Bribery, or other high Crimes and Misdemeanors.

ARTICLE III

Section 1. The judicial Power of the United States, shall be vested in one supreme Court, and in such inferior Courts as the Congress may from time to time ordain and establish. The Judges, both of the supreme and inferior Courts, shall hold their Offices during good Behaviour, and shall, at stated Times, receive for their Services, a Compensation, which shall not be diminished during their Continuance in Office.

Section 2. The judicial Power shall extend to all Cases, in Law and Equity, arising under this Constitution, the Laws of the United States, and Treaties made, or which shall be made, under their Authority;—to all Cases affecting Ambassadors, other public Ministers and Consuls;—to all Cases of admiralty and maritime Jurisdiction;—to Controversies to which the United States shall be a Party;—to Controversies between two or more States;—between a State and Citizens of another State;—between Citizens of different States;—between Citizens of the same State claiming Lands under Grants of different States, and between a State, or the Citizens thereof, and foreign States, Citizens or Subjects.[8]

In all Cases affecting Ambassadors, other public Ministers and Consuls, and those in which a State shall be Party, the supreme Court shall have original Jurisdiction. In all the other Cases before mentioned, the supreme Court shall have appellate Jurisdiction, both as to Law and Fact, with such Exceptions, and under such Regulations as the Congress shall make.

The Trial of all Crimes, except in Cases of Impeachment, shall be by Jury; and such Trial shall be held in the State where the said Crimes shall have been committed; but when not committed within any State, the Trial shall be at such Place or Places as the Congress may by Law have directed.

Section 3. Treason against the United States, shall consist only in levying War against them, or in adhering to their Enemies, giving them Aid and Comfort. No Person shall be convicted of Treason unless on the Testimony of two Witnesses to the same overt Act, or on Confession in open Court.

The Congress shall have Power to declare the Punishment of Treason, but no Attainder of Treason shall work Corruption of Blood, or Forfeiture except during the Life of the Person attainted.

ARTICLE IV

Section 1. Full Faith and Credit shall be given in each State to the public Acts, Records, and judicial Proceedings of every other State. And the Congress may by general Laws prescribe the Manner in which such Acts, Records and Proceedings shall be proved, and the Effect thereof.

Section 2. The Citizens of each State shall be entitled to all Privileges and Immunities of Citizens in the several States.

A Person charged in any State with Treason, Felony, or other Crime, who shall flee from Justice, and be found in another State, shall on Demand of the executive Authority of the State from which he fled, be delivered up, to be removed to the State having Jurisdiction of the Crime.

[No Person held to Service or Labour in one State, under the Laws thereof, escaping into another, shall, in Consequence of any Law or Regulation therein, be discharged from such Service or Labour, but shall be delivered up on Claim of the Party to whom such Service or Labour may be due.]9

Section 3. New States may be admitted by the Congress into this Union; but no new State shall be formed or erected within the Jurisdiction of any other State; nor any State be formed by the Junction of two or more States, or Parts of States, without the Consent of the Legislatures of the States concerned as well as of the Congress.

The Congress shall have Power to dispose of and make all needful Rules and Regulations respecting the Territory or other Property belonging to the United States; and nothing in this Constitution shall be so construed as to Prejudice any Claims of the United States, or of any particular State.

Section 4. The United States shall guarantee to every State in this Union a Republican Form of Government, and shall protect each of them against Invasion; and on Application of the Legislature, or of the Executive (when the Legislature cannot be convened) against domestic Violence.

ARTICLE V

The Congress, whenever two thirds of both Houses shall deem it necessary, shall propose Amendments to this Constitution, or, on the Application of the Legislatures of two thirds of the several States, shall call a Convention for proposing Amendments, which, in either Case, shall be valid to all Intents and Purposes, as Part of this Constitution, when ratified by the Legislatures of three fourths of the several States, or by Conventions in three fourths thereof, as the one or the other Mode of Ratification may be proposed by the Congress; Provided [that no Amendment which may be made prior to the Year One thousand eight hundred and eight shall in any Manner affect the first and fourth Clauses in the Ninth Section of the first Article; and]10 that no State, without its Consent, shall be deprived of its equal Suffrage in the Senate.

ARTICLE VI

All Debts contracted and Engagements entered into, before the Adoption of this Constitution, shall be as valid against the United States under this Constitution, as under the Confederation.

This Constitution, and the Laws of the United States which shall be made in Pursuance thereof; and all Treaties made, or which shall be made, under the Authority of the United States, shall be the supreme Law of the Land; and the Judges in every State shall be bound thereby, any Thing in the Constitution or Laws of any State to the Contrary notwithstanding.

The Senators and Representatives before mentioned, and the Members of the several State Legislatures, and all executive and judicial Officers, both of the United States and of the several States, shall be bound by Oath or Affirmation, to support this Constitution; but no religious Test shall ever be required as a Qualification to any Office or public Trust under the United States.

ARTICLE VII

The Ratification of the Conventions of nine States, shall be sufficient for the Establishment of this Constitution between the States so ratifying the Same.

Done in Convention by the Unanimous Consent of the States present the Seventeenth Day of September in the Year of our Lord one thousand seven hundred and Eighty seven and of the Independence of the United States of America the Twelfth. IN WITNESS whereof We have hereunto subscribed our Names,

George Washington,
President and
deputy from Virginia.

New Hampshire:	John Langdon,
	Nicholas Gilman.
Massachusetts:	Nathaniel Gorham,
	Rufus King.
Connecticut:	William Samuel Johnson,
	Roger Sherman.
New York:	Alexander Hamilton.
New Jersey:	William Livingston,
	David Brearley,
	William Paterson,
	Jonathan Dayton.
Pennsylvania:	Benjamin Franklin,
	Thomas Mifflin,
	Robert Morris,
	George Clymer,
	Thomas FitzSimons,
	Jared Ingersoll,

	James Wilson, Gouverneur Morris.
Delaware:	George Read, Gunning Bedford Jr., John Dickinson, Richard Bassett, Jacob Broom.
Maryland:	James McHenry, Daniel of St. Thomas Jenifer, Daniel Carroll.
Virginia:	John Blair, James Madison Jr.
North Carolina:	William Blount, Richard Dobbs Spaight, Hugh Williamson.
South Carolina:	John Rutledge, Charles Cotesworth Pinckney, Charles Pinckney, Pierce Butler.
Georgia:	William Few, Abraham Baldwin.

[The language of the original Constitution, not including the Amendments, was adopted by a convention of the states on September 17, 1787, and was subsequently ratified by the states on the following dates: Delaware, December 7, 1787; Pennsylvania, December 12, 1787; New Jersey, December 18, 1787; Georgia, January 2, 1788; Connecticut, January 9, 1788; Massachusetts, February 6, 1788; Maryland, April 28, 1788; South Carolina, May 23, 1788; New Hampshire, June 21, 1788.

Ratification was completed on June 21, 1788.

The Constitution subsequently was ratified by Virginia, June 25, 1788; New York, July 26, 1788; North Carolina, November 21, 1789; Rhode Island, May 29, 1790; and Vermont, January 10, 1791.]

AMENDMENTS

AMENDMENT I

(The first ten amendments were ratified December 15, 1791.)

Congress shall make no law respecting an establishment of religion, or prohibiting the free exercise thereof; or abridging the freedom of speech, or of the press; or the right of the people peaceably to assemble, and to petition the Government for a redress of grievances.

AMENDMENT II

A well regulated Militia, being necessary to the security of a free State, the right of the people to keep and bear Arms, shall not be infringed.

AMENDMENT III

No Soldier shall, in time of peace be quartered in any house, without the consent of the Owner, nor in time of war, but in a manner to be prescribed by law.

AMENDMENT IV

The right of the people to be secure in their persons, houses, papers, and effects, against unreasonable searches and seizures, shall not be violated, and no Warrants shall issue, but upon probable cause, supported by Oath or affirmation, and particularly describing the place to be searched, and the persons or things to be seized.

AMENDMENT V

No person shall be held to answer for a capital, or otherwise infamous crime, unless on a presentment or indictment of a Grand Jury, except in cases arising in the land or naval forces, or in the Militia, when in actual service in time of War or public danger; nor shall any person be subject for the same offence to be twice put in jeopardy of life or limb; nor shall be compelled in any criminal case to be a witness against himself, nor be deprived of life, liberty, or property, without due process of law; nor shall private property be taken for public use, without just compensation.

AMENDMENT VI

In all criminal prosecutions, the accused shall enjoy the right to a speedy and public trial, by an impartial jury of the State and district wherein the crime shall have been committed, which district shall have been previously ascertained by law, and to be informed of the nature and cause of the accusation; to be confronted with the witnesses against him; to have compulsory process for obtaining witnesses in his favor, and to have the Assistance of Counsel for his defence.

AMENDMENT VII

In Suits at common law, where the value in controversy shall exceed twenty dollars, the right of trial by jury shall be preserved, and no fact tried by a jury, shall be otherwise re-examined in any Court of the United States, than according to the rules of the common law.

AMENDMENT VIII

Excessive bail shall not be required, nor excessive fines imposed, nor cruel and unusual punishments inflicted.

AMENDMENT IX

The enumeration in the Constitution, of certain rights, shall not be construed to deny or disparage others retained by the people.

AMENDMENT X

The powers not delegated to the United States by the Constitution, nor prohibited by it to the States, are reserved to the States respectively, or to the people.

AMENDMENT XI (RATIFIED FEBRUARY 7, 1795)

The Judicial power of the United States shall not be construed to extend to any suit in law or equity, commenced or prosecuted against one of the United States by Citizens of another State, or by Citizens or Subjects of any Foreign State.

AMENDMENT XII (RATIFIED JUNE 15, 1804)

The Electors shall meet in their respective states and vote by ballot for President and Vice-President, one of whom, at least, shall not be an inhabitant of the same state with themselves; they shall name in their ballots the person voted for as President, and in distinct ballots the person voted for as Vice-President, and they shall make distinct lists of all persons voted for as President, and of all persons voted for as Vice-President, and of the number of votes for each, which lists they shall sign and certify, and transmit sealed to the seat of the government of the United States, directed to the President of the Senate;—The President of the Senate shall, in the presence of the Senate and House of Representatives, open all the certificates and the votes shall then be counted;—The person having the greatest number of votes for President, shall be the President, if such number be a majority of the whole number of Electors appointed; and if no person have such majority, then from the persons having the highest numbers not exceeding three on the list of those voted for as President, the House of Representatives shall choose immediately, by ballot, the President. But in choosing the President, the votes shall be taken by states, the representation from each state having one vote; a quorum for this purpose shall consist of a member or members from two-thirds of the states, and a majority of all the states shall be necessary to a choice. [And if the House of Representatives shall not choose a President whenever the right of choice shall devolve upon them, before the fourth day of March next following, then the Vice-President shall act as President, as in the case of the death or other constitutional disability of the President.—][11] The person having the greatest number of votes as Vice-President, shall be the Vice-President, if such number be a majority of the whole number of Electors appointed, and if no person have a majority, then from the two highest numbers on the list, the Senate shall choose the Vice-President; a quorum for the purpose shall consist of two-thirds of the whole number of Senators, and a majority of the whole number shall be necessary to a choice. But no person constitutionally ineligible to the office of President shall be eligible to that of Vice-President of the United States.

AMENDMENT XIII (RATIFIED DECEMBER 6, 1865)

Section 1. Neither slavery nor involuntary servitude, except as a punishment for crime whereof the party shall have been duly convicted, shall exist within the United States, or any place subject to their jurisdiction.

Section 2. Congress shall have power to enforce this article by appropriate legislation.

AMENDMENT XIV (RATIFIED JULY 9, 1868)

Section 1. All persons born or naturalized in the United States, and subject to the jurisdiction thereof, are citizens of the United States and of the State wherein they reside. No State shall make or enforce any law which shall abridge the privileges or immunities of citizens of the United States; nor shall any State deprive any person of life, liberty, or property, without due process of law; nor deny to any person within its jurisdiction the equal protection of the laws.

Section 2. Representatives shall be apportioned among the several States according to their respective numbers, counting the whole number of persons in each State, excluding Indians not taxed. But when the right to vote at any election for the choice of electors for President and Vice President of the United States, Representatives in Congress, the Executive and Judicial officers of a State, or the members of the Legislature thereof, is denied to any of the male inhabitants of such State, being twenty-one years of age,[12] and citizens of the United States, or in any way abridged, except for participation in rebellion, or other crime, the basis of representation therein shall be reduced in the proportion which the number of such male citizens shall bear to the whole number of male citizens twenty-one years of age in such State.

Section 3. No person shall be a Senator or Representative in Congress, or elector of President and Vice President, or hold any office, civil or military, under the United States, or under any State, who, having previously taken an oath, as a member of Congress, or as an officer of the United States, or as a member of any State legislature, or as an executive or judicial officer of any State, to support the Constitution of the United States, shall have engaged in insurrection or rebellion against the same, or given aid or comfort to the enemies thereof. But Congress may by a vote of two-thirds of each House, remove such disability.

Section 4. The validity of the public debt of the United States, authorized by law, including debts incurred for payment of pensions and bounties for services in suppressing insurrection or rebellion, shall not be questioned. But neither the United States nor any State shall assume or pay any debt or obligation incurred in aid of insurrection or rebellion against the United States, or any claim for the loss or emancipation of any slave; but all such debts, obligations and claims shall be held illegal and void.

Section 5. The Congress shall have power to enforce, by appropriate legislation, the provisions of this article.

AMENDMENT XV (RATIFIED FEBRUARY 3, 1870)

Section 1. The right of citizens of the United States to vote shall not be denied or abridged by the United States or by any State on account of race, color, or previous condition of servitude.

Section 2. The Congress shall have power to enforce this article by appropriate legislation.

AMENDMENT XVI (RATIFIED FEBRUARY 3, 1913)

The Congress shall have power to lay and collect taxes on incomes, from whatever source derived, without apportionment among the several States, and without regard to any census or enumeration.

AMENDMENT XVII (RATIFIED APRIL 8, 1913)

The Senate of the United States shall be composed of two Senators from each State, elected by the people thereof, for six years; and each Senator shall have one vote. The electors in each State shall have the qualifications requisite for electors of the most numerous branch of the State legislatures.

When vacancies happen in the representation of any State in the Senate, the executive authority of such State shall issue writs of election to fill such vacancies: *Provided,* That the legislature of any State may empower the executive thereof to make temporary appointments until the people fill the vacancies by election as the legislature may direct.

This amendment shall not be so construed as to affect the election or term of any Senator chosen before it becomes valid as part of the Constitution.

AMENDMENT XVIII (RATIFIED JANUARY 16, 1919)

Section 1. After one year from the ratification of this article the manufacture, sale, or transportation of intoxicating liquors within, the importation thereof into, or the exportation thereof from the United States and all territory subject to the jurisdiction thereof for beverage purposes is hereby prohibited.

Section 2. The Congress and the several States shall have concurrent power to enforce this article by appropriate legislation.

Section 3. This article shall be inoperative unless it shall have been ratified as an amendment to the Constitution by the legislatures of the several States, as provided in the Constitution, within seven years from the date of the submission hereof to the States by the Congress.[13]

AMENDMENT XIX (RATIFIED AUGUST 18, 1920)

The right of citizens of the United States to vote shall not be denied or abridged by the United States or by any State on account of sex.

Congress shall have power to enforce this article by appropriate legislation.

AMENDMENT XX (RATIFIED JANUARY 23, 1933)

Section 1. The terms of the President and Vice President shall end at noon on the 20th day of January, and the terms of Senators and Representatives at noon on the 3d day of January, of the years in which such terms would have ended if this article had not been ratified; and the terms of their successors shall then begin.

Section 2. The Congress shall assemble at least once in every year, and such meeting shall begin at noon on the 3d day of January, unless they shall by law appoint a different day.

Section 3.[14] If, at the time fixed for the beginning of the term of the President, the President elect shall have died, the Vice President elect shall become President. If a President shall not have been chosen before the time fixed for the beginning of his term, or if the President elect shall have failed to qualify, then the Vice President elect shall act as President until a President shall have qualified; and the Congress may by law provide for the case wherein neither a President elect nor a Vice President elect shall have qualified, declaring who shall then act as President, or the manner in which one who is to act shall be selected, and such person shall act accordingly until a President or Vice President shall have qualified.

Section 4. The Congress may by law provide for the case of the death of any of the persons from whom the House of Representatives may choose a President whenever the right of choice shall have devolved upon them, and for the case of the death of any of the persons from whom the Senate may choose a Vice President whenever the right of choice shall have devolved upon them.

Section 5. Sections 1 and 2 shall take effect on the 15th day of October following the ratification of this article.

Section 6. This article shall be inoperative unless it shall have been ratified as an amendment to the Constitution by the legislatures of three-fourths of the several States within seven years from the date of its submission.

AMENDMENT XXI (RATIFIED DECEMBER 5, 1933)

Section 1. The eighteenth article of amendment to the Constitution of the United States is hereby repealed.

Section 2. The transportation or importation into any State, Territory, or possession of the United States for delivery or use therein of intoxicating liquors, in violation of the laws thereof, is hereby prohibited.

Section 3. This article shall be inoperative unless it shall have been ratified as an amendment to the Constitution by conventions in the several States, as provided in the Constitution, within seven years from the date of the submission hereof to the States by the Congress.

AMENDMENT XXII (RATIFIED FEBRUARY 27, 1951)

Section 1. No person shall be elected to the office of the President more than twice, and no person who has held the office of President, or acted as President, for more than two years of a term to which some other person was elected President shall be elected to the office of the President more than once. But this Article shall not apply to any person holding the office of President when this Article was proposed by the Congress, and shall not prevent any person who may be holding the office of President, or acting as President, during the term within which this Article becomes operative from holding the office of President or acting as President during the remainder of such term.

Section 2. This article shall be inoperative unless it shall have been ratified as an amendment to the Constitution by the legislatures of three-fourths of the several States within seven years from the date of its submission to the States by the Congress.

AMENDMENT XXIII (RATIFIED MARCH 29, 1961)

Section 1. The District constituting the seat of Government of the United States shall appoint in such manner as the Congress may direct:

A number of electors of President and Vice President equal to the whole number of Senators and Representatives in Congress to which the District would be entitled if it were a State, but in no event more than the least populous State; they shall be in addition to those appointed by the States, but they shall be considered, for the purposes of the election of President and Vice President, to be electors appointed by a State; and they shall meet in the District and perform such duties as provided by the twelfth article of amendment.

Section 2. The Congress shall have power to enforce this article by appropriate legislation.

AMENDMENT XXIV (RATIFIED JANUARY 23, 1964)

Section 1. The right of citizens of the United States to vote in any primary or other election for President or Vice President, for electors for President or Vice President, or for Senator or Representative in Congress, shall not be denied or abridged by the United States or any State by reason of failure to pay any poll tax or other tax.

Section 2. The Congress shall have power to enforce this article by appropriate legislation.

AMENDMENT XXV (RATIFIED FEBRUARY 10, 1967)

Section 1. In case of the removal of the President from office or of his death or resignation, the Vice President shall become President.

Section 2. Whenever there is a vacancy in the office of the Vice President, the President shall nominate a Vice President who shall take office upon confirmation by a majority vote of both Houses of Congress.

Section 3. Whenever the President transmits to the President pro tempore of the Senate and the Speaker of the House of Representatives his written declaration that he is unable to discharge the powers and duties of his office, and until he transmits to them a written declaration to the contrary, such powers and duties shall be discharged by the Vice President as Acting President.

Section 4. Whenever the Vice President and a majority of either the principal officers of the executive departments or of such other body as Congress may by law provide, transmit to the President pro tempore of the Senate and the Speaker of the House of Representatives their written declaration that the President is unable to discharge the powers and duties of his office, the Vice President shall immediately assume the powers and duties of the office as Acting President.

Thereafter, when the President transmits to the President pro tempore of the Senate and the Speaker of the House of Representatives his written declaration that no inability exists, he shall resume the powers and duties of his office unless the Vice President and a majority of either the principal officers of the executive department or of such other body as Congress may by law provide, transmit within four days to the President pro tempore of the Senate and the Speaker of the House of Representatives their written declaration that the President is unable to discharge the powers and duties of his office. Thereupon Congress shall decide the issue, assembling within forty-eight hours for that purpose if not in session. If the Congress, within twenty-one days after receipt of the latter written declaration, or, if Congress is not in session, within twenty-one days after Congress is required to assemble, determines by two-thirds vote of both Houses that the President is unable to discharge the powers and duties of his office, the Vice President shall continue to discharge the same as Acting President; otherwise, the President shall resume the powers and duties of his office.

AMENDMENT XXVI (RATIFIED JULY 1, 1971)

Section 1. The right of citizens of the United States, who are eighteen years of age or older, to vote shall not be denied or abridged by the United States or by any State on account of age.

Section 2. The Congress shall have power to enforce this article by appropriate legislation.

AMENDMENT XXVII (RATIFIED MAY 7, 1992)

No law varying the compensation for the services of the Senators and Representatives shall take effect, until an election of Representatives shall have intervened.

NOTES

Source: The Constitution of the United States of America, as Amended, House Document No. 106–214 (Washington, D.C.: Government Printing Office, 2000).

1. The part in brackets was changed by section 2 of the Fourteenth Amendment.

2. The part in brackets was changed by the first paragraph of the Seventeenth Amendment.

3. The part in brackets was changed by the second paragraph of the Seventeenth Amendment.

4. The part in brackets was changed by section 2 of the Twentieth Amendment.

5. The Sixteenth Amendment gave Congress the power to tax incomes.

6. The material in brackets has been superseded by the Twelfth Amendment.

7. This provision has been affected by the Twenty-fifth Amendment.

8. These clauses were affected by the Eleventh Amendment.

9. This paragraph has been superseded by the Thirteenth Amendment.

10. Obsolete.

11. The part in brackets has been superseded by section 3 of the Twentieth Amendment.

12. See the Nineteenth and Twenty-sixth Amendments.

13. This amendment was repealed by section 1 of the Twenty-first Amendment.

14. See the Twenty-fifth Amendment.

U.S. PRESIDENTS AND VICE PRESIDENTS

President and political party	Born	Died	President's term of service	Vice president	Vice president's term of service
George Washington (F)	1732	1799	April 30, 1789–March 4, 1793	John Adams	April 30, 1789–March 4, 1793
George Washington (F)			March 4, 1793–March 4, 1797	John Adams	March 4, 1793–March 4, 1797
John Adams (F)	1735	1826	March 4, 1797–March 4, 1801	Thomas Jefferson	March 4, 1797–March 4, 1801
Thomas Jefferson (DR)	1743	1826	March 4, 1801–March 4, 1805	Aaron Burr	March 4, 1801–March 4, 1805
Thomas Jefferson (DR)			March 4, 1805–March 4, 1809	George Clinton	March 4, 1805–March 4, 1809
James Madison (DR)	1751	1836	March 4, 1809–March 4, 1813	George Clinton[a]	March 4, 1809–April 12, 1812
James Madison (DR)			March 4, 1813–March 4, 1817	Elbridge Gerry[a]	March 4, 1813–Nov. 23, 1814
James Monroe (DR)	1758	1831	March 4, 1817–March 4, 1821	Daniel D. Tompkins	March 4, 1817–March 4, 1821
James Monroe (DR)			March 4, 1821–March 4, 1825	Daniel D. Tompkins	March 4, 1821–March 4, 1825
John Q. Adams (DR)	1767	1848	March 4, 1825–March 4, 1829	John C. Calhoun	March 4, 1825–March 4, 1829
Andrew Jackson (D)	1767	1845	March 4, 1829–March 4, 1833	John C. Calhoun[b]	March 4, 1829–Dec. 28, 1832
Andrew Jackson (D)			March 4, 1833–March 4, 1837	Martin Van Buren	March 4, 1833–March 4, 1837
Martin Van Buren (D)	1782	1862	March 4, 1837–March 4, 1841	Richard M. Johnson	March 4, 1837–March 4, 1841
William H. Harrison[a] (W)	1773	1841	March 4, 1841–April 4, 1841	John Tyler[c]	March 4, 1841–April 6, 1841
John Tyler[c] (W)	1790	1862	April 6, 1841–March 4, 1845		
James K. Polk (D)	1795	1849	March 4, 1845–March 4, 1849	George M. Dallas	March 4, 1845–March 4, 1849
Zachary Taylor[a] (W)	1784	1850	March 4, 1849–July 9, 1850	Millard Fillmore[c]	March 4, 1849–July 10, 1850
Millard Fillmore[c] (W)	1800	1874	July 10, 1850–March 4, 1853		
Franklin Pierce (D)	1804	1869	March 4, 1853–March 4, 1857	William R. King[a]	March 24, 1853–April 18, 1853
James Buchanan (D)	1791	1868	March 4, 1857–March 4, 1861	John C. Breckinridge	March 4, 1857–March 4, 1861
Abraham Lincoln (R)	1809	1865	March 4, 1861–March 4, 1865	Hannibal Hamlin	March 4, 1861–March 4, 1865
Abraham Lincoln[a] (R)			March 4, 1865–April 15, 1865	Andrew Johnson[c]	March 4, 1865–April 15, 1865
Andrew Johnson[c] (R)	1808	1875	April 15, 1865–March 4, 1869		
Ulysses S. Grant (R)	1822	1885	March 4, 1869–March 4, 1873	Schuyler Colfax	March 4, 1869–March 4, 1873
Ulysses S. Grant (R)			March 4, 1873–March 4, 1877	Henry Wilson[a]	March 4, 1873–Nov. 22, 1875
Rutherford B. Hayes (R)	1822	1893	March 4, 1877–March 4, 1881	William A. Wheeler	March 4, 1877–March 4, 1881
James A. Garfield[a] (R)	1831	1881	March 4, 1881–Sept. 19, 1881	Chester A. Arthur[c]	March 4, 1881–Sept. 20, 1881

President	Born	Died	Term of Service	Vice President	Term of Service
Chester A. Arthur[c] (R)	1830	1886	Sept. 20, 1881–March 4, 1885		
Grover Cleveland (D)	1837	1908	March 4, 1885–March 4, 1889	Thomas A. Hendricks[a]	March 4, 1885–Nov. 25, 1885
Benjamin Harrison (R)	1833	1901	March 4, 1889–March 4, 1893	Levi P. Morton	March 4, 1889–March 4, 1893
Grover Cleveland (D)	1837	1908	March 4, 1893–March 4, 1897	Adlai E. Stevenson	March 4, 1893–March 4, 1897
William McKinley (R)	1843	1901	March 4, 1897–March 4, 1901	Garret A. Hobart[a]	March 4, 1897–Nov. 21, 1899
William McKinley[a] (R)			March 4, 1901–Sept. 14, 1901	Theodore Roosevelt[c]	March 4, 1901–Sept. 14, 1901
Theodore Roosevelt[c] (R)	1858	1919	Sept. 14, 1901–March 4, 1905		
Theodore Roosevelt (R)			March 4, 1905–March 4, 1909	Charles W. Fairbanks	March 4, 1905–March 4, 1909
William H. Taft (R)	1857	1930	March 4, 1909–March 4, 1913	James S. Sherman[a]	March 4, 1909–Oct. 30, 1912
Woodrow Wilson (D)	1856	1924	March 4, 1913–March 4, 1917	Thomas R. Marshall	March 4, 1913–March 4, 1917
Woodrow Wilson (D)			March 4, 1917–March 4, 1921	Thomas R. Marshall	March 4, 1917–March 4, 1921
Warren G. Harding[a] (R)	1865	1923	March 4, 1921–Aug. 2, 1923	Calvin Coolidge[c]	March 4, 1921–Aug. 3, 1923
Calvin Coolidge[c] (R)	1872	1933	Aug. 3, 1923–March 4, 1925		
Calvin Coolidge (R)			March 4, 1925–March 4, 1929	Charles G. Dawes	March 4, 1925–March 4, 1929
Herbert Hoover (R)	1874	1964	March 4, 1929–March 4, 1933	Charles Curtis	March 4, 1929–March 4, 1933
Franklin D. Roosevelt (D)	1882	1945	March 4, 1933–Jan. 20, 1937	John N. Garner	March 4, 1933–Jan. 20, 1937
Franklin D. Roosevelt (D)			Jan. 20, 1937–Jan. 20, 1941	John N. Garner	Jan. 20, 1937–Jan. 20, 1941
Franklin D. Roosevelt (D)			Jan. 20, 1941–Jan. 20, 1945	Henry A. Wallace	Jan. 20, 1941–Jan. 20, 1945
Franklin D. Roosevelt[a] (D)			Jan. 20, 1945–April 12, 1945	Harry S. Truman[c]	Jan. 20, 1945–April 12, 1945
Harry S. Truman[c] (D)	1884	1972	April 12, 1945–Jan. 20, 1949		
Harry S. Truman (D)			Jan. 20, 1949–Jan. 20, 1953	Alben W. Barkley	Jan. 20, 1949–Jan. 20, 1953
Dwight D. Eisenhower (R)	1890	1969	Jan. 20, 1953–Jan. 20, 1957	Richard Nixon	Jan. 20, 1953–Jan. 20, 1957
Dwight D. Eisenhower (R)			Jan. 20, 1957–Jan. 20, 1961	Richard Nixon	Jan. 20, 1957–Jan. 20, 1961
John F. Kennedy[a] (D)	1917	1963	Jan. 20, 1961–Nov. 22, 1963	Lyndon B. Johnson[c]	Jan. 20, 1961–Nov. 22, 1963
Lyndon B. Johnson[c] (D)	1908	1973	Nov. 22, 1963–Jan. 20, 1965		
Lyndon B. Johnson (D)			Jan. 20, 1965–Jan. 20, 1969	Hubert H. Humphrey	Jan. 20, 1965–Jan. 20, 1969
Richard Nixon (R)	1913	1994	Jan. 20, 1969–Jan. 20, 1973	Spiro T. Agnew	Jan. 20, 1969–Jan. 20, 1973
Richard Nixon[b] (R)			Jan. 20, 1973–Aug. 9, 1974	Spiro T. Agnew[b]	Jan. 20, 1973–Oct. 10, 1973
				Gerald R. Ford[c]	Dec. 6, 1973–Aug. 9, 1974
Gerald R. Ford[c] (R)	1913	2006	Aug. 9, 1974–Jan. 20, 1977	Nelson A. Rockefeller	Dec. 19, 1974–Jan. 20, 1977
Jimmy Carter (D)	1924		Jan. 20, 1977–Jan. 20, 1981	Walter F. Mondale	Jan. 20, 1977–Jan. 20, 1981

continued

U.S. PRESIDENTS AND VICE PRESIDENTS *(continued)*

President and political party	Born	Died	Vice president	Vice president's term of service	President's term of service
Ronald Reagan (R)	1911	2004	George Bush	Jan. 20, 1981–Jan. 20, 1985	Jan. 20, 1981–Jan. 20, 1985
Ronald Reagan (R)			George Bush	Jan. 20, 1985–Jan. 20, 1989	Jan. 20, 1985–Jan. 20, 1989
George Bush (R)	1924		Dan Quayle	Jan. 20, 1989–Jan. 20, 1993	Jan. 20, 1989–Jan. 20, 1993
William J. Clinton (D)	1946		Albert Gore Jr.	Jan. 20, 1993–Jan. 20, 1997	Jan. 20, 1993–Jan. 20, 1997
William J. Clinton (D)			Albert Gore Jr.	Jan. 20, 1997–Jan. 20, 2001	Jan. 20, 1997–Jan. 20, 2001
George W. Bush (R)	1946		Richard B. Cheney	Jan. 20, 2001–Jan. 20, 2005	Jan. 20, 2001–Jan. 20, 2005
George W. Bush (R)			Richard B. Cheney	Jan. 20, 2001–	Jan. 20, 2005–
George W. Bush (R)			Richard B. Cheney	Jan. 20, 2005–Jan. 20, 2009	Jan. 20, 2005–Jan. 20, 2009
Barack Obama (D)			Joseph R. Biden, Jr.	Jan. 20, 2009–	Jan. 20, 2009–

Sources: "Table 6-1 Presidents and Vice Presidents of the United States." In *Vital Statistics on American Politics 2009–2010*, edited by Harold W. Stanley, and Richard G. Niemi, 233-35. Washington, DC: CQ Press, 2009. http://library.cqpress.com/vsap/vsap09_tab6-1.

Note: D—Democrat; DR—Democratic–Republican; F—Federalist; R—Republican; W—Whig.
a. Died in office.
b. Resigned.
c. Succeeded to the presidency.

Year	No. of states	Candidates	Party	Electoral vote	Popular vote
1789[a]	10	**George Washington**	**Fed.**	**69**	—[b]
		John Adams	Fed.	34	
1792[a]	15	**George Washington**	**Fed.**	**132**	—[b]
		John Adams	Fed.	77	
1796[a]	16	**John Adams**	**Fed.**	**71**	—[b]
		Thomas Jefferson	Dem.-Rep.	68	
1800[a]	16	**Thomas Jefferson**	**Dem.-Rep.**	**73**	—[b]
		Aaron Burr	Dem.-Rep.	73	
		John Adams	Fed.	65	
		Charles Cotesworth Pinckney	Fed.	64	
1804	17	**Thomas Jefferson**	**Dem.-Rep.**	**162**	—[b]
		George Clinton			
		Charles Cotesworth Pinckney	Fed.	64	
		Rufus King			
1808	17	**James Madison**	**Dem.-Rep.**	**122**	—[b]
		George Clinton			
		Charles Cotesworth Pinckney	Fed.	64	
		Rufus King			
1812	18	**James Madison**	**Dem.-Rep.**	**128**	—[b]
		Elbridge Gerry			
		George Clinton	Fed.	89	
		Jared Ingersoll			

continued

Year	No. of states	Candidates	Party	Electoral vote	Popular vote
1816	19	**James Monroe** ***Daniel D. Tompkins***	**Dem.-Rep.**	**183**	—[b]
		Rufus King *John Howard*	Fed.	34	
1820	24	**James Monroe** ***Daniel D. Tompkins***	**Dem.-Rep.**	**231**[c]	—[b]
1824[d]	24	**John Quincy Adams** ***John C. Calhoun***	**Dem.-Rep.**	**99**	**113,122 (30.9%)**
		Andrew Jackson *Nathan Sanford*	Dem.-Rep.	84	151,271 (41.3%)
1828	24	**Andrew Jackson** ***John C. Calhoun***	**Dem.-Rep.**	**178**	**642,553 (56.0%)**
		John Quincy Adams *Richard Rush*	Nat.-Rep.	83	500,897 (43.6%)
1832[e]	24	**Andrew Jackson** ***Martin Van Buren***	**Dem.**	**219**	**701,780 (54.2%)**
		Henry Clay *John Sergeant*	Nat.-Rep.	49	484,205 (37.4%)
1836[f]	26	**Martin Van Buren** ***Richard M. Johnson***	**Dem.**	**170**	**764,176 (50.8%)**
		William Henry Harrison *Francis Granger*	Whig	73	550,816 (36.6%)
1840	26	**William Henry Harrison** ***John Tyler***	**Whig**	**234**	**1,275,390 (52.9%)**
		Martin Van Buren *Richard M. Johnson*	Dem.	60	1,128,854 (46.8%)

Year		Candidates	Party	Electoral Vote	Popular Vote
1844	26	**James K. Polk** / ***George M. Dallas***	**Dem.**	**170**	**1,339,494 (49.5%)**
		Henry Clay / *Theodore Frelinghuysen*	Whig	105	1,300,004 (48.1%)
1848	30	**Zachary Taylor** / ***Millard Fillmore***	**Whig**	**163**	**1,361,393 (47.3%)**
		Lewis Cass / *William O. Butler*	Dem.	127	1,223,460 (42.5%)
1852	31	**Franklin Pierce** / ***William R. King***	**Dem.**	**254**	**1,607,510 (50.8%)**
		Winfield Scott / *William A. Graham*	Whig	42	1,386,942 (43.9%)
1856[g]	31	**James Buchanan** / ***John C. Breckinridge***	**Dem.**	**174**	**1,836,072 (45.3%)**
		John C. Fremont / *William L. Dayton*	Rep.	114	1,342,345 (33.1%)
1860[h]	33	**Abraham Lincoln** / ***Hannibal Hamlin***	**Rep.**	**180**	**1,865,908 (39.8%)**
		Stephen A. Douglas / *Herschel V. Johnson*	Dem.	12	1,380,202 (29.5%)
1864[i]	36	**Abraham Lincoln** / ***Andrew Johnson***	**Rep.**	**212**	**2,218,388 (55.0%)**
		George B. McClellan / *George H. Pendleton*	Dem.	21	1,812,807 (45.0%)
1868[j]	37	**Ulysses S. Grant** / ***Schuyler Colfax***	**Rep.**	**214**	**3,013,650 (52.7%)**
		Horatio Seymour / *Francis P. Blair Jr.*	Dem.	80	2,708,744 (47.3%)
1872	37	**Ulysses S. Grant** / ***Henry Wilson***	**Rep.**	**286**	**3,598,235 (55.6%)**
		Horace Greeley / *Benjamin Gratz Brown*	Dem.	—[k]	2,834,761 (43.8%)

continued

Year	No. of states	Candidates	Party	Electoral vote	Popular vote
1876	38	**Rutherford B. Hayes** **William A. Wheeler**	**Rep.**	**185**	**4,034,311 (47.9%)**
		Samuel J. Tilden *Thomas A. Hendricks*	Dem.	184	4,288,546 (51.0%)
1880	38	**James A. Garfield** **Chester A. Arthur**	**Rep.**	**214**	**4,446,158 (48.3%)**
		Winfield S. Hancock *William H. English*	Dem.	155	4,444,260 (48.2%)
1884	38	**Grover Cleveland** **Thomas A. Hendricks**	**Dem.**	**219**	**4,874,621 (48.5%)**
		James G. Blaine *John A. Logan*	Rep.	182	4,848,936 (48.2%)
1888	38	**Benjamin Harrison** **Levi P. Morton**	**Rep.**	**233**	**5,443,892 (47.8%)**
		Grover Cleveland *Allen G. Thurman*	Dem.	168	5,534,488 (48.6%)
1892[1]	44	**Grover Cleveland** **Adlai E. Stevenson**	**Dem.**	**277**	**5,551,883 (46.1%)**
		Benjamin Harrison *Whitelaw Reid*	Rep.	145	5,179,244 (43.0%)
1896	45	**William McKinley** **Garret A. Hobart**	**Rep.**	**271**	**7,108,480 (51.0%)**
		William J. Bryan *Arthur Sewall*	Dem.	176	6,511,495 (46.7%)
1900	45	**William McKinley** **Theodore Roosevelt**	**Rep.**	**292**	**7,218,039 (51.7%)**
		William J. Bryan *Adlai E. Stevenson*	Dem.	155	6,358,345 (45.5%)

Year	States	Candidates	Party	Electoral Vote	Popular Vote
1904	45	**Theodore Roosevelt** / ***Charles W. Fairbanks***	**Rep.**	**336**	**7,626,593 (56.4%)**
		Alton B. Parker / *Henry G. Davis*	Dem.	140	5,028,898 (37.6%)
1908	46	**William Howard Taft** / ***James S. Sherman***	**Rep.**	**321**	**7,676,258 (51.6%)**
		William J. Bryan / *John W. Kern*	Dem.	162	6,406,801 (43.0%)
1912[m]	48	**Woodrow Wilson** / ***Thomas R. Marshall***	**Dem.**	**435**	**6,293,152 (41.8%)**
		William Howard Taft / *James S. Sherman*	Rep.	8	3,486,333 (23.2%)
1916	48	**Woodrow Wilson** / ***Thomas R. Marshall***	**Dem.**	**277**	**9,126,300 (49.2%)**
		Charles E. Hughes / *Charles W. Fairbanks*	Rep.	254	8,546,789 (46.1%)
1920	48	**Warren G. Harding** / ***Calvin Coolidge***	**Rep.**	**404**	**16,133,314 (60.3%)**
		James M. Cox / *Franklin D. Roosevelt*	Dem.	127	9,140,884 (34.2%)
1924[n]	48	**Calvin Coolidge** / ***Charles G. Dawes***	**Rep.**	**382**	**15,717,553 (54.1%)**
		John W. Davis / *Charles W. Bryan*	Dem.	136	8,386,169 (28.8%)
1928	48	**Herbert C. Hoover** / ***Charles Curtis***	**Rep.**	**444**	**21,411,991 (58.2%)**
		Alfred E. Smith / *Joseph T. Robinson*	Dem.	87	15,000,185 (40.8%)
1932	48	**Franklin D. Roosevelt** / ***John N. Garner***	**Dem.**	**472**	**22,825,016 (57.4%)**
		Herbert C. Hoover	Rep.	59	15,758,397 (39.6%)

continued

Year	No. of states	Candidates	Party	Electoral vote	Popular vote
		Charles Curtis			
1936	48	**Franklin D. Roosevelt**	**Dem.**	**523**	**27,747,636 (60.8%)**
		John N. Garner			
		Alfred M. Landon	Rep.	8	16,679,543 (36.5%)
		Frank Knox			
1940	48	**Franklin D. Roosevelt**	**Dem.**	**449**	**27,263,448 (54.7%)**
		Henry A. Wallace			
		Wendell L. Willkie	Rep.	82	22,336,260 (44.8%)
		Charles L. McNary			
1944	48	**Franklin D. Roosevelt**	**Dem.**	**432**	**25,611,936 (53.4%)**
		Harry S. Truman			
		Thomas E. Dewey	Rep.	99	22,013,372 (45.9%)
		John W. Bricker			
1948[o]	48	**Harry S. Truman**	**Dem.**	**303**	**24,105,587 (49.5%)**
		Alben W. Barkley			
		Thomas E. Dewey	Rep.	198	21,970,017 (45.1%)
		Earl Warren			
1952	48	**Dwight D. Eisenhower**	**Rep.**	**442**	**33,936,137 (55.1%)**
		Richard M. Nixon			
		Adlai E. Stevenson II	Dem.	89	27,314,649 (44.4%)
		John J. Sparkman			
1956[p]	48	**Dwight D. Eisenhower**	**Rep.**	**457**	**35,585,245 (57.4%)**
		Richard Nixon			
		Adlai E. Stevenson II	Dem.	73	26,030,172 (42.0%)
		Estes Kefauver			

Year	States	Candidate	Party	Electoral Vote	Popular Vote
1960[q]	50	**John F. Kennedy** / ***Lyndon B. Johnson***	**Dem.**	303	**34,221,344 (49.7%)**
		Richard Nixon / *Henry Cabot Lodge*	Rep.	219	34,106,671 (49.5%)
1964	50[w]	**Lyndon B. Johnson** / ***Hubert H. Humphrey***	**Dem.**	486	**43,126,584 (61.1%)**
		Barry Goldwater / *William E. Miller*	Rep.	52	27,177,838 (38.5%)
1968[r]	50[w]	**Richard Nixon** / ***Spiro T. Agnew***	**Rep.**	301	**31,785,148 (43.4%)**
		Hubert H. Humphrey / *Edmund S. Muskie*	Dem.	191	31,274,503 (42.7%)
1972[s]	50[w]	**Richard Nixon** / ***Spiro T. Agnew***	**Rep.**	520	**47,170,179 (60.7%)**
		George McGovern / *R. Sargent Shriver Jr.*	Dem.	17	29,171,791 (37.5%)
1976[t]	50[w]	**Jimmy Carter** / ***Walter F. Mondale***	**Dem.**	297	**40,830,763 (50.1%)**
		Gerald R. Ford / *Robert Dole*	Rep.	240	39,147,793 (48.0%)
1980	50[w]	**Ronald Reagan** / ***George H. W. Bush***	**Rep.**	489	**43,904,153 (50.7%)**
		Jimmy Carter / *Walter F. Mondale*	Dem.	49	35,483,883 (41.0%)
1984	50[w]	**Ronald Reagan** / ***George H. W. Bush***	**Rep.**	525	**54,455,074 (58.8%)**
		Walter F. Mondale / *Geraldine Ferraro*	Dem.	13	37,577,137 (40.6%)

continued

Summary of Presidential Elections, 1789–2004 *(continued)*

Year	No. of states	Candidates	Party	Electoral vote	Popular vote
1988[u]	50[w]	**George H. W. Bush** ***Dan Quayle***	**Rep.**	**426**	**48,881,278 (53.4%)**
		Michael S. Dukakis *Lloyd M. Bentsen Jr.*	Dem.	111	41,805,374 (45.6%)
1992	50w	**Bill Clinton** ***Al Gore***	**Dem.**	**370**	**44,908,233 (43.0%)**
		George H. W. Bush *Dan Quayle*	Rep.	168	39,102,282 (37.4%)
1996	50[w]	**Bill Clinton** ***Al Gore***	**Dem.**	**379**	**47,402,357 (49.2%)**
		Robert J. Dole *Jack Kemp*	Rep.	159	39,198,755 (40.7%)
2000[v]	50[w]	**George W. Bush** ***Richard B. Cheney***	**Rep.**	**271**	**50,455,156 (47.9%)**
		Al Gore *Joseph I. Lieberman*	Dem.	266	50,992,335 (48.4%)
2004[x]	50[w]	**George W. Bush** ***Richard B. Cheney***	**Rep.**	**286**	**62,025,554 (50.7%)**
		John Kerry *John Edwards*	Dem.	251	59,026,013 (48.3%)
2008	50w	**Barack Obama** ***Joseph R. Biden, Jr.***	**Dem.**	**365**	**69,459,909 (52.9%)**
		John McCain *Sarah Palin*	Rep.	173	59,930,608 (45.7%)

Source: "Table 1-7 Popular and Electoral Votes for President, 1789–2008." In *Vital Statistics on American Politics 2009–2010*, edited by Harold W. Stanley, and Richard G. Niemi, 17-21. Washington, DC: CQ Press, 2009. http://library.cqpress.com/vsap/vsap09_tab1-7.

Note: In the elections of 1789, 1792, 1796, and 1800, each candidate ran for the office of president. The candidate with the second highest number of electoral votes became vice president. For elections after 1800, italic indicates vice-presidential candidates. Dem.-Rep. = Democratic-Republican; Fed. = Federalist; Nat.-Rep.= National-Republican; Dem. = Democratic; Rep. = Republican.

a. The elections of 1789–1800 were held under rules that did not allow separate voting for president and vice president.

b. Popular vote returns are not shown before 1824 because consistent, reliable data are not available.

c. Monroe ran unopposed. One electoral vote was cast for John Adams and Richard Stockton, who were not candidates.

d. 1824: All four candidates represented Democratic-Republican factions. William H. Crawford received forty-one electoral votes, and Henry Clay received thirty-seven votes. Because no candidate received a majority, the election was decided (in Adams's favor) by the House of Representatives.

e. 1832: Two electoral votes were not cast.

f. 1836: Other Whig candidates receiving electoral votes were Hugh L. White, who received twenty-six votes, and Daniel Webster, who received fourteen votes.

g. 1856: Millard Fillmore, Whig-American, received eight electoral votes.

h. 1860: John C. Breckinridge, Southern Democrat, received seventy-two electoral votes. John Bell, Constitutional Union, received thirty-nine electoral votes.

i. 1864: Eighty-one electoral votes were not cast.

j. 1868: Twenty-three electoral votes were not cast.

k. 1872: Horace Greeley, Democrat, died after the election. In the electoral college, Democratic electoral votes went to Thomas Hendricks, forty-two votes; Benjamin Gratz Brown, eighteen votes; Charles J. Jenkins, two votes; and David Davis, one vote. Seventeen electoral votes were not cast.

l. 1892: James B. Weaver, People's Party, received twenty-two electoral votes.

m. 1912: Theodore Roosevelt, Progressive Party, received eighty-six electoral votes.

n. 1924: Robert M. La Follette, Progressive Party, received thirteen electoral votes.

o. 1948: J. Strom Thurmond, States' Rights Party, received thirty-nine electoral votes.

p. 1956: Walter B. Jones, Democrat, received one electoral vote.

q. 1960: Harry Flood Byrd, Democrat, received fifteen electoral votes.

r. 1968: George C. Wallace, American Independent Party, received forty-six electoral votes.

s. 1972: John Hospers, Libertarian Party, received one electoral vote.

t. 1976: Ronald Reagan, Republican, received one electoral vote.

u. 1988: Lloyd M. Bentsen Jr., the Democratic vice-presidential nominee, received one electoral vote for president.

v. 2000: One District of Columbia elector left the ballot blank.

w. Fifty states plus the District of Columbia.

x. 2004: One Minnesota elector voted for "John Edwards" (*sic*) for president.

Index

A

Abbott, Lyman, 259*n*13
Adams, John
 Alien and Sedition Acts (1798), 94–96
 election and presidency, 88, 90–96, 102,
  107–108, 488–489
 executive power controversy, 73–74, 75,
  78, 95–96
 French conflict, 91–94
 judiciary power, 104
 party conflicts, 84, 87–88, 92–94
 presidential etiquette, 74–75
 on the rule of secrecy, 11
 1796 election, 88, 90–91, 102, 488–489
 treaty-making power, 80
 as vice president, 486, 488, 494
 XYZ Affair, 92
Adams, John Quincy
 election and presidency, 120–122, 126, 491
 on government, 120
 National Republicans, 117, 126
 popular leadership approach, 111
 Whig Party, 131
Adams, Samuel, 9
Adams, Sherman, 325
Adarand Constructors, Inc. v. Pena (1995),
  431
Addams, Jane, 257
Advisory legislative powers, 50
Affirmative action, 354, 431
Afghanistan, 386, 445, 474–475
African Americans, 109, 171–172, 177,
  181–185, 193, 311–312
 see also Lincoln, Abraham; Obama,
  Barack; Slavery
Age requirements, 53–54
Agnew, Spiro T., 363, 375*n*99, 499, 501–502,
  504, 508, 510
Agricultural Market Act, 280

Aidid, Mohammed, 418
Aid to Families with Dependent Children
  (AFDC), 294, 413
Air Pollution Control Act, 345
Alabama, 164, 312
Albert, Carl W., 375*n*99
Aldrich, Nelson, 207, 223, 237
Alien Act (1798), 94–96
Alito, Samuel A., 457
Allgor, Catherine, 74, 120
Allison, William B., 207
Altgeld, John P., 209
Ambassador-related duties, 51, 64
American Plan, 131, 144
American Recovery and Reinvestment Act
  (2009), 469
Americans Coming Together (ACT), 453,
  460*n*42
AmeriCorps program, 424
Amnesty program, 364
Anderson, John B., 378, 424
Angola, 366, 386
Annapolis Convention, 8–9
Anti-Federalists, 59–61, 65
Appointments and commissioning power,
  48–50, 63–64
Arch-Federalists, 92–96
Arkansas, 172, 181, 324–325
Armey, Richard K., 437
Arms race, 338–339, 380, 400
Arms sales, 302, 310, 386–387
Arthur, Chester A., 197–202, 373*n*58, 486,
  491, 493, 512*n*13
Article I (U.S. Constitution), 83, 394, 429
Article II (U.S. Constitution), 42, 48–49, 58,
  83, 111–112, 143–144, 298, 347
Articles of Confederation, 5–6, 9, 15, 18
 see also Enumerated powers
Ashcroft, John, 447

Aspin, Les, 414–415
Atlantic Monthly, 225
Axelrod, David, 498

B
Babbitt, Bruce, 414
Babcock, Orville E., 193
Bailey, Josiah, 301
Baird, Zoë, 414, 433*n*9
Baker, James A., III, 397, 398, 457
Baker, Ray Stannard, 247
Balanced Budget Act (1997), 426
Balz, Dan, 420
Bancroft, George, 148
Bank Holiday Proclamation (1933), 291–292
Banking crisis, 291–293
Bank regulation, 472–473
Barbash, Fred, 34
Barkley, Alben W., 502
Baruch, Bernard, 254
Bates, Edward, 164
Battle of New Orleans (1815), 115
Bayard, James A., 103
Bayh, Birch, 349–350
Bay of Pigs invasion, 338
Beard, Charles A., 71
Bechloss, Michael, 418
Beeman, Richard, 22, 30, 79
Begin, Menachem, 368–369
Bell, John, 162
Belz, Herman, 174
Benton, Thomas Hart, 148, 149
Bentsen, Lloyd, 414–415, 498
Berkin, Carol, 35
Berman, Larry, 367
Biddle, Nicholas, 131
Biden, Joseph, 465, 487, 498, 501, 505–506, 508
Binkley, Wilfred E., 145, 153, 182, 197, 275
Bipartisan Campaign Finance Reform Act (2002), 460*n*42
Black Codes, 183, 186
Black, Hugo, 293, 305, 314
Blaine, James G., 199, 200, 202, 216*n*70
Blair, Francis P., 135, 137–138
Blumenthal, Sidney, 390, 428
Blum, John Morton, 226
Board of Economic Warfare, 495
Boland Amendment, 98*n*70, 386–387
Booth, John Wilkes, 181
Borah, William E., 264*n*136, 268

Bork, Robert H., 391, 392–393, 404
Bosnia, 423
Boumediene v. Bush (2008), 449
Boundary disputes, 7
Bourbon Democrats, 202–203
Bowen, Catherine Drinker, 9
Boxer Rebellion, 212
Branch, Taylor, 312
Brandeis, Louis, 392
Brauer, Carl M., 335, 339
Brearley, David, 21
Breckinridge, John, 106, 162
Brezhnev, Leonid, 360
Bricker Amendment, 326
Bricker, John, 326
Brinkley, Douglas, 504
Bristow, Benjamin H., 193
British Petroleum (BP) oil disaster, 477–478
Brock, William, 390
Broder, David, 346
Brookhiser, Richard, 87
Broom, Jacob, 36
Brownlow Committee, 296–298, 316, 325
Brownlow, Louis, 296
Brown, Scott, 471
Brownstein, Ronald, 420
Brown v. Board of Education of Topeka (1954), 324
Bryan, William Jennings, 208, 209, 210, 218, 240, 250
Bryce, James, 207, 365
Buchanan, James, 139, 148, 153
Buchanan, Pat, 439–440
Budget and Accounting Act (1921), 205, 271, 273
Budget Bureau, 271, 296, 298, 315, 345, 356
Budget reconciliation process, 471, 472
Budgets and fiscal control
    Cleveland administration, 205
    Clinton administration, 415–417, 419, 426–427
    George H. W. Bush administration, 402–403
    Harding administration, 271
    Obama administration, 468–470, 473
    Polk administration, 147
    Reagan administration, 381–383, 385
    Taft administration, 238–239
Bully pulpit, 259*n*13
    see also Rhetorical presidency
Bundy, McGeorge, 337

Burger, Warren, 360–361, 391, 394
Burleson, Albert S., 249, 250
Burnett, John D., 204
Burnham, Walter Dean, 389, 414
Burns, James MacGregor, 344
Burr, Aaron, 88, 102–103, 111, 489
Bush Doctrine, 451
Bush, George H. W.
    domestic policies, 401–405
    election and presidency, 396–405, 411,
        487, 507–508
    foreign policy, 397–401
    judiciary appointments, 403–404
    political philosophy, 401–402
    presidential pardons, 400–401
    and Reagan, 510
    as vice president, 389, 498, 503
Bush, George W.
    administrative presidency strategy,
        475–476
    approval ratings, 445–446, 455
    and Cheney, 504–505, 507
    domestic policies, 451–452
    election and presidency, 437–458,
        500–501, 509
    executive power doctrine, 355, 448
    foreign policy, 451
    judiciary appointments, 456–457
    military tribunals, 304, 447–449
    partisan politics, 442–443, 455–457
    party-building activities, 451–456
    political philosophy, 440, 442–445, 468
    and the Republican Party, 442–445,
        451–456
    unitary executive strategy, 446–451
    war on terrorism, 445–451, 454
Bush, Jeb, 441
Bush v. Gore (2000), 440–442
Butler, Benjamin F., 188
Butler, Elizur, 136–137
Butler, Pierce, 40–41, 45, 54
Byrd, Robert, 429

C
Calhoun, John C.
    nullification crisis, 128, 131
    Petticoat Affair, 135
    political philosophy, 117, 126
    Polk administration, 148
    Texas annexation treaty, 146
    as vice president, 374n59, 491

Califano, Joseph, 345, 369
California, 148, 150, 151
Cambodia, 355, 358, 365
Camelot mythology, 371n7
Cameron, Simon, 192
Camp David Accords (1978), 368–369
Canada, 114–115
Cannon, Joseph, 223, 226, 238, 362
Caribbean foreign policies, 232–233
Carranza, Venustiano, 251–252
Carter, Jimmy, 98n70, 366–370, 377–378,
        407n41, 420, 498, 500
Carwardine, Richard, 174
Case Act (1972), 362
Cass, Lewis, 148, 150
Castro, Fidel, 338
Cato, 60, 65
Catt, Carrie Chapman, 255
Central High School (Little Rock, Arkansas),
        324–325
Central Intelligence Agency (CIA), 316, 448
Chadha, Jagdish Rai, 394
Chafee, John, 419
Chase, Salmon P., 164
Chase, Samuel, 105
Cheney, Richard B.
    presidential nominations, 508
    responsibilities, 504–505
    as secretary of defense, 397, 408n66
    as vice president, 438, 442, 456, 487, 498,
        500–501, 507
Chernow, Ron, 16
China, 212, 233–234, 260n54, 356
Cholera epidemic, 151, 157n75
Christopher, Warren, 500
Churchill, Winston, 305–307
Cincinnatus myth, 66n5, 72
Citizenship requirements, 53–54, 68n80
Civil rights
    Andrew Johnson administration, 185
    Eisenhower administration, 324
    George H. W. Bush administration, 403,
        404, 409n79
    Lyndon Johnson administration, 341–344,
        372n39
    Nixon administration, 354
    Truman administration, 311–312
    Wilson administration, 249–250
Civil Rights Act (1866), 184
Civil Rights Act (1964), 343
Civil Rights Act (1991), 403, 404, 409n79

Civil Service Commission, 194, 202, 229
Civil service reform, 194–197, 201–203,
    205, 229
Civil War, 166–170, 181
Clark, James Beauchamp (Champ), 240
Claybrook, Joan, 369
Clay, Henry
    American Plan, 131, 144
    1824 election, 121
    1840 election, 140–141
    Jackson presidency, 134
    National Republicans, 117, 126
    Speaker of the House position, 114
    Texas annexation treaty, 146
    veto power, 145
    Whig Party, 131
Clayton Anti-Trust Act (1914), 248
Clean Air Act (1990), 403
Cleveland, Frederick, 238–239
Cleveland, Grover, 202–210, 227, 373n58,
    512n13
Clifford, Clark M., 311
Clinton, Bill
    administrative presidency strategy, 431
    approval rating, 438–439
    election and presidency, 410–432, 453, 500
    executive power doctrine, 415
    foreign policy, 417–418, 423
    and Fred Korematsu, 305
    and Gore, 503–504
    and John Kennedy, 413
    1992 election, 405, 410, 411–414
    1994 election, 420
    1996 election, 410, 420, 423–426
    partisan politics, 396
    political philosophy, 412–413, 415
    triangulation strategy, 420–423, 425
Clinton, George, 4, 9, 60, 374n59, 491
Clinton, Hillary Rodham, 419, 462, 464, 474
Clinton v. City of New York, 429
Clinton v. Jones (1997), 432
Coal strike, 227, 260n32, 314
Cohen, William, 407n35
Coletta, Paolo E., 235, 237
Colfax, Schuyler, 491
Collier, Christopher, 6, 11
Collier, James Lincoln, 6, 11
Colombia, 230–231
Commander in chief, 44–45, 63, 330n102
Commission on Economy and Efficiency,
    238–239, 271

Committee of Detail, 18–19, 29, 35, 37–38
    see also Enumerated powers
Committee of Style, 22–23
Committee of the Whole, 14–16, 30, 35, 37
Committee of Thirteen, 5
Committee on Postponed Matters, 21–22,
    29, 33–34, 35
    see also Enumerated powers
Committee on Public Information (CPI),
    256–257
Committee to Re-elect the President
    (CREEP), 357
Communism, fall of, 398–399, 402
Compassionate conservatism, 440, 443–444
Compromise of 1850, 151
Compromise of 1877, 195–196, 215n56, 312
Conference on Inflation, 364
Congress
    Arthur administration, 201–202
    Carter administration, 366–370
    Cleveland administration, 203–204, 206,
        209
    Clinton administration, 415–432
    Coolidge administration, 275–276
    Eisenhower administration, 320–326
    electoral commission, 195
    executive power controversy, 205–206
    Ford administration, 364–366
    foreign policy, 268–269
    Franklin Roosevelt administration,
        292–294, 297–303
    George H. W. Bush administration,
        396–405
    George W. Bush administration, 442–455
    Grant administration, 182–191, 194–195
    Harding administration, 266–269, 271
    Harrison administration, 206–208
    Hayes administration, 196–198
    health care reform, 470–472
    Hoover administration, 279–283
    internal conflicts, 238, 267, 312, 395–396
    Johnson administration, 182–189
    Kennedy administration, 340
    legislative veto, 393–395, 429
    Lincoln administration, 181–182
    Lyndon Johnson administration, 343–348
    McKinley administration, 211–213
    1910 election, 239
    1912 election, 240–242
    1946 election, 309, 319
    1948 election, 309–310, 312

1980 election, 378
1994 election, 419–420
1996 election, 425
Nixon administration, 352–357
Obama administration, 463, 468–481
partisan politics, 427–428
post-Civil War legislative activity, 191
presidential power legislation, 362
Reagan administration, 380–391
Taft administration, 236–238
Theodore Roosevelt administration,
    223–228, 232–233
Truman administration, 308–317
Twentieth Amendment, 283–284
2002 election, 452–453
2004 election, 453–455
2010 election, 478–479
Twenty-fifth Amendment, 348–351
Twenty-seventh Amendment, 331n110
Wilson administration, 243–258, 266
Congressional Budget and Impoundment
    Control Act (1974), 362, 381
Congressional Budget Office, 362
Congressional committees, 114
Congressional party caucus, 102, 113–114,
    124n46, 130
Conkling, James C., 171
Conkling, Roscoe, 194, 197–201
Connecticut, 15
Connecticut Compromise, 17
Conservation programs, 228, 236–237, 270
Constitution
    Article I, 83, 394, 429
    Article II, 42, 48–49, 58, 83, 111–112,
        143–144, 298, 347
    Fifteenth Amendment, 177, 193, 195–196
    Fourteenth Amendment, 177, 184,
        185–186, 195, 441
    Nineteenth Amendment, 255
    ratification debates, 59–65
    Seventeenth Amendment, 267
    Thirteenth Amendment, 172
    Twelfth Amendment, 91, 111–112, 489
    Twentieth Amendment, 283–284, 298, 496
    Twenty-fifth Amendment, 348–351, 363,
        373n57, 501, 502, 506–507
    Twenty-second Amendment, 317–320,
        508
    Twenty-seventh Amendment, 331n110
Constitutional Convention, 1–26
    background information, 8–9

clause-by-clause evaluation and debate,
    16–18, 19–21
Committee of Detail, 18–19, 29, 35, 37–38
Committee of Style, 22–23
Committee of the Whole, 14–16, 30, 35, 37
Committee on Postponed Matters, 21–22,
    29, 33–34, 35
controversies, 20–21
delegates, 9–10
draft modifications, 19–20
executive design, 27–69
final adjustments, 22–24
Hamilton's Plan, 15–16
legislative design, 13–21
New Jersey Plan, 15, 16, 18
ratification debates, 59–65
rules and procedures, 10–12
stages, 12–24
vice presidential role, 55–59
Virginia Plan, 13–14, 15, 26n29
see also Enumerated powers
Constitutional monarchies, 2–3
Constitutions, state, 4–5, 26n29
Continental Congress, 5–9
Contract with America, 419, 421
Contract with America Advancement Act
    (1966), 394
Contra rebels, 386–387
Convene and adjourn Congress, 51
Coolidge, Calvin
    election and presidency, 270, 275–278,
        286n43, 287n48, 493
    executive power doctrine, 266, 278–279
    political philosophy, 275–276, 379
    popularity, 275–278
    as presidential successor, 487
    as vice president, 494
Cooper, John Milton, Jr., 255
Cornell, Alonzo B., 197–198
Cornwallis, Charles, 6
Cornwell, Elmer E., Jr., 236, 247, 266,
    274, 282
Corruption, 269–270
Corwin, Edward S., 166, 169, 254, 264n119
Council of Economic Advisers (CEA),
    315–316
Council proposal, 31–32, 45–46
Court-packing conflict, 298–300, 384
Cox, Archibald, 360
Cox, James M., 265
Cramer, Charles F., 269

Crawford, William, 117, 120
Creek Indian treaty, 80
Creel, George, 256
Crenson, Matthew, 144, 168–169, 337
Cresson, W. P., 119
Crittenden, John J., 165
Cuba
    Bay of Pigs invasion, 338
    Cuban missle crisis, 338–339, 372n27
    Spanish-American War, 212
Cumberland Road controversy, 117–118
Cunliffe, Marcus, 28
Currency crisis, 7
Curtis, Charles, 494
Curtis, George William, 194
Customhouse investigation, 197–198
Customs Service, 450
Czechoslovakia, 311

D

Dahl, Robert A., 33, 479
Dallas, George M., 491–492
Dallek, Robert, 373n58
Daniels, Josephus, 249
Davie, William R., 65
Davis, David, 168
Davis, John W., 278
Dawes, Charles G., 271–272, 494, 512n18
Dayton, Jonathan, 10
Dean, Howard, 465, 471
Debates, political, 439
Debs, Eugene V., 210, 242, 262n83, 265
Debs, In re, 210, 227
Declaration of Independence, 3, 176–177
Declaration on Liberated Europe, 306
Delaware, 8
DeLay, Tom, 437
Democratic Leadership Council (DLC), 413
Democratic National Committee, 421,
    433n17, 460n42, 463, 465
Democratic Party
    1840 election, 140–143
    1848 election, 150
    1864 election, 173–175
    1880 election, 199
    1884 election, 202–203
    1894 election, 209
    1896 election, 210–211
    Carter administration, 366–370
    Clinton presidency, 416–417, 427–429,
        433n17

Franklin Roosevelt administration,
    300–301
Grant presidency, 193
Jackson presidency, 131
Kennedy administration, 340
national conventions, 130
1910 election, 239
1912 election, 240
1932 election, 288, 319
1936 election, 295–296
1938 election, 300–301
1946 election, 309, 319
1948 election, 309–310
1964 election, 344
1968 election, 351–352, 356–357
1980 election, 378
Nixon administration, 357–358, 359
origins, 126
party press, 137–138
philosophical changes, 384
Pierce presidency, 152
Progressive era, 239–241
reform efforts, 351–352
slavery controversy, 150
Texas annexation treaty, 146
2008 election, 462–465
war on terrorism, 445–446
Wilson presidency, 247–250
Democratic-Republicans
    dissolution, 120, 122
    Jefferson presidency, 100–113, 488–489
    Madison presidency, 113–117, 124n46
    Monroe presidency, 117–119
    national bank charter, 116
    political philosophy, 129
    Washington presidency, 82, 84–96
Denby, Edwin, 270
Department of Defense (DOD), 316
Department of Homeland Security (DHS),
    449
Department of Housing and Urban Devel-
    opment (HUD), 345
Department of Transportation (DOT), 345
Deputy governors, 55
Desch, Michael, 475
Detainee Treatment Act (2005), 448
Dewey, Thomas E., 309, 500
Dewitt, David Miller, 187
Dickinson, John, 33, 38–39, 46, 50
Diem, Ngo Dinh, 338
Direct primaries, 240–241, 245

Dirksen, Everett, 343, 372n39
Disability Benefits Reform Act (1984), 388–389
Disability proposals, 38–39, 348–350, 373n58, 507
Divided government, 351–353, 367, 392–393, 395–399, 404–405, 408n66, 418–419
Dixiecrats, 312
Dodd, Christopher, 473
Dodd-Frank bill, 473, 477
Doheny, Edward L., 270–271
Dole, Robert J., 384, 409n79, 416, 422, 424–425
Dollar Diplomacy, 251
Domestic Council, 345, 356
Domestic economic crisis, 139–140
Donald, David Herbert, 163–164
Donelson, Andrew J., 135
"Don't Ask, Don't Tell" policy, 415
Dorgan, Byron, 427
Douglass, Frederick, 185
Douglas, Stephen A., 152, 161, 162
Douglas, William O., 314
Dowd, Matthew, 454, 455
Draft, military, 168
Dred Scott v. Sandford, 153, 161, 164, 172
Drew, Elizabeth, 504
Duane, William J., 133, 134
Dukakis, Michael, 396, 500
Dunne, Finley Peter, 486, 494
Duskin, George M., 204

E
Eagleton, Thomas, 499, 511
Early, Steve, 307
Eastern Europe, 306–307, 310–311, 398–399
East Germany, 398
Eaton, John, 135
Eaton, Margaret, 135
Economic and social security
    Clinton administration, 413, 416–417, 421–422, 426–427
    Eisenhower administration, 321–324
    Franklin Roosevelt administration, 293–295, 465–466
    George W. Bush administration, 443, 450–451
    Kennedy administration, 339
    Nixon administration, 353–354
    Obama administration, 466–467

see also New Deal program; Nixon, Richard M.; Roosevelt, Franklin D.
Economic Defense Board, 495
Economic stimulus package, 466, 468–470, 478
Edmunds, George F., 204
Educational reform, 440, 443–444, 451–452, 459n17
Edwards, John, 500, 501
Ehrenhalt, Alan, 384
Ehrlichman, John, 353, 356
Eightieth Congress, 309, 316–320
Eighty-ninth Congress, 344
Eisenhower, Dwight D.
    civil rights initiatives, 324
    disabling illnesses, 348, 373n58
    election and presidency, 320–326, 334, 453
    executive power doctrine, 321–326
    executive reorganization program, 325
    foreign policy, 322–323
    legacy, 323–324
    military powers, 324–325
    and Nixon, 356–357, 501–502, 509–510
    political philosophy, 320–326, 353
    popularity, 323–324
    on the presidency, 510
    on Vietnam, 338
Eisenhower, Edgar, 321
Eisenhower, Milton, 323
Elections
    1796, 88–91, 102, 488–489
    1800, 102–103, 111, 122n6, 489
    1824, 120–122, 130
    1836, 511n10
    1840, 140–143
    1848, 150–151
    1860, 162–164
    1864, 173–175
    1866, 185–186
    1872, 193
    1876, 195, 441
    1880, 199
    1882, 201
    1884, 202
    1888, 206
    1890, 209
    1892, 208
    1894, 209
    1896, 210–211
    1908, 234–235
    1910, 239

1912, 240–242, 262n83, 411
1918, 256–258
1920, 258, 265–266
1924, 277–278
1928, 279
1930, 281
1932, 288, 319
1936, 295–296, 318
1938, 300–301
1940, 301, 318
1944, 301, 318
1946, 309, 319
1948, 309–310, 312
1960, 334–335, 337, 510
1964, 344
1968, 351–352, 356–357, 424, 510
1972, 357
1975, 365
1976, 366
1980, 370, 377–378, 424
1982, 383, 388
1984, 383–384
1988, 396, 401, 507, 510
1992, 397, 400, 404–405, 410, 411–414,
    424
1994, 419–420
1996, 410, 420, 423–426
1998, 429–430
2000, 437–442, 510
2002, 452–453
2004, 453–455
2006, 455, 457
2008, 462–464, 505
2010, 463, 478–479
Twentieth Amendment, 283–284
Electoral College
    1800 election, 102–103, 111, 122n6, 489
    1824 election, 120–121, 130
    1860 election, 162
    1864 election, 174
    1876 election, 195, 441
    1880 election, 199
    1888 election, 206
    1896 election, 210
    design and functional role, 21, 29, 32–36,
        56, 60, 66n25, 66n28
    1920 election, 265
    1924 election, 278
    1932 election, 288
    1980 election, 378
    1992 election, 414

    presidential election process, 111–112, 489
    Twentieth Amendment, 284
    2000 election, 510
    2004 election, 453
Electoral Count Act (1887), 441–442
Elementary and Secondary Education Act,
    345
Elk Hill oil reserve (California), 270
Elkins, Stanley, 10, 28, 77
Ellis, Joseph J., 85
Ellis, Richard J., 31, 37, 49
Ellsworth, Oliver, 18, 33, 65
Emancipation Proclamation, 170–173
Emergency Banking Bill (1933), 292
Emmerich, Herbert, 271
Endara, Guillermo, 398
Engler, John, 500
Enron, 450
Entitlement programs, 413, 419, 422, 451,
    465–466
Enumerated powers
    advisory legislative powers, 50
    appointments and commissioning power,
        48–50, 63–64
    commander in chief, 44–45, 63, 330n102
    Committee of Detail, 18–19, 42–43
    convene and adjourn Congress, 51
    executive design, 29
    executive power, 43–44
    Federalist defense, 63–64
    general versus specific powers, 41–42
    pardons, 46–47
    receive ambassadors, 51, 64
    "require the opinion" clause, 45–46
    rights of the people, 26n43
    "take care" clause, 51
    treaty-making power, 47–48, 63, 98n70
    veto powers, 42–43, 63
Environmental Protection Agency (EPA),
    477
Equal Employment Opportunity
    Commission (EEOC), 343, 372n39
Equal rights, 184–185
    see also Civil rights
Espionage Act (1917), 257
Ethics in Government Act (1978), 396,
    400–401, 427, 430
Executive design
    council proposal, 31–32, 45–46
    enumerated powers, 29, 41–51, 63–64
    executive salary, 40, 62–63

institutional separation, 39–41
number of the executive, 29, 30, 62
oath of office, 52–53
overview, 27–32
qualifications, 53–55, 68*n*80
removal from office, 36–39
selection and succession, 32–35, 55–59
term of office, 29, 35–36, 62
title designation, 29, 52
Executive Office of the President (EOP),
    296–298, 315, 356, 381
Executive Order 8248, 297–298
Executive Order 11246, 354, 431
Executive Order 11478, 354
Executive Order 12291, 389
Executive Order 12498, 389
Executive Order 13087, 431
Executive Order 13198, 459*n*17
Executive Order 13199, 443, 459*n*17
Executive privilege, 360–362, 428, 432
Executive Reorganization Act (1939),
    297–298
Ex parte Milligan, 168–169, 303, 314
Ex parte Quirin, 303–304, 447

F
Fahey, Charles, 312
Fairbanks, Charles W., 494
Fair Deal program, 308
Fair Employment Board, 312
Fairey, Shepard, 467
Faith-based initiatives, 443, 451, 459*n*17,
    476
Fall, Albert B., 270–271, 285*n*21
Fallows, James, 369
Faubus, Orval, 324–325
Fausold, Martin L., 279, 281
Federal Emergency Management Agency, 450
Federal Farm Board, 280
Federalist Papers, The
    Electoral College, 111
    executive power controversy, 78–79
    foreign policy conflicts, 83
    impeachable offenses, 61
    impeachment process, 430
    institutional separation, 39
    presidential defense, 61–64
    presidential election process, 111
    presidential qualifications, 54
    presidential reeligibility, 36
    treaty-making power, 47

Federalists
    Adams presidency, 90–96, 488–489
    demise, 119–120
    Jefferson presidency, 100–113
    Madison presidency, 115–116
    Monroe presidency, 119
    political philosophy, 129
    presidential defense, 61–62
    presidential election process, 489
    Washington presidency, 85–88
Federal Reserve Act (1913), 248
Federal Reserve Board, 403, 473
Federal Trade Commission Act (1914), 248
Feerick, John D., 64, 65
Ferling, John, 90, 94
Ferraro, Geraldine A., 499, 511
Fifteenth Amendment, 177, 193, 195–196
Fifty-first Congress (1889-1891), 209
Filibusters, 343, 416, 456, 457, 472
Fillmore, Millard, 151, 486, 492
Financial reform, 472–473, 477
Fiorina, Morris P., 396
Fireside chats, 292, 294, 298, 327*n*17
First Congress, 71
Fiscal control and budgets
    Cleveland administration, 205
    Clinton administration, 415–417, 419,
        426–427
    George H. W. Bush administration,
        402–403
    Harding administration, 271
    Obama administration, 468–470, 473
    Polk administration, 147
    Reagan administration, 381–383, 385
    Taft administration, 238–239
Flexner, James Thomas, 79
Florida, 164, 195, 440–442, 465
Food and Drug Administration (FDA),
    477
Forbes, Charles, 269
Ford, Gerald R., 363–366, 377, 487, 493,
    501–503, 508, 514*n*63
Foreign policy, 82–84, 88–90
Forrestal, James, 316
Fort Sumter, 165, 166
Forty-second Congress (1871-1873), 191
Fourteen Points peace program, 255–256
Fourteenth Amendment, 177, 184, 185–186,
    195, 441
Frank, Barney, 473
Frankfurter, Felix, 295

Franklin, Benjamin
  age, 10
  and the Constitutional Convention, 12,
    23–24
  council proposal, 46
  executive design, 30–31
  executive salary, 40
  impeachment proposal, 37
  property requirements, 55
  veto powers, 42
Franklin, John Hope, 312
Freedman's Bureau, 183–184
Freeman, Joanne B., 73, 103
Free Soil Party, 150
Frémont, John C., 152–153
French conflict, 91–94
French Revolution (1789), 82
Frist, Bill, 456
"Front porch" campaigns, 211
Fugitive Slave Act, 151

G
Gabler, Ted, 417
Gaddis, John Lewis, 380
Gaither, James, 345
Gallatin, Albert, 89, 107, 113, 147
Gang of 14, 456, 457
Garfield, James A., 198–201, 373n58, 374n59,
    491, 493, 512n13
Garment, Leonard, 354–355
Garner, John Nance, 486, 494–495, 502
Garner-Wagner relief bill, 283
Garraty, John A., 206, 207
Gates, Robert, 474
Gays and lesbians in the military, 415
General Accounting Office (GAO), 271
Genet, Edmond, 83
Geneva Conventions, 448, 449
George III (King), 3
Georgia
  Constitutional Convention, 15
  1918 election, 256
  secession, 164
  Worcester v. Georgia (1832), 136–137,
    155n34
Germany, 232, 253, 255, 301, 303–304, 307,
    398
Gerry, Elbridge
  and the Constitutional Convention, 22, 23
  council proposal, 32
  deaths in office, 374n59, 491

  French conflict, 91
  impeachment proposal, 37
  military matters, 45
  presidential qualifications, 53
  presidential succession, 58
  veto powers, 42
Gerry, Peter, 301
Gershwin, George and Ira, 486
Gettysburg Address, 176–177
Giglio, James N., 336
Gilmore, James S., III, 443
Gingrich, Newt, 419, 420, 422, 423, 429
Ginsberg, Benjamin, 144, 168–169, 337
Ginsburg, Douglas H., 393
Glass-Steagall Act, 427, 473
Globe, 137–138
Goldsmith, William M., 86, 90, 231, 234
Gold standard, 191, 209, 210, 223
Goldstein, Joel K., 498
Goldwater, Barry, 344
Goldwater-Nichols Act (1986), 330n102
Gonzales, Alberto, 457
Good Morning America, 412
Gore, Al
  and Clinton, 509, 510
  1996 election, 423
  presidential nomination, 508
  2000 election, 437–442
  as vice president, 417, 418, 422–423, 487,
    498, 499–500, 503–504
Gorham, Nathaniel, 14, 18, 48, 58
Gould, Lewis L., 338, 430
Government spending issues, 147
Graham, Lindsay, 449
Gramm-Leach-Bliley Act (1999), 427
Grant, Ulysses S., 186, 189–195, 196, 318
Grassroots campaigns, 453–454, 462–464
Great Britain
  boundary disputes, 7
  government structure, 2–3
  Jay Treaty (1794), 88–90
  Latin American foreign policies, 232,
    251–252
  Lend Lease program, 302–303
  naval arms race, 268
  Treaty of Washington (1871), 192–193
  War of 1812, 114–115
  World War II, 302, 307
  Yalta summit meeting, 305–306
Great Depression, 279, 289 see also Hoover,
    Herbert C.

Great Society program, 343–346, 358, 378
Greece, 310
Greeley, Horace, 137, 160, 168, 194
Greenstein, Fred, 82, 109, 122, 309, 321, 327n4, 333, 366, 383, 389
Grenada invasion, 385
Grier, Robert C., 153
Griggs v. Duke Power Company, 409n79
Guantánamo Bay prison, 473, 474, 476
Guiteau, Charles J., 201
Gulf of Tonkin Resolution, 347
Gulf oil explosion, 477–478
Gulick, Luther, 296, 297, 298

H

Habeas corpus, suspension of, 166, 167–168, 169
Hagerty, James, 323, 336
Hale, Eugene, 223
Half-breed Republicans, 199, 202, 216n70
Hamby, Alonzo L., 308, 361, 390
Hamdan, Salam Ahmed, 449
Hamdan v. Rumsfeld (2006), 448–449
Hamilton, Alexander
    Annapolis Convention, 8
    appointments and commissioning power, 49
    death, 489
    executive design, 36
    executive power controversy, 73–74, 75, 78, 83–84, 221
    foreign policy conflicts, 82–84, 256, 302
    Hamilton's Plan, 15–16
    on impeachment, 430
    and Jefferson, 103, 107
    pardon power, 46–47
    party conflicts, 81–86, 92–93, 97n43
    presidential defense, 61–65
    presidential succession, 57
    residency requirements, 54
    as Treasury Secretary, 75, 81, 147
    treaty-making power, 47
    veto powers, 42, 79
    Whiskey Rebellion, 85
Hamilton, Lee, 457
Hamilton's Plan, 15–16
Hamlin, Hannibal, 492
Hancock, Winfield Scott, 199
Handlin, Oscar, 322
Hanna, Mark, 211, 220, 231
Harding, Warren G.
    and Coolidge, 494
    death, 270, 274, 374n59
    disabling illnesses, 373n58
    election and presidency, 258, 265–274, 276
    executive power doctrine, 266–267
    foreign policy, 268–269
    national budget system, 271–272
    political philosophy, 266–267, 271–272
    public relations, 273
    removal power judgment, 272–273
    rhetorical presidency, 274
Hargrove, Erwin C., 368, 370
Harlow, Ralph Volney, 113
Harriger, Katy, 401
Harris, Katherine, 441
Harrison, Benjamin A., 206–208, 211
Harrison, William Henry, 126, 140–143, 373n57, 374n59, 492, 512n13
Harris, Patricia Roberts, 369
Harsch, Joseph C., 321
Hawley, Ellis, 298
Hayden, Carl, 349
Hayden, Jay C., 287n48
Hayes, Rutherford B., 195–198, 205, 441, 492
Hay-Herran Treaty, 98n70, 230
Hay, John, 217n116, 230, 232
Health care reform, 418–419, 470–472, 477–478
Heclo, Hugh, 379
Helvidius, 83, 84
Hendrick, Burton J., 251
Hendricks, Thomas A., 374n59, 491
Henry, Patrick, 9, 59–60
Hepburn Act (1906), 223–224, 226
Herran, Thomas, 230
Hill, Anita, 403
Hinsdale, B. A., 200
Hoar, George F., 191
Hobart, Garret A., 374n59, 491, 492
Hodges, Albert G., 165
Hoffman, Paul, 311
Hoff-Wilson, Joan, 353
Hofstadter, Richard, 96, 100, 219
Holmes, John, 118
Homestead Act, 176
Hoover Commission, 316–317, 325, 331n112
Hoover, Herbert C.
    bank holiday proclamation, 291–292
    as cabinet appointee, 269, 279, 280
    election and presidency, 279–283, 288, 290
    executive power doctrine, 266, 291–292

executive reorganization program,
      316–317
   political philosophy, 279–283
   and Wilson, 254
Hopkins, William, 293
House of Representatives
   see Congress
Hovey, Alvin P., 168
Howard, Oliver O., 183
Huerta, Victoriano, 251
Hughes, Charles Evans, 269
Humphrey, Hubert H., 349, 351–352,
      358–359, 487, 508
Humphrey's Executor v. United States, 299
Hunt, Gaillard, 115, 124*n*46
Huntington, Samuel, 1
Hurricane Katrina, 455
Hussein, Saddam, 399, 418, 447, 451, 504
Hyman, Harold M., 173

I
Illinois, 241
Immigration and Naturalization Act (1952),
      394
Immigration and Naturalization Service, 450
*Immigration and Naturalization Service v.
      Chadha*, 393–395, 429
Impeachment
   Andrew Johnson, 188–189, 430
   basic principles, 37–38, 46–47, 56–57, 61
   Bill Clinton, 410, 429–430, 432
   constitutional design, 18, 22
   John Tyler, 145
   judiciary branch, 13
   Richard Nixon, 361, 430
   vice presidential role, 35
   Virginia Plan, 13, 14
Imperial presidency, 357–359, 364, 366–367,
      446
Income tax, 176
Industrial development, 218–220
Inflation Bill (1874), 191
Inland Waterways Commission, 228
In re Debs, 210, 227
Intermediate-range Nuclear Forces (INF)
      Treaty, 389
Internet-based campaigns, 464
Internment camps, 304–305
Interrogations, terrorist, 448–449, 473, 474
Interstate Commerce Commission (ICC),
      223–224

Iran-contra affair, 386–387, 400–401,
      407*n*34, 407*n*35
Iran hostage crisis, 370
Iraq Study Group, 457–458
Iraq War
   George H. W. Bush administration, 399,
      402
   George W. Bush administration, 454, 455,
      457–458, 504
   Obama administration, 473–475
   2008 election, 464
Italy, 232

J
Jackson, Andrew
   cabinet status, 134–136
   Congressional conflicts, 131–134
   1824 election, 121
   1840 election, 140–141
   election and presidency, 122, 126–139, 491
   executive power controversy, 138–139
   kitchen cabinet, 135–136
   legacy, 136–139
   national bank charter, 131–133, 139–140
   nullification crisis, 128, 137, 155*n*34
   partisan politics, 138–139
   Petticoat Affair, 134–135
   political philosophy, 126–139, 154*n*5
   popular leadership approach, 128–130,
      133, 137–139, 222
   Senate censure, 133–134
   spoils system, 138–139, 155*n*45
   and Van Buren, 510
   veto powers, 131–133, 136
   War of 1812, 115
Jackson, Robert, 305, 314, 361
Jackson, William, 11
Jacobson, Gary C., 419
Japan, 233–234, 260*n*54, 268, 301, 303, 307
Japanese-American relocation camps,
      304–305
Jardine, William M., 280
Jaworski, Leon, 360
Jay, John, 54, 61, 68*n*80, 88, 103
Jay Treaty (1794), 88–90
Jefferson, Thomas
   Democratic-Republican Party, 100–113
   1800 election, 102–103, 111, 122*n*6, 489
   election and presidency, 100–113
   embargo policy, 106, 107, 110–111
   on executive and legislative power, 4

executive power controversy, 81–82, 112–113
foreign policy conflicts, 82–83, 88–90
and Hamilton, 103, 107
institutional separation, 107–108, 113
Jay Treaty (1794), 89, 90
judiciary power, 104–105, 123n17
legacy, 112–113
Massachusetts rebellion, 9
on Missouri statehood, 118
partisan politics, 100–108, 110, 113
party conflicts, 81–82, 85–86, 97n43
political philosophy, 221
popular leadership approach, 107–111, 113, 174–175, 222
presidential critiques, 61
presidential etiquette, 74–75, 108
on the rule of secrecy, 11–12
1796 election, 88, 90–91, 102
slavery controversy, 161
State Department appointment, 75
two-term tradition, 317–318
as vice president, 91, 92, 488–489
on Washington, 72
Jeffords, James M., 443
Jennings, Malcolm, 268
John, Richard, 127
Johnson, Andrew, 181, 182–189, 222, 486, 491, 492, 511n10
Johnson, Dick, 148
Johnson, Hiram, 264n136
Johnson, Lyndon B.
election and presidency, 341–348, 487, 493, 508
executive power doctrine, 346, 355
and Humphrey, 510
political philosophy, 344–346
as presidential successor, 487
as senator, 341
task force concept, 345–346
as vice president, 498, 502
Vietnam conflict, 338, 346–348
Johnson, Richard M., 491
Johnstone, Robert M., Jr., 106
Joint Chiefs of Staff (JSC), 316, 330n102
Jones, Paula Corbin, 432
Jordan, Len, 504–505
Jordan, Vernon, 428
Judiciary Act (1789), 105
Judiciary Act (1801), 104–105
Jungle, The (Sinclair), 225

K
Kansas-Nebraska Act (1854), 152, 159, 161
Katzenbach, Nicholas, 347
Kefauver, Estes, 319, 498
Keller, Morton, 194, 196
Kemp, Jack, 382
Kendall, Amos, 135, 137
Kennedy, Anthony M., 393
Kennedy, David M., 282, 283, 303, 306
Kennedy, Edward M., 370, 444, 459n17
Kennedy, Jacqueline, 371n7
Kennedy, John F.
appointments and commissioning power, 337
assassination, 334, 341, 348–349, 374n59
disabling illnesses, 373n58
election and presidency, 334–341
executive power doctrine, 333
legacy, 337–341
military powers, 325
political philosophy, 334–335
popularity, 334–336
presidential personalization, 336–337, 341
as senator, 319, 326
televised speeches, 335–336
term limit debate, 319
and Vietnam, 338, 341
Kennedy, Joseph P., 319
Kennedy, Robert F., 337, 338, 351
Kent, William, 237
Kerrey, Bob, 500
Kerry, John, 453, 454, 465, 500, 501
Ketcham, Ralph, 117, 124n54
Kettl, Donald F., 417
Key, David M., 196
Khrushchev, Nikita, 338–339
King, Rufus, 32
King, William R., 374n59, 491, 493
Kissinger, Henry, 355, 356, 357, 364
Kitchen cabinet, 135–136
Knox, Henry, 75, 80
Kohut, Andrew, 424
Korea, 234
Korean intervention, 313, 347
Korematsu, Fred, 304–305
Korematsu v. United States (1944), 304–305
Kosovo conflict, 431
Krock, Arthur, 290
Ku Klux Klan, 193
Kuwait, 399

L

Labor unions, 295, 309, 330n79, 354, 453, 460n42, 463
Laffer, Arthur, 382
La Follette, Robert, 240–241
LaGuardia, Fiorello, 282
Lame-duck Congress, 283–284
Landon, Alfred M., 500
Lansing, Robert, 373n58
Laracey, Mel, 111
Larry King Live, 412, 418
Latin American foreign policies, 230–233, 251–252
League of Nations, 255, 264n136, 268–269, 445
Leahy, William, 306
Lee, Charles, 93
Lee, Richard Henry, 5, 9, 65
Legislative design, 13–21
Legislative veto, 393–395, 429
Lend Lease program, 302–303
Leuchtenburg, William E., 296, 322, 342, 379
Lever, A. F., 254
Lever Food and Fuel Control Act (1917), 253–254
Lewinsky, Monica, 410, 428, 432, 500, 509
Lewis, William B., 135
Liberal Republicans, 194
Libya, 385
Lieberman, Joseph, 499, 500
Lieutenant governors, 55
Light, Paul, 422
Lincoln, Abraham
  assassination, 181, 182, 374n59
  election and presidency, 162–177
  Emancipation Proclamation, 170–173
  executive power usage, 158–159, 166–170, 259n11
  and Hamlin, 492
  judiciary power, 153
  legacy, 176–177
  political philosophy, 159–177, 208, 221, 294
  popular leadership approach, 174–175, 222
  Reconstruction policies, 172, 181–182, 187
  slavery controversy, 159, 160–162, 164–166, 170–173, 177
  wartime measures, 158–159, 166–173
Lindsey, Bruce, 423, 428
Line Item Veto Act (1966), 299

Line Item Veto Act (1996), 428–429
Link, Arthur S., 246, 250, 252
Lippmann, Walter, 280–281, 282
Lipset, Seymour Martin, 28
Little Rock crisis, 324–325
Locke, John, 39, 44
Lodge, Henry Cabot, 257, 266, 269, 498
Log cabin-hard cider campaign, 141–143
Lombardo, Steve, 478
Long, Russell, 367
Louisiana, 164, 172, 181, 195, 312
Louisiana Purchase, 106, 109, 126
Lowi, Theodore J., 176
Luce, Henry, 323
Lute, Douglas, 474

M

Maclay, William, 80
MacPherson, Harry, 346
Madero, Francisco I., 251
Madison, James
  age, 10
  Annapolis Convention, 8
  appointments and commissioning power, 49
  and the Constitutional Convention, 11–12, 22
  council proposal, 32, 46
  disabling illnesses, 373n58, 512n13
  election and presidency, 113–117, 124n46, 124n54, 491
  on the Electoral College, 66n25
  executive design, 29, 30
  executive power controversy, 78, 81–82
  foreign policy conflicts, 82–84
  on Hamilton, 16
  institutional separation, 39
  Jay Treaty (1794), 88–89
  judiciary power, 104–105
  Massachusetts rebellion, 9
  military matters, 45
  national bank charter, 116
  oath of office, 52
  party conflicts, 85–86, 97n43
  popular leadership approach, 111
  presidential defense, 61
  presidential etiquette, 74–75
  presidential succession, 57
  property requirements, 55
  ratification debates, 65
  on the rule of secrecy, 12

"take care" clause, 51
treaty-making power, 48
Virginia Plan, 13–14, 29
Mansfield, Harvey, 100
Manufacturing production and growth, 218–220
Marbury v. Madison (1803), 104–105, 132
Marbury, William, 104–105
Marcus, Maeva, 315
Marcy, William L., 138, 147
Marroquin, José Manuel, 230
Marshall, George C., 311
Marshall, John, 91, 94, 104–105, 132, 136–137
Marshall Plan, 310–311
Marshall, Thomas R., 373n58, 486, 487, 494, 512n18
Martin, Luther, 47, 60, 65
Maryland, 241
Mason, George
and the Constitutional Convention, 22, 23
council proposal, 32, 46
on the Electoral College, 34, 60
impeachment proposal, 37, 38
oath of office, 52
popular election proposal, 32
presidential succession, 58–59
property requirements, 55
ratification debates, 65
term of office, 36
treaty-making power, 48
veto powers, 42
Massachusetts, 6, 8–9, 15, 241
Mass-circulation press, 224–225
Mayaguez (merchant ship), 365
Mayer, Kenneth R., 354
May, Ernest R., 255
McAdoo, William Gibbs, 250, 254
McCain, John, 437, 438, 448, 449, 464–465, 468, 499
McCarthy, Eugene, 351
McCarthy, Joseph, 322–323
McClarty, Thomas F. (Mack), 414
McClellan, George B., 173, 175
McClure's, 225
McClurg, James, 36
McCormack, John W., 349
McCulloch v. Maryland (1819), 132
McCurry, Michael, 423
McDonald, Forrest, 89, 103
McDonald, John A., 193

McFarlane, Robert C., 386
McGovern-Fraser Commission, 351–352
McGovern, George, 499
McHenry, James, 51, 54, 93, 94
McKinley Tariff (1890), 207
McKinley, William
assassination, 219–220, 493
deaths in office, 373n58, 374n59
election and presidency, 208, 210–213, 219–220, 222–223, 232, 267
and Hobart, 492
McKitrick, Eric, 10, 28, 77
McLane, Louis, 133
McPherson, James M., 160
McVeigh, Timothy, 422
Meacham, Jon, 138
Meat Inspection Act (1906), 225
Medicaid, 345, 413, 421
Medicare, 339, 340, 343, 413, 421, 426, 452
Mellon, Andrew, 268, 275
Mellon tax reduction plan, 275, 276
Melnick, Shep, 362
Mercer, John, 41
Merit system, 229, 249, 269
Merriam, Charles E., 296
Merrill, Horace Samuel, 203
Merritt, E. A., 198
Merry, Robert W., 148
Mexico
civil war, 251–252
Mexican-American War (1846), 147, 148, 149, 150
Michel, Robert, 382
Middle East conflict, 399
Midnight appointments, 104–105
Midnight rules, 407n41
Miers, Harriet, 456–457
Mifflin, Thomas, 85
Miles, Edwin, 155n34
Military Commissions Act (2006), 449
Military expenditures, 380, 385–386
Military powers
Andrew Johnson administration, 186
Cleveland presidency, 209–210, 227
Clinton administration, 431
Eisenhower administration, 324–325
enumerated powers, 44–45, 330n102
Franklin Roosevelt administration, 302–305, 314
George H. W. Bush administration, 398–400

George W. Bush administration, 445–449, 455, 458
Harding administration, 268
Kennedy administration, 325
Lincoln administration, 158–159, 166–170
Lyndon Johnson administration, 346–348
McKinley administration, 212–213
Obama administration, 473–475
Polk administration, 148–150
Reagan administration, 385–386
Theodore Roosevelt administration, 227, 314
Truman administration, 313–315, 347
Wilson administration, 251–255
Military Reconstruction Act, 186, 214n17
Military tribunals, 168–169, 303–304, 314, 447–449
Milligan, Ex parte, 168–169, 303, 314
Milligan, Lambdin P., 168–169
Mills, Ogden, 291
Milosevic, Slobodan, 423, 431
Minerals Management Service (MMS), 478
Miroff, Bruce, 336
Mississippi
    1918 election, 256
    1948 election, 312
    Reconstruction policies, 215n56
    secession, 164
Missouri Compromise (1820), 118, 152, 161
Mitchell, George, 419
Mitchell, John, 227, 359
Modern presidency
    Clinton administration, 410–432
    Eisenhower administration, 320–326, 353
    executive characteristics, 327n4, 479–480
    executive power doctrine, 333–334
    Ford administration, 365
    Franklin Roosevelt administration, 296–298, 327n4
    George H. W. Bush administration, 411
    George W. Bush administration, 442–458
    isolation issues, 341
    Kennedy administration, 334–335
    legislative actions, 362
    Lyndon Johnson administration, 342–343, 346
    Nixon administration, 355–359
    Obama administration, 462–481
    Reagan administration, 379–387
    Theodore Roosevelt administration, 289–291
    Truman administration, 313, 315–317

Modern vice presidency
    activities, 501–506
    political status, 507–510
    presidential succession and disability, 506–507
    selection criteria, 497–501
Moley, Raymond, 293
Monarchy fears, 59–62
Mondale, Walter F., 385, 487, 498, 499, 503, 508
Monroe Doctrine, 118–119, 232
Monroe, James, 61, 111, 117–119
Montesquieu, Charles de Secondat, baron de, 39
Moore, Frank, 368
Morison, Samuel Eliot, 215n55
Morris, Dick, 420–421
Morris, Gouverneur
    advisory legislative powers, 50
    age, 10
    and the Constitutional Convention, 23
    council proposal, 32, 46
    executive design, 30, 36–37
    impeachment proposal, 37–38
    presidential succession, 57, 58
    vesting clauses, 44
Morris-Pinckney plan, 46
Morton, Levi P., 199
Mowry, George W., 227–228, 234, 235
Muckrakers, 225, 259n25
Mullen, Mike, 474
Mundt, Karl, 319
Murphy, Charles, 240
Murray, Robert K., 274
Murray, William Vans, 93
Myers, Frank S., 272
Myers v. United States (1926), 272, 299
Myers, William Starr, 266

N
Nader, Ralph, 440
Nathan, Richard P., 356
National bank charter, 116, 128, 131–133, 139–140
National Constitutional Union, 162
National Country Life Commission, 228
National debt, 6–7
National Labor Relations Act (1935), 295, 296, 298
National Military Establishment (1947), 316
National party conventions, 130, 290, 327n10, 351–352, 366

National Performance Review (NPR), 417, 419, 422
National Recovery Administration, 299
National Republicans, 117, 126, 136
    see also Whig Party
National Security Act (1947), 316, 449
National Security Agency (NSA), 447
National Security Council (NSC), 315–316, 386, 449
National Union Party, 185
Natural resources management programs, 228, 236–237, 270
Naval arms race, 268–269
Neustadt, Richard E., 333, 377
Neutrality Proclamation (1793), 82–83, 170, 302
Nevins, Allan, 163
Newburgh Conspiracy, 72
New Covenant program, 413, 420
New Deal program, 293–301, 308–309, 321–322, 335, 377–379, 390, 465–466
New Federalism initiative, 353–355, 358
New Foundation program, 466, 473
New Freedom program, 248–250, 255
New Frontier program, 335, 339, 343
New Jersey, 8
New Jersey Plan, 15, 16, 18, 41, 57
New Mexico, 148, 150
New Nationalism program, 241–242, 248
New Panama Canal Company, 230–231
New York, 4–5, 6
New York Stock Exchange, 289, 293
Nicaraguan contra rebels, 386–387, 398
Nineteenth Amendment, 255
Ninety-fifth Congress, 368
Nixon, Richard M.
    administrative presidency strategy, 355–357
    election and presidency, 351–361, 377, 453, 487, 499, 508
    executive power doctrine, 353–360
    executive reorganization program, 356–357
    political philosophy, 345, 379
    presidential pardon, 364–365
    resignation, 361, 363
    as vice president, 323, 501–502
    Vietnam conflict, 355–356
    Watergate scandal, 359–361, 363
Nobel Peace Prize, 234
No Child Left Behind Act (2002), 443–444, 451
Non-Intercourse Act (1809), 111

Nonpartisanship, 80–81, 86–87
Noriega, Manuel, 398
Norris, George W., 238, 271, 283–284
North American Free Trade Agreement (NAFTA), 400, 417–418
North Atlantic Treaty Organization (NATO), 310, 322
North Carolina, 15, 465
North Korea, 313
North, Oliver, 407n34
Nuclear missle buildup, 338–339
"Nuclear option", 456
Nuclear test ban treaty, 339
Nullification doctrine, 128, 137, 155n34
Nunn, Sam, 415

O
Oath of office, 52–53
Obama, Barack
    administrative presidency strategy, 475–478
    and Biden, 498, 505–506
    election and presidency, 462–481
    foreign policy, 473–475
    and Franklin Roosevelt, 465–466
    and Lincoln, 465
    partisan politics, 462–463, 466–475
    political philosophy, 465–468
O'Brien, David M., 392
O'Brien, Lawrence, 340
Occupational and Safety Health Administration (OSHA), 477
O'Connor, Sandra Day, 391, 456
Office of Congressional Relations, 340
Office of Economic Opportunity (OEO), 358–359
Office of Federal Contract Compliance, 354
Office of Homeland Security, 445, 447, 449–450
Office of Information and Regulatory Affairs (OIRA), 477
Office of Management and Budget (OMB), 356, 362, 381, 389
Office of Public Liaison (OPL), 368
Ogle, Charles, 142
Ohio, 241
Oklahoma City terrorist bombing, 422
Old age insurance, 294–295
Older Americans Act, 345
Old Guard Republicans, 223, 226, 239, 240, 242

104th Congress, 421–422, 423, 424
O'Neill, Thomas P. (Tip), 367, 368, 381, 388
Open Door trade policy, 212, 217n116, 233–234, 260n54
Operation Desert Shield, 399
Operation Desert Storm, 399, 402
Operation Just Cause, 398
Oregon, 195
Oregon Territory, 148
Organizing for America (OFA), 463, 479–480
Osborne, David, 417
O'Sullivan, John L., 129
Oswald, Lee Harvey, 334

P

Pacificus, 83, 84, 221, 256, 302
Palin, Sarah, 499, 501, 505
Palmer, A. Mitchell, 242
Paludan, Phillip Shaw, 172
Panama Canal, 98n70, 230–231, 368
Panama invasion, 398
Panetta, Leon, 423
Panic of 1837, 139–140
Panic of 1873, 191
Panic of 1893, 209
Pardons, 46–47
Party conflicts
   Adams presidency, 92–94
   Harding administration, 267
   Reagan administration, 395–396
   Taft administration, 238, 240
   Truman administration, 312
   Washington presidency, 81–88
   see also Divided government
Party conventions, 130, 290
Party press, 137–138
Paterson, William, 15
Patronage system
   Cleveland administration, 202–204
   Grant administration, 193–194
   Harding administration, 269
   Hayes administration, 196–198
   Jackson administration, 138–139, 155n45
   Johnson administration, 185
   Roosevelt administration, 229, 269
   Wilson administration, 249, 269
PAYGO, 402, 470
Payne-Aldrich tariff bill, 237, 239
Peace Corps, 339
Peace of Portsmouth (1905), 234
Pelosi, Nancy, 475, 480

Pendleton Act (1883), 201–202, 203, 229, 269
Pendleton, George Hunt, 201
Pennsylvania
   Constitutional Convention, 15
   direct primaries, 241
   Whiskey Rebellion, 84–85
Pentagon attacks, 438, 504
Perot, H. Ross, 411–412, 418, 424, 425, 439–440, 503
Pershing, John J., 252, 254
Persian Gulf War (1991), 399, 445
Persons, Wilton B. (Jerry), 325
Pertschuk, Michael, 369
Peterson, Merrill D., 108
Petraeus, David, 458, 474
Petroleum reserves, 270
Petticoat Affair, 134–135
Philadelphia Plan, 354
Philippines, 212–213, 233
Phillips, Howard, 358
Pickering, Timothy, 93, 94, 95
Pierce, Franklin, 68n74, 139, 152–153
Pinchot, Gifford, 228, 237
Pinckney, Charles
   age, 10
   council proposal, 46
   institutional separation, 41
   oath of office, 53
   Pinckney Plan, 18, 26n29
   property requirements, 55
   "take care" clause, 51
Pinckney, General Charles Cotesworth, 19, 20, 51, 55, 91, 114
Pinckney Plan, 26n29
Pinckney, Thomas, 88, 102
Pious, Richard M., 43–44, 70, 347, 387, 399–400
Platt, Thomas C., 200
Plumer, William, 489
Pocket vetoes, 43, 132, 186
Poindexter, John M., 386
Poland, 306–307, 398
Political debates, 439
Polk, James K., 145–150, 156n65, 159, 491
Populism, 218, 262n83
Porter, Roger, 365
Posner, Richard, 391
Postal system, 139
Post-Civil War legislative activity, 191
Powell, Colin, 397–398, 415, 438

Presidency
  antecedents, 2–8
  Anti-Federalist critique, 59–61, 65
  deaths in office, 374n59
  disabling illnesses, 348, 373n58, 507,
    512n13
  election process, 111–112, 129, 245, 489,
    495
  enumerated powers, 29, 41–51, 63–64
  executive power, 29–30, 70
  executive salary, 40, 62–63
  Federalist defense, 61–62
  imperial presidency, 357–359, 364,
    366–367
  institutionalization, 296–298, 315–317,
    325, 345–346
  institutional separation, 39–41
  number of the executive, 29, 30, 62
  oath of office, 52–53
  Progressive era, 218–223, 230, 258
  qualifications, 53–55, 68n80
  rating polls, 327n5
  removal from office, 36–39
  rhetorical presidency, 222, 224–225
  selection and succession, 29, 32–35, 55–59,
    143–145, 348, 373n57, 373n58
  term of office, 29, 35–36, 62
  title designation, 29, 52
  treaty-making power, 98n70
  Twelfth Amendment, 111–112, 489
  Twentieth Amendment, 283–284
  Twenty-fifth Amendment, 348–351
  Twenty-second Amendment, 317–320, 508
  two-term tradition, 317–318, 508
  veto powers, 29, 42–43, 63
  see also Enumerated powers; Modern
    presidency
Presidential Power (Neustadt), 333
Presidential primaries, 245
Presidential Succession Act (1947), 349
President's Committee on Civil Rights
  (PCCR), 311, 312
President's Council on Bioethics, 444
President's Emergency Plan for AIDS Relief
  (PEP-FAR), 444
Press conferences
  Clinton administration, 414
  Coolidge administration, 276
  Eisenhower administration, 336
  Harding administration, 273–274
  Kennedy administration, 336, 371n17

Prize Cases, 167
Progressive era, 218–223, 230, 239–241,
  247–249, 258, 265
Progressive Party, 241–242, 262n83
Property requirements, 55
Public Accounting and Oversight Board, 450
Public relations
  Coolidge administration, 275–277
  Harding administration, 273–274
  Hoover administration, 282
  Roosevelt administration, 224–225
  Wilson administration, 246–247, 257–258
Public Utility Holding Company Act, 296
Publius, 61
Pullman railroad strike (1894), 209–210, 227
Pure Food and Drug Act (1906), 225
Purge campaign, 300–301

Q
al Qaeda network, 438, 445, 504
Quayle, Dan, 403, 499–500, 503, 511
Quirin, Ex parte, 303–304, 447

R
Racial discrimination, 249–250, 304–305,
  311–312, 324, 343–344, 372n39
Radical Republicans, 181–187, 189, 190
Radio broadcasts
  Coolidge administration, 277–278, 292
  Franklin Roosevelt administration, 292,
    294, 298, 327n17
  Hoover administration, 292
  Truman administration, 309
Railroad shipping rates, 223–224, 226
Rakove, Jack N., 12, 23
Randall, James, 158, 175
Randolph, Edmund
  age, 10
  Attorney General appointment, 75
  Committee of Detail, 18
  and the Constitutional Convention, 22
  executive design, 4, 30
  impeachment proposal, 37
  pardon power, 47
  presidential succession, 57, 58
  Virginia Plan, 13
Randolph, John, 113–114
Rasmussen, Nick, 474
Ratification debates, 59–65
Rayburn, Sam, 307, 340
Read, George, 50

Reagan Doctrine, 386–387
Reagan, Ronald
  administrative presidency strategy,
    384–390, 475–476
  and Bush, 510
  and Carter, 380–381
  congressional relationship, 380–391
  and Coolidge, 406n9
  disabling illnesses, 373n58, 507
  election and presidency, 377–396, 412,
    419–420, 453, 500
  foreign policy, 384–390
  and Franklin Roosevelt, 379
  judiciary appointments, 391–393
  legacy, 391–393
  1976 election, 366
  1980 election, 370, 377–378
  1984 election, 383–384
  political philosophy, 377–390
  popularity, 381, 384–385, 389–390
  treaty-making power, 98n70
Receive ambassadors, 51, 64
Reconstruction Finance Corporation (RFC),
    282, 283
Reconstruction policies, 172, 181–187,
    215n56
Red Cross, 282–283
Redeemers, 196
Reed, Thomas B., 207
Reedy, George E., 351
Reform Party, 412, 439–440
Regulatory agencies, 477–478
Rehnquist, William H., 391–392, 456
Reichley, A. James, 359, 406n25
Reid, Harry, 480
Reid, Whitelaw, 200
Reinventing government (REGO) program,
    417, 422
Relief and Reconstruction Act (1932), 283
Religious affiliation, 52–53
Remini, Robert V., 131
Removal power, 272–273, 286n21
Reorganization Act (1949), 317
Reorganization Plan No. 8, 317
Repeal Act (1920), 266
Republican National Committee, 453
Republican Party
  1864 election, 173–175
  1880 election, 199
  1884 election, 202
  1888 election, 206

1896 election, 210–211
and Coolidge, 277–278
and Eisenhower, 320–322
George W. Bush administration, 442–445,
    451–457
and Grant, 190–195
Harding administration, 266–267
and Harrison, 206–208
Hoover administration, 280–281
internal conflicts, 238, 240
and Johnson, 182–184
Kennedy administration, 340
and Lincoln, 159, 163–165, 172, 176–177
Lyndon Johnson administration, 343
1910 election, 239
1912 election, 240–242
1920 election, 265–266
1932 election, 288, 319
1946 election, 309, 319
1964 election, 344
1968 election, 351–352, 356–357
1972 election, 357
1980 election, 378
1994 election, 419–420
origins, 152–153
political philosophy, 206–208, 383–387
Progressive era, 239–241
Reagan administration, 383–385, 390
Reconstruction policies, 181–187
reform efforts, 351–352
slavery controversy, 172
and Taft, 236–239
and Theodore Roosevelt, 220, 223,
    225–226
2002 election, 452–453
"Require the opinion" clause, 45–46
Residency requirements, 53–54
Reston, James, 340
Resumption Act (1875), 191
Revolutionary War, 6–7
Revolution of 1875, 215n56
Rhetorical presidency
  Harding administration, 274
  Reagan administration, 378–385, 390
  Roosevelt administration, 222, 224–225
  Wilson administration, 246–247, 257–258
Rice, Condoleezza, 438
Richardson, Elmo, 326
Ridge, Tom, 447, 450, 500
Ritchie, Thomas, 137
Roane, Spencer, 103, 123n17

Roberts, John G., Jr., 456
Robertson, William H., 200–201
Roberts, Paul Craig, 382
Roche, John P., 9
Rockefeller, Nelson A., 364, 501, 503, 505, 508, 513n45
Rockman, Bert A., 387, 390
Rogers, William, 356
Roosevelt Corollary, 231–233
Roosevelt, Eleanor, 307
Roosevelt, Franklin D.
    bank holiday proclamation, 291–292
    death, 307, 374n59, 497
    disabling illnesses, 373n58
    election and presidency, 288–308, 329n49, 335, 412, 500
    executive power doctrine, 291, 299, 302–303
    executive reorganization program, 296–298
    foreign policy, 301–307, 445
    and Garner, 494–495
    New Deal program, 293–301, 308–309, 335
    1920 election, 265
    1932 election, 288–290
    1936 election, 295–296, 318
    1938 election, 300–301
    1940 election, 301, 318
    1944 election, 301, 318
    political philosophy, 291–298, 465–466
    popularity, 291, 293, 296, 328n32, 336–337
    purge campaign, 300–301
    two-term tradition, 318
    on the vice presidency, 494
    wartime measures, 302–305, 314, 447
    World War II, 301–307
    Yalta summit meeting, 305–307
Roosevelt, Theodore
    campaign tactics, 493
    civil service reform, 229
    election and presidency, 226–235, 240–242, 260n32, 314, 411–412, 493–494
    executive power doctrine, 220–221, 224–230, 235, 243–244, 266, 289
    foreign policy, 229–234, 250, 256, 445
    mass-circulation press, 224–225
    1908 election, 234–235
    1912 election, 240–242, 262n83, 411–412
    policy leadership, 226–234, 260n32, 314

    political philosophy, 219–221, 224–226, 241–244, 262n83, 465–466
    popular leadership approach, 221–223, 246
    as presidential successor, 487, 493
    rhetorical presidency, 222, 224–225, 246
    term limits, 318
    as vice president, 493–494
    and Wilson, 256, 257
Root, Elihu, 219
Rosenman, Samuel and Dorothy, 220–221, 308
Rossiter, Clinton, 9–10, 14, 33, 169, 290, 323
Rove, Karl, 443, 451, 452–453, 454
Rudalevige, Andrew, 34, 394–395, 446
Rudman, Warren, 407n35
"Rugged individualism" concept, 282–283
Rule of secrecy, 11–12, 25n23
Rumsfeld, Donald H., 438, 458
Rusk, Dean, 339
Russia, 233–234, 260n54
Russo-Japanese war, 233–234, 260n54
Rutledge, Edward, 89, 92
Rutledge, John, 18, 55

S
Sadat, Anwar, 368–369
Safire, William, 286n32
Salary, executive, 40, 62–63
Salinger, Pierre, 371n17
Sandanistas, 398
Santo Domingo, 192, 232–233
Sarbanes-Oxley Act (2002), 450–451
Saturday night massacre, 360
Savage, James D., 116
Sawyer, Charles, 313
Scalia, Antonin, 391–392
Scandals
    Grant administration, 193–194
    Harding administration, 269–271, 276
    Nixon, Richard M., 359–361, 363
    vice presidents, 491
Scaturro, Frank J., 191
Schechter Poultry Corp. v. United States (1935), 299, 303
Schlesinger, Arthur M., Jr., 338, 358
Schurz, Carl, 176, 196
Scigliano, Robert, 41
Scott, Dred, 153
Scott, Winfield, 149
Scowcroft, Brent, 397

Secession of the states, 164–165

Secret Service, 450

Securities and Exchange Act, 296

Securities and Exchange Commission, 450, 477

Security Council (UN), 306, 313, 329n63, 418

Sedition Act (1798), 94–96, 105–106

Sedition Act (1918), 257, 265

Segregation policies
 Eisenhower administration, 324
 Johnson administration, 185
 Truman administration, 311–312
 Wilson administration, 249–250

Senate
 see Congress

Senate president, 56

Separation of power, 39–41

September 11, 2001 terrorist attacks, 438, 445, 504

Serbia, 431

Seventeenth Amendment, 267

Seventy-fifth Congress, 384

Seward, William H., 160, 163–164, 165

Sharpe, George H., 197–198

Sharp, James Roger, 120

Shays, Daniel, 8

Shays's Rebellion, 8–9

Sherman Antitrust Act, 209

Sherman, James S., 374n59, 493

Sherman, John, 196–197, 206

Sherman, Roger
 Connecticut Compromise, 15, 17
 executive design, 30–31, 33, 35
 military matters, 45
 pardon power, 47
 presidential succession, 58
 ratification debates, 65
 veto powers, 42

Sherman Silver Purchase Act, 209

Sherman, William Tecumseh, 174, 263n119

Shipping blockade, 167

Shultz, George, 354

Signing statements, 404, 448, 477

Silver standard, 209, 210

Sinclair, Harry F., 270–271

Sinclair, Upton, 225

Slavery
 Buchanan presidency, 153
 Compromise of 1850, 151
 draft constitution, 20

1848 election, 150–151

Freedman's Bureau, 183–184

Fugitive Slave Act, 151

Kansas-Nebraska Act (1854), 152, 159, 161

Lincoln's philosophy, 159, 160–162, 164–166, 170–173, 177

Missouri Compromise (1820), 118, 152, 161

Pierce presidency, 152

presidents as slaveholders, 109, 151

Texas annexation treaty, 146

Smith, Al, 279

Smith, Hedrick, 381

Smith, Jean Edward, 191, 192–193

Smoot-Hawley tariff, 280

Snake River (Idaho) Potato Growers, 429

Social and economic security
 Clinton administration, 413, 416–417, 421–422, 426–427
 Eisenhower administration, 321–324
 Franklin Roosevelt administration, 293–295, 465–466
 George W. Bush administration, 443, 450–451
 Kennedy administration, 339
 Nixon administration, 353–354
 Obama administration, 466–467
 see also New Deal program; Nixon, Richard M.; Roosevelt, Franklin D.

Socialist Party, 242, 265

Social Security Act (1935), 293–295, 298

Social Security Administration (SSA), 388

Social Security benefit changes, 388–389

Social Security reforms, 452

Soft money donations, 424, 435n41, 460n42

Somalia, 400, 418

Souter, David, 403

South Carolina
 civil rights initiatives, 312
 1876 election, 195
 New Jersey Plan, 15
 1918 election, 256
 1948 election, 312
 nullification crisis, 128, 137, 164
 presidential election process, 129
 secession, 164–165
 taxation policies, 6

South Dakota, 241

Southeast Asia Treaty Organization (SEATO), 324

South Korea, 313

Soviet Union, 306, 310–311, 325, 338–339, 379–380, 398–399
Spain, 7, 212
Spanish-American War, 212
Sparkman, John, 498
Sparks, Jared, 12
Speaker of the House position, 114, 238
Specie Circular, 139–140
Speechwriters, 274, 286n32
Speed, Joshua A., 161
Spitzer, Robert, 98n70
Spoils system, 138–139, 155n45
Square Deal program, 226–227
Stalin, Joseph, 305–307, 310
Stalwart Republicans, 194, 196, 199, 201, 216n70
Stanton, Edwin, 185, 186, 188
Starr, Kenneth W., 428, 432
State Children's Health Insurance Program, 426
State constitutions, 4–5, 26n29
State legislative governments, 6–9
States' Rights Party, 312
Steel mill crisis, 313–315
Stem cell research, 444–445, 476
Stevens, John Paul, 429, 442
Stevenson, Adlai, 500
Stevens, Thaddeus, 181, 187
Stewart, David, 189
Stiles, Ezra, 28
Stimulus package, 466, 468–470, 478
Stockman, David, 381, 382, 388
Stock market crash, 279
Stoddert, Benjamin, 93
Stone, Harlan Fiske, 303–304
Story, Joseph, 118
Strategic Arms Reduction Treaty (START II), 400
Strategic Defense Initiative (SDI), 380
Subtreasury proposal, 140
Summers, Lawrence, 427
Sumner, Charles, 162–163, 181, 184, 187, 192
Sunstein, Cass, 477
Sununu, John, 402
Supply-side economics, 382
Supreme Court
    Adarand Constructors, Inc. v. Pena (1995), 431
    Boumediene v. Bush (2008), 449
    Brown v. Board of Education of Topeka (1954), 324
    Bush v. Gore (2000), 440–442
    Clinton v. City of New York, 429
    Clinton v. Jones (1997), 432
    court-packing bill, 298–300
    Dred Scott v. Sandford, 153, 161, 164, 172
    Ex parte Milligan, 168–169, 303, 314
    Ex parte Quirin, 303–304, 447
    Griggs v. Duke Power Company, 409n79
    Hamdan v. Rumsfeld (2006), 448–449
    Humphrey's Executor v. United States, 299
    Immigration and Naturalization Service v. Chadha, 393–395, 429
    Korematsu v. United States (1944), 304–305
    Marbury v. Madison (1803), 104–105, 132
    McCulloch v. Maryland (1819), 132
    Myers v. United States (1926), 272, 299
    New Deal program, 298–299
    presidential actions, 313–315
    Prize Cases, 167
    Reagan administration, 391–393
    In re Debs, 210, 227
    Schechter Poultry Corp. v. United States (1935), 299, 303
    United States v. Belmont (1937), 302
    United States v. Curtiss-Wright Export Corp., 302
    United States v. Nixon, 360–361
    Wards Cove Packing Co. v. Atonio, 409n79
    Worcester v. Georgia (1832), 136–137, 155n34
    Yakus v. United States (1944), 303
    Youngstown Sheet and Tube Co. v. Sawyer, 313–315, 361
Surge, military, 475
Suspension of habeas corpus, 166, 167–168, 169
Sutherland, George, 302
"Swing around the Circle" rhetoric, 187, 222

T
Taft-Hartley Act, 309, 313–315, 330n79
Taft, Robert A., 310, 322
Taft, William Howard
    executive power doctrine, 235–239, 266
    1910 election, 239
    1912 election, 240–242, 411
    political philosophy, 236–239
    as Supreme Court justice, 272
    and Theodore Roosevelt, 224, 235
Taggart, Samuel, 489
"Take care" clause, 51

Taliban regime, 438, 445, 504
Talleyrand, C., 91–92
Tammany Hall, 215n55, 240
Taney, Roger B., 133, 134
Tariff reform
    Cleveland administration, 206
    Hoover administration, 280–281
    Polk administration, 148
    Roosevelt administration, 226
    Taft administration, 237
    Van Buren administration, 156n65
    Wilson administration, 247, 248
Task Force on National Health Reform,
        418–419
Task Force on Regulatory Relief, 389
Taxation
    Clinton administration, 415–417,
        426–427
    Coolidge administration, 275–276
    Grant administration, 193
    Harding administration, 268
    imported goods, 6
    Jefferson administration, 106
    Lincoln administration, 176
    Reagan administration, 382–383, 385
Tax Reform Act (1986), 385
Taylor, Zachary, 126, 148, 149, 150–151,
        157n75, 374n59, 492
Tea Party movement, 479–480
Teapot Dome scandal, 270–271
Television broadcasts
    Carter administration, 367
    Clinton administration, 414
    Eisenhower administration, 326, 335
    Kennedy administration, 335–337
    Perot campaign, 412
    Reagan administration, 378, 382
Tennessee, 172, 181–182, 186, 265
Tennessee Valley Authority (TVA), 296,
        328n32
Tenure of Office Act (1867), 186, 188, 190,
        197, 203–205, 214n30, 272
Term limits, 317–320
Term of office, 29, 35–36, 62
Territorial expansion, 106, 109, 118, 127,
        148–150, 192, 230
Terrorist interrogations, 448–449, 473, 474
Texas
    annexation treaty, 146, 148
    1918 election, 256
    secession, 164

Thach, Charles C., Jr., 7–8, 29, 44, 70, 71
Thirteenth Amendment, 172
Thomas, Clarence, 403–404
Thompson, Charles, 72
Thorpe, Merle, 289–290
Throttlebottom, Alexander, 486
Thurmond, Strom, 312
Ticket splitting, 352
Tilden, Samuel J., 195, 196, 441
Title designation, 29, 52
Tocqueville, Alexis de, 100, 129, 139
Today, 412
Tompkins, Daniel D., 491
Total war, 253–255, 263n119
Tower Commission, 386–387
Tower, John, 386, 408n66
Toynbee, Arnold J., 289
Transfer of the capital, 108
Treasury Act (1789), 147
Treaty-making power, 47–48, 63, 88–90,
        98n70, 302
Treaty of Ghent (1814), 115
Treaty of Paris (1783), 7, 25n10
Treaty of Versailles (1919), 255, 257, 268
Treaty of Washington (1871), 192–193
Trevelyan, George, 235
Triangulation strategy, 420–423, 425
Tribble, Paul, 407n35
Troubled Asset Relief Program (TARP), 469
Trout, Robert, 327n17
Troy, Gil, 210, 211
Truman Doctrine, 310
Truman, Harry S.
    civil rights initiatives, 311–312
    election and presidency, 307–317, 493,
        502, 508
    executive power doctrine, 311–317, 355
    executive reorganization program,
        316–317
    foreign policy, 310–311, 313–317
    international security policies, 313–317
    modern presidency, 313, 315–317
    1948 election, 309–310, 312
    political philosophy, 311–312
    popularity, 308
    as presidential successor, 487, 497
    as vice president, 496–497
    wartime measures, 313–315, 347
Trumbull, Lyman, 183–184, 189
Tulis, Jeffrey K., 327n4, 342, 377, 382
Tumulty, Joseph, 373n58

Turkey, 310, 365
Tweed, William Marcy (Boss), 195, 215n55
Twelfth Amendment, 91, 111–112, 489
Twentieth Amendment, 283–284, 298, 496
Twenty-fifth Amendment, 348–351, 363,
    373n57, 501, 502, 506–507
Twenty-one-point message, 308–309
Twenty-second Amendment, 317–320, 508
Twenty-seventh Amendment, 331n110
Tyler, John, 141, 143–145, 373n57, 486, 492
Tyrell, Sir William, 251

U
Ultra-Federalists, 92–96
Underwood, Oscar W., 269
Underwood Tariff Act (1913), 248
Unemployment, 289, 403
Unionization, 295, 309, 330n79, 354
Unitary executive, 30–31
United Mine Workers, 227, 260n32
United Nations Participation Act (1945), 313
United Nations (UN), 305–306, 313, 445
United States v. Belmont (1937), 302
United States v. Curtiss-Wright Export Corp.,
    302
United States v. Nixon, 360–361
Universal white manhood suffrage, 129–130
Unrestricted presidential reeligibility,
    317–320

V
Van Buren, Martin
    1840 election, 142
    election and presidency, 139–140, 156n63
    Free Soil Party, 150
    Panic of 1837, 139–140
    political philosophy, 127
    Polk cabinet position, 148
    Texas annexation treaty, 146
    as vice president, 135, 137, 491
Vance, Cyrus, 369
Vandenberg, Arthur H., 311
Van Riper, Paul, 269, 352
Venezuela, 232
Veterans Bureau scandal, 269
Veto power
    Cleveland presidency, 205
    Clinton presidency, 428–429
    enumerated powers, 29, 42–43, 63
    Ford presidency, 365
    George W. Bush presidency, 444–445, 455

Grant presidency, 191
Harding presidency, 285n11
Hayes presidency, 205
Hoover presidency, 283
Jackson presidency, 131–133, 136
Johnson presidency, 184, 186
legislative veto, 393–395, 429
Monroe presidency, 117–118
Truman presidency, 309
Tyler presidency, 144–145
Washington presidency, 79, 97n37
Vice presidency
    background information, 55–56
    Committee on Postponed Matters, 29
    deaths in office, 374n59, 491, 492–493
    early twentieth century, 493–497
    founding period, 487–490
    functional role, 35, 58, 487–488, 491–492,
        494–496, 502–505
    modern vice presidency, 497–511
    nineteenth century, 490–493
    presidential election process, 489
    presidential succession, 55–59, 143–145,
        348, 373n57, 373n58, 487–488, 492,
        496
    ratification debates, 64–65
    selection criteria, 510–511
    Senate president, 56
    1796 election, 88, 102, 489
    significance, 486–487
    ticket-balancing policies, 490–491, 494,
        496
    Twelfth Amendment, 111–112, 489
    Twentieth Amendment, 283–284, 496
    Twenty-fifth Amendment, 348–351, 501,
        502, 506–507
    Twenty-second Amendment, 317–320,
        508
Vietnam amnesty program, 364
Vietnam conflict, 338, 341, 346–348,
    355–356
Villa, Francisco (Pancho), 251–252
Virginia, 8, 15, 465
Virginia Plan
    appointments and commissioning power,
        49
    council proposal, 31–32, 45–46
    enumerated powers, 41–42
    executive design, 13–15, 26n29, 29–33
    executive salary, 40
    institutional separation, 39–41

legislative selection, 33
presidential succession, 57
term of office, 35
Volcker, Paul, 382
Voting rights
Hayes administration, 195–196
Johnson presidency, 184–185
Wilson administration, 255
Voting Rights Act (1965), 345, 384

W

Wade, Benjamin, 182, 189
Wade-Davis Bill (1864), 171, 182
Wade-Davis Manifesto, 182
Wagner Act (1935), 295, 296, 298
Wagner, Robert F., 296
Walker, Robert J., 148
Walker Tariff (1846), 148, 156n65
Wallace, George C., 351, 424
Wallace, Henry A., 310, 495–496, 512n15
Wall Street Reform and Consumer
    Protection Act, 472–473
Walsh, Lawrence, 400–401
Walsh, Thomas J., 270
War bonds, 257
Wards Cove Packing Co. v. Atonio, 409n79
Warner, John, 449
War of 1812, 114–115
War on Poverty, 345, 358
War on Terrorism, 445–451, 454, 473–475
War Powers Resolution (1973), 362, 365,
    385, 394
Warren, Earl, 304
War veterans, 268, 285n11
Washington, George
    appointments and commissioning power,
        75–77
    and the Constitutional Convention, 11, 12
    election and presidency, 71–90, 107–108
    executive branch (cabinet) formation,
        75–78
    executive power controversy, 78–79, 82
    foreign policy conflicts, 82–84, 88–90
    institutional separation, 79–80
    leadership role, 28, 31, 72–73
    Massachusetts rebellion, 9
    Newburgh Conspiracy, 72
    nonpartisanship, 80–81, 86–87
    oath of office, 68n74
    party conflicts, 81, 84–88
    presidential etiquette, 74–75

presidential qualifications, 68n80
public contact, 73–74
retirement, 87–88
treaty-making power, 79–80, 88–90
veto powers, 79, 97n37
Whiskey Rebellion, 84–87
Watergate scandal, 359–361, 363
Watson, James E., 277
Weapons sales, 302, 310, 386–387
Weaver, James B., 262n83
Weber, Max, 28
Weber, Vin, 385
Webster, Daniel, 131, 132, 134, 140–141, 145,
    490
Weinberger, Caspar, 358, 400
Welfare Reform Act (1996), 422, 426
Welfare state, 288, 293–295, 353–354,
    465–467
    see also New Deal program; Nixon,
        Richard M.; Reagan, Ronald;
        Roosevelt, Franklin D.
Welles, Gideon, 190
Welliver, Judson, 274, 286n32
Western territories, 6
Wexler, Anne, 368
Wheeler, William A., 492
Whig Party
    collapse, 152
    1840 election, 140–143
    1848 election, 150–151
    Jackson presidency, 131, 136
    and Lincoln, 159
    national conventions, 130
    origins, 126
    political philosophy, 136
    Texas annexation treaty, 146
    Tyler presidency, 144–145
    see also Republican Party
Whiskey Rebellion, 84–87
Whiskey Ring scandal, 193–194
"Whistle-stop" campaigns, 210
White, Byron R., 394
White House News Photographers'
    Association, 273
White House Office, 296–297, 315, 325, 337,
    356, 381
White House tapes, 360, 361
White, Leonard D., 76, 94, 110, 114, 118, 149,
    155n45, 202
White, Theodore H., 339, 344, 371n7
Whitewater investigation, 427–428

White, William Allen, 270, 278, 288
White, William S., 307
Wilentz, Sean, 92, 102, 115, 127, 137, 480
Will, George F., 411
Williams, John Sharp, 247
Williamson, Hugh, 22, 37, 56, 57
Willkie, Wendell, 318
Wills, Garry, 73, 160
Wilson, Henry, 374n59, 491
Wilson, James
    appointments and commissioning power,
        49, 50
    Committee of Detail, 18
    and the Constitutional Convention, 11
    council proposal, 46
    on enumerated powers, 26n43
    on executive and legislative power, 3, 4
    executive design, 30–31
    institutional separation, 41
    oath of office, 52
    pardon power, 47
    popular election proposal, 32–33
    as Supreme Court justice, 85
    veto powers, 42
Wilson, Major L., 128
Wilson, Woodrow
    Congressional relationship, 243–258, 266
    election and presidency, 242–258
    executive power doctrine, 242–255,
        262n88, 272, 289
    foreign policy, 250–258, 445
    on legislative supremacy, 206, 212
    1912 election, 240, 242, 411–412
    1918 election, 256–258
    party reform efforts, 245
    political philosophy, 243–248, 333
    popular leadership approach, 245–247,
        256–258, 336–337
    presidential succession, 373n58
    removal powers, 272
    rhetorical presidency, 246–247, 257–258
    on Taft, 238
    term limits, 318
    on the vice presidency, 493
    wartime measures, 251–255, 266
Windom, William, 199–200
Winter, Ralph K., 391
Wise, H. A., 134
Wolcott, Oliver, 93
Women's suffrage, 255
Woodbury, Levi, 147
Wood, Gordon S., 4, 11, 14, 72
Wood, Kimba, 414, 433n9
Worcester, Samuel, 136–137
Worcester v. Georgia (1832), 136–137, 155n34
WorldCom, 450
World Court treaty, 275, 276–277
World Trade Center attacks, 438, 504
World War Adjusted Compensation Act,
    285n11
World War I, 253–255
World War II, 301–307, 313
Wright, Jim, 382

X
XYZ Affair, 92

Y
Yakus v. United States (1944), 303
Yalta summit meeting, 305–307
Yeltsin, Boris, 400
Youngstown Sheet and Tube Co. v. Sawyer,
    313–315, 361

Z
Ziegler, Ron, 359